China at the Center

The Transformation of Modern China Series
James E. Sheridan, General Editor

The Fall of Imperial China
Frederic Wakeman, Jr.

China in Disintegration
The Republican Era in Chinese History, 1912–1949
James E. Sheridan

Mao's China
A History of the People's Republic
Maurice Meisner

Intellectuals and the State in Modern China
A Narrative History
Jerome B. Grieder

China at the Center
300 Years of Foreign Policy
Mark Mancall

China at the Center,

300 Years of Foreign Policy

Mark Mancall

Fp | THE FREE PRESS
A Division of Macmillan, Inc.
NEW YORK

Collier Macmillan Publishers
LONDON

The Free Press
A Division of Macmillan, Inc.
866 Third Avenue, New York, N. Y. 10022

Collier Macmillan Canada, Inc.

Printed in the United States of America

printing number

1 2 3 4 5 6 7 8 9 10

Library of Congress Cataloging in Publication Data

Mancall, Mark.
  China at the center.

  (Transformation of modern China series)
  Bibliography: p.
  Includes index.
  1. China—Foreign relations—1644-1912. 2. China—
Foreign relations—1912-1949. 3. China—Foreign
relations—1949-   I. Title   II. Series.
DS754.18.M36   1983   327.51   83-47981
ISBN 0-02-919810-0

For John King Fairbank

and

for my students,

teachers all

Contents

Acknowledgments

THE CONTRIBUTIONS of scholars who, before now, have written on one or another aspect of Chinese foreign relations provide the indispensable basis upon which this book rests. It would be impossible for me to acknowledge all of them. At best, I can indicate my indebtedness to those upon whom I have relied most directly by including their works in the Suggested Reading at the end of this volume. I hope I can discharge my debts to them by encouraging readers to seek them out in the pursuit of more and more profound knowledge. Because the citations in this book are restricted almost entirely to quotations, it is impossible to recognize in any other fashion my colleagues' influence on this text and on the speculative reflections that gave rise to it.

Two colleagues who are also friends deserve special recognition. James E. Sheridan provided me with many detailed comments that saved me from more errors than I care to admit. More than that, he constantly goaded me to complete this book, and its appearance testifies to the array of encouragements he has in his repertoire. Lyman Van Slyke read the manuscript and, with his usual thoughtfulness, led me to rethink some problems. Neither of them, nor any of those upon whose work I have relied, bears the slightest responsibility either for the views expressed here or for the errors I may have committed.

Friends and students bore with the writing of this work over too long a period of time, and their good will benefited me greatly. Particular recognition is due Daryl Sawyer and the staff of Stanford Overseas Studies, Bonnie Senko, Michael Doran, and my colleagues in the Stanford Program in Structured Liberal Education, who frequently relieved me of responsibilities that made it possible for me to read and write. Michael Carter and Pentti Kanerva, both of Stanford's Center for Information Technology, introduced me to word processing, which I approached with the temper of a Luddite; their kind guidance and ministrations transformed that temper into the zeal of a convert. Amy Sims, Phyllis Brown, and Nancy Winbigler criticized the manuscript into improvement, but infelicities of style are all my own.

Finally, my parents, Boone and Olga Mancall, constantly called me back to work when I strayed, for which more than gratitude is due.

Introduction

THE COMMON WISDOM of the second half of the twentieth century is that the world would be a better place if its peoples communicated more, and more often, than they do. In light of this presupposition, the discipline of international relations—the formulation and execution of foreign policy and the study thereof—has developed around a congeries of problems. These problems arise from differences—political, economic, social, and, equally important if at times overlooked, ethnic, geographical, and ecological—many of which actually constitute contradictions. Students of international relations study these contradictions, their resolution, and the means to their resolution, focusing to no little extent on the problem-solving processes that diminish the threat of using war to achieve policy objectives. Thus, hopeful that an understanding of both the processes of problem-solving and the sources of national behavior will foster peace among nations, international relations explores and tries to explain the reasons why particular countries behave in the international arena as they do.

Because the problems are disparate, international relations approaches the objective of peace through a variety of disciplines; however, it always harks back to the core belief that increased knowledge will lead to better communication and that better communication will promote peace. Immediately, however, problems arise in this rather idealistic endeavor. In order to be an effective discipline (or interdiscipline), international relations must rest upon a set of value-free assumptions. Unfortunately, the students of international relations tend unconsciously to conceptualize the problems to be studied not from a neutral point of view but rather from the point of view that seems natural to them because it reflects the political, economic, social, ethnic, geographical, and ecological structures with which they are most familiar. Therefore, practitioners of international relations in the field we call intelligence often believe that the more knowledge we have of our enemies or potential enemies, the less threatened we will feel; at the same time, intelligence experts tend not to believe the converse, that the more knowledge our enemies have of us, the less threatened they will feel.

The language used to discuss international relations is more telling yet, although less immediately slanted. In its very name, international relations assumes the existence and legitimacy of nation-states as the appropriate units of analysis and action. This position can lead to two major errors of analysis and judgment, not to mention mistakes in policy formulation. First, it assumes that the *significant* actors in the field are nation-states; it does not allow for the adequate analysis and evaluation of other social, cultural, economic, and political elements and their associated values. Second, it reads nineteenth- and twentieth-century Western European and North Atlantic institutions and values back into the past and over into other cultural areas. In making this assumption, international relations imposes cognitive structures on various actors and cultural domains in what may be inappropriate circumstances. To some extent this tendency is the consequence of history. In Africa, for example, both analytical and real problems arise out of the imposition of the Western nation-state structure on an environment foreign to it. This happened, to no small extent, because of the presumed correctness of giving geographical and institutional expression to a population not on the basis of those ethnic considerations whereby it distinguished itself from other populations but rather on the basis of the consequences of rivalries among European imperialist powers in the nineteenth century. In order to resolve this contradiction, Western social sciences have defined ethnic identities and the accompanying demand for their institutional expression in Africa as "tribalism" and have attached to that term a negative value. In the Far East, the same assumptions on the part of the aggressive Atlantic powers in the nineteenth century led to armed conflict between the Chinese empire and the West and to the defeat of the former, with consequences we are still experiencing.

The investigation of another culture's views and attitudes toward foreign policy further illustrates how far international relations actually is from being a value-free discipline. Specifically, the history of China's foreign policy, including the assumptions about the world upon which it was based and the institutions that have been its formal expression, demonstrates that the Chinese have not always considered the nation-state to be the basic unit in international affairs or international togetherness to be the best approach to peace. For example, prior to the middle of the nineteenth century, the objective of China's foreign policy was not to solve problems but to prevent problems from arising in the first place. China believed this goal was best accomplished not by bringing peoples together and increasing their mutual understanding but by keeping peoples apart and providing structures for interaction that would maintain a safe distance between them. Consequently, unique institutions and practices were developed to control what contact was deemed essential to implementing this policy. A certain distance and a certain level of activity between peoples were considered optimal for the maintenance of peace through ignorance and awe; when optimal conditions failed to obtain, problems arose. Thus, for the Chinese the emergence of problems was a sign of failure, not their solution a sign of success.

Further increasing the distance between the assumptions on which Western and Chinese foreign policies are based is a lack of distinction between foreign and domestic policy in traditional Chinese philosophy and practice. The idea that the conduct of international relations obeys, or ought to obey, rules that are distinct from the rules of the cultures and states that participate in international relations is distinctly modern and Western. The so-called tribute system, which constituted the structure of China's interaction with the rest of the world, was itself a manifestation of the Great Tradition, the mainstream of Chinese culture, recognized as such by its participants and its observers alike, and, for both, the policy of controlled apartness was central to all the philosophical assumptions, cognitive perceptions, customs, and institutions that were established and developed in the Ming (1368–1644) and Qing (1644–1912) dynasties. Furthermore, for the traditional Chinese, the world was a coherent whole; their assumptions and presuppositions about the world were part of a conceptual and institutional continuum and were themselves an integral part of the structure of Chinese institutions and behaviors. This unified vision conceptually resolved contradictions inherent in the Empire's physical and political environment and in the interplay of the world view of traditional China with the world views of those with whom traditional China came into contact and conflict. The institutions and behaviors, and the assumptions upon which the institutions and behaviors rested and from which they grew, can be separated only by an act of historical analysis.

Thus, the Empire was culturally, institutionally, and geographically a world system until the middle of the nineteenth century, when all this changed. What was changing, of course, was the West, not the Empire. The West had been a precapitalist collection of socioeconomic-political units integrated, at least theoretically, into a hierarchical structure headed by the duumvirs, emperor and pope; it was becoming a congeries of nation-states bound into a headless system that in turn was held together by the very relationships and contradictions that were capitalism, based in the market and expressed in the ideology of the newly dominant bourgeois class. The feudal system—more accurately, mercantilism, which marked the transition from feudalism to merchant and industrial capitalism—was becoming the capitalist Oikoumene. None of this is to suggest that the Empire, for its part, was unchanging; far from it. Changes in the West, however, were of a type and magnitude to overwhelm the changes through which the Empire was passing, changes rooted in Chinese history, economy, and society. Western technology overcame the limitations and structural imperatives directing China's interaction with other societies. The growth of capitalism in the West, most particularly in Great Britain, required ever expanding markets, or commercial intercourse, not controlled separation. Therefore, what became a necessity for the West directly clashed with what the Empire perceived as its own necessity. Conflict was the unavoidable result. It was not the Empire's "backwardness" but the West's new aggressiveness and modernism that led to this conflict. Geography and technology, hitherto factors protecting the integrity of separate societies, now became, as technology conquered geography, instruments for intercourse and gradual integration into a world system.

In the face of the Oikoumene's onslaught—and an onslaught it was, for in the middle of the nineteenth century the West defeated the Empire three times in less than twenty years—the coherent view of the world that had guided China's external interactions began to break down. As time passed, officials concerned with foreign policy realized that traditional assumptions no longer applied. They learned, often painfully, that the strategies and tactics that had characterized the Empire's external interaction before the West's attack were now ineffective. China's coherent world view was decreasingly able to resolve the contradictions between China's world and the world of its invaders.

The Oikoumene's defeat of the Empire in the three successive Opium wars (1839–1842, 1856, 1858–1860) initiated the disintegration of traditional coherence. The second half of the nineteenth century, particularly after 1860, witnessed various attempts to restore coherence. All the while, the imperial bureaucracy, or at least some of its members, were trying to learn how to live with the new world impinging upon the consciousness of the traditional scholar-bureaucrats. The traditional view, for example, allowed for "barbarian" victory and conquest; indeed, it almost required barbarian rule as a vehicle for absorption. When the barbarian became so strong that other mechanisms failed to hold him at bay, he would conquer China, thereby becoming its victim, for to rule China the barbarian had to become Chinese. The Manchus, who conquered the Empire in the middle of the seventeenth century, ultimately became the most conservative guardians of Chinese tradition. What the system could not tolerate, however, was rule by barbarians who refused to pay proper obeisance to the Chinese tradition. In this sense, the Chinese cultivation of foreigners with a taste for things Chinese or the attention paid to the Westerner who fell victim to the charms of Peking extended a traditional strategy on an individual level rather than on a broad, cultural one; the strategy endured, but it was no longer an instrument of imperial survival.

The Boxer Rebellion of 1900 marked the final failure of the attempted restoration of coherence in China's external interactions. Fierce nativism (a precursor of Third World revolts against westernization-modernization), combined with a rejection of the realities of the material world inhabited by the Westerners, particularly the military, led directly to disaster. The abolition of the Confucian examination system in 1905 symbolized the utter fragmentation of the world as experienced by traditional Chinese. The great leaders of the last dynasty's end—the Zeng Guofans, the Li Hungzhangs, the Zhang Zhidongs—men dedicated to the tradition and the Empire, began to disappear from the scene. The tradition in the East Asian Empire's external affairs, as embodied in imperial institutions and policies, and the disintegration of that tradition in the face of the Oikoumene's onslaught, form the focus of the first part of this book.

The crumbling of tradition initiated a new period in the Empire's relations with the outside world. The years 1900–1949 are the focus of the book's second section. In this period, a new breed of men such as Yuan Shikai, Duan Qirui, and Chiang Kai-shek supplanted the statesmen of the Empire. The new leaders equaled their predecessors in dedication, but they turned that dedication toward their own narrowly defined interests. From 1911 to 1949, what little Chinese foreign policy existed revealed those same characteristics of disorientation and chaos that were manifested by China's internal social, economic, political and cultural life. The primary objective of the government's activity on the international scene was survival pure and simple—not necessarily survival of the nation but survival of the individual or the elite group in power. In this view, the corruption so characteristic of Chiang Kai-shek's regime during World War II was not produced by any defect in the Chinese character; rather, it was a natural, even if unacceptable, consequence of the necessity to act in a world in which the only conceivable objects of loyalty were oneself, one's family, and one's friends. By the same token, the shifting alliances among opponents to Chiang's Nationalist Party regime, ranging from liberal-left collaborators of the Japanese to Marxist and populist nationalists, all sought to actualize a vision of a revitalized China that necessarily included the reestablishment of a center of coherence based, depending on point of view, in one or another conceptual structure: liberal (Western) reformism, geopolitical and anticapitalist Asianism centered on the Japanese idea of the Greater East Asia Co-prosperity Sphere, or populist nationalism rooted in the peasantry and informed by an adaptation of Marxist historical and social theory to Chinese society. The dialectic of opposition between the officially recognized holders of state power and those who sought the creation of a new coherence and, with it, a fundamental change in Chinese society took the form of the Chinese Revolution.

The third section of this book discusses the present period, initiated by the victory of the Chinese Communists in 1949. The revolution brought to power a new group that, despite the vicissitudes of ideology and personnel, has continued to hold a coherent view of the world, which is the basis of Chinese foreign policy. Like the pre-1900 coherence, this new coherence does not imply any lack of change; quite the contrary, it is characterized by great creative energy within the system. Indeed, this very combination of energy, change, and system provides the conceptual, institutional, and political basis for China's foreign policy. A world view with horizons broader than immediate self-interest was reestablished in Peking. But there were profound ironies in this reestablishment of order. Like its predecessors, the new coherence advanced separation, at times bordering on isolation, and controlled interaction as objectives of the new China's foreign policy. This came precisely when the West began to move at an accelerated speed in the direction of international integration, a trend particularly evident in trade and cultural interaction. The irony was compounded by the reestablishment of institutions of the tribute system type, such as the symbolic and ceremonial visits of foreign governmental and party leaders to Peking, a modern avatar of the old tribute mission, or the Canton trade fair, which sharply recalls the regulated frontier trade that was a central element in the tribute system. There is further irony in the fact that when, in the late 1970s, China's leadership decided that a new opening to the West from a position of strength was possible, and even necessary for China's growth, the West itself apparently had lost its resilience and was suffering from internal economic difficulties that limited its ability to respond to China's needs.

The discussion of the three consecutive periods in the history of China's foreign policy that are the subject of this book takes place in a primary perspective that begins with a paradox. The world view established in Peking after 1949 must be defined, if we are to assess it within the context of Chinese history, without reference to the immediate vocabulary of its expression. In other words, we must study the structure of the new world view and make comparisons with the traditional world view if we are to understand why our own perceptions of Chinese foreign policy today seem somehow to be echoes of a memory. In the third section of this volume, I argue that what to outsiders appear to be contradictions in China's international behavior are indeed contradictions, but contradictions that are resolved within the coherent system of China's cognitive perception of the world today. Contradictions need not stand over against coherence; they may be a very part of the structure of it, and this is as true of the premodern tradition as of the postmodern.

The history of China's interactions with other cultures and political entities is intrinsically interesting in a world in which China looms larger and larger as a power whose immediate decisions and long-range policies are increasingly decisive in human affairs. That does not exhaust the subject's value, however; this inquiry can also give us a necessary perspective on our own international behavior. We may discern more easily in another what is equally true of ourselves, which is that foreign policy is made neither in a vacuum nor in an external reality that we can perceive and analyze directly. Policy is made and executed by people who define the world and themselves in terms provided to them by the world view within which they lead their daily lives. The intellectual assumptions, emotional predispositions, cognitive maps, and perceptual structures of the foreign policymaker are all rooted in the prevailing world view of his society; moreover, they are reinforced by a system of education supported by a hierarchy of expectations. Precisely because Chinese, American, and Soviet diplomats are themselves members of the cultures they represent, their meetings are interactions in which different worlds must come to terms with each other. It is an error to read differences in behavior rooted in differences in culture as acts of dishonesty or deception (indeed, deception itself may be culturally advantaged in some contexts), and it is equally dangerous to assume the same degree of sincerity among statements of friendship made by representatives of diverse cultures.

The world viewed from Peking is different from the world viewed from North America or Western Europe. Successful diplomacy in the cause of peace depends on our recognition of this difference rather than on our hopes for a world increasingly re-created in our own image. As nations outside the West—with world views rooted in their own cultures and experiences—become international powers, appreciation of such differences and the consequent displacement of our own concept of international reality may become both moral and political necessities. The need to recognize differences in world views is the vital issue raised by the study of both traditional and contemporary Chinese foreign policy from the Chinese perspective.

In order to encourage a reconceptualization of the international arena and at the same time to help develop a vocabulary better suited to a world in which Western concepts are being called into question by the rise to great power status of other than Western politico-social units, I have adopted a modified vocabulary to speak about the world as perceived not from London or Washington but from Peking. In the history of China's foreign relations since the middle of the seventeenth century, the two major actors have been the Empire and the Oikoumene. The use of the term "Empire" is intended to indicate that China conceived of itself, and continues to conceive of itself, as a highly centralized, bureaucratically and hierarchically organized society summarized, as it were, in the person of the emperor or, later, the party and its chairman. In this view, the interregnum that began with the fall of the Qing dynasty in 1911 and ended with the victory of the Chinese Communist revolution in 1949 emphasized the fundamental nature of the Empire by the absence during those years of a state apparatus of the imperial type. The term "Empire" is used, therefore, not to suggest continuity between premodern Chinese ideology and Chinese Communist ideology; rather, it refers to a view of the world in which one of the major actors, the speaking subject of this history, is, and sees itself as, a unitary power of world dimensions. The term "Oikoumene" refers to the other major actor in this story, the West, viewed here as a collection of greater and lesser powers without a single head or a formal interpower organization. The West is characterized predominantly by its economic system, capitalism, which sets it apart from the rest of the world, and by its shared policy interests vis-à-vis those of the rest of the world, even if such shared interests also involve rivalry and conflict within the Oikoumene. Indeed, the most important problems faced by the Empire were to comprehend the nature of the Oikoumene from the perspective of a hierarchically organized, unitary universe and to deal with a multifaceted opponent that apparently had no head. In a very real sense, these two concepts of Empire and Oikoumene are as valid today as they were three hundred years ago, and it is in this observation that the continuity in China's views of, and interactions with, the non-Chinese world needs to be found.

The adoption of Empire and Oikoumene to refer to the two major actors in China's foreign policy during the Qing, Republican, and Communist periods led to slight revisions in the use of a few common terms. In this analysis, "interstate" refers not only to relations between nation-states but also to relations between any *formal* political units. Similarly, "international" denotes relationships between any interacting elements or units, a usage that more accurately reflects current reality, as well as the reality of Chinese foreign relations, than does the historically circumscribed use of the term to reflect only, or at least primarily, interstate relations. Finally, "foreign" means that which is external to, and different from, the speaking subject—in this case the subject conceptualizing the world. The last usage should focus the reader's attention on the primary issue of China's relations with the West, namely the development of a *modus vivendi* not between different powers but between different worlds, each organized according to its own principles and perceiving the other in terms of the only reality it can know, itself.

The Setting of China's Foreign Relations

IT IS COMMONPLACE to state that East Asian civilization, with China at its center, developed autonomously because oceans, forests, deserts, high mountains, and jungles isolated it from the other major areas of the development of Asian civilization, such as India, Mesopotamia, and Egypt. In saying this we tend to forget that Western civilization, surrounded by the deserts of Africa and the Middle East, the steppes of southern Russia, the forests of Europe, and the waters of the Atlantic, developed no less autonomously. In the East Asian world, as we shall see, one culture came to predominate among the elite, allowing great latitude for local cultures among the people. But the same situation characterized the Mediterranean, where, for example, Greek and later Latin were the languages of the official and intellectual elite, while the local populations from the Hebrew- and Aramaic-speaking Middle Easterners to the Iberian speakers of the farthest West had their own richly local cultures. In both China and the West, a dialectical tension existed between the centrifugal tendency toward the unity of the Great Tradition and the centripetal tendency toward disunity of the small, local traditions. This observation becomes extremely important for an understanding of the origins of international relations in both China and the West. Both ancient China and the modern Anglo-Saxon world clearly show that many states may exist within the boundaries of a single culture area. Under one Empire, with whatever degree of unity and centralization that politics and technology permit, several cultures may exist, as the ancient Greek and Roman empires and the comparatively modern Austro-Hungarian empire demonstrate. China differs from the West, however, in that centrifugence predominated over centripetence, and therefore a discussion of China's foreign relations must be grounded on an understanding that as a policy-formulating subject China is not a nation in the ordinary Western sense of the term. To understand the nature and quality of China's foreign relations, we must first survey the geographical, historical, material, and cultural bases of China's foreign relations. The division and classification of the sections is merely to facilitate the analysis, for in fact all are closely interrelated factors in the development of China's policies.

The Geographical Setting

Unlike the Mediterranean countries, Northern Europe, Northern India, and North America, where physical features of the land facilitated communications, the spread of culture, and therefore unity, the geography of China contributed to differentiation and disunity. The North China Plain, extending from Peking in the north, south to the Changjiang (the Yangtze River) and from the ocean in the east to the mountain ranges of China's midwest, was the original center of Chinese cultural growth. Here the two rivers flowing from west to east—the Changjiang and the Huanghe (the Yellow River)—were the main foci of settlement and provided an easy means of communication that distinguished this region from the areas surrounding it, all locked in by mountains, high plateaus, or thick forests. However, despite numerous tributaries, especially of the Changjiang, which helped extend both culture and commerce, identifiably distinct "states" began to emerge at the end of what is called the Shang dynasty, states defined to no small extent by the geographical characteristics of the land. Similarly, the political units of the "Warring States" period (approximately 403–221 B.C.E.) were defined to a recognizable extent by geographical characteristics. That these states were more than simple administrative subdivisions of a united country can be demonstrated in a variety of ways. For example, the *Book of Odes*, the great Confucian classic collection of poetry, is an anthology of verses collected from many of these states, and their linguistic and stylistic differences suggest that local cultures were not submerged in a homogenizing national culture. Further evidence for the "stateness" of these political units is the fact that, according to one scholar, in the 242-year period from 463 to 222 B.C.E. there were only 89 years of peace, while over 450 major military campaigns were fought[1] among the states, and the size of the armies involved reached the hundreds of thousands. In 260 B.C.E., for example, as many as 450,000 men may have lost their lives in a major war; after that war, the state of Zhao could raise only 130,000 men to resist invasion by another state whose army numbered 600,000. All this suggests a world in which the state, as an organism capable of marshalling significant numbers of men and fielding them for military purposes, had already emerged. Thus the geography of the North China Plain imposed barriers that were conducive to the development of autonomous cultures but that were ultimately surmountable, as the evidence of the wars demonstrates.

Just as the geography of the North China Plain militated against unity but allowed enough communication for war to result, similarly, geography contributed to the simultaneous existence and perpetuation of economic, sociological, linguistic, and political differences among the states and regions—differences that, in fact, survive right down to the modern period—but did not prevent the emergence of a common elite culture that can be characterized as Chinese. Scholars call this culture and the system of customs and beliefs, as well as the written languages and literary traditions on which it was based, "the Great Tradition." It is great because of its cultural impact over the centuries, providing China with a basis for the definition of itself over and against the surrounding peoples who did not share in it and great because it provided the framework for a common discourse among the upper classes of the various states and regions. It was this culture that Confucius and his disciples began to codify and elaborate in the sixth and fifth centuries B.C.E. Local cultures were "lesser traditions," rooted in the daily life of the people, surviving alongside and enriching the Great Tradition and, in turn, being enriched by it. With the passage of the centuries, this distinction between the Great Tradition and the lesser, local traditions marked class distinctions, and assimilation of the Great Tradition was a primary vehicle for, and characteristic of, upward social mobility in China's strongly hierarchical society.

By about 200 B.C.E., Chinese cultural expansion reached, in various directions, geographical limits beyond which lived peoples who linguistically, socially, culturally, and politically were different from the Chinese. This frontier was a line that was not fixed geographically and did not separate permanently one people and its culture from another. It was, rather, a transitional zone that demarcated one ecological-cultural region from another and which shifted according to climatological considerations. Depending upon the population's degree of adjustment to the particular ecological situation in which it found itself at a given time, a given people might be found on one or another side of this frontier. For example, the line between sedentary peasants and nomadic herders, each with their own culture, was not immutable geographically; it was not necessarily fixed from the point of view of population either, for a given people could be sedentary or nomadic, depending upon the ecological conditions in which it found itself.

The Chinese culture area was surrounded by six such regions in all. In the farthest east was the ocean, inhabited by a variety of different peoples, ranging from the Ryukyuans and the Japanese, of whom the Chinese had some slight immediate knowledge, to strangers who came from afar, such as Arabs and Persians, and, later, Western Europeans. From the point of view of Chinese culture, the ocean with its inhabitants formed a single ecological region by virtue of the fact that deep-seated in Chinese culture was, and is, a continental orientation accompanied by an apparently equally deep-seated thalassophobia which through long stretches of history prevented China from becoming a major sea-going power, even though she possessed the geographical and technological ability to become one. To the northeast, in what is today Manchuria, the Chinese encountered forests and steppes, inhabited largely by hunting and fishing tribes with a certain basic agriculture. The classic example of the society of this frontier was the Manchus, who themselves conquered China in the middle of the seventeenth century and succeeded in ruling China for 268 years by becoming more Chinese than the Chinese themselves. To the west the Chinese faced, from the earliest times, the steppes and deserts of Mongolia, inhabited by pastoral nomads who organized their society around the necessity to seek sufficient forage for animals by seasonally ranging over wide territories. Still further to the west, in Central Asia proper, were the desert cultures of Turkestan, characterized by small-scale agriculture based upon oases, a limited amount of nomadism, and long-distance trade along caravan routes. To the southwest, the high Tibetan plateau contained a society based upon a combination of agriculture and nomadism, in part organized around feudal kings and in part around the Lamaist Buddhist church. Finally, to the south, in what is today South China and Southeast Asia, the geography consisted of mountain ranges, fertile valleys, and jungles. The culture there differed sharply from, and at the same time—especially in the lowlands with village-based sedentary agriculture—was in some ways similar to, North China; therefore, it assimilated the north Chinese Great Tradition more easily than the other five surrounding regions did.

In all six regions, however, linguistic, cultural, and religious differences created a distinctly "foreign" environment that met the encroachment of the northern culture with hostility. Evidence of the genius of Chinese culture lay in China's ability to extend the system developed for the conduct of relationships among political units within China proper to incorporate societies and peoples as culturally and ecologically diverse as the hunting and fishing tribes of Manchuria, the theocratic-feudal semisedentary/semi-agricultural society of Tibet, and the bourgeois society of Dutch merchants coming to China to trade by sea. By insisting upon the universalistic and "civilized" qualities of Chinese culture, the Empire succeeded in constructing a system for the conduct of intercultural and interstate relations that parochialized, in its eyes, the cultures of all who came to treat with it.

The Historical Setting of China's Foreign Relations

The dialectical tension between the Great Tradition and the little traditions, between the ideal of a state that was isomorphic with the culture of the Great Tradition and the reality of local power and the little tradition, found its objectively real expression in Chinese history. Periods of unity, dominated by the imperial state, alternated with periods of disunity, characterized by the reemergence of a polycentric multistate system. Ideologically, the same dialectical tension was expressed in terms of the heavy priority assigned to a unified Empire and the negative affects attached to disunity and its causes. This primacy placed upon the value of unity is not surprising in view of the fact that those who gave formal leadership to the society and expressed its values were the literati. As literati, they were members of that group in Chinese society whose culture was the Great Tradition, adhesion to which was the source of their power as individuals and as a class. Thus, for example, the complicated Chinese system for counting historical time and the grand design of Chinese history as interpreted by Chinese official scholars was expressed in terms of dynasties that were considered an almost natural feature of the historical landscape. Periods of dynastic decline and social or cultural disunity were counted as aberrational, as the product of moral decline.

However, there is an alternative and equally valid scheme for the organization of Chinese history. This alternative suggests that the norm is a pattern of fluctuation between warfare and the search for peace, between fragmentation and unification, in a multistate system. If one considers as part of the periods of disunity the years when a dynasty was on the path to unification and the years when it was gradually losing control over some of its territory, then one sees that the periods when a strong dynasty held real power over the broad reaches of the Chinese culture area were only one aspect of the long stream of Chinese history.

Both models have some validity. The dynastic cycle—the appearance of a new dynasty and its unification of the Empire, its period of flourishing, its decline, the emergence of a multistate polycentric system, the appearance of a new dynasty—for long years has provided the structure for the interpretation of Chinese history by Western as well as Chinese scholars. This impulse to adopt the Chinese scheme of periodization and explanation of history, which emphasizes the unity of the culture and tradition, may well be rooted not only in the human desire to see order in the events of man but also in the West's desire for a unity that, somehow, always seems to elude it. The historian's choice of one or the other model must depend upon his or her focus and philosophical perspective. However, the simultaneous recognition of both models encourages certain distinctions that may be valuable in the analysis of the history of China's foreign relations. For example, the purpose for which certain kinds of public works were undertaken and their significance for foreign relations can be ascertained within the context of one or the other model. The Qin dynasty's standardization of roads, weights, measures, and written language or, at a later period, the construction of the Grand Canal are bureaucratic and technological measures taken to overcome the natural tendency, encouraged by geography, toward a polycentric or multinational system. Conversely, the construction of the Great Wall, initially in parts and later as a connected system of defense, demarcated the entire Chinese culture from an ecological, social, and cultural region of foreignness. Behind the Great Wall, the processes of Chinese history could work themselves out as Chinese processes, leading sometimes to unified empires, at others to multistate systems. The Great Wall itself was not a defense mechanism against the barbarians; both Chinese and barbarian dynasties of unity originated beyond the Great Wall, and barbarians often as not encouraged, consciously or unconsciously, the disintegration of unified imperial systems and the development of multistate systems in which they themselves could be participants. The historical dialectic of unity and disunity in China was accompanied to a certain extent by a dialectic of technology and geography. The disunifying influences of China's geography have been met at various times in its history with technological modifications such as the the standardization of axle lengths and the construction of the Grand Canal, but at no time prior to the middle of the twentieth century was the technology available to the Chinese leadership sufficient to tip the scales of Chinese history permanently in the direction of unity. It remains to be seen whether the Chinese Communists will be more successful in this endeavor.

In the history of China the model of a multistate international system found its first clear application in the second part of the Zhou dynasty in the "Spring and Autumn" period (722–481 B.C.E.) and the "Warring States" period (403–221 B.C.E.), particularly in the latter. These were centuries in which there was growing awareness of an identity shared by the various parts of what was to become China and of common cultural, social, and linguistic traits, as demonstrated by wandering scholars such as Confucius and the demand for such men to serve as teachers in many states. (The Middle Ages in Europe offer an example of a similar development.) However, the degree to which the Zhou dynasty in its early years or its predecessor, the Shang dynasty, can be considered a unified and centralized state is open to question. What is incontrovertible is the fact that in the last two periods of the so-called Zhou dynasty, and particularly in the last period, a multinational system had developed within the Chinese culture area. This system of large and small states engaged in almost constant warfare. Alliances, both bilateral and multilateral, dynastic intermarriage as a form of alliance, interstate peace conferences, all were part of a multistate system that, in retrospect, had a peculiarly modern cast to it.

As the states multiplied and population growth made it possible to increase the scope and ferocity of warfare and, finally, as the tendency of larger, particularly barbarian, states to overcome small Chinese states became more clearly recognized, an international system or order began to take form. Faced in the south with increasing danger from the state of Chu, a growing barbarian power, the smaller states of the center of the Chinese culture area, the North China Plain, met in 651 B.C.E. and organized a confederation under a hegemon (called the *Ba*). This confederation for mutual defense and for the establishment of some form of stability on the international scene can best be understood, perhaps, by an analogy with the United Nations. The strength of the confederation depended almost entirely upon the strength of personality of the hegemon, and the shift of the balance of power within the confederation was such that within a century the king of Chu himself became the third hegemon of the confederation, which had been created originally as a defense against Chu. Sporadic efforts to maintain some degree of peace in the world failed, and by the middle of the fifth century B.C.E. three great powers had emerged as the chief contenders on the international scene: Qi, Qin, and Chu. By 221 B.C.E., Qin succeeded in conquering all the states in the multinational system and in unifying all of the Chinese culture area for the first time in any real sense. In the world as the Chinese of that age knew it, a single power finally had achieved world domination.

Two characteristic Chinese ideas about foreign relations can be traced directly back to this period. First, the belief that order on the international scene is both possible and highly desirable finds institutional expression in the hegemonic system of the latter part of the Zhou dynasty. Second, the concept that order must be based upon a certain set of values and the institutions and rituals that give direct expression to, and in turn reinforce, those values was a clearly stated proposition in the works of the dominant philosophers of the period, including Confucius, Mencius, and the Legalists. By way of an historical observation, we should note that the development of a multistate system within a single culture area, that identified itself as civilization and in terms of explicit values and that saw itself as opposed to the world of the foreign, which is to say the barbarian, who was not civilized because he did not possess those civilized values, permitted the Chinese to conceptualize the international order in terms of value systems as well as systems of power. Alliances could be based upon adherence to a value system and its symbols. Ironically, the primacy given to a specific, but quite different, value system on the international scene at a much later date, in the nineteenth century, was to inhibit creative Chinese interaction with societies and cultures that possessed different systems of values and that were unwilling, for various reasons, even to appear to adhere symbolically to the Chinese system.

The Material and Cultural Bases of China's Foreign Relations

Two factors that contribute in a significant fashion to the development of international relations are economic and cultural differentiation. Economic differentiation may take one or more of several different forms: differences in endowment of raw materials and labor, differences in price structure, differences in quality of production, and the like. The great division of labor operates in international society just as it does within any given society. Cultural differentiation also has many possible facets, among which may be differences in style, the strangeness that attaches to a foreign product, the superiority or greater efficiency of one cultural artifact or technique over another, the attitudes of superiority or of·inferiority of one people toward another, the need within one society for legitimacy derived from another.

The earliest known form of exchange between peoples is the so-called silent trade that took place in forest clearings in Siberia. One tribe or group of people would leave trade goods in a clearing and withdraw to the forest, and another tribe or group of people would approach the clearing, take what goods it wished or needed, and leave an appropriate amount of its own. This kind of exchange without personal contact would continue until the needs of each were satisfied. Obviously, this was a primitive barter arrangement in which the deposit in the clearing of an insufficient quantity of goods or of goods of unacceptable quality would result in the nonappearance of the other partner in the trading situation. This most primitive form of peaceful interaction between peoples was already based upon a division of labor and differentiation among material cultures. Although the structure of intergroup relationships grew more complex, the factors leading to such relationships remained principally the same.

The emergence of an interstate system in the Chinese cultural world (722–221 B.C.E., more particularly 403–221 B.C.E.) was characterized by economic and social development that sharply differentiated the Chinese peoples and the regions they inhabited from the surrounding non-Chinese peoples. Some growth in agricultural production, brought about by the construction of dams and irrigation systems and, perhaps, by the initial effects of the introduction of iron in limited quantities, together with the use of fertilizer and the beginnings of soil science, contributed to the expansion of the society's economic base. Ancient cultural differentiation and the existence in China of an economic base sufficient to support foreign trade is indicated by the evidence of very early importation into China of such indigenously scarce goods as jade and cowrie shells.

Another differentiating factor was the growth of cities. Relatively small settlements whose purpose was primarily military in the Spring and Autumn period expanded in the Warring States period in size and function to include industrial, residential, and commercial quarters. Some Warring States cities seemed to have housed a considerable population of remarkable density. A great variety of commercial activities were pursued in these cities, and a proto-urban culture began to emerge which differentiated such population centers from the surrounding countryside, on the one hand, and, on the other, the Chinese culture area from surrounding non-Chinese peoples. Indeed, some of those peoples with whom the Chinese were to come into direct contact did not develop recognizably urban cultures until the twentieth century.

The growth of Chinese material culture continued during the first great imperial period, the Qin (221–206 B.C.E.) and Han (206 B.C.E.–220 C.E.) dynasties. Indeed, during this time China became the most advanced area in the world. Techniques in textile production, iron casting, pottery production, and many other fields were far in advance of those found elsewhere. Technological invention ranging from the Zhou dynasty's development of the crossbow to the invention of paper sometime during the Later Han dynasty increased the gulf between China and her neighbors and, therefore, increased the potential for international relations on all levels.

Because the superiority of Chinese material culture made its goods attractive to other peoples, the development of trade networks beyond the Chinese cultural area proceeded rapidly. The trade routes of Central Asia and the maritime routes through the Indian Ocean carried Chinese goods to the Roman East and to India. A port for trade with South and Southeast Asia was located in the region of the present city of Hanoi, and later the city of Canton developed as the point of departure for trade with West and South Asia. Indeed, Han records indicated some knowledge of, and occasional interaction with, the Roman East, and Chinese silk from that period has been found in the Middle East. Trade with China was an extremely attractive proposition for non-Chinese peoples and has remained so down to the present day, though the reasons for this attractiveness changed with the industrialization of the North Atlantic states beginning in the late eighteenth century.

The very same material and cultural superiority that made trade with China so attractive to non-Chinese peoples made it somewhat less interesting for the Chinese themselves, and this tendency was reenforced by the Chinese consciousness of their own superiority. Nonetheless, there was a definite Chinese demand for some foreign goods, and the impact of foreign trade on China and its culture was profound indeed. The demand ranged from luxury products and strange and peculiar items that would titillate the fancies of a jaded aristocracy to horses from Central Asia. The latter is a fine example of the division of labor: horses were most efficiently produced in the Central Asian steppe by nomadic peoples whose economy and society were based upon animal husbandry, whereas China's sedentary and village-based population specialized in agricultural production that required intensive use of arable land and left relatively little pasturage for the grazing of herds of horses or cattle.

The importation of goods and animals was not the only form of foreign trade that had an impact on China. Musical instruments were imported along with music; decorative designs accompanied *objets d'art* and *objets de curiosité*. Horsemanship and horses came together. Scientific and other forms of knowledge came in with trade. Most important of all, perhaps, Buddhism, with its profound impact upon the intellectual, spiritual, social, and architectural life of China, was imported through the same far-flung networks of trade routes that were the means for China's commercial interaction with the rest of the world.

The pattern in which Chinese goods were in greater demand abroad than foreign goods were in China (in contemporary terms an unequal balance of trade) was already discernable in the Han period and was to be characteristic of China's commercial relations with the outside world down until the middle of the nineteenth century. Indeed, as we shall see later, it was within the context of this structure of trade that changes were to take place that would, in the middle of the nineteenth century, result in the destruction of the traditional pattern of Chinese foreign relations.

The greatest trade commodity of all, however, was Chinese culture itself, and its export was based upon China's recognized superiority in intellectual and material culture. Once a degree of synonymity was established between the concept of civilization and the reality of Chinese culture, and once this synonymity was buttressed by the real superiority of China's material culture, the importation of various aspects of Chinese culture by the rulers and elites of the peoples surrounding China was a logical development. The adoption of the Chinese written language as the official and cultural language in Japan, Korea, the Ryukyu Islands, and Annam, for example, is an example of the export of Chinese culture, as is the adoption of the Chinese calendar, Chinese literature, and so forth. It should be noted here (see below for further discussion) that Chinese culture was exported primarily to those areas that ecologically resembled China itself and that it continued to be an active element in some of those areas and cultures down into the twentieth century.

Three primary factors inhibited the spread of Chinese culture and Chinese artifacts beyond a limited area, however. First, the technology of transportation did not encourage the movement of large numbers of people or large quantities of goods over a great distance at economical speeds. Years were required before Chinese goods reached Western Asia, and the hardships of travel overland to India were well known. The difficulties of transportation within China were magnified many times abroad by difficulties of terrain and hostility of populations, which made trade routes dangerous, and by a technological level that was insufficient to overcome these factors. Although Chinese were present along the Southeast and South Asian shipping routes and were versed in the maritime arts, the bulk of long-distance maritime trade was, from earliest days, carried in non-Chinese bottoms manned by non-Chinese crews and merchants. This also inhibited the spread of Chinese culture outside of East and Southeast Asia.

The second factor inhibiting the expansion of China's foreign relations was the existence of hostile environments. In Southeast Asia, as Chinese culture began to penetrate the eastern and southern coasts, Indian culture, with its own powerful center in the subcontinent and its own aesthetic, intellectual, and material achievements, was spreading eastward through Burma, eventually reaching Thailand, Cambodia, Laos, and parts of the Indonesian Archipelago. Indian culture also had a major influence in Tibet, to the northeast of India. Chinese culture and cultural products, therefore, met Indian culture along a line that extended from Indonesia in the southeast through Southeast Asia and along the Sino-Tibetan border, and neither technological nor cultural development suggested the possibility of a further expansion of Chinese culture into the Indian area.

A third factor, one much more difficult to describe, is the sinocentric quality of Chinese culture itself. Having created its own image of itself as the center of the world, the Chinese state and population were for the most part, though not completely, disinterested in the twilight world of non-Chinese cultures. This remained true down through the middle of the nineteenth century. Foreign trade developed not because the Chinese thirsted after foreign goods but because foreign merchants came to China to trade. China's knowledge of the outside world developed not because Chinese fanned out across the trade routes to gather information but, by and large, because foreigners coming to China brought information that struck the Chinese as delightfully quaint. This intellectual and cultural self-satisfaction paralleled closely the self-sufficiency of Chinese material culture. In the Ming dynasty (1368–1644), for example, the far-ranging maritime expeditions captained by the eunuch and imperial favorite Cheng He between 1405 and 1433, which reached the Middle East and the coast of East Africa, did not lead to further exploration or development because of the lack of any cultural or commercial impetus in that direction. The lack of such an impetus supported the dynasty's basically anti-foreign commerce policies (see below).

Conclusion

The factors that inhibited the expansion of Chinese culture and its influence beyond East and Southeast Asia and those parts of Central Asia bordering on China proper clearly inhibited the development of an East Asian Chinese imperialism in the modern sense of the term. China's sense of its own civilization did not include an aggressive mission either to civilize the rest of the world or to shoulder its burdens; the Chinese did not feel the need to bring the blessings of their technology, religions, or governmental system to other peoples. When other peoples adopted and adapted elements of Chinese culture, they did so for their own reasons, and the Chinese were always welcoming to those who wished to transform themselves into members of civilization, but they did not, like the French,

English, and Americans in the nineteenth and twentieth centuries, try to civilize the world by subduing it and turning it into a replication of themselves. Nor did the Chinese traditional economy develop a voracious appetite for the products, the raw materials, or the cheap labor of other economies. The technology of the Chinese economy was far advanced over European technology until the late eighteenth century, but it combined with China's own particular structure of social relationships to impel the economy and society in the direction of self-sufficiency, not foreign expansion through trade or distant conquests.

Within the context both of these inhibitions and of a coherent view of the world that constituted the ideology of the state and of the elite ruling groups of Chinese society down to the beginning of the twentieth century, China developed a system for the conduct of its foreign relations that was the institutional expression of its social ideology, on the one hand, and, on the other, the direct reflection and consequence of the political and economic needs of Chinese society and the technological level that that society had reached. This system, which evolved through the centuries, reached its classical form in the Ming and Qing dynasties. The so-called tribute system functioned, and functioned well, until the middle of the nineteenth century, when economic, social, technological, and ideological changes in the world outside China reached a point where the system had to give way before them. It is to the description of that system that we will now turn.

The World Ordered

BETWEEN 1368, WHEN the Chinese Ming dynasty was founded, and 1842, when the English victory over the Manchu Qing dynasty (1644–1912) in the First Opium War initiated the disintegration of traditional Confucian society, China's foreign political, economic, and cultural relations were conducted in a world it ordered by, and experienced through, the tribute system. Any Western attempt to describe this complex traditional system faces three intellectual problems at the outset.

First, the system cannot be explained in nineteenth- or twentieth-century Western terms. It is dangerous to find modern Western equivalents for traditional Confucian institutions or concepts: they may resemble each other in structure or function and yet have quite different significances when examined within the contexts of traditional Confucian and modern Western societies. The tribute system must be understood, in all its ramifications, in terms of the vocabulary and institutions of traditional China itself.

Second, it must be constantly borne in mind that the concept of the tribute system is a Western invention for descriptive purposes. The Confucian scholar-bureaucrat did not conceive of a tribute system (there is no Chinese word for it) as an institutional complex complete within itself or distinct from the other institutions of Confucian society. Consequently, although a whole series of definitions and descriptions of the structures and functions of the tribute system exists for various countries' relations with China, none is complete in itself or related structurally or functionally to other definitions and descriptions for other countries; each, like a link in a chain, may be discrete, but all joined together they become a definition and description of a whole because the chain exists only by virtue of this combination. The tribute system is merely the observer's simultaneous

13

conceptualization of a large number of distinct but structurally and functionally interdependent political and social processes that took place through time in an extended geographical area.

Third, a sharp analytic distinction must be made between the form and the function of any institution. Historian-observers, like the actors themselves—the Confucian scholar-bureaucrats and the barbarian chieftains—recognize the tribute system by its forms, which are consciously described in documents and represented in symbolic acts. But the empirical function of the whole complex of institutions can be described only as a result of abstract conceptualization based on documentary research against the background of the total society and culture of China after the Mongols' Yuan dynasty (1279–1368). This function cannot be deduced merely from the forms of the institutions as described in the documents.

The Tribute System

The phenomena of the tribute system were, like all social phenomena, neither unique nor discrete. The tribute system contained all the threads of which the traditional Chinese social fabric was composed between the middle of the fourteenth and the beginning of the twentieth century. Chinese and Confucian concepts of philosophy, morality, economics, politics, and war found expression in the tribute system. It even had an aesthetic aspect; the correct performance of ritual was aesthetically pleasing, and unusual *objets d'art* often were presented as tribute. Moreover, geographical and technological conditions interpenetrated with the tribute system's social structure. In any society, all phenomena interact and are related by virtue of the fact that each individual is a carrier of his own culture and lives with others who carry the same, or almost the same, traits. Consequently, the institutional conduct of traditional Chinese foreign relations can be grasped intellectually only if the entire tribute system is analyzed as a complex of concrete " 'total' social phenomena" from which, for convenience, some abstractions are made in the study of specific parts.[1] The patterns of behavior that constituted the tribute system must be studied through the examination of individual and discrete historical acts revealing historically derived patterns and arrangements that add up to part of the unique tradition of Imperial China, a tradition that served the needs of that particular society in its contacts with all other societies approaching it, whether by land or by sea. The tribute system was of a high order of generality, and its patterns of behavior themselves summarized, symbolized, and evaluated the historical, economic and social development of Chinese civilization, instantly recognizable as such by the carriers of Confucian civilization but not by Westerners, whose own behavior patterns derived from a different tradition.

The tribute system functioned to intermesh rather than to integrate the Central, East, and Southeast Asian societies that were derivative of, or peripheral to, China and the region's preponderant Confucian society and tradition. The intermeshing of one or more societies or cultures with China involved, broadly speaking, patterns of behavior and institutions through which material goods, political positions, and ideological statements were communicated between otherwise discrete societies, that is, societies between which the system functioned to maintain a prescribed and optimal distance. This intermeshing was more than mere contact because it was highly institutionalized and simultaneously took place along several dimensions, such as the economic, the political, and the cultural. The existence at any given moment of a wide variety of mechanisms for intermeshing allowed participants in East Asian international society a choice of means to achieve their ends. For instance, through the medium of trade, Central Asia's nomadic animal-husbandry economy intermeshed with China's sedentary agricultural economy. Since societies apparently consist of an aggregate of disparate actions and structures, however, intermeshing also took place in forms that were institutionally less clearly defined than, say, the marketplace; nevertheless, these were equally important for the definition of an East Asian international order. Thus, economic intermeshing took place at certain times not through trade but through warfare in the form of either predatory raids or permanent conquest; while permanent conquest, as when the Manchus conquered China in the seventeenth century, had clear political implications, raids did not. On the other hand, frontier trade and frontier military defense—the one primarily economic and the other political—merged into one system of interdependent actions and structures that included the dispatch of tribute bearing missions to the capital, Peking, some distance from the frontier, and the issuance of patents of office by Peking to rulers tributary to China's emperor but located far beyond China's political frontier. In one sense the tribute system was simply the recognizable, stable recurrence of discrete social phenomena that shared certain characteristics. Between 1662 and 1911 well over five hundred tribute missions called at Peking from sixty-two different countries. Each mission was unique, but at the same time each was part of a larger pattern that implied a theoretical potential for infinite repetition and stability.

The tribute system served other functions in addition to the intermeshing of China and its neighbors. The system, boundary mechanism between the barbarian world and Confucian China, played a role analogous to that of a boundary mechanism between nature and its fluctuations, on the one hand, and the society of man, on the other. The "mandate of heaven" (*tian-ming*) usually has been defined as heaven's granting the right to rule to a wise and virtuous emperor, who could lose his mandate if he failed to follow the precepts of Confucianism. The emperor's failures, in turn, would cause natural disasters that symbolized the emperor's, or his dynasty's, loss of the mandate. The mandate functioned as a means of legitimizing both a dynasty's rule and a successful rebellion against it. However, it may also be viewed as what the economic historian Karl Polanyi[2] called a "boundary mechanism," an institution that functions at the boundary between society and nature or between two societies (regardless of their geographic proximity) in order to communicate and explain changes in a society's natural or social environment. The concept of the mandate of heaven provided an ideological explanation for what happened to the economy or to society when floods or famines occurred and people were dislocated, as often took place in China. In other words, this notion translated natural into social fluctuations by placing both under one ideological canopy or system of explanation.

The tribute system operated as a boundary mechanism in "social nature": it translated barbarian impingements on Chinese society into social terms comprehensible to the Confucian Chinese, thus minimizing fluctuations like a kind of conductor-reductor that filtered barbarian pressures into a Confucian conceptual context. The system functioned as an ideational process within the "boundary sphere" between the "purely barbarian" and the "purely Chinese." In this capacity, it maintained the line separating the processes that were internal to Chinese society (and composed it) from the barbarian processes that while external to Chinese society were causally related to certain Chinese social processes. The tribute system performed this function by keeping the fluctuations in the barbarian environment from impinging on Chinese society in forms, or to degrees, not taken into account by Confucian Chinese institutionalized expectations. Thus, for instance, continual barbarian raids on China's frontiers could be interpreted as symbolic of the dynasty's loss of the mandate of heaven, particularly when such raids resulted in drains on the state treasury, rises in taxes, and losses of personnel. But the raids could not challenge China's view of itself as the central kingdom since the tribute system explained the raids in terms of the emperor's personal lack of virtue rather than in socioeconomic terms that might require a revision of China's institutional relations with the barbarians. This may explain the remarkable persistence of certain institutions within the Sino-Confucian tradition.

The organization of the tribute system's major formal institutions, which were more refined and more differentiated under the Qing than under the Ming, reflected the system's buffer function. During the Ming, tributary relations were supervised by the Reception Department of the Board of Ceremonies (also known as the Board of Rites), the high government office charged with responsibility for the maintenance and correct execution of the rituals that were so central to Confucian theory and Chinese social practice. Only relations with certain tribes of aborigines along China's cultural frontiers (which were not necessarily coterminous with the area of the emperor's effective power) were managed by a department of the Board of War, the government's military office. Although the statutes of the Ming dynasty contained a clear geographical distinction for purposes of description between, for instance, northern barbarians and others, the law did not distinguish between them in the organization of formal tributary mechanisms. The Manchus, however, modified and refined this system even before their conquest of China Proper in 1644. An office was created to handle Manchu relations with the Mongols probably before the official establishment of the Manchus' Qing dynasty at Mukden in 1636, and in 1638 this Mongolian Office became the "Li-fan Yuan," usually translated "Mongolian Superintendency" or the "Court of Colonial Affairs" but perhaps more properly translated, in view of both the exact meaning of the title and the nature of the institution, as the "Barbarian Control Office." After the Manchu entry into China in 1644 and the transfer of the dynastic capital to Peking, the Manchus integrated the Li-fan Yuan into the tribute system, which they inherited from their Ming predecessors, and this office used the rites and forms of the traditional Confucian Chinese system to conduct relations with the so-called barbarians. With the expansion of the Manchu dominions, the Li-fan Yuan managed relations with Xinjiang and Tibet, as well as with Mongolia.

The establishment of the Li-fan Yuan was originally predicated on the specific nature of the Manchu relationship with the Mongols. The latter were the Qing dynasty's first allies and vassals. Like the Manchus, the Mongols were a frontier people essentially peripheral to China, the center of East Asian civilization. From China they wished to draw luxury goods and political benefits by raid or by trade, and they participated in the Manchu conquest of China as an auxiliary military force. The Mongols were Lamaists, Buddhists who looked toward Tibet as their spiritual center, not Confucians facing the emperor's throne. The Manchu alphabet derived from the Mongolian, and the Manchu language contained many borrowings from Mongolian, the result of long contact. Once the Manchus had conquered China, included it in their empire, and moved their capital to Peking, it was to their advantage to maintain the Li-fan Yuan as the instrument for handling the problems they faced in Central Asia, problems common to all continentally oriented dynasties in the North China Plain throughout Chinese history: the control of the Central Asian peoples, through techniques of divide-and-rule, and the prevention of attacks along other frontiers.

The inclusion of Xinjiang, Tibet, and Mongolia under the tributary jurisdiction of the Li-fan Yuan, rather than under the Board of Rites, indicates that the preconquest Manchu-Mongol alliance was not the sole reason for the division of the essentially single Ming tribute system into two by the Manchus. The existence during the Qing of two tributary institutions, the Board of Rites and the Li-fan Yuan, that did not overlap in their geographical responsibilities though they used the same ritual procedures, suggests that the Manchu image of the East Asian world differed from that of the Ming. Under the Ming, the world was divided into two distinct parts: China and non-China. In a conservative Confucian Chinese reaction to barbarian domination under the Yuan dynasty of the Mongols, the Ming raised high barriers between itself and the outside world, regardless of the nature of any particular part of that world. The Qing, however, lived in a perceptually more complex environment. The Manchus themselves came from an economy that was originally a mixture of hunting, fishing, and animal husbandry, technologically far different from the sedentary grain-growing economy of China. That the Manchus clearly recognized a difference between themselves and the Chinese was evident throughout their dominion in China, where strict regulations prohibited marriage to Chinese and where Manchus did not become peasants but remained fairly strictly within the structure of their own martial society. The Qing court went so far as to attempt the preservation of the difference by means of ritual hunts recalling the Manchus' original way of life. Mongolia, Xinjiang, and Tibet, forming a crescent astride China's northern frontier, shared certain fundamental characteristics. With the partial exception of the precarious, oasis-based agriculture of portions of Xinjiang and Tibet, they were regions suited more to extensive, nomadic animal husbandry than to intensive agriculture. Where cities existed at all, as at Urga in Mongolia or Lhasa in Tibet, they were based primarily not on the control of the agricultural hinterland, as in China, but on particular religious and commercial functions, from which they derived their livelihood. In this fashion the societies of the northern crescent more resembled the Manchu homeland in Manchuria than they did China Proper, and this resemblance was emphasized by Manchu prohibitions on Chinese emigration to any of these areas. None of these regions, including most of Manchuria before 1636, had accepted Confucianism and other aspects of Chinese culture as the organizing principles of their own societies.

On the other hand, the regions to the east, southeast, and south of China were sharply different from the northern crescent that extended from Manchuria through Central Asia to Tibet. Like China they were dominated, or presumed to be dominated, by sedentary grain-growing economies. They had adopted, or were supposed to have adopted, Confucian principles for the organization of government. They used the Chinese calendar and employed the Chinese language in addressing themselves to the emperor (and in Korea, Annam, or Vietnam, and Liuqiu, even within their own governments). Their rulers were understood to be traditional Confucian monarch-vassals of the emperor of China. Japan, Korea, and Annam may, in fact, have fitted this pattern of expectation fairly closely, and if Siam, Burma, and Sulu did not they were still agricultural economies somewhat resembling China. All the organized states in this southeastern crescent, which extended from Japan and Korea through Southeast Asia to Burma, shared with China details of environment, military and civil technology, and economic organization. Consequently, the world as viewed by the Manchu conquerors of China was also divided in two, but not along the China—non-China axis of the Ming. China Proper and East, Southeast, and South Asia appeared to belong to one ecological system, and the only region in East Asia that exhibited distinctive environmental characteristics was the northern crescent of societies. While all the others were primarily grain-producing and intensively settled regions, the northern crescent was *neither* grain producing nor intensively settled. Furthermore, it differed from China in its cultural symbols. Beyond China and its two surrounding crescents lay wasteland, deserts, high mountains, impenetrable forests, and water, the existence of which contributed to the unity and autonomy of East Asia and made it an almost closed international socioeconomic system. Beyond the wasteland, in Western Europe and the Western Hemisphere, lived peoples in outer darkness, and though they eventually impinged on the world of East Asia they were not institutionally recognized by it until 1842.

The organization of the tribute system reflected this Manchu perception of the Empire's environment. The societies of East, Southeast, and South Asia were included within the jurisdiction of the Board of Rites, which was also charged with the performance of that broad spectrum of rites that transmitted Confucian culture inside China. Ritually, therefore, these regions were an extension of China Proper beyond the immediate control of the emperor. The societies of the northern crescent, however, were under the jurisdiction of the Li-fan Yuan, whose sole function was the conduct of intercourse between them and the Qing.

Though ritual practice in the Li-fan Yuan was the same as in the Board of Rites, the northern crescent was institutionally set off from the main body of China by the Li-fan Yuan's very existence. In other words, the Board of Rites and the Li-fan Yuan functioned in different social, economic, and ecological environments. This divergence was reflected in the forms and degree of intermeshing required for the maintenance of relations between China and nomadic Asia, on the one hand, and China and agricultural Asia, on the other. Granted, economic similarity between communities may well give rise to disunion; social cohesion depends to a large extent on economically or ecologically *necessary* exchanges, not merely on the exchange of marginal items. For instance, trade between China and Southeast Asia may have been economically convenient for Peking since the transportation costs on Siamese rice brought to the China coast by sea were lower than those on rice brought to the coast from certain interior Chinese provinces. However, rice *was* available in the interior of China and the state could survive without the importation of rice from Southeast Asia. In contrast, China and the societies of the northern crescent were engaged in exchanges that were considered necessary for the stability of Chinese society. The imperial power in China needed horses and other products of Central Asia's animal-husbandry economy that were not available locally in sufficient quantities to satisfy the Empire's requirements. The Central Asians, for their part, needed Chinese tea, other agricultural products, and handcrafted goods. Therefore, this exchange relationship was more one of necessity than of convenience. The Li-fan Yuan, the Qing response to this necessity, represented a significant modification of the Ming dynasty's institutions for intercourse with Central Asia and a more sophisticated approach to the institutionalization of exchange relationships between differing ecologies. In this respect, the Li-fan Yuan can be considered one of the instruments for the exploitation of the natural resources of the East Asian resource complex, particularly the northern crescent. While not necessarily the most efficient instrument in purely economic terms, the tribute system, of which the Li-fan Yuan was one element, brought to China Proper the products of the entire resource system in East Asia. In effect, then, the tribute system was a total system for the conduct of *all* international relations. The intermeshing of China and the surrounding communities took place on several levels: ideological, ritual, and economic.

The Ideology and Politics of the Tribute System

Behind the immediately observable phenomena of the traditional East Asian world order stood certain presuppositions that, as ideology or philosophy, helped shape the system. These presuppositions concerned not only the nature of the universe, on the broadest level, but the political tools and moves available to the policymakers as well.

To paraphrase Gregory Bateson,[3] the Chinese were constantly simplifying and generalizing their perceptions of their physical and sociocultural environment and constantly imposing their constructions and learning on it. Because their environment included societies and ecological systems different from and peripheral to the region dominated by Chinese culture and imperial power, the Chinese (and, later, the Confucianized and sinicized Manchus) imposed on the entire universe of observable phenomena constructions that were characteristic of Confucian culture. China's physical location in the universe and level of technological development conditioned the Chinese interpretation and perception of their social environment. In other words, the societies of Mongolia, Tibet, Siam, and Burma were all observable phenomena because East Asian technology, both Chinese and barbarian, permitted travel of personnel in sufficient numbers to allow an accumulation of information about these peoples at Peking.

Russia and England were not observable phenomena in the same sense except insofar as their citizens came to China, where epistemologically they fitted into the system of premises that were part of the Sino-Confucian cultural tradition. The sinocentric world order disintegrated when the tribute system's ideology could no longer account for the observable phenomena of the East Asian environment, such as the new and at first but dimly understood technology of English sea power in Eastern waters at the beginning of the nineteenth century, and when the exercise of the traditional Chinese instruments of persuasion, politics, and power failed to bring England into conformity with the tribute system.

The cornerstone of the Confucian world view was a concept of the universe—the entire cosmos—as an unbroken, orderly stasis-continuum. Unlike the Judeo-Christian chiliastic image of time as a process, the Confucian view conceived of the world as *being*, which, as Joseph Levenson[4] pointed out, "is by definition different from becoming." Process, change, and progress were all concepts unnatural to the Confucian; they were either deviations from the norm or unthinkable notions. Although the phenomena of the universe were interrelated in the continuum, every phenomenon had its uniquely correct name, which was its essence. Only by giving every thing its correct name, by recognizing the essence of every phenomenon in his universe, could man assimilate himself to the order that was the natural state of the universe. Consequently, relativism had no place in the Confucian universe. Virtue, for instance, was absolute, not relative; moreover, it was described and defined in the Confucian classics and the accepted commentaries thereto. These classics, which significantly included no epics or figures of epic proportions, were textbooks on the nature of the continuum, and when events or actors appeared, as in the *Classic of History*, they were important as illustrations of virtue, not as historical causes of effects. Consequently, history was concerned not with change through time but with virtuous action in a universe that was essentially timeless because it was phenomenally endlessly cyclical.

Human society, a part of the continuum, was hierarchical; equality did not exist, only hierarchically arranged ranks of social classes and men. The hierarchy was symbolized in official ideology and sumptuary laws. Stability and order, which were the highest virtues in the cosmological continuum, were secured through the maintenance of hierarchy and the performance of rituals. Man, however, was the basic source of evil because neglect or incorrect performance of ritual, which arose from man's failure to perceive the true nature of the universe, resulted in natural and social disorder. For instance, the emperor's failure to perform correctly the annual fertility rite of plowing a sacred furrow might result in crop failure, famine, and mass dislocation, leading to rebellion. It must be emphasized, however, that ritual was not a causative factor in the universe but rather a part of the continuum. The incorrect performance of ritual introduced a note of discord into the harmony of the continuum that could have far-reaching consequences since all parts of the continuum resonated to changes in any one part. These Confucian philosophical abstractions concerning the nature of the universe were not, in the Ming and Qing dynasties, simply hypotheses offered for debate but were the official description of nature and, as such, they directly influenced the Chinese perception of the world order.

Neither China nor Chinese civilization existed from the Confucian point of view. There was only civilization and barbarism, which were conceptually related in that they defined each other. Civilization was "an empire without neighbors."[5] In this sense the Chinese state was not a state in the conventional Western mold; rather, it was the administration of civilized society *in toto*, and the emperor, far from being the ruler of one state among many, was the mediator between heaven and earth, a cardinal point in the universal continuum, the apex of civilization, unique in the universe. In other words, the emperor was both a temporal political ruler and a figure of cosmic dimensions. The rituals he performed, or those performed about him, were not particularistic but universal. He plowed the sacred furrow not so that Chinese crops would grow but so that crops *per se* could grow.

The emperor possessed two distinct but related formal personalities. As a point in the cosmos he was the embodiment of virtue; by his very nature he carried out the rites required for the continuing harmony of the universe in both its natural and its social aspects. This personality was identified by the title *tianzi*, "son of heaven," a son not in a biological but in a holistic sense. His second personality was human. As the man at the apex of organized civilization, the emperor was styled *huangdi*, or "emperor." In this personality he could stray from the path of true virtue, betraying his role as son of heaven and causing disharmony in the universe.

Presentation of tribute to the emperor was the ritual appropriate to maintenance of the world order; it was recognition not simply or even necessarily of *China's* superior civilization but of civilization itself, whose highest point was the emperor of China, whoever he was (regardless of ethnic origin, he had to be "civilized," that is, Chinese in culture). As the son of heaven, the emperor connected human society to the rest of the cosmos. Entry into the emperor's presence or court required recognition of these principles through the correct performance of the rituals and through tribute presentation. Refusal to perform the rituals was tantamount to an insult to the universal scheme of things, an unnatural act that could not be tolerated by the emperor since it was his role to maintain the harmony of the cosmos. Because the Chinese conception of the universe was devoid of relativity, the rituals could not be compromised, and no barbarian could be admitted to the emperor's presence unless he performed the prescribed rituals. This did not mean, of course, that he could not visit or even reside at Peking. Russians, for instance, lived in Peking almost continuously after 1727, but because they did not seek entry into the emperor's presence they were not required to perform the rituals. The British in the late eighteenth and the early nineteenth century mistook what was a ritual with politico-philosophical intent for a purely political act and therefore were unable to gain access to the emperor's person. What in Europe was a political issue was in China by very definition a moral issue.

The Confucian world view gave rise to other discontinuities between Western and traditional Chinese diplomatic practice. For instance, in the Far East the written word assumed primacy over all other forms of communication. In part this was because as an ideographic script the Chinese written language could be understood by the initiated regardless of the ability to speak Chinese. A given character had the same meaning in Peking, Seoul, Tokyo, and Hanoi regardless of its pronunciation. Equally if not more important, however, was the role of the written word as the conveyor of virtue. Textual criticism of the classics was more than a simple scholarly pursuit, and even in popular religion the written word assumed ritual importance that it lacked in the West. Consequently, in diplomacy an ambassador's credentials and the letters he carried from his master were valued more highly, and treated with greater reverence, than the person of the ambassador. Time and again in Russian and British relations with Peking, and even in British relations with Confucian Annam, which was not Chinese, the relative value of the ambassador's person and his documents was a source of contention. In the West the ambassador as the personal representative of his master partook of his master's official personality. International law even today recognizes the physical and legal immunity of the ambassador and his embassy. In the East Asian diplomatic scheme of things, however, the ambassador was fundamentally a messenger conveying his master's letters. His own person was not inviolate and he might, in fact, be harshly treated. Western envoys to Peking before 1842 often complained that they were ill handled by their hosts and, significantly, that such mistreatment was not simply unpleasant but constituted, they felt, a personal insult to the envoy's master.

On the plane of social philosophy, the tribute system was considered the extension of the social structure of civilization into the realms beyond the immediate power of the emperor. The five Confucian relationships—ruler and subject, father and son, husband and wife, elder brother and younger brother, friend and friend—often provided the vocabulary for specific tributary relationships. Moreover, the emperor constantly used the terminology that expressed his relationship to his Chinese subjects to describe his relationships with the tributary states; he showed them compassion, encouraged them, and nourished them.

The tribute system was a bilateral, never a multilateral, relationship in which one partner was always the ruler of China. When discontinuities

threatened the system it was often because China's partner in the relationship could not accept, ideologically or institutionally, necessary elements
of the system itself. Conversely, however, when continuity of relationship
existed, through both time and space, the non-Chinese power was able to
find in its own presuppositions some factor or factors that enabled it to fit
the tribute system into its own political and intellectual universe. In other
words, within the tribute system any power's relationship with China depended in large measure on the partner's cultural tradition; the structure
and content of the particular relationship could not be a glaring exception
to either side's tradition. The ideological intermeshing of tributary states
with China varied from complete acceptance of Confucianism as the tributary state's own ideology, as in Annam (Vietnam), to parallel sets of assumptions, as in the case of Siam, to total political cynicism in the search
for survival, as among the Turks in Central Asia.

   Vietnam, like Korea and Ryukyu, was a Chinese tributary state participating in the East Asian world order on the basis of its own Confucian
heritage, the product of centuries of direct Chinese control and indirect
political and cultural influence. The structure of Vietnam's government,
the cultural life of the elite and the court, and Vietnam's literature were
all patterned on Chinese models; its written language was pure Chinese,
and its spoken tongue was strongly influenced by the latter. Confucianism,
along with its characteristic examination system, dominated the country's
political and intellectual life. The degree to which the Vietnamese kings
themselves accepted the Confucian world view is apparent in an official
nineteenth-century document that describes an event that took place in
179 B.C.E., during the Han dynasty, long before the East Asian world order achieved its classic form under the Ming and the Qing. The report
clearly illustrates Vietnam's full acceptance of Confucian institutions on
their own terms. When Emperor Wendi of the Han ascended the throne
in 179 B.C.E., he sent a letter to the Vietnamese king in which he discussed frontier affairs, particularly referring to some recent disturbances.
Assuring the king of Vietnam that he had no interest in occupying Vietnamese territory, the emperor wrote:

> Although you govern independently you have changed your title from king to
> emperor. When two emperors appear simultaneously, one must be destroyed;
> sending an ambassador to communicate the "way" [of this] may cause a strug-
> gle. Struggling and not yielding is not the way of a person endowed with
> humanity.

   The emperor concluded that he was sending an ambassador to Vietnam
bearing gifts and that he thought it suitable for the Vietnamese king to
submit himself to the will of the emperor.
   The king of Vietnam informed the Chinese envoy that he respectfully
submitted to the emperor's will "as a tributary subject" and promised to

send tribute in the proper fashion. He then issued a proclamation to his people in which he declared that

> I hear that two heroes cannot appear together, that two sages cannot exist in the same generation. The Han emperor (*huangdi*) is the sagacious son of heaven (*tianzi*). Henceforth I shall suppress my own imperial edicts, imperial cart, and the [imperial] banner of the left command.

Finally, the Vietnamese king wrote the Han emperor a letter, which is worth quoting extensively because it fully expresses his understanding and acceptance of the tributary philosophy:

> I, the great chief of the barbarians, with temerity worthy of death, worshipping twice, present [this] to His Majesty the Emperor. I was formerly an official of Viet. [Han] Gaodi deigned to confer on me the seal and ribbon [attached to the seal] and invested me as king of Nam-viet. When the August emperor [Han] Huidi ascended the throne, he in justice did not dismiss me and treated me extremely generously. When the empress Gao retained power, she divided the Chinese from the barbarians (i.e., civilized from barbarian) and issued a decree saying, "It is forbidden to send to Nam-viet agricultural implements made of iron, and if horses, oxen, and sheep are to be sent, there should be sent only males and not females." I live in a remote region, and my horses, oxen, and sheep were already very old. I thought that having performed the rituals incorrectly, I was being subjected to the death penalty. I sent Phien, president of my secretariat, and Cao, the general of my army, and Binh, my censor, officials of three classes, to present a letter, confessing the past. None returned. Moreover, I heard rumors that my parents' tombs and sepulchers had already been despoiled and that my brothers and relatives had already been put to death. I conferred with my ministers who advised me saying, "Now, if inside you are unable to shake [yourself free] from the Han, outside you will have no means of rising and distinguishing yourself." That is why I changed my title, calling myself emperor. I governed my country as emperor but did not dare harm the empire (i.e., *tianxia* all under heaven, the Chinese empire). When Emperor Gaodi heard this, he was exceedingly angry and erased the Nam-viet ambassadorial list (i.e., cancelled the tribute regulations as applied to Nam-viet). Ambassadors were not exchanged. I furtively suspected I had been slandered by the king of Truong Sa. That is why I sent troops to attack his frontier. Moreover . . . the chiefs of Dong Nam and Tay An called themselves kings; I called myself emperor for the purpose of giving myself pleasure. How would I dare to inform the Heavenly King (i.e., the emperor)? I have lived in Viet for forty-nine years. Now I carry in my arms my grandchildren. Still, I rise early and bed late. I lie down and find no peace on my mat. I eat and find no flavor. My eyes do not perceive the brilliant colors. My ears do not hear the sounds of bell and drum, all because I could not serve the Han. Now your Majesty graciously restores my old title and communicates through an ambassador as of old. Therefore, when I die my bones will not rot. I change my title and dare not call myself emperor. . . . (Here follows a list of tributary goods sent to the emperor.) . . . With a temerity worthy of death I twice worshipfully inform Your Imperial Majesty of all this.

    The author clearly intended to create the image of a hierarchical trib-
utary relationship between the king of Vietnam and his superior, the emperor of China. Not only did the king state that he held his office at the
pleasure of the Chinese ruler; he went much further and declared that the
very well-being of Vietnam depended upon the good will of the Chinese,
without whose benediction even the horses, oxen, and sheep could not
reproduce. In a hierarchical world, he acknowledged, one disturbance
inevitably leads to another: incorrectly performed rituals lead to death and
retribution even beyond that; a change in titles leads to further changes in
titles; and an unimaginable expression of equality can lead to the disruption of daily life. It is no wonder that, according to reports, the Han emperor was pleased with this letter of confession and normal relations were
reestablished between China and Vietnam. The report concludes: "Afterwards, whenever the king sent ambassadors, if it was to the Han he called
himself king, and in [imperial] audiences he was ranked as a feudal prince.
Inside his own country he used his ancient title."[6] Whatever titles were
used *inside* Vietnam between ruler and ruled, the hierarchical harmony of
the universe was maintained by the use of correct titles between the ruler
of Vietnam and the emperor of China. In the Qing, the Vietnamese were
required to send tribute to Peking every two years and an envoy every
four years.
    This institutionalization of hierarchy, a central feature of Confucianism,
also influenced Vietnam's dealings with its own neighbors. In 1813, for
instance, Vietnamese troops drove the Siamese out of Cambodia at the
request of the Cambodian king. It was reported: "Our troops built two
walls and constructed a Pavilion of the Pacified Frontier [at Phnom Penh,
Cambodia], and on this pavilion they built a structure called the Yuyuan-
tang to be a place where the barbarian king (i.e., the Cambodian king) will
look toward Hue (the Vietnamese capital), worshipping."[7] This passage is
particularly interesting because it uses Chinese terminology for barbarians
when referring to Cambodians, i.e., the Vietnamese called the Cambodians *fan*, or "barbarians," though they referred to themselves in the same
terms in correspondence with the Chinese. Moreover, the Cambodians
were not Confucians and were outside the domain of influence of Chinese
culture. In fact, the Cambodians were well within the direct cultural
sphere of the Siamese and therefore within the broader cultural sphere of
India, whose influence on the Cambodians was mediated through Siam.
The Cambodians were Hinayana Buddhists and belonged to quite a different social and political philosophical tradition. The Vietnamese, for their
part, were Mahayana Buddhists and Confucian in their philosophy. And
yet, like the Chinese in their description of their relationship with the
Vietnamese, the Vietnamese described of their relations with Cambodia in
strictly Confucian terms, and the Cambodian king could fit himself into
this culturally alien structure.

Siam, like Cambodia but unlike Annam, was not Confucian. Although Rama I, who founded the Chakri dynasty in 1782, was part Chinese, the Siamese king was in no fashion a Confucian monarch. On the contrary, he was considered, in Siamese political theory, a reincarnated deity, a *chakravartin*. Moreover, he was a *bodhisattva*, a being destined to be a Buddha. His authority was absolute and his person was both sacred and unapproachable. His country was not influenced by Chinese culture, as was Vietnam: Siamese was written with an alphabetic script; the country's dominant religion was Hinayana Buddhism, and Brahmanic Hindus rather than Confucian literati dominated the ceremonial and intellectual life of the court. The Indian epic, the *Ramayana*, not the Confucian classics, was Siam's greatest literary monument. Mongkut, one of the most important of the Chakri kings (and the hero of *Anna and the King of Siam*), styled himself, in English, "by the blessing from the highest superagency of the whole universe, the first King of the Siamese kingdom and sovereign of all its dependent tributary countries lying around in adjacent states"[8]—indeed, Siam's king received tribute from various minor princes in Malaya, Laos, Cambodia, and Burma, when his strength was sufficient to demand it.

Siam's traditional foreign policy had one primary objective: accommodation with the region's dominant power. Until the arrival of the Europeans in Southeast Asia in force, this dominant power was China. Siam's accommodation with China was entirely within the context of the Confucian tributary system. During the Qing dynasty Siam sent forty-nine official tribute missions to Peking, almost three-fourths of them after the accession of the Chakri dynasty to the throne in Bangkok. This tribute system relationship was possible, however, not because Confucianism dominated Siamese thought, as it did Vietnamese, but because, first, Siamese political theory could accommodate Confucian pretensions without serious conflict and, second, because Bangkok's court ritual resembled, or was influenced by, Peking's.

A description of the coronation of King Prajdhipok of Siam in 1926, using forms that were characteristic of the Chakri court, reports that the king received the Great Crown of Victory from the hands of the Brahmanic high priest of Siva and placed it on his own head. A member of the Lord Chamberlain's Department of the Court of Siam remarked that "although he received the Crown from the hands of a representative of the god Siva, it is quite natural that a divine or priestly king would not tolerate the idea of actually being crowned by mortal hands."[9] The entire ceremonial, in fact, stressed the divine nature of the king, his identity with the godhead.

Paradoxically, it was precisely the king's divinity that enabled him to participate in the Chinese Confucian tribute system. The Siamese king, like the Chinese emperor, theoretically had two personalities, in this case a religious personality and a political one. In his religious personality the king of Siam was a *chakravartin*, or "universal emperor," as the Sanskrit title is sometimes translated. In ancient Hindu political theory, the *chakravartin* was not the head of state in any political, military, or bureaucratic sense; rather, he was an overlord or overking—the world emperor as it were. In this role he was the lord of the entire cosmic order. He was the extraordinary man who, because of his complete mastery of himself, could master the world in a very historical sense and could save it from decay and destruction. The kingship of the *chakravartin* had about it a universal quality that was largely spiritual, and the *chakravartin* was not necessarily a unique cosmological figure from the viewpoint of political philosophy. More than one *chakravartin* could exist in the world simultaneously and, consequently, the emperor of China did not constitute a challenge to this aspect of the Siamese king's kingship. Indeed, in the cosmological order of things, the Siamese could have considered the emperor of China a *chakravartin* and therefore incorporated him into their own political philosophy. China, in fact, was irrelevant.

In his political personality, on the other hand, the Siamese king found himself in a hierarchical situation in which, depending upon Siam's power at any given moment, he was either the giver or the recipient of tribute, or both. Siam's view of its position in the tribute system was not Confucian; instead, it was an extension of the king's objective political position, and his receipt of tribute from lesser princes did not necessarily preclude his presenting tribute to a prince greater than he, the emperor of China. At the same time, Siamese court ceremonial was strongly influenced by Chinese practice, particularly in the reception of ambassadors, which was a nonreligious, sociopolitical ceremony. In Siam as in China, the issue of foreign ambassadors' access to the ruler was complicated by the ceremonial demands of the court, and the right of foreign ambassadors to the Siamese court to follow their own customs was established only in the Bowring-Parkes Treaty of 1856. The Siamese, like the Chinese, prostrated themselves at state audiences until Chulalongkorn's accession to the throne in 1868, when the reforming king abolished that practice in Siam. Consequently, Peking's court practices were not so different from Bangkok's as to disturb the tributary relationship, and by the time prostration was ended at the Siamese court traditional tributary relationships with Peking had already been terminated (the last Siamese tributary mission visited Peking in 1853). Siam, therefore, fitted into the tributary pattern on the basis of secular state practice without disturbing its traditional non-Confucian religious and political world views.

In the north, along the crescent of Central Asian peoples, no dynasty based on the sedentary, bureaucratic society of China could tolerate the molestation of its frontier by nomadic raiders; they not only disturbed the bureaucratic process but also challenged the legitimacy of the dynasty in Confucian terms by suggesting that the emperor's inability to control the barbarian meant that the emperor had lost the mandate of heaven. Consequently, Central Asia, and not sedentary Southeast Asia, was always the primary focus of dynastic foreign policy, at least until the middle of the nineteenth century. China constantly sought to dominate the Central Asian steppes and deserts by demonstrating its military strength, trying to force the barbarians to recognize Chinese primacy within the context of prescribed Confucian rituals. While Confucian China was at most a military-political threat to the grain-growing societies of Southeast and East Asia, it posed a direct threat to the very way of life of the Turkish and Mongolian Central Asian nomads. And when the Manchu Nurhachi, who organized the Manchu state and founded the Qing dynasty, proposed an alliance to the Mongols, he implicitly recognized societal differences between the nomads and the sedentary Confucian Chinese as a basis for a joint military offensive against China:

> Although the two nations Dai-ming (the Ming dynasty) and Solongkha (Korea) have different tongues, the clothes they wear and the hair upon their heads are similar, and therefore those two nations live as one nation. Although we two nations [Manchus and Mongols] have different tongues, the clothes we wear and the hair upon our heads are similar. If you are an intelligent person, saying [to yourself] "at the moment when my elder brother, the Khan, is making war against the Dai-ming whom I have hated from ancient times; Father Heaven and Mother Earth favor him, and he breaches the cities in a great manner and is continuously overcoming the great enemy," then you send envoys [to me] saying, "I shall be of one accord with my elder brother, the Khan, whom the gods have favored, and shall make war against the hated Dai-ming nation." Would that not be right?[10]

Perhaps the clearest expression of nomadic suspicion of the Chinese appears in an ancient Turkish Orkhon inscription of the eighth century. The epitaph of the Turkic khan, Koltegin, written as if he himself were speaking, reads in part:

> In the Otukan fastnesses there was no real leader, but the Otukan fastness was just such a country in which it was possible to create a tribal alliance, and it was in this very country that having settled down, I joined my life with the Chinese. The Chinese people, giving us limitless amounts of gold, silver, alcohol [grain], and silk always had a sweet speech and luxurious treasures, and seducing us with this sweet speech and luxurious treasure they so strongly attracted faraway peoples to themselves, who settled close by, and then absorbed their evil practices. The Chinese and their allies could not divert the good and wise people, the noble heroes [from the true path]. But if [individuals] from among the Turks [did allow themselves to be seduced], whole clans did not turn away [from the true path]. . . .Having given yourselves over to seduction by their sweet words and precious gifts, you, O Turks, have perished in large numbers. Turks! When one part of you said, "I want to settle down not only on the right (i.e., on the south, towards China), in the Chogai fast-

nesses, but in the valley of the Tiun," then evil people so instructed a part of the Turks, saying, "To him who lives far away, the Chinese give poor gifts, but to him who lives close by, they give fine gifts." By these words they instructed you, and now you, people, not possessing true wisdom, have heeded their words, and having approached right up [to China] have perished there in great numbers. Thus, O Turks, when you go into that country you come to the edge of death, but when, on the other hand, you stay in your Otukan fastnesses, and only send caravans [for trade or tribute], you have no woes at all; when you remain in the Otukan fastnesses, establishing your eternal tribal union, you, O Turks, are sated.[11]

The clarity with which this document describes the threat China posed to the nomadic way of life is striking, as is the Khan's warning. It was only when Chinese military power was demonstrably greater than the nomads' ability profitably to raid the frontier that Confucian China could force the nomadic Turks and Mongols into the tribute system. That particular bilateral relationship rested on the relative strength of Chinese and nomadic military forces and on Mongol cynicism, which derived, on the one hand, from long conflict with China and, on the other, from conscious recognition of social and ideological incompatibility with China. This apparent cynicism persisted down to the twentieth century.

Thus, shared tradition was not essential to symbolic communication between China and other powers. In fact, the genius of the system was the extraordinary variety of Chinese political strategies: China's strength was not simply military. For analytic purposes, traditional Chinese strategies of intersocietal contact can be divided into four groups. Derived, respectively, from dynastic military power, dynastic weakness, Confucianism, and Chinese (but not necessarily Confucian) cultural superiority, the strategies largely reflected the paradoxical potential of China's strength, when dynastic vigor infused the Empire's frontiers, and of its weakness, when dynastic decline weakened the imperial frontiers and, often as not, encouraged a dangerous intellectual, aesthetic, and emotional introspection among courtiers and bureaucrats alike. There was always an interaction among these categories, and indeed by far the most important strategies were based on dynastic possession of military power, but there was no absolute correlation between the success of a particular strategy and the military power at the disposal of the dynasty. Dynastic policy planning was carried out almost entirely on a discrete, *ad hoc* basis, at any given moment representing a variety of the four strategy types.

The problem of establishing and guarding a boundary was fundamental. In the Chinese world view, legal boundaries could not exist between societies since all societies were part of a socially and culturally hierarchical, not a legal and egalitarian, universe; boundaries had to be given objective physical existence. The Great Wall, for instance, did not mark a boundary; it *was* the boundary. Erecting boundary markers at specified points, rather than merely drawing them on a map, was a more sophisticated expression of the same process. Given sufficient military power, the Great Wall, or a series of frontier stations, could be garrisoned. Frontier military colonies, for instance, defended the boundary they themselves formed.

However, the Chinese East Asian universe contained another form of boundary that could not be garrisoned: the outer limit of actual military power. While the latter might be coterminous with the physical boundary established on the ground, it was not necessarily so since the boundary on the ground had only a physical and not a legal existence. It was along this boundary of real power that strategies based on military strength developed that were more intensive than the simple garrisoning of a line of fortresses. Dynastic armies might, for example, conquer territory from which they would then withdraw, having exerted political power through the demonstration of military might. Such an area might then submit and enter the tribute system as, for instance, the Khalkha region of Outer Mongolia or Nepal in the Himalayas did at certain moments during the Qing dynasty. However, the memory of conquest could be erased by the rise of, say, new powers on the nether frontiers of the region in question, such as the development of Oirat power on the Khalkha frontier with Turkestan or of British power on the Nepalese frontier. Therefore, the dynasty might seek to organize the administration of the conquered region before withdrawing its troops, and the memory of the conquest would be perpetuated in the administration of the country despite the absence of Chinese forces. The presence of Qing officials (*ambans*) in Tibet, for instance, was meant as a constant reminder of the Qing military power that had conquered Tibet, even though the *ambans* exerted no real influence. The only actual extension of the Empire's political boundaries, and in fact the most intensive expression of China's military power, was the conquest, permanent garrisoning, and direct administration of a region.

Certain non-Confucian institutions of intersocietal contact were based on, but ancillary to, the demonstration of dynastic military might. For instance, barbarian rulers might be ennobled in the Qing dynastic table of ranks as a form of sino-barbarian administrative interpenetration that rested more on symbolism than upon actual administration. Thus, on several occasions in the seventeenth and eighteenth centuries the Khalkha Mongolian rulers made formal submission to the Qing emperor not in the context of the Confucian tradition but in that of their own nomadic-feudal tradition. Similarly, the dynasty issued to barbarian rulers and officials the same patents of office that in other situations had Confucian significance and in doing so legitimized the ruler's position among his own people by implying the availability of Chinese or Manchu power to protect his position. The marriage of imperial daughters to barbarian chieftains fell into this institutional genre, for the value of such marriages depended upon their serving as the human, indeed familial, vehicle of an alliance with a physical power mightier than the husband's. Marriage's role as a vehicle for alliance with military power, rather than with the Confucian emperor, is emphasized by the relative unimportance of the duties owed by the son-in-law to his wife's father in Confucian Chinese society.

Dynastic weakness did not necessarily leave the Empire strategically impotent. The famous policy of "using the barbarian to control the barbarian" by intricate diplomatic maneuvers was based on the need to defend a weak, not a strong, dynasty. Under duress, weak dynasties could avail themselves of a variety of strategies. The distribution of gifts, showing the emperor's benevolence and generosity toward his vassals, was the payment, in either cash or kind, of protection money intended to buy off potential barbarian predators. This was a particularly useful strategy during the Northern Song dynasty (960–1126), for example. At times, a Chinese dynasty was prepared to recognize the hierarchical superiority of the barbarians. When the barbarians conquered North China, the Song dynasty not only used this strategy but also surrendered territory and even recognized, in familial terms, the power superiority of the barbarians. The Southern Song (1127–1279) went so far as to present tribute to the barbarians. While this was an apparent reversal of the imperial view of China's own hierarchical centrality in the world, the presentation of tribute to a barbarian ruler maintained the order of the universe even if it cost China its position at the apex.

Total weakness gave rise to its own strategy, surrender. The West recognized this strategy in expressions such as the inappropriate and inexact "China always conquers her conquerors." The continuity of Chinese institutions even at the imperial level was guaranteed by China's vast size in comparison to that of the relatively few barbarian groups, which in any case required China's bureaucracy to rule China. Though this policy was not necessarily conscious, the barbarian conqueror of China fell victim to Chinese political techniques, without which he himself was administratively impotent over a long period of time. The strategy worked because the object of allegiance was the emperor, not the Chinese nation; try as he might, the emperor of China could not escape the influence of the institutions he needed to rule except through physical flight. Thus, while the Mongols, defeated by the Ming, returned to Mongolia and avoided sinification, the Manchus, despite elaborate institutional safeguards for their cultural integrity, inevitably fell victim to their own conquest of China through assimilation.

Confucianism, so dominant on the Chinese cultural scene, surprisingly gave rise to only one distinctive strategy: the ritual integration of Confucian non-Chinese into the Sino-Confucian world order through grants of patents of authority that rested on the mutual acceptance of Confucian hierarchical principles and the performance of certain ritual acts. Korean kings, for instance, accepted investiture in office from the Chinese emperors and sent them tribute missions regardless of the dynasty's military might, and they did this almost solely on the basis of Confucian principles, backed up by commercial advantage and the cultural and traditional image, though not necessarily the physical reality, of power.

Finally, several strategies derived from the cultural and material wealth of China. Trade, certainly the most important single strategic instrument at the disposal of the emperor, included, as in Outer Mongolia, the "corruption" of barbarian vigor through the introduction of sedentary luxuries into nomadic societies; these items, purchased on credit, meant ever increasing debt. This strategy, which was embedded in the very features that distinguished the Chinese economy and its goods from the barbarians', was not a consciously employed instrument of policy, yet it was remarkably effective. After 1860, for instance, Outer Mongolia's relationship with China was almost entirely that of a debtor. The debt was too large for the Chinese merchants to collect, but they kept the Mongolian aristocracy in a perpetual round of payment of interest on the debt, the collection of which was supported by the presence of Qing troops at urban centers in Mongolia. Barbarian chieftains, or their sons, also might be brought to the dynastic court and raised in the Chinese tradition, thus removing them from their own people and tying them by bonds of habit and custom to the imperial throne. Barbarian loyalty could be purchased with gifts, frontier trade, and the recognition of a barbarian ruler's honor and influence that was inherent in his reception of a dynastic embassy or imperial commissioner. Finally, Chinese or Chinese trained bureaucrats at times became key figures in the bureaucracy of a non-Chinese ruler and served as a moderating influence on him. The most striking example, of course, is the Mongolian employment of Yelu Chucai, who reputedly persuaded Chinggis Khan to pursue a more humane policy in his conquest of China than he had in his conquest of Central Asia.

The Tribute System
in the World

The Chinese behavior patterns or strategies in the international domain were mechanisms for the fulfillment of the tribute system's primary function; that is, they were intermeshing mechanisms that bridged the cleavages that separated Han Chinese society and its rulers from the surrounding social environment. The system can be located in visual terms in two perspectives. First, if we take the Chinese at their word and conceive of the traditional East Asian world order horizontally as a series of tangential rings with China at the epicenter (*zhongguo*, or "middle kingdom"), the tribute system was a mechanism for communication at the points of contact of the rings or over the cleavages between them. Second, viewed vertically, the Peking-centered tribute system was itself only the uppermost and most solemn part of a vast system of hierarchical relationships that seemed to embrace the entire intergroup and even interpersonal life of East Asia. The presentation of tribute to the emperor of China was the crowning episode of East Asian life. This practice was the gathering point of diverse institutions and subsystems at all levels of Asian life (even the peasant presented tribute, in the form of taxes delivered to the bureaucracy, to the emperor). One factor was common to all strategies and institutions: in East Asia the emperor sat at the center or apex of the international system not by law but by virtue of a prestige that was born of philosophy and power, as well as culture. The institutions that constituted the tribute system functioned, in their respective spheres, in the reflection of the emperor's prestige, but as institutions their functional (as opposed to their political or intellectual) legitimation did not depend directly on the emperor's real physical power but rather on their ability to perform certain tasks.

East Asian society was not simply a collection of minor potentates grouped around the emperor of China. While to the Chinese their emperor was both cosmologically and politically unique in the system, the rulers of the other parts, or sections, were not. There were, in fact, numerous lines of rulers both inside and outside China in descending order from the unique emperor. While the kings (*wang*) and khans were inferior to the emperor, there were princes inferior to kings, tribal chieftains inferior to civilized monarchs, and heads of innumerable institutions of local administration throughout the autonomous East Asian universe, all inferior to their superiors. But relative hierarchical position did not exhaust the social value of these dignitaries. Each ruler or administrator, regardless of his vertical position in the universal hierarchy, stood also for the identity and unity of his section as against like segments on an equal plane of the hierarchy. Just as in China the governor or governor-general of one or more provinces stood for the identity and interests of his region against other governors or governors-general, so too, for instance, the kings of Vietnam and Cambodia each stood for the identity of his own region against the other, as did the various levels of nomadic-feudal officials of the Central Asian steppe. The sedentary societies of East and Southeast Asia and the nomadic groupings of Inner Asia were all part of a pyramidal structure topped by the emperor, and the structure's intermeshing mechanisms (other than trade in its purely commercial facet) ran through the leadership positions of all the groups and connected each position vertically to the ones above and below it.

The role and the position of each group head varied however, because he was related to his subjects by ties different from those that linked him to the emperor of China. Far and away one of the most distinctive aspects of the East Asian traditional international order, this feature led in the middle and late nineteenth century to much Western confusion over the nature of the tribute system, particularly in the case of Korea's relations to China. In the West all governments were conceived as resting on law, regardless of the particular form law took in each state; therefore, all sovereigns were equal. Moreover, international relationships and even organizations existed on the basis of, or strove toward the creation of, international law. (States, particularly certain forms of dictatorship, that flout the law both internally and externally are thought of as political aberrations even today.) In traditional East Asia, on the other hand, the international system consisted of ties that were quite distinct from internal political links. Sectional leaders on the same hierarchical level might all recognize the emperor of China as the apex of the political universe while fighting each other and demoting a defeated enemy in the hierarchical system. Korea, in other words, functioned internally as a completely independent country, with all the attributes of internal independence that were normally a part of Western concepts of the state, but externally Korea deferred to China in international politics. The West, seeking to open Korea after the middle of the nineteenth century, had difficulty determining whether Korea was an independent country or a Chinese dependency. In the West, independence was a legal concept in the international domain; in East Asia, independence was a description of the real freedom of action of a ruler within a polity.

Chinese power intruded into the internal affairs of tributary states only when developments threatened the position or person of the segment's leader in his relations with the emperor. This distinction between the political structure of each segment and the ties that bound the various segments to the international order permitted China to "use the barbarian to control the barbarian"—China could create tensions between inferior members of the universal hierarchy without endangering the hierarchy itself.

This, then, is the context within which the great variety of tribute institutions and political strategies that constituted China's premodern (pre-1842) foreign relations must be understood. It is insufficient, for instance, to see the emperor simply as the Confucian pinnacle of human society or the tangent point between man and the cosmos. The emperor was, or was supposed to be, the political head of the most powerful state in civilization, and his ritual value in both Confucian and non-Confucian relationships throughout the world (*tianxia*, "all under heaven") arose in large part from the very conflicts aroused by his (and China's) power over subordinate or weaker societies. Human society as a whole, and interstate relations in particular, were pyramidal in form, but the categories of social relations that were knit together at each level varied radically. The tribute system encompassed a large variety of strategies and institutions because the intermeshing mechanisms that offset economic, political, social, military, and

cultural cleavages did not necessarily coincide. Moreover, the inter-societal cleavages that derived from ecological or social or political differences
in East Asia were not, functionally, breaches of normative patterns of behavior; that is, they were not dysfunctions. In fact, they were normal, predictable phenomena that emerged directly from the structural differentiation of each society and its environment, and they were resolved in a new
balance through ritual collaboration, military action, trade, and so on—in
short, through the tribute system.

The administrative institutions of the tribute system—the Board of
Rites and the Li-fan Yuan—were more than simple organizing mechanisms
for the political universe. They were structural elements of the universe
itself, interlocking "variant and congruent systems" with China, "with ritual values acting as pins at crucial points."[12] Moreover, ritual functioned
even in relations with non-Confucian societies, because it constantly and
periodically reestablished a unity that transcended the mobility and conflicts inherent in the East Asian world order.[13] To put it another way, the
periodic presentation of tribute by a non-Confucian potentate to the emperor functioned as a reminder of the former's inferiority in power and
culture. In this respect, the tribute ritual was a means of expressing universal cohesion and impressing the values of civilization and its social sentiments on non-Chinese. Seen from a slightly different angle, the stren-
uous exercise of the kowtow ritual—three kneelings and nine prostrations
before one's superior—exaggerated China's power (even when China was
in fact weak) and exaggerated real conflicts and cleavages between the emperor (China) and the tribute presenting potentate, who affirmed by kow-
towing that there was universal harmony and unity through submission to
the emperor *despite* the reality of Chinese power and despite conflicts of
interest. In the kowtow ritual and other tributary forms, the emperor's
subject from inside China or the barbarian ruler from outside the frontiers
insisted that he himself was unworthy and, in theory, he demanded his
own rejection by the emperor in Confucian or diplomatic terms. In turn,
the emperor signified his acceptance of the petitioner by presenting him
with gifts and food from the imperial table. The tribute ritual was a paradox, therefore, because it was a periodic recollection of rebellion or conflict that resulted in the periodic strengthening of the centrality, and the
recognition, of China's power, particularly the power of the emperor and
his dynasty.

The exchange of tribute and gifts, which was the crucial activity of the
entire tributary relationship, was highly symbolic. *Gong,* the word used to
designate the presentation of tribute to the emperor, meant the presentation of anything to him regardless of who presented it. Consequently, inclusion of barbarian tribute under the rubric *gong* served to reinforce the
emperor's role as *paterfamilias* of all civilization and to equate this ritual
with that of the emperor's own subjects inside civilization (the expression

"turning toward civilization") was used to indicate the barbarians' recognition of China and its emperor). The symbolic meaning of the tribute was further extended by the fact that the emperor's gifts were usually more valuable than the tribute he received, indicating that the emperor, as the apex of the entire system, could not be outdone in generosity and reinforcing, through the obvious exhibition of abundance and wealth (in contrast to the implied paucity of the tributary's treasure), his apexical role. In many societies, merit and even social power may be gained by the presentation of gifts so costly that the receiver cannot reciprocate and is therefore placed in the debt of the donor: East Asia was no exception.

In traditional East Asia, gift giving was more than simply a means of obtaining power. Because of the close relationship that existed between the objects that were exchanged and those who exchanged them, gift giving was a crucial part of the entire social process, providing the excuse for visits or serving as a necessary opening for a relationship. (This close relationship is implicit, for instance, in the idea that we must display the ugly vase Aunt Mary gave us as a wedding present because she will be insulted if she drops by and does not see it. Aunt Mary will feel that it is not just the vase but she herself that we are rejecting.) The exchange of objects between the tributary and the emperor established bonds that were highly complex indeed, again irrespective of the Confucian content of the ceremonial. This institution was particularly important in an international community in which no abstract law was universally recognized but in which relationships depended upon custom.

The emblematic recognition of the emperor's superiority and uniqueness was a crucial element in the intermeshing processes of the East Asian world order. The emperor as a man had no supernatural powers as does, for instance, the pope, who can create saints, give indulgences, and so on. The emperor's role in society was emblematic (supported, of course, by strength whenever possible) and therefore intermeshing. The political units of traditional East Asia were all politically independent internally if they were not actually occupied by China, but they were not, as in the West, politically isolated. The traditional order was a polity, a league of parts; the periodic recognition of the emperor's superiority served to maintain that polity as an integrated system. (In this regard, the ancient Zhou dynasty's interstate system was clearly the tribute system's antecedent.) Consequently, when barbarians like the Mongols and Manchus conquered China they sought not to destroy it or to substitute their own form of society or government for China's. Quite the contrary, their interest was to seize the emblem of power and unity for themselves (always recognizing that it carried material advantages), and the barbarian emperor's zealousness in maintaining Chinese forms in relations with other barbarians did not occur simply because he was sinified (how does one measure, say, the Mongolian Kublai Khan's or the Manchu Kangxi's sinification?) but because these were the universally recognized emblems of power in East Asia. For instance, as long as the center of the Mongol empire remained in Mongolia, the Empire as a whole could be held together by force and administration, but once it was moved by Kublai to Peking and Chinese imperial symbols were adopted as the primary instrument of domination, the Empire fell apart, not just because communication difficulties or dynastic rivalries existed but because, in part, the Chinese emblems of imperial power and social unity that were recognized in East Asia were not so similarly recognized in Russia or Persia.

The emperor's emblematic role in societal interpenetration in East Asia was also apparent in his role as the font of political sanctions. These sanctions were notable because of the relative unimportance of military force or political influence *per se* and because of their diversity, which no doubt reflected the diversity of the allegiances in East Asian society: to one's ancestors, to the emperor, to the king or khan, to the local prince, governor, or military leader, to the elders of one's own family, etc. The emperor himself ruled by the mandate of heaven; yet he, too, was an example of the importance of allegiance to one's ancestors for he announced to them his accession to the throne and all other major events of his reign. Whereas this allegiance might appear to be an invocation of his ancestors' protection, in fact rebels were pacified not by the power of the emperor's ancestors but by secular might. Actually his ancestors played no role in sanctioning either his secular or his cosmological status; the performance of ceremonies to his ancestors, normally the responsibility of the senior family member, established the emperor as the *paterfamilias* of all mankind and therefore resolved any role conflict that otherwise would have arisen if he had older relatives, who ordinarily would have been due allegiance from him. Because there was no rule of primogeniture in China, the emperor might not be his father's eldest son or even the senior member of his kinship lineage. Kangxi's successor, for instance, was his fourth son.

Because the sanction for the emperor came solely from Heaven, he was in a position to sanction the political positions and powers of his tributaries who also found themselves in situations in which family or kinship relations did not provide power sanctions and who needed sanctions based on concepts into which such considerations did not intrude. Where used to express a political relationship, kinship terms pointed only to hierarchical values. In Japan the imperial clan's power was sanctioned by its own divinity; in Tibet, political power was sanctioned by the uniqueness of the Dalai Lama's spiritual position in a fundamentally theocratic society. But in societies that required a high sanction for rule from nondomestic sources, that is, where ancestors sanctioned family headship but not political power, the emperor of China could play the sanctioning role through the issuance of patents of office. A reciprocal relationship existed between the emperor and his tributaries. They required his sanction as the only force greater than themselves who was not limited by family or ancestral connections in their own societies. He, in turn, required their recognition of his possession of the mandate of heaven as insurance against his loss of the mandate through the revolt of tributary powers on the empire's frontier.

The issuance of patents of office by the emperor of China to his tributaries was roughly equivalent to modern diplomatic recognition in the West, where political entities that have no international diplomatic status are not considered to exist legally. However, the imperial patents did not themselves affect the constitutional structure of the tributary societies. The divergent interests of each tributary or of groups within each tributary were to a certain extent balanced by their common acceptance of the emperor of China's primacy within the international order and by the emperor's power to recognize local political authority through the patent system. The emperor's executive authority within the international order lessened as geographical distance from his capital increased and local political power intervened, but his ability to issue patents of office to tributary potentates gave him at least a symbolic role to play not only in international politics but also in the internal affairs of the tributaries. Intriguers for power primarily needed popular support, but China's military or economic ability to interfere, particularly in Confucian states directly on the frontiers, either in behalf of the ruler who already possessed the emperor's patent or in behalf of a usurper who promised fealty to the emperor as against a ruler who had rebelled, was symbolized in the patent itself and in the accompanying seals of office. This device allowed the resolution of conflicts for power by changing the individuals occupying office without changing the structure either of the office or of its relation to China. In other words, rebellion against China traditionally could be resolved by the accession of a new ruler without affecting the international system, or, put in another way, internal strife experienced by a tributary power did not challenge the emperor's hegemony.

Traditional Trade

THE TRADITIONAL SINOCENTRIC international order in East Asia enabled its participants to gain economic advantages through almost ceaseless warfare or, in times of peace, through ritual and political means. This international economic system was the functional, but not necessarily the structural, equivalent of, first, the modern world's international trade and, second, recognition under international law according to the diplomatic practice of the nineteenth and twentieth centuries in the West.

The premodern East Asian international economy differed ideologically from the modern capitalism that was to overwhelm it after the middle of the nineteenth century. The former required noneconomic sanctions for the same acts that constitute the modern capitalist economy and require, in the nature of capitalism, actual or theoretical economic sanctions. Conversely, the very existence of noneconomic sanctions for economic activities in the international arena leads to the conclusion that the East Asian international economy was organized along noncapitalistic lines since the sanctions, as ideas and institutions, were themselves real elements in the world order, not arbitrary, self-conscious explanations for quaint practices. Support is lent this conclusion by the fact that the tribute system was organized in dual, parallel forms; in other words, trade and tribute were neither synonymous nor completely independent activities. Approached from either direction, the conclusion remains the same: a description of the traditional international economy in East Asia requires the suspension of assumptions derived from our own experience.

Trade and Tribute

Trade and tribute were both aspects of the Confucian universal continuum and were intricately, but not necessarily directly, related. Three patterns characterized commerce between China and the barbarians. In the first, trade followed immediately upon the presentation of tribute to the emperor at the capital. Merchants usually accompanied tribute missions and were permitted to trade at Peking for a specified number of days immediately after completion of the tributary rituals. In these cases, trade was also permitted along the frontiers as part of the tribute arrangement. There were marketplaces on the Sino-Korean and Sino-Mongolian frontiers, for instance, and along the China coast. In the second pattern, trade took place at Peking without the presentation of tribute. The Russians, for instance, visited Peking very frequently for trade between 1695 and 1755, but court documents from that period record only one tribute mission, in 1728. In the third pattern, trade also took place along the frontier without the presentation of tribute. The British East India Company traded at Canton regularly until the Opium wars, but for the years 1644–1842 only four English tribute missions appear in official documents and two of these references are to one embassy. The presentation of tribute by a specific country was not, therefore, a prerequisite for commercial exchange between that country and China. When small barbarian kingdoms sought to present tribute at court, or when Central Asian merchants pretended tributary status in order to present tribute to the emperor, they did so largely because the presentation of tribute was itself a commercially profitable act; the court bore the expenses of a tribute mission while it remained at Peking and exchanged gifts with it to the profit of the tributary.

Although presentation of tribute to the emperor was not necessarily related to the broad exchange of the international marketplace in a causal or even purely permissive manner, these activities were connected in several ways. Though of secondary importance to the establishment of the social context of the relationship between the emperor and his vassals, the tribute-gift exchange, which was at the heart of the tribute ceremonial, represented an economic exchange of real value. The objects offered in tribute or received in gift were often rare in the society of the recipient and consequently would have commanded a high price on the market had they been offered for sale as luxury goods; their value, of course, was enhanced by their connection with the imperial household. What is clear, however, is that the tribute-gift exchange was by no means either purely symbolic or purely commercial. In other words, on several levels ceremony and commerce were so intertwined as to be separable only for analytical purposes. Feasts and dinners had ritual value, but at the same time they possessed economic importance as a means of defraying the costs of an embassy's sojourn in Peking. The greater value of the emperor's gifts as against the tribute he received had, in addition to social, psychological, and moral significance, a strictly economic value: the difference between tribute and gift functioned as a subsidy toward the costs of the tribute mission itself.

At its most simple, the commercial significance of the tribute ceremonial derived from the fact that it did away with conflict and muted hatred so that trade could take place between friends or, at least, nonenemies. On a slightly more complex level, the Peking-centered tributary institutions—the tribute embassies and their appurtenances—provided an opportunity for the exchange of goods at Peking itself. But even here it must be clearly perceived that the presentation of tribute was the primary value in the emperor's eyes, even if the tributary used the ceremony to obtain nothing more than access to the Peking market. Tribute, from the point of view of the East Asian order, was the principal activity in the tribute-trade duality. However, just as tribute was presented to the emperor at Peking, so missions went from Peking to the tributaries to invest them with symbols of ranks and patents of office, on which occasions trade also took place. This was not simple reciprocation; the presentation of tribute kept movement going in both directions. It is true, of course, that there were no *periodic* visitations by imperial representatives to vassal capitals, but such a vehicle existed to be used when required. In this light, the foreign expeditions led by the eunuch Cheng He during the Ming dynasty were, commercially, not exceptions to the tribute-trade system but prime examples of it.

At the most complex and fundamental level, tribute was related to trade because tribute was the ritual appropriate to commercial activities in the universe. Tribute was, in this sense, a sanction for commercial activity, but it was neither a specific sanction for a specific act nor a permissive sanction. Rather it was a *sine qua non*: man's trading activity required the presentation of tribute to the emperor by someone at some point in time, and preferably, though not necessarily, the act was carried out by the representative of the chief of the power trading with China. Russia, for instance, traded in Peking without presenting tribute partly because the Russian merchants did not seek access to the emperor, but more importantly because the Peking court chose to assume that certain individuals and groups that did present tribute were envoys or embassies from the Russian court. In all instances, the presentation of tribute and the receipt of gifts were ceremonial barter cosmologically required for trade. The emperor, paraphrasing Dostoevski's grand inquisitor, might have remarked, "We have given them order, legitimacy, and bread, and they have given us their power and recognized our position in the cosmos."

In another dimension, trade and tribute were important, linked aspects of traditional Chinese diplomacy. This is patently clear in a memorial written in the 1570s by Wang Chonggu, governor-general of Xuanfu and Datong. Discussing a Mongolian chieftain's request for entitlement and trade, Wang listed eight subjects for the court's consideration, including trade. "The northern barbarians depend entirely on China for their supply of cooking pots, iron, and textiles," Wang memorialized. "Now that they have foresworn invasion of China, their envoys have requested the opening of markets for trade so as to prevent the occurrence of theft and robbery."[1]

What is significant is that Wang specifically related trade to the prevention of incursions into China by barbarians who had agreed not to transgress on Chinese soil. While the agreement may have been symbolized or consummated by the presentation of tribute, trade followed upon the agreement, not upon the tribute.

In a slightly different perspective, trade and tribute were related aspects of a process of exchange that included not only tribute goods and things of economic value, but political recognition, military aid, courtesies, entertainments, ritual, women, and feasts. All these exchanges constituted "a wide and enduring contract"[2] in which groups, not individuals, were bound by mutual obligations. The individuals represented in the contractual situation were social bodies rather than distinctive personalities. The tributary chieftain and the emperor were intermediaries, symbols, points in the universe; they were not simply individual personalities engaged in mutually profitable business. The marketplace was only one element in this exchange. Furthermore, while both the presentation of tribute and the exchange of goods in the marketplace appeared voluntary, in reality they were distinctly obligatory for each side, under the sanction of warfare or natural disaster.

Trade and tribute were also related as paired mechanisms for intermeshing. Both functioned to bridge the antagonisms between Han China and its neighbors, but paradoxically trade, which economically intermeshed ecologically different societies, was itself a socially disintegrative element in the international order, which in turn required reintegration through either the tribute ritual or war. One means of obtaining goods not available on the spot, trade belonged to the same genre of social activity as hunting, raiding, war, and robbery. Trade's distinctive characteristic was two-sided movement. Value moved in two directions, though not necessarily simultaneously, giving this form of exchange a fairly regular and comparatively peaceful character. On a spectrum of economic relationships including tribute, pilfering, raids, and war, trade was toward the tribute end, where hostility was resolved through ritual, while at the war end symbolic interaction gave way to violence.

However, in the traditional sinocentric international order trade was hostile, rather than friendly, because haggling was the basic, almost ritualistic, form of exchange on all levels of the universal East Asian market. Negotiated bartering by its nature involves a specific and intrinsically antagonistic relationship between the partners to the exchange; usually, the tribute system served a reintegrative function, removing or dissolving the antagonisms that arose from the commercial process and that might lead to conflict, but it was a delicate balance. In Central Asia, for instance, when the tribute system broke down through imperial weakness, the antagonistic elements in frontier market haggling grew because the peaceful integrative mechanisms had failed and a new integrative mechanism, war, took over. In other words, when tribute's reintegrative role failed, the maximizing of one side's economic self-interest required moving up the spectrum from trade into seizure. War, however, was only marginally profitable and the risks were high. Consequently, trade and its concomitant war were not simply commercial activities but conditions for survival, with trade the more preferable by far. Only in these terms does the trade-tribute relationship become intelligible. To misread tribute as a cover for trade and to understand trade as a purely commercial activity is to distort the nature of the traditional institutions of the sinocentric international order.

The consequences of systemic differences between the trading partners were felt in the immediate organization of the commercial situation. The quality of the economy from which the traders came determined their general expectations and institutional assumptions. The malfunctioning of the institutions of the marketplace often led to war, for instance, between the British and the Chinese in the middle of the nineteenth century, and was in large measure the result of each side's failure to understand the structure of the other's economy and its implications for commerce across cultural frontiers. The tribute system could be modified and stretched as an intermeshing mechanism but only to a point; beyond that point its destruction was implicit in any further adjustment to the institutional peculiarities of the non-Chinese partner. This point of tension was reached when the economic institutional expectations of the English in the nineteenth century passed beyond the ability of the tribute system to mediate between English concepts of free trade and traditional Chinese concepts of the proper economic organization of the universe. To the English, moreover, economic institutions were explicit, well-defined, independent structures whose activities were justified by the search for profits. The British East India Company, for instance, had been comprehensible to the traditional Sino-Manchu policymakers because one and the same agency wanted both to engage in trade and to send ambassadors to Peking (though not under conditions acceptable to the emperor). The end of the East India Company's monopoly in 1834 and the development in the marketplace of competing independent companies that were not representatives of the British government severely curtailed the possibilities and opportunities for the institutional intermeshing of English and Chinese trading economies in the marketplace. This lack of means for ritual integration led to conflict. English, not Chinese, institutions had changed, and China's ancient trading system became incomprehensible and irrational in terms of Western nineteenth- and twentieth-century capitalist assumptions.

The Structure of China's Traditional Economy

In 1793 the Qianlong emperor (1736–1795) wrote England's King George III that "there is nothing we lack, as your principal envoy and others have themselves observed. We have never set much store on strange or ingenious objects, nor do we need any more of your country's manufactures."[3] China's vaunted self-sufficiency and, from the point of view of Western observers, the backwardness of China's economic system perplexed Western traders along the China coast in the nineteenth century. That the Manchu empire could meet the needs of its people from its own resources was, by and large, true. However, at the time it was not clear why, for instance, given European commercial and economic theory, advantageous prices on European goods should not have promoted their sale in China. In fact, England obtained a favorable balance of trade with China only upon introducing opium to the China market. Opium had the special property of causing addiction, with the consequence that demand expanded with supply and price did not fall with increased supply. The Manchu government, opposed to opium consumption on moral, economic, and political grounds, tried to prevent the narcotic's distribution through the normal mechanism of the economy. Consequently, the illegal development of the opium trade contributed to the breakdown of the regular economy.

European goods found a wider demand inside China only as the traditional economy began to disintegrate, at first along the coast and in the urban centers. China's apparent self-sufficiency and unreceptiveness to European goods before the introduction of opium derived not from fixed wants or limited purchasing power but rather from the fact that the society's wants (as opposed to strict needs), particularly in foreign trade, were met through distributive arrangements other than the market-price exchange mechanism familiar in the West. Moreover, the Western merchant's failure to understand the Chinese economy was compounded by his inability to recognize that no necessary relationship existed between economizing action and the economy itself. In fact, as some scholars have recognized, "the institutional structure of the economy need not compel, as with the market system, economizing actions."[4] What the Westerners did not realize was that while all societies have both certain material requirements for survival and socioeconomic structures to maintain the necessary supply, the institutions and mechanisms of supply differ from society to society, resembling each other functionally but not structurally. Traditional China was no exception.

All economic systems fall into one of two categories. In the "subsistence economy," a "single social unit performs the economic functions relating to production and distribution as well as consumption." The second category is the "exchange economy," in which goods and services are transferred between social units by mechanisms embodied in the larger social unit that is defined by the economy. The principles of exchange may be as varied as the mechanisms through which exchange takes place. The definition of exchange economies can be further refined in terms of price and nonprice economies. Exchanges in a "nonprice economy" are carried out with reference to some principle other than equivalence in standard value among the goods themselves. This system specializes the roles of production and consumption of its members, and the consumers of particular goods and services are not the same as the producers. Such specialization may be embodied in society's structure, as well as in particular skills, or it may be geographically defined. Moreover, the allotment of production and consumption roles may be either diffuse or centralized. If diffuse, then traditional principles and practices determine economic roles and the conditions of exchange. If centralized, then policy, rather than tradition, regulates economic behavior, and policy is made by specific institutions that may not be strictly economic in nature. For instance, the decision making power may be embedded in an institution that, from the viewpoint of twentieth-century analysis, would not be a strictly economic agency.

The centrally directed nonprice exchange economy may be called a *redistributive economy*. In such an economy the goods and services produced by any social unit are distributed to other units through a central agency according to either traditional principles or arbitrary decisions. Obviously, some governing mechanism is a *sine qua non* in a redistributive economy, and governments always exercise redistributive functions. The redistributive relationship resembles hostile economic intercourse because both require the employment or potential employment of force. In fact, the redistributive function depends upon a monopoly of power, and the redistributive agency attempts to suppress competition from any other source, such as criminal activities or enemy raids, since its redistributive function within society is one of the sources of its power. This is particularly true in societies in which the redistributive function is embedded in a social, rather than a purely economic, institution. The institutional relations within a society upon which the redistributive agency's functions rest may, in some instances, be based on ritual forms of integration. In any case, redistributive agencies are not concerned with individual rights or interests, and exchanges take place not in terms of equal value but in reference to specifically defined obligations.[5]

In addition to the diffuse nonprice exchange economy and the centrally directed nonprice exchange economy, there is a third type, the "price (or market) economy," in which goods and services have measurable values according to some common standard and are exchanged on the basis of equivalences between values, or prices. "Barter economies" exist when there are "numerous different and incommensurable standards of value for different kinds of goods," and they are not really subject to market principles. Barter economies, characteristic of societies in which the volume of trade is small and only a few standard items are exchanged, may run the gamut from the basic and primitive "silent trade" to the complex social situation of the Kyakhta emporium (on what is now the border between Siberia and Mongolia) in traditional Sino-Russian trade. Such systems often appear as the institution for economic contact between cultures or societies with different levels of technological development. Tradition, as well as fluctuating needs, determines amounts exchanged.

A full market economy has no preconditions for exchange in terms of social status, policy, or tradition. Exchange takes place on the basis of prices, or equivalence in a common medium of exchange, at rates determined by fluctuations in supply and demand. Relations between producer and producer, as well as between producer and consumer, are determined by, and goods and services tend to flow freely in response to, price in both production and consumption. Advantage determines choice between products that resemble each other functionally, and producers may compete in functionally equivalent products. Barter differs from the full market economy in that it does not provide mechanisms for the allocation of resources and labor in terms of comparative advantage or competition among firms, and although barter may take place in a marketplace it does not provide a regulative device such as the supply-demand-price mechanism of the market economy. The market economy is the classical economy described by nineteenth- and twentieth-century Western economic theorists, but of course it hardly ever existed in the form of perfect competition or total self-regulation.

For our purposes one further distinction is useful in the definition of economies. Exchange relations are always symbiotic, but the symbiosis takes two forms. The first is the *obligate*, in which the "symbiotic relation is essential to the survival of the organism"; the second is the *facultative*, "in which the organism may take advantage of a symbiotic relationship, but may survive without it quite well." Although these terms are derived from ecology, they are useful in generalizations concerning types of economies. It must also be stressed that, beyond a very crude minimum of food, clothing, and shelter defined only in generic terms, what is essential is not biologically but culturally determined.[6] The difference between obligate and facultative relationships provides the basis for a distinction between the Chinese and British economies in the first half of the nineteenth century that may explain the Chinese concept of self-sufficiency. The Chinese economy was facultative on the international scene—it could satisfy all its wants internally or through the tributary relationship with Central Asia (the Southeast Asian economies supplemented, rather than complemented, China's) and could survive quite well without commerce with the West. Britain, on the other hand, with a growing population based on industrialization, had become an obligate economy requiring exports and imports to survive. Conflict was almost inevitable: China did not need Britain but Britain did need China and other countries as well. Because the transformation of Britain back into a facultative economy would have been not only impossible but suicidal for British society as it was then structured, Britain, with its superior technology, initiated the transforma-

tion of China (and other areas in other ways) from a facultative into an
obligate economy through the introduction of opium and, after the Opium
wars, through the introduction of foreign capital and Western made or
Western style goods.

All economies between subsistence and pure market economies may be
considered transitional in nature, but in fact pure subsistence economies
are rare and pure market economies probably even rarer. In reality, all
economies combine reciprocative (diffuse nonprice exchange), redistributive, and market mechanisms: each institutional type can be clearly recognized, but they are not mutually exclusive. Redistributive and market
mechanisms almost always appear together since taxation is itself redistribution. One may go so far as to suggest that different economic systems
coexist within one economy in time and space and interact with each other
to provide for the wants of the social units bound by the economy. In
contemporary Taiwan, for instance, the government collects agricultural
products in kind from the peasant in the form of taxes and service payments. Government servants receive emoluments in kind (rice, oil, housing, transportation, etc.) in amounts varying with their social function
(civil, military, etc.) and status (hierarchical position). However, the government servant will have to go into the market to satisfy other wants or
additional wants in the same goods received from the government. This is
an example of the coexistence of different economic systems even within
one household. In accord with the definition of a redistributive economy,
government allotments are fixed neither in terms of identified wants nor in
terms of cash equivalences on the basis of the supply-demand-price market
mechanism but, rather, in terms of contractual or traditional fixed
amounts. Moreover, within any society economic dependence in obligate
and facultative terms may vary from individual to individual or group to
group. For instance, a Chinese peasant in traditional society could feed
himself without the services of administrators, soldiers, or artisans. His
obligate relationship was with the small group that joined him in the production of his livelihood, his family. On the other hand, almost the entire
bureaucratic structure of traditional China (perhaps excluding only a small
group of soldier-peasants), with its abhorrence of physical labor, was completely dependent upon the redistributive system that provided it with a
portion of the peasants' production. Thus, the bureaucracy and, in fact, the
entire gentry class were in obligate relationship with the peasantry, which
in turn was in facultative dependence upon the gentry.

In broad terms, the traditional Chinese economy, which had trade-
tribute relations with surrounding societies, was redistributive in character. The state subsisted on the basis of the economy's redistributive mechanisms. Land was theoretically subject to redistribution at the will of the
emperor. Grain tribute and taxes flowed into the state, which redistributed
the income on contractual and traditional bases to other social units. Labor

was distributed through the corvée, and when labor was commutable into cash payments commutation was made at fixed rates, not on the basis of the market value of labor. Redistributive mechanisms, working through a vast system of state graneries, bridged the discrepancy between harvest and consumption or between good and bad harvests. The same principle predominated in all these activities: collecting into and distributing from or by a center on the basis of concepts other than equivalences set by the market's price mechanism. Moreover, the economic decisionmaking power in China's broad social economy was embedded essentially in a noneconomic agency, the emperor, together with the Confucian state bureaucracy. The emperor's prestige operated as a noneconomic, or nonmarket, factor in channeling economic activity into socially useful (as defined by tradition and the will of emperor and bureaucracy) patterns rather than toward private gain, which was, in the Confucian ethic, socially and morally disadvantaged. This prestige rested not on economic power or the emperor's wealth but, rather, on his power and ability to provide political and military public stability. (Many of Wang Anshi's eleventh-century economic reforms appear today to have a socialist cast about them not because Wang foreshadowed modern socialist economic theory but because of the precise opposite: both traditional China's economy and modern New Deal and socialist economies are primarily redistributive and therefore resemble each other in general problems and solutions.)

It is highly significant that even the traditional rural standard marketing structures, or standard marketing community, as described by anthropologist G. William Skinner, exhibited the characteristics of a redistributional rather than a primarily market economy. Competition, considered so essential to the workings of the market mechanism, was inhibited by the periodicity of markets, to which peasants were spatially attached by tradition. In the main, demand was influenced not by supply and price but by "general poverty, value emphasis on frugality, and traditional consumption norms . . . self-sufficiency was a virtue." Moreover, petty merchants and transportation personnel usually were attached by tradition to a specific marketing structure, and merchants who serviced more than one marketing system to take advantage of price differentiation were relatively few. Even weights and measures, the standardization of which is vital to competition in a market system, differed from marketing community to marketing community. In short, producers, consumers, and merchants were associated within a traditional marketing structure whose conditions of exchange were largely determined by tradition rather than by supply and demand. Rarely did one leave his traditional market community, with all its social, economic, religious, linguistic and kinship implications, in order to take advantage, as producer or consumer, of price differentials in another, adjacent, community.

Economic exchange, the marketplace (as the physical location of the act of exchange), and the market (as an exchange-price mechanism that was, within limits, self-regulating based on supply and demand) were all distinguishable in traditional China, as they were in most other archaic societies, and were by no means coterminous. The existence of marketplaces in contemporary traditional or in historical societies is often thought to prove the existence of a market system in the classical capitalist sense of price-making markets (whether for consumer goods, the means of production, or the medium of exchange—that is, the money market) and, moreover, to imply that modern economic theory is relevant to the analysis of the economy in which the marketplace exists. However, the existence of a meeting place where goods are transferred from one individual or social unit to another does not support the assumption that a supply-demand-price mechanism governs the exchange. Exchange, functionally defined as the transfer of goods and services, may take place in different places under varied conditions and circumstances. In China, the standard market town may "lack a single marketplace altogether. Instead there is a multitude of petty marketplaces, one for each product." Moreover, these marketplaces may be widely dispersed in a town. Intermediate and central market towns, which trade over larger areas including several standard markets, may provide different facilities. And exchange may take place outside any marketplace, like the tribute-gift exchange at Peking's imperial court, without losing its significance as an economic act.[7]

Furthermore, exchange in the marketplace does not necessarily produce market prices that regulate the supply of goods in relation to the demand and channel the demand for goods in relation to the available supply; that is, the marketplace does not necessarily operate in terms of a supply-demand-price mechanism. Prices might be fixed by some governmental agency or simply be traditional; the market might not involve price, or even barter, at all, as in silent trade, where exchange takes place on entirely different principles.

In traditional China, as in other archaic or traditional societies, a price system characteristic of redistributive economies and administered trade, rather than of price markets and free trade economies, appears to have operated alongside a primitive supply-demand-price mechanism. "Administered trade" is trade carried out under the supervision of government officials who, representing the government, fix prices and other conditions of trade, such as the scheduling of the market and the collection of taxes. In the Ming and Qing dynasties, "it is a reasonable hypothesis that . . . a given market's transactions were more likely to be regulated and taxed by bureaucratic officials the higher its position in the functional hierarchy of central places," and, it goes without saying, the tribute exchange in Peking was the highest of all.[8] Since intermediate and central markets traded over wider areas than standard markets and since the communities attached to the higher markets were by and large strangers to each other, traditional sanctions imposed by society itself were weaker and bureaucratic sanctions had to take their place. In other words, where self-administration was weak, centralized bureaucratic administration took its place.

In premarket economies, price is the result not primarily of the interplay of supply and demand but of government fiat and/or tradition. The setting of prices was, in traditional Confucian theory, a government's proper function. According to the *Rites of Zhou*, "When there is a natural calamity, selling at high prices should be prohibited, so that prices will remain stable. This should be applied also to scarce goods throughout the year."⁹ In Ming civil law, "commodity prices were fixed by the government and could not be changed at will."¹⁰ In order to stabilize prices, the government might encourage or even order merchants to transport rice, for instance, to regions of rice shortage in order to prevent a price rise. Consequently, there could be no market in the modern sense of that word. If we take the money market as an example, in medieval Europe usury, the charging of interest on money, was considered immoral and was theoretically not permitted. China, in contrast, had a traditional interest rate on money that did not fluctuate in response to changing supply and demand (just as there was a traditional rent that did not fluctuate). Functionally, a traditional zero percent interest rate and a hundred percent interest rate are equivalent—interest rates do not vary in either case. In China, prices (like interest rates) were set, depending on product and quality, by tradition or fiat. In many sectors of the economy, consumption was often controlled by considerations of biology, tradition, and legislation. Caste and class were also determinants of consumption levels, both by tradition and by legislation.

Preindustrial societies lack true standardization or interchangeability of goods; therefore, no real competition on the market is possible. Prices may be set on the basis of certain assumed standards, but no particular item fits the standards completely; quality control is distinctly a development of industrialized societies. Consequently, haggling, which was fundamental to the exchange mechanism in traditional China, did not take place either in terms of relative prices on comparable goods as set by the interplay of supply and demand or in terms of a variety of interchangeable products (say, lard and oil). Rather, haggling took place over the quality of a particular item, over deviations from the standard product as traditionally or legislatively defined and priced, over measure, etc. In advanced traditional societies like China, money existed and fluctuated in value, but such fluctuations did not depend on money's purchasing power in terms of the supply and demand of products as much as on the value of the coin, based on the amount of precious metal actually present in it. Logically, for instance, sixteen ounces of copper would be worth 160 copper cash if the metal were coined into cash at the rate of ten percent pure copper per coin, but not at the rate of one percent pure copper per coin. Paper currency fluctuations reflected bad fiscal policies; the indiscriminate introduction of paper money into the economy debased the currency because "no one seems to have understood the basic principles of paper money . . . to have grasped the fact that the basis of paper money was 'credit.' " For this reason, paper money never succeeded in traditional China and went out of use during the Qing, when it was discountenanced as a bad administrative practice. However, from the beginning of the Ming in 1368, while paper currency was still in use, commodity prices were periodically revaluated and fixed; Ming price fixing "had no apparent connection with the question of paper currency." Price fluctuations, in other words, were more apparent than real since currency, not prices, fluctuated.[11]

Etymological evidence also suggests that exchange in traditional Chinese society was not characterized by purchase and sale in an open price market. In Mandarin Chinese the words meaning "purchase" and "sale" are distinguished orally only by tone. Visually they are distinguished by a minor change: the addition of the three-stroke character *shi*, or "scholar, gentleman, official, soldier," to the character for "sale." The implications of this in a centralized redistributive economy are obvious. More significant, however, is the fact that what is now translated from the Chinese as "to buy" originally may simply have indicated the direction of transfer in ego's direction, while "to sell" originally indicated transfer from ego to someone else. Such evidence exists in English, too: "to buy" derives from the Anglo-Saxon *bugan*, which originally meant "to compromise in bartering," while "to sell" derives from the Anglo-Saxon *sellan*, meaning "to give, offer." Evidently, none of these words originally connoted sale and purchase in a price market but, rather, exchange.

Significantly, long-distance trade, particularly foreign trade, was distinguished by the absence of the use of paper money. (In neither pre-Columbian Mezoamerica, for example, nor in China, is there any indication of the use of money in long-distance trade.) In China, money was used on local markets and occasionally in the long-distance movement of value within the country, particularly to the government treasury at Peking. But the East Asian international economy had no generally accepted coinage or currency in premodern times. Indeed, in Anglo-Chinese trade after the introduction of opium, when China's balance of trade became unfavorable, silver flowed out of China as a precious metal, not as currency or coinage.

The Structure of the Economy
of the Tribute System

In China, the only goods that moved in impressive quantities over great distances were the tribute grains for the capital and, perhaps, grain especially shipped to frontier posts in non-grain-growing regions. Tea also moved over great distances, but the movement of tea from South to North China was a highly specialized activity resulting from ecological differentiation within China. Petty trade was very localized. In other words, long-distance trade had its primary *raison d'etre* in the needs of the central imperial power, not the consumption needs of the local populace. Moreover, the conditions of trade over long distances in China must have differed according to the kinds of goods carried, the distances to be traveled, the geographical obstacles to be passed, and the political and ecological conditions of the venture. In premarket societies, however, where prices are fairly static and profits are not necessarily the result of maximizing advantages by carrying goods over long distances, the emphasis tends to fall on the acquisition of goods from a distance rather than on the transportation of goods to a distance. In traditional China external trade aimed primarily, although not exclusively, at the acquisition of luxury items, not the exploitation of foreign markets and the potential to make a profit. Therefore import, albeit in a limited amount, not export, was considered important (whereas in nineteenth-century capitalism in the West, export predominated). Accordingly, British and Chinese merchants did not compete to carry goods between England and China. While the British merchants recognized the advantages that would accrue to them by assuming the costs and burdens of transportation and thereby gaining control over British prices on Chinese goods, Chinese merchants, who were anyway disciplined not to venture out to sea, did not understand the value of competitive prices in an export market at a distance from their own shores. For the same reason, the British merchants understood the economic value of a carrying trade; the Chinese did not.

Because China had no desire for a large export business or a carrying trade, it never developed an efficient, unified, and standardized transportation system either inside China or between China and its trading partners. This lack had important consequences. First, there was little long-distance trading in general, and most trading ventures that did occur were discontinuous affairs. What continuity existed was not a commercial or accounting phenomenon but rather was an administrative one—established over time by the state itself through the tribute system. Frontier or coastal markets and caravans to Peking were concrete undertakings or events, circumscribed by two moments in time, with amounts to be traded fixed by the year or season. When continuity did develop, as at Kyakhta or Canton, it was administrative. Until well into the nineteenth century, the accounting of each venture was accomplished separately. Russian caravans to Peking, for instance, or trading ventures at Kyakhta, were conducted, as were their Chinese counterparts, on a seasonal basis, with accounting performed for each venture separately. Within the administrative continuity of the British East India Company's trade at Canton, each ship was invested in and accounted for separately. On the Chinese side, enterprises at Canton were continuous only as long as the merchant himself remained unchanged, and his admission to the market was closely controlled by the government. (Such discontinuous commercial activities are still well-known today, such as the annual Leningrad fur market, for example.) The discontinuity of trade on the Chinese side was enhanced by the fact that export goods were required to acquire import goods but, at least as far as the Peking market was concerned, the processes of the collection of export goods and the distribution of import goods differed. For instance, goods collected as taxes through the Board of Revenue might be given to the Li-fan Yuan to export in trade for import goods that would be distributed through the emperor's own household.

The second consequence of the absence of an efficient transportation system, and therefore of the absence of great long-distance trade, was the remarkable social polarization of the personnel engaged in long-distance or external commerce. The two polar groups can be characterized by their primary motivations. First were the officials who at Peking administered the tributary and caravan trade and at the frontiers administered the markets. As officials, their primary motivation was duty or public service; their status at the top of society as members of the gentry-bureaucracy placed them at the state's disposal, and they were assigned to commercial functions. Their status motives were quite often reinforced by material gains from corruption or even from indirect participation in commerce, but these were secondary to their bureaucratic functions. In fact, commercial service was often regarded with distaste, almost as a form of exile or punishment, and pecuniary concerns only softened the disgrace but did not erase it. Had an independent long-distance trade existed apart from the state, this bureaucratic class might not have entered the commercial lists at all. At the other end of the Confucian social spectrum were the merchants and, even lower, the transportation workers, all of whom were attracted to commerce by pecuniary interests and were therefore socially disadvantaged. Because premarket China did not recognize the productive role long-distance trade played in economic growth, the merchant was considered a nonproductive social element and was therefore held in social contempt. The economic risks involved in trade were compensated by material gains, but material gains did not necessarily carry with them social mobility. Profits might be used to purchase higher social status, but that was problematical.

A further, though more indirect, consequence of a comparatively underdeveloped transportation technology and of the absence of a developed transportation system was the two-sided nature of China's external trade, a bilateral activity between China and a second power. Transportation routes were discrete and usually defined in terms of the geographical proximity of the second trading party to one of China's frontiers. China traded with Portugal through Macao, the East India Company at Canton, the Koreans on the Korean frontier, and the Russians at Kyakhta. Similarly, China traded discretely with the caravans that came to Peking along established routes and did not consider them to be competing with each other. The bilateral structure of the Canton market broke down at the end of the eighteenth and beginning of the nineteenth century, when American and continental European merchants arrived to compete with the British, introducing a new and probably unexpected element into the commercial scene. Nevertheless, Kyakhta remained a bilateral market since all European goods funneled through it still came under Russian control, more often than not passing through Russian hands.

Three main types of trade occurred in two-sided commerce, each resting on a different integrative principle. Gift trade, based on simple reciprocity according to certain accepted behavior patterns, appeared in China's external commerce both at Peking in the form of the tribute-gift exchange and at the frontier in the form of certain concessions, such as gifts and entertainment in return for barbarian tranquility. In the second form, market trade, the supply-demand-price mechanism was the integrative factor, but to all appearances this form played a fairly subsidiary role until the nineteenth century, when it made its first important appearance at Canton as a result of the growth of the market mechanism in European economies. The third type, and by far the most important, was administered trade.

Administered trade was the reflection in external commerce of China's fundamentally redistributive internal economy, and it was perhaps the most efficient mechanism for exchange between societies that differed in economic assumptions but were not prepared to press their case against each other too vigorously. This trade, like the tribute system, rested on contractual relationships between the partners in any bilateral trade situation. The contract could take many forms: in Russia's case, for instance, it was an explicit diplomatic treaty, while in China's trade with England before 1839 it took the form of England's agreement, albeit tacit and at times most unwilling, to operate within the so-called Canton system. Regardless of the form the contract took, the structure of the administered trade was fairly uniform, differing only slightly to accommodate the peculiarities of each of China's partners. Administered trade presupposed the existence of relatively permanent trading bodies, like governments or government chartered companies. Trade was carried on by administrative methods through channels controlled either by the government or by a company. While in market trade the individual traders and merchants haggle to establish prices, in administered trade formal negotiations between officials of government or company establish equivalences by either tacit or explicit agreement. In China's case, bargaining occurred over matters other than price, though it might be expressed in terms of exchange ratios (which is different from price) since exchange was made, theoretically, in terms of units on a basis of one for one. When required, adjustments took place in terms of units exchanged, but redress of commercial grievances came through appeal to an official, not through bargaining between traders. Depending on the relative strength of the trading partners, prices might be set by Peking itself, as in China's trade with Central Asia, or by mutual agreement, as at Kyakhta. Therefore, administered trade required specific marketplaces at which commerce could take place, to which the trading partners could control access, and in which the partners' official representatives could enforce compliance with the fixed price.

China's traditional external trade took place primarily in locations that may be classified generically as "ports of trade" and that were the product of two distinct traditions. On the one hand, China's ports of trade were analogous to markets in the ancient Eastern Mediterranean, in Mezoamerica, and along the West African coast. On the other hand, the ports were the application of China's traditional commercial practices to external commerce. The port of trade was a major organ of administered trade that persisted in several parts of the world "from antiquity almost to the threshold of modern times." Its existence through time reflects the fundamental role the port of trade played in contact between societies under the conditions of premodern technology and statecraft. Probably arising from a tradition of politically neutral meeting places that stemmed from primitive silent trade, the ports of trade were "towns or cities whose specific function was to serve as a meeting place for foreign traders." Traditional authorities usually feared the penetration of their territories by foreigners who might disrupt carefully balanced societies based on the common acceptance of certain social and mythic forms of control; strangers in premodern societies tended to shun territories that were incorporated into militarily strong, but foreign, hinterland empires. Consequently, ports of trade as a rule developed either on the frontiers of a state or empire or in the politically neutral territory of a small and weak independent potentate. Trade in the ports of trade was based on contracts and administered by special organs of the host authority. Competition was excluded and prices were set through negotiations. Within the confines of the port of trade special administrative organs might develop out of the cooperation of the various authorities whose traders met there.[12]

The port of trade itself was the product of a universal experience, but the Chinese articulated this institution within the context of their own traditional patterns of commercial behavior and located it, as one would expect, at the outer edges of imperial power. Port-of-trade practices were analogous to practices inside the Empire; for instance, the ports of trade were well within the Chinese tradition of extramural markets, that is, of markets located outside a town's or city's walls, and decree and custom set their trading periods much as they did for markets within the Empire. The existence of such an analogous tradition may explain why the Ming and

Qing dynasties permitted Chinese trade with foreigners within the ports of trade but did not allow Chinese merchants to travel abroad for trade: abroad the government could not define behavior patterns for the merchants.

Kyakhta, on the Russo-Mongolian frontier, other frontier trading posts for commerce with the barbarians, and seaports like Canton were all ports of trade, located in Chinese territory over which Peking's central control was, at best, limited. While the Ming and Qing dynastic authorities were prepared to permit foreigners to come to Peking under the rubric of tributary missions, their penchant for avoiding foreign visits outside the strictly structured tributary situation and their constant effort to remove trade to the frontier must be understood in terms of the port-of-trade concept. For instance, when in 1405, during the Ming dynasty, Peking received a request from a frontier garrison in Manchuria for permission for Manchus to sell horses at the capital, the court decided to refuse the request and, instead, ordered the establishment of markets at two places in the Liaodong region of Manchuria. In 1571 four markets were opened in Central Asia for trade with the Mongols. In 1727 the Qing and the Russians negotiated the Kyakhta trade settlement and the removal of all Sino-Russian trade from Peking to the frontier. And Peking constantly rejected English requests for permission to trade outside Canton. In fact, the treaty port system that was born along the China coast in the middle of the nineteenth century with the midwifery of British guns was really a modern modification of the ancient port of trade concept.

China's Inner Asian frontier markets and seacoast ports were functionally equivalent inasmuch as both were at the outer edge of imperial power, and this shared characteristic was more significant than environmental differences between inland and coastal ports of trade. The existence of seacoast ports of trade did not mean that China had tendencies to engage significantly in ocean-going commerce. Northern China's failure to follow logically down the rivers and early become a sea-going power, which would have given the Chinese a better means of communication even with South China than overland routes afforded, can be explained only in terms of an almost mesmerizing continental orientation born of constant danger from nomads in Inner Asia, while the sea posed comparatively little danger and therefore was not an object of bureaucratic interest. However, only a deep-seated cultural thalassophobia, which was reinforced by the Central Asian security problem, can explain the mythic organization of maritime powers into a separate category of barbarians. The same factors may explain why "extraterritoriality," the right of foreigners to be self-governing inside China, developed functionally along the coast at an early date, at least as early as the Arab visits during the Tang, but with minor exceptions never really developed in Inner Asia. Lack of dynastic concern with the coast, transforming it into a weakly controlled frontier region in contrast to the tightly regulated coasts associated with Western maritime powers, was apparent during the reign of the Qing emperor Kangxi. Since Siamese rice was cheaper than rice transported from inland China to the coast (in no small measure a result of lower transportation costs), Kangxi ordered the importation of rice from Siam to feed his coastal garrisons. But this practice inevitably placed the provisioning of the coastal garrisons on a far less sure footing than the use of Chinese rice would have done: China controlled its internal transportation routes but not the routes in Southeast Asia. Even in the middle of the nineteenth century, when the West was pressing hard along the China coast, the Qing did not, as they could have done, overwhelm the small foreign contingents by sheer numbers. Instead, they chose surrender, which in the historical record contrasts sharply with their resolute behavior forty years later in the Ili valley in Central Asia, where they faced a continental Russian incursion. The coast was simply less important than Inner Asia, which is why it constituted a frontier along which ports of trade were located. This is not to say that in Chinese history naval power was never a source of dynastic concern. In the Song, Yuan, and early Ming dynasties tentative moves were made in the direction of the development of naval strength, but China's failure to progress in this area must be understood as part of the pattern of continentally oriented power.

Commerce in the ports of trade in Inner Asia or along the China coast was administered, at least theoretically, in accordance with regulations that implicitly precluded the development of a supply-demand-price market mechanism. Such a mechanism could not exist in the presence of regulations controlling access to the market and the rate, or price, at which exchanges were to take place. During the Ming strict regulations existed for the operation of horse markets, for instance, according to which only authorized persons were permitted to participate in the commerce on market days; additionally, private trade between Chinese and Mongols outside the market was strictly forbidden. Later regulations, issued in 1608 to govern certain markets, also reflected the concept of administered trade: Chinese sales to Mongols were limited to textiles and foodstuffs; Chinese garrison officers were to control the quality of Mongolian horses offered for purchase; business was to be conducted with dispatch and barbarians were not to be permitted to tarry in the marketplace; official interpreters were to keep the number of Mongolian envoys, or merchants (within the tribute system context), at the proper level; and, perhaps most significant, the regulations specified that "once the trade regulations had been fixed, the least increase in the number of horses or in price was to be strictly forbidden." Tribute itself was a form of trade and was subject, therefore, to the practices of administered trade in a redistributive economy. A memorial from the 1570s concerning the establishment of trade with the Mongols says quite clearly concerning tribute:

> There should be one tribute annually. . . .In toto the number should not exceed 500 horses and 150 envoys. Let the horses be divided into three grades. Thirty of the best grade should be presented for Palace use, but the rest should be paid for according to the worth of each horse. Old and lean ones should not be accepted as tribute. Each year sixty of the barbarian [envoys] should be allowed to enter the capital, and the rest should be made to wait at the border. When the envoys depart they should be allowed to use the proceeds from the horse sales to purchase textiles for presentation as gifts for their chiefs.[13]

However the memorialist understood trade processes, he was not referring to any kind of market that could be identified in terms of the supply-demand-price mechanism. The licensed traders at Kyakhta, the designated "hong merchants" of Canton, and the caravan merchants officially recognized for trade at Peking were all participants in an administered trade within the context of a premarket or nonmarket economy.

At Peking itself, and not only in the frontier ports of trade, the principles of the nonmarket economy operated in the tribute situation. When, in addition to the formal tribute presentations, the court demanded goods at low prices, it was not trying to get something for nothing or for less than the market price, as many Western observers thought. On the contrary, the court was trying to obtain, as was its due within its own system, goods for which it had already paid in part or in whole, at a just price, by providing housing and other services in connection with a tribute mission's sojourn at the capital. From another viewpoint, such demands could be considered, functionally, a tax for permission to trade. The caravans, especially the Russians, often failed to recognize this pattern of interaction; only the eventual transfer of trade to the frontier could resolve the resulting conflict.

Two final questions remain to be asked in this description of the tribute system's economy. First, what was the degree of risk for the merchants in the tribute trade? The chief difference between administered and free market trade lies in the activities of the traders themselves. Because the empire had no fluctuating price-making market, price risk was excluded, and profit depended on turnover rather than on price differentials. For this reason, accounts of the Russian trade with China speak of the turnover of the merchants' investment rather than of profits on price fluctuations. Furthermore, since traditional accounting procedures did not necessarily include the cost of transportation or of administration of the market, participation in the trade was tantamount to participation in its profits. In this trade, there was apparently no risk of debtor's insolvency either, since the state or the company assumed the risks of transportation and administration and, at worst, the merchant was left with his goods and only those minor costs against them that were required for his own subsistence. Consequently, in the 1720s, when Russian furs did not sell well on the Peking market, the Russian merchants returned to Siberia with the pelts rather than risk their sale at a loss in the capital. Equally, the merchant to whom public goods were entrusted for sale had to produce, upon return home, either the goods or their equivalent, but he did not incur the risk of costs on the failure of trade.

Second, what was the difference between taxes and tribute? Tribute was a fixed sum or quantity of specified goods required by fiat or by tradition, regardless of the producer's productivity. The same statement often applied to taxes in traditional China, while in a modern market economy taxes can be defined as percentages of production, either uniformly applied or scaled to profit and income increases. Tribute defined by imperial edict was statutory in the same sense that taxes were. Consequently, while various taxes and tribute were called by different terms, the terms referred to the person receiving the tax or tribute, not to the source. The emperor received tribute; his officials collected taxes. Functionally, tax and tribute were economically indistinguishable in China's premodern economy.

Early Qing Foreign Trade Policies

The Manchus, a frontier nonsinitic people, were influenced strongly by the Chinese Ming dynasty and adopted traditional Sino-Confucian institutions after 1636, when they founded their Qing dynasty, and more particularly after 1644, when they began their conquest of China. But in the beginning the Manchus infused the newly adopted institutions with their own "barbarian vigor." The official public disdain for foreign commerce and the institutional identification of trade with tribute were absent in the early years of the Qing dynasty. In fact, the three emperors Taizong (1626–1644), Shunzhi (1644–1662), and Kangxi (1662–1723) were actively interested in the development of certain forms of foreign trade and, to an extent, understood the economic implications of commerce. Not yet subjected to the full weight of Confucian orthodoxy by sinification, these emperors were fairly pragmatic in the solution of their economic and diplomatic problems; their pragmatism allowed the continuation of the Ming dynasty's multiport trade policy. Early Qing trade with Korea and along China's southeastern coast showed the institutional vigor that the dynasty later applied in developing the institutions of the Sino-Russian treaty system, the first such arrangement with a non-Asian power.

The Manchus entered into active commercial relations with Korea at least fifteen years before beginning their conquest of China in 1644. The development of their armies required food and other materiel for which Korea was the best source. As early as January 15, 1628, the Taizong emperor ordered two officers to accompany a Korean envoy back to Korea in order to deliver a letter to the Korean king. The letter was a detailed proposal for the opening of trade between Manchuria and Korea. Taizong was quite willing for Manchu merchants to go to the Korean capital for trade. He also indicated that he understood the relationship of demand and supply and the role of foreign trade in development. Although insisting that his own grain supplies were sufficient to feed his people, he claimed that they were insufficient to feed a population that was growing larger through the adherence of vassal tribes. Consequently, he sought trade in Korea.

The correspondence between Taizong and the Korean king following the Manchu request for trade points to the existence of conscious conceptual distinctions between trade and tribute. In a letter dated March 3, 1628, and entered in the Qing dynasty's official records, the Korean king agreed to open trade in order to alleviate Manchuria's grain shortage; moreover, he permitted the establishment of a market in one of his frontier cities, but he stipulated that trade there be conducted freely. A second letter, dated March 7, 1628, was delivered on the occasion of the presentation of ritually required annual spring gifts. The style and terminology of this second letter seem more ceremonial and traditional than that of the first: trade, the Korean king said, was based on the exchange of surplus commodities and would prosper provided it was unrestricted.[14]

During the next five years Korean-Manchu commerce grew, though not without disputes. In 1633, Taizong sent a mission to Korea to trade ginseng for silk and to present a formal complaint to the Korean king concerning price changes made by Korean merchants for their commodities. Later that same year, Taizong sent a letter in which he discussed his desire for economic self-sufficiency and the need for protectionist policies to achieve that goal.[15] He complained that the Koreans were capricious in the setting of prices. Consequently, in order to diminish his dependence on foreign trade and to increase the internal production of such items as cotton, the Manchu ruler announced a five-year development program and the adoption of a protectionist policy prohibiting the weaving of silk or its importation from Korea, since silk competed with cotton. Taizong concluded by warning the Korean king that the breaking of commercial agreements could have serious political consequences. After 1644, Manchuria's economic difficulties were obviously eased by the conquest of China. By the end of the seventeenth century, China, a grain exporter, was part of the Manchu empire; as late as 1698 the Qing, formerly purchasers of Korean grain, were able to send thirty thousand *shi* of rice to Seoul.[16]

The Manchus continued Taizong's non-Confucian, non-Chinese positive approach toward trade after the conquest of China and this posture became part, but only part, of the background to Kangxi's trade policies. For the Manchus, Kangxi's reign was a period of adjustment to China and to the institutions they needed to govern their newly won empire. An intellectual tension developed between traditional Sino-Confucian commercial attitudes and the vigor that characterized Taizong's dealings with the Koreans. This tension expressed itself, on the policymaking level, in a general doubt as to whether foreign trade should be encouraged and, if so, to what extent it should be controlled beyond already existing mechanisms. Manchu policymakers, whether they were dispensing edicts at the capital or proposing policies from the provinces, were remarkably aware of the economic problems they faced in China after their wars of conquest. The tension between various possible attitudes toward trade was clear in the development and vagaries of policy along the southeastern coast, where trade had a definite economic value for the Qing above and beyond the simple supply of necessary commodities China did not itself produce.

Kangxi, at the age of thirteen *sui*, assumed the throne in 1662 in the midst of the struggle against the Ming loyalist Zheng Chenggong (Koxinga) and his successors. In that same year, Hong Wu, a former Ming general who had surrendered to the Manchus, recommended the removal of the inhabitants of the coastal provinces of Shandong, Jiangnan, Jiejiang, Fujian, and Guangdong inland to a distance of thirty to fifty *li*.[17] This measure was intended to deny Zheng opportunities for supply raids along the coast. In May 1668, the emperor approved a suggestion from the Board of War that, for the same reason, foreign trade should be prohibited "if it is not a time for the presentation of tribute." This edict is particularly interesting because it states that a search of the records was made for mention of "foreign traders who come when it is not a time for the presentation of tribute"; the absence of records of such traders was used to justify the new interdiction against nontributary trade.[18] This close identification of trade and tribute is absent in Manchu documents before 1644, but the lack must not be misconstrued since probably the only trade that would have received official mention in the records of the imperial court was trade that took place during the visits of tribute missions to the capital.

Although practical considerations of defense dictated recourse to traditional Sino-Confucian trade policies in 1668, in 1684, when the Rebellion of the Three Feudatories in the south and southwest and Zheng's rebellion in the southeast had been overcome and the Manchus sat firmly on China's throne, an edict issued to the Grand Secretaries indicated a sharp return to the original Manchu view of the value of foreign trade. The emperor stated explicitly that maritime trade would benefit the coastal regions of Fujian and Guangdong by increasing commodity circulation and purchasing power. Furthermore, the proceeds from a light tax on foreign trade could be used to support the Fujian and Guangdong garrisons, in lieu of the transportation of rice from the interior. This step, in turn, would benefit the interior provinces by decreasing exactions for military supplies and transport.[19] In order to encourage trade, the emperor prohibited the collection of taxes from maritime trade at coastal bridges, ferries, ports, and customshouses, beyond the light garrison tax he himself proposed.

The emperor reaffirmed Qing support of foreign trade in February

1708. Lao Zhiban, a censor (an official charged with the task of criticizing government operations), had memorialized that the price of rice in Jiejiang and Jiangsu had suddenly risen because "evil merchants" were exporting rice from the interior overseas, and he recommended the complete cessation of foreign trade. Kangxi opposed this move vigorously and ordered, instead, closer surveillance of ports.[20] However, the development of an export trade in ships seriously endangered the continuity of the emperor's pro-trade policy. In 1717, during a southern progress, Kangxi had noticed extensive shipyards at Suzhou, and upon inquiry he learned that annually some one thousand or more ships went abroad to trade but that only fifty or sixty percent returned; the remainder were exchanged overseas for silver. The Suzhou ship merchants had told him that the ships that did not return from abroad were destroyed by storms. The use of ironwood for the construction of keels particularly disturbed the emperor. Ironwood was available only in Guangdong, he believed, and if ships with ironwood keels were sold abroad China would lose control of the shipbuilding industry (which, of course, China did not control in the first place). "Herein is something irregular. A stop should be put to it," he concluded. Kangxi's overriding concern was not to increase the inflow of silver (as would have been the case had he been guided by the mercantilist ideas then prevalent in Europe) but to prevent the export of a valuable wood. Consequently, he forbade Chinese ships to sail to Southeast Asia, thus reverting to dependence on Southeast Asian bottoms and traders for commerce with that region. One month later, in March 1717, the emperor approved a strict set of regulations designed to prevent active Chinese trade with Southeast Asia, but the following year he modified these at the request of the governor-general of Guangdong and Guangxi to permit Chinese vessels to trade directly with Vietnam.[21]

Up to the very end of his life, Kangxi continued to encourage those forms of foreign trade he considered beneficial for the Chinese economy. As late as 1722 he issued an edict encouraging the importation of cheap rice from Siam to his southeastern provinces. Fujian, Guangdong, and Ningbo were each to receive 100,000 *shi* of rice, but in accord with his policy of 1717, Siamese ships were to carry the rice. The emperor's death at the end of 1722 marked the end of experimentation and encouragement in the field of foreign trade for well over a century and began a period of increasing restriction and inhibitory policies.[22] In 1727 Kangxi's successor, Yongzheng (1723–1736), ordered the strict control and, if possible, outright prevention of Chinese emigration abroad or the return of Chinese emigrants to their homes. In general, policy returned to strict Sino-Confucian attitudes toward commerce. Where necessary, however, Yongzheng extended existing institutions to new areas: when Li Wei, the governor-general of Jiejiang, an official high in the emperor's favor, requested the application to his province of the rules permitting and governing rice imports from Southeast Asia, the new emperor agreed.[23] The reasons why the emperor approved this request, granting Jiejiang ships permission to engage in foreign trade can only be surmised. One Gao Qizho held various governorships in South China between 1723 and 1738. It was rumored that Cai Wan, his mother, had been a concubine of Wu Sanguei, who first cooperated with, and then led, a great rebellion against the Manchus. Whether for this or other reasons, Li Wei was ordered, as part of his work, to report on Gao's activities to the emperor. It may well be that the privilege of being allowed to participate in the controlled rice trade with Southeast Asia, from which the governor could himself undoubtedly hope to profit, was granted Li Wei as a sign of the emperor's personal favor. It should be noted, in this regard, that the emperor did not grant the privilege on the basis of economic need but rather on the basis of Jiejiang's proximity to Fujien and the consequent difficulties expected in enforcing the general prohibitions. The emperor's permission was granted by virtue of his approval of Li Wei's memorial.[24]

Kangxi's trade policies, which to some extent influenced the early years of his successor's reign, were only a reflection, in one specific area of state activity, of the general vigor that characterized his entire era. The favor shown the Jesuits (whose position, for political reasons, began to decline toward the end of Kangxi's long years on the throne) and the emperor's keen curiosity and inquiring mind about things foreign demonstrate that the dynasty had not yet become sinified. The contrast with a later monarch of equally long reign, Qianlong, is striking. Kangxi could never have written Qianlong's famous 1793 edict to King George III of England, which, as one commentator remarked, is composed in "powerful and elegant Chinese, drafted by a master hand."[25] The categories of thought from which the document proceeded show clearly the influence of the rigid Sino-Confucian tradition at work.

This, then, was the Chinese world of international relations into which the Europeans came, both by chance and by design, during the seventeenth century. We cannot say simply that in that world the tribute system was a reflection of Confucian ideas on the international scene. On the contrary, as we have seen, the tribute system *per se* did not exist except as a complex of many institutions interacting with each other. Had the particular set of institutions that we call the tribute system not resulted in important or unexpected increments, both physical and political, it would have been changed or abandoned. The system existed not because Confucianism dictated its existence but because it provided the mechanisms for dealing with the universe on the basis of prior, detailed observation. The eighteenth century saw the development of a compromise between the tribute system and a new element in the traditional East Asian world, the Russians; however, when the English, in the nineteenth century, were unprepared to compromise, worlds came into conflict. China is still adjusting to its defeat.

Alone No More

THE TRIBUTE SYSTEM constituted the institutional and ideational infrastructure of an empire that was sinocentric and whose center we call China. The Empire was ruled by the Han Chinese Ming dynasty from 1368 to 1644 and, from 1644 to 1912, by a sinicized dynasty of barbarian origin, the Manchu Qing. The distinction between the Chinese Ming and the Manchu Qing dynasty is significant both in the history of China itself and in the history of China's foreign interactions within the context of the international order that developed autonomously in East Asia from the Zhou dynasty to the Ming, when this institutional complex assumed its classical form as the tribute system. The Empire occupied the whole of its world, or at least the only important part of it, and those regions that were beyond its ken lay in outer darkness. The appearance of the West in East Asia in the sixteenth century opened a new chapter in the history of the sinocentric world-empire. Although the rulers of that empire and their subjects did not realize it at the time, the arrival of the Western barbarians signaled the expansion of the effective world to encompass the entire planet. The Westerners also represented a new system, the capitalist world economy, which itself was in the process of emergence and whose core was in Western Europe.

The East and the West: The Old Order and the New

China was the center of a world empire, which is to say that the tribute system in its entirety—beginning with its focus on the emperor and extending through Chinese society out into the areas peripheral to China itself—defined an empire that occupied the geographical, social, and political space of the East Asians' known world. In this view, the very term *zhong-guo* ("China," or "central kingdom") refers not to a culture or a historical nation in the modern Western sense but rather to the ideational and spatial center of this world empire. The history of China in its international relations with the West is, to no small extent, the story of the transformation of the center of the world empire into the Western and more parochial concept and reality of a national culture and state such as emerged in the West beginning in the seventeenth century.

The geographical space of the world empire was quite clearly circumscribed. Within that area, the parts were articulated into a whole (on the basis of political and military power, culture, and ideology) that consisted of a well-defined center, subsidiary centers, and outlying regions. A broad and socially distinct bureaucracy provided the personnel structure of this Empire, and this bureaucracy grew thinner the further away one drew from the imperial center. Its existence beyond China depended upon the incorporation of local rulers and ruling groups into the cultural constructions of the imperial center, and that incorporation depended either upon internal acceptance of the Empire's culture or upon external compliance with those of its customs that were appropriate to interaction with the Empire.

Throughout the Empire, culture and social occupation were linked; within both China Proper and the outlying areas of the Empire, the ruling groups were assimilated into some form, or adopted various aspects, of Han Chinese culture. In the nonsinicized regions of the Empire, that is, in those areas removed from of the heavy influence of Han culture, compliance with the forms of the imperial Han culture was expected along the interface with China Proper even if the ruling groups rejected China's Han culture for themselves. Outside China Proper, therefore, the upper reaches of local bureaucracies or social structures participated in a culture that transcended, and knew no specific reference to, particular boundaries or geopolitical institutions. Areas, groups, and even individuals moved into or out of the Empire depending upon the degree to which they were prepared, or forced, to accept the cultural definition of imperial status. Within the Empire, the economy was embedded in the thoughts, customs, and behaviors that constituted the articulation of the Empire's infrastructure. That is why in China-centered East Asia, trade and tribute were facets of a single jewel.

The Portuguese, Spanish, and Dutch merchants who intruded into the Empire presaged a society emerging in Western Europe that would engulf the East Asian world order, through the agency of English power, after the middle of the nineteenth century. The causes of the rise of capitalism and even its very definition continue to be the foci of an intense debate that itself has a long history and, undoubtedly, a future as well. The purpose here is not to engage in that debate but briefly to sketch some of the outstanding characteristics of the new system emerging in the West so that it can be perceived in contrast to the sinocentric imperial system.

Capitalism as an economy encompasses not one but a multiplicity of political systems. It is noteworthy that despite numerous attempts at transnational unification, social and political unity remains an elusive goal of capitalist world society. Neither the Papacy nor the Holy Roman Empire—two remnants of a noncapitalist imperial era in European history that was institutionalized in the Roman Empire, which tended more toward a sense of universality than any other polity in Western history—could inhibit the development of mutual rivalry, religious schism, and other institutions that deflected the focus of public attention. Perhaps capitalism, rooted in a world view that asserts the primacy of competition and contention in human relationships, negates the very possibility of a harmonious world system. In this way, capitalism contrasts sharply with the sinocentric imperial system in East Asia, a political system that encompassed many economies that were carefully articulated through the rituals and ideology of the tribute system and, at the same time, through the ports of trade and commercial caravans. While in the West the center declined and eventually disappeared—the Holy Roman Empire officially dissolved in 1806—in East Asia the emperor remained the theoretical and often real center of both policy and style. Even when a weak emperor sat upon the throne, his court was the necessary font of all legitimacy in the system. This remained true until the beginning of the twentieth century and was resumed, in a new form, in 1949 after a relatively short period of polycentric disunity.

The capitalist world economy is characterized by the assumption that no political entity can, or should try to, control economic factors entirely. The ideological basis of capitalism presumes that control over any part of the economy is difficult and unnatural even if necessary. Moreover, in this system various economic factors operate over a territory that is larger than any political unit can control. Ideologically this view is supported by, and reflected in, the concept of the worldwide interdependence of economies. Historically, it allowed for the economic expansion of the system to the limits of the planet. In the process of development at home and expansion abroad, the relationship between the state and the economy was such that the state often supported the growth of the private economy by absorbing losses that private capitalists sustained while, at the same time, it insured that gains from economic activity were distributed to that same sector of the population. The use of monopolies granted by the crown to groups of merchants on the basis of which private capital could become more firmly established is well known. The state often supported the foreign expansion of the capitalist system by absorbing the costs of conquest and pacification to allow the operation of private capital in economically advantageous conditions. In one way or another, therefore, the state tended to support the bourgeois class. In the sinocentric Empire, however, the state did not support the bourgeois class: in Confucian ideology the merchant occupied the bottom rung of the social ladder, operating under many legal, customary, and social restrictions. Likewise, the state did not encourage or support economic expansion. Chinese merchants often emigrated overseas, particularly to Southeast Asia in the eighteenth and nineteenth centuries, but they did so in contravention of established policy.

Extensive division of labor on a broad geographical basis also characterizes the capitalist system. Even in the sixteenth and seventeenth centuries, economic activities were not evenly distributed throughout the capitalist world order. For example, in Western Europe some areas remained primarily agricultural and supported more industrial areas in a symbiotic relationship. One area served as a source of the raw materials that the industrial centers in another area turned into commercial products, and an increasingly ramified communications network distributed these products, again unevenly, throughout the system. This division of labor had ecological foundations, but it was also a function of the social organization of labor and of intersectional competition within the capitalist world economy. Here, too, that economy stood in contrast to the sinocentric Empire. In the latter, nothing approaching a systemwide market developed until very late, and regional self-sufficiency, not systemic interdependence, was the norm. Constraints imposed by geography and transportation technology inhibited the development of a systemwide market. The only significant good to be transported over great distances was grain; by and large the various economic regions of China were self-sufficient in food (the tremendous regional differentiation in Chinese cuisine reflects this characteristic of the economy). In the Empire, the full range of economic activities was distributed differentially throughout the system, but except in very specific areas, such as grain production, division of labor was social rather than regional. Not until Western commerce and industry made serious inroads into China in the latter part of the nineteenth and early part of the twentieth century did regional division of labor develop, with the growth of great commercial centers along the coast and in industrialized areas in the Northeast.

A division of the system's constituent parts into core states and peripheral areas closely accompanied the geographical division of labor in the capitalist world system. Industrialism and advanced commercial institutions and techniques characterized the core states, while the peripheral areas were less industrialized, if at all, and served the core states commercially. The state was strong in the core states and relatively weak in the peripheral areas, allowing metropolitan exploitation of the resources, both natural and human, of the peripheral (colonial and semicolonial) areas. The sinocentric Empire had a culturally identifiable core area in China Proper, more especially in the capital, but the relationship between core area and peripheral regions was not one of exploitation. Moreover, the differentiation in potential power among the units in the Empire depended on size and available resources rather than on internal strength, with only one exception: institutional weakness within the larger China permitted smaller and relatively weak peoples, such as the Mongols and the Manchus, to conquer the vaster territory and population. The expansion of the capitalist world economy to its planetary limits transformed China—the core area of its own system—into a peripheral area of the capitalist world system. Capitalism, through the agency of its Western governments, merchants, and military forces, imposed severe limitations on the sovereignty of the Chinese state, at times using it as an instrument of the capitalist world system.

Economic activities and institutions provide the primary forms and loci of articulation between groups in the capitalist world economy, both within a given state and throughout the system. This explains why economic questions tend to dominate politics and foreign policy in the modern, or Western, world. In the sinocentric Empire, however, trade was only one form of articulation among groups, and not necessarily the most significant; ritual, for example, provided an important form of articulation, as we have seen. This profound difference between the world capitalist system and the sinocentric Empire became a source of major conflict in the second part of the nineteenth century.

In the capitalist economic system, culture and geographical location have become closely linked. As the Middle Ages waned and the Renaissance faded into the Modern Age, and as the vernacular replaced Latin as the primary vehicle of discourse, the horizontally shared culture of the European ecclesiastical and secular elite, which distinguished it from the lower social orders, was replaced by vertical political and cultural identification. We observe this development most clearly in the emergence of the nation-state and nationalism, which are rooted in the consciousness of geographical, ethnic, and linguistic differences. Even in Prussia and Russia, where the aristocracy spoke French in preference to German or Russian during a large part of the eighteenth century, the Napoleonic wars resulted in the primacy of German and Russian as nationalism and culture-centrism replaced a broader European outlook in the upper reaches of society.

In the sinocentric Empire, the link of culture to class remained stronger than the link of culture to geography, which is to say that the principal locus of culture tended to be social rather than spatial. The Han Chinese, the Mongols, the Manchus, the Tibetans, the Turks—all these and other ethnic groups of the Empire differed fundamentally from each other in language, custom, and social structure. And within the Han culture area, the ruling class was identifiable culturally as well as sociopolitically; while it shared a great deal with the masses (among whom regional differences were very strong, in many areas including mutual linguistic incomprehension), it was distinguished from them by its own culture. Similarly, the ruling classes in the other states of the Empire learned a language and literature they did not share with the populace. The more these ruling classes were integrated into, or influenced by, the culture of the Han ruling class of China Proper, the more distinctive they became. This class based cultural differentiation certainly inhibited the growth of nationalism in East Asia. In the capitalist West, the growth of the national state as an expression of, and reinforcement for, ethnic differentiation encouraged competition among systemic units within the Oikoumene, that centerless community of nation-states that was (and is) the capitalist world system, and this development was considered healthy for the system. Such competition had no place, systemically or ideologically, in the sinocentric Empire.

Technology has played a significant role in the development of the capitalist world economy. It is an accepted but unwarranted assertion that technology, which is what we mean by the Industrial Revolution, was the basis for capitalism's emergence. More correctly, the emerging capitalist world economy and technology were mutually reinforcing and symbiotic factors in a process of historical change called modernization or industrialization. The sinocentric Empire's court and bureaucracy, for their part, found China's transportation and communications technology adequate to the needs of the imperial system and did not encourage the development of technology, which, in turn, might have led to profound structural changes in the system.

Finally, the world capitalist system is geographically and economically expansionist. Europe expanded to the Western Hemisphere in the sixteenth century, and, as Ferdinand Braudel pointed out, "the gold and silver of the new world enabled Europe to live above its means, to invest beyond its savings."[1] Population growth accompanied capitalism and, whether as a consequence or a concomitant, production expanded as well. The expansionism of capitalism contrasted sharply with the stability of the sinocentric Empire and brought first Portuguese and then other Western merchants into the zone of the East Asian sinocentric imperial system, an intrusion whose consequences were to change the world.

The Barbarians Who Came by Sea

The characteristics that differentiated the growing capitalist world system from the sinocentric Empire delineated the domain in which the specifics of China's foreign relations took on their primary significance. The history of the foreign relations of the Qing dynasty is the history, first, of the parochialization of the universal culture of the sinocentric world and, second, of the transformation of that world's core area into a peripheral region within the new capitalist world economy. Westerners who arrived along the China coast by sea were the first agents of this transformation.

THE PORTUGUESE ARRIVE

The sinocentric Empire's first continuing contact with the new society of Europe occurred through the medium of the Portuguese empire, more particularly its merchants in the Far East. The Chinese did not realize the significance of the Portuguese arrival, but it initiated a process that would end by destroying the Empire and engulfing China.

The sudden expansion of the Portuguese in the fifteenth century and the emergence of the capitalist world economy are historically one process; the same factors account for both. By the middle of the fourteenth century, Portugal possessed an internal market but experienced limitations imposed upon it by geography. Portugal expanded into the Atlantic in search of agricultural lands to provide grains and wine for the Iberian Peninsula and the rest of Europe. The search for sugar, new fishing grounds, and gold also played a role. Portugal itself belonged to the Mediterranean world, and its economy was more monetarized than the economies of the other areas of Europe. As a society bridging the Mediterranean and Atlantic zones, Portugal also participated in the commerce of the Islamic world and therefore could take advantage of the geographical knowledge the latter possessed.

These and other factors, including Christian missionary zeal, account for the almost annual expeditions dispatched by Portugal's Prince Henry the Navigator between 1421 and 1460. By 1488, the Portuguese had rounded the Cape of Good Hope; the Indian Ocean and the Far East lay before them. In 1498, Vasco da Gama reached the southwest coast of India, and after 1509 the Portuguese, having defeated a Moslem fleet at Diu, found themselves a major power in the Indian Ocean. They secured a base on the island of Goa on the west coast of India in 1510 and established themselves at Malacca in the Malay Archipelago in 1511. From there, they sailed to the east and also north to China, arriving there in 1514. The speed with which the Portuguese economy expanded to include commercial outposts and ventures half a world away reflected the maritime technological superiority Portugal had developed in the course of its Atlantic explorations. Changes in ship design permitted longer voyages, more maneuverability and greater firepower.

Technological innovations facilitated the establishment of stations across the Indian Ocean, which then enabled the Portuguese to pursue their objectives in a coherent fashion. Controlling the entrance to the Red Sea in the west and the advantageously narrow Straits of Malacca in the east, they established three great markets at Malacca in the East Indies, Calicut in India, and Ormuz in Persia. At the entrance to the Red Sea, Aden served as a subsidiary entrepôt. Two squadrons—one in the western area around the Red Sea and one in the Indian Ocean, both under a governor-general at Goa—protected these markets. In addition, a series of small trading posts fed into the larger markets.

The Portuguese faced important military and administrative problems from the outset since their intrusion into the area took place along trade routes previously controlled by the Arabs, whose defeat at the hands of the Portuguese opened the door for European expansion. Indeed, throughout the period of their predominance in the Indian Ocean, the Portuguese clashed with rivals, including, eventually, competitors from Europe itself. In the final analysis, however, the Portuguese in Asia were unable to reach that critical mass of population and power that would have permitted them to maintain over time more than a limited number of distant outposts.

PORTUGAL AND CHINA

En route to China, the Portuguese began to penetrate into the periphery of the sinocentric Empire in a fashion that was well in accord with the latter's traditional structure of expectations. In Burma, Siam, and Southeast Asia, they entered local conflicts as mercenaries, pirates, and advisors; on occasion, a Portuguese even became a local potentate. When the Portuguese first arrived in China in 1514, at the entrance to the Xi River in Southwest China not far from the city of Canton, they came as barbarians from the sea and were considered, despite their vulgarities, "a harmless sort of people."[2]

Three years later, an embassy arrived from the king of Portugal to visit his equal, the "king of China." This, of course, was an impossibility from the Chinese point of view. When the embassy reached Canton, it fired a salute, outraging the Chinese sense of propriety and leading to a demand for an apology, but the Portuguese ambassador, carrying gifts for the emperor, appeared to the Chinese to be a tribute bearer and was treated accordingly. In the meantime, other Portuguese had established a fort on Lintin Island at the entrance to the bay that is the mouth of the Xi River, and they began to behave like pirates. The official Chinese description of the affair accuses them of being cannibals with a special taste for small children. This first Portuguese embassy ended badly, particularly for the ambassador, who died in a prison in Canton. The Portuguese aggravated the situation by engaging Chinese junks in a series of naval battles, and the king of Malacca, who was a tributary of the emperor's, complained to Peking about Portuguese behavior in his domain.

This first Western attempt to establish formal diplomatic contact with the sinocentric Empire failed, but the Portuguese continued to be a presence in the Far East during the next three decades. Finally, in 1557, they obtained the permission of local Chinese authorities to establish a permanent trading post on Macao, a small peninsula south of Canton. This was the first Western colony in the Far East, and it survives to this day. In Macao, the Portuguese ruled a mixed population, instituted their own form of government, and pursued their own commercial objectives. Macao was an example of the application of the port of trade concept to a new group of barbarians, thereby incorporating them into the imperial system.

ENTER SPAIN

Chinese contacts with the capitalist world economy expanded with the appearance of Spain on the Southeast Asian scene. The international rivalry between Spain and Portugal for the division of the world was resolved by the papal bull *Inter Coetera* of 1493 and the Treaty of Tordesillas of 1494. These documents, with later minor modifications, stipulated that Portugal could evangelize and colonize Brazil, the islands of the Atlantic Ocean, and all the lands to the east as far as the other side of the world. Spain received the same rights in the Caribbean, the rest of the Americas, and the Pacific. Subsequent modifications of the arrangement honored Spanish claims to the Philippine islands, which the Portuguese explorer Magellan had visited in his circumnavigation of the globe while in Spanish service.

In 1571, the Spaniards established the city of Manila in the Philippines. Manila became the basis for the Christianization of most of the Philippine islands and, at the same time, a major entrepôt in the developing trade between Europe and China. Manila was, in effect, a port of trade within the institutional structure of the sinocentric sphere of influence. As an entrepôt, Manila was a political extension of the Spanish administration of Mexico and a commercial outpost of the extractive economy of the New World. From the beginning of the seventeenth century to 1815, galleons made annual voyages between Mexico's western port of Acapulco and Manila, carrying silver extracted from the Mexican mines to Manila, where it was used to purchase Chinese silks and Southeast Asian spices, particularly pepper, for export to Spain back across the Pacific, through Mexico, and across the Atlantic. Manila itself became a community inhabited to a large extent by Chinese who emigrated to the Philippines in order to engage in steady commerce; they dominated the economy of the city. Spanish-Chinese conflicts occurred, sometimes with great loss of life. Junks annually visited Manila to supply silks for the galleons, and the flow of silver from Mexico to China was so significant that the Mexican dollar in time became the primary silver currency on the China coast. Eventually, of course, the China trade through Manila came under sharp criticism from Spain itself, for the outflow of silver to China contradicted the prevailing mercantilist ideology.

The tribute system functioned in the Philippines, too. The king of Luzon entered the imperial system in 1575, after the arrival of the Spaniards; undoubtedly he was seeking support against the intruders. After the Spanish massacred the Chinese population of Manila in 1662, the following description of the Spaniards appeared in the imperial records:

> These Fo-lang chi people have cat's eyes (blue pupils) and eagle noses (high noses) and curly hair and red beards. They are the most treacherous people in the world. No matter what the country, as long as it has never been visited by them (Fo-lang chi) it is peaceful and quiet. Once they (Fo-lang chi) arrive they immediately plot to conquer that country. Luzon also was annexed by their conspiracy.[3]

Critical of the Spaniards though the Chinese were, the system functioned to mediate between the two world systems by filtering information about the Spaniards in the Philippines into the Chinese world-view.

THE DUTCH

European commercial politics pitted the Dutch against the Portuguese and Spaniards in the Far East. In the course of the sixteenth century, Amsterdam overtook the Iberian commercial centers as the core community of the expanding European capitalist world economy. Amsterdam was a major port and the chief city of the Low Countries, whose foreign trade in manufactured woolens provided capital for economic development. The Dutch increasingly engaged in the Baltic and North Sea trade and developed a vigorous fishing and shipping tradition, which led to the growth of nautical skills among Dutch sailors. The impact of the Protestant Reformation and the long years of Dutch struggle against Spanish control between 1568 and 1648 further stimulated the natural tendency within the capitalist world economy for culture to develop on spatial rather than social bases. The profound intra-European rivalry intensified when the Spanish took over Portugal in 1580 and excluded the Dutch from the Lisbon spice market in 1594.

The Portuguese attempt at the end of the sixteenth century to prevent the publication in Europe of information concerning the trade routes and spice trade in the East failed, and in 1595 a Dutch expedition reached the island of Java. By 1601, the Dutch were active throughout the Far East, including Japan, and in 1619 they established a permanent settlement at Batavia on Java. East of India the Dutch maintained a system of bases and successfully fought the Spaniards and Portuguese for the control of maritime trade routes. In 1641, they seized Malacca and established themselves permanently in the Indies. This widespread and energetic commercial activity on the periphery of the world economy hastened Amsterdam's growth as the commercial center of the system. By the end of the seventeenth century, Dutch commerce and shipping provided a model for the development of such peripheral areas as Russia.

By 1622 the Dutch had established a small fort in the Pescadores, islands between Taiwan and the Chinese mainland, whence they had been driven by Chinese military forces after an unsuccessful attempt to settle on the mainland. In 1624 they established fortified positions on Taiwan itself. They traded there until Koxinga, the Ming loyalist, expelled them in 1661. In June 1662, Batavia sent twelve ships to attack Koxinga's outposts and ships along the China coast in retaliation for the expulsion from Taiwan. In 1663 and 1664 the Dutch cooperated with the Manchus in their military activities against the Ming loyalists, and beginning in 1656 they sent tributary missions to Peking. According to Qing records, the tributary missions served as the appropriate occasions for the conduct of trade, even though the Dutch did not succeed in establishing a permanent trade relationship with the Manchus. A certain pragmatism prevented the Dutch from making a frontal assault on the imperial system, though they themselves represented the core area of the new emerging world economy.

The Portuguese, Spaniards, and Dutch stood at different stages in the development of the capitalist world economy. Seaborne barbarians all, they intruded upon the periphery of the sinocentric Empire as quaint and somewhat unsavory types with whom the system could deal because they posed it no challenge.

The Russians Come by Land

During the seventeenth century, Russia was a "reservoir of grain and forest products" for the Western European core area of the developing capitalist world economy. For example, Russia exported to England essential materials for the navy. Moscow exchanged Russian raw materials and semifinished products for the manufactures of Western Europe, which is why it is possible to speak of Russia as a peripheral area in the world economy of the time.[4]

Several important factors combined to distinguish Russia from Western Europe, including that country's size and potential for continental expansion. Russia had a frontier that faced unorganized and economically unintegrated territory in Siberia all the way to the Pacific. This land was potentially a great source of raw materials for Russian development. Russia's external trade with the Near East and the Turks and Persians of Central Asia and the Middle East was as important as its trade with Western Europe. Finally, to the south and east Russia faced organized societies that had reached a high level of bureaucratic and cultural development but that lay outside the Christian, even the orthodox Christian, context of Europe.

While the Western Europeans approached the sinocentric Empire by sea, the Russians approached China by land. As a consequence, the Empire dealt with the Russians through the same mechanisms used for continental barbarians. In effect, the Empire incorporated the Russians into its structure in the same way it did Central Asians. Beginning in 1579, when the first Cossacks raided western Siberia, Russian explorers crossed Siberia to the Pacific with remarkable speed, reaching the ocean at the Sea of Okhotsk in 1639. In sixty years, Russia created a basis for its future as an Asian and Pacific power. Economic exploitation and incorporation of the territories through which they passed accompanied the Russians' expansion eastward. Local tribes were russified, or at least their rulers were brought into a ritualistic and juridical relationship with the Russian state, while Russian settlements were established, first military and then civilian, across the face of Siberia.

Russia's thrust into the Amur River valley in Northern Manchuria in the 1640s occurred at precisely the same time that the Manchus, having organized the Qing dynasty in Manchuria itself, vigorously invaded China Proper. The appearance of the Russians at their backs and by land led to a series of significant armed conflicts in which the Manchus mounted a concerted campaign to control Russian incursions and the Russians mounted a less concerted but no less committed campaign to establish a permanent presence in the area.

As they penetrated the Manchu dominated Empire in the Far East, the Russians also began to appear as a factor in Central Asia to the west, where the Manchus faced a serious challenge from the Mongolian and Turkish tribes of the region. Though the Manchus at first did not associate the Russians in Manchuria with those in Central Asia, they were aware that crises in both areas would weaken their position in China Proper.

While the Russians approached China territorially, they also attempted to make direct contact with China diplomatically and commercially through a series of missions to Peking. Russian authorities clearly believed that trade with Peking would benefit Moscow commercially, and preliminary efforts seemed to support their expectations. It was only in the 1670s that the Manchus recognized that the missions and the caravans came from essentially the same source as the intruders into the Amur River valley. After several unsuccessful diplomatic encounters and a relatively successful Manchu military campaign against the Russians in the 1680s, negotiations led to the signing of China's first treaty with a Western power, the Treaty of Nerchinsk of 1689. Concluded against the background of mounting Mongol pressure on the Manchus in Central Asia, the treaty represented a compromise between the positions assumed by Moscow and Peking. The body of the treaty consists of a fairly detailed delineation of a significant part of the frontier between Russian and Manchu territories, and the document promulgated regulations and created institutions to establish and maintain peaceful contacts between the two polities.

Several details of the treaty deserve note. It defined a juridical frontier in geographical terms, which was something of a departure from traditional Chinese practice since the Empire did not conceptually recognize the existence of juridical frontiers. It established the right of one or the other side to be present in specific territories, and it contained agreements concerning hunting rights and other commercial activities. It explicitly recognized that the past was passed and should not influence the present, and it implicitly recognized that the future held the possibility of increased Russo-Chinese interaction by including clauses on the conduct of trade and the exchange of personnel. It also provided for the possibility of the reception of Russian embassies and caravans at Peking on a triennial basis. From the Manchus' point of view, the treaty made the Empire's domination of Central Asia possible since it inhibited the growth of Russian relations with the Central Asian enemies of Manchu power.

After 1689, Russian trade caravans regularly visited Peking; this caravan trade easily fit the expectations of the imperial tribute system. The leaders of the caravans, who often carried the rank of ambassador, agreed to follow the prescribed rituals of the tribute system, and regulations similar to those governing the commercial ventures of other land based barbarians in Peking governed the Russians as well. The Li-fan Yuan was responsible for the Russians while they were inside imperial territory, and in Peking they were housed in the Russian Hostel, which closely resembled the Hostel for Tributary Envoys. The Manchus organized a small group of Russians, who had emigrated to Peking after Russia's first defeat in the Amur River valley, into a Russian company within the structure of Manchu military society. The court donated land for the establishment of a Russian church in Peking, with a Russian priest to serve the Russian community that was becoming a part of the capital's regular population, and the Li-fan Yuan established a Russian-language school in the capital. These measures assured the Manchu court personnel who knew Russian or had access to Russian residents in Peking who could serve as interpreters.

A revival of the crisis in Central Asia and Russian involvement in it, combined with the institutional inability of the treaty's caravan system to satisfy Russian commercial interests, exposed the weakness of the arrangements made at Nerchinsk. The caravan trade declined in importance as Russian goods began to glut the Peking market. The Nerchinsk arrangements did not inhibit a vigorous tsar from pursuing a forward policy in Central Asia. The Manchus tried several approaches to a resolution of their continuing Russian problem. Military action in Central Asia against the Qing's indigenous enemies accompanied diplomatic moves intended to prevent a Russian-Mongol alliance against the Manchus in that area. This suggested the necessity to delineate further the frontier between those areas of immediate interest to Russia and the sinocentric Empire. In pursuit of its diplomatic objectives, the Manchu court sent an extraordinary mission led by a court official, Tulishen, to visit a western Mongol tribe settled on the Volga River. Traversing Siberia and eastern Russia between 1712 and 1715, this embassy gathered significant information about Siberia and Russia for the use of the Qing court and may have been instrumental in preventing further Russian encroachments on Manchu interests in Asia.

For its part, Russia sought a more precise definition of the frontier, a commercial structure that would permit Sino-Russian trade to grow, and ways to remain in fruitful contact with the sinocentric Empire. It was in the interest of both parties to reach an accommodation, and difficult and complex negotiations ended in the Treaty of Kyakhta of 1728, which was more comprehensive, more sophisticated, and more farseeing than the Treaty of Nerchinsk had been.

In eleven articles, the new treaty carefully covered all aspects of Sino-Russian relations and established a context within which those relations could continue in a fashion not prejudicial to either party. The heart of the treaty was the commercial system it established: trade by caravan on a controlled triennial basis and a frontier trade to take place at two regular ports of trade along the Sino-Russian frontier. The treaty specified the conditions under which both kinds of trade would take place. The Empire made certain religious concessions to Russia in exchange for the frontier settlement. The Manchus reaffirmed the specific functions of the Russian Hostel in Peking and gave permission for the construction of a church on the hostel's premises. The treaty also provided for the appointment of a court official to manage relations with Russia and permitted the Russians to organize a religious establishment in Peking to serve the church. This was the origin of the famous Russian Ecclesiastical Mission in Peking, which functioned over the decades as an unofficial embassy.

The Kyakhta agreement projected the Sino-Russian relationship into the future by creating machinery for the resolution of disputes and by describing in detail the forms for the conduct of diplomatic intercourse. It stipulated the manner in which correspondence would be written, diplomatic personnel exchanged, documents legitimated, and caravans and embassies conducted. The treaty further stipulated appropriate punishment for crimes officially recognized as such by the authorities on each side; moreover, the punishments were to be appropriate to the culture of the culprit. Finally, there were provisions whereby either side could take action to force the other to observe the treaty.

The various parts of the Treaty of Kyakhta became operative in the years immediately after its conclusion. The Russians established two frontier ports of trade: one failed to develop while the other, located at

Kyakhta, flourished. The caravan trade prospered for a while, but the Kyakhta entrepôt quickly eclipsed it, and the last Russian caravan went to Peking in 1755, after which this particular form of trade ceased to be of commercial interest to the Russians. The provisions compelling observance of the treaty's stipulations were invoked only three times between 1728 and 1860, demonstrating the stability of the Sino-Russian system created by the treaty. In effect, the expanding Russian state and the sinocentric Empire established a relationship of peaceful coexistence that endured more than one hundred thirty years.

The success of the settlement reached by the Russians and Manchus at Kyakhta derived from a flexibility built into the system by diplomats cognizant not only of cultural and historical differences but of systemic differences as well. The institutions created at Kyakhta intentionally eschewed those areas of ideological, cultural, and customary conflict that previously had troubled Russian-Chinese relations just as they were troubling China's relations with other Western nations. The treaty system allowed for the development and modification of commercial institutions, which encouraged commercial continuity rather than sporadic contact through caravans alone. Most important, the treaty established a culturally neutral system of institutions that allowed for interpretation of the acts of intercourse in accord with the political, ideological, and ritual requirements and perceptions of each side. Russia's commercial caravans to Peking could be listed in the official records of the dynasty as tribute missions if the Qing court so wished, but the court was not required to treat the caravans as tribute missions. From the Russian perspective, they were commercial caravans and nothing more. Criminals were to be punished according to the expectations instilled in them by their own culture, but they would be punished by the side that caught them. The treaty did not stipulate a level of contact that had to be maintained, thus allowing the relationship to fluctuate as conditions warranted: trade could increase or decrease as necessary, and frontier officials could correspond with each other when they felt the need to do so.

This system rested on the equation of dissimilar cultures on the international scene. Faced with the problem of cross-cultural communications, the Sino-Russian relationship depended upon an ability to develop a system that recognized the superiority of each culture in its own view. At the same time, each culture had to be free to perpetuate its own perceptions of the other and the international scene, and that depended upon the cultural neutrality of the system that the treaty established.

The Treaty of Kyakhta demonstrated the flexibility of the sinocentric imperial order. With its assumptions left unchallenged and intact, China helped create a pragmatic institutional arrangement that permitted productive interaction with a radically different culture. Testimony to the Empire's flexibility came in 1731 and again in 1732, when two Qing diplomatic missions visited Moscow, where the envoys were received as ambassadors, ceremonially saluted, presented at court, and asked to perform the short kowtow. These first Chinese missions to a Western power were also the last until the latter part of the nineteenth century. The Manchus maintained their ideological purity by failing to enter these missions in their own imperial records, a procedure to which the Russians neither could nor would object. In the end, as we shall see shortly, changes in the West, not in the Empire, brought about the increasing debility and eventual destruction of the sinocentric world order.

The Jesuits

Diplomacy and commerce were two facets of the sinocentric imperial system. A third concerned the adherence of individuals to the system and their employment by it. In a world in which culture is a dimension of social rather than of spatial location, there is no real possibility for the development of the type of nationalism characteristic of the European capitalist world economy, particularly in the nineteenth and twentieth centuries. Furthermore, in such a world the state is not the organic expression of the nation or of the people's ethnicity; nor is it the instrument of one social class in its struggle with similar social classes in other countries. Indeed, there is no room for the very concepts of nation, country, or citizenship as these terms are used in the political language of bourgeois capitalism.

The inhabitants of a world that is dichotomized between civilization and barbarism will not perceive the emblem of civilization to be the nation with its flags and titles; rather, they will perceive the emblem to be the palpable form of civilization, which is culture in the sense of manners, morals, and arts, including the foods eaten and the clothes worn. All those varied characteristics that in the twentieth century's social sciences and humanities define a particular culture were in the world of the sinocentric Empire the characteristics of culture *per se*.

In a dichotomized world like the Empire's, an individual also was defined in terms of this same pair of concepts, civilization or barbarism, although the individual could be "turning toward civilization," or in transit from barbarism to culture. This is not to say that an individual's identity was not also defined socially in terms of class, sex, or a multitude of other characteristics. But it is clear from records that those characteristics that cluster around the twentieth-century Western concept of culture in both the humanistic and the anthropological sense provided a primary set of features for individual identification in China. In the capitalist world system, a person's allegiance is assumed to be attached, in some natural fashion, to his sovereign or his government and to be expressed by his ritual participation in activities directed at or around the emblem of his sovereign or government. Indeed, the power of this attachment and the degree to which it is considered a *natural* phenomenon can be perceived in bourgeois society's response to its negation. The traitor is guilty of a crime so heinous in the eyes of the bourgeois nation-state that death is widely considered to be the only appropriate punishment, and the crime is so profoundly "against nature" that it is difficult to comprehend.

In the sinocentric Empire, as in most of the nonbourgeois world historically, an individual's loyalty was primarily to his master, not to his people or to the sovereign of his homeland. His service was the more acceptable or sought after if he were also civilized. For example, Yelu Chucai, who served the Mongols and purportedly saved China from depredation by advising them to utilize China's wealth for their own purposes, is accounted at least a worthy gentleman and perhaps even a hero in Chinese historical annals. In the bourgeois world, defense of treasonable acts in terms of their possibly beneficial effects on society does not hold much credence in courts of law.

The universality of the sinocentric world empire allowed for the employment of foreigners in the upper reaches of the bureaucracy as long as the foreigner could be incorporated into the institutional and conceptual structure of civilization without challenging it directly. The story of the Jesuits in China is a good example of this.

THE ARRIVAL OF THE JESUITS

The Catholic church in Europe was both a spiritual and a temporal empire, and it belonged even in the sixteenth century to an era and social system that antedated the rise of the European capitalist world economy. Expansion of the church into the non-European world paralleled and took advantage of, but was not identical with, the expansion of Portuguese and Spanish interests. Often dependent upon the beneficence of the temporal rulers of Portugal and Spain and their officials, the missionaries' primary concern was their god and the expansion of the Catholic church. If the church and the secular authority could cooperate in a symbiotic relationship in the expanding world, that was all to the good, but the representatives of the church were quite capable of striking out on their own and in their own interests.

Ignatius of Loyola (1491–1556) fashioned the Society of Jesus on the basis of self-discipline and a nonmonastic, quasi-military organization under the absolute control of a "general." This "army of Christ," which combined disciplined membership in a semimilitary organization with a high concern for intellectual accomplishment, became an order of the church in

1540. In the missionary field, their discipline enabled the Jesuits to withstand the rigors of cultural and social transplantation, and their learning made them attractive to non-Western rulers as technical advisors.

The Jesuits entered Asia in the person of St. Francis Xavier (1506–1552), one of the founders of the Society of Jesus. In 1540 he arrived at Goa, where the Franciscans had set up their own Asian headquarters in 1517. There he established a training center before traveling on to the East Indies and the Far East. In 1549, six years after the Portuguese first reached Japan, Francis Xavier arrived in southern Kyushu on a Chinese junk from Malacca, accompanied by some Japanese Catholics who had been converted to the new religion in Southeast Asia. The importance of China in the sinocentric world of East Asia did not escape Francis Xavier, who believed that the conversion of the Chinese emperor to Catholicism was a crucial step in the Christianization of the Far East. He himself, however, never gained entrance to China, and attempts by other Jesuits and by Augustinians to penetrate China at about the same time failed. In 1576 the pope created a diocese in Macao under Portuguese patronage.

The Jesuits quickly learned that the key to the successful penetration of China required knowledge of the language and culture of the ruling scholar-gentry class, from which the imperial bureaucracy drew its members. Accordingly, they established a training center at Macao in 1580, which educated, among others, the greatest Jesuit in the history of the order in China, Matteo Ricci (1552–1610). By approaching China through the mastery of its dominant class's language and culture, the Jesuits prepared to fulfill the expectations of the sinocentric world order and the conditions that system laid down for membership in it. The success of the system in incorporating the Jesuits and the way in which the Jesuits, as other foreigners before them, became participants are best seen in the record of the activities of Matteo Ricci and his immediate successors.

Ricci's background prepared him for his tasks. An Italian by birth, he was broadly educated in the sciences of his day and he evidently possessed a photographic memory that served him in the study of both written and spoken Chinese. Among his first contributions to the Chinese scene were a large clock of his own making and a map of the world, which was published, with notes, in eight editions during his lifetime. The degree to which Ricci had already absorbed the nature of the system he was beginning to penetrate is illustrated by his notes to the map: in them, he told his Chinese readers that Europe's Catholic countries highly respected China's Confucian ethics. He himself was already "turning toward civilization."

The Jesuits, under Ricci's leadership, adapted themselves to China's culture as the only way of gaining access to the dominant class in society. They lived in Chinese style houses, wore the traditional gowns of a Confucian scholar, ate Chinese food, avoided open contact with the Portuguese merchants at Macao, and became proficient in Chinese. They eschewed preaching in favor of cultivated conversation with Chinese scholars, and they used Western inventions in combination with allusions to Chinese classics to win favor with the scholar-gentry officials. Through these efforts, Ricci and his colleagues in thirteen years moved north from the environs of Canton in the southeast to the Changjiang valley. It was only in 1598 that Ricci gained permission to visit Peking for two months, but in 1601 he finally received permission to establish a permanent residence there.

Once in the imperial capital, Ricci immediately thrust himself into the frenetic life of the imperial court. In the course of his sojourn there, Ricci succeeded in changing his identity from tribute bearer to resident scholar with an imperial income. Both categories were well within the Chinese system, but only after the change of identity could the Jesuits establish a position at court on a continuing basis. By the time Ricci died in 1601, there were over two thousand Christians in the Ming empire.

Ricci's successors continued to play a marginal but increasingly interesting role in the capital. They were involved primarily in the application of Western knowledge to China, much as their distant descendents, foreign technical advisors, were to be in the twentieth century. They helped revise the Chinese calendar through their knowledge of astronomy, and they succeeded in introducing the Copernican system to the court even though it was under interdiction in Europe. They introduced into Peking a Western library of seven thousand volumes, which they themselves used as a source of information for writing in Chinese. By the end of the seventeenth century, they had published 380 books in Chinese, mostly about Christianity but including a large number of titles ranging through the various fields of knowledge from astronomy to zoology. The marriage of Christianity and scientific knowledge that the Jesuits accomplished was to be a potent factor in the conversion of Chinese to Christianity in succeeding centuries.

The apparent ease with which the Jesuits made the transition from the Ming to the Qing dynasty after the Manchu conquest in 1644 testifies to more than self-interest. They had become in behavior and thought increasingly Chinese. In the 1630s, the Jesuit leader Johannes Adam Schall von Bell (1591–1666) established a foundry to aid in the Ming defense against the Manchus. During the collapse of the Ming, some members of the ruling house who had been baptized by the Jesuits appealed, in vain, to the pope for aid against the Manchu invaders. But when the Manchus conquered China, they kept Schall as chief court astronomer. In retaining his position, Schall demonstrated his loyalty to the system rather than to the dynasty, as was the case with many Ming officials. Schall's successor as head of the Jesuits, the Belgian Ferdinand Verbiest, also aided the defense of the Empire and advised the Manchu emperor in his capacity as court astronomer. Other Jesuits served the dynasty as interpreters, diplomats,

and advisors in a myriad of fields. They administered medicines to the
emperor, mapped the entire Qing empire, and contributed to China's
knowledge of the outside world. Until the Sino-Russian Treaty of Kyakhta
(1728), which established a permanent Russian presence at Peking, the
Jesuits were the only continuing point of contact between China and the
developing European world economy.

The Jesuits presented Europe with an image of China that stressed
compatibility and compromise rather than conflict and difference, that is
to say, themes they also stressed in presenting Christianity to the Chinese.
Ricci's major theological work in Chinese was a dialogue between a
Chinese and a Western scholar that avoided direct contradiction of classical
Confucianism and suggested that Christianity was a completion of Confucianism. The Jesuits rejected Buddhism and those forms of Confucianism
influenced by it and emphasized, rather, a classical interpretation of the
Confucian canon as a form of ancient wisdom. They honored Confucius as
a philosopher without venerating him as a deity. They considered Confucianism to be a system of ethics that was not at all incompatible with
Christianity.

In assuming the position of interpreter of East to West and West to
East, the Jesuits contributed, perhaps unwittingly, to the growth of the
belief in deism in Europe and to the search for alternatives to orthodox
Roman Catholic theology among the leading thinkers of their time. This
unanticipated consequence of their Chinese activities led to their downfall
and to a radical shift in the structure of China's relations with the West.

THE RITES CONTROVERSY

As the army of the church, the Society of Jesus was a non-national
entity in a world of growing nationalism. Its missionaries in China were
drawn from many countries, including Italy, Portugal, and Belgium.
France and Spain, on the other hand, were relatively poorly represented
among the Jesuits in China. In order to correct this imbalance and to
broaden the national character of the missionary effort in the Far East, the
papacy sent French Jesuits and Spanish Franciscans and Dominicans. Secular priests were dispatched by the French Society for Foreign Missions.
By the beginning of the eighteenth century, therefore, although the Jesuits
were the most significant group of Christian missionaries in China, they
were no longer alone. Furthermore, the missionaries had had no little success. The Christian community in China may have numbered as many as
300,000, and the Jesuits alone maintained seventy residences and over two
hundred churches or chapels. However, international rivalries stemming
from competition within the expanding capitalist economy were directly
reflected in, and profoundly influenced, the rivalry among the various orders active inside China.

The intrachurch controversy that centered on the Jesuits focused on their interpetation of China to the West. As the Jesuits became more assimilated to the Chinese scene, which is to say, as the sinocentric order increasingly dominated the Jesuits, their interpretations of Chinese thought became more defensive in the sense that ambiguity developed in their writings between the church *in* China and the church *of* China. If they had been concerned primarily with the church *in* China, the Jesuits would have argued for the direct and unmediated transplantation of Catholic practice to the Chinese landscape. However, their primary concern was for the church *of* China, that is, a synthesis that would permit the Catholic faith to flourish in China within the context of the dominant civil system and philosophy.

The broad outline of the conflict, not the fine details of theological controversy, will suffice to indicate the nature of the dispute. A group of Jesuits in China professed to see in the classical Confucian texts a precognition of Christian truths; their suggestion that this precognition was proof of the universality of Catholicism did not prevent European perceptions that this idea was heterodox and had to be rejected for publication. Nonetheless, the theory spread through private correspondence. Briefly, this was the question: did China demonstrate that morality was possible without the Christian revelation? In their interpretation of China to Europe, the Jesuits presented a non-Christian system of morality that included a concept of god the creator without a dependent messiah. This image provided comfort and support for anti-Christian and anti-Catholic philosophers and deists. By 1700 the debate had reached such proportions that the Chinese Jesuit position was condemned as "false, scandalous, and injurious."[5]

Ritual was another subject of debate. Was ancestor worship before the family altar, with its name tablets, a civil rite, or a pagan practice? If the former, such observances were allowable within the Christian tradition, but if the latter, they had to be rejected. In China, with its heavy traditional emphasis upon veneration of ancestors, the answer to this question would have tremendous consequences for the future of conversion. The Jesuits insisted that the absence in Confucianism of idol worship or of doctrines concerning life after death demonstrated the civil nature of Confucian thought. Confucianism, they argued, was in fact a state religion. The controversy demonstrated the problem that Westerners faced in confronting a system of thought that did not fit the definitions available within their own conceptual schemes. In Western eyes, if Confucianism were not a religion, it had to be a civil philosophy, or vice versa: there were no other possibilities. From the Christian point of view, if Confucianism were defined as a religion, it had to be placed in the category of deism since it had no knowledge of Christ and eschewed revelation. However, this position automatically made it an enemy of the institutionalized Catholic church.

The controversy over rites in China raged for another century both in

Europe and in the Far East. Eventually, the issue arose between the Manchu emperor in Peking and the pope in Rome. Despite the high esteem in which the emperor held the Jesuits, he was, when all was said and done, the ruler of the sinocentric world empire, sitting at the apex of civilization. And just as within the context of Chinese thought the emperor was unique in the world, so within the context of Catholic thought the pope in Rome was the unique representative of Christ on earth. In 1700, when the Jesuits in Peking sought and obtained an edict from the emperor supporting their own interpretation of Confucianism, they in effect secured a theological pronouncement from the emperor. Within Catholicism, however, theological pronouncements were the prerogative of the Roman pope and no one else. Consequently, in 1704 the pope condemned participation by Christians in Chinese rituals and declared himself in favor of the Franciscans and Dominicans in certain controversial questions. In addition, he sent a special legate to China to settle the dispute, thus introducing himself with all his unique qualities, in the person of his representative, into the Empire, where only the emperor was unique.

The rivalries that surrounded the papal legate contributed to the demise of the Christian cause in the Empire. The emperor received the pope's representative properly, but as befitted the representative of Christ's vicar on earth the legate was disrespectful and uncompromising. The pope and emperor, now pitted against each other, each universally unique according to his own system, could not reach a compromise. In 1706, the emperor decided to expel from China missionaries who did not accept the Jesuit position and who did not agree to remain within the Empire for the rest of their lives. This would have given the emperor both theological and practical primacy over the pope in the thought and governance of the church *of* China. The pope's representative forbade acceptance of this offer. Some missionaries accepted the emperor's conditions; others were forced to leave. The emperor, in his turn, sent some Jesuits to Rome as his representatives; they carried documents to argue their position, which had now become his own. The pope rejected the arguments of the emperor and *his* Jesuit representatives in 1715. Between then and 1742, several missions were sent by both pope and emperor to each other's courts in an attempt to resolve the debate, but the pope could not compromise his ecclesiastical institutions and the emperor could only defend the members of his own bureaucracy even though they were European and Christian.

The atmosphere in the Empire changed with the accession of the Yungzheng emperor in 1722. Having come to the throne through bloody competition with many rivals, the new emperor suspected anything he perceived as a threat to his position. The European missionaries, as members of the court and bureaucracy, were involved in the succession struggle, and this, together with the continuing dispute among the Christians in his

Empire, led the new emperor to an active anti-Christianism. In 1724 he issued an edict condemning Christianity as a heterodox sect; thereafter, he refused to discuss Christianity with foreigners. For his part, the pope in 1742 rejected all Christian participation in "the Rites and Ceremonies of China," which made it virtually impossible for active members of the Empire's bureaucracy to convert to Catholicism.[6]

During the reign of the Qianlong emperor (1736–1795), missionaries continued their service to the imperial court in their own accepted roles as architects, astronomers, mapmakers, interpreters, painters, etc. In the provinces, however, persecution grew, and the number of Christians fell dramatically. A popular anti-Christian folklore, feeding on xenophobia, developed in many parts of the country. Even the court began to reject knowledge introduced by the Jesuits. In the end, by the time the pope dissolved the Jesuit order in 1773, the history of the Catholic attempt to penetrate the Empire could be read only as a record of failure in communication between highly different systems. It was the insistence of the pope in Rome and the anti-Jesuit Catholic orders on the rectitude of their own position that led to the Christian debacle. Until the Jesuits brought the emperor himself into the picture, they were able to engage in all manner of disputation with their Christian confreres without endangering their position in the sinocentric order. Once the emperor entered the scene, choice became a necessity. But even with the rejection by emperor and pope of each other's positions, the Jesuits could continue their bureaucratic functions in Peking as defined by the imperial order. The sinocentric Empire was catholic, but would not become Catholic; the pope's church was Catholic, but would not become catholic. Worlds remained intact, and apart.

By the middle of the eighteenth century, as the Catholic church cut the ground from under itself in China, the sinocentric Empire's relations with the West entered a new phase in a new context.

The English and the Canton System

England entered the Indian Ocean and eventually reached the periphery of the East Asian Empire in tandem with, or, more accurately, as an adjunct to, the Dutch. This was part of the general process of displacement of the most highly developed center of the European world economy from Iberia to Holland and England.

Several reasons may be suggested for England's ability to surpass its rivals from the Iberian Peninsula and Holland and to achieve primacy in the Asian trade. Inside England itself, industrial development and social structure depended upon the world market. The city-based bourgeois merchant class had won its autonomy from the landed aristocracy and gentry.

Economic growth based on industrialization, particularly in textiles, had become an end in its own right and required markets if it were to achieve the growth potential that would assure future investment. Indeed, even political stability required the expansion of markets. Another reason for England's rise was that nation's gradual but definite liberation by about 1600 from the economic tutelage of the Dutch. This encouraged competition between the Dutch and the English overseas. A third factor was the economic crisis at the end of the first quarter of the seventeenth century. Plague and resumption of the Spanish war led to economic difficulties and a commercial crisis. Faced with the choice of deindustrialization or social unrest at home, on the one hand, or the development of new industries that, in turn, would require new markets, on the other, the English chose the latter. This stimulated interest in colonial expansion and intensified Anglo-Dutch rivalry in foreign markets. These markets themselves became more available to the English as the Spanish empire faltered. The Dutch and English, advantaged by seafaring skills and a growing weakness on the part of the Portuguese, profited not only from trade but from their plundering of Portuguese ships as well. In fact, they did not bring a new element to the Asian market; rather, they continued the Portuguese role by replacing the Portuguese.

The expansion of English activity into Asian waters had two more immediate and specific causes. First, the spice trade greatly interested the English, and it was to their advantage to engage in it directly. There was not one but two spice trades. The first, sometimes called the "Asian contract," brought spices from Asia to Lisbon, Venice, or, later, Amsterdam; its profits derived from the sale of these spices in the Mediterranean, the Iberian Peninsula, and elsewhere. The second spice trade, sometimes called the "European contract," involved the resale of these same spices to England and Northern Europe. Lisbon did not possess a trade network in Europe of sufficient ramification to allow Portugal to become the primary supplier of spices throughout the continent, nor did Portugal have sufficient military power on the continent to protect such a network. Venice's market was limited. Amsterdam, however, had both the capital and the land- and sea-based trade networks necessary to play the role of middleman between the first and second spice trades. From the point of view of the English, direct participation in the spice trade from the Indies either would bring profit to the English merchants or, conversely, would bring down prices in England. In 1600, Queen Elizabeth chartered a joint-stock company, the Governor and Merchants of London Trading into the East Indies, and granted it a monopoly of all trade between the Cape of Good Hope and the Straits of Magellan. The future British East India Company, in other words, was to monopolize English trade in the Indian and Pacific oceans.

THE EAST INDIA COMPANIES

The creation of joint-stock companies of the East India Company type was an important step in the development of the capitalist world economy. They operated in the interstices between crown and merchant, on the one hand, and national economy and international economy, on the other. As commercial organizations, they were more effective than previous entities had been because they provided a structure that could maximize the use of capital from a variety of merchant sources and focus it on a particular venture. Thus, they were instrumental in the development of capitalist investment. From the point of view of the crown, these companies represented a potential source of funds through the sale of monopoly rights or through the transfer to the merchants in the company of the noncommercial costs associated with long-distance commercial ventures, such as the provision of military protection. From the point of view of the merchant class, such companies provided more protection and limited rivals' access to markets. For example, a royal charter would limit the rights of non-Englishmen to import goods into England and would require the use of English shipping. By providing a monopoly for the benefit of private merchants, the state aided the rise of an independent urban capitalist class and avoided the costs associated with commercial expansion.

In the Indies, the Dutch East India Company, not the state, defeated the Portuguese at Malacca in 1641. The company's activities extended from India to Japan, its ships sailed in fleets, and its power was such that it could reinforce its European monopoly by controlling production in the East Indies. In that territory, the company became a territorial government that gradually spread its control through direct conquest and indirect treaty relationships over the entire archipelago. The relationships the company established with those rulers it left in place were similar to the tributary relationships that obtained within the sinocentric Empire. Only in 1799 did the Dutch government take over the company, together with its debts, converting the territory into a crown colony.

Just as the Dutch company made the East Indies its primary concern, the British East India Company made the Indian subcontinent its base. The British arrived in India when the Mongol empire was on the decline, and over the course of the eighteenth century the company's outposts, established as early as 1639, became administrative centers and sources of territorial expansion. The British East India Company defeated the French East India Company in the Seven Years' War and entered into occupation and direct rule of Bengal in northeastern India. As the British company's control spread over India, through both direct and indirect rule, India became the base from which the company expanded its commercial activities into the sinocentric Empire.

THE CANTON SYSTEM

The first British trading ships visited Canton as early as 1637, and between 1685 and 1759 the English and other Europeans traded along the China coast at several points, including Canton, Xiamen (Amoy), Fuzhou (Foochow), and Ningbo (Ningpo). Continuous trading in one location began only in 1699, however, when a British East India Company ship established a trading post at Canton. The "Canton system," that is to say, the institutional and procedural structure of Anglo-Chinese commerce within a port of trade, gradually developed over the next six decades. By 1760, the Empire's need to establish firm control over the trade led to the closing of all coastal ports besides Canton to European access. Several features of the Canton system deserve particular note.

As the Anglo-Chinese trade developed, it became more restricted in the range of goods exchanged. At first, European commerce with China covered exports and imports that were characteristic of China's traditional Southeast Asian trade: silk, tea, copper, zinc, sugar, rhubarb, musk, camphor, chinaware, handicraft products, and lacquerware. When the English adopted tea as their national drink in the eighteenth century, the merchants at Canton concentrated increasingly on the purchase of tea and, in second place, silk. Tea, in fact, became the major source of profit for the East India Company and an important source of revenue for the crown. China, however, was relatively uninterested in foreign goods. The necessity to pay for Chinese goods with silver quickly became a problem because this meant an unfavorable balance of trade for Britain, and that ran counter to all economic theory. Thus, the financing of the Anglo-Chinese commerce constituted a serious issue for the British.

The Structure of the Commercial System

China's maritime trade with Southeast Asia increased rapidly after the Manchu conquest, but it fell outside the traditional trade-tribute system because it did not involve foreign merchants and envoys coming to China but, rather, Chinese merchants going abroad. The imperial bureaucracy had to regulate this activity through other devices, albeit traditional ones. Merchant firms, or *hangs* ("hong" in English transcription), were officially licensed as brokers responsible for the conduct of the trade. At least three groups of such merchants existed at Canton, and collectively they were known as *yang-hang* ("merchants in maritime commerce"). These groups were functionally defined in geographical terms: one was responsible for trade along the coast to the north of Canton, a second for trade with Southeast Asia, and a third for trade with the Europeans. This arrangement strongly resembled the chartered joint-stock company system of Europe; the *yang-hang* was the functional equivalent of the East India Company though it differed structurally and culturally from its European counterpart since it was embedded within the traditional sinocentric imperial system.

The third group of licensed merchants, those responsible for trade with the Europeans who came by sea, was organized into a merchant guild that Westerners called the "Cohong," an anglicized version of the Chinese term *kung-hang* ("officially authorized merchants"). This group, which included between six and twelve firms, held a monopoly over, and was fully responsible for, all trade with the West. The Cohong represented the application to European trade of the very type of regulatory arrangements that the government utilized to control trade within China Proper; at the same time, it was an appropriate institution for the conduct of trade with the British East India Company because they were analogues of each other. The essence of this system was control and responsibility, not free trade and free enterprise; the doctrines of free trade and free enterprise had not yet gained center stage in Europe, much less in the Empire. At this time the Chinese and English systems still meshed.

The chief imperial officials in Canton were the governor-general (the Europeans called him "viceroy"), the governor, and after 1685 an official known to the Westerners as the "Hoppo," whose full title meant "superintendent of maritime customs for Kwangtung." The Hoppo controlled foreign trade at Canton, directly represented the imperial household at Peking, and collected the duties on foreign trade and dispatched them to the Board of Revenue at the capital. The Hoppo also controlled the customs at Macao and five other ports in the Canton delta region. The Hoppo's office represented the intrusion of the imperial central power into the local bureaucratic scene and, in the absence of a highly articulated centralized bureaucracy for the conduct of trade with the Europeans, the office was constantly sensitive to the unavoidable friction between the capital and the local bureaucracy at Canton. Nevertheless, the Hoppo found his own position lucrative since it afforded him many opportunities for both legitimate and illegitimate gain.

The Cohong, or merchant guild, was next in line of responsibility after the Hoppo. Its members, the hong merchants, paid the authorities significant amounts for the privilege of bearing the responsibility for trade with the Europeans and for the commercial and personal behavior of Europeans in the Canton harbor. The guild members took a blood oath to obey a thirteen-article code that governed Chinese commercial activities. The code made it possible for the merchant members of the guild to maintain a monopoly over dealings with the foreigners, and in turn they assumed responsibility for each foreign ship entering the harbor.

On the British side, the Canton committee of the British East India

Company took responsibility for British vessels and merchants, thus accommodating to the analogous Chinese institutional system. The foreign merchants trading at Canton found themselves laboring under numerous restrictions: they could not enter the city proper, ride in sedan chairs, or bring wives to Canton; they were required to remain in the area known as the "thirteen factories," or in earlier days at Macao during the off-season; they could not trade with other than hong merchants; they were subject to Chinese law, which differed dramatically from Anglo-Saxon law in both theory and practice; finally, and perhaps historically most significant, they were subject to the Chinese concept of collective responsibility.

The system successfully isolated the foreign merchants from the life of the Empire. They learned little of Chinese culture or language, and the Chinese encouraged them in their ignorance. A local patois, or pidgin, developed, with a limited vocabulary of English words strung together according to Chinese grammatical rules, and this sufficed for commercial purposes. (Similar "contact languages" developed in other areas in which cultures came into contact on a limited basis, as at Kyakhta, where a pidgin Russian developed for use between Russian and Chinese merchants.) Thus, from 1760 to 1834, European trade with China fitted well into the Chinese system of control and organization. The traditional sinocentric order contained the outposts of Europe's developing capitalist world system.

English behavior and interests reinforced the Sino-Western institutional symbiosis at Canton, particularly in the early years of the commerce. The British East India Company functioned as a merchant enterprise there and carried out its activities without raising the question of official contact between Peking and London on a basis of equality. That issue would have brought Western international diplomatic practice and the imperial tribute system into sharp conflict; by avoiding the issue, the English fitted into the tribute system and helped to perpetuate it. Commercially, too, the East India Company found the Canton system advantageous. As the trade increasingly concentrated on tea, the company established a monopoly over exports to England. The high prices it charged, together with the taxes the British government collected (often approaching one hundred percent of value), encouraged the growth of smuggling from the continent, but the British company gradually eliminated competition from rival European East India companies and, as it did so, found the monopolistic Canton system more and more to its liking.

While the British East India Company was content, by and large, with the Canton system, the English government's interest in expanding the China trade mounted. The government was strongly influenced by the growing industrialization of the economy at home and by the new free enterprise and free trade theories that were gradually gaining ground against mercantilism. As British industrial production and export, particularly in textiles, increased, private merchants at home began calling for the abolition of the company's monopoly and for the government's intervention in the commerce in the interest of market expansion. This, of course, would require modification if not the eventual disappearance of the traditional sinocentric world order. The first tentative signs of crisis began to appear at the end of the eighteenth century.

THE MACARTNEY EMBASSY

In 1793 the British government sent the Earl of Macartney, an experienced diplomat, on an embassy to the court at Peking to request the expansion of trade to other cities along the China coast and the establishment by the Chinese authorities of a tariff system to protect the interests of both the imperial government and the British merchants; the latter believed themselves to be suffering at the hands of unscrupulous Chinese customs officials. The East India Company bore the costs of the mission, but Macartney was an ambassador from the king to the emperor. He arrived at Tianjin on the northeastern coast in a ship of war, accompanied by ninety-five persons including two Chinese Catholic priests from Naples who were fluent in Latin and Italian and by an artillery guard of fifty soldiers in red coats. Macartney was an experienced diplomat, having been an envoy to the Russian court at St. Petersburg and a governor of Madras in India.

The Macartney embassy, in sharp contrast to the Company, found it impossible to approach the imperial court without participating in the tribute system, which it could not do. The embassy had brought six hundred bales of gifts, which required ninety wagons, two hundred horses, and three thousand coolies for transport up to Peking. The imperial officials called these gifts tribute presents and instructed Macartney to practice the traditional tributary presentation ritual of the kowtow. The British ambassador refused to perform any rituals other than those he would have performed to his own sovereign, namely, kneeling on one knee; this condemned the embassy to failure. A Dutch embassy's regular participation in the tribute ritual in 1795 gave additional emphasis to the failure of the Macartney embassy; moreover, it highlighted the problem that the tribute system presented to the Europeans in their desire for more intensive contacts with the Empire.

The Macartney mission failed, but the Canton system continued unchanged because both the Chinese system and the company's interests were best served by a stable relationship. In 1816, a second British embassy to Peking, led by Lord Amherst, failed even more completely because it arrived in the imperial capital at the time of the British war with Nepal, a Himalayan country tributary to China. Amherst was unceremoniously dispatched from Peking by order of the emperor. Thereafter, the company and the hong merchants both strenuously opposed any diplomatic efforts that might complicate the Canton trade. The system would survive until the blood of war washed it away.

THE CRISIS IN THE SYSTEM

By the 1830s the Canton system was in trouble. Three primary factors contributed to the system's crisis, which quickly became mortal. First, the British company's monopoly could no longer contain the so-called country trade, which, together with the non-English traders who were entering the Canton market, made continuation of the existing system of control practically impossible from the Chinese point of view and troublesome from the point of view of the British East India Company. Second, the introduction of opium into the China trade constituted a political, institutional, economic, and moral challenge to the Empire that the tribute system could not encompass and that the Empire could not manage, given the forms of administrative control and the technology available to it. Third, the growth in the West of the free enterprise and free trade ideology of burgeoning capitalism logically led to demands by Western merchants that the system be dismantled in favor of free access to the Chinese market.

The term "country trade" indicated the type of trade carried on by private individuals within the territory covered by the monopoly of the East India Company. Such activity originally sought to connect the monopoly company's commercial system with local Asian commercial systems, though it developed out of human desire to maximize advantage rather than any plan conceived in the boardroom of the East India Company in London. The country trade developed in and around the Indian subcontinent, where, for example, private merchants traded between Bengal in the northeast and Bombay in the northwest, exchanging textiles, silk, and sugar for raw cotton. The British moved on to existing East Indian trade routes and profited from the commercial and nautical knowledge of the indigenous merchant class and those who served it. The company found the indigenous trade advantageous because it profited by selling bills of exchange to private merchants as a way whereby the latter could remit funds over long distances. Individual officials of the company also profited through private investments in the local trade. Beginning from India, then, the country trade moved eastward. The company, which controlled the supply of opium from Bengal, auctioned it off to private European country traders, who in turn exported the opium to the East Indies and traded it for Javanese sugar; they also carried Javanese sugar westward and it soon supplanted Bengal sugar in the important market of western India. The expansion of the country trade to the East Indies and eventually to China seriously (and permanently) hurt the Bengali economy.

The country traders, primarily Englishmen and Scotsmen, operated as agents or as agency houses. They themselves invested in cargoes and ships, but they also operated as agents for the chartering of ships (gradually they began to own and charter ships themselves), the purchase, transport, storage, and sale of cargoes, and the sale of insurance. The traders represented companies in India and London and performed these services on a commission basis. This type of commerce was attractive because it required little start-up capital and relied heavily on imagination, initiative, and skill. With time non-British merchants, such as Parsees from Bombay and Jews from Iran and Iraq, entered the country trade, and their descendents are still important businessmen in such entrepôts as Hongkong and Singapore.

From the East Indies, the country trade expanded north to Canton, where the first private British merchants arrived in the 1780s and acquired legal status outside the company monopoly by becoming the commercial representatives of various European governments such as Sweden, Denmark, and Sardinia. Here their function as agency houses expanded, and they became true middlemen, outside the scope of the British monopoly but within the framework of the imperial system.

The country trade had worldwide ramifications for the survival of the British East India Company's China monopoly. As the Canton representatives of English merchant houses in India that were, in their turn, outposts of British firms in London, or as merchants with their own access to the London market, the private merchants who were involved in the country trade between India and China played an increasingly important role in British-Chinese commerce, often out of proportion to their numbers. They did this in a variety of ways in addition to performing such agency operations as representation and remittance of funds. After the 1820s, three-quarters of British imports to China came through the country trade, beginning with cotton, which gave way to silver and, eventually, to opium. The trade had many side effects, which made it useful to all concerned. It provided an outlet for Indian products in China and a means for remitting profits from the Canton market back to India. Through the remittance system, which involved the purchase from the company of bills of remittance that would be honored in London, the company could use the profits from the sale in China of Indian goods to purchase Chinese teas. Tea brought great profits in London, which the government taxed, also most profitably. However, the country trade had a negative consequence for the company: with the connivance of merchants on the Chinese side, the country traders broke the company's absolute monopoly both through smuggling and through legitimate but uncontrolled commerce.

By the 1830s, the Canton trade had changed significantly. Institutionally, the country trade had come to dominate the Canton market, and the British East India Company's monopoly was broken; the company itself now depended heavily upon the "private sector." On the Chinese side, official corruption and private smuggling undermined the hong merchants' monopoly and hamstrung the imperial government's attempts to control both the commerce and the officials locally responsible for it. Commercially, Chinese demand for Indian raw cotton and, later, opium, together with the vast and growing English demand for Chinese teas, had reached proportions beyond the capacity of the company or the Chinese officials to control. The Canton system was about to burst the bonds of institutional control and expectations on both the British and the Chinese side.

THE OPIUM TRADE

The cultivation and sale of opium became increasingly attractive to the British East India Company late in the eighteenth century. Two kinds of opium were grown in India: Patna opium was produced in Bengal, cultivated directly under the company's control by peasants who received advances from the government, purchased by an official agency at a fixed price, processed by the company, and sold at auction in Calcutta at stated intervals, again by the company. The company's increasing dependence upon the revenues from the Patna opium industry was significant in that industry's expansion: at the turn of the nineteenth century, three percent of the company's revenues in India came from opium; within fifty years it rose to twelve percent. Malwa, the second kind of opium, was grown in western India. Malwa competed with the company's Patna opium until the company gained control over the former by various means. In 1843 the company conquered the Sind in western India, a primary source of Malwa.

The opium trade in India was profitable for the company, as it was, too, in the Malay Peninsula and the western islands of the East Indian archipelago. The British entrepôt at Singapore was the primary distribution point for British Indian opium in the East Indies. The most remarkable market for British Indian opium, however, was China. Opium was no novelty in the Empire, but it was used more as a medicinal drug than as a narcotic. In fact, smoking opium as a narcotic may have started in China only after the Chinese began to smoke tobacco, which came from North America. In the late eighteenth century, British exports of Indian opium to China amounted to approximately 133,000 pounds per annum, but by 1838 forty times this quantity was being imported yearly.

For the British, the growth of the opium trade with China was an important development. The flow of silver into China, which was necessary to pay for the teas and silks the British exported from China but was considered bad economically, was supplanted by imports of opium; this led to a reversal in the balance of trade. Opium was an attractive product economically because, being addictive and lacking substitutes, demand for it was likely to rise rather than diminish. Furthermore, although general prices fluctuated in response to supply, great profits could be made in the opium trade, a speculative and intensely competitive commerce. Opium merchants used the most modern ships to speed their ware to the China market, and the cargoes were delivered to floating warehouses, or receiving ships, that were heavily armed in order to protect them from raiders.

The Chinese side of the trade was carried on by brokerage houses composed of partners whose combined funds allowed them sufficient capital to engage in the opium business. They owned smuggling boats that received opium from the floating warehouses and brought it to land, where distribution took place along established routes. The trade, originally localized at Canton, spread north along the China coast as foreign ships developed routes beyond the reach of Chinese government forces but accessible to the smuggling boats. The opium trade could exist because of the active participation of Chinese merchants and officials, both of which groups profited either by smuggling or by receipt of bribes.

The opium trade escaped the control of imperial institutions and traditional commercial practices and harmed society and human beings. Opium smoking spread rapidly through the Chinese population, including government servants, soldiers, and even members of the imperial household. Opium may have been associated with a decline in living standards among those who consumed it, and it contributed to the general demoralization of significant segments of Chinese society. By the 1830s China had between two and ten million habitual smokers of opium. Because so many bureaucrats and court officials were involved in the trade or were addicted, the imperial government could not even define a coherent policy toward the problem. And when the government tried to curtail the trade, vested interests in many social sectors combined to defeat the government's efforts. As early as 1729 the government had forbidden the sale and smoking of opium, and in 1796 it forbade importation and domestic production. The frequency with which these prohibitions had to be repeated in the first part of the nineteenth century is testimony to their ineffectiveness. When officials in one area were able to combine to drive the opium trade from their region, it simply moved to another area. This pattern accounted for the spread of British opium commerce north along the China coast, in turn further weakening the Canton system.

COMMERCIAL IDEOLOGY AND POLITICS

The Canton system, although efficacious for the British East India Company in its earlier years, never fully satisfied either the company or the private merchants in the Canton trade. The British craved more open trading ports along the coast even if they were open to private commerce as well. They also wanted a regularized tariff system to replace the complex and often capricious payments the Chinese customs officials at Canton exacted.

The growth in volume of trade and the increasing complexity of the market's commercial structure led to grievances, a situation complicated by what appeared to the Westerners as Chinese corruption. For example, Qing officials often forced the hong merchants to make contributions to them. Accordingly, the merchants, with limited capital available to them because of the nature of the Chinese economy, often had to go into debt to the company.

The debtor relationship grew out of structural differences between the traditional Chinese and European commercial economies. It was further complicated by differences between their legal cultures. No Chinese legal or administrative machinery existed to insure the company's or private merchants' ability to collect the debts the hong merchants owed them. Consequently, Chinese indebtedness to the British in the local market increased over time. This difference in legal and administrative culture had broader implications. Westerners often found China's judicial customs (which included group responsibility for individual behavior, arbitrary arrest, and torture) repugnant. As early as 1784, the British refused to accept Chinese jurisdiction in murder cases, and the Americans took this position after 1821. These circumstances excluded any mediating institutions that could permit the survival of the Canton system despite the difficulties it was encountering. In this light, the growth of conflict had structural causes, and the opium problem was not the source but merely an exacerbating factor.

The immediate intercultural conflict at Canton was aggravated by the growth in the West of the ideology of Manchester liberalism as the mainstay of an increasingly aggressive commercial capitalism. The Western liberals argued for free trade and for the reform of existing commercial law and practices. They applied their ideas to the international market as well, demanding reforms in foreign commerce and the abolition of all restrictions on free trade abroad. The new ideology grew in strength as it acquired the status of a science, economics, and as its advocates increased their political power inside England.

Influenced by the new ideology, as well as by practical political and economic considerations, the British government abolished the East India Company's monopoly on trade with India in 1813; the company's rapidly weakening monopoly on British trade with China was abolished in 1834. The government then appointed an official superintendent of trade at Canton, who, in Chinese eyes, appeared to be the counterpart of the Hoppo. The first government-appointed superintendent was Lord William Napier, a Scotsman who strongly supported Manchester liberal reformism. Napier had neither Asian nor commercial experience, nor did he receive from the

British foreign secretary, Viscount Palmerston, instructions adequate to the satisfaction or modification of Chinese ideological and procedural expectations. Palmerston's, and therefore Napier's, sole objective was the reorganization of the China trade and of China's own commercial policies and procedures to bring them into conformity with the free trade theories and practices that dominated England. Napier's behavior when he arrived at Canton, however, was so repugnant to the Chinese that they not only refused to receive him but also prohibited further trade with the British in the hope that this move would bring Napier under control. Napier, for his part, sought to subvert the official bureaucracy by denouncing the Qing officials in Chinese-language propaganda broadsheets that he ordered distributed directly to the populace. In retaliation, the Chinese cut off supplies to the commercial and residential area inhabited by the British merchants and officials. Napier then ordered the two frigates that had accompanied his mission to fire on the Chinese. Displaying nothing but disdain and arrogance toward the Chinese, Napier also sent to India for reinforcements, planning to force the Empire to acquiesce and accept British policies and ideology. The emperor ordered Napier expelled from the Empire by force if he did not submit. The issue was joined. The hong merchants and the British private traders, however, feared that open warfare between the Empire and the British in India would utterly destroy their commercial interests, and they negotiated a compromise that permitted Napier to retire to Macao. The trade was reopened.

The disastrous Napier mission exposed the critical issues that underlay the conflict between the Empire and the West. Push had come to shove, and it was only a matter of time before the sinocentric imperial order and the expanding capitalist world system came into armed conflict. The use of armed force in support of the spread of capitalist ideology and institutions was legitimate according to the tenets of Manchester liberalism, which was reinforced by concepts of progress that relegated noncapitalist, non–North Atlantic societies to a lower position on the ladder of human development. In the years after 1834, the British colony at Canton itself split over these issues. Some wanted to force free trade upon the Empire by military means or, at the very least, to open more ports of trade; others wanted to continue to operate within the imperial system. The Empire, for its part, demanded that the British appoint a merchant, not a government official, to supervise British commerce. London, however, was not prepared to respond, and it did not act.

The Canton system thus fell apart. Commerce had expanded beyond the geographical confines of the Canton area, and the institutions evolved by each side to control the trade were no longer adequate to the purpose. British self-interest dictated the introduction into the trade of a commodity, opium, that was justified in real and theoretical terms by capitalist ideology. However productive the opium trade may have been for the

British opium traders and their Chinese collaborators, the Qing government could not but condemn it and seek to destroy it. For both sides, traditional diplomacy, institutions, and strategies had failed.

Inside the Empire

The sinocentric world empire did not wait until the breakdown of the Canton system to react to the appearance and growing importance of Western commerce and merchants along the China coast, particularly at Canton. The Empire was neither unaware of, nor insensitive to, the challenge this new and aggressive element in its foreign relations presented. Nonetheless, it could respond only in terms of its own experience, and for historians to condemn the Empire for failure to do otherwise is only Western arrogance.

FOREIGN TRADE AND THE IMPERIAL ECONOMY

An immediate consequence of the growth of the Empire's trade with the West was the increase in the quantity of bullion available within the Empire. Lacking goods that appealed to Chinese taste or satisfied Chinese needs (with the exception of opium late in the period), Westerners used silver to make their purchases along the periphery of China, and it is estimated that some 350 million Mexican dollars' worth of bullion was imported into the Empire in the two-and-a-half centuries before the First Opium War (1839–1842).

Foreign trade stimulated the growth of the tea industry. It also stimulated, through increased demand for these products, the traditional Chinese handicraft industry that produced silk and cotton textiles in central and south China. The Chinese market itself, however, was so vast that it absorbed considerable amounts of raw cotton from India to supply its own cottage based textile industry. Therefore, the growth of trade with the West meant that to a certain extent the Empire's economy developed a symbiotic relationship with distant economies that lay beyond its control. The Canton trade encouraged the accumulation of capital and the development of commercial instruments within the Empire that provided the basis for the growth of Chinese trade with the West in later decades. At Canton itself, the hong merchants were the precursors of a class of merchants with considerable experience in commerce with the West, and they would have a profound influence on the whole course of Chinese history.

KNOWLEDGE AND ATTITUDES

The Empire possessed limited and inaccurate knowledge of the West and its customs because the bureaucratic system held out little reward for those who would have wished to acquaint themselves with the world beyond. Undoubtedly, some information was available through personal experience with foreigners, for example, from individuals in and around the imperial court who had had direct contact with the Russians in the Amur valley or at Kyakhta. Foreigners, like the Russians and the Jesuits living in Peking, also provided the court with some, albeit limited, knowledge.

Though sparse and often erroneous, the written record contained certain information, too. The journal of the Manchu mission to the western Mongols between 1712 and 1715 carried a considerable amount of information about the areas traversed in Siberia and eastern Russia. Another work, the *Record of Things Seen and Heard about the Overseas Countries (Haiguo Wenjian Lu)*, written about 1730, became a standard reference for the next hundred years. These and similar accounts yielded just enough information to develop stereotypic images of the foreigner, much as the foreigner in the same period used stereotypes to envision the Chinese. In these works, Westerners were depicted as mercurial, opportunistic, and materialistic. They spoke an odd language, smelled strange, and dressed peculiarly. Moreover, they used their clothes strangely, as when they lifted their hats as a sign of politeness. They also had peculiarly fashioned facial features, strange colored skin, and an abundance of hair on their bodies. Barbarian marriages, according to one report, were the result of mutual agreement between the partners, obviously a most unsatisfactory and unsatisfying situation. The *Maritime Record (Hai-lu)*, another important source of information, published in 1820, was dictated by an aged blind interpreter who purported to have sailed abroad in his youth. The author was struck by the multistoried houses of England, the bridges across the Thames, the prostitutes in London, the soldiers' dressing in red, and the odd shape their clothes gave Englishwomen. It was this kind of information that was available to the imperial officials whose responsibility it was to make policy toward the West.

Sometimes chance observations were translated into official policy. For example, noting that the Dutch and the Russians who visited Peking in the seventeenth century knew about each other's countries, the Manchus concluded that Russia and Holland were neighbors in Western Europe. Similarly, having observed that the Dutch ate considerable quantities of fish, the court assumed that the Russians did likewise. Since the Russians imported significant amounts of rhubarb from China, the Manchus concluded that the Russians, after consuming so much fish, required rhubarb in order to assure the movement of their bowels; the Manchus drew the policy conclusion that prohibition of the rhubarb trade with Russia would quite literally bring the Russians to their knees and force compliance with Manchu wishes.

Official publications also carried strange information: for example, Portugal was located in the South Seas, England and Holland were the same country, France was Buddhist before it became Catholic, Christianity was a form of Buddhism, and France was the same place as Portugal. This confusion reflected the fact that, just as all foreigners looked alike, so their countries' names all seemed the same. For example, the term "Folangji," which came to China via the Arabs at the time of the Crusades, was applied to the medieval Franks, after which it was applied to the Portuguese; when Spain absorbed Portugal, Spain acquired the same name. The French, when they arrived, were called "Falanxi," which soon became "Folanxi," a variant of the earlier "Folangji (Fo-lang chi)." Conversely, western countries multiplied in the Chinese mind as foreign envoys coming successively from the same country used different characters or different versions of a name to identify themselves or to be identified in the official records.

THE DEVELOPMENT OF IMPERIAL POLICY

Ignorance of the West did not mean that the imperial bureaucracy was not profoundly concerned with the development of policy toward the West. On the contrary, the Westerner presented the imperial bureaucrat with the need to make policies that would advance the interests of the Empire as the bureaucracy perceived them under the guidance of the emperor. After the debacle of the Catholic church in China, Christianity acquired the status and character of a secret society, which is to say that imperial policy toward it fluctuated between lack of interest and persecution. As internal disturbances spread toward the end of the eighteenth century, Christianity came to be viewed by the court with increasing suspicion as a foreign element intruded into China to the Empire's disadvantage. Persecution of the sect intensified. Between 1801 and 1829, no new missionaries were permitted to enter the Empire, with the exception of a Protestant missionary who came under the protection of the East India Company. Missionaries, who often had to keep on the move in order to avoid persecution, were not alone in suffering from this new attitude. Chinese Christians were arrested and pressured, at times by torture, to abandon Christianity or face the consequences, which ranged from exile and torture to death.

Christians constituted only a small group in the vast population of the Empire, but this group had particular interests of its own and stood between Chinese society and the West. Christians often were merchants, scholars with a heterodox interest in things foreign, or bureaucrats who in some fashion or other had inherited an affiliation with Christianity that reached back to the end of the Ming dynasty. All this only increased official suspicion of the Christians at the time the Canton crisis was brewing. The future of Christianity in the Empire became a political issue between the governments of the West and the Empire when they entered the era of negotiations after the First Opium War.

OPIUM POLICY

The opium trade, which the bureaucracy officially viewed negatively, required the formulation of policy toward the outside world. Here again, the policy planners could work only with the ideas and information available to them. The economic and fiscal consequences of the trade in opium, not the moral distaste for the narcotic that official pronouncements often voiced, were the source of the most urgent considerations for the imperial government. The smoking of opium threatened the Empire's economy in general and the court's finances in particular. The reversal of the balance of trade and the outflow of silver from China became an immediate and practical policy issue.

The imperial economy used a bimetallic currency system in its accounting and remittance procedures. The government received taxes in silver and copper and used both currencies in its expenditures at a ratio of three parts of copper to seven parts of silver. Silver was not produced in great quantities inside China; therefore, any serious fluctuation in the use of silver in foreign trade was likely to have a direct consequence inside the Empire. In both foreign and domestic trade, significant commercial transactions were made in silver because it was more valuable and because, being more valuable, it was more efficient than copper. As long as silver flowed into China in exchange for tea, the imperial economy flourished and the public benefited. However, as we have seen, the British found this arrangement disadvantageous. Their substitution of opium for silver resulted in a reversal in the flow, and large quantities of silver left China. Imperial officials perceived an apparent drain of silver by 1822 and became alarmed by 1830. In the next decade, China may have lost as much as ten million ounces of silver per annum. The outflow of silver led to its growing scarcity within the Empire and to a rise in its price, which created considerable panic in government circles. As early as the 1820s, imperial edicts forbade the export of silver. Had these directives been heeded, China's trade with the West would have been brought to a virtual standstill. In fact, they had no more success than the policy of attempting to stem the outflow of silver by inhibiting the importation of opium.

As the 1830s drew to an end, the Empire's efforts to control the trade through those mechanisms it knew and understood had failed. The inability to solve the crisis of the Canton system and to check both the importation of opium and the export of silver exposed the weakness of the tribute system in the new age: it was unable to absorb the representatives and commercial practices of a culture that flatly rejected the centrality of China and the world empire and the validity of imperial institutions and procedures. In the same way, Western (specifically British) policy toward the Empire had also failed. The West had undergone such changes that its cognition of the world and its real and imagined needs, formulated in the ideology of capitalism and in the policy of free trade, required that the world, and the sinocentric Empire with it, change to meet its terms. Self-assurance, combined with technological progress, gave the West the confidence to attempt to cut the Gordian knot of China's world empire.

Whether it was Chinese conservatism and inability to respond or Western radicalism and aggressiveness that led to war is a matter of judgment and interpretation. In any case, open warfare between the Empire and Great Britain resolved the crisis of the Canton system to the Empire's disadvantage. The First Opium War, beginning in 1839, may have been an Anglo-Chinese conflict on the field of battle but historically it was a war in which world systems clashed.

The Way
the World Changed

THE COLLAPSE of the Canton system in the late 1830s and the inability of the sinocentric Empire's traditional tribute system to encompass that failure or to arrive at new institutional arrangements with the expanding and increasingly aggressive European capitalist world economy led to more than a half century of confrontation in which the two worlds faced each other over a gulf of ignorance, misunderstanding, and misinterpretation. Between the First Opium War (1839–1842) and the Boxer Rebellion (1900), the sinocentric Empire and the European world economy interacted dialectically: the Manchu dynasty and its Han Chinese personnel sought to adjust to the West's new world while retaining as many of its traditional institutions and values as possible. But none of the proposed formulas brought a satisfactory resolution of the conflict. For its part, the West sought to change China so that the new capitalist economy's commerce could be conducted with and in the Empire and so that the West's equally aggressive religious groups, both Catholic and Protestant, could pursue their salvationist purposes among the heathens. These objectives required the establishment within the Empire of stability. Moreover, the cost of such security would be better and more economically borne by the Chinese themselves than by the foreigners. This led to a logical conclusion, sometimes doubted but never abandoned: the interests of the imperialists were best served in China not by the destruction of native institutions but by the maintenance of the Qing dynasty in power.

The structure of the interaction between the Empire and the West quickly assumed a recognizable pattern: war led to negotiations, which led to attempts at adjustment on the part of the Empire and to its officials' reflection upon, and response to, the new situation; this led, in turn, to internal reaction and a resumption of war. In the meantime, and throughout the same period, the Empire was assaulted on other fronts as well. These included Mongolia, Turkestan, and Tibet; in these areas the Empire was, at first, the imperialist power, but with the passage of time its outposts in their turn fell under the same kind of attack the Empire was suffering at the hands of the outside world along the China coast.

Imperial-oikoumenical conflict in the middle of the nineteenth century resulted directly in the destruction of the tribute system as a means for accommodation between the Empire and the societies that surrounded or were approaching it. This conflict also resulted in the erosion of China's assumptions about itself, so that not only Chinese perceptions of the world but also Chinese perceptions of the empire's own nature changed; China and its world did not coincide with the reality that the Western world economy was creating. Survival became the primary objective of imperial foreign policy. By the beginning of the twentieth century, however, it had become apparent that even the Empire's attempts to adjust to the new world, however creative those attempts may have been, were doomed to failure. China would continue to exist as an entity on the international scene only if the Empire itself were dismantled.

Aggression, Response, and Defeat

Concern over the outflow of silver to pay for increasing opium imports combined with moral indignation and worry over the socially and morally unacceptable consequences of the opium habit to produce considerable uncertainty within the imperial government. An intense debate ensued over the appropriate policy to adopt. As early as 1832 the governor-general and governor of Canton memorialized the emperor, advocating the legalization of the opium trade in order to diminish the outflow of silver and keep prices at a manageable level. In 1836 another memorial recommended that soldiers be forbidden opium but that others be permitted to smoke it at their own risk. The objective of this proposal was to safeguard the health of the military as a defense priority. Both petitions pointed toward a policy of compromise, a possibility that fell well within the capacity of the system to absorb so long as the compromise derived its legitimacy from imperial decree rather than from submission to external pressure and force.

The 1836 memorial attracted the attention of the foreigners at Canton but encountered considerable opposition in the ensuing debate among the government bureaucrats. One opponent, for example, said that

> Opium is nothing else but a flowing poison; that it leads to extravagant expenditure is a small evil, but as it utterly ruins the minds and morals of people, it is a dreadful calamity. The people are the foundations of the empire; and all wealth is produced by their labor; the state of an impoverished people may be changed and improved, but it is not in the power of medicine to save a debilitated people, enervated by luxury and excess.

This concern for the health of the people was not purely moral: the memorialist cited an occasion in 1832 on which troops were sent to fight rebels, but "in consequence of smoking opium, of all the effective corps, although they mustered many in numbers, few were fit or strong enough to take the field." Consequently, the legalization of the trade and the domestic production of opium in order to inhibit the outflow of silver was not a satisfactory response. The emperor was persuaded.[1]

The high officials at Canton now instructed the hong merchants to investigate the nine most notorious foreign opium dealers to develop information necessary for the formulation of policy against the commerce. In November 1836, the government ordered the dealers to leave the city. This was not the first time that strong measures were taken against the opium trade, nor was it to be the last. Eventually the dealers were allowed four months to prepare for their departure, but in the meantime the trade increased, silver continued to flow out of the Empire, and corruption spread.

The debate continued. During the following months, many officials sent memorials to the court recommending pressure against the foreigners. Only a minority perceived that since the trade had developed its own market within the Empire, it was within the market that the trade had to be confronted. Among the clearest and most reasoned presentations of this point of view was a memorial written by Lin Zexu, governor-general of Hubei and Hunan provinces. He had studied the issues carefully and recommended a six-point policy that would attack the trade through the Chinese market and its middlemen, dealers, and consumers. He even proposed a program of detoxification and a system of justice for violators of the imperial policy. So persuasive was Lin's argument that at the end of 1838 he was appointed imperial commissioner at Canton with specific instructions to eradicate the sources of the opium traffic. The new commissioner arrived at Canton in March 1839, and in June the emperor promulgated a statute of thirty-nine articles intended to combat opium.

The foreigners were not passive during the debate. Hoping for legalization but fully aware of the possibility that the imperial court would oppose this policy, the responsible British official at Canton, Captain Charles Elliot (the queen's representative), was in constant contact with the rulers of British India. Elliot recognized that the Qing government might take action against the foreigners and that, in any event, a show of strength would be useful; as early as February 1837 he requested that British men-of-war from India visit Chinese waters. By September, London had ordered such a visit and further suggested that it be a regular event. The forces requested by Elliot arrived in the seas off Canton in July 1838, but they only further excited the antagonism of the imperial authorities.

Inside Canton, an anti-opium crusade was developing. By the time Lin was appointed imperial commissioner, the government had put over two thousand opium dealers, brokers, and smokers in prison, executions had become a daily event, and the opium traffic had come to a standstill. Peking accompanied its dispatch of Lin Zexu to Canton with reprimands to local officials for being too lenient. The winter of 1838–1839 promised to be a watershed in the Empire's relations with the West.

The Imperial Commissioner

Lin Zexu (1785–1850), perhaps the main actor in the conflict brewing at Canton between the Empire and the expanding capitalist world system, was the quintessential representative of imperial society and culture. He represented the best and the brightest the Empire in its classical form produced. It is more than ironic, then, that he became the stormy petrel around whom the events that heralded the end of the Empire swirled.

The future imperial commissioner, whose family had been prominent in the earlier Ming dynasty, was an experienced and capable administrator who had earned the confidence of the emperor through his able management in a variety of posts. Lin Zexu had attained the high position of governor-general of Hubei and Hunan provinces and was known for his serious concern for the welfare of the people, his attention to detail, and his direct participation in both the planning and the execution of policy. Moreover, his membership in a poetry group and other intellectual activities brought him into close association with a group of progressive and intelligent colleagues who shared his interests in administrative reform and suppression of the opium trade. This group, adhering to the so-called modern text school of thought, which perceived Confucius as a reformer rather than a conservator of tradition, also shared a desire to learn as much as possible about the world beyond the Empire. The appointment of this intelligent, progressive, and experienced administrator was an imaginative and appropriate response to the developing crisis in Canton.

The commissioner arrived at Canton on March 10, 1839 and plunged into his work. Lin was guided by a set of assumptions that correspondence and conversations with sympathetic colleagues had clarified in his mind. They included three principles, three supplementary rules, three arguments, and one general maxim, summarized as follows:

    I. Principles
        A. The Empire could not afford a further loss of silver.
        B. Opium was an "edible demon"; civilian consumers should be strangled, military consumers and traffickers in the drug beheaded.
        C. The traffic could not be stopped at its source because the controls necessary for such a policy were beyond the means of the Empire; both foreigners and Chinese would rebel.
    II. Supplementary Rules
        A. In addition to opium, imported woolens and other goods, includ-

ing luxury items, injured Chinese industry and should be
forbidden.

    B. Foreigners should be expelled from Canton and restricted to Macao within a specified time.

    C. China should study and improve the manufacture of weapons.

III. Arguments

    A. Stemming the outflow of silver had priority over every other policy objective, including improvement of the food supply, though in the long run the latter was primary.

    B. In foreign trade, only food imports benefited the Empire, and customs revenues were relatively unimportant.

    C. Severity in policy toward the opium traffic was justified because it was defensive, not offensive, and the Empire harbored no aggressive designs.

IV. General Maxim: Beware of Spies![2]

Lin's policy perspective was comprehensive, including broad assumptions concerning priorities, immediate anti-opium measures, and tentative suggestions for improvement of the Empire's military position vis-à-vis that of the West. Furthermore, he was aware of the problems involved in dealing with another culture, as indicated by his suggestion to expel, rather than punish, the foreigners.

The imperial commissioner's first need upon his arrival in Canton was intelligence information; accordingly, he organized a staff that included English and Latin speakers and began to collect newspapers and books that contained information about the West. He also needed specific data about the internal market, primarily the Chinese merchants who engaged in the drug traffic and the addicts who depended upon it. Lin therefore ordered local officials to begin the compilation of lists of suspects, to develop the evidence implicating them, and to arrest and prepare them for trial. In addition, he ordered the arrest of addicts who were members of the scholar-gentry class in and around the city of Canton.

Lin's opium suppression program required more than administrative and legal measures against participants in the trade. It needed positive support from the local gentry, so he began to mobilize this class by introducing questions concerning the opium trade and policies for its suppression into the local preliminary civil service examinations. Students could write their answers anonymously, and through these responses Lin gathered important information not only about the drug traffic but about official connivance as well. Finally, he was aware that an active suppression program would excite the foreigners to retaliation. In order to prepare for this eventually he reorganized the local defense forces. Lin's approach to policy formulation and preparation for its execution was steady and discerning.

In the mobilization of local society against the opium trade and the development of policies against Chinese traffickers and addicts, Lin was on familiar ground. The foreigners presented him with a different problem, however. They represented the new and aggressive Western commercial capitalist class, with which he was unacquainted, and they came from a world of which he had little indirect and no direct knowledge. Here he found himself on less firm ground. In the beginning, for example, he accepted the Chinese bromide that tea and rhubarb were vital to the health of the foreigners and constituted a tool to use against them. He did not understand the nature of international trade. Within the framework of the traditional assumptions of the tribute system, he noted that the opium trade had developed with a rapid increase in the numbers of foreigners at Canton and therefore concluded that intensity and frequency of trade was directly related to the opium traffic and to instability. Lin had little or no knowledge of the new science of economics and did not understand that the opium trade was a response to Britain's need to develop a favorable balance of trade with China; he believed, contrary to experience, that without opium the trade could be profitable to the foreigners. Moreover, Lin failed to realize that his analyses rested on moral distinctions between legal and illegal trade that were not shared by the Westerners, at least not in their dealings with the Empire. What was illegal in the Empire made economic sense in the capitalist world system (indeed, what was immoral or illegal in Great Britain sometimes was considered economically advantageous and, therefore, acceptable abroad). Lin's policy objectives with regard to the foreigners were clear: support legal commerce, suppress illegal trade, and insure the continuation of the *status quo* as defined by the tribute system. Confucian administrative theory and Lin's own bureaucratic experience suggested that a primary tool for the achievement of policy objectives was ethical persuasion in the form of entreaties to cooperation and reprimands for misbehavior, and it was to these that he turned first, most importantly in the form of two letters he wrote to Queen Victoria.

The first letter was written in the traditional superior-to-inferior style that the Empire's representatives customarily used in addressing barbarians and their rulers. Lin's arguments, however, were sincere and cogent. He began by insisting that, according to natural law, one could not permit others to be harmed for one's own profit. He reminded the queen that the emperor had benevolently permitted the foreigner to trade in tea, rhubarb, silk, and other goods, without which the foreigner would be in serious jeopardy. In light of the imperial benevolence, he asked the queen to bring an end to the cultivation of poppies and the manufacture of opium: "We are of the opinion that this poisonous article is clandestinely manufactured by artful and depraved people of various tribes under the dominion of your honorable nation. Doubtless you, the honorable sovereign of that nation, have not commanded the manufacture and the sale of it." Lin obviously did not understand the relationship between the state and commerce in the capitalist world economy. His tone throughout was utterly conciliatory: "We now wish to find, in cooperation with your honorable sovereignty, some means to bring to a perpetual end this opium, so hurtful to mankind: we in this land forbidding the use of it and you, in the nations of your dominion, forbidding its manufacture." He did not refrain from suggesting, however, that failure to respond positively could lead to other measures, more precisely to the end of commerce altogether: "Is it not far better to turn and seek other occupations than vainly to labor in the pursuit of a losing employment?" Lin concluded that the illegal trade would undermine legal commerce, and the letter ended politely if not gently: "Let it not be said that early warning of this has not been given." Having written the letter, Lin now faced the problem of delivering it, since he lacked any formal means of communication with the queen and did not trust her representative in Canton. In the hope that at least one copy would reach London, he ordered many copies of the document printed and distributed to all ships and foreigners at Canton.[3]

Lin sent Queen Victoria a second letter in December 1839. He repeated the argument from natural law and declared that persons "who only care to profit themselves, and disregard their harm to others, are not tolerated by the laws of heaven and are unanimously hated by human beings." He informed Victoria that the emperor was "in a towering rage" over the opium traffic. Reminding her that foreigners cannot live without tea and rhubarb, he asked: "If China cuts off these benefits with no sympathy for those who are to suffer, then what can the barbarians rely upon to keep themselves alive?" The letter informed the queen of the new imperial policies and the measures taken against the opium trade. "The emperor," Lin wrote, "cannot bear to execute people without first having tried to reform them by instruction. . . .This may be called the height of kindness and the perfection of justice." Lin concluded by asking for a prompt reply. This second letter was distributed just as the first had been. Lin now believed that if he were forced to take strong measures against the foreigners, no one would be able to accuse him or the court of having failed to give ample warning of the empire's policies and of the consequences of refusal to comply.[4]

Differences between the political and economic cultures of the Empire and the West, exhibited by both the style and the content of Lin's letters to Victoria, doomed his policy of restraint and leniency to failure from the start. The recalcitrance of the foreigners and their refusal to surrender their opium stocks forced him to adopt coercive measures, and on March 24, 1839 the commissioner ordered the foreigners, some three hundred fifty men, including Captain Elliot, the queen's own representative, confined to the so-called thirteen factories. He withdrew their Chinese servants but permitted them to receive necessary supplies. After six weeks of confinement in uncomfortable conditions, the British delivered their opium stocks, twenty thousand chests, to the authorities, who promptly burned them in public. From Lin's point of view, this measure and the result it achieved was a clear application of the traditional concept of collective responsibility to barbarians, in this case to a foreign community in which individual initiative, not collective responsibility, was the norm. Captain Elliot, on his part, accepted on behalf of the British crown full responsibility for the surrender of the opium supplies. In his view, Lin's actions were completely illegitimate, involving as they did the confiscation of private property and the infringement of the right of free trade as it was understood in the expanding universe of the capitalist world economy.

The conflict between the Empire and the West at Canton worsened in July 1839, when a group of drunken English sailors killed a Chinese peasant, raising, albeit unintentionally, the entire question of legal jurisdiction and the problem of the conflict inherent in two systems of law that derived from such different cultures. There was no question of the guilt of the English sailors. Only jurisdiction and punishment were at issue. Both sides conducted investigations, and Captain Elliot sought to give financial compensation to the victim's family. In Chinese law murder was punishable by execution, and the authorities repeatedly requested the surrender of the murderer. English policy and practice, on the other hand, held that no British criminal could be handed over to the Chinese for trial, regardless of his crime. Captain Elliot even refused to receive relevant documents from the Chinese authorities. In an effort to placate the Chinese, he tried six suspects in mid-August: they were found guilty of riot and assault but none was convicted of murder; condemned to short-term confinements and small fines, the sailors were sent back to England, where they were set free. This failure to resolve a conflict between systems of law and justice added another dimension of profound disputation to a situation in which accommodation was becoming increasingly difficult if not impossible.

The British community had retreated, under pressure from the imperial commissioner, from Canton to Macao, and in August 1839 it gathered on the island of Hong Kong, which at the time was mostly uninhabited. The island was superbly located for trade to Canton and along the China coast. With one of the world's best deep-water ports between it and the Kowloon Peninsula on the mainland, Hong Kong quickly became the chief warehouse for British commerce and the primary base for the British population, which by that time included several thousand. Sufficiently beyond the reach of Commissioner Lin's real power, the island could serve as both a refuge and a base for military operations.

In the middle of September 1839 Lin memorialized the emperor to report that he had drawn up secret plans for military action and was prepared for war, should the situation develop to that point. He would take such measures only if compelled to do so by circumstances, however, and even then only with the greatest reluctance. Lin proposed a defensive strategy on the assumption that, if war came, the foreign forces would be exhausted by the long journey and could be overwhelmed easily by fresh Chinese troops. This proposal won the emperor's complete approval.[5]

The British, on the other hand, decided to go on the offensive. On October 18, 1839, Lord Palmerston, the foreign secretary, who had been contemplating military action in China for some time, secretly instructed Captain Elliot that London had decided "to place Britain's relations with China on a proper footing"; an expeditionary force would arrive in China by March 1840 to blockade Canton and other areas. To friends and associates, Palmerston argued that this move was necessary to obtain satisfaction and reparation for injuries inflicted by the Empire on British subjects.[6]

THE TWENTY-ONE YEARS' WAR

The events of 1838–1839 along the China coast ushered in a period of intermittent armed conflict that constituted the first war between the sinocentric Empire and the new and still expanding capitalist world economic system. It was a twenty-one years' war, although historians are wont to identify this struggle as the Opium wars, of which there were one, two, or three, depending upon how the commentator classifies the events involved. The Twenty-one Years' War was marked by alternating periods of conflict and nonconflict, separated by negotiations. The war falls into the genre of premodern, or traditional, warfare; that is to say, it was the type of war characteristic of society before industrialization (the concomitant reorganization of society made possible the efficient and focused system we call modern, or total, warfare). Traditional armed conflicts often dragged on for thirty or even a hundred years; twenty-one years was not a particularly long time as things went in those days.

England alone originally represented the Oikoumene in the war, but other nations joined Britain at different stages. All the major powers of the West were involved in the final treaty settlement that ended the conflict in 1860–1861.

The Twenty-one Years' War radically altered the relationship between the Empire and the capitalist world system. When the war began, the traditional tribute system was still in place, even if it was under strong pressure from outside. When the war ended, the tribute system no longer operated in the Empire's relationship with the West. The conflict also radically altered the world in which the sinocentric Empire perceived itself to be the center or apex. When the struggle began, the emperor was still first among unequals, and his commissioner in Canton could write to the queen of England as a superior to an inferior. When the war ended, the Empire's very survival was in question; it was no longer the center of its world, and the emperor, far from being first among unequals, was no longer even counted in the first rank of the mighty. The Twenty-one Years' War must be considered, therefore, one of the pivotal conflicts in world history: the changes it brought about in the East were profound and its effects were permanent.

For a conflict fraught with such implications and consequences, the war began in an almost trivial way. Commissioner Lin's prohibition against the delivery of supplies to the growing and increasingly military English population of Hong Kong led Captain Elliot to repeated protests. For example, on August 25, 1839, he dispatched four armed vessels with over eighty men into the Bay of Kowloon to deliver a protest to Chinese officials. That afternoon, the English encountered two imperial government junks and carried out their mission with no bloodshed. The Twenty-one Years' War began on September 4, 1839, when Captain Elliot himself led a small fleet to Kowloon. At noon that day this force arrived off the town of Kowloon, where it encountered three imperial war junks and a strong battery in place. Infuriated over the refusal to accept his letter of protest, Captain Elliot presented the imperial officials with an ultimatum at 2:00 P.M., stating that he would sink the junks if the English did not receive provisions within a half hour. The deadline passed, no provisions arrived, and the English immediately fired on the junks. In the battle that ensued, two imperial soldiers were killed, two were wounded seriously, and more were wounded slightly; on the English side, the captain of one of the ships suffered a flesh wound in the arm, and two crewmen were more seriously injured. Blood had been shed, and the war began.[7]

Negotiations to prevent the spread of the conflict failed. Trade could not be resumed because the British continued to refuse to surrender the murderer of the Chinese peasant. This and related issues fed Lin's impatience and made further conflict inevitable. The first major battle of the war erupted at Chuanbi in November 1839, when, ironically, imperial naval vessels were trying to protect British merchant ships that intended to trade at Canton on imperial terms, while British ships were attempting to prevent the merchants from trading on other than British terms. It was traditional in the Far East for commerce to continue in spite of, and in the midst of, war. Between October 1839 and June 1840, over twenty-six million pounds of tea were shipped to England, and the tea trade with the United States and the European continent exceeded expectations. Moreover, despite the imperial commissioner's efforts to the contrary, the coastal trade in opium continued to flourish.

The ships of the British expeditionary force began to arrive in Chinese waters in June 1840. Soon Canton was declared blockaded, which constituted the formal opening of a war that had actually begun nine months earlier. On July 4 a British fleet of six ships arrived at Chusan Island, south of Shanghai, and British soldiers landed and occupied the city of Dinghai on July 6. The *London Times* reported, "The British flag waves over a portion of the Chinese empire for the first time! Chusan fell into the hands of the English on Sunday, the 5th of July, and one more settlement in the Far East was added to the British Crown."[8] As the British proceeded north and the war spread, Lin Zexu was dismissed and disgraced because he had failed to eradicate opium, because war had broken out, and because the court, in any event, needed a scapegoat. The Empire's attempts at resistance were doomed to failure. The imperial forces, numerous though they were, were no match for the very much smaller but very much better trained and equipped English. The imperial army was corrupt and weak. As one official said, the soldiers knew neither how to ride nor how to shoot, and the sailors could neither sail nor fire a cannon. Officers were able only to keep accounts. The junks, equipped with archers, ancient cannon, and stinkpots, were totally ineffective. Between 1840 and 1842, small British forces, numbering only a few thousand men but possessed of the most modern military equipment, significantly reduced the imperial forces along the coast between Canton and Shanghai.

Throughout the war, military activity and diplomatic negotiations were intricately intertwined. As befitted a new world system whose primary foundations were self-consciously economic, Britain, the standard bearer of the Oikoumene, had no territorial ambitions with regard to the Empire save the barest minimum necessary for trade, to wit, a commercial base. England already had found this on the island of Hong Kong, though British possession of that island was not yet legitimated by international agreement. Britain's basic objective, therefore, was the imposition of change upon the Empire, particularly change that would bring the Empire into a cooperative relationship with the new world economic system. Therefore, victory in the Twenty-one Years' War was never defined as defeat of the Qing dynasty but, rather, as a change in Qing policy. The Chinese tradition that permitted the continuation of commerce and negotiations in the midst of conflict was reinforced here by a tacit British understanding that the objective of the use of force was to change, not to defeat; therefore, force was a support for, not an alternative to, negotiations.

In 1840–1841, the war's first period, Captain Elliot carried on negotiations outside Tianjin and, later, at Canton. After Commissioner Lin's dismissal, these negotiations continued with his successor, Qishan. In January 1841 they succeeded in concluding the Chuanbi (Chuenpi) Convention, which ceded Hong Kong to England, established diplomatic equality between the two powers, provided an indemnity for Britain, and reopened Canton for trade. However, both governments rejected this settlement, which ultimately led to Qishan's dismissal and Elliot's recall. Meanwhile, in May 1841, after the close of the tea trading season, Elliot prepared to lead a force of twenty-four hundred troops in an assault on Canton. Attack was avoided when the city was ransomed for $6 million. At the same time, the regional gentry had mobilized a local militia that was threatening the British, which suggested the growth of antiforeignism in the Canton area.

A shift in the relationship between negotiation and the use of force by the British characterized the second period of the war, 1841–1842. The British, dissatisfied with the Elliot-Qishan agreement, decided they would not stop short of a complete restructuring of their relationship with the

Empire. Consequently, they determined to force the Qing government, by military means, to negotiate the total restructuring desired. This policy meant military campaigns *before* negotiations rather than *with* negotiations. In the fall of 1841, therefore, the British landed and established garrisons all along the coast, at Xiamen, on Chusan Island (which they had previously evacuated), and at Ningbo (Ningpo), after which they halted action for the winter. In the spring of 1842, reinforcements arrived from India, and the British forces captured a position in Hangzhou Bay, occupied Shanghai, and took Jinjiang (where the Grand Canal crosses the Changjiang River). They also advanced into the outskirts of the city of Nanjing. This was full, though not total (in the modern sense) warfare, and the imperial response, including a surprise but vain attack on the British occupied city of Ningbo in March 1842, was to no avail. The imperial forces often fought courageously, but they were inferior in training, equipment, and tactics. Western technology and organization enabled the British to fight and win, with very small forces, a war on the other side of the world, on the home territory of the world's largest geographically unified Empire.

The settlement negotiated between the British and the Qing government in August 1842 began, but only began, the reconstruction of the Empire's relationship with the West. Still contending with severe imperial restrictions that ran counter to British and capitalist expectations, the British felt compelled to continue the use of force to achieve their objectives. In 1847, for example, British forces attacked Canton in order to wrest from the government access to the city for Western merchants, and they withdrew only when access was promised. In the early 1850s fear of disturbing the China trade at a time when turmoil within the Empire was already giving the foreign merchants difficulties was all that prevented the British from attacking the Empire again. Meanwhile, Great Britain had become involved in war with Russia, and this occupied England's attention until 1856. In that year, London found a new excuse to reopen hostilities with the Empire when the governor-general of Canton refused to apologize for a supposed insult to the Union Jack: imperial officials had lowered the British flag from a Chinese owned boat registered at Hong Kong, the *Lorcha Arrow* (this phase of the Twenty-one Years' War is often called, therefore, the Arrow War). At approximately the same time, a French missionary in Guangxi province, accused of being a subversive working for rebels, was arrested, judicially tortured, and executed. The French, under Napoleon III, used this event as an excuse to join the British in the war, thus widening Western participation in the process of expanding the world economic system to East Asia.

The immediate causes for the resumption of hostilities—the *Arrow* incident and the demise of the French missionary—could not mask the fact that the war was continuing because the West had not yet achieved its objectives. In October 1856, Harry Parkes, the British consul, ordered the navy to attack Canton. It succeeded in bombarding the governor-general's office, but the Chinese would not capitulate. In May 1857, the great Sepoy mutiny broke out in India, which delayed the arrival of the expeditionary force sent from England. Canton was captured only at the beginning of 1858, therefore, and the governor-general, who was captured at the same time, was sent to Calcutta while the British consul appointed a Chinese puppet to govern the city under orders from an Anglo-French commission. The allies fully recognized, however, that the emperor and his court were the key to the settlement the West wanted. Therefore, Lord Elgin and Barron Gros, the British and French negotiators, led the allied Western forces to Tianjin, where they concluded treaties in June 1858 that permitted Western ministers to live at Peking within a context of equality as understood in Western diplomatic practice.

It now appeared that victory belonged to the West, and its fleets and negotiators departed. The imperial court, however, was not ready to surrender as completely as implied by the treaties. In June 1859, when the British and French ministers arrived off the China coast at Tianjin in order to go to Peking for the exchange of ratifications of the treaties, they were not permitted to proceed. They attempted to use force to reach the capital but were defeated by the forts at Taku, with a loss of four gunboats and many casualties.

The war continued. In 1860, Lord Elgin and Barron Gros returned with 41 British warships, 143 troop transports, 10,500 soldiers, both cavalry and foot (mostly Indian), and a corps of 2,500 Cantonese coolies from the occupied city; the French contribution consisted of 6,300 troops and more than 60 ships. The imperial court fielded far more numerous forces than the allies could muster, but the Chinese were defeated and the allies entered Peking in October 1860. The emperor fled to Jehol, which lies beyond the Great Wall in the direction of Manchuria.

The allied forces' capture of Peking opened the way for the complete reorientation of the Empire's foreign relations. The process was complicated, however, by long-standing Anglo-French rivalries in Europe that now found an echo in the Far East. France had no major commercial interests in East Asia; Paris sought, rather, to enhance French glory. Lord Elgin, representing England's primarily commercial interests, was forced to restrain the rambunctious French at the same time that he had to contain England's own "old China hands," whose objectives were expansionist. Harry Parkes, the British consul, was not the least troublesome of these. Further complications developed when the imperial representatives seized Parkes, who had been negotiating under a flag of truce. They held the consul prisoner for three weeks and executed twenty-three members of his party. In reprisal, Lord Elgin burned down the emperor's summer palace, the famous "Yuan Ming Yuan," to the northwest of Peking.

The approach of winter forced the allied troops to withdraw; they were short of ammunition and had no wish to remain in occupation of the capital during the harsh winter of North China. Elgin and Gros finally succeeded in exchanging the ratifications of the 1858 treaties and in signing new agreements with Prince Gung, the emperor's brother, who represented the dynasty in the emperor's absence. With these documents, the West accomplished three things. First, it completed the first major step in the dismantling of the traditional apparatus whereby the sinocentric Empire conducted its foreign relations. Second, it reoriented the Empire's foreign policy and created new institutions for the structuring of China's relations with the countries of the expanding capitalist world system. Third, it placed the Empire in a position inferior to that of the West and, unconsciously, set loose forces and processes whose consequences are still being felt today.

The Unequal Treaty System

The Twenty-one Years' War concluded with the dismantling of the tribute system and its replacement by a new structure in Sino-Western relations, the "unequal treaty system." Like the tribute system before it, the unequal treaty system was multinational. Its basic forms and structures were established in one bilateral treaty, but various diplomatic mechanisms were used to extend these features to other nations through a whole series of bilateral treaties; the same structural relationships established with one country were replicated in relationships with others. The unequal treaty system was also like the tribute system in that it described a set of unequal relationships, except that now the Oikoumene was superior to the Empire. To be sure, the treaties used a language of equality, but the reality they described was quite otherwise.

The first step in the construction of the unequal treaty system was taken on August 29, 1842, when the British plenipotentiary, Sir Henry Pottinger, signed the Treaty of Nanjing with Qiying, the imperial commissioner who had replaced Lin Zexu. This document abolished the Cohong monopoly in the Canton trade, recognized British possession of Hong Kong, opened five ports to British residence and commerce (Canton, Xiamen, Fuzhou, Ningbo, and Shanghai), and promised the establishment of a fair and regular tariff. In addition, the treaty required the Empire to pay Britain an indemnity of twenty-one million Mexican dollars, which was intended to cover the debts the hong merchants owed the British, the value of the opium Lin Zexu had confiscated, and the cost of the war to the British Indian government. This payment was also considered a sign of the Empire's guilt in the war. Britain's superiority and China's inferiority in a new relationship that reversed the Empire's traditional view of inequality was manifest in the treaty's provisions denying Peking the exercise of sovereignty in specific areas: the organization of trade with other countries, tariffs, and the determination of where foreigners could live and work. Three more treaties added to the structure of the unequal treaty system in 1843–1844. On October 8, 1843, the British signed the Supplementary Treaty of the Bogue; the Americans signed the Treaty of Wangxia on July 3, 1844; and the French signed the Treaty of Whampoa on October 24, 1844. These four treaties, together with others signed in the course of the Twenty-one Years' War and later, constituted a system because they included the famous "most favored nation" clause. According to this provision, any privilege granted one power was automatically granted to all powers. This meant that a single system was formed of a series of independently negotiated bilateral treaties. (The tribute system also had consisted of a series of a discrete bilateral relationships resembling each other so strongly that we can speak of a system.)

This first stage in the construction of the new system included the appointment of British consuls and the creation of consular establishments in the treaty ports; British nationals lived and worked under their protection and legal jurisdiction. According to this principle of extraterritoriality, foreigners living abroad, in this case in the Empire, were subject to their own laws and courts, not to those of the host country. Under the unequal treaty system, this protection covered foreigners of certain nationalities whatever their occupation, together with their property and goods and, sometimes, their Chinese employees. Originally British, the "most favored nation" clause extended this privilege automatically to the nationals of any other country maintaining a treaty with the Empire. In addition, Peking was now required to establish a treaty tariff on all imported goods, which meant the imposition of free trade theories that were the core of the expanding capitalist world-economic system. This regulation, in turn, was reinforced by the treaty prohibition against the organization of trade on the Chinese side. This first settlement, therefore, established the pattern for later settlements, including inequality, the extension of the system in any of its given regulations to all participating countries, and the restriction of imperial sovereignty over particular classes of residents within the Empire's own borders.

The unequal treaty system grew incrementally throughout the period of the Twenty-one Years' War. For example, after the first round of treaty settlements opened Shanghai to foreign residents and commerce, foreigners began to settle outside the city walls in an area that later came to be known as the International Settlement and French Concession. In July 1854, after the capture of Shanghai by the Taipings (the Taiping rebellion lasted from 1850 to 1864), the British, French, and American consuls obtained the local government's consent to the establishment of foreign self-government in these areas, including rights of self-protection, taxation, etc. In one respect, the foreigners thought they needed these arrangements for self-defense in an Empire in the throes of rebellion; in another respect, however, this development represented an expansion of the concept of extraterritoriality to include foreign municipal governments on imperial territory. The British, French, and Americans also cooperated in persuading the local government to accept their appointees as customs collectors. From this agreement grew, eventually, the Foreign Inspectorate of Customs. After 1855, this service was managed by a foreigner, employed by the imperial government, and it was he who had the responsibility for collecting duties established by treaty for China's foreign trade.

By the 1850s, the West (particularly Britain) was convinced that the treaty system would fall apart if it were not reaffirmed and extended. This belief was encouraged by imperial recalcitrance in granting foreigners the full measure of privileges the foreigners believed was their due from the treaties. The Westerners believed the seal of permanence would be placed upon the treaty system only when Western ministers took up residence at the imperial capital on the same terms of equality that they enjoyed in Western capitals. The imperial court resisted this move mightily, being fully aware that granting the West this privilege would mark the public admission of the Empire's loss of centrality in the world, its defeat at the hands of the West, and the end of the traditional tribute system. The Westerners achieved their objective with the treaties negotiated at Tianjin in June 1858, but these were rejected by the court. The Treaties of Peking of 1860, negotiated after a resumption of East-West hostilities, confirmed the 1858 agreements, increased the indemnities owed the West, and expanded the list of concessions. Britain now obtained possession of the Kowloon Peninsula, across from the island of Hong Kong, and France obtained the right for Christian missions in China's interior to possess property.

Thus, by 1860 the unequal treaty system existed in all its important aspects. Although the British and French had carried the major responsibility for achieving the objectives of the West, the Americans, Russians, and other Westerners all participated in the benefits of the system through the "most favored nation" clause. The system would be amended from time to time, but it would survive almost to the middle of the twentieth century along the lines worked out in the course of the Twenty-one Years' War.

THE RUSSIANS

The Russian caravan trade with Peking ended in the middle of the eighteenth century, but the frontier trade thrived, and the religious mission in Peking continued to function as a semi-official diplomatic office and a center for Chinese studies within the context of the tribute system. Nevertheless, just as the unequal treaty system replaced the tribute system and the Canton system, that particular form the tribute system took in relations between the Empire and Great Britain, so, too, it replaced the Kyakhta system.

Although Russia lay outside the core area of the world capitalist economic order, Russia's geographical relationship with the sinocentric Empire conjoined it to the imperialist powers in the Far East. The treaties of Nerchinsk (1689) and Kyakhta (1728) had established a structure for Russia's relationship with the Empire that kept the Russians out of the Amur valley and along the farther frontier of Mongolia. However, these treaties did not prevent the extension of Russian interests in Siberia and North America. Rapidly expanding through Siberia, they reached Alaska in 1741. The Russians established outposts throughout the region, and in 1799 the Russian-American Company was created to monopolize and expand Russian trade in the Pacific in competition with the British East India Company.

Russia's natural geographical interest in the North Pacific and in Northeast Asian trade was rooted in, and reinforced by, Russia's great rivalry with Britain throughout the nineteenth century. As the British presence expanded in the Middle East and India, the Russians perceived the possibility of a growing British interest in Central Asia, which would constitute a direct threat to Russia proper and to Moscow's interests in the region. As a consequence, the Russians themselves began concertedly expanding into the area east of the Caspian Sea and west of the Pamir Mountains. This steady move to the south and east brought them into commercial contact with the sinocentric Empire in Central Asia, in the area where Chinese Turkestan (Xinjiang) and the khanates of Central Asia meet. Consequently, in 1861 a new Sino-Russian treaty was signed, the Treaty of Kuldja, which essentially extended to Central Asia the regulations governing Sino-Russian intercourse at Kyakhta. Now, however, in light of the developments along the China coast, the Russians obtained the right to establish a consulate at Kuldja, in the Ili region, which would have charge over Russian citizens in the area.

The appointment in 1847 of Nikolai Muraviev as governor-general of eastern Siberia brought renewed Russian interest in that region. Muraviev sent a flotilla of barges down the Amur River in 1854 and established posts along its northern bank. Settlers and troops began to move into the region from which they had been excluded by the Treaty of Nerchinsk in 1689. The Empire proved incapable of expelling the Russians this time, and on May 16, 1858, Russia and the Empire signed a treaty at Aigun, on the Amur River, granting Russia the northern bank of the river and declaring the two countries' joint possession of the region between the Ussuri River and the Pacific Ocean. This settlement in effect postponed any decision about the disposition of this territory. Meanwhile, in June of that same year, the Russians signed their own Treaty of Tianjin with Peking, gaining thereby all the privileges granted the other Western powers along the China coast.

When in 1859 the imperial court rejected the treaties concluded with the Western powers the previous year at Tianjin, it also rejected the Aigun treaty. Consequently, Russia's interests coalesced with those of the other Western powers, and Nikolai Ignatiev, one of Russia's great nineteenth-century diplomats, promoted Russia's interests by placing himself in a position to negotiate between the defeated Qing court and the victorious allies. His reward for serving as mediator was the Russian Treaty of Peking, signed in November 1860 after the departure of the French and the British from the capital. This treaty confirmed the agreements made at Aigun, and Russia gained sole possession of the region between the Ussuri and the Pacific Ocean. This territory became the Maritime province; in July 1860, even before the conclusion of the treaty, Muraviev had established Vladivostok, destined to become Russia's primary urban settlement on the Pacific.

The Empire in the New System

One of the principal effects of the tribute system was the incorporation of the foreigner, once he had "turned toward civilization," into the Empire. The unequal treaty system had a similar effect, but whereas previously the foreigner had entered the imperial system upon his recognition of its superiority, under the unequal treaty system the foreigner participated in the Empire on the basis of his own superiority. This reflected the same reversal of roles achieved under the unequal treaty system itself. The West now began to play the role in China that China previously had played in the peripheral areas of the sinocentric Empire. This shift brought profound changes to China that were a direct consequence not of internal change but of the impact of the West on China's interior life.

FURTHER WESTERN EXPANSION

The Treaties of Peking of 1860, which marked the end of the Twenty-one Years' War, also opened a new period of Western expansion in China that was to last until, with the Boxer Rebellion of 1900–1903, Sino-Western relations reached a new plateau. As Western penetration of China proceeded, the number of ports open to foreign trade and settlement increased from the five that had been established in the 1840s to the 115 that existed when the unequal treaty system was abrogated in 1943. The freedom with which Western merchants and missionaries could move throughout the Empire improved dramatically, foreign goods began to compete successfully with Chinese products, opium was legalized, and Chinese converts were brought under the protection of foreign governments.

By the 1860s "concessions" had developed in at least seven Chinese cities. These were large tracts of land leased in perpetuity by foreign governments for a small, symbolic rent. These concessions, centered around a foreign consulate, gradually developed into self-sufficient communities independent of imperial sovereignty in matters of taxation and legal jurisdiction. In Shanghai, for example, the British and American concessions together formed the Shanghai International Settlement, governed by the Shanghai municipal council, which levied taxes against Chinese residents in its jurisdiction, as well as against its two thousand foreign residents. Foreign communities in treaty ports such as Shanghai developed a culture of their own, publishing newspapers and maintaining libraries, hospitals, schools, sewage systems, etc. These foreigners lived in China as a privileged class superior in power to the traditional Chinese upper classes. But most important, these communities were living examples of Western society, culture, and civilization. They were power centers in their own right and provided seedbeds of change within Chinese society.

THE TRADE SYSTEM

The treaty ports served as the centers for a growing commercial activity. Western technological advances such as ironclad ships, steamships, and the trans-Atlantic telegraph network all tied China into the international market, increasingly subjecting the Empire to the vagaries of the West's complex economic system. However, as an importer of foreign goods, China never matched Western expectations, and while initially exports of tea and silk rose dramatically, China did not keep pace with Western industrialization and, over the course of the nineteenth century, became less and less able to compete with Western products.

When China's internal market for Western goods failed to develop, many foreign merchants blamed the Chinese economic and social system; however, this failure probably had more to do with both the poverty and the self-sufficiency of the Chinese peasant society. Even opium imports, which had doubled over the course of the Twenty-one Years' War, declined after 1879, when the Chinese began producing the drug themselves.

China's export trade also started to decline around this time, as Japanese tea began to compete successfully for the American market and the Indian and Ceylonese tea industries were modernized. Nor could the Chinese silk industry compete with Japan's modernized technology, and China's cotton manufacture never developed beyond the cottage handicraft stage. In fact, since machine-spun yarn from India could be sold in China more cheaply than handspun Chinese yarn, this native industry was destroyed.

In addition to the Chinese market's inability to absorb Western goods or to compete with Western products, China's lack of a modern and stable currency further inhibited its participation in trade. In an attempt to remedy this situation, the government adopted an artifical unit of exchange, the *tael*, in 1857. But as the production of silver increased around the world and more and more countries went on the gold standard, the *tael* declined steadily against gold.

The failure of the China market to develop and China's inability to participate more actively in trade raise an interesting question of values. Whose interests, after all, would have been served by the growth of the China market and the China trade? In the West, the U.S. labor market feared competition from cheap Chinese labor and the import of cheaper Chinese goods. The British textile industry, while it might have profited from a better Chinese market for its goods, could well have been threatened had the Chinese textile industry became sufficiently modernized to compete. From the point of view of the Empire, even the limited participation of China in the world economic system had undermined the traditional imperial establishment. In the nineteenth century, industrialization would have required, in a country as densely populated as China, a growth of urban centers and consequent urban poverty of almost unimaginable proportions. Conditions in a city like Calcutta suggest that the potential horrors of industrialization for China far outweighed even those real horrors experienced by British, continental, and American workers of that era. The question of the value of foreign trade to the Empire must be a matter of judgment; we can observe its consequences and project possible implications, but we must be careful lest we judge the Empire by its failure to develop as an international economic power.

SOCIAL CHANGE

One noteworthy development of Sino-Western trade in the nineteenth century was the establishment of a new class of Chinese called "compradors." The compradors, who took their name from the Portuguese word for "buyer," managed the Chinese side of a Westerner's commerce and served as a cultural and social bridge between West and East. Never large, this class had no status in traditional Chinese society but existed as an out-group specializing in foreign matters, having its children educated in Western languages, and serving foreign governments and firms. The existence of these pioneers in the small, "modern" sector of Chinese society suggested profound possibilities for social change.

The Chinese merchants who acted as agents for Western companies and as wholesalers and retailers of Western goods were also influenced by the culture and economic system they served. Like the compradors, they began to accumulate capital through savings. Western banks emerged in China to serve their needs, as well as the needs of the foreigners, and entered into the imperial economy. These banks also functioned between China and overseas Chinese communities, occasionally even issuing their own currency.

The compradors and Chinese merchants gradually moved away from traditional land investments and became sources of capital for Chinese industrialization in partnership with government officials, thereby aiding the development of the emerging modern sector of which they were a part.

SUPPRESSION OF REBELLION

As internal revolution increasingly disturbed the Empire, the growth of Sino-Western relations began to have effects beyond the commercial sector. To suppress the rebels, central government and provincial officials first turned to Western guns and ships and then to Western mercenaries. Frederick Townsend Ward of Massachusetts, for example, led a group of foreign adventurers in the pay of Chinese merchants involved in Western trade. When the Taiping rebels reached the suburbs of Shanghai early in 1862, Britain and France joined forces with the imperial dynasty. Although the Taipings had pretensions to Western mythology and echoed certain Christian words, ideas, and practices, the Westerners felt their interests lay in the preservation of the weak Qing dynasty rather than in the uncertainties of the possibly hostile Taipings.

The western states became more active in China's internal struggles, and Ward moved from being the leader of a group of foreign adventurers to becoming the leader of a group of four thousand Chinese, the highly effective Ever-Victorious Army, trained in Western tactics, armed with Western guns, and inspired with a high level of morale from their close connection with foreigners. When Ward died in 1862, his place was taken by Major Charles George Gordon, the Englishman who became known as "Chinese Gordon" and, later, "Gordon of Khartoum." Both Ward and Gordon were given Chinese military rank and were incorporated into the system as they could not have been into that of a sovereign Western power. It was precisely because the sinocentric imperial system continued to survive alongside the Western world economy that men like Ward and Gordon could participate so directly in the military affairs of the Empire.

SPREADING THE FAITH

Another important consequence of the unequal treaty system was the rapid growth in the number of missionaries, both Catholic and Protestant:

the Roman Catholics, who had retained a base after the expulsion of the Jesuits toward the end of the eighteenth century, had some 400,000 converts served by 250 priests in 1870; the Protestants, by contrast, had 6,000 converts and 350 missionaries, supported by donations from hometown missionary societies.

Like the compradors, the missionaries and their converts became a cutting edge for social change inside China; they studied each other's books, languages, art, and philosophy and sought to apply to Chinese life the rubrics that governed personal and group behavior in the West. Through their schools and hospitals, the Protestants particularly became agents for modernization and change; many of China's twentieth-century leaders were products of a complete Western educational system, from kindergarten through college, transplanted to the Empire.

Once again, the evaluation of this activity is a matter separate from the record of its existence. Few other countries in the world were subjected to the religious and intellectual offensive that the Western churches carried out against China. The offensive was based upon the arrogance of Westerners who believed that their faith and way of life was innately superior to any other. To the extent that they were able to persuade some Chinese of the validity of this proposition, they represented a frontal attack upon another tradition, about which they knew relatively little and whose successes and failures they were in no position to judge. Some of the best and some of the worst of modern China's leaders were the products of Western education and of the Sino-Western culture to which it gave rise in China. The record of this interaction, however, is at best mixed. Perhaps judgment of it should begin with the observation that what the Westerner perceived to be the conservatism of Chinese culture was really the refusal of the Chinese to accept Western evaluations of Chinese culture.

WESTERN STUDIES

The institutions of the treaty ports and the personnel of marketplace, church, and school expanded the possibility for Western studies by Chinese in China. Early Chinese studies of foreigners, such as Wei Yuan's *Illustrated Gazetteer of the Countries Overseas (Haiguo Tuzhi)*, which appeared in 1844 and was republished in expanded editions in 1847 and 1852, did not lead necessarily to positive responses to the West. Wei Yuan, for example, criticized Christianity for being inherently irrational.

Probably the first coherent attempt to study and appraise Western countries in China was Xu Jiyü's *A Brief Survey of the Maritime Circuit (Yinghuan Zhilue)*, published in 1850. The author, a governor of Fujian province, examined each country separately, described it in a summary fashion, and presented maps as illustrations. Although a major step forward in Western studies, the book, along with its author, was denounced by conservatives. The imperial defeat in the Twenty-one Years' War led to a different kind of Western studies. Interest in Western languages began to develop, and special schools were opened in Peking, Shanghai, Canton, and Fuzhou, but results were disappointing because the students selected to study in them were not equal to the task.

Arsenals, machine shops, and shipyards were established to make Western arms and ships, and these, too, became centers of foreign learning and even of translation of Western scientific and technological works. Obviously, the products of these latter institutions primarily interested military and naval authorities.

In addition to all these activities inside China, students of the Empire began to go abroad to study. Yung Wing (1828–1912) was one of the earliest and most famous. Born into a poor family in Macao, he had learned English in missionary schools and was sent by the missionaries to the United States. Becoming both a Christian and an American citizen, he graduated from Yale in 1854. Yung Wing believed that "through Western education China might be regenerated, become enlightened and powerful," and he wanted to send Chinese students to the United States on an educational mission.[9] In 1872, 120 Chinese boys, mostly from poor families in the southeast, went to Hartford, Connecticut, where they began what was planned to be a fifteen-year program of Western education that would prepare them to serve the imperial government in international relations. The boys, living with American families, studied English and America, but they also continued their traditional Chinese studies. Yung Wing himself became a Congregationalist and married an American; he encouraged the Chinese boys to become more and more Americanized. Responding to negative reactions on the part of the traditional Chinese officials, the growth of anti-Chinese sentiment in the United States, and the feeling in Peking that it would be cheaper to educate such students at home, the Qing suspended the mission in 1881. Some of the students were admitted to West Point and Annapolis, however. When they returned to Shanghai, the students found that they no longer fitted into the imperial system, as the traditional examinations were still the primary road to government service. Some went into naval service, some into other modern sectors, such as mining or telegraph or railroad administration, and others entered the diplomatic corps. Of the original group, only twelve became regular government officials. Despite this rather undramatic beginning, however, the mission opened the way for further Western education of Chinese; Yung's project was, in fact, the first step down the path that was to end with the abolition of the traditional examination system in 1905.

OVERSEAS CHINESE

One more development must be mentioned in connection with the growth of Sino-Western intercourse during and after the Twenty-one Years' War. Overseas Chinese communities in Southeast Asia had existed for some time; indeed, some of the earliest significant contact between Westerners and Chinese had taken place in and around Chinese communities in the Philippines, the Dutch East Indies, and Indochina. The spread of the treaty ports and increasing awareness overseas of the availability of cheap Chinese labor, together with ships of a size and speed capable of transporting significant numbers across the ocean, led to the development of what can only be called the export of humans from China.

Chinese and foreign merchants together began to arrange for the shipment of male workers from China, particularly from the southeast coast, to such places as Southeast Asia, Hawaii, Peru, and Cuba, where cheap labor was in great demand. The international effort to abolish slavery and the slave rebellions in the Americas contributed to this demand. The discovery of gold in California and Australia in 1848 and 1851, respectively, and railroad construction in the American west and along the Pacific coast of South America also stimulated this human commerce. Initially, Chinese laborers went overseas under contract; later, as knowledge of opportunities abroad began to filter back home, more and more free emigration took place. As the years passed, some of these Chinese laborers returned home to marry and then went overseas again; gradually, women began to emigrate as well, actually or potentially contracted for marriage. The large Chinese communities in the United States, Peru, Cuba, and Trinidad, to mention but a few outside East and Southeast Asia, are the result of this commerce. These communities never lost interest in their homeland, and most particularly in their home regions; as China began to undergo revolutionary change, Chinese revolutionaries sought aid and support among the overseas communities. Therefore, even while the West was confronting and defeating the sinocentric imperial system, Chinese society was establishing outposts, as it were, far beyond the traditional reaches of Chinese culture and imperial power.

The Failure of the Treaty System

Both the tribute system and the unequal treaty system had operated not for the coexistence of two radically different worlds but, rather, for the modification of one by the other. After the disintegration of the tribute system and the conceptual structures that institutional complex implied, the unequal treaty system left the Empire with neither the institutions to protect its own interests nor the means to modify the conceptual world in which it interacted with the foreign powers. The weak position of the Empire, combined with the technological strength of the West, seemed to force the Chinese to become modernized, that is, westernized, to survive in the expanding world capitalist system.

Both Western and imperial officials hoped that a policy of cooperation and modernization would allow the Empire to adjust without a recurrence of external warfare or internal disruption, and leading foreigners in China sometimes even submitted proposals for reform to the court. But the terms of adjustment were always unequal: no one spoke of the need for the capitalists to adjust to the Empire. In 1868, however, the Qing court went so far as to appoint Anson Burlingame, the American minister to the Empire, who was retiring from that post, the first imperial emissary to the Western world. Appointed to high civil rank in the bureaucracy, Burlingame orated his way through Washington, London, Paris, St. Petersburg, and a host of other capitals, portraying an Empire on the eve of both westernization and Christianization: he played to his audience and not always in the interests of the Empire.

The policy of cooperation had opponents in both camps. Throughout the Empire, strong forces opposed any concessions to foreigners, and among the Westerners, calls for a more aggressive policy could be heard on every side, as capitalists, militarists, and jingoists all sought to press their interests with little regard for the consequences to the Empire itself.

In 1869 the British rejected a revision of the Treaty of Tianjin initiated by the British minister, Rutherford Alcock, and Robert Hart of the Customs Service. This was a serious setback for moderates of both sides because the Alcock Convention, as it was called, had provided enough minor, face-saving modifications to be acceptable to the imperial negotiators, while leaving intact such major provisions of the earlier treaty as extraterritoriality, tariff restrictions, and the legalization of opium. But British commercial interests, basically unconcerned with the interests or stability of the Empire, violently attacked the convention because it did little to extend their privileges or strengthen their position.

THE TIANJIN MASSACRE OF 1870

On June 21, 1870, the French consul fired on a patriotic, antiforeign demonstration. Trying to hit the local magistrate, he missed and was, in turn, torn to pieces by the demonstrators. They then killed twenty more foreigners (mostly French), including ten nuns. Some Catholic buildings were also destroyed. This incident, dramatic in both origins and consequences, exposed as a sham the policy of cooperation that was intended to protect the Empire's interests only so long as the Empire did not assert them.

The entire treaty system rested upon a particular set of assumptions that, if realized, would have required that the Qing government involve itself in perpetual self-contradiction. British policy in 1860s intended to force the imperial government to take responsibility for the enforcement of the treaty system both along the coast and inside the country. At the same time, the British meant to support the imperial government in this endeavor by contributing to the modernization of its administrative apparatus. However, the very treaty system that the British expected the Qing government to enforce allowed foreigners privileges within the Empire that both undermined the traditional institutional bases of the government's authority and attacked the cultural foundations of its legitimacy. The treaty restricted the freedom of action of a government that traditionally had enjoyed almost unrestricted freedom, and it granted groups within the Empire privileges that had no foundations either in the state or in the society. The treaty permitted proselytization by resident Christian missionaries whose primary objective had to be, by definition, the transfer of popular loyalty from the Confucian tradition, which was the foundation of the state, to a wholly foreign religion. Indeed the treaty system's protection of missionary rights exposed the system for what it really was.

The treaty system granted foreign governments the right to extend protection to their own citizens engaged in missionary activity in the Empire. Thus, for example, in the late 1860s the British minister, Alcock, sent four gunboats to Nanjing to force Zeng Guofan, the great Hunanese general and scholar-official, to dismiss local authorities in the Yangzhou region, on the Grand Canal, because in 1868 a British missionary had been assaulted by elements of the local population. Moreover, Alcock insisted that the imperial government make restitution for the missionary's losses. The disclaimers of historians, politicians, and churchmen to the contrary, imperialism was imperialism, no matter how enlightened.

French behavior in the Empire' was even more outrageous. France used its treaty-given right to protect Christian missionaries as a means to expand French influence in the Empire despite a lack of commercial interests that required protection. Early in 1870, for example, Count Julien de Rochechouart, the particularly bellicose French representative to the Empire, sailed up the Changjiang to negotiate with local authorities about cases involving missionary interests. His maneuver undermined the authority of the imperial regime in the districts through which he passed, and his gunboats quickly brought the results he wanted.

These were but two of many incidents in which the representatives of the Western powers pursued the interests of their own countries with little or no thought for the consequences of their actions. They served only to increase popular outrage and xenophobia, which, in turn, fueled further conflicts.

The incident at Tianjin was simply the culmination of Western postwar policy in the Empire. French Sisters of Charity in that city publicly offered to pay for orphans who were given to them for care. Tianjin's people believed this practice would encourage kidnapping, and rumors began to spread that behind the walls of the orphanage children's eyes and hearts were being removed from their bodies. Agitation developed, and the demonstration on June 21 was a direct consequence of the nuns' unseemly offer. The spark that lit the flame was the action of the French consul, and the massacre that ensued was a response born of long accumulated resentment.

The foreign powers gathered their gunboats off Tianjin, while Chinese conservatives and reformers alike thought they saw in the uprising a new force that could tame the outrageous Westerners. The strength of the public outcry against the foreigners showed that the policy of conciliation had little popular support.

Zeng Guofan, now old and ill, was asked to resolve the crisis, and toward that end he conducted an investigation and announced the unpalatable results: he could find no evidence of kidnapping or of mutilation of children by the missionaries. Paris, however, was threatening military action and only defeat in the Franco-Prussian War in Europe seemed to prevent France from gathering its resources to attack the Empire. Nonetheless, when Li Hungzhang became governor-general of Zhili province and took charge of the situation at Tianjin, he continued to prepare for an attack by France. If the treaty system had held out any hope for coexistence—and this is questionable—French behavior at Tianjin in 1870 destroyed that possibility.

China in Asia

The expansion of the world capitalist system in the person of British, French, American, and Russian nationals was not limited to seaborne trade, warfare, and treaty negotiations with the imperial center in China Proper. As the states of the West sent expeditions into territories peripheral to the sinocentric Empire and established outposts there, they encountered the traditional power of the Empire in those areas too, but with a difference: while along the coast the two systems met head-on, the societies in the Empire's peripheral regions, highly conscious of their own cultural traditions and sociopolitical and economic organization, became both onlookers and players in the game. Influenced and buffeted by the forces coming from the outside, these peoples were concerned mainly with survival in the face of two antagonistic and incompatible imperialisms: the imperialism of the Empire and the imperialism of the Western economic system.

Twentieth-century North Atlantic peoples are accustomed to traversing great distances by air and sea. Consequently, they do not think in the terms of a continentally oriented society for which a long coastline is of relatively little concern compared to vast stretches of sparsely inhabited land in the interior of the continent. The interiors of continents—the heart of Africa or Inner Asia—tend in North Atlantic consciousness to seem mysterious and elusive and by virtue of being relatively unknown constitute a source of unease. For the sinocentric Empire, almost the reverse was the case: the Empire's frontier with Mongolia and, to only a slightly lesser extent, the frontier with Turkestan and Tibet were throughout China's long history regions of primary concern, while the ocean and its inhabitants were relatively unknown and thought to be of little importance. The reversal in imperial orientation that resulted from the Twenty-one Years' War affected geography as well, for gradually—but only gradually—the Empire turned its attention away from Inner Asia and toward the maritime barbarians and the ocean across which they came. Nonetheless, Mongolia, Tibet, and Turkestan continued to be vastly important to the Empire, and throughout the second half of the nineteenth century they attracted the attention of the West as well. The collapse of the tribute system and the traditional relationships and expectations that had characterized the Empire's dealings with its periphery also transformed its relationship with such traditional sociocultural dependents as Korea and Vietnam.

THE INNER ASIAN CRESCENT

Mongolia is a vast area of desert and grasslands (steppe) whose boundaries over the ages were defined more ecologically than politically. The division between Mongolia and China Proper depended as much on rainfall as on any other factor. When rain was insufficient, marginal areas under cultivation were unable to sustain agriculture and became pastoral. Conversely, when rainfall was sufficient, areas that were only marginally pastures were cultivated by agriculturalists and became sites of sedentary life. The assumption that the sedentary life represents a later and more advanced stage in the development of human society and that the sedentary farmer and his later avatar, the sedentary city dweller, are superior to the wandering inhabitant of the steppe is a product of the conceit of the sedentary. Actually, the determination between nomadism and sedentarism is solely an ecological matter and concerns the most efficient use of available resources for sustaining human life in groups.

In the grasslands, sheep and horses, not crops, were the mainstay of life, providing the nomad with food, clothing, and materials for lodging in the form of felt for tents; even dung was collected and used for fuel. Although grain was needed as a dietary supplement, and there was occasionally a demand for luxury items such as tea, metal, and textiles, the nomad was basically self-sufficient; he maintained a symbiotic relationship with sedentary society based on mutual advantage, not necessity. The nomad migrated, but his migration was not aimless. In the summer, the herds and flocks grazed on the open grassland, but they had to be led to winter shelter in valleys or other protected regions. In the spring, the direction was reversed. Distances might range up to many hundreds of miles, and the entire society was mobile, but each group had assigned summer and winter regions, and property in animals usually included rights to pasturage and movement. An existence so closely dependent upon, and defined by, the ecological advantages of a given region is precarious. The nomadic lifestyle did not permit much accumulation of surplus to provide for luxuries or to insure against disasters.

Nomadism does not imply lack of change. Quite the contrary, nomadic society changes as do all others, but it changes in response to conditions and imperatives that are characteristic of nomadism. In both Mongolia and Tibet, a social relationship between leader and led, major and minor tribal chieftains, and warrior class and other classes developed that strongly resembled feudalism as it was known in the West, but these relationships were based upon animals rather than land. The society was highly mobile, precisely because it was nomadic and horsed, and the skills of horsemanship closely related to those of hunting and fighting, pursuits that were also highly developed in these societies. In both Mongolia and Tibet, the introduction of Buddhism, particularly in its Lamaistic form, led to the establishment of monasteries, around which small urban centers sometimes grew. As the secular authority of the Lamaist church increased, these monastery villages became administrative centers from which the church's state power reached out to the nomadic tribes. In both Mongolia and Tibet, too, the church itself became an element in the secular society as landlord or herd owner in a feudal structure. In both societies, the church, on the one hand, and the nomadic tribes and sedentary villages, on the other, were integrated socially through the large number of males who became monks for varying periods of time or for life. In Tibet, the primacy of the Dalai Lama, whose capital was at Lhasa, was constantly challenged by the Tashi Lama, a more purely spiritual leader, whose capital lay in the south near India, and by secular lords. In Mongolia, the primacy of the church was supported by the Qing dynasty; the religious apparatus was organized under the Living Buddha at Urga, an ecclesiastical-secular leader like the Dalai Lama.

Xinjiang (Chinese Turkestan), located between Mongolia and Tibet, included many different peoples—Uighurs, Kazakhs, Kirghiz, Uzbeks, and others—who lived in oasis settlements and depended for their livelihoods upon limited agriculture, extensive trading, and grazing. Moslems rather than Buddhists, they spoke Turkish and had strong ties to other Turkish tribes and peoples to the west.

All three regions were part of the Qing empire and had close commercial relations with China Proper, but at the same time each was highly dependent upon long-distance trade with economies and polities that lay beyond the immediate periphery of the Empire: Tibet with India, Xinjiang with Russia and Central Asia, and Mongolia with Russia (after the middle of the nineteenth century). Because each region had its own characteristic society and culture, the Han Chinese or Manchu imperial culture had only a limited ability to penetrate into, and significantly change or control, the indigenous societies. Moreover, in each area the Qing had to contend with a rival in the form of the real or potential influence and even authoritative presence of the area's other chief trading partner. Consequently, these regions became primary foci of the Empire's foreign policy rather than its domestic policy (if such a distinction was ever valid for the Empire).

Mongolia. The inclusion in the Empire of Outer Mongolia—the part of Mongolia that, from the perspective of China Proper, lay toward the outer edge of the Empire (Inner Mongolia, the part of Mongolia that lay closer to China Proper, was part of the Qing empire almost from its inception)— began gradually almost as soon as the Manchus had settled themselves in Peking in 1644. The Mongols formally recognized Qing suzerainty in 1691, after the Kangxi emperor defeated Galdan, a tribal leader who had threatened Manchu power in Central Asia. The Mongols now entered the tribute system, presenting tribute to the court and receiving titles, validation of rank and office, gifts, and other perquisites in return. The entire structure reinforced the nomadic feudalism characteristic of Mongol society because the Qing incorporated the traditional Mongol social unit (*aimak*) into a hierarchical structure that led naturally to the tribute system as the link between Mongol society and the emperor; the latter functioned as the apex of local Mongol society just as he did of the world in general. Roughly a dozen military officials, whose headquarters were located at strategic points throughout the country, exercised immediate Manchu control within Mongolia. The Manchus extended the imperial system of dividing responsibility among top administrators to Mongolia, where an imperial resident or agent (*amban*) at Urga represented the Empire's civilian presence; military governors were headquartered at Uliasutai and Kobdo. Imperial control over Mongolia was further strengthened by appointing Mongols to the imperial administrative system, both civil and military, elsewhere in the Empire and by bringing young Mongols to the imperial court for education. Strong imperial support for the Lamaist church perpetuated the division between secular and ecclesiastical society in Mongolia, and the Qing were careful to maintain this distinction so as to prevent a coalescence of Mongols that might threaten Manchu power. The memory of the military capacity of a united Mongol people, which had been amply demonstrated under the leadership of Chinggis Khan throughout Asia and Europe in the thirteenth century, was still very much alive in both Manchu and Chinese minds.

Outer Mongolia, inhabited by the Khalkhas, a major cultural subdivision of the Mongolian people, was thus a distinct ethnic and geographical area within the sinocentric Empire but located on a periphery that was exposed to immediate contact with the expanding West in the form of the Russian empire. After the disintegration in the fourteenth century of the

Mongol empire, which incorporated vast areas of the Russia of those days, the Russians again began to learn about Mongolia only toward the end of the sixteenth century. The first commercial contact between Russia and Mongolia probably occurred in the course of the sixteenth century through travelers, itinerant merchants, or permanent settlers. According to Chinese historical records, the Khalkhas presented tribute to the Shunzhi emperor in 1645, including among the gifts some Russian firearms. The same records indicate that from time to time a Khalkha prince or chieftain was admonished or even punished for entering into unapproved bilateral trade with Russians, but Khalkha-Russian commercial contacts were insignificant at first and what contacts continued were a by-product of the Russian caravan trade to Peking. The caravans passed through Mongol territory, entering into trade with Mongol officials en route. By 1721, this type of interaction had become sufficiently important that the Qing gave the *amban* at Urga responsibility for overseeing relations with Russia. After the signing of the Treaty of Nerchinsk in 1689, which regularized the Russian caravan trade with Peking along the Mongolian route, Russian merchants succeeded in penetrating as far as Urga and establishing trade operations at that center. This trade was sufficiently important that in 1723 St. Petersburg dispatched an official to Urga with the responsibility for governing the merchants and their commercial transactions. He was to concern himself particularly with activities that were illegal under the treaty lest the Russian merchants endanger the trade relationship between the two empires.

The Treaty of Kyakhta (1728), which led to the establishment of twin trading centers at Kyakhta on the Russian side and Maimaicheng on the imperial side, sought to restrict trade to the frontier and to the caravans. Inevitably, however, the imperatives and characteristics of the trade increased the influence and even the real presence of the Russians in Mongolia. Along the caravan routes and in the urban centers such as Urga, a significant proportion of the population became economically dependent upon the trade, especially as carriers of goods to and from the frontier. The number of Russians at Urga and other centers in Mongolia grew to the point that toward the end of the eighteenth century a special court had to be established at Urga to deal with them. Similar developments took place in the western part of the country, particularly around Kobdo and along the trade route that ran from Central Asia through Mongolia to China. Thus, while Russian penetration of Mongolia differed in terms of environment and details from English penetration of the China coast, the structure was similar; it included, for instance, managed trade, appointment of local officials with special responsibilities over the foreigners, and a limited but growing system of extraterritoriality. The Chinese merchants at Maimaicheng were even organized in the same fashion as the *hong* merchants at Canton.

Just as China Proper was opened up to Western penetration by certain treaties consequent upon the Twenty-one Years' War, so Mongolia was opened to Russian settlers by the same treaties. The first to come, in 1858, were the long-persecuted Old Believers, members of a peasant religious sect, very quickly followed by small-scale merchants. In the steppe, these newcomers tended to live in Mongol yurts or in Chinese style buildings, while in towns they built two-story Russian style houses. Though they came prepared to settle permanently in the region, these peasants and merchants were largely illiterate, rarely learned much Mongolian or Chinese, and commonly sent their children to Russia for schooling. However unrepresentative of Russian culture they may have been, these colonizers, who by 1910 numbered perhaps eight thousand in some fifty settlements, were one of the two major modernizing forces in that vast land.

A second source of foreign influence was the Buriats, Mongols speaking a dialect somewhat different from Khalkha, who lived in the region around Lake Baikal in Siberia. Although Mongolian in culture and Lamaist in religion, the Buriats were Russian subjects and largely agriculturalists, in contrast to the Khalkhas, who were imperial subjects and largely nomadic. Russian culture had penetrated deeply among the Buriats, and they had achieved a fairly high level of education, particularly in Russian. Mongolia felt the full impact of Buriat influence after the Chinese Revolution, but even before 1911 the Buriats came into Mongolia as traders and artisans who brought knowledge of foreign things already filtered through a recognizably Mongolian screen. In 1895, a Buriat in Urga began to publish the first Mongolian newspaper, including examples of Western literature. For instance, he published translations of Russian translations of American novels about the Wild West, with which Mongols could identify. Mongolia knew of the Russian Revolution of 1905 through these Buriats, and the Russian revolutionary tradition had a significant impact on Mongolia itself.

Although the Mongolian market never loomed large in overall Russian foreign trade, it was important to Russia as a source of meat for Siberia and, until the completion of the Trans-Siberian Railway, as the primary route for the importation of Chinese tea. Inside Mongolia the Russian trade laid the groundwork for political developments that were eventually to lead to the complete separation of Mongolia from the Empire.

With the growth of imperialist activity along the China coast, and with the appearance of Russians in Mongolia and other border regions, Chinese merchants began to overcome their traditional disdain for the barbarians and to move out into the steppe in search of markets. Taking tea, basic utensils, luxury silks, and manufactured products such as yurt frames, they traveled through Mongolia along well-established routes and extended their commercial network by trading on credit, particularly with Mongolian princes, to whom they loaned large sums of money at very high rates of interest. The Mongol princes often mortgaged their peoples' revenues and resources to the Chinese merchants, who on occasion used imperial military units to collect the debts owed them.

With the completion of the Trans-Siberian Railway, Russian penetration of Mongolia and Manchuria picked up speed, and the imperial government became alarmed at this threat to the Empire's security. Therefore, in 1902 Peking officially opened Mongolia to Chinese settlement, adding another dimension to China's secondary imperialism in Central Asia. Having already lost their economic independence to the Chinese merchants, the Mongols now began to fear that their animal-husbandry economy and nomadic way of life would be fundamentally altered by the Chinese influx. Completion of the Chinese Peking-Kalgan-Suiyuan Railway in 1909 facilitated Chinese immigration, particularly into areas of Mongolia adjacent to China Proper. As a consequence, when revolution came to the Empire, that particular part of Mongolia would remain under Chinese administration and would be absorbed by the China that was to succeed the Empire. In Outer Mongolia, the fear of culture conflict, added to the loss of economic independence, exacerbated an already strong feeling of antagonism toward the Empire, and the revolution was accompanied there, in 1912, by Mongol pogroms against Chinese living in the country's few and small urban centers.

While Russia and the Empire were pursuing their own interests in Mongolia, the region was also developing a broader international significance in consequence of Russo-Japanese relations in the Far East. As conflict between Russia and Japan approached in Manchuria, the Japanese sought contact with the Living Buddha at Urga, both because Mongolia was economically significant to the Russian forces in the Far East as a source of meat and other animal products and because strategically Mongolia provided access to Russia's only line of communication with the Far East, the railway. Japanese efforts met with no success, probably as much because of Mongolian ignorance of the outside world as for any other reason. In 1907, as part of the general long-term settlement of Russian and Japanese conflicts in the Far East, Mongolia was included in the division of Manchuria into spheres of influence. Outer Mongolia, along with Northern Manchuria, was assigned to Russia, and Eastern Inner Mongolia was assigned to Japan along with Southern Manchuria. The Empire, weakened by decades of internal decline and Western (and Japanese) depredation, had little choice but to accept this state of affairs.

The world had grown unimaginably complex for the Mongols. The disintegration of the Empire, and of the traditional safeguards provided the Mongols by the tribute system, left them exposed to forces of which they had little knowledge and over which they had no control. Russia was both powerful and far away, a combination considerably more attractive to the Mongols than the growth of Chinese settlements and indebtedness to Chinese merchants. The need for protection was obvious. Moreover, the eighth Living Buddha at Urga (1870–1924) was a Tibetan with strong ties to his homeland, which had been invaded by the British in 1905. Although reputedly an alcoholic and a syphilitic, the Living Buddha was an intelligent and sophisticated leader. When, in 1910, Peking began to insist upon administrative reforms and debt payments, the Living Buddha appealed to Russia for aid. The geographical disintegration of the Empire had begun, and Outer Mongolia was about to be permanently lost to China.

Xinjiang and the Ili Crisis. Xinjiang, or Chinese Turkestan, is located between Mongolia and Tibet. This region played a most important role historically as a zone through which communication routes between East Asia and the West passed. This ethnically complex region was inhabited by western Mongols in the east and eastern Turks in the west, with an admixture of Persian speakers. Distant from the center of the Empire, Sinkiang was both a region difficult to administer and a potential source of danger if local rulers acquired too much independence of action.

Late in the seventeenth century, Galdan, a leader in the northern part of Chinese Turkestan, began to unite his people, the Jungars, who were western Mongols and Lamaists. He raided as far as the Kerulen River to the east of Urga, the Khalkha Mongol capital in Outer Mongolia (he may have contemplated marching on Peking itself), and thus posed a direct threat to the Qing empire. The great Kangxi emperor led an army of 800,000 across Mongolia to the Kerulen, where he destroyed Galdan's power and expanded Manchu dominion more firmly over Outer Mongolia, as far west as Hami. Defeated in the east, the Jungars moved west and south and, in 1717, they occupied Lhasa, the capital of Tibet and the spiritual center of Lamaist Buddhism. The Jungars were such a major power in Central Asia that Peter the Great contemplated an alliance with Tsewang Araptan (1643–1727), Galdan's successor. Exchanges of embassies took place and Russian and Scandinavian military experts helped train and advise the Jungar forces. Greatly fearing a Russian-Jungar alliance, the Manchus sent a mission in 1712–1715 to the Torguts, a western Mongol tribe living on the Volga, in an effort to construct a countervailing alliance. Kangxi died in 1722, and his successor, the Yongzheng emperor, continued to try to prevent an anti-Manchu alliance in Central Asia. To this purpose he negotiated the Treaty of Kyakhta with the Russians, to keep Russian influence out of Chinese Turkestan.

Xinjiang continued to create unease in Peking until, on three separate occasions between 1755 and 1757, imperial forces under a Manchu general occupied the Ili region in the western part of Chinese Turkestan. Located beyond Hami, Turfan, and Urumchi, the population centers of Turkestan, Ili was an important region from which the Manchus could master the invasions and counterinvasions, assassinations and usurpations, and general tribal conflict that threatened the stability of the Empire's Central Asian frontier. In 1760, the Qing established a permanent military presence in

Ili and along the main caravan routes leading to it, and in 1762 Peking gave jurisdiction over all of Xinjiang to a military governor headquartered in the Ili region. In Xinjiang, as elsewhere in areas periperhal to, but part of, the sinocentric Empire, the Manchus respected local culture, tradition, and religion and bound the people and their leaders to the Empire through the instruments of the tribute system. Imperial control of Xinjiang, therefore, was effected through a kind of dyarchy, in which the territory was administered by Qing officials through traditional local officials.

The Ili crisis in the 1870s was the consequence of developments within Xinjiang and competition among imperialist powers in the region. In 1862, a Moslem rebellion in Northwest China led to a sympathetic uprising in Xinjiang. The uprising in Xinjiang was supported by descendents of a group of politically and economically significant fugitives from the Qing pacification campaigns of the previous century who had settled in Khokand in what is now Soviet Central Asia. In the middle of the nineteenth century one of them, Yakub Beg, became commander-in-chief of the Khokandian army. In 1865 he led the army into Kashgaria, his ancestral home in Xinjiang, in support of the Moslem rebellion. An adventurer with considerable military and political skill, Yakub Beg quickly established his own leadership of the rebellion and declared Kashgaria independent; he first placed a relative on the new throne but soon declared himself king. By 1870 he ruled all of southern Xinjiang and a good portion of northern Xinjiang, too, with a total population well over a million.

This new Central Asian power was a threat both to the Russians, who were expanding into the region, and to the Qing, who hoped to maintain stability and control over Xinjiang's affairs. An independent and volatile Central Asian power presented a continual encouragement to Moslems in their respective territories. To complicate matters further, the British, with their great dominions in India and interest in Tibet, saw in Yakub Beg's Kashgarian kingdom the potential for an anti-Russian Anglo-Islamic united front. To bolster this opportunity and to secure freedom for commercial expansion, the British recommended that Peking recognize Kashgaria's independence, but the Empire rejected this proposal, arguing that Xinjiang was an integral part of its territory, not a tributary state like Korea or Annam.

The Russians moved to establish their primacy in the region in August 1870, when the governor-general of Russian Turkestan sent an army to occupy a key mountain pass in order to preserve Russian access to the Ili region. In May 1871, he sent a military force further into the area, ostensibly to punish the Moslems for raiding the Russian frontier. Within weeks, the Russians occupied the entire Ili River Valley and the strategic commercial center of Kuldja, where they had a consulate and conducted regulated trade with the Empire under the Treaty of Kuldja (1851). The local Russian general declared the Ili region a permanent part of Russia.

The Russians completed their occupation of the region early in July

1871, but so remote was the area and so primitive the communications that London did not learn of the occupation until the end of August; the British minister in China did not hear of it until December. The Manchu court itself did not learn of the Russian move until the Russian minister in Peking notified the Qing of the occupation on September 1, 1871. The court immediately initiated discussions aimed at recovering the territory for the Empire. The Russians claimed that Manchu inability to control the area made their occupation of the Ili region an act of self-defense; moreover, they insisted, their presence was an act of kindness toward the Empire since Peking could not control its own territories. Nevertheless, they agreed to return the territory once imperial authority was reestablished in Xinjiang. Fully believing that the Empire could not reconquer Xinjiang, and wishing to establish a legitimate basis for retaining the region under their own control, the Russians now found that Yakub Beg, who previously had been a source of great discomfort to them, might become a support. In April 1871, they negotiated a commercial treaty with him and recognized him as the leader of the Moslem areas of Xinjiang, in return for which Russian merchants were allowed freedom of trade within Xinjiang upon payment of a small tariff. Worried about these Russian activities, the British viceroy in India received Yakub Beg's nephew in March 1873 and in October of that same year sent a mission to the new state, accompanied by three hundred soldiers. The British delegation brought the Moslem ruler a letter from Queen Victoria and several thousand old-fashioned muskets from the viceroy. As a consequence, the British, too, signed a treaty with Yakub Beg, officially recognizing him in return for the right to set up a legation and consulate in his capital. Yakub Beg now proceeded to broaden his own international base by establishing diplomatic relations with Turkey, which he honored both as a Turkish and as a Moslem state. The Turkish sultan sent him three thousand rifles, thirty cannons, and officers to train his troops.

The Ili problem was only part of a larger crisis confronting the Empire in the mid-1870s. In the northwest, Chinese-speaking Moslems were in rebellion and on the coast Japan threatened Formosa. A great foreign policy debate arose over which situation was the more critical: proponents of a coastal defense, seeing Britain, France, and the United States as the real threat to the Empire, argued that Xinjiang was remote and unproductive; proponents of a strong Central Asian policy focused on the double threat posed by Russia, with its long common frontier with the Empire and its access by sea. Already in occupation of imperial territory, Russia posed an immediate threat that had an import beyond the purely military: permanent loss of territories won by the dynasty threatened the dynasty's internal position. These arguments swayed the court, which still granted Central Asia the primacy characteristic of the sinocentric Empire's strategic thinking, and in 1876 Zuo Zongtang, a general who earlier had suppressed a Moslem uprising in Northwest China, used a combination of imperial funds and foreign loans to marshall an army of sixty thousand. By 1878 Zuo had recovered all of Xinjiang except the Ili region itself.

This spectacular demonstration of military capability enabled the imperial court to demand that the Russians evacuate the Ili region. When the ambassador sent to Russia to conclude the necessary settlement came back with a treaty that was highly unsatisfactory to the court, both sides again mobilized their troops. Negotiations were reopened, however, and war was averted. In 1881, the Treaty of St. Petersburg awarded most of the Ili region and the strategic passes to the Empire in exchange for a large indemnity paid to the Russians.

In 1884, Peking declared Chinese Turkestan a full province of the Empire and included in it the Ili region and the Tarim basin. An imperial administration was organized throughout the region and staffed by Zuo Zongtang's followers, but the populace continued to be ruled through the local ruling classes. Chinese bureaucrats, military personnel, agriculturists, and merchants began to move into the area, as did Chinese-speaking Moslems from the northwest. The military reconquest and administrative incorporation of the area into the Empire combined with growing Chinese settlement to inhibit further Russian advance into the Empire's territory in Central Asia.

Tibet. Like Mongolia, Tibet was an area peripheral to, but incorporated into, the sinocentric Empire. Also as in Mongolia, ecological conditions severely influenced the structure of society. Most of Tibet is a cold, dry, windy, and treeless plateau located above sixteen thousand feet. The mountain ranges that ring the country on the south and west rise in at least one spot to twenty-nine thousand feet and include some of the world's highest mountains. This plateau is inhabited by nomads, who until recently lived off animals and raiding. Much of the country's agriculture and its primary urban center, Lhasa, are located in the south, at about twelve thousand feet. In the east, toward China, the plateau descends into forested and cultivable land, with sedentary agricultural centers. Tibet is crossed by important north-south and east-west trade routes. Ancient and medieval Chinese pilgrims sometimes traveled to India along these routes, along which Buddhism was introduced into Tibet, where it absorbed indigenous beliefs and practices and became the particular form of Buddhism known as Lamaism. During the Yuan dynasty, Lamaism became popular among the Mongols, who patronized the church. During the Ming, which succeeded the Yuan, Tibet became a tributary of the Empire, and emperors like the great Yongluo entertained Tibetan envoys and lamas at court.

Tibetans and Mongols belong to quite different cultural and linguistic groups but share religion and lifestyle. Historically, ties between the Tibetan church and Mongol khans were irregular but close. The fourth Dalai

Lama was a Mongol, for example, who appointed a Tibetan (together with all his successive incarnations) the Living Buddha of Urga, that is, the head of the Lamaist church in Mongolia. It was the Mongols who, having invaded Tibet in the middle of the seventeenth century, affirmed the Dalai Lama's primacy in the spiritual life of Tibet and the Lamaist religion. Any occupant of, or aspirant to, the throne of the Empire had to take into account his relations with, and the intentions of, the political, military and religious powers that ranged along the Empire's Inner Asian frontiers in the region embraced by Tibetan-Mongolian interests. For example, two years before the Manchu invasion of China, the Dalai Lama sent a mission to the Manchu capital at Mukden, in Manchuria, and in 1652, only eight years after the Manchu invasion, he himself visited Peking, where he presented tribute and received great gifts and honors, including his official investiture. The structure of the tribute system was sufficiently elastic to permit the Tibetans to maintain a symbiotic, rather than a subservient, relationship with the Qing, all the while using tributary forms for that purpose.

The Jungar invasion of Tibet in the second decade of the eighteenth century and the attendant disruptions of the country's internal stability posed a threat to the Manchus not only in the Tibetan frontier region but in Mongolia and Xinjiang as well, since the influence of events in Tibet was felt throughout the Lamaist regions and the possibility of an anti-Qing Tibetan-Mongolian combination was something to be avoided. Consequently, the Manchus sent several pacification missions into Tibet and established a Qing administration over the Tibetan hierarchy. After the middle of the eighteenth century, the Qianlong emperor granted the Dalai Lama full temporal as well as spiritual power in Tibet in order to provide a focus for internal stability, and two imperial residents, backed up by a small military garrison of fifteen hundred men, supported this arrangement. At the same time, the Panchen Lama, the abbot of the great monastery of Tashi-lumpo, located at Shigatse to the southwest of Lhasa, who claimed to be the reincarnation of an important early Tibetan religious leader, provided an alternative focus of ecclesiastical and even temporal loyalties.

Tibet attracted the attention of expanding British interests in India and the Himalayan states, potentially offering both a market and a means of access to China. British commercial envoys visited Tibet in the 1770s and 1780s, but these tentative probes ended when the Gurkhas, who earlier had conquered Nepal, invaded Tibet in 1788 and 1791. The Qianlong emperor responded to Tibetan pleas for help by sending two armies that made a forced march across Tibet and drove the Gurkhas back into Nepal. The Gurkhas now became tributaries to the Empire and sent regular missions to Peking. The English maintained neutrality throughout the conflict because they did not want to create any pretext for Qing interference with the Canton trade; they won the amity of both sides because they had been in a position to help either and had helped neither. The Empire now closed Tibet to foreigners and its long years of isolation from the rest of the world began. However, British interest in the country did not flag: the commercial advantages of Tibet's market and position along the trade routes between India and China continued to whet the appetites of British merchants and government officials alike. This interest grew as the British position in the Himalayas strengthened. Tibet's relations with the Himalayan states largely replicated those the Qing dynasty maintained with Tibet. Consequently, there was considerable trans-Himalayan commercial and political intercourse, of which the British were well aware. British inability to penetrate Tibet, combined with that country's exclusion of foreigners, namely Westerners, contributed to the growth of a mystique about Tibet and particularly its capital, Lhasa, which made both the country and the city a magnet for explorers and adventurers during the latter half of the nineteenth century. However, almost none reached this goal.

The Qing policy of excluding foreigners from Tibet was intended to maintain security both inside the country and along its frontiers. As the Empire well knew from experience, the presence of foreigners meant change, and this was precisely what neither the Dalai Lama nor his Qing overlords wanted. Even the wheel was prohibited, lest it upset the traditional socioeconomic balance. The British were prepared to acquiesce to exclusion as long as the policy applied to all Westerners, particularly the Russians. In 1886, they signed an agreement with the Manchus whereby they recognized the Empire's control over Tibet's foreign relations in return for the Empire's recognition of British rule in upper Burma. In 1890 Peking released Sikkim, now a British protectorate, from the tribute system, and in 1893 an agreement established regulations for the control of trade between Tibet and India through one of the Himalayan mountain passes. British recognition of the Empire's control of Tibet depended upon the Empire's ability to exert that control and to conclude meaningful agreements with the British governing their mutual interests in the region. In the 1890s, however, the British began to find that agreements made with the Empire were unenforceable in Tibet as a consequence of Peking's growing inability to exert control over the country. This was a source of unease in both London and Delhi.

British disquiet about political conditions in Tibet and the Himalayas increased markedly at the end of the nineteenth century as they began to realize that Tibet was about to become one of the arenas of the Anglo-Russian rivalry that spanned Asia. The incumbent Dalai Lama was young, and a Buriat Mongol named Dorjiev, a Russian subject who had studied in Lhasa for some twenty years, was one of his most important tutors. Dorjiev used his position to promote communication between the Dalai Lama and the Russian tsar. In 1900 and again in 1901 the Buriat traveled through

India to Russia, and rumors about him and a Russian sponsored arsenal in Lhasa spread. The viceroy of India feared that a Tibet under Russian influence would be a springboard for the expansion of Russian influence into the Himalayas and would constitute a threat to the British position in India. Delhi was aware that the Empire's control over Tibet was weakening and that Peking could not be depended upon to keep the Russians out of Lhasa. British attempts to communicate directly with the Tibetans failed. A sense of impending crisis grew, particularly after the British became convinced that the Manchus and the Russians had signed a secret treaty about Tibet in 1902. The viceroy in Delhi decided to intervene by sending a military mission to Lhasa to "negotiate" with the Dalai Lama. Led by Francis Younghusband, by whose name the expedition has become known in the historical record, eight thousand troops fought their way to Lhasa in 1904 and, in September, forced the Dalai Lama to sign a convention with the British. The agreement's stipulations resembled those of the unequal treaty system the Oikoumene had imposed upon the Qing along the China Coast more than half a century before. The convention severely limited both the Empire's sovereignty in Tibet and Tibet's internal autonomy.

The Younghusband expedition demonstrated to all concerned, not least to the Tibetans themselves, the tenuousness of the Empire's control over the region. By the time the expedition returned from Lhasa, however, British interests had shifted, and London now wanted to resolve its Himalayan concerns not by direct intervention in Tibetan affairs but by an understanding with St. Petersburg. A new Anglo-Chinese convention was negotiated, restoring some autonomy to Tibet. Meanwhile, however, the Dalai Lama had fled to Mongolia and was unable to avail himself of the change in British policy. In 1906 the British recognized, yet again, the Empire's suzerainty over Tibet and in 1907 the two powers signed a non-intervention agreement. Both these agreements were part of a broader settlement of great power rivalry in Central Asia. By 1910, however, the situation had reversed itself once more. The Empire tried to introduce reforms into Tibet and sent an army to enforce its policies in Lhasa. This time the Dalai Lama fled to India, accompanied by Dorjiev. It was too late. The Chinese Revolution in 1911 marked the end of the Qing era in Tibetan and Himalayan affairs, and China was unable to assert its power until after the Communist Revolution in 1949. Meanwhile, Tibet moved into the British sphere of influence.

THE MARITIME CRESCENT

The Empire's limited success in keeping the imperialists at bay along its Inner Asian frontiers was not reflected among its traditional tributaries Korea, in the northeast, and Vietnam, in the south. The historian must note a certain irony here: those areas on the sinocentric Empire's periphery that were most different from China Proper remained within the imperial penumbra, while those that had adopted and adapted significant aspects of Chinese culture fell away earlier and more completely. The cause, of course, is not to be found in China's culture but, rather, in the aggressiveness of the maritime powers' approach to the Empire. This view is borne out by the fact that the Empire's first major loss of territory (to Japan in 1895) that could conceivably be considered to be Han Chinese in culture, Formosa, is located in the maritime, not the Inner Asian, crescent.

Korea. The Japanese revolution of 1868, called the Meiji Restoration, was a turning point in, not the beginning of, Japan's surprisingly rapid modernization. Aware of the consequences of weakness in the face of Western imperialism, the new Japanese leadership resolved not only to develop the internal political, economic, and military resources necessary to fend off the West but also to establish for Japan a geopolitical base in East Asia that would make Japan a power to be reckoned with. Even during the imperial confrontation with Russia in Central Asia and with growing awareness of the French threat in the south, Li Hungzhang and others believed that the primary threat to the Empire came from the peoples who arrived on China's shores by sea; the dynasty carefully observed the increasing power of the Japanese. Korea, long one of the Empire's most faithful tributaries, became an object of Japanese attention in the 1870s, and Japan's influence in the peninsular "hermit kingdom" significantly eroded the basis of the tribute system, upon which Korea's entire relationship with the Empire rested.

Until the middle of the nineteenth century, the Empire constituted Korea's primary, and almost sole, external contact. The Empire acted on behalf of Korea in almost all its external relations, and the relationship between the two was often described as that of an older and a younger brother. Just as an older brother would protect his younger sibling, so the Empire helped maintain Korea's isolation by providing Korea with a political excuse to avoid dealing with other powers and by controlling Korea's access to China Proper. Korea's annual tribute missions to Peking, which continued into the 1860s, were its only active external contacts, with the exception of an occasional diplomatic mission to the shogunal capital at Edo, Japan. Throughout Korea's seclusion, Japanese were permitted to trade on a limited basis at Pusan, just as the Dutch were permitted to trade at Nagasaki during the period of Japan's seclusion.

The growth of Western activity in Far Eastern waters led to increased barbarian awareness of Korea. If Western ships sailing along the China coast or to Japan were shipwrecked on the Korean coast, the Koreans would care for the survivors, but they were always deported to China. Korea resisted all attempts to open negotiations or trade, even when such attempts were made forcefully.

The successful opening of Japan by the American Commodore Matthew

Perry suggested an approach to Korea. In 1871 F. F. Low, American minister in China, was directed to proceed with five warships to the river mouth below Seoul, the Korean capital. When his scouts moved on upriver, two were wounded. The minister could not obtain an apology from the Korean authorities; consequently, the American fleet attacked and destroyed five forts, killing perhaps as many as two hundred fifty Koreans. No one had invited the Americans to Korea in the first place, the Koreans continued to refuse to enter into negotiations, and the Americans had to leave, having achieved nothing. Japan, however, constituted a great threat to Korea. Leaders of the samurai class sought a foreign war as a means of promoting their own power in the midst of internal strife in Japan, and Korea was a convenient target. Although this plan was frustrated in 1873, the opening of Korea became a major Japanese policy objective. Earlier, Peking had told the British that the Empire could not open Korea for foreign trade because Korea was not part of the Empire; at the same time, the argument continued, because Korea was not an independent country it could not open itself to foreign trade. This seeming paradox was not at all illogical; the Korean and imperial conceptual maps did not allow for trade with powers outside the sinocentric tribute system. In reality, however, that system was no longer capable of fending off the rising interests of such powers as America and Japan.

Although the Japanese government continued to oppose a samurai invasion of Korea, a group of Japanese landed on the Korean coast in 1875, supposedly without military intentions, and the Koreans fired upon them. Tokyo decided to take this as a challenge and to open Korea, as Commodore Perry had done in Japan, by making demands for commerce with Korea and using a show of force to back them up. The Japanese asked Peking to intervene in Korea on their behalf, but the imperial government responded by again defining Korea as a tributary: "Though Korea is a dependent country of China, it is not a territorial possession; hence in its domestic and foreign affairs it is self-governing."[10] Finally, however, the Qing court advised Seoul to enter into negotiations with Japan. In February 1876, under the threat of Japanese warships sailing off the port of Inchon (near Seoul), the Japanese forced the Koreans to sign an unequal treaty modeled after the treaties the West had imposed earlier on China and Japan. The Koreans opened three ports to Japanese commerce, and Korea was declared an independent state. Korea was now outside the tribute system. The Empire institutionally recognized this development in 1880 by transferring management of its relations with Korea from the Board of Rites to the Zongli Yamen, which was responsible for the Empire's relations with the West under the new diplomatic dispensation.

Li Hungzhang, the great Qing statesman, continued to advocate an active foreign policy toward the threat from the maritime powers and now tried to apply that policy to Korea. He wanted to employ the traditional strategy of "using the barbarian to control the barbarian." To this end he sought to bring Korea into treaty relationships with as many foreign powers as possible on the ground that multilateral commerce would create a situation in which the natural self-interest of each of the several powers would protect Korea against any one of them. To build Korea's own defense, he encouraged a policy of modernization in both the political and the military sector. All of these steps aimed at the protection of the Empire, of course, and consequently Li also tried to maintain imperial influence at the Korean capital by replacing the traditional tribute relationship with a more modern great power–client state relationship. When the United States tried to negotiate a treaty with Korea through Japan and failed, it approached Li Hungzhang. Li negotiated for Korea and signed a treaty with the Americans in 1882. He had hoped to insert in the treaty a clause describing Korea's new relationship with the Empire as that of a dependent state, but he failed, and the United States recognized the independence of Korea. Subsequently, the treaties Korea signed with other foreign powers also recognized its independence, but only the United States and Japan opened legations in Seoul, the other powers apparently recognizing the Empire's superiority by placing their representation in Seoul under their legations in Peking. Li Hungzhang's attempt to translate the traditional tributary relationship into terms more suitable to the new age while still maintaining the traditional (and real) structure of superior-inferior in Far Eastern international relations ultimately failed because the ideology of the West insisted upon the sovereign equality of nation-states regardless of their respective power relationships. The West still maintains this ideological position today, despite an intrusive reality that contradicts it.

Korea now found itself surrounded by three great powers, each of which wanted to exclude the other two from influence in the peninsula's affairs. The Empire, with British support, hoped to oppose both Russia and Japan. As the competition among the three continued, St. Petersburg withdrew from the fray, leaving the field to Peking and Tokyo. Inside Korea itself, Sino-Japanese competition was mirrored in the struggle between conservatives and reformers, and as Japan's modernization program moved ahead more rapidly than the Empire's, the Korean modernizers began to advocate closer relations with Tokyo.

In the summer of 1882, during a popular antiforeign uprising in Seoul, a mob attacked the Japanese legation. This incident provided both the Empire and Japan with a pretext for intervention. The Empire sent in larger forces than the Japanese, who therefore accepted an indemnity from Seuol in lieu of attempting to occupy Korea. From the advantageous position of having an imperial military presence inside the Korean capital, Li Hungzhang now attempted to translate his concept of a dependency relationship between Korea and the Empire into reality by obtaining for the Empire preferential treatment in trade and by forcing the Korean government to accept imperial advisors who, once in place, would dominate policy development and realization. What Li was proposing, whether he knew it or not, was the same structure with which the British exercised their power indirectly in India. It was a reasonable attempt, supported by precedent but not by reality. Continued disorders in Seoul, including an attempted coup and the kidnapping of the king, met with vigorous imperial action, but they exposed the shallowness of the Empire's strength in the country. Consequently, in 1885, a Sino-Japanese convention was signed in Tianjin; according to this agreement, both Peking and Tokyo were to abstain from intervention in Korean affairs, withdraw their troops and military advisors, and consult each other about developments in the peninsula.

Li Hungzhang now began to assume the same position toward Korea that Britain had assumed toward the Empire. He encouraged modernization and development of those institutions that would enable Korea to defend itself; in his eyes this meant the transfer to Korea of many of the developments that had taken place inside the Empire, a position dictated by the great power–client state relationship. For example, a Korean customs service was established, directed by Westerners who were seconded to Seoul from the British-directed Chinese maritime customs. The telegraph and modern military training were introduced, and Li encouraged the Koreans to appoint an American advisor for foreign policy. All of this took place under the direction of an imperial resident in Seoul. Between 1885 and 1894, this official was Yuan Shikai (1859–1916), who was to play a crucial role in the history of the Empire and of China in the early twentieth century. In the decade after 1885, however, Japanese influence in Korea, particularly among the youth, steadily grew as Japan outdistanced the Empire in the modernization process and as the Empire's policies foundered on the rocks of Korean internal developments. In 1894, a complex series of events—including an uprising led by a radically antiforeign, and increasingly antigovernment, semi-religious movement and the brutal assassination in Shanghai of a pro-Japanese Korean leader and the dismemberment and public display of his body upon its return to Korea aboard an imperial warship—resulted in disturbances and a request by the Korean king for imperial aid. Peking dispatched a small force; in turn, Japan refused to accept the Empire's assertion of suzerainty over Korea and sent a larger force. The situation was aggravated when the Japanese sank a British ship carrying imperial reinforcements to Korea. The Empire then rejected Japanese demands for reforms in Korea that would have led to Japanese domination of the peninsula, and the Japanese, in retaliation, captured the conservative Korean court and forced it to declare war on the Empire. The imperial resident fled Seoul, and Peking and Tokyo declared war on August 1, 1894. In the Treaty of Shimonoseki (April 17, 1895), which ended the war, the Empire recognized Korea's independence in Western terms, thus ending any semblance of a traditional relationship between Peking and Seoul. Korea was fully and formally annexed by Japan ten years later, in November 1905, and remained a colony of Japan for fifty years, until, in the wake of the Japanese defeat in World War II, Korea regained its independence in the context of a great power–client state relationship with the United States.

Imperial policy toward Korea as defined by Li Hungzhang failed because it rested upon the assumption that the historical depth of the tribute system and Korea's geographical proximity to the Empire made possible the redefinition of the traditional relationship in terms that were suitable to the new age. Li Hungzhang clearly recognized that Japan's modernization program posed a threat to the Empire, when he wrote that "in about ten years, the wealth and strength of Japan will be admirable. This is China's future, not present, source of trouble."[11] Japan, on the other hand, was learning the lessons the West had to teach very well indeed. Ito Hirobumi, the great Japanese statesman and sometime Prime Minister, understood the modernization process and realized that Japan needed time to reach the point at which it could fight the Empire successfully without the danger of a stalemate, which would only benefit Russian interests in the area. In the Sino-Japanese War of 1894–1895, Japan demonstrated its skills as a student of the West by carrying out in Korea the same policy that Western nations had successfully pursued in South and Southeast Asia. The Empire, on the other hand, was no more successful against Japan than it had been, fifty years earlier, against the British and the French.

Formosa. Lying one hundred miles off the coast of Fujian province, Formosa was sparsely inhabited, until the late fourteenth or early fifteenth century, by indigenous head-hunting tribes related to the mountain peoples of Luzon in the Philippines. A few Chinese fishermen, pirates, and adventurers lived on small islands offshore or in established fugitive villages along Formosa's west coast. There is evidence that the Japanese maintained a small settlement on the southwestern coast of the island, serving both pirates and Japanese trading illegally along the China coast. Although by and large ignored by the continentally oriented Empire, the island soon attracted the attention of Europeans arriving in the Far East. In 1628, for example, the Spaniards, who at the end of the sixteenth century had charted Formosa's coastline, established a garrison, together with a missionary and trading center, in the northern part of the island. The Spaniards hoped to use this coastal settlement for the penetration of China, the Ryukyus, and Japan.

In 1622, the Dutch from Java landed on the Pescadore Islands, off the Formosan coast, where they found a well-established Chinese fishing village under the jurisdiction of Fujian province. Imperial forces succeeded in expelling the Dutch two years later. Nevertheless, in 1624, the Dutch established Zelandia near the Japanese village on the southwestern coast of the island; the Dutch town, protected by a fort, was intended to serve as a base for the development of the island. From there they proceeded to explore the interior, establish control over more and more territory, institute a territorial system of government, develop a writing system for the indigenous languages, establish schools and churches, and expand agriculture by introducing exogenous flora and fauna. The Dutch produced and exported sugar, rice, and various other goods, including coal, to East and Southeast Asian, as well as European, markets. Dutch commercial and economic activities needed a population socially capable of serving an essentially extractive economy; the population also had to be able to support itself. Fujian across the Straits was fairly impoverished and subject to both internal disorders and the depredations of pirates. Consequently, in spite of imperial bans on immigration, poor peasants and fishermen from the mainland began to move to Formosa, where they established farms and stockaded villages and sometimes married indigenous women. They developed a society that resembled the one they had left but that had a distinct frontier quality. Zelandia, as the center of the growing Sino-Dutch community, became a transshipment point for Dutch trade among China, Java, and Europe. The Dutch succeeded in establishing their primacy on the island when the Japanese withdrew and the Dutch themselves drove the Spaniards away.

The very characteristics that had attracted the Dutch and poor Fujianese settlers to Formosa also attracted Koxinga (Guoxingye), a maritime marauder and Ming loyalist, who, when driven from the mainland by the Manchus in 1662, took refuge on Formosa with his followers, forcing the Dutch off the island within eight months. In 1683, a Manchu expedition occupied the Pescadore Islands, defeated Koxinga, and established an imperial garrison on Formosa. Renewing the Ming dynasty's somewhat ineffectual prohibition against Chinese immigration, the imperial government now declared the island a Fujianese dependency and, fearful that the island could again become a source of difficulty, did everything it could to prevent Formosa's development.

Formosa came to the attention of foreign powers again in the nineteenth century. As they extended their activities in Far Eastern waters, the Western powers recognized the island's potential hazards, with its unmarked and unlighted coast, disorganized administration, and head-hunting aborigines. On the other hand, properly developed Formosa represented a potential haven and valuable transshipment point; England, France, Germany, and the United States all urged Peking to make reforms on the island. Commodore Perry suggested that the United States establish a colony at the northern end of the island and join with the Empire in a program of economic development leading to eventual annexation by the United States, and Townsend Harris, the first American representative in

Japan, recommended that Washington purchase the island from the Empire.

From this point, Peking's approach to Formosa began to parallel in certain respects its attitude toward Korea at about the same time. The Qing government claimed no responsibility for the island beyond the coast, where the Chinese settlements were located. When, in the 1870s, Japan showed an interest in Formosa similar to its interest in Korea, Peking protested; in response, Japan, fearing the occupation of Formosa by a Western colonial power, insisted that the Empire declare in writing its sovereignty over the entire island and accept responsibility for the actions of its inhabitants. At British urging the Empire took this action, paying the costs of an expedition the Japanese had sent against the island's inhabitants to punish them for mistreating Japanese sailors shipwrecked on the island's shores. Japan withdrew in December 1874, but, as with Korea, the crisis was only postponed.

Once the entire island was imperial territory, Peking's concerns about foreign incursions into the Empire embraced Formosa as well. The court's response was the same it had given to its continental periphery: in 1875 the traditional prohibitions against Chinese immigration to the island were removed and the traditional imperial policy of economic neglect was changed into a policy of economic development. Ding Zhizhang, an energetic and reform-minded official, was dispatched to Formosa to establish an administration for the island that would carry out the court's intentions. However, he soon resigned in bitterness because he was unable to overcome the corruption and self-interest that governed the behavior of the island's provincial bureaucrats. The capital's good intentions did not include strong support for Ding's mission in real terms.

War with France (1884–1885) again brought Formosa to the court's attention. In 1884 the French seized the Pescadores, blockaded Formosa, and occupied the northern port of Keelung. When the French withdrew at the end of the war, the new governor, the remarkable and modern-minded Liu Mingchuan, determinedly introduced broad and profound reforms and innovations. In 1887, Peking removed the island from the Fujian provincial administration and declared it a province in its own right. The governor quickly initiated a program that included the establishment of railroad and telegraph systems, the development of modern mining, the improvement of harbors, and the laying of a telegraph cable connecting the island with the mainland. He made Taipei, the main urban center in the northern part of the island, the capital and tried to turn it into a modern city.

Under Governor Liu, Taiwan was soon transformed from one of the most backward regions of the Han part of the sinocentric Empire into its most progressive element; indeed, Formosa was a model of what proper leadership could have accomplished on the mainland. The nature of the local population also contributed significantly to this transformation: less bound by the traditions that governed life on the mainland and descended from immigrants who had left China Proper because of harsh political and economic conditions, the Taiwanese Han population, with a frontier mentality and comparatively long experience with foreigners, was more aware of the broader world and more open to innovation. The island had prospered as foreigners settled there after 1855 and stimulated the production of a variety of goods. The years 1870–1890 witnessed a very noticeable improvement in the island's economy, and foreign missionaries opened schools, hospitals, and social service programs, which found greater response on the island than similar efforts did on mainland China. Far from hindering their activities, Governor Liu encouraged foreigners and employed them in his own administration, even establishing schools for the study of technology and foreign languages. However, in the end he, too, fell victim to the conflict between reformism and conservatism that was raging in the imperial bureaucracy, and in 1891 he returned to the continent. Liu's successor reversed his progressive policies and diverted to his own interest funds required for the upkeep and expansion of the institutions and programs Liu had introduced. Nonetheless, history, distance from the mainland, and the achievements of the reform program had begun to give Formosans a consciousness of themselves as Formosans rather than as displaced Fujianese.

Japan did not forget Formosa after 1874. Though Korea was the primary focus of the Sino-Japanese War (1894–1895), Formosa was an important part of the peace settlement, both politically and militarily. During the beginning of the peace negotiations, Tokyo discovered that Peking had secretly appealed for aid to Russia, England, and Germany and that the Empire was even prepared temporarily to transfer the Pescadore Islands to French control. Japan felt forced to take action because of its determination to preclude East Asian colonization by the West. Tokyo sent a naval force into the South China Sea to forestall an agreement between Peking and any other power, but no direct action was required. The Empire's defeat by Japan had exposed the failure of the attempt to reform and modernize Formosa within a traditional context, and Japan was able to exact a heavy penalty for the Empire's weakness. This included the cession to Japan of the Liaodong Peninsula, the Pescadore Islands, and Formosa, as well as an indemnity. Quick intervention by Russia, France, and Germany forced Japan to relinquish claims to the Liaodong Peninsula in return for a greatly increased indemnity.

The Empire's island province was notified of its new status by telegram from Peking two days after the signing of the Treaty of Shimonoseki, and imperial officials and officers were ordered to return to the mainland immediately. Formosan protests, including the declaration of an independent republic, came to nothing, and the Japanese landed in the northern part of the island on May 30. By June 17, they felt in sufficient control to hold ceremonies at the capital, Taipei, celebrating their assumption of authority over Formosa and the Pescadores. By the end of 1895, the entire island was under Japanese control. The Treaty of Shimonoseki provided a two-year grace period during which the residents of the island could move to the mainland if they wished. Those remaining were given a choice between imperial nationality, in which case they would be registered as resident aliens, or Japanese nationality. Those who made no choice would automatically become Japanese subjects on May 1, 1898.

The description of Formosa's historical and legal status within the Qing empire and the Chinese republic has been a matter of controversy. Chinese leaders, particularly in the republican period, were wont to claim the island as an inalienable part of China Proper, but during both the Qing and the republic the central government's attitude toward Formosa suggested that the island's status was somewhat more ambiguous than the claims suggested. Its transformation from a loosely administered frontier region into a Qing province, which occurred under the pressure of international developments, did not necessarily make the island an integral part of China, as Peking itself indicated when it encouraged the establishment of a republic in Taiwan in opposition to Japanese occupation in 1895. Even as a province, Formosa was peripheral in the Empire's vision. Imperial policy along the Central Asian frontier was "secondary imperialism," inspired and impelled both by Western examples and by fear of the West. Peking's belated attempts to incorporate Formosa into the imperial system were part of that same secondary imperialism. Imperial policy was still primarily continentally oriented, however, and though fairly successful in Central Asia, the empire's tactics failed in Formosa.

Vietnam. Often called the "lesser dragon" to indicate its imitation of Han Chinese culture, Vietnam—known in the West in the nineteenth and early twentieth centuries as Annam—was the most sinicized of the states that were peripheral to the sinocentric Empire. Not only did the court, bureaucracy, and official culture imitate the Chinese, Vietnamese society was sinicized to no small extent even at its lowest levels: village and family structure both resembled Han models. As we have seen, the Empire's suzerain-vassal relationship with Vietnam was replicated in Vietnam's relationship with Cambodia and other territories peripheral to Vietnam. The close relationship between the Empire and Vietnam, together with the geographical proximity of Annam and, just to the north, Tonking to China Proper, made the region an object of the West's attention since it seemed to hold out the possibility of an alternative land route into China Proper and, more particularly, into that part of China beyond the penumbra of the commercial system on the Chinese coast.

France's intrusion into Southeast and East Asia was motivated not by a desire for trade—indeed, France had no colonial interests in the region—but, rather, by a psychological need to keep pace with Great Britain, which with enormous territorial and commercial interests in Asia was the primary personification of the West in that area. The French were also motivated by a sense of their own civilizing mission in the world and by their concern to promote the interests of Roman Catholicism, a peculiar motive in light of ambiguous French feelings toward the papacy and the church but less surprising in light of the Protestantism of France's main rival, Great Britain.

Vietnam's earliest contacts with the West occurred when Portuguese traders based in Macao followed traditional Chinese and Japanese trade routes to Vietnamese ports in order to purchase raw silk. The Jesuits followed and arrived in Vietnam in 1615. Prohibited from proselytizing in the northern region of Tongking, which was under the rule of the Trinh family, they succeeded in establishing relations with the Nguyen family, which ruled in Annam, south of Tongking. The Nguyen, the great rivals of the Trinh, were interested in Western trade and, more particularly, in the acquisition of Western arms.

The internal history of Vietnam lies outside the scope of this book, but it is important to note that Vietnam was profoundly influenced by the West from its earliest contacts. At the same time, however, it continued to maintain a close tributary relationship with the sinocentric Empire. For example, while a writing system developed by the Jesuits was used for popular literature and Western texts, Chinese language and writing were used for all official, scholarly, and literary purposes.

Following the initial Jesuit penetration of Vietnam, French missionaries persevered in their attempts to establish a broader base. When a peasant uprising divided the country under three brothers in 1771, the French allied themselves with the Nguyen family, which had been ousted from the south. Predictably, the Empire, through the tribute system, recognized the northern brother, but he died in 1792, having proved himself unable to control his country. A priest, Pigneau de Behaine, mustered support at the French court at Versailles for Nguyen Anh, the scion of the ruling family, and for his reconquest of Vietnam, which was completed in 1802; the Nguyen dynasty survived until 1945.

Vietnam was now unified for the first time. Nguyen Anh, who took the reign title Gia-long, soon shook off the influence of the Western power that had helped him and modeled his government on that of the Qing, from the design of cities down to reliance on the traditional examination system. Minh-Mang, Gia-long's successor, adhered even more rigorously to Confucian tradition. Moreover, he became increasingly xenophobic and anti-Western, prohibiting foreign trade and persecuting Christians, policies that were continued by his successors, Thien-tri (reigned 1841–1847) and Tu-duc (reigned 1848–1883).

The Twenty-one Years' War hurt Vietnam primarily because of the country's place in the sinocentric imperial system. The inflation of silver, brought about by the outflow of that metal from the Empire to pay for opium, created an economic crisis in Vietnam. The war itself disrupted the trade routes upon which Vietnam depended for a significant amount of its commercial contact with the Empire, and exposed to the Vietnamese the weakness of the Empire. Consequent upon a major debate at the Vietnamese court, which the emperor not unexpectedly won, the local bureaucrats more actively promoted the development of programs for studying the West, and at a relatively earlier date, than did their colleagues inside the Empire. The court at Hue encouraged Western trade and sought to learn something about Western technology, but adherence to Han Chinese tradition and institutions betrayed these attempts and opened the way for a more active French penetration of the region.

Repeated anti-Christian persecutions, such as the execution of the Spanish bishop of Tongking in 1857, and rebuffs of foreign overtures like those that had been successful in Japan provided France with both a pretext and a challenge; during its mid-century alliance with Britain, brought about by similar persecutions in China, France also sent forces to Vietnam. Compelled to withdraw from Danang in 1858, the French turned south to Saigon, where by the close of the Twenty-one Years' War they were firmly established. Tu-duc, who was facing rebellion within his domains, was forced to sign the Treaty of Saigon in 1862, which granted the French Cochin China, promises of freedom of religion and trade, and vague control of Vietnam's foreign relations. Spain, which had aided the French with troops, received an indemnity.

Rebellion against the French in the south and the flight of the members of the Vietnamese bureaucracy from the affected region forced the French to establish a system of direct rule. In 1863–1864, they extended their power to include a protectorate over Cambodia, which was tributary to Vietnam and Siam. Cambodia had traditionally used its position as a vassal of both states to play them off against each other, thus preserving its own independence. The French forced the Cambodians to end their relationship with Siam, thus tying them closer to the expanding French system. In 1867, they completed their absorption of Cochin China. With a firm base in southern Vietnam, the French began to explore the region, seeking a direct riverine route into South China, but this proved to be a disappointment. Their attention, therefore, turned back to Indochina itself, and the construction of a French empire in Indochina became an ever more absorbing interest after the blow dealt French pride by defeat in the Franco-Prussian War of 1870. In the early 1870s, a force of French irregulars succeeded in capturing the Hanoi citadel and other strongholds in Tongking; the purpose of the action was to seize control of the entire region. The French were forced to withdraw, but the Vietnamese government's inability to prevent the original incursion led to growing disorders within Tongking and to increasing friction between France and the Empire.

Imperial suzerainty over Vietnam was continually reaffirmed by tribute missions, such as those that arrived in Peking in 1877 and 1881. The tribute system, however, was disintegrating in the south just as it was in the east. France now claimed sovereignty over Vietnam on the basis of a treaty it had signed with Hue in 1874, and this claim was supported materially by France's colonial status in Cochin China and great influence in the Vietnamese capital. Conflicting imperial and French claims over Vietnam made armed conflict likely. Events in Tongking provided the immediate cause for the outbreak of war. Remnants of the Taiping and Panthay rebels, the so-called Black Flag irregulars, penetrated Tongking, where there was already considerable opposition to the Nguyen dynasty; consequently, the region was in a state of turmoil. The French found themselves unable to exercise their recently acquired treaty rights to commerce in the Red River valley, Tongking's most populous region. Furthermore, the Vietnamese court tried to play all sides against the middle by encouraging the Black Flags to resist the French and then asking the Empire to send an army to fight both the Black Flags and the French. The French, not to be outdone, captured Hanoi in 1882, signed a treaty with Vietnam establishing a protectorate over that country, and, finding themselves unable to control the situation, sent for reinforcements. Peking supported the Black Flags and in 1883 sent regular forces overland into Tongking to oppose the French. The Sino-French War was, quite simply, a direct consequence of French imperialism.

In a very real sense, the Sino-French War of 1884–1885 was a continuation of the Twenty-one Years' War. It was caused by the bellicose activities of an intruder into the East Asian sinocentric imperial system, activities that were unacceptable to the Empire. The war itself imbricated hostilities and negotiations in the same way that the Twenty-one Years' War had. On the French side, both popular and official imperialism, represented most nakedly by Jules Ferry's two governments (1880–1881, 1884–1885), made the war possible. The internecine rivalries between the French foreign office and navy were a complicating factor. Indeed, French negotiations with the Empire before, during, and after the war were carried on by teams that included both diplomatic and naval personnel.

In Peking, willingness to mount active opposition to the French in Tongking grew out of a sense of optimism rooted in the Empire's success in suppressing the rebellions of the 1850s, 1860s and 1870s, and in confronting with the Russians in Central Asia. A war party had emerged, and by the beginning of the 1880s the imperial court and the upper reaches of the bureaucracy were prepared to assume an activist posture in foreign relations. Known as the "purification clique," the activists came to power briefly in 1884, when French victories in Tongking led to the dismissal of the great Prince Gong, the emperor's brother and leading representative of the dynasty.

Li Hungzhang had attempted to avoid war by working out an agreement with the French minister in Peking late in 1882. Negotiations broke down in 1883 and, as we have seen, gave way to war, but in 1884 Li again entered into negotiations with the French. In May Li and a French naval officer signed the so-called Li-Fournier Convention. The Empire would withdraw its troops from Tongking, permit France to trade with China from Tongking, and recognize France's suzerainty over, and treaty rights in, Vietnam. The Empire would pay no indemnity to France. The Qing court, still under the influence of the war party, rejected the agreement, and hostilities and negotiations continued in tandem. A French fleet attacked Northern Formosa and French land forces advanced into Guangxi province, across the border from Tongking. In 1885, Robert Hart, the Englishman employed by Peking to head the Imperial Maritime Customs Service, dispatched his London agent to Paris, where the English employee of the Maritime Customs Service and the imperialist premier of France agreed on terms for a peace settlement, based on the Li-Fournier Convention of the previous year. The peace treaty was signed by Li Hungzhang in June 1885.

The Sino-French War and the agreement with which it was concluded dealt two great blows to imperial foreign policy. Ironically, both traditionalists and reformers suffered. Imperial recognition of French suzerainty over Annam removed it from its ancient position within the tribute system and exposed the growing decay of the traditional relationship. Ten years later, as we have seen, both Korea and Formosa would be lost. Second, the war showed that the policies of the reformers, both those who sought to defend the Empire aggressively and those who sought to defend it by negotiating limited acquiescence, were insufficient to prevent further deterioration of the Empire's international position. Traditional management and bureaucratic behavior were inadequate to the control and use of modern implements of war. On the other hand, the war led to a growing popular consciousness of the foreigner as a real enemy, particularly in Guangdong province, which had almost from the very beginning of contact with the West been influenced by that contact and which now was the primary staging area for the imperial efforts in Tongking. Popular fears of an attack by the French and official measures such as the governor-general's offer of rewards for dead Frenchmen encouraged rioting and pillaging of foreign establishments, particularly of Christian missions. The Empire's inability to defeat the French led to peace terms unfavorable to the Empire; unfortunately, this result did not promote a reconsideration of imperial foreign policy.

The Scramble for Concessions, 1894–1901

The unification of Italy and of Germany, the new Germany's late entry into the race for colonies, the growing rivalry between Britain and France, the optimism of a burgeoning industrial system, and the arrogance spawned by Social Darwinism and most varieties of Christianity (many of which were highly nationalist in orientation) intensified the rivalry among the imperialist powers in the last decades of the nineteenth century. The opening of the Suez Canal in 1869 and the completion of the telegraph cable links between Europe and the Far East in 1870–1871 made transportation and communication between Europe and Asia much easier and allowed the European powers to fight with greater resources among each other for control of the Far East. The Sino-French War of 1884 was but a continuation of this process. The Sino-Japanese war of 1894–1895 showed that an Asian power could enter the fray with hope for a modicum of success, provided only that it accepted the West's rules of the game. If anyone had lingering doubts, the Empire's inability to defend itself militarily or to develop diplomatic strategies that would prevent disaster was exposed by China's defeat at the hands of Japan, which was viewed both by the West and by the Empire as a land of upstarts. The scramble for concessions, the competition among the Western powers to dismember the Empire, was a consequence of the realization that the Empire had become a mere observer of its own fate.

The growth of maritime trade between the Far East and Europe, the sale of Alaska to the United States in 1867, and the decline of the Pacific fur trade had all weakened Russia's position in East Asia, but Russia's temporary passivity did not blunt its desire for expansion. Tsar Alexander III concluded that connecting European Russia with the Pacific was a necessary step to becoming a major Far Eastern power. To this end, with the help of a remarkably powerful and energetic minister of finance, Sergei Witte, he began to plan the construction of the Trans-Siberian Railway. Although the other foreign powers were always suspicious of Russia's intentions, France preferred to see Russia's attention diverted from Europe and therefore helped finance the project; Germany, from similar motives, encouraged Russia's pretensions to a historical mission to liberate the oppressed Asian hordes by bringing them Western culture.

Russia's aggressive foreign policy in the late 1800s led to other developments. In 1895 Russia brought France and Germany together in the so-called Triple Intervention to persuade Japan to restore the Liaodong Peninsula to the Empire after Japan's victory in the Sino-Japanese War. Next,

Witte organized French and Russian banks in a loan to the Empire to help pay its indemnity to France, and by the end of the year he had established the Russo-Chinese Bank, which used French capital to finance industrial, commercial, and railway ventures in the Empire. Successful negotiations with Peking opened the way for lengthy extensions of the Trans-Siberian Railway. First Russia added a 950-mile spur, called the Chinese Eastern Railway, across Manchuria to Vladivostok; later, having obtained a twenty-five-year lease for the southern tip of the Kwangtung Peninsula, Russia added the 650-mile South Manchurian Railway to connect this leasehold to the system.

Russia's rapid and aggressive expansion of its interests in the Far East led to the creation of a "sphere of influence," a territory in which a foreign power possessed primacy of interest over all other powers, including the titulary sovereign power, and in which this primacy of interest was exercised through a variety of instruments, including the possession of leases covering the sphere of influence and the right to exercise local jurisdiction and police power within it. Depending upon the particular concerns of the foreign power, it also possessed special rights to construct railroads, to engage in mining and other extractive industries, and to engage in commerce under privileged conditions. Finally, a power might obtain its sphere of influence by a judicious use of military force or a threat of force, by political maneuvering, and/or by the extension of loans to the imperial government. The extension of loans was particularly efficacious because these advanced the foreign power's influence in the imperial central government. The sphere of influence was an especially pernicious form of colonialism because the foreign power obtained vast rights and privileges in a defined local territory, while responsibility for the behavior of the inhabitants of the territory remained with the central government and its local representatives.

It is impossible within the scope of this book to describe the complex maneuvers and agreements that constituted the scramble for concessions. What is important is the recognition that through a series of maneuvers, Russia, France, England, Germany, and even Belgium carved up the Empire into a patchwork of spheres of influence that were, by international agreement, assigned to one or another power along with rights to build railroads, lend money to the imperial and provincial governments, engage in mining, etc. The scramble brought the Empire close to destruction.

This development demonstrated that the treaty system had not only failed to function in the Empire's relationships with the West but it also had failed to structure the relationships among the Western powers in the Far East. From almost the very beginning, the treaty system had rested upon the "most favored nation" clause, according to which any power signing with the Empire a treaty that contained the clause would receive the same privileges as those obtained by the most favored nation. The drive to establish exclusive spheres of influence in which one power could deny access to other powers was the antithesis of the "most favored nation" strategy. Moreover, the unequal treaty system had been unequal, but it had assumed the independence of the Empire and its sovereignty over its own territory. The scramble for spheres of influence, which quite often were colonies in everything but name, and the reduction of the imperial government to the role of spectator, was tantamount to a declaration by the Western powers of China's dependency status. The Empire's independence and sovereignty had become, to all intents and purposes, a fiction. Finally, the unequal treaty system was based upon the assumption that the West's primary business with the Empire was trade and commerce. Now, however, a new form of imperialism, finance capitalism, had entered the picture, rivaling commerce, if not supplanting it, as the substance of the West's business in the East. The treaties were not constructed to deal with this novel development.

Finance Imperialism

In the initial period of the development of the world capitalist economic system, imperialism meant the Western powers' domination over, and acquisition of, territories outside Europe and North America that were useful or profitable to the capitalist powers for reasons of commerce, cheap labor, new markets, raw materials, etc. As the world capitalist system began to mature, however, and as financial capital increasingly replaced commercial capital as the dominant element in the system, it was natural that imperialism would change its character from territorial to financial exploitation. The new imperialism was, in some respects, more pernicious than the old because it could leave its client the appearance of independence and sovereignty while dominating and exploiting its financial and economic structures. First used during the scramble in the Qing empire, this tactic became the rule rather than the exception in areas such as Latin America, where with certain qualifications U.S. imperialism exercised itself through finance capitalism and exploitation rather than territorial expansion.

In China "finance imperialism" early took on the form of railway construction, which permitted Western capitalists to invest in China and at the same time to attempt to control a significant part of the Empire's modernizing economic infrastructure. The first railroad built by foreigners was a short line between Shanghai and Wusung that opened in 1876, but almost immediately the governor-general of Nanjing bought and dismantled this railway. The Qing government recognized the danger posed both by foreign construction and ownership and by foreign financing of railroads in the Empire. By 1896 there were only about two hundred forty miles of railroad in China Proper and a short line on the island of Formosa; nevertheless, railroads provided an important means for the penetration of Western capital into the Empire.

By 1893, twenty-five or more foreign loans had been made to various imperial government agencies. These loans came from both official and private sources, and the agencies to which they were made (or some financial institution under that agency's control) were put up as collateral and insurance for repayment of the loans. For example, a loan from the Hong Kong and Shanghai Banking Corporation to the superintendent of customs at Shanghai in 1886 was secured on the revenue from the Imperial Maritime Customs Service. The making of such loans was, under the conditions that prevailed before 1894, fairly safe and quite profitable, and the Empire's total indebtedness up to that time was relatively small.

The large indemnity Japan extracted from Peking for the Sino-Japanese War and for the return of the Liaodong Peninsula to imperial sovereignty produced a financial crisis in China. In order to pay the indemnity, the imperial government was forced to accept loans from foreign banks on extraordinarily disadvantageous terms, including, for instance, receipt of less than the full value of the loan as contracted and high interest rates over the long periods in which repayment installments would come due. In other words, the Empire was constrained by international action to accept loans from foreign powers and banks at rates that in any Western country would have been considered usurious. The Empire's international indebtedness after the turn of the century was so large that, according to a repayment schedule established by an international commission of bankers, China's annual remittance on all its foreign debt was fixed at a figure larger than the Empire's annual revenue in the first part of the preceding century. The most exploitative element in finance imperialism as it applied to the Empire was the extraction of indemnities, which constituted an utter loss, depriving Peking of revenues badly needed for modernization, industrialization, and defense. Not only the income from maritime customs, but also provincial revenues, revenues on domestic trade, and revenues on monopolies were considered available by foreigners as sources for security and repayment on loans.

In the end, the Empire was saved by events that were beyond the control of the imperialist states. World War I brought about the disappearance of some powers, such as tsarist Russia and imperial Germany. Changes in policies in other Western countries led to reductions or cancellations of portions of the debt, though in 1935, for example, the Republic of China was still making payments on part of the Boxer indemnity that had been forced upon the Qing dynasty. In other instances, the imperialist powers, having obtained a sphere of influence, failed to pursue their advantages for reasons of their own. None of this mitigates the fact that by

1900 the Empire lay prostrate at the feet of the imperialists, almost all pretense to respect for territorial and institutional independence and sovereignty having been cast to the winds.

The United States joined the ranks of the imperialists relatively late but by 1899 found itself in a position similar to that of Britain and France. Having expanded across the Pacific, engulfing the Hawaiian Islands, the Philippines, and various territories in the South Pacific, the United States became a Far Eastern power by virtue of its colonial possessions. The expansionist American economy, seeking its share of the spoils, needed to develop a strategy to contest the established position of the European powers.

Secretary of State John Hay took his cue from the British, who at one time had considered insisting on equality of opportunity in commerce as a principle that transcended spheres of influence. The British chose the alternative and joined the scramble for concessions, but a policy of equality of opportunity suited the Americans very well. The Open Door policy, as it came to be called, was born from the understanding that American interests would be best served by maintaining the integrity of the Empire. Inspired by the unequal treaty system, Hay sought to reaffirm the "most favored nation" clause of the original treaties. In addition, he stated in a diplomatic circular outlining the new policy that treaty tariffs should be collected only by imperial government agencies and that no power should benefit from preferential harbor dues or railway charges. The Russians, however, insisted on maintaining the favorable rate they had obtained for their Manchurian railway project and intially demurred; but in the face of the Boxer Rebellion, all the allies embraced a solution that would insure the Empire's safety and peace, "preserve Chinese territorial and administrative entity, protect all rights guaranteed to friendly powers by treaty and international law, and safeguard for the world the principle of equal and impartial trade with all parts of the Chinese empire."[12] Thus was the United States assured equal access to the China market, from which otherwise it might have been excluded.

The Boxers

The events of 1900, which centered around the activities of a secret society—the Society of Righteous and Harmonious Fists, or the Boxers—often are presented as an uprising and, indeed, are referred to in literature as the Boxer Rebellion. This, of course, immediately raises the question: a rebellion against whom? Although Boxer slogans originally contained anti-dynastic elements, the society soon turned to support of the dynasty. Moreover, before the story was played out, the dynasty supported and provided leadership for the Boxers. In effect, the Boxer movement is more accurately described as the next in a series of anti-Western and anti-imperialist wars that began with the Twenty-one Years' War and moved on through the Sino-French and Sino-Japanese wars; or it can be described as a colonial or semicolonial uprising by Han Chinese (eventually with Manchu support and even leadership) against the foreign imperialist, that is, the capitalist-colonialist power in the Empire, whether the foreign imperialist appeared in the guise of Englishman, Frenchman, German, or American, merchant, government official, or missionary. It is important to note that by perpetuating the terms "Boxer Rebellion" or "Boxer Uprising," Western historians, however anti-imperialist they think they may be, are suggesting that the Boxers engaged in an action against legitimate authority instead of a war against the West, as the presence of dynastic support and leadership suggests. The only legitimate authority against which the Boxers could have been rebelling would have been the authority of the Western imperialists themselves, which qualifies as legitimate only in Western eyes.

The Boxers arose in the context of the general disintegration of the imperial system at the end of the nineteenth century. The entire Empire was caught in a vicious circle. Foreign depredations upset normal behavior and expectations, leading to popular activism, such as banditry, riots, and local rebellions, which were traditional responses to social, economic, political, and cultural disruptions. These conditions in turn provided the foreigners with the pretext for further intervention on the local Chinese scene, which led to further disruptions and responses. The intrusion of Christianity into the local scene in China Proper exacerbated the situation by undermining the common man's expected pattern of life and intellectual and psychological assumptions. The social disintegration of China was paralleled, particularly in North China in 1898 and 1899, by havoc wrought by natural disasters and by the consequent physical suffering of masses of people. Famine and hunger were widespread, and the corruption and inefficiency of a demoralized bureaucracy hampered the dynasty's meager relief efforts.

The seriousness of these conditions was signaled when the court instructed imperial princes to burn incense and ordered monks and priests to pray for relief. In the context of this extreme situation, the intrusion of foreign secular, particularly military, power into the local scene contributed to the rapid growth of a widespread fear that the Empire was about to dissolve. In Kiaochow, for example, the Germans at the slightest provocation marched troops into some Han Chinese villages, which they burned down. In South Manchuria, Russian troops fired upon Han Chinese who refused to accede to Russian demands in the vicinity of Port Arthur: 96 Chinese were killed, 123 wounded. Interventions such as these fed the mounting antiforeignism of the people and produced extraordinarily volatile conditions throughout China. Secret societies, often with a his-

tory of traditional opposition to oppression of the people, grew in strength
and increased their activities.

The empress dowager, who now wielded the real power in Peking,
apparently recognized that there was a relationship between the Empire's
internal condition and the intrusion of foreigners. In September 1898 she
announced a policy of no further concessions to the imperialists, and in
March 1899, when an Italian fleet appeared to press Rome's demand for a
lease in the province of Zhejiang, the Qing court rejected the request and
began to prepare for war in the south. A standing order was sent to all the
provinces to resist foreign aggression of any kind and to take military measures where necessary. To bolster this position, the government in November 1898 ordered the organization and training of militia forces in North
China. At the same time, and as part of the general attempt to reassert the
Empire's control over its own affairs, the court ordered, in March 1899,
the absorption of the foreign missionaries into the traditional sociopolitical
structure by granting them imperial rank, emblems, and honors. This resembled earlier attempts to assimilate Buddhist, Moslem, and Jesuit
clergy. The measure is interesting not because it was effective but because
it illustrates the attempt to use traditional means to resolve nontraditional
problems; it also shows the extent and subtlety of the dynasty's attempt to
reverse the situation in which it now found itself.

The Boxers became more and more active in 1898–1899. In Shandong
and Zhili provinces, they distributed handbills calling for the death of
Christians, and they attacked the houses of Han Chinese Christians and
forced their families to flee. They started riots, burned down churches,
and resisted attempts by the local authorities to control them. Just as their
anti-Christianism focused on manifestations of Christianity in the midst of
Han Chinese daily life, so their antiforeignism aimed at the most visible
representations of the foreigner. They attacked railroads, cut telegraph
lines, and burned railway stations, factories, and foreign style bridges. Despite initial imperial attempts to control the movement, it expanded rapidly and by the middle of 1899 Boxer activities began in the region of
Peking itself. Early in 1899, the primary Boxer slogan was "Overthrow the
Qing; destroy the foreigner." By the end of the year it had changed to
"Support the Qing; destroy the foreigner."

The remarkable difference between the first and the second slogan can
be explained by a combination of events and policy developments. As information about the Boxer doings reached the court, somewhat belatedly
in the spring of 1898, the conservatives around the throne found the Boxers' anti-Christianism and antiforeignism to be a support for their own position. This congeniality of views found political expression when, in March
1899, Yuxian, a Manchu, was appointed governor of Shandong; he was a
conservative who not only supported Boxer activities but even went so far
as to incorporate groups of Boxers into the militia organization. While the

conservatives at court grew stronger, the threats and actions of the foreigners weakened the court moderates, who wanted an accommodation with
the imperialists. The foreigners succeded in obtaining the dismissal of the
pro-Boxer governor of Shandong, and he was replaced in December 1899
by Yuan Shikai. While he acted against the Boxers in Shandong with some
success, the movement grew in neighboring Zhili province.

The foreign diplomats in Peking began to demand resolute government
action against the Boxers. The government's response, as early as January
1900, took the form of edicts insisting upon the ambiguity of the situation
and instructing local officials to distinguish between good and bad organizations. In effect, the court had abandoned cooperation with the West under the unequal treaty system and was creating a space in which its local
representatives, the bureaucrats, could encourage and direct the popular
antiforeign movement. This position became patently obvious with the appointment of the antiforeign former governor of Shandong, Yuxian, to be
governor of Shanxi province in March 1900. The court protested its cooperation with the foreign powers and took such measures as would make
the foreigners believe in its protestations, but it actively encouraged the
Boxers. Troops were sent to quell disturbances, for example, but they
were instructed, like the bureaucrats, to distinguish between good and evil
elements. That such gaps should exist between official words and actions
or between the appearance and the reality of action should come as no
surprise to anyone who has lived in the twentieth century.

The Boxer War reached its final definition and climax in Peking in the
middle of 1900. The foreign diplomatic corps, alarmed by events in the
countryside and the killing of Han Chinese Christians, decided that they
themselves would take action against the Boxers. Seventeen naval ships
were anchored off Tianjin, and 426 foreign guards were brought to the
legation quarter in the capital at the beginning of June. When the Boxers
attacked imperial forces that were protecting the Peking-Tianjin Railroad,
the diplomats' lifeline, the general in charge returned their fire, but he
was reprimanded by the court for having done so. On June 8, the pro-
Boxer imperial commissioner withdrew the imperial armies that had been
sent against the Boxers. On June 10, an international relief expedition of
twenty-one hundred men, led by a British admiral, started out from Tianjin for Peking to protect the legations. On June 13, the Boxers entered the
capital, where they burned foreign buildings outside the legation quarter
and massacred Han Chinese Christians. At this moment, the real nature of
the conflict and the true alignment of forces became clear: the court declared that the so-called international relief expedition constituted a foreign invasion and ordered the Boxers to resist. The expedition was caught
halfway between Tianjin and Peking, leaving the foreigners in both cities
exposed; the next day, June 14, Boxers laid seige to the foreign settlements
in Tianjin. On June 17, the empress dowager was informed by some of her

courtiers that the foreigners were demanding her retirement and, though false, this information strengthened her determination to fight. The next day the relief column, stuck on the railroad, was attacked by imperial forces using modern weapons. The column was not only unable to proceed into Peking but had to fight its way back to Tianjin. On June 20, the German minister in Peking was killed in the street on his way to the Zongli Yamen. Finally, on June 21, the dynasty itself declared war on the foreigners.

THE SIEGE OF THE LEGATIONS

The legation quarter in Peking, three-quarters of a mile square, contained 11 foreign legations, 475 foreign civilians, 455 guards, 3,000 Han Chinese Christians, and 115 racehorses. The presence of the Chinese Christians and the horses was fortuitous: as the people inside organized to fight, the Chinese provided the labor, the horses the meat. Across the Forbidden City from the quarter, the French bishop, 43 French and Italian sailors, and 3,400 others were beseiged in the Roman Catholic North Cathedral; the cathedral was inadequately supplied to survive the siege and as time passed many starved. Outside Peking, 250 foreigners and many more Han Chinese Christians died during June and July.

Almost immediately the moderate Li Hungzhang began seeking a way out of the conflict, but the Empire's very size and lack of strong central control made it possible for the Empire to wage war in the north while pursuing a settlement in other regions. Such a course also lent credence to the interpretation, which the moderates were trying to advance, of the conflict as a rebellion. It served the purposes of both moderate Chinese and foreigners to maintain the current dynasty in power. The rebellion that was really a war helped to remind the foreigners of the potential threat to their interests posed by an antiforeign imperial government, reinforcing the necessity of avoiding direct conflict between the current dynasty and the Western powers. No wonder, then, that the empress dowager was represented to the foreigners as wanting peace, while she continued to pursue a war against them; it was a surreal sort of strategy, however, which stopped short of an all-out effort to win.

On July 14, an international contingent of twenty thousand troops, half Japanese and half allied, including more than a thousand British-recruited Chinese, ended the siege of the foreign concession in Tianjin and placed that city under the control of an international provisional government. The siege of Peking itself was delayed, however, by fierce competition among the allied powers, each of which wanted its troops to enter the imperial capital first. On August 15, the day after the siege of Peking was finally lifted by British Indian troops, the emperor and empress dowager fled the capital in disguise, remaining in Xian under the pretext of making a western tour, thereby maintaining the fiction that the war had been an antidynastic rebellion. Li Hungzhang now took charge of negotiating a settlement.

The only German killed in the war had been the minister to Peking, but the kaiser demanded and received the right to name the commander-in-chief of the allied forces, who arrived in the capital on October 17. By the end of the year, some forty-five thousand foreign troops were stationed in North China, and the German commander-in-chief spent the next six months sending these foreign troops on punitive expeditions against northern Chinese cities. Moreover, Russia was in full occupation of Manchuria. The war ended in disaster for the Empire.

THE RESOLUTION

By December 1900 the main outlines of a settlement of the conflict had been reached with the imperial court. However, rivalries among the Westerners prevented any final conclusion, and the Boxer Protocol was not signed until September 1901. This document could not be called a peace treaty, given the fiction of the rebellion, but it stipulated the execution of ten high officials, including the pro-Boxer Yuxian, and the severe punishment of one hundred others. It also required the Qing government to make formal apologies to the Western powers. The other stipulations of the document clearly showed that the Western powers did not see the Boxer War as a warning about structural problems in the relationship between the Empire and the Oikoumene. Quite the contrary, the West dictated a settlement that took into account only its own interests; this move was guaranteed to lead, over time, to further disintegration of the relationship. The protocol insisted that retribution for the war be carried directly to the Chinese population; for example, it called for the suspension of the traditional examinations—the primary route whereby the government recruited new talent—in forty-five cities, half of which were located in Shanxi province, and it subjected the gentry class to special penalties. In Peking, the legation quarter was expanded in size, and it was to be fortified and permanently garrisoned by foreign troops. Some twenty-five imperial forts were to be destroyed, and the protocol stipulated the foreign occupation of several railroad centers to insure permanent foreign access to the capital from the sea. Import duties were to be raised, and the imperial government had to pay a huge indemnity, equal to about $333 million (in 1900 dollars), from a variety of sources, including gold, over forty years at interest rates that, in the final analysis, practically doubled the amount of the indemnity. These measures, which constituted a further foreign incursion into the Empire and promised to strangle it financially and, therefore, economically, could not but fuel further the fires of antiforeignism. The indemnity represented the furthest advance of finance imperialism to that time.

The Boxer War and the Boxer Protocol effectively marked the end of any possibility of an imperial foreign policy that would recover the ground lost to the foreigners. In January 1902, the empress dowager and her court returned to the capital, where she received the members of the foreign diplomatic corps and their wives in audience, indicating the court's total capitulation to foreign demands. In August 1902, the Empire recovered the administration of Tianjin. Attempts in succeeding months and years to build a basis for national recovery and a forward foreign policy were in vain. Indeed, the dynasty itself soon fell.

China and the Russo-Japanese War

The Boxer War and the settlement terms imposed upon the Empire by the allied powers dissolved to all intents and purposes any hope that might have lingered for a revival of the Empire's fortunes and an accommodation between a gradually modernizing sinocentric Empire and the capitalist-imperialist West. Neither the Empire nor the treaty system, weak and insufficient to the task as both were, could survive, and the Western powers struggled among themselves like carrion birds preparing to feed on the corpse of the dying Empire. In the moiling and toiling of the Western powers, a new threat to the interests of Japan and the Western powers, as well as to the territorial integrity of the Empire, or what was left of it, appeared in Russia's attempt to bring Manchuria under control.

ALLIANCES

Russia's construction of the Chinese Eastern Railway and the South Manchurian Railway posed for St. Petersburg the serious problem of maintaining control over the territory through which the railways passed. Finance Minister Witte wanted to extend Russia's power by expanding its economic activities; the Russian military, on the other hand, wanted to occupy the country and incorporate it permanently into Russia, thereby guaranteeing that the railways would be able to operate without interruption. The Japanese saw either policy as a threat and debated between negotiating and preparing to fight. The Germans, hoping to scare the British into an Anglo-German alliance, encouraged the Russians. The British, preoccupied with the Boer War in South Africa, found that their interests lay in accommodating Russia rather than Germany, Britain's chief rival in Europe. British primacy in the Changjiang valley was recognized in an Anglo-Russian agreement in April 1899 and in an Anglo-German agreement in October 1900. However, neither dealt with the question of constraining Russian advances in Manchuria.

The imperial forces at first scored successes against the Russians in

Manchuria during the Boxer War, even forcing them to retreat from several major centers, but by October 1900 Russian forces had returned to Mukden. Backed by 175,000 soldiers in the Far East, the Russians sought an agreement with Li Hungzhang outside the Boxer Protocol; they wanted to legitimate their position in Manchuria without involving the other powers in the negotiations, which would not have been to Russia's benefit. Faced with such a large Russian military force and with no hope of aid from Peking, the imperial governor-general of Manchuria, Zeng Qi, signed a broad agreement with the Russian governor-general of the Liaodong Peninsula, Vice-Admiral Evegeni I. Alexiev. This agreement, which the imperial governor-general signed under duress, essentially handed over control of Manchuria to the Russians, though it recognized, for cosmetic reasons, imperial sovereignty in the region. The boldness and completeness with which Russia asserted itself in Manchuria, and the threat that Russia's position there posed to the other powers, led to the strongest protests from Great Britain, Japan, and the United States, so that Russia finally withdrew the agreement. (The court wished to punish Zeng Qi for signing the agreement and decreed his dismissal and demotion, but Russia intervened, warning that such action would be taken as an insult by St. Petersburg. Consequently, the decree of punishment was withdrawn and the governor-general was ordered to remain at his post.) In January 1902, Great Britain and Japan signed an alliance that Russia saw as a dangerous development vis-à-vis its own interests in the Far East. Japan and Great Britain agreed that, in the event of conflict, each alone would fight against a third power, but that if a fourth power entered the conflict they would come to each other's support. In other words, if Japan and Russia went to war, Great Britain would come to Japan's aid if another power, Germany for example, helped Russia. This alliance aimed at the isolation of Russia in the Far East.

THE RUSSO-JAPANESE WAR

Russia's construction of railroads in Manchuria was an expensive operation. Large purchases of land and equipment, the employment of a huge force of Chinese workers, the building of cities as administrative and commercial centers, and the development of forest and mining resources to support railroad construction all involved great expenses that were not compensated by increases in Russian trade with the Far East. The first train from European Russia reached Dairen in March 1903; the trip over six thousand miles of track took almost one month. In light of these frustrations, St. Petersburg delayed the evacuation of Russian troops from Manchuria. Moreover, the tsar dismissed Witte from office in August 1903 and established a vice-royalty of the Far East. All these steps portended the resumption by Russia of an aggressive policy; indeed, St. Petersburg tried to reopen negotiations leading toward the strengthening of its Manchurian position. When Peking refused, the Russians turned to Japan. Japan had become, both militarily and economically, the strongest power in the Far East, and St. Petersburg needed its acquiescence if Russia were to maintain its position in Manchuria. In a very real way, these maneuvers showed how unimportant the foreign powers considered the Empire's interests in its own territories to be. They negotiated over imperial territory as if the imperial government were not a factor.

Between August 1903 and February 1904, the Russian and Japanese governments engaged in negotiations over parts of the sinocentric Empire, the former tributary state of Korea, and the dynasty's own homeland of Manchuria. Japan obtained Russian recognition of Japan's freedom of action in Korea but refused to recognize similar rights for Russia in Manchuria: Japan was prepared only to recognize Russia's privileged position in the railroad rights-of-way and insisted on recognition and preservation of the territorial integrity of the Qing empire. As the negotiations went on, St. Petersburg strengthened Russia's Far Eastern forces, sending about seven thousand troops a month over the newly completed Trans-Siberian Railway. This policy, not unnaturally, raised Japanese suspicions and the Japanese broke off negotiations with Russia on February 6, 1904. On February 8, they succeeded in immobilizing a Russian fleet at Port Authur. Two days later, they declared war on Russia. In May, Japanese forces crossed the Yalu River from Korea into Manchuria, laid siege to Port Arthur, and occupied Dairen. Port Arthur surrendered in January 1905, and the Japanese forces continued to force the Russians to withdraw toward the Siberian border. In March 1905, the Japanese defeated the Russians at Mukden, which battle lasted more than two weeks. By this time, both Russia and Japan were exhausted by the war, and the Russian government was confronting revolution at home. To make matters worse, the Russians' Baltic fleet, which had been dispatched to the Far East in October 1904, did not even reach its objective, Vladivostok; on May 27, 1905, it was destroyed by the Japanese navy in the Tsushima Straits in an almost classic naval confrontation.

Fearful that continued Japanese victories would leave Tokyo utterly ascendent in the Far East, the American President, Theodore Roosevelt, invited the Russians and the Japanese to meet at Portsmouth, New Hampshire, to negotiate a settlement. The Treaty of Portsmouth, which was signed on September 5, 1905, was concerned primarily with the disposition of territories belonging to the Qing empire, but no Qing representatives were present. After paying lip service to the recognition and restoration of Qing sovereignty and administration in Manchuria, the treaty gave Japan "paramount interests" in Korea, together with the Russian lease on the Liaodong Peninsula in South Manchuria and the Russian built South Manchurian Railway as far north as the city of Changchun. In addition, Japan received the southern half of Sakhalin Island, but Russia did not have to pay an indemnity. Even before the signing of the Treaty of Portsmouth, Japan and Great Britain in August 1905 had renegotiated and renewed their treaty of alliance, according to which the two powers would fight together against any fourth power. Moreover, India now came under the protection of the alliance, so that a Russian threat to India would be countered by Japanese action against Russia in the Far East.

Japan's remarkable victory in the war with Russia and growing difficulties among the powers in Europe ended the competition among the imperialist powers in East Asia. This new stability was recognized in a series of agreements by means of which the powers formally acknowledged the Empire's independence and integrity but settled China's affairs among themselves without reference to its interests. France and Japan signed a treaty in June 1907 in which they recognized each other's spheres of influence inside the Empire. In July 1907, Russia and Japan signed a series of agreements in which they secretly settled upon a division of Manchuria into two spheres, the north for Russia and the south for Japan. In August 1907, an agreement between Russia and Great Britain established their respective spheres of influence in Persia, Afghanistan, and Tibet, which was a part of the Qing empire. Japan completed its domination of Korea by annexing the kingdom in August 1910.

New Institutions for Old

The structures of the traditional tribute system, whose disintegration was hastened if not actually caused by the Twenty-one Years' War, could not account for, or provide a means for dealing with, the permanent presence in Peking of official representatives of barbarian rulers. Although Russians had resided in the capital on a permanent basis since the first part of the eighteenth century, their status and position could be either accommodated by traditional concepts or ignored entirely. But one of the foreigners' primary demands on the imperial government, even before the beginning of the Twenty-one Years' War, had been imperial acquiescence in the permanent residence of foreign representatives at the capital and the imperial government's reception of them as such. This demand, formulated time and again as one of the imperialists' objectives in the war, was a principal condition imposed upon the Qing in the treaties that ended the war. By the summer of 1862, the French, English, Russian, and American ministers not only had arrived in Peking but had also begun to acquire residences and office buildings and to organize the legation quarter.

No experience and no conceptual predispositions enabled the imperial government and its leaders to account for this development. Quite the contrary, the Empire's prewar experience with the Western barbarians to no small extent had pointed to the viability of the traditional methods of dealing with the barbarians. The Canton system itself, while troublesome, was accommodated within the tribute system: the adjustments that were necessary to accommodate the foreigners and their peculiar ways at Canton were minor and did not themselves constitute a challenge to traditional structures and institutions. Moreover, the habit, imposed upon the Empire by the imperatives of distance and premodern means of communication, of leaving the conduct of foreign relations to the improvisation of provincial officials was reinforced by the experience of the Canton system. The barbarians may have been obstreperous, weird, and hazardous to the economic and moral well-being of civilized society, but no Manchu or Chinese experience of them would have led the government to question its own institutions or ways of conducting business. Now that all had changed. Different institutions were required for new tasks.

THE ZONGLI YAMEN

The permanent presence of foreign diplomats in Peking and the establishment of permanent legations there led to the creation of the Office for General Management of Matters Concerning the Various Countries, which in Chinese was known as the "Zongli Yamen" and in English as the Foreign Office, though we shall see this latter appellation was a misnomer.

Instinct molded by tradition suggested, at the beginning, that the barbarians be kept at a distance and, if possible, persuaded to leave the capital. In early January 1861 Prince Gong proposed the appointment at Tianjin of a new commissioner for foreign trade who would so organize matters that the foreigners would be bored in Peking: since their business would be in Tianjin, they would want to leave the capital. He wrote: "If Tianjin can manage properly, then, even though the barbarian chieftains live in the capital, they must be depressed with having nothing to do and finally think of returning home. Hence the Tianjin commissionship is most important."[13] The imperial court considered this suggestion so clever that it appointed a trade commissioner not only for Tianjin but another for Shanghai as well. The latter had responsibility for trade in the southern ports. The court ordered provincial authorities to deal directly with the foreigners and not to refer issues to Peking, so that foreigners would have less occasion to come to the capital. In the end, this tactic succeeded only in annoying the barbarians.

The British early recognized that the court intended the establishment of the port commissioners to avoid the conduct of foreign relations at the capital. In contrast, Prince Gong and other imperial officials did not realize that the creation in Peking of an institution that foreigners could interpret as a foreign office would attract the foreign diplomats and fix them there. Moreover, they were insufficiently aware of the attractions the social, cultural, and aesthetic pleasures of Peking's famed lifestyle held for foreigners who, indeed, quickly began to enjoy life at the imperial capital.

Although the foreigners perceived the Zongli Yamen to be a kind of foreign office, and although the court intended it to manage the Empire's relations with "the various countries" and to enter into regular interaction with the foreign legations in the capital itself, at first the Zongli Yamen consisted only of an informal group of prominent statesmen. At the very beginning of 1861, Prince Gong, supported by two other officials, sent a memorial to the throne in which he said that new circumstances required a new foreign policy. On January 20, 1861, the court instructed him to establish a permanent office for foreign relations; he informed the foreigners of this fact and was congratulated by them. Prince Gong now proceeded to institutionalize the Zongli Yamen.[14]

In the beginning, the Zongli Yamen consisted of Prince Gong and the two officials who had supported his memorial. However, by 1869 their number had increased to ten. In effect, the Zongli Yamen was a subcommittee of the Grand Council, and its members were high officials who had primary appointments elsewhere in the bureaucracy at the capital but who met to manage foreign affairs. The office had jurisdiction over the superintendents of trade for the northern and southern ports. As the office's responsibilities began to be defined, it developed a staff of about fifty minor officials.

The Zongli Yamen certainly was not a Western style foreign office. Rather, it was an ad hoc structure intended to accommodate the unexpected outside of the usual institutions, and its position in the bureaucracy and its style of work remained fairly undefined. On the one hand, the Zongli Yamen was charged with the management of foreign affairs. However, other officials and bodies involved in the actual conduct of relations with the foreign powers—superintendents of trade, high provincial officials, and boards such as the Board of War—were all free to consult among themselves; moreover, they could memorialize, that is, communicate in writing with, the court directly. The Zongli Yamen received copies of all pertinent correspondence, but nothing required other personnel concerned with foreign relations to consult the Zongli Yamen before memorializing the throne or taking action. The staff of the Zongli Yamen, which grew with time, tended to remain small and to conduct its work secretly. Even the secretaries were considered specialists who would not need to rely on clerks or other menial officials. None of these features encouraged the development of a foreign office in any Western sense of the term, but this setup reflected the Qing desire to insulate the conduct of foreign relations from the rest of the processes of government, a hope that, in the end, proved vain.

By 1864 the Zongli Yamen had developed sufficiently to require reorganization and formalization, and it was given the shape that it would re-

tain until 1901, when it would be replaced by a more recognizable foreign
office. Its budget remained small, but this did not inhibit its activities because a considerable proportion of its expenditures derived from the budg-
ets of other government agencies. Since the members of the Zongli Yamen
were officials in these other agencies, the latter paid their salaries and
expenses. The Imperial Maritime Customs Service paid many of its expenses, too.

Even though the Zongli Yamen never became a central institution of
the Qing administrative structure, the court attempted to assure the importance of the office by instructing the Zongli Yamen to come to its own
decisions on specific issues of foreign relations, or at least to make the
foreigner think that it was doing so. Consequently, foreigners began to
accept the Zongli Yamen as a policymaking agency, and imperial officials
in the provinces sometimes complained that foreign representatives no
longer would treat with them but communicated directly with Peking.

As the Zongli Yamen began to develop a personality of its own, it became an advocate, inside the imperial government, of a flexible foreign
policy. Consequently, it often found itself at odds with more conservative
agencies of the Qing government. Moreover, because the foreign envoys
in Peking were its responsibility, the Zongli Yamen and the foreigners
began to develop a set of common interests, which pitted them against
advocates of more aggressive policies on both sides. This was the beginning of a phenomenon observed in foreign diplomats who served in China;
namely, some of them often seemed to become not their own nations'
representatives to China but China's advocates to their own governments.
That the barbarian Anson Burlingame, former American minister to Peking, became the imperial minister to Europe and the United States, fitted
both the traditional pattern of employing barbarians and the new spirit of
communal interests growing up between the Zongli Yamen and the foreign
envoys in the capital. The conduct of foreign relations did not depend on
the Zongli Yamen alone, however, and for the rest of the dynasty's existence, foreign policy was made by the men most concerned with it, regardless of their official position. Traditional patterns of administrative decentralization survived into the twentieth century; as we have seen, this
served the interests of both the foreigners and the Empire. The myths
upon which the Empire's survival depended were themselves supported
by this system.

THE IMPERIAL MARITIME CUSTOMS SERVICE

Another institution of sino-foreign contact that fitted neither traditional
imperial nor Western models was the maritime customs service, which
had its origins in the Twenty-one Years' War, more particularly in initiatives taken by British representatives to resolve problems of commercial

intercourse with the Empire in the midst of the Taiping rebellion and the incursion of rebels into Shanghai.

Once the foreigners had imposed a treaty tariff on the Empire, it became necessary to collect that tariff, particularly if foreign goods were to be free from internal customs collections, as the treaties stipulated. Shanghai was quickly becoming the major entrepôt on the China coast, but it had no imperial customshouse; consequently, in 1853 Rutherford Alcock, the British consul, himself began to organize the collection of duties as defined by the treaties. However, it became clear that some more systematic approach to customs collection was necessary. In July 1854 the British, French, and American consuls obtained the agreement of the Shanghai *daotai*, the chief local official, for their appointment of customs collectors who would be in the service of the *daotai* and would assure the payment of the legal revenues to the government. This led to the creation of the Foreign Inspectorate of Customs. After 1855, Horatio Nelson Lay, an Englishman, was employed by the imperial government, not by the foreign governments, to manage the assessment and collection of customs duties from the Empire's foreign trade. Lay, the son of one of the earliest British consuls in the Empire, was thoroughly familiar with Sino-Western relations and evidently knew the Chinese language well. As an Englishman in the employ of the imperial government—a traditional situation—Lay had played an important role in the negotiations that brought the Twenty-One Years' War to an end. In the aftermath of the war, Lay was instrumental in developing plans for the new customs service that was now required, and in January 1861, as one of the measures taken to reorganize Qing foreign relations, he was appointed inspector-general of customs.

In the meantime, an Irishman, Robert Hart, had arrived on the China coast in 1854 and, between 1858 and 1861, had served as the secretary of the Anglo-French commission that ruled Canton during the occupation. Canton, like Shanghai before it, had to move toward the regularization of customs collections, and Hart was appointed foreign inspector of customs at Canton in 1859. In 1863, he succeeded Lay as inspector-general of the Imperial Maritime Customs Service, which now operated in eleven ports along the coast and up the Changjiang. The Imperial Maritime Customs Service's role as intermediary between the Empire and the West acquired definition, however haltingly, from the very beginning of its existence. For some time, the imperial government had sought to obtain, in one way or another, foreign steamships that it could use to strengthen its position vis-à-vis the foreigners. Finally, Prince Gong agreed to purchase gunboats, which were considered the ultimate weapon of the era. When Lay went on leave to England in 1861, he was empowered to make such a purchase for the government, and he bought a fleet of eight gunboats; with the approval of the British government, he also hired British crews to man them. However, Lay informed the British commander of the fleet that he himself would transmit to the commander any imperial orders sent down and would exercise his own discretion in doing so. The fleet reached China in 1863, and the court immediately rejected this arrangement. It could not and would not permit Westerners to control its armed forces; besides, the high officials wanted possession of this new weapon for themselves. Consequently, Lay received a large sum of money in compensation, the British disposed of the fleet, and Lay left the Imperial Maritime Customs Service. Lay "considered himself to be working *for* the Chinese authorities, not *under* them. 'The notion,' he said, 'of a gentleman acting *under* an Asiatic barbarian is preposterous.'"[15] Hart, on the other hand, saw himself as a servant of the imperial government and therefore logically a brother officer of other imperial officials. He impressed this attitude upon the foreigners he employed in the customs service, and he and the service performed many valuable tasks for the imperial government.

Under Hart, who remained in the imperial service right down to the end of the dynasty, the Imperial Maritime Customs Service grew from eighteen hundred employees, of whom four hundred were Westerners, to approximately forty-two hundred in 1895, of whom seven hundred were Westerners (half of these were British). The customs service, the first modern civil service in the Empire, placed the Empire's foreign trade on a sound administrative basis, provided the Empire with a regular source of income, albeit income that debt payments eventually absorbed, and contributed both by example and by action to whatever modernization the Empire underwent.

Charged with providing the imperial government with revenues to pay off indemnities and debts owed foreign governments and financiers, the customs service engaged in other activities related to commerce. For instance, it was active in the campaign against corruption and smuggling. Hong Kong had become a center of smuggling of salt, opium, and other goods into imperial territory. Two steps were taken to prevent this illegal trade. Macao, long a Portuguese port, was recognized officially as Portuguese territory in 1887; Macao's status as a foreign territory meant that intercourse between it and the Chinese hinterland could be controlled by the customs service. The service also replaced traditional customs offices in those areas so that it could assume regular and direct control over trade.

The collection of customs duties depended upon foreign commerce, which in turn required the creation and maintenance of conditions conducive to trade. Hart directed the customs in completing the charting of the China coast and in establishing lighthouses and other navigational aids both on the coast and along the rivers, and he took over the management of port facilities and activities, such as piloting, berthing, and quarantine. The service also maintained and published statistics on commerce and conducted research about its growth.

BARBARIAN SPECIALISTS

Although institutions like the Imperial Maritime Customs Service served the imperial government well, the so-called barbarian experts of the traditional system were not suited to the new tasks that faced the Empire in the development and execution of foreign policy. Moreover, many of the leading officials upon whom the court had relied during the Twenty-One Years' War, such as Lin Zexu, were either dead or incompetent. In the 1860s, however, several leading imperial officials, including Prince Gong, began to develop knowledge of, and competence in, the conduct of foreign relations, and a rudimentary knowledge of the strange barbarian world and of its affairs began to spread throughout the bureaucracy and the court.

The character of the experts in the Zongli Yamen also changed with the passage of time. In the office's first year, most members were Manchus, reflecting the predominance of Manchus at the court. These men often were highly skilled in their own fields, and they were certainly experienced bureaucrats and court politicians, but they possessed no preparation or training for their work in foreign affairs. The appointment of Han Chinese to the Zongli Yamen initiated a change. The first, Tung Xun, held a variety of other positions concurrently, one of which required that he be well acquainted with the documentation of all aspects of recent imperial history, including foreign affairs. In 1865, the great geographer Xu Jiyü was appointed to the Zongli Yamen. He and his famous work on foreigners and their customs had been ignored two decades before, and he had been demoted and later dismissed from public office and disgraced. Xu's appointment to the Zongli Yamen in 1865, however, which was accompanied by the republication of his book, indicated the seriousness with which the Qing government now approached the mustering of resources for foreign affairs.

As the Zongli Yamen developed, it cast its net wide in the search for staff members. In 1864, it issued a general invitation to all government offices to recommend candidates for the staff, and thirty Han Chinese and thirty Manchus were eventually appointed. Service on the staff constituted training for higher positions at a later time. Promotion within the Zongli Yamen itself also was possible, as was concurrent or subsequent appointment to other government agencies. Not surprisingly, some members of the staff later served as ministers overseas.

THE TONG-WEN GUAN

The Empire was fortunate that a number of officials trained in the tradition were sufficiently capable of shifting perspectives to help develop new institutions and policies in foreign affairs. However, the need for specialists knowledgeable in Western languages and technology becme increasingly urgent, particularly when Sino-Western treaties stipulated that the authoritative treaty texts were those written in the relevant foreign language. Prince Gong and his supporters, in their memorial proposing the establishment of the Zongli Yamen, had pointed out the need for information about foreigners and for translators, noting that "in any negotiations with foreign nations, the prerequisite is to know their nature and feelings. At present, their speech cannot be understood and their writing can hardly be deciphered. Everything is impeded."[16]

In 1863, Li Hungzhang pinpointed the Empire's needs:

> When China has contact with foreigners, we should first understand their ambitions, be aware of their desires, and thoroughly know their points of strength and weakness, their honesty and dishonesty, before we can expect to secure just treatment. During the last twenty years of trade relations there have been quite a few of their leaders who have learned our written and spoken language and the best are able to read our classics and history. . . .Whenever we have a discussion between Chinese and foreign high officials, we depend entirely upon the foreign interpreters to transmit the ideas; it is difficult to guarantee that there is no such thing as prejudice or misinterpretation. . . .
>
> After the language students have become numerous, men of ability will emerge. . . .Are Chinese wisdom and intelligence inferior to those of Westerners? If we have really mastered the Western languages and, in turn, teach one another, then all their clever techniques of steamships and firearms can be gradually and thoroughly learned."[17]

In response to Prince Gong's memorial of 1861 and the broad support it received from those officials directly concerned with foreign relations, the court authorized the establishment in Peking of the "Tong-wen Guan" (School of Combined Learning, or "Interpreters' College") to train selected young Manchus in foreign languages. It quickly became a model for other schools, such as the ones established in Shanghai in 1863, in Canton in 1864, and in Fuzhou in 1866. The curriculum of the latter included navigation and engineering in addition to English and French.

At first, the Zongli Yamen intended to use Han Chinese and Manchus as instructors in the Tong-wen Guan, but the lack of competent teachers of Western languages soon led to a decision to employ foreigners, despite considerable fear that foreign teachers would attempt to propagate Christianity. The students were to be tested on a regular basis and, after one year's study, would continue to develop their knowledge by translating official documents.

It was but a short jump from instruction in Western languages to instruction in other Western subjects. In January 1867, for example, the Zongli Yamen suggested the establishment of an additional school for the study of engineering, astronomy, and mathematics. Science was the basis of Western technology, it was argued, and therefore the Empire needed science if it were to develop the technology necessary for self-defense. The Tong-wen Guan expanded to include the new subjects, and Xu Jiyü was appointed director. The rubric "astronomy and mathematics" covered the following subjects: anatomy, astronomy, biology, chemistry, geology, mathematics, mechanics, metallurgy, mineralogy, physics, physiology, political economy, and international law. This strange conglomeration of subjects was not a peculiar product of traditional perceptions of the West; rather, it was a conscious attempt on the part of Prince Gong and Xu Jiyü to neutralize conservative opposition to the development of the institution. Early in 1867 a debate began in which the conservatives strongly attacked both the new institution and the Western knowledge it sought to teach. The throne supported the liberals, however, and the way was open for the expansion of education in foreign subject areas.

By 1869, the school had one hundred students, and an American missionary, W. A. P. Martin, another of those enterprising foreigners who served the imperial regime in its final decades, was head. Martin had the responsibility for developing an eight-year curriculum in Western language and science studies. In the end the school failed for reasons that are not entirely clear. Undoubtedly, its decline was part of the malaise and growing weakness that the Empire experienced after the middle of the 1870s.

The Tong-wen guan, however, was important for two reasons. First, the school was the first concerted attempt on the part of the imperial government actively to prepare experts in foreign relations. Second, this experiment showed that, for a while at least, the imperial government recognized the importance of Western studies and made room for them in the traditional curriculum. The school opened the way for the establishment of other institutions, such as arsenals, naval yards, technical schools, and foreign schools and universities on imperial soil, all of which increased the flow of information about the West to the Empire and educated increasing numbers of Chinese and, to some extent, Manchus, too, in fields whose importance the dynasty now began to recognize.

THE DISPATCH OF MISSIONS ABROAD

The Empire was accustomed to sending embassies beyond its frontiers on diplomatic missions. Some went to invest local rulers with the insignia of office; some went to show the flag and, perhaps, to develop trade, like Cheng He's missions in the middle of the Ming; others went to explore the possibility of alliances, such as Tulishen's mission to the Mongols of the Volga, which sought an alliance against the Russians; and some, like the two imperial missions to Russia after the Treaty of Kyahkta, were required for purposes of diplomacy. Not all such missions were recorded in the annals of the dynasties, particularly if they fell outside the rubrics of accepted imperial behavior. Obviously, the concept of permanent resident envoys abroad was not foreign to the Qing: Western ministers resided in Peking after 1861. Nonetheless, despite all the other efforts to come to grips creatively with the new situation in foreign relations, no imperial diplomatic mission was established abroad until 1877.

Following the Twenty-one Years' War, the first mission sent overseas was the Burlingame embassy of 1868–1870, headed by the former American minister to Peking. Another mission went to France to apologize for the Tianjin massacre of 1870. Peking accepted, under duress to be sure, the presence of Western missions in the capital and was even prepared to explore Western knowledge and to teach its officials Western languages, but the establishment of permanent missions abroad lay too far outside traditional thought and behavior for the court to take that step. Furthermore, foreign relations seemed to some a rather humiliating field of endeavor in light of the defeats and restrictions suffered by the Empire at Western hands. Consequently, few officials were prepared to live abroad as envoys. In addition, the establishment of diplomatic missions in foreign capitals would have contributed to the arguments of the conservatives, against whom the moderates sometimes had difficulty holding their own.

Two incidents helped change opinions about this matter. The first was the Japanese punitive expedition to Formosa in 1874. Li Hungzhang and his supporters believed the presence of an imperial envoy in Japan might have avoided the entire affair because Peking could have been forewarned of Japanese intentions and undertaken negotiations to forestall action. The second incident was the murder of a British interpreter, A. R. Margary, by armed Chinese or tribesmen in Southwest China. Margary was in the area preparing the way for a British expedition traveling overland to China from Burma. According to international law, no one could be held responsible for the death of an individual who voluntarily exposed himself to danger. The British minister to Peking, however, had been looking for an opportunity to pressure the imperial government to expand British trade and influence in the Empire, and he now demanded an indemnity, an investigation, an apology, and a modification of the rules governing trade and diplomatic intercourse between the Empire and the West. He also demanded that an imperial mission carry the apology to England. The minister, Mr. Thomas Wade, was not known for his reasonableness.

The imperial government accepted the demand for payment of an indemnity and for an investigation but objected to the British minister's other requests. Wade and his legation withdrew from Peking and moved to Shanghai, hoping thereby to frighten the government. Peking, for its part, feared yet another diplomatic confrontation with a Western power; its fears were compounded by a rumor that the British and Russian ministers had entered into a secret agreement according to which England would invade Yunnan from India and Russia would invade Turkestan through Ili. The court capitulated and in August 1875 instructed Guo Songtao (1818–1891) to prepare for a mission of apology to England. In September 1876 some, but not all, of Wade's demands were formalized in the Chefoo Convention, which Li Hungzhang, with the support of Robert Hart, negotiated with the British minister.

Guo Songtao, an advocate of modernization and an eager student of all matters pertaining to the barbarians, was an appropriate choice for the mission, although he had little desire to make the trip. He was well trained in Confucian studies and had been pursuing a traditional bureaucratic career when the Empire's defeat in the Twenty-one Years' War turned his attention to barbarian studies, which he pursued, during a term as acting governor of Guangdong province, through direct contacts with foreigners. For this Guo was widely attacked both in Peking and in the provinces, but the court prevailed over his critics and he sailed from Shanghai on December 1, 1876. Guo presented the Emperor's letter of apology to Queen Victoria in February. The Margary affair and the Chefoo Convention convinced Li Hungzhang that the time had arrived to establish permanent imperial missions abroad, and Guo was instructed to remain in England as resident minister after the presentation of the emperor's letter of apology. By 1879, imperial missions had been established in London, Paris, Tokyo, Washington, and St. Petersburg.

These imperial missions provided another point of contact between the Empire and foreign governments and also served as sources of knowledge about the West. Furthermore, officials who served overseas often became advocates of modernization at home. Guo Songtao's letters from London carried a great deal of information concerning the West, and he strongly advocated acquisition of Western knowledge and of self-help. As he said, "My idea is that if everything must be done by foreigners it cannot last long. We should first make the Chinese thoroughly familiar with their methods. The state of Egypt is in Africa, and when she builds railroads, she first sends some people to England to study and then builds them by imitation. This is the best example."[18]

The Empire Thinks about the West

Until the full impact of the new international world began to be felt within the Empire as a consequence of repeated policy failures and military and political disasters, the West was at best peripheral to court and public consciousness. This may be illustrated by reference to Ruan Yuan (1764–1849), a well-known classical scholar and bibliophile who served as governor-general at Canton between 1817 and 1826, precisely at the time that the Canton system began to collapse. He was extraordinarily well educated and was widely active in the establishment of libraries and academies and the publication of scholarly works. During the decade he served at Canton, while the conflict leading to the Twenty-one Years' War was already a matter of concern, Ruan Yuan founded yet another academy, edited the provincial gazetteer of Guangdong, and published a collection of commentaries on the classics in 366 volumes, an anthology of poets from Jiangsu province in 183 chapters, and about 50 chapters of his own writing, including poetry, prose, and bibliographical annotations. In addition, he contributed to the study of Chinese painting, ancient stone and bronze inscriptions, and mathematics and served as the chief official in charge of imperial relations with the West. Though Ruan Yuan was neither unintelligent nor lazy, he did not turn his mind to the study of those foreigners and their things that were under his jurisdiction. His policy toward them was generally one of passivity and avoidance of conflict through compromise.

As the conflict approached, the standard work of reference about the outside world was a small book published around 1730 entitled *Record of Things Seen and Heard about the Overseas Countries* (*Haiguo Wenjian Lu*). But the West had changed drastically. Against this background, the tone of condescension and ignorance about the outside world that marked Lin Zexu's decree to Queen Victoria in 1839 concerning opium comes as no surprise. Commissioner Lin himself, however, recognized the need to collect information about his opponents, and he amassed translations and other material that came to hand and published some information himself. The information he gathered, and his experience with the barbarians at Canton, led him to a clear recognition, perhaps the first among imperial officials, of the military superiority of the barbarian:

> After all, ships, guns, and a water force are absolutely indispensable. Even if the rebellious barbarians had fled and returned beyond the seas, these things would still have to be urgently planned for, in order to work out the permanent defense of our sea frontiers. Moreover, unless we have weapons, what other help can we get now to drive away the crocodile and to get rid of the whales?[19]

After his dismissal, Lin turned his materials over to his friend, Wei Yuan, who completed and published Lin's work in 1844 as the *Illustrated Gazetteer of the Countries Overseas* (*Haiguo Tuzhi*). This work, enlarged and republished in 1847 and 1852, was the first serious attempt to provide a description of the outlanders and a discussion of the policy problems they raised. Both Lin Zexu and Wei Yuan recognized that the Empire needed to learn "the superior skills of the barbarians,"[20] while they opposed policies that derived from the experience of the Empire in another age and with other peoples. But they advocated the policy of "using the barbarian to control barbarian," which in the present case meant attempting to create conflict between Russia and Britain so that the British would have to withdraw from the Empire. According to Wei Yuan:

The enemy countries of which the British barbarians are afraid, are three: Russia, France, and America. The vassal states of our country of which the British are afraid are four: the Gurkhas (i.e., Nepal), Burma, Siam, and Annam. The methods for attacking England are, first, from the land; and second, from the ocean. The method of attacking her from the land lies in India. The countries which are close to India are Russia and the Gurkhas. The Russian capital and the English capital are separated by a few countries and not connected by land routes.[21]

Wei Yuan also proposed using the Americans and the French against the British. Ignorance of geography and contemporary politics does not negate the fact that this was the first attempt to deal creatively with new problems.

In 1850, the governor of Fujian, Xu Jiyü, published a geography of the world entitled *A Brief Survey of the Maritime Circuit (Yinghuan Zhilue)*, which was based on atlases and other information he had acquired from foreigners. This book represented another step in the search for knowledge because it was a systematic synthesis of information accompanied by relatively up-to-date maps. Xu, in his turn, was denounced and dismissed because of his connections with foreigners. Nonetheless, the information he published was now available.

In the course of the Twenty-one Years' War the policy alternatives that would be available to the Empire in the years after the war began to appear clearly. The arguments of men like Lin Zexu and Wei Yuan for the acquisition of Western technology foreshadowed the *ziqiang* ("self-strengthening") policy by which the Empire sought to acquire Western technology, through learning and through purchase, in order to fortify itself against the foreigners. Also in this period the basis of the so-called cooperative policy was laid, according to which small compromises would buy time for self-strengthening. As Qiying suggested in his proposals for negotiating with the foreigners in 1844:

The methods by which to conciliate the barbarians and get them under control similarly could not but shift about and change their form. Certainly we have to curb them by sincerity, but it has been even more necessary to control them by skillful methods. There are times when it is possible to have them follow our directions but not let them understand the reasons. Sometimes we expose everything so that they will not be suspicious, whereupon we can dissipate their rebellious restlessness. Sometimes we have given them receptions and entertained them, after which they have had a feeling of appreciation. And at still other times we have shown trust in them in a broad minded way and deemed it necessary to go deeply into minute discussions with them, whereupon we have been able to get their help in the business at hand.[22]

Cooperation, however, did not mean intimacy: "We must give them some sort of entertainment and cordial reception; but we are on guard against an intimate relationship in intercourse with them."[23]

THE POLICY OF SELF-STRENGTHENING

By the end of the Twenty-one Years' War, it was apparent to the more enlightened members of the imperial bureaucracy that the disaster was a consequence, on the one hand, of internal weakness and, on the other, of the Empire's lack of a technology equal to that of the west. Zeng Guofan, who had developed the policy and led the campaigns that defeated the Taiping rebellion, clearly recognized the relationship between foreign affairs and domestic affairs. In 1862, he wrote to Li Hungzhang:

> The barbarian affairs are fundamentally difficult to manage. . . .when you have contacts with foreigners, there are four important sentences to keep in mind, namely: your words must be faithful and sincere; your conduct must be earnest and respectable; you should cooperate with them in defense, but not in attack; and you should keep at a distance from them at first, but later on become close. . . .This last phrase means that we must earnestly strive to make our military power adequate so that we can stand on our own feet.

But, he goes on, quoting Confucius, "'If you can rule your own country, who dares to insult you?' If we are unified, strict, and sober, and if hundreds of measures are fostered, naturally they will not insult and affront us without reason."[24] Thus, while Prince Gong and the dynasty tried to keep the foreigner at bay diplomatically, the time so bought had to be used for self-strengthening, which meant internal reform and acquisition of technology. The two, in fact, were related: foreign military technology could be used against domestic rebellion just as easily as it could be used against foreign incursions. Gradually the fact that the world had changed was clearly recognized. "The world today," wrote Feng Gueifen, one of the great theorists of foreign affairs, "is not to be compared with that of the Three Dynasties (of ancient China). . . .Now the globe is 90,000 *li* around, and every spot may be reached by ship or wheeled vehicles."[25] The truth of this point, of course, was demonstrated by the experience of the Ever-Victorious Army, which employed Western weapons against internal rebels. "I feel deeply ashamed that the Chinese weapons are far inferior to those of foreign countries,"[26] wrote Li Hungzhang to Zeng Guofan in February 1863. In a very real sense, therefore, the entire process of modernization and industrialization, to which many officials and others devoted themselves in the years after 1860, was part and parcel of foreign affairs insofar as it was brought about by failure in the face of the Western onslaught and the desire to find alternatives. As we have seen, the effort was too little and came too late. Disaster followed disaster, and the decline of the Empire's fortunes continued.

The defeat of the Empire in the Sino-Japanese War of 1894–1895 only served to confirm the bankruptcy of the self-strengthening concept. The reforms introduced into military and naval affairs, the schools, the post office and telegraph, the factories, and all the other measures taken under the rubric of self-strengthening did not change the Empire's international position. And the worst blow yet was the defeat of the Empire at the hands of another Asian nation. Moreover, the forces of conservatism, which feared the erosion of Sino-Confucian virtues in the face of reform and modernization, no matter how successful, had become, for a while at least, the preponderant influence at Peking. They were even able to frustrate the attempt of the Hundred Days reform, which had the support of the throne. In this context Zhang Zhidong (1837–1909), the great liberal official who rivaled Li Hungzhang, sought to reformulate the self-strengthening position in such a way that the interest of both conservatives and reformers would be served. Advancing the slogan "Chinese learning for the fundamental principles, Western learning for practical application" (*zhongxue wei ti; xixue wei yong*), he sought to reaffirm traditional virtues and revive Confucianism as the basis of an attempt to use education and industrialization to save the Empire. His essay "Exhortation to Study" is a stirring statement, but it did not point in any new directions.[27] The Boxer movement and Boxer War in the following years provided further evidence of the failure of the self-strengthening program.

Younger members of the official bureaucracy, or candidates for appointments, produced more radical proposals. For example, Kang Youwei (1858–1927) from Canton, leading twelve hundred provincial candidates who were in Peking to take advanced exams, presented in May 1895 the "Ten Thousand Word Memorial" (also called the "Memorial of the Examination Candidates"). Kang and his followers advocated profound reforms aimed at combating the foreigner. As his thought developed, Kang argued that the Confucian classics sanctioned westernization and included the concept of progress as the West understood it. This was a deeply anti-orthodox position, which Kang augmented by suggesting the establishment of a Western style national religion focused on Confucius as a vehicle for sanctioning change. Kang's radicalism was exceeded by that of his student Liang Qichao (1873–1929), who moved beyond Chinese classical learning to develop a view of China within the context of world history, drawing upon Western ideas such as Social Darwinism. Kang and Liang were only the most prominent members of the reform movement that sought to legislate change in the Empire during the famous Hundred Days, from June to September 1898, when it enjoyed the favor of the emperor. Their attempt to change the Empire from within the system, using the established bureaucracy as their vehicle, was brought to an abrupt end by the empress dowager, who carried out a *coup d'etat* on September 21, 1898, and, with the aid of the top Manchu military commanders, seized the emperor and began a new regency.

One person alone seemed to perceive the truth. Tan Sitong (1865–1898), one of the reformers of 1898, was an intelligent and original thinker who was prepared to speak out. Only by breaking the mould of tradition, he argued, would the Empire be able to save itself, and that required "complete westernization" (*quanpan xihua*). Writing to a friend Tan said:

> Your letter says that during the last several decades Chinese scholars and officials have been trying to talk about "foreign matters", but that they have achieved absolutely nothing and, on the contrary, they have been driving the men of ability in the empire into foolishness, greed, and cheating. Sitong thinks that not only do you not know what is meant by "foreign matters", but also that you are ignorant of the meaning of discussion. In China, during the last several decades, where have we had genuine understanding of foreign culture? When have we had scholars or officials who could discuss them? If they had been able to discuss foreign matters, there would have been no such incident as we have today (the defeat of China by Japan). What you mean by foreign matters are things you have seen, such as steamships, telegraph lines, trains, guns, cannon, torpedos, and machines for weaving and for metallurgy; that's all. You have never dreamed of nor seen the beauty or perfection of western legal systems and political institutions. . . .all that you speak of are the branches and foliage of foreign matters, not the root.[28]

But this was a voice in the wilderness. Tan was executed in the aftermath of the empress dowager's coup.

ABOUT INTERNATIONAL LAW

The failure of the self-strengthening movement and the dimming of the lights lit by such men as Lin Zexu and Wei Yuan does not mean that no attempt was made to understand how foreign nations conducted their international relations. Lin Zexu realized as early as 1839 that the Western powers possessed something called international law, on the basis of which they organized their relationships, and that this law differed profoundly from the customs and legislation of the Empire. In 1839, the imperial commissioner asked Peter Parker (1804–1888), an American medical missionary, to translate three paragraphs of Vattel's *Droit des gens*. The paragraphs, which were later published by Wei Yuan, concerned the right of nations to control imports of goods into their own territories. The translation left a great deal to be desired and, evidently, Lin had difficulty understanding it. He requested a second, and better, translation from Yuan Dehui, a translator on his staff, who had first brought Vattel's book to his attention. This interest in international law was no more than a glimmer, however, and with Lin's dismissal in 1840 and the end of the first stage of the Twenty-one Years' War in 1842, no one in the Empire evinced further interest in the subject.

After the war, however, this situation changed. In 1864, for example, Prince Gong informed the court: "We have learned that there is a book called *Wanguo Luli* (Laws and Precedents of All Nations). Yet when we wanted to seek it directly, and entrust its translation to the foreigners, we were afraid that they might wish to keep it confidential and not have shown it to us."[29]

The Empire's first real exposure to the concepts of international law came through the translation of Henry Wheaton's *Elements of International Law* (1830), well known in the West. The U.S. State Department had sent a copy of the book to the American commissioner in China in 1855, but it was lost in transit. The American minister, William Reed, purchased another copy in 1857. Robert Hart, when he was still chief assistant to Horatio Nelson Lay, the inspector-general of the customs, translated twenty-four sections of the work into Chinese for the Zongli Yamen. These sections dealt with the rights of legations, and Hart hoped to use them to persuade the Zongli Yamen to send diplomatic missions to foreign capitals.

W. A. P. Martin, the educational missionary who later became head of the Tong-wen Guan, began a complete translation of Wheaton's book in 1862 with encouragement from Hart, who was now the inspector-general of the maritime customs. At Hart's suggestion, the Zongli Yamen appointed a commission of four scholars to work with Martin on the translation, and the completed Chinese version, with a preface written by Tung Xun, was presented to the throne on January 7, 1865.

Martin believed that law, in this case international law, was the finest product of Christian civilization; therefore, by making this work available to the imperial government, he somehow was bringing it closer to Christianity. Martin hoped the project would "bring this atheistic government to the recognition of God and his eternal justice; and perhaps impart to them something of the spirit of Christianity." In his own preface to the Chinese translation, Martin remarked that international law would not be foreign to the Chinese mind:

> To its (international law's) fundamental principles, the Chinese mind is prepared to yield a ready assent. In their state ritual as well as their canonical books, they acknowledge a supreme arbiter of human destiny to whom kings and princes are responsible for their exercise of delegated power; . . . The relations of nations, considered as moral persons, and their reciprocal obligations as deduced from this maxim, they are thoroughly able to comprehend.[30]

The court's response to the Wheaton volume was very pragmatic. Prince Gong, reading the work in translation before final editing for presentation to the throne, remarked that "examining this book, I found it generally deals with alliances, laws of war, and other things. Particularly, it has laws on the outbreak of war and the check and balance between states."[31] The traditional taste for finely reasoned documentation was fed by Western international legalisms, and the Zongli Yamen quickly began to use lessons learned from, and about, international law for the defense of the Empire's interests. Indeed, foreign residents of the Empire began to regret that the Chinese had discovered "those flowery means of diplomacy where they so highly excelled" and admitted that "we must make up our minds to see the Chinese in future contesting acts to which they are opposed on grounds which we ourselves recognize."[32]

The introduction and growth of knowledge about international law was one further element in the construction of a new set of institutions and assumptions for the Empire's conduct of foreign relations. However, this candle did not light much of the darkness. In the end, might was stronger than right, particularly in a situation in which the two sides could not agree on what was right. International law did not save the Empire, and it was certainly no bar to the imperialists' pursuit of their own interests in East Asia.

The Broken Wall, The Burning Roof and Tower: 1911–1949

THE IMPACT OF THE WEST on the history of modern China can be measured by the extent to which the Oikoumene disassembled the Empire, transformed China Proper into a semicolonial region, and separated off many of the Empire's non-Han regions, subjecting them to direct and indirect exploitation. The revolution of 1911 and the fall of the Qing dynasty closed the history of the traditional Empire. The disappearance of Manchu power—or, more accurately, the remaining shadows of Manchu power—was merely one more step in the West's exploitation of Chinese society. Beyond that, the Empire's disappearance was an event of universal importance because it signaled the inability of traditional institutions and ways of life to withstand the assaults of the Oikoumene. Thereafter, things fell apart at great speed in the Empire, and they were never to be the same again. Only the victory of the Chinese Communists in 1949 halted the processes of exploitation from without and decay from within and began the reassembling of the world into an intelligible order.

From 1911 to 1949, the period of the Republic, imperial history conjoined Western history. What was a particular event in the former—the fall of a dynasty—was an instance of a general event in the latter—the expansion of the Oikoumene and the transformation (and often destruction) of cultures and societies that stood in its way or differed from it. In the first decade and a half of the twentieth century, Europe became aware that it had changed in ways it was only beginning to recognize. The optimism characteristic of nineteenth-century industrialization and expansionism was becoming tinged with pessimism and uncertainty. The world market was expanding, the metropolitan countries were profiting, the traditional rivalries that were endemic within the Oikoumene were sharpening, and war loomed upon the horizon.

The barbarities of World War I shocked Westerners and non-Western-
ers alike and created doubts in non-Western minds concerning the moral
or spiritual superiority of the West. Although fought almost entirely among
the members of the Oikoumene, the war was a world war to the extent
that it involved the direct and indirect dependencies of the Oikoumene.
Indians fought for Great Britain; Great Britain and France fought Turkey,
a Middle Eastern ally of the Central powers. Chinese workers labored in
French factories augmenting the French work force.

The war changed everything. In 1917, even before the war's end, Russia broke away from the Oikoumene and began the construction of what
many believed, and hoped, was an alternative to capitalism. Japan, a rapidly industrializing ally of the Allies, now became a full-fledged participant
in the Oikoumene. The two interwar decades saw extraordinary political,
social, economic, and cultural dislocations and changes in many parts of
the world, followed in some countries by attempts to order chaos through
rigidification and to seek relief and purification through the "cleansing"
action of racial, social, and political purgation. The national rivalries and
class conflicts characteristic of the Oikoumene led to attempted resolutions
such as fascism in Central and Eastern Europe and Stalinism in the Soviet
Union; political and social movements in the Western democracies were
sharply influenced by these phenomena.

Like World War I, World War II was a conflict within the Oikoumene
(now including Japan). It was climactic, cataclysmic, and climacteric. Afterward, the Oikoumene discovered that the world it had constructed in its
own image no longer existed. Surrounded by its many "clients" in Europe,
Asia, Africa, and Latin America, the United States was not the uncontested
leader of the world it thought itself to be. The Soviet Union, with its "satellites," challenged the Oikoumene and America's dominant position in it.
In the Far East, China began to expel the Oikoumene from its soil and,
shortly, fought in Korea the first war with the West in which it did not
suffer defeat.

The republican period in Chinese history can be variously defined. Dynastic cycle theorists call it an interregnum, similar to earlier periods in
China's history (this leads logically to calling the period beginning in 1949
a new dynasty). Certainly Yuan Shikai's short-lived attempt at imperial restoration and the devolution of the Empire into a congeries of small, constantly battling, and ever shifting warlord states would tend to support this
view. A variation of this approach interprets the period as a prolonged
government crisis, in which the state experienced rapid and unpredictable
changes; the central but weakened power of the Manchu dynasty became
the prize sought by those who wanted to become the new rulers of a unified China. A third interpretation, and the one that constitutes the point
of departure for this survey of modern China's foreign relations, sees the
years 1911–1949 as a period in which the system of the sinocentric cen-

tralized Empire gave way, dialectically, to an international system of states, similar to the arrangement in earlier eras of Chinese history such as the periods of the Warring States, the Three Kingdoms, the Sixteen Kingdoms, the Ten Kingdoms and the Five Dynasties. These were multistate or polycentric periods. This characterization privileges neither a centralized dynastic power nor a decentralized political-social system; it also avoids having to account for the fact that the model of a strong, centralized, and centralizing dynasty that retains power for a significant period of time is valid for only about half the Empire's recorded history. Moreover, the characterization of the years 1911–1949 as a return to a sinocentric international system in the Far East—for throughout the period China remains the central issue, it can be argued—permits us analytically to incorporate the Oikoumene, in the person of the various competing and/or cooperating states as well as individuals and nonstate institutions, as an actor in that international system. At the same time, this model is dynamic, permitting us to observe both the impact of the Oikoumene on the Empire, particularly on China, and the functioning of China as a peripheral subsystem of the Oikoumene.

Many of the warlords, who were the power centers in the society during the period of polycentrism, particularly in the first half of the period, began as officers of the now defunct imperial armies or as military governors in one or another region of the Empire. Their status depended upon their possession of military forces that were loyal to them personally, and they and their armies required a source of revenues and supplies, such as a city, a province, or a region. Consequently, a warlord's power was based not on a population but on the ecology of a region of a nature and size sufficient to provide him with a population from which taxes could be exacted and supplies collected. Recognizable institutions, ideologies, slogans, and politicians constituted, on the one hand, a means to legitimate military power and, on the other, a means to exercise it among the people. The disappearance of the Empire, which such military types would have served and in whose service they would have found their legitimacy, itself created a legitimization problem. The warlords, singly or in rapidly shifting alliances, sought control of a central government whose existence as an effective element in the country was largely a myth. Nonetheless, this myth was itself a source of legitimacy, defining the central government both as the successor to the Qing dynasty and as the appropriate organ in China with which the foreign powers should have dealings. The foreigners, therefore, by validating the myth through their recognition of the central government, irrespective of the person or group holding power, themselves became a primary source of legitimacy inside China. The attempts by one or another group of warlords to seize the central power did not signify their assumption that a central Chinese state continued to exist in theory, if not in fact; quite the contrary, provinces all too easily declared their

independence from each other and from China in the years immediately
after the revolution of 1911. The existence of a state was a myth that
served the interests of the warlords, not an ideal to which they felt they
owed allegiance. As we shall see, this myth also served the interests of the
foreigners.

By the early 1920s political forces within China began to coalesce
around some limited commitment to ideology and party. The parties were
defined by both the internal and the international context within which
they developed. Like the warlords, the politicians were deeply rooted in
the conditions that surrounded the fall of the Qing dynasty. Some were
revolutionaries in groups that resembled traditional Chinese secret societies; others had been traditional bureaucrats. Two conditions in particular
defined the quality of Chinese politics in the first part of the 1920s. First,
the Soviet Union, more especially the Communists' Third International,
provided ideological and organizational content to fill the void created, on
the one hand, by the decline of traditional values and institutions and, on
the other, by the irrelevance of Western liberal ideas to Chinese reality.
The noncommunist Guomindang (Nationalist Party, abbreviated KMT) was
reorganized, and the Chinese Communist Party was organized, under the
aegis of Moscow, which sent both political and military advisors to China.
The Communists joined the Guomindang as individuals, providing the basis for an aggressive, albeit short-lived, alliance between the two parties.
In this fashion the Oikoumene's successor on Russian territory, the Soviet
government, itself became a participant in Chinese politics by virtue of its
own rejection of, and opposition to, capitalism and imperialism. Warlordism was the second factor conditioning the evolution of Chinese politics in
the 1920s. When internal political and military power were almost synonymous and military conquest was the primary avenue to political power,
nonmilitary politicians could not afford not to develop their own military
organizations. Here again the Soviets filled a role the Oikoumene was unable, or unwilling, to fill. With Soviet aid the Nationalist-Communist alliance established a military academy at Whampoa, near Canton, and organized an army to seek power in competition with the warlords and on their
own ground. In effect, the parties became warlords in their own right and
used military tactics to seize territory. When the Nationalist-Communist
alliance broke apart in 1927, the two parties continued to pursue their
objectives within the context of the Chinese political culture of the time,
and the politico-military conflict between them lasted for decades and itself
became an issue in world politics.

The first even partially effective central government in China since
1911 was Chiang Kaishek's Nanjing government. Established in 1928, this
administration extended its control over large parts of the former Manchu
empire by a combination of military conquest and compromise with local
warlords. The Communists became one more participant in a struggle

whose other participants were the central government and the remaining recalcitrant warlords. This civil war ended only in 1949, with the victory of the Communists and the flight of the Nationalists to Formosa. Throughout the period, various powers in the Oikoumene, as well as the Soviet Union, played roles in Chinese politics by supporting one or another contestant. This transformed what, in other contexts, would have been an internal affair into an integral part of international politics on the periphery of the Oikoumene.

The Japanese were already part of the Oikoumene when they invaded Manchuria in 1931 and, soon thereafter, China Proper. Now they became direct actors on the Chinese scene and began to play roles that resembled, in both action and intention, those being played by the warlords and politicians. Japan's legitimacy as an actor in Chinese politics stemmed, its advocates insisted, from Tokyo's vision of the world and of Japan's and China's places in it. World War II in China, therefore, was a drama played out among three groups contesting for the role of successor to the Empire: the KMT, the Chinese Communists, and the Japanese. In this three-sided struggle, the foreigners—the United States and the Soviet Union in particular—functioned much as foreigners customarily did in China, acting to maximize their own advantages.

Throughout the years of polycentrism, the social and economic disintegration that accompanied the growth of power of the Oikoumene in China elicited an increasingly sharp recognition of the need for social and economic change. Nationalism, particularly among the more progressive sectors of society, was a direct response to the imperialism of the foreign powers. The reformist political theories of the dying years of the Empire quickly gave way to programs for reorganization and reform that sought to restore to the Chinese control over their own destiny and to reject foreign power from China. The Qing self-strengthening and modernization programs had rested on a perception of international affairs as a matter purely of relative armed power and modernization. Now new political theories such as Marxism offered alternative tools for interpreting the systemic sources of imperialism in the West. Thus, China's perceptions of its foreign relations changed in the course of the multistate period.

The interaction between polycentric China and the Oikoumene constituted, ironically, a symbiosis grounded in each side's pursuit of its own interests. The need of various Chinese groups for legitimation found a counterpart in the need of the foreign powers for a legitimate government inside China to guarantee the minimal security and structure required for commerce. Foreign powers wanted to influence internal Chinese affairs in their own interests while the warlords and political groups wanted to use this foreign influence to strengthen their own positions. But whereas the West wanted a government in China that would not be quite strong enough to threaten the interests of the Oikoumene, the Chinese wanted a strong government that would take its internal problems in hand. And while the West sought to maintain access to China, China itself sought to reconquer the sovereignty lost through the unequal treaty system.

Throughout the polycentric period, the foreign presence in China remained a primary issue around which the political and military struggle inside the country raged. Revision of the unequal treaty system, the Oikoumene's desire for the law and order inside China that would favor its commercial interests, and debt collection were among the problems that continued to plague the period of polycentrism, just as they had the dynasty's last decade. Only the reestablishment of a strong central authority throughout almost the entire extent of the Empire, under the Communist regime after 1949, restored to the discourse of China's foreign relations the essential outlines that had prevailed before the onslaught of the Oikoumene began in the middle of the eighteenth century.

The Collapse of the Traditional Imperial State

Dynastic disintegration had occurred many times in China's history without occasioning the disappearance of the traditional state. This development arose primarily because of a new factor, the presence in the Far East of the Oikoumene, which had a continuing impact upon the Empire. Early in 1901, in the aftermath of the Boxer War, the empress dowager declared from her exile in Xian that she, and therefore the dynasty, was in favor of reform. The Empire, she said, must "adopt strong points of foreign countries in order to make up China's shortcomings." She recognized that the study of foreign languages and the use of foreign machines were not "the fundamental source of Western government," and, therefore, not the source of that power that was overwhelming the Empire.[1] Now she was prepared to follow the recommendations of Zhang Zhidong and Liu Kunyi, both viceroys in the Changjiang valley, who in a series of memorials called for a profound reorganization of the Empire's political structure.[2] Zhang and Liu recommended, in addition to the creation of new military and civil schools and the reformation of the traditional Confucian civil service examination system, the great expansion of personal contact with foreign countries by the dispatch of diplomats, officials, and students abroad, the increase of translations of foreign works, and the official collection of opium duties. In almost all their recommendations they made direct reference to conditions in England, France, Germany, the United States, or Japan. The Empire itself was looking overseas for models of change.

CONSTITUTIONALISM

Against the background of commitment to reform, the spectacle of Japan's victory over Russia in the war of 1904–1905, a perception of Japan's

strengths as deriving in part from her adoption of Western style governmental institutions, and the continuing growth of nationalism within the
Empire, the court sent two missions to study the constitutional governments of the foreign powers: one visited Japan, England, and France; the
other went to the United States and Germany. Toward the end of 1906,
two of the commissioners, one a traditional Confucian bureaucrat and the
other a reputedly open-minded Manchu official, analyzed in a long memorial to the throne the nature of Western government and its applicability
to the Empire. Taking their point of departure from a lecture given them
by Prince Ito, one of the leading Japanese statesmen of the day, they recommended the adoption of a constitution that would increase the Emperor's powers by encouraging support for the throne through limited public participation in government. The Emperor should be "beyond the reach
of adverse criticism and discussion" and should be assisted by ministers
who could "be blamed for not doing their duty" if matters did not go well.
Their interpretation of responsible government is a most interesting adaptation of a Western political concept to a different society: "Consequently,
the high ministers of the government must take the responsibility on behalf of the monarch. This is called the system of responsible ministers,
which had been clearly provided for in the constitutions of the various
nations." Nonetheless, it was a brave attempt at understanding.[3]

In November 1906 steps were taken to establish a central government
in the Western mode by converting the traditional six boards into eleven
ministries, including a Ministry of Foreign Affairs. In 1908 the empress
dowager published a set of principles that were intended to lay the
groundwork for a program that would lead to constitutional government at
the end of a nine-year period. The program would begin with the establishment in 1909 of consultative assemblies in the provinces. Throughout
the whole process, the dynasty sought guidance by observation of, and
direct contact with, the foreign powers. The empress dowager died in the
middle of November 1908, however, and the death of the Guangxu emperor was announced the same day, although officially it had taken place
the day before. Consequently, the throne fell to the empress dowager's
three-year-old grandnephew. The child was hardly equal to the tasks the
dynasty faced; his father was named regent but was incompetent. To make
matters worse, Sir Robert Hart, so central to the processes of accommodation and reform through which the dynasty already had passed, retired
and returned to England that same year, and the leaders of the dynastic
reform attempt of 1898 were either dying or were to be dismissed the
following year. The end was near.

FINANCE IMPERIALISM

The construction of foreign owned railroads to extract natural resources
and agricultural products from the Empire's interior was one of the most

important aspects of the scramble for concessions. The French railroad in Yunnan, the Russian and Japanese in Manchuria, and the German in Shandong all provided access to markets and sources of cheap labor. Even where the Empire itself was titular owner, the railways were built with loans from foreign banking consortia, which then managed and directed the rail service. Thus, the government itself became a vehicle for the penetration of finance imperialism.

"Railroad imperialism" elicited two primary responses inside the Empire. One suggested that the construction of railroads required centralized planning, financing, and management. The other had a different focus, the provinces, where the gentry and their bureaucratic allies were increasingly demanding the recovery of railroad ownership; to this end they formed provincial companies for the purchase and further construction of railroads. The provincial gentry were motivated as much by the desire for profit as by patriotism, and local control promised no greater degree of honesty or efficiency than did centralization. Both responses suffered from the same weakness, however: unlike the Oikoumene, the Empire lacked the resources, institutions, and discipline or state of mind necessary for the accumulation of capital; social structure and cultural formations all pointed to the use of available funds for the purchase of rank and security, not for risk investments. The Empire's economy may have produced a surplus, but it was unable to transform that surplus into capital available for investment. Advocates of both responses were dependent upon foreign financing. For example, in 1905 Zhang Zhidong obtained British financing for the purchase of an American contract for the construction of a railroad between the cities of Canton and Hankou. The lack of domestic capital left the field open to foreign investment.

Not yet *primus*, nor even *primus inter pares*, among the nations of the Oikoumene, the United States was determined not to be left behind. Using the so-called Open Door policy as a cover for "dollar diplomacy," Philander Knox, the American secretary of state, suggested in November 1909 the "neutralization" of the Russian and Japanese railroads in Manchuria. Since 1907, however, Great Britain had agreed to Russian and Japanese expansion in Manchuria in return for freedom for the expansion of British interests elsewhere in the Empire, particularly in the Changjiang valley and in the coastal provinces north and south of the mouth of the river. The American proposal led only to the reaffirmation of Russia's and Japan's positions in Manchuria. The United States pursued similar policies elsewhere in the Empire. In July 1909, for example, the American president demanded the "equal participation by American capital" in negotiations for railway loans for the construction of the railroad between Hankou and Canton. His objective, he said, was the promotion of "the welfare of China and . . . her territorial integrity," with the consequence that a four-power banking consortium was created in 1910 for the purpose of making a railway loan. The consortium, which included German, French, and British interests and the Morgan banks from the United States, signed a loan agreement in 1911.[4]

The railway loan of 1911 illustrates the role of finance imperialism in the sociopolitical life of the Empire. At the same time that Peking signed the four-power loan, it ordered the centralization, through purchase, of all provincial railroads and railroad construction projects. The loan may have been intended to finance this centralization policy. Be that as it may, the adoption of a centralization policy immediately led to movements in the provinces, particularly in Sichuan in the southwest, for "rights recovery" and "railway protection." Patriots thought the imperial government was selling the Empire to the foreigners. The gentry feared the loss of a great opportunity for profit. They made common cause in mass meetings and vainly petitioned the court. In Sichuan, the movement gained momentum as taxes were withheld, schools and shops were closed, and the peasants were mobilized by the gentry. This movement's leaders were members of the gentry and merchant classes and many of them had studied abroad, particularly in Japan; these men were both wealthy and well placed in the traditional social and bureaucratic systems. By September 1911, the situation in Sichuan had become so volatile that Peking dispatched imperial troops to reassert central control; in the process, they shot demonstrators and arrested members of the gentry leadership group. The efficacy of the central institutions of the Empire already eroded by the assaults of imperialism, the local gentry in Sichuan and elsewhere increasingly were identifying their interests not with the dynasty but with their own provinces. The end of the Confucian examination system and the disintegration of the links that the traditional bureaucracy had provided between the local gentry and the imperial centralized power removed the ideological superstructure and institutional infrastructure that were the *sine quibus non* for the maintenance of centralized power in the sinocentric Empire. By 1911, little was required for the shattering of the fragile imperial structure and the recrudescence of the sinocentric multistate system in continental East Asia. That little something was provided by the rebellion of some soldiers in the Changjiang city of Wuhan on October 10, 1911, which led almost immediately to the abdication of the dynasty.

REVOLUTIONARIES AND FOREIGNERS

Imperialist penetration of the Empire was not restricted either to intergovernmental relations or to military power and economic development. Foreign countries, particularly Japan, provided Qing government and Chinese reformers alike with models for development and change. Reformers and revolutionaries studied in Japan, for example, and Japan's own successful modernization, defeat of Russia, and acceptance by the European powers as an equal, made it a symbol of successful resistance whose impact was felt throughout Asia.

Japan did not hesitate to use this preeminence to its own advantage. Japan's occupation of Taiwan and Korea and the establishment of a sphere of influence in Manchuria demonstrated Japan's imperialist intentions. Various private and semiprivate organizations were established to pursue Chinese studies and promote Japanese interests on the continent. The "Toa Dobun Kai" ("East Asian Common Culture Society") and the various research centers established in Shanghai, Manchuria, and on the island of Taiwan provided training for China specialists and conducted research that was intended to be useful to the Japanese. Societies such as the ultrapatriotic Amur River Society (better known as the Black Dragon Society, from the Chinese name for the Amur River), founded in 1901, promoted a more activist approach on the continent by sending businessmen, students, and tourists to prepare the ground for Japanese expansion in the north against Russia. Inevitably, the society and its agents became involved in Chinese affairs as well. The growth of research and of activist organizations as agencies of imperialism, though fairly recent, was not a novel development, having precursors in the geographical societies of England and France, for example. The relationship between scholarship and politics, so marked in the post–World War II environment in the United States, was evident in Japan before 1911.

In its pursuit of a dominant position on the continent, Japan was prepared to encourage reformers and revolutionaries at the same time that it dealt with the imperial government. Japan sought a government on the mainland that would accept Japanese guidance and recognize the primacy of Japanese interests in East Asia; the specific structure of the government was a secondary question. Consequently, when, after the failure of the reform movement of 1898, some of its leaders, including Kang Youwei, sought refuge in Japan, they received official encouragement. Indeed, Kang, for example, was a guest in the home of Okuma Shigenobu, leader of the Progressive Party and sometime prime minister, who himself provided the ideological rationale for Japan's interest in China: Japan's cultural debt to China could be repaid by Japanese guarantees of China's freedom and sponsorship of Chinese modernization. Sun Yat-sen was also in Japan, and Inukai Ki, one of Okuma's assistants and much later a prime minister himself, actively encouraged cooperation among the leaders of the various Chinese factions in Japan. Unity among the antidynastic reformers and revolutionaries, particularly the two groups led by Kang Youwei and Sun Yat-sen, respectively, would have been in Japan's interests. Inukai failed, and Sun, Kang, and Liang Qichao all began to travel through the overseas Chinese communities in Southeast Asia, the Pacific, and North America, as well as Europe, to seek support. Among the powers, however, it was Japan that most actively promoted Chinese revolutionaries who would respond to Tokyo's concerns, and in the first decade of the twentieth century Japan continued to be their primary refuge and support. Moreover, many leaders of the postdynastic period, including Chiang Kaishek, were educated in Japan.

THE POWERS AND THE REVOLUTION

Within weeks of the revolutionary outbreak of October 10, 1911, the Empire dissolved into a polycentric system. By the middle of December, the provinces in south and central China and even in the northwest declared their independence; in most areas a dynastic military officer or military governor shared power with gentry leaders. The dynasty, technically still in power, summoned Yuan Shikai, commander of its best armies, to protect the dynasty and to reassert its authority; at his own insistence Yuan was appointed both premier and commander of the armed forces. The confusion grew as the provinces that had declared themselves independent and Sun Yat-sen's revolutionaries together established a provisional government at Nanjing in the Changjiang valley. Now the dialectical tension between unitary Empire and polycentric system was at full play: Sun Yat-sen, abroad when the revolution began, proceeded to England to seek a British loan and other aid to inhibit Japanese military and financial support for the tottering dynasty. He returned to China in time to be inaugurated provisional president of the Chinese republic at Nanjing on January 1, 1912. However, he announced that he was prepared to resign if Yuan Shikai agreed to support the republic.

Amid this confusion, individuals of many different political persuasions agreed that national unity was necessary to prevent foreign intervention, which most likely would come from Japan. Foreign relations, therefore, became a primary focus of internal politics. In order to promote unity, the dynasty abdicated in February 1912, Sun Yat-sen resigned the presidency, and Yuan Shikai was elected president at Nanjing and inaugurated at Peking on March 10.

CODA TO EMPIRE: YUAN SHIKAI AND THE
FAILED RESTORATION

Numerous questions remained unanswered in the midst of China's confusion. Many politicians, both Chinese and foreign, understood that national unity was necessary to prevent Japanese intervention, but who was to provide that unity? With the disintegration of the Manchu empire, what territories did China encompass? What form of government was appropriate to China's circumstances? Yuan, as president of the republic, asserted China's claims over all Qing territory, even though some areas, such as Mongolia and Tibet, rejected the republic as the successor to the Qing.

More important, Yuan tried to bolster his internal position by seeking legitimation and financial support among the imperialists, thus bringing them directly into China's internal politics. In April 1911, the Empire had borrowed £10 million from the British, French, German, and American banking consortium to support currency reform and economic development, and the debt did not disappear with the dynasty. In June 1912, Japan and Russia joined the consortium. Finance imperialism now presented a united front to China and monopolized China's access to the international money market. Yuan wanted large foreign loans, but the consortium insisted that he promise China's salt taxes as security and that the administration and collection of the salt tax be placed under a sino-foreign administration modeled on the Imperial Maritime Customs Service. Claiming that these conditions constituted a direct threat to China's independence, President Woodrow Wilson forced the American bankers to withdraw from the consortium. Nevertheless, in April 1913, after months of protracted negotiations, the remaining members of the consortium agreed to lend Yuan's government £25 million. This so-called reorganization loan consisted of bonds sold at ninety percent, from which six percent was the banks' commission. Therefore, China received only eighty-four percent of the loan but was obligated to pay the full principle plus five percent interest until 1960. In other words, China received only £21 million of a loan valued at £25 million but was obligated to repay nearly £68 million. This was only the beginning of accelerated imperialist incursions into postdynastic China.

Control of the Empire's borderlands began to slip from China's grasp. The republic maintained at least its nominal sovereignty over the Manchus' homeland in the northeast and over Inner Mongolia, where the railroad constructed between Peking and Kalgan in 1909 facilitated Chinese trade and agriculture in the region. Outer Mongolia, however, declared its independence from China in December 1911, and the government's troops in Lhasa, the capital of Tibet, were forced to withdraw in the wake of the 1911 revolution. Russia became the primary external influence in Mongolia and Britain in Tibet. Yuan Shikai paid for Russian and British recognition of his government on November 7, 1913, by accepting this situation. Russian, Outer Mongolian, and Chinese representatives negotiated a formula whereby China admitted Mongolian autonomy while Mongolia accepted nominal Chinese suzerainty. This left Russia a free hand in the area. The same formula was applied to Tibet in parallel Anglo-Chinese negotiations.

China also increasingly lost power over its own revenues. By November 1911, foreign commissioners were empowered to collect the customs revenues, which were now pledged for the repayment of foreign loans and indemnities and were transmitted directly to an international banking commission in Shanghai rather than indirectly through the government. In the treaty ports, particularly Shanghai, foreign power expanded to fill the vacuum left by the collapse of central authority. It was argued that these developments helped China: financially, the growth of foreign control over its revenues preserved China's international credit and the efficiency of revenue collection; domestically, the expansion of foreign power in the treaty ports improved municipal administration. However, a different gloss can be put on the situation: the expansion of foreign control over China's revenues and cities was utterly self-serving since the revenues went directly to the foreigners; moreover, maintenance of China's international credit status was in the interests of the imperialists, who could obtain whatever security from China they wanted for their loans.

With the outbreak of World War I, which diverted the attention of the European members of the Oikoumene from the Far East, Japan took over the field. China declared neutrality as soon as war broke out. Japan, however, declared war on Germany and thus claimed the right to land troops in Shandong province, Germany's sphere of influence. In November 1914 Japanese troops, with British help, captured Qingdao, the Chinese city that was the German administered port in Shandong. Now in occupation of the province, Japan placed its own military police in its railway zones. Japan quickly followed up its advantage in Shandong by presenting Yuan Shikai, on January 18, 1915, with what came to be known as the "Twenty-one Demands." These demands reflected the need of Japanese industrialists for foreign expansion, most conveniently into China. Japan's objective was the establishment and protection of the primacy of its interests in China. The demands, divided into five groups, had two primary foci. First, they staked out extended Japanese claims to dominance in specific geographical regions and over specific industries. Second, and more important, they called for the establishment of a system of Japanese advisors throughout the Chinese government, Japan's assumption of control over China's police, arsenals, and purchases of military equipment, and control over the development of Fujian province (opposite Formosa). In effect, Japan wanted to establish a protectorate over China. Yuan Shikai received no support from the Western members of the Oikoumene and had to face Japan alone. He succeeded in postponing a decision on the fifth set of demands, which outlined the protectorate, but was forced to agree to most of the others. On May 25, 1915, a series of treaties was signed and notes exchanged that formalized China's acquiescence to Japan's claims over territory and industry.

Inside China, the Japanese demands led to an angry nationalism that found expression in mass rallies, boycotts of Japanese goods, strikes, and shows of support for Yuan Shikai, who was known as an opponent of Japanese expansionism. At this moment, however, another and different foreign intrusion resulted in a strange, almost theatrical, entertainment. F. J. Goodnow, an American political scientist serving as Yuan's advisor on constitutions, proposed the reestablishment of the monarchy as insurance for China's survival. The throne, he believed, would unify the Chinese as neither republicanism nor democracy could. Yuan, who had his own imperial ambitions, ignored the qualifications that Goodnow had attached to his proposal and declared himself emperor in December 1915. This curious affair lacked all majesty and romance, and the attempted restoration came to naught. Yuan died on June 6, 1916. His own military supporters had begun to desert him and he had received no help from the foreigners, who may have feared the emergence of a strong government under his leadership. After all, Chinese weakness and disunity served the Oikoumene in China better than did strength and unity. Yuan's death marked the failure of both Empire and republic. Nevertheless, throughout the next decade and a half Peking and the Oikoumene together sustained the myth of the existence of a central Chinese government with power over the entire country. Western concepts of international relations required a government in China with which the Oikoumene could deal. The myth of a central government, therefore, served the interests of the foreign powers, but in reality China had become a decentralized society within an international system.

The Foreign Relations of a Decentralized Society

Yuan Shikai's failure to restore the throne, together with his death, removed the last impediment to the final devolution of real political power into the hands of local rulers. The period between 1916 and 1928, when the Guomindang, under Chiang Kaishek, established the Nationalist government at Nanjing, is usually called the "warlord period." This term emphasizes, of course, the argument that centralized unity is the natural state of Chinese society. A more useful model for understanding the international relations of this period, however, may be provided by Renaissance Europe. During the Renaissance, Europe consisted of numerous states of varying size, independent of each other in every practical way but joined in ever shifting alliances that covered the gamut of interstate relations, ranging from active cooperation to outright warfare. Over the whole of Western European society reigned emperor and pope. Each claimed his own prerogatives and engaged in conflicts with the other, but each personally ruled only limited territories as a participant in the same interstate system that embraced all the other states. Although each region of Europe had its own language or dialect and its own culture, the upper class, particularly its educated members (including the clergy), participated in a common European culture served by Latin.

With appropriate changes to account for geography and titles, and with the substitution of Mandarin Chinese and the Chinese written language for Latin, the same model that serves for Renaissance Europe can serve for China after the fall of the Qing dynasty. Indeed, many of the factors that worked for disunity and the survival of the interstate system in Renaissance Europe were at work in China in the first half of the twentieth century. Geographical constraints and the lack of modern means of communications encouraged polycentrism in the absence of a central authority strong enough to overcome the cultural, historical, social, and economic factors that led toward disunity. The difference between Europe and continental East Asia lay in the presence in China of a tendency toward unity that was sufficiently strong to overwhelm its negation for very significant periods of time, while in Europe the dominant tendency was toward disunity.

In China, the swing toward decentralization and fragmentation had become apparent after the middle of the nineteenth century, as the Empire wrestled with its declining fortunes and the new problems presented by the Oikoumene's strength. The Oikoumene, in fact, greatly inhibited the development of forces for unity within China after the death of Yuan Shikai. The Western powers already dominated different areas of the country, and their spheres of influence sometimes embraced whole provinces or more. Regions under Japan's sway became industrialized at a faster rate than, for example, British dominated Canton, and many areas of China escaped modernization almost completely.

The treaty ports, with their foreign concessions, also contributed to decentralization; they provided competitors for political power on both the regional and the national scene with sanctuaries from their opponents and with resources for building their strength. Finance imperialism was a further factor: neither central nor regional governments possessed sufficient tax bases to pay the costs of obtaining and possessing power. Consequently, the Oikoumene, particularly its constituent powers' banks, could prevent or encourage the growth of one or another contestant by withholding or granting loans, restructuring debt payments, and the like.

New ideas from the West that attacked the intellectual, emotional, and psychological supports of the traditional social system further encouraged decentralization. The modernist philosopher Hu Shi's "Ibsenism" placed the individual and his or her own interests above those of the family; Western education liberated youths from the control of their elders; anarchism called into question the traditional bonds that held sinitic society together; and Marxism constituted a different world from that of traditional Confucian and Western liberal constructions of reality and provided a basis for political action that offered hope for better lives to peasants who believed that tradition stood in the way of the improvement of their lot. The impact of imported ideas and ideologies was not uniform throughout China; traditionalism continued to be more powerful in some areas than in others. Finally, the availability to the warlords of Western arms contributed to decentralization by increasing their ability to wage war on each other and to maintain their positions within their regions.

The period 1912–1949 was extraordinarily confused and can only be summarized briefly here:

1912–1927. Numerous rulers, appearing and disappearing, were engaged in almost constant warfare with each other. Seizure of Peking, which would have allowed the visitor to participate in the myth of a central government and, therefore, to benefit from certain advantages of intercourse with the foreign powers, was one of the prizes sought in this warfare; another was survival. Although Sun Yat-sen and his followers tried to participate in the political and military activities of the early part of the period through alliance with the regional authority in the southeast, this attempt came to naught. However, both the Guomindang and the Communist Party became participants in the interstate system after 1921 by establishing territorial political power. The military dimension of both parties' organizational structure and activity derived from the fact that to pursue their objectives they themselves had to become like the warlords. Until 1927, the Guomindang and the Communists were in alliance, however uneasy. The Guomindang expanded its territorial control both through direct conquest and through alliances with other warlords.

1928–1936. The Guomindang dominated central and south China; for longer or shorter periods, the KMT asserted suzerainty over other areas and exercised an indirect influence, particularly in Manchuria and Xinjiang. The Nationalists succeeded in forcing the Communists to resort to the warlord strategy of building territorial political power and continued to use the instruments of an international system—treaties, agreements, or conquests—to maintain themselves inside China and to build an international position. In 1931, Japan, beginning in Manchuria, assumed by its aggression the role of another warlord on the Chinese scene.

1937–1945. By 1937, three primary groups were contending for power inside China: the Guomindang, under Chiang Kaishek, with a territorial and political base primarily in the Changjiang valley, the southeast, and the southwest; the Communists, who, after the Long March, were building their territorial and political base in the northwest; and the Japanese, who were expanding their territorial and political base from Manchuria down into Northeast China and along the coast, following the river valleys and railroads inland. This tripartite conflict was carried out primarily by military means, but it included considerable political interaction among the three groups. Victory in the struggle meant the ability to unify China in the interests of the victor. By the end of 1945, Japan was eliminated from the scene, and the two remaining powers, the Guomindang and the Communists, were left facing each other.

1946–1949. The polarization of Chinese politics that had been developing since 1928 reached its climax in this period, when the Nationalists and the Communists engaged in a protracted civil war, ending when the

Communists were victorious in 1949 and the Nationalists fled to the island of Taiwan.

Throughout this period, international relations were a principal and often decisive factor in the internal affairs of China. In fact, as often as not it is impossible to distinguish between the two. Foreign affairs and internal affairs, foreigners and Chinese, and Chinese overseas and Chinese at home all constituted a structure of symbiosis in which the demarcation between inside and outside was unclear.

The Treaty System and Treaty Revision

The scramble for spheres of influence and for concessions, finance imperialism, and the disappearance of effective central authority combined to change the context and, therefore, the meaning of the unequal treaty system. The treaty system consisted of a set of bilateral agreements between the Empire and foreign powers. In each case, the foreign power had recognized the Empire's sovereignty while the Empire had accepted limitations imposed on its sovereignty by the foreign power. The bilateralism characteristic of the treaty structure did not, however, reflect reality. The powers either competed with each other for preference in the Empire or cooperated with each other in pursuit of their mutual objectives; no power came to the aid of the Empire or, later, of China: even the American Open Door policy, which paid lip service to the Empire's integrity, had as its primary objective the inclusion of the United States in the China market. From the Empire's and China's point of view, therefore, bilateralism was largely a myth that reflected diplomatic practices required by the nation-state structures of the Oikoumene and their internal politics. The banking consortium clearly demonstrated the essential unity of the Oikoumene's approach to China, even if that unity sometimes took the form of competition. China, after all, did not gain from that competition; nor was China a party to it.

The myth of bilateralism allowed for the possibility of China's full recovery of its sovereignty, while the reality of the treaty system did not. Finance imperialists and foreign capitalist merchants could see nothing but disadvantages arising from abrogation of the treaty system, no matter when that might be accomplished.

The governments of the Oikoumene thus were caught in the tension between the myth inspired by their own legal fictions and a reality whose substance was defined and represented by their own bankers and citizens in China. But there was more: President Wilson had proclaimed the self-determination of peoples to be an objective of the Allied powers in World War I. To the structural tension was now added an ideological tension between the lofty idealism of that objective and a realistic assessment of its applicability to China. The Versailles peace conference and its aftermath did little to convince Chinese patriots of whatever political persuasion that anything but rank cynicism, however clothed in high-sounding phrases, governed Western policy toward China.

CHINA AT VERSAILLES

China declared war on Germany and Austria-Hungary on August 14, 1917, not out of any commitment to the Allied cause but, rather, for the gains one group of Chinese hoped to obtain thereby. Although Sun Yat-sen in the south opposed the move, the northern warlords believed that a declaration of war against the Central powers would bring them financial gain in the form of foreign aid, a hope encouraged by the American minister to China, Paul Reinsch. They also believed that such a declaration would provide them with a rationale for the expansion of their power to other areas of the country. The diplomats of the putative central government in Peking saw the declaration as the necessary means for their participation in international negotiations at the end of the war. While the Western powers sought China's entry into the war as a means to limit the scope of German and Austro-Hungarian activities, the Japanese saw in the possibility of internal disturbances resulting from opposition to Chinese participation in the war an opportunity for Japanese intervention. Tokyo's minister in Peking even went so far as to promise Japanese aid in suppression of local disturbances, a promise the Peking government did not receive happily.

China's declaration of war against the Central Powers occasioned the first real breach Peking was able to make in the relatively solid wall of the unequal treaty system. Given the new state of war, China declared:

> All treaties, agreements, (and) conventions, concluded between China and Germany and between China and Austria-Hungary, as well as such parts of the international protocols and international agreements as concern the relations between China and Germany and between China and Austria-Hungary are, in conformity with the law of nations and international practice, all abrogated.[5]

Technically, therefore, China recovered from Germany and Austria-Hungary those regions earlier surrendered to them within the context of the treaty system. Actually, of course, Japan already occupied the portion of China, in Shandong province, that Germany claimed as a sphere of influence. Nonetheless, the cancellation of the extraterritorial position enjoyed by German and Austro-Hungarian nationals in China was more than nothing. It was, however, less than something. The Allied powers were unwilling to see the German and Austro-Hungarian concessions revert to

Chinese control lest that impugn the legitimacy of their own positions; accordingly, they suggested that these be reorganized into international concessions, a suggestion the Chinese tried to reject.

Just before the end of the war, the Allied governments accused China of making less than adequate contributions to the war. Internal conflicts and seeking after advantage had, they said, taken precedence over the war effort. How the Allied powers could have expected China's devotion to the prosecution of a war that was primarily a fratricidal conflict among China's exploiters is not clear; nor is it clear how they could have expected other behavior from the China they knew. However, the accusation showed that the Oikoumenical powers had no intention of granting China a prominent role in the upcoming peace negotiations. Any lingering hopes concerning Allied intentions that an optimistic Chinese may have entertained would have been smashed when the Allied powers gave China only two seats at the peace conference; moreover, although permitted to appear before either the Council of Ten or the Council of Four, China could do so only as a petitioner and only upon invitation. China's position at Versailles was not strengthened by the fact that its delegation had to represent the two most significant centers of power in China's polycentric political system, the governments of both Peking and Canton. The delegation was united in its objectives, however: the abolition of extraterritoriality and other foreign rights and privileges in China; the restoration of urban concessions and leased territories to China's control; the abolition of the restrictions imposed on Chinese sovereignty by the Boxer Protocol; and the restoration of complete tariff autonomy to China. In short, the united Chinese delegation asked for the complete abrogation of the unequal elements of the sino-foreign treaty system.

The Versailles peace conference did not accede to China's wishes. The Chinese had laid great store by President Wilson's Fourteen Points, which they believed would be a basis for China's recovery of full sovereignty. However, while Wilson may have been committed idealistically to China's cause, his practical commitment was no match for the opposition of the other powers. Moreover, China's position encountered opposition within the American delegation itself. Paul Reinsch, the American minister to China, often criticized for having been too pro-Chinese, stated unequivocally:

> Unfortunately, there does not appear to be the determination to bring about that reform of China's judicial and administrative departments which alone would justify the abandonment of the peculiar privileges now enjoyed by foreign residents. Not only is the present provincial administration the worst since foreign intercourse with China first began, but even where China has had a special opportunity to demonstrate her fitness to assume the rights and duties which she claims, she has failed to do so.[6]

International equality and Woodrow Wilson's self-determination of peoples made nice theory, and lip service was paid these sentiments at Versailles and later. But China's equality with the Western powers was only a potential, and they declared that China had not yet earned its realization.

In the end, the Western powers proved unable to curb their Japanese ally's aggressive geographical, political, and economic expansion in China. Moreover, not only had they rejected China's claims at Versailles, but they had both publicly and secretly recognized Japan's. As a consequence, China refused to sign the Versailles treaty. Later, the United States refused to ratify it, partly, but only partly, for the same reason.

Political changes in Germany and the disappearance of Austria-Hungary prevented the restoration of those nations' extraterritorial positions in China. Indeed, German and Austrian merchants now found themselves without treaty privileges. Nor were they subject to the restrictions to which the treaty system formally subjected foreign nationals, restrictions that were, in practice, a dead letter anyway. Therefore, abrogation of Germany's and Austria-Hungary's privileges had less import than apologists for Western policy in the Far East claim. This was confirmed in June 1918, when a new Chinese-Swiss friendship treaty granted Swiss citizens in China extraterritorial privileges until such time as the other treaty powers agreed to the abolition of extraterritoriality. In April 1919, the Chinese unilaterally declared that nations not covered by the treaty system would have to accept equality as the basis for treaty relations with China. Nonetheless, a Chinese treaty with Bolivia signed in December 1919 contained the "most favored nation" clause. Bolivia was not about to breach the unity of the Oikoumene. However, given the fact that Bolivian citizens did not reside in China in significant numbers, China and Bolivia agreed, in an accompanying note, that the treaty's "most favored nation" clause did not mean that Bolivians in China had extraterritorial rights. Only in June 1920 did a Chinese-Persian treaty specifically exclude extraterritoriality and place Persian subjects involved in civil proceedings in China under the jurisdiction of Chinese law and Chinese courts.

China's refusal to sign the Treaty of Versailles occasioned an anachronistic act that demonstrated how slowly deeply ingrained patterns of thought and behavior disappear. The problem was: how was China to make peace with Germany outside the Versailles treaty? For an answer, Peking did what came naturally, and on September 15, 1919, an edict issued in the name of the President of the Chinese Republic (since there was no longer an emperor or a dynasty) declared simply that "the state of war between Germany and the Republic of China is at an end. Let all take note of this." The edict was issued unilaterally; China had undertaken no prior consultations with Germany. As the American chargé d'affaires remarked, the edict was "curiously reminiscent of the earliest days of foreign intercourse with China, when China quite genuinely assumed to regulate the affairs of the universe by Imperial Edict."[7]

THE CASE OF RUSSIA

The argument that the unequal treaty system was the structure whereby the Oikoumene imposed its collective will on the Empire and sustained its will against the republic is supported by reference to the behavior of the one major power that withdrew from the Oikoumene. Soviet Russia, born in the revolution of October 1917, declared that it was the harbinger of a new age in international affairs. The Soviet government gave reality to its declaration by eschewing the policies and privileges of the imperialists and by expelling foreign financial interests from Russian territory. Indeed, Soviet Russia itself was soon at war with the Oikoumene, which invaded its territories in the person of British, French, and Japanese interventionists, the latter under American "observation" on the ground in Siberia. The core members of the Oikoumene were following their natural propensity to defend themselves from potential threats to their interests by aggression against any power that rejected the world of the Oikoumene.

In spite of the Russian Revolution and the accession to power of a new government that declared itself very different from its predecessor, the putative national government in Peking continued to recognize the tsarist ambassador and his diplomatic and consular staff as the legal representatives of Russia in China. This situation continued until the end of September 1920. This meant that tsarist Russia's extraterritorial position in China, which, of course, was most significant in Northern Manchuria, continued as a legal-diplomatic fiction even though the governments that had negotiated the treaties no longer existed and even though Russia was no longer prepared to come to the aid of its citizens inside China should that have been necessary.

This state of affairs reflected neither reality nor logic. Moreover, in the increasingly nationalistic atmosphere that followed the Versailles conference, it would have been unreasonable to expect the Peking government to continue to acquiesce in it. On September 8, 1920, therefore, the Russian minister was informed that the Peking government no longer recognized the status of the tsarist Russian legation in Peking or of the Russian consulates elsewhere in China and expected their offices to be closed immediately. The U.S. reaction, as expressed by the American minister in China, betrayed more than a hint of paranoia: "This is the first tangible victory in China of the bolshevik emissaries who have been arriving in Peking of late from different parts of Russia." The U.S. State Department voiced fears that the action of the government in Peking might "lend itself to the construction that China is entertaining the proposals of the bolshe-

viks who are reported to be offering a renunciation of Russian treaty of
rights in China," and it further stated that the American government "feels
it to be an obligation of good faith towards Russia and of friendship towards
China to invite the attention of the Chinese government to the necessity
of so ácting as to not lay that government open to the charge of having
connived with the bolsheviks to violate or ignore the treaty rights of the
Russian people."[8]

The U.S. government's position reflected the peculiar assumption that
the acts of the tsarist government were more representative of the interests of the Russian people than were the acts of the new government; the
United States feared the consequences for extraterritoriality of Chinese
rejection of the claims of a government that, though it had ceased to exist,
had been a member of the Oikoumene. In this context, the Chinese action
must have appeared to Washington as a potential threat to the American
position in China. (The situation was complicated, of course, as antirevolutionary refugees fled to China and as antirevolutionary armed forces began to use Chinese territory as a base from which to attack the Soviets in
Siberia.) The foreign powers clearly recognized that the issue of Russian
representation provided Peking with an opportunity to assert its sovereignty. As one commentator put it, "The thin edge of the wedge, which
entered when China took over the German and Austrian concessions. . .
was now opening up a considerable breach in the old extraterritorial
rights."[9]

For a power that frequently proclaimed its concern for the preservation
of China's sovereignty and integrity and had declared one of its cardinal
policy objectives to be the self-determination of peoples, the United
States, in approaching the problem of Russian representation, showed remarkable disregard for China's interests. Time and again the Americans
attempted to protect extraterritoriality from potential ambiguities that
might arise from China's actions with regard to Russian claims. Peking
rejected an American proposal that the Oikoumenical powers establish an
international trusteeship to take over and protect Russia's rights and interests. The U.S. State Department then proposed that the legal interests of
Russians in China be dealt with institutionally in a setting similar to the
mixed court in Shanghai, a proposal the Chinese considered unnecessary
since China had no intention of denying individual Russians their rights.

In the end, the complete victory of the Russian Communists and shifting political configurations inside China made the Oikoumenical powers'
argument outdated: there was no longer a Russia whose interests in China
needed championing. Nevertheless, China's action removed some 300,000
Russians resident in China from the protection of extraterritorial privileges. It also left the status of Russian possessions on Chinese territory,
such as the Chinese Eastern Railway, ambiguous, particularly in view of

Soviet offers in 1919 and 1920 to surrender unilaterally the privileges claimed by the defunct tsarist regime.

THE WASHINGTON CONFERENCE

The relationships of various powers in the Far East clearly needed to be restructured in light of these unsettling shifts of power and the continuing absence of a strong central authority in China to protect imperialist interests. The United States called a conference (November 12, 1921 to February 2, 1922) to reorganize the treaty system and stabilize the international situation in the Far East. Belgium, China, France, Great Britain, Italy, Japan, and the Netherlands—were invited to Washington. Soviet Russia, despite its obvious interests in the region, was not; Moscow could only observe from a distance through an unofficial delegation from the Far Eastern Republic, a theoretically autonomous regime established by the Soviets in Eastern Siberia.

The participants adopted the American objectives for the conference, pledging themselves in the first article of the Nine-Power Treaty "to respect China's sovereignty, independence, and territorial and administrative integrity"; to provide China with the best opportunities for development of "an effective and stable government"; to establish and maintain equal commercial and industrial opportunity for all countries everywhere in China; and, finally, to maintain a common front in China for the equal advantage of the citizens of all "friendly states" and the security "of such states."[10] It is striking, in view of these objectives and American professions of concern for China's sovereignty and integrity, that the issue of extraterritoriality appeared nowhere on the agenda. The Chinese delegation, of course, fully expected the question to be raised.

The Washington conference issued stirring words concerning China and its development, but the powers had no intention of surrendering any of their privileges and did not do so. The true American position was perhaps best expressed by the American minister at Peking, Jacob Schurman, who cabled to the American secretary of state:

> Even were Government thoroughly reformed extra-territoriality should not be abolished till China has not merely adopted modern codes and procedure but developed sound habits of judicial administration and practice which would prevent return to system of delay, improper influence, squeeze and corruption all but universal today.[11]

That modernization and stabilization really meant westernization of China's legal system and practices was suggested by the American consul in Nanjing:

In Kiangsu, which is one of the leading provinces of China, and in the famous city of Nanking itself, it is impossible for American interests to receive justice at the hands of the so-called reformed judiciary. The judge who has rendered the decisions quoted is not an old style, ignorant, Mandarin, but a man who received his legal training in Japan.[12]

Besides avoiding any action that would modify, much less abolish, the inequality imposed upon China by the treaty system, the Oikoumenical powers regulated their own relationships in the Far East. The Anglo-Japanese alliance, which had failed to serve Britain's intention to constrain Japanese action, was abrogated and not replaced. The powers agreed to limit naval armaments on the basis of the famous "five-five-three ratio," which gave an apparent advantage to Great Britain and the United States over Japan. One provision of this particular agreement inhibited the development of any new British or American naval bases west of Hawaii or east of Singapore; this stipulation gave Japan some sense of security for its newly acquired (formerly German) island possessions in the Pacific north of the equator but clearly established Anglo-American superiority on the China coast. This superiority was further reinforced by Japan's agreement to end its occupation of Shandong province and to withdraw from Eastern Siberia, the Maritime province, and Northern Manchuria, where Japanese forces had been sent as part of the Oikoumenical intervention in the Russian Revolution. Japan retained its primary interest only in Southern Manchuria, Korea, and Taiwan. These agreements, taken together, represented a successful maneuver on the part of the Western powers, primarily the United States and Great Britain, to deny Japan the advantages it had gained since 1905, including all those that resulted from Japan's adherence to the Allied cause in World War I, and to reestablish the *status quo ante* in China. Japan proceeded to withdraw from Shandong and Britain, eventually, from Weihaiwei; China recovered possession of the port of Qingdao.

The Washington conference called for a tariff conference to modify the system of foreign control over Chinese tariff collections and revenues. Meeting in Peking on October 26, 1925, the powers came to no agreement, suggesting only that under suitable conditions China might lay claim to tariff autonomy by 1929. The Washington conference also had provided for the establishment of a commission on extraterritoriality in China, which finally met in Peking on January 12, 1926, to investigate China's legal administration and judicial system in order to recommend changes the Oikuomenical powers would find acceptable. This session also produced no results. The Oikoumene's protestations of interest in furthering China's economic development also proved empty when, in 1920 and afterward, the United States was unable to reestablish the international banking consortium for the purpose of extending aid to China.

SOME TREATY SYSTEM MODIFICATIONS

Whether failure to modify the unequal treaty system at the Washington conference and the two subsequent Peking conferences reflected the Oikoumene's unwillingness or inability to find grounds for common action is a matter of opinion; the consequences for China were the same in either case. Certainly the absence of a central authority and the presence of chaotic conditions in warlord China were major factors influencing the Oikoumene. As the Chinese Revolution proceeded and Chiang Kaishek and the Guomindang moved toward national unification, whose achievement was symbolized by both the capture of Peking in June 1928 and the general international recognition accorded the Nanjing regime by the end of the year, some significant modifications of the treaty system began to develop. It must be noted, of course, that these modifications represented a form of support by the foreign powers for the new Nationalist regime.

Growing nationalism in China, however, helped force the Oikoumenical powers to concede greater participation to the Chinese in the processes of their own society. For example, after the May Thirtieth movement, a national wave of strikes, demonstrations, and boycotts that developed when British police in Shanghai killed thirteen anti-imperialist demonstrators, Shanghai's municipal council was expanded to include Chinese representatives, municipal parks were opened to Chinese residents, and the Shanghai mixed court was replaced by a Chinese district court with jurisdiction over Chinese citizens. In Canton, the powers permitted the Chinese to collect customs dues, and in Hankou and Jiujiang the British surrendered their concessions when Chinese occupied them in 1927. Very slowly but surely, the powers were teaching the Chinese that the Oikoumene would surrender privileges only if threatened with violence.

The success of the Nationalists' "northern expedition," the military campaign that was intended to unify the country politically and administratively, led, in the middle of 1928, to a Sino-American tariff treaty that recognized the new Nanjing government. Under this government, particularly under the leadership of an American educated elite, China took steps to prepare for the recovery of its rights, that is, the end of extraterritoriality. By 1930, with the help of American advisors, China succeeded in negotiating new treaties removing the citizens of many minor powers from extraterritoriality; however, these successes were somewhat hollow since no Peruvians and only sixteen Brazilians were living in China at the time. Still, serious advances were made on other fronts: by 1933, the Nanjing government had recovered full tariff autonomy and control over maritime customs, the salt revenue administration (which maintained a state monopoly over the sale of salt), and the post office; in the same period, the number of foreign concessions was reduced from thirty-three to thirteen.

China's rapid progress in modifying the unequal treaty system slowed in the 1930s as a consequence of Japanese aggression against China. The Nanjing government, pressed in Northern and Eastern China by Japan, felt at first that the foreign concessions and the extraterritorial privileges enjoyed by foreigners helped protect Chinese interests against the Japanese. After 1937, the situation deteriorated as Japanese military action spilled over into foreign concessions, damaged foreign property, and endangered and injured the citizens of foreign powers. In December 1938, for example, the American ambassador to Japan protested some two to three hundred cases of Japanese bombings of American property in China, and in March 1939 he again protested at least twenty-nine new attacks on American lives and property. To compound the difficulty, Japan established its own puppet governments in Manchuria in 1932, in Peking in 1937, and in Nanjing in 1940. The latter, which was intended to be the national government of the Republic of China and to subsume other governments in China Proper, excluding Manchuria, initially was recognized only by Japan and Manchuria. Japan attempted to provide the puppet regime in Nanjing with legitimacy by having it adopt the Guomindang flag, by establishing the same form of government that the Guomindang had set up under Chiang Kaishek, and by appointing as president Wang Qingwei, a former leading member of the Nationalists' Nanjing government. Japan's intention was now clear. Tokyo planned to use this "legal" Chinese regime to expel all powers other than Japan itself from China. By the time of the Japanese attack on Pearl Harbor on December 7, 1941, extraterritoriality and the treaty system had become virtually inoperative under conditions of Japanese occupation. Only Great Britain and the United States were in a position to oppose Japan. France had been defeated, and Italy and Germany were Japan's allies.

THE END OF THE UNEQUAL TREATY SYSTEM

By the end of 1941, twelve countries, all of them associated with, or occupied by, Germany or Japan, had recognized the puppet Nanjing government. Operating as Japan's agent, Nanjing, for example, negotiated with the German sponsored Vichy regime in France and recovered jurisdiction over some one million Chinese and twenty-five thousand foreigners who had been under French protection in the French concessions. This agreement also gave the Nanjing regime control over the courts, which meant that American citizens residing in the concessions now came under Japanese authority through the jurisdiction of the puppet Nanjing government.

Faced, on the one hand, with the increasing meaninglessness of treaty privileges in China, and, on the other, with the necessity to bolster Chinese opposition to Japanese aggression, the British government proposed, in April 1942, that London and Washington begin negotiations with Chiang Kaishek's government to abolish extraterritoriality. A tripartite declaration was issued on October 10, China's national day, announcing the start of the negotiations. A treaty relinquishing extraterritorial rights was signed in Washington on January 11, 1943; in notes exchanged with the treaty, the United States gave up many special rights it had acquired over time, including those enjoyed by American vessels along China's inland waterways.[13]

On January 9, 1943, in light of the imminent conclusion of the new treaty, the puppet Nanjing government declared war on both the United States and Great Britain and signed an agreement with Japan whereby all foreign concessions and settlements in China, including the Japanese, were supposedly returned to Chinese control. The two governments also announced their intention to achieve the early abolition of Japanese extraterritorial privileges. The Japanese now proceeded to turn over foreign concessions, including their own, to the puppet regime; by the middle of 1943, Italy and Vichy France had signed similar agreements with the Nanjing regime. Thus, both sides in World War II found it useful, if only for propaganda reasons, to put an end to the unequal treaty system. For both the Allied and the Axis powers, the action was, for the moment, meaningless. Because the Japanese occupied significant areas of China, the Allied powers were unable to exercise their treaty privileges; because of that same occupation, Japan was able to establish a puppet regime in Nanjing with which it could negotiate an end to the unequal treaty system as a means of reinforcing the apparent legality of its own privileged position in China. By 1945, the system had become obsolete, and by 1947 its last legal vestiges had disappeared with the conclusion of a series of treaties between China and those countries that previously had enjoyed the privileges accorded by the treaty system. By this time, China was in the final throes of its revolution and rejection of the Oikoumene.

Finance Imperialism

The new, nonterritorial form of imperialism that emerged in the years just before World War I, after the scramble for colonies in Africa and certain parts of Asia was over, depended upon financial penetration of another society, as we have seen, and was the outreach of the most highly developed form of capitalism. Finance imperialism required that the institutions and policies of a country become dependent upon external financing, which meant, of course, external control; it also required that the dependent country ideologically recognize as natural both the role foreign capital played in its national development and the structure of the relationship the foreign powers maintained with it. (Indeed, the ideologists and practitioners of capitalism display a seemingly mortal fear of Marxist theory and practice precisely because it provides both an alternative analysis of the relationship between imperialist powers and semicolonial countries and potentially an alternative approach to development.)

Yuan Shikai's dependence upon foreign loans, discussed earlier, fitted the model of finance imperialism. Non-Marxist revolutionaries, primarily Sun Yat-sen and his followers, also adopted the prescriptions of finance imperialism for China. Sun published his own plan for economic reformation entitled, in English, *The International Development of China*. He accepted as natural, and called for, foreign investments throughout China. Sun wanted foreign capital to construct a railroad network that would cover the country. He had no difficulty accepting the idea of financial control of China by foreigners as necessary and valuable for Chinese economic development. It is important to note that Sun Yat-sen understood imperialism in almost purely political terms; he did not see the connection between imperialism and capitalism. He opposed the political oppression of one nation by another, but he did not understand the Marxist concept of class struggle, either as a factor internal to a given country or as a factor in international relations. This attitude was shared by his followers; indeed, it was fostered by the imperialists themselves, who were then, as they are today, prepared to welcome national political independence as long as the nation achieving independence would remain economically dependent upon one or another of the Oikoumene's core nations. Sun Yat-sen's concept of the relationship between foreign capital and internal development strongly influenced the economic policies of the Nanjing regime after 1928, no doubt both because it was politically advantageous for the leadership and because it was accepted theoretically by the regime's financial and economic experts, many of whom had received their training in the United States. There is no necessary relationship between capitalism and democracy, so it should cause no surprise that Nanjing's models of development were not the advanced capitalist democratic states like the United States and Great Britain but, rather, Japan, Nazi Germany, and the Soviet Union. Indeed, the Guomindang's own concept of a "tutored democracy" must have made those three countries even more attractive as potential models for China.

However, the Nanjing regime never had sufficient control over China's economy to promote serious economic growth. The League of Nations provided China with technical support in fields like public health and flood control, but the resources necessary for genuine economic development were lacking. The Oikoumene after 1929 was overwhelmed by its own economic crises and could not help China even if it had wanted. The question of Oikoumenical intentions remains, since economic development might have rendered China less attractive as a source of cheap labor or as a controllable market.

Under the Nanjing regime, the foreign banks located in the treaty ports remained the primary source of financing for foreign trade. More important from the point of view of China's economic development, they were the principal repository for the private capital of those groups in China that had funds available for saving, such as businessmen, high military officers, higher level bureaucrats, and politicians. In Shanghai alone, the foreign banks sometimes controlled more than half the available silver in an economy whose primary medium of exchange was silver. Moreover, some of these banks were of sufficient size and independence to issue their own currencies. The British-owned Hong Kong and Shanghai Banking Corporation was the largest foreign bank in the country; its capital had increased tenfold between 1864 and 1930, and it had reserves of 100 million Hong Kong dollars (equal to $50 million) and assets of ten times that sum. This fund represented an immense amount of financial power in a society at China's level of economic development. In addition, China's customs and salt revenues were, as noted, assigned to foreign debt payment. Privately owned Chinese banks simply could not compete, and the Nanjing government, which had foregone revenues from land taxes in order to purchase support from provincial authorities, was capital poor. The government owned four major banks, which dominated the Chinese banking scene, but they were no real match for the local representatives of foreign finance capital.

Nonetheless, under the imaginative leadership of the highly influential T. V. Soong, the first manager of the Central Bank of China (established in 1924 at Canton), who was the minister of finance of the Nanjing government until 1933, the government carried out reforms of the currency system and succeeded in obtaining tariff autonomy. China readjusted its foreign debts, increased its customs revenues, and carried out similar reforms, so that for a time it was able to maximize the advantages of even a limited economic base. However, since land taxes were unavailable to the government and it did not possess the mechanisms to insure itself a significant source of domestic income, the Nanjing regime had to rely for fifty percent of its annual income upon revenues that derived from precisely that economic sector most dependent upon foreign relations, the maritime customs service. The internal taxes the government did control (mostly consumption taxes) were highly regressive and, therefore, a source of real and potential difficulty within the country. So insufficient were these revenues that the government had to borrow approximately twenty-five percent of its annual expenditures from the four banks it itself owned, and by the mid-1930s service on foreign and domestic debts consumed about one-third of the government's annual expenditures.

Still, some progress was made. By assigning Chinese revenues to the construction of railroads and using foreign sources to purchase equipment, China began to participate in the ownership of its own railroads. Total railroad mileage in China amounted to roughly ten thousand miles in 1935, hardly sufficient for the country, particularly since about one-third of this service was in Manchuria under Japanese control. The government built about fifty thousand miles of roads suitable for motor transport, but the very wealthy southwestern province of Sichuan was still joined to the rest of China largely by river transportation (and in the mid-1930s some forty percent of China's total tonnage flew the British flag).

The deep penetration of Chinese society by finance imperialism is well illustrated by the Nishihara loans. Duan Qirui, the warlord from the Changjiang province of Anhui who was premier in 1917 and again in 1918 and who was primarily responsible for the Chinese declaration of war on Germany in August 1917, borrowed great sums of money from Japan in order to finance the warfare by means of which he conducted his domestic politics. These so-called Nishihara loans were borrowed on the pretense of the war with Germany. However, the loans actually provided the basis for an alliance between Duan and Japan, which meant that he received Japanese military advisors and benefited from the political support of Japanese politicians and pro-Japanese Chinese politicians. Just as Duan was trying to use Japan and its military and financial resources to establish his own power inside China, so the Japanese were obviously using him to establish themselves there. The Nishihara loans, totaling about 188 million Chinese dollars, were given to Duan without security. Admittedly, this was not common international banking practice, but it did show the extent to which the Japanese were prepared to use finance capital directly to influence internal Chinese politics.

Foreign Trade and Foreign Aid

Although the Oikoumenical powers tried to maximize their economic advantages in China during the period of polycentrism, China's foreign trade remained at a low *per capita* level and, in fact, declined during the period. In the 1920s the foreign trade of China Proper may have amounted to approximately $2.00–$2.50 per capita in value, but by the mid-1930s, in the midst of the worldwide depression, this had declined to about $1.00, or six to eight percent of the estimated gross national product.[14]

Foreign trade was the obvious link between the internal economy and the rest of the world and therefore is considered by some a factor contributing to the drive to modernize China's economy. But between 1921 and 1937 the annual value of imports exceeded, often significantly, that of the value of exports, so that China's foreign trade produced a consistently unfavorable balance of trade. This accounts, however, only for trade that was officially recorded. After the Nationalist government succeeded in raising import duties and, eventually, in recovering tariff autonomy, smuggling increased remarkably; one estimate suggests that in 1935, for example, the total value of imports into China was twenty-five percent greater than that reported, with smuggling accounting for the difference. With Japanese expansion in China after 1937, smuggling into Chinese controlled parts of the country became significantly easier and greater.

Although the country's foreign trade remained largely in foreign hands, financing through the Bank of China, with branches in London, New York, Singapore, and Hong Kong, increased China's share in its own trade. Basic foreign goods, foodstuffs, and raw materials could be sold more cheaply, particularly in coastal areas, than comparable Chinese products because inland transportation costs were high. This made much of China's nascent industry in the treaty ports and along the coast dependent upon foreign rather than domestic supplies. A typical semi-colonial economy, China exported mostly agricultural and mineral products.

The distribution of China's foreign trade among its major partners shifted significantly during the period in question. Trade with the British Empire, including both Great Britain and Hong Kong, fell from 42.5 percent of China's total foreign trade in 1921 to 27.8 percent in 1937, and China's trade with Japan fell between the same years from 24.9 to 12.9 percent. On the other hand, China's trade with the United States increased from 17.3 to 23.7 percent and with Europe from 5.9 to 21.5 percent. China's trade with Japan is particularly interesting in light of the special role Japan played in China. The drop in Japan's portion of China's foreign trade from 24.9 percent in 1921 to 12.9 percent in 1937 is explained by the fact that after Manchuria became the independent puppet state of Manchukuo in 1931, trade with Manchuria was eliminated from China's customs statistics. In addition, increasing anti-Japanese sentiment in China led to boycotts, while rising tariff rates encouraged smuggling of Japanese goods, particularly from Formosa, so close to the China coast. Consequently, Japan's real portion of China's foreign trade was much larger than the official statistics indicate. At the same time, Japanese figures suggest that Japan's trade with China constituted approximately one-fifth of Japan's total foreign trade; this was second only to Japan's trade with the United States. In this, as in other areas, Japan occupied a special position vis-à-vis China.[15]

TRADE AND INDUSTRY

Foreign investment and trade affected Chinese industrial development in two significant ways. First, traditional Chinese handicraft industries could not compete with the modern sector of the economy, and the former's share of the country's industrial production declined. Second, foreign investments became the single most important factor in the development and control of modern industry. Transportation, communications, utilities, and services were all largely in the hands of foreign capital. Foreign capital accounted for about 1/3 of the cotton industry's product in 1933, and in that same year foreign-owned companies accounted for about thirty-five percent of China's total industrial production. Statistics for 1933 concerning factories throughout China, including Manchuria, employing more than thirty people and using power, show that foreign investment controlled more than fifty percent of the industry in woodworking, transportation, water, gas, and electricity; more than twenty-five percent of machine tool production, electrical instruments, bricks, earthenware, chemicals, textiles, paper, and printing; and almost twenty-five percent of leather and rubber production. Moreover, most modern industry was concentrated in the treaty ports, which offered many advantages, including greater security and better communications. This uneven distribution of industry in the country was paralleled by an undue emphasis on consumer production, not on the heavy industry that was necessary for the healthy development of the Chinese economy. Under these conditions, industrial development by and large had a negative impact on the country's economic independence, perpetuating finance imperialism and semicolonialism.

RAILWAYS

By the mid-1920s, China, including Manchuria, had only 7,683 miles of railroad, some sixty percent of which had been built by foreign capital. The existing railways mostly served the heavily populated and more advanced regions of the country, and they were more profitable than manpowered wheeled vehicles for the transportation of goods. Only man-powered canal and river boats were competitive. Of course, the railroads were often commandeered by the warlords, which increased both cost and depreciation. While important lines of considerable length were built between the mid-1920s and the mid-1930s with Chinese provincial capital, supported by central government resources after 1928, most of the new railway mileage was constructed with foreign capital; this was the case both in Manchuria, where Russian and Japanese investment predominated, and in China Proper. In China Proper alone, in the decade 1928–1937, railway mileage increased forty-seven percent, or by about twenty-three hundred miles. Foreign capital not only participated in railway construction but also financed China's purchases abroad of rolling stock; for example, the Export-Import Bank was prepared to aid the purchase of locomotives, and European capital was deeply involved in financing railroad development.

ROADS

In 1920 China possessed about one hundred miles of motor roads outside its cities. As a consequence of various foreign interests, including those of famine relief workers who needed to transport goods to stricken areas, the quantity of roads suitable for motor traffic had increased by the outbreak of the Sino-Japanese War in the mid-1930s to sixty-nine thousand miles, including motor roads in Manchuria and Mongolia. Another forty thousand miles of road were under construction or projected. By and large, construction radiated out from Shanghai, the country's most important entrepôt and the area most securely under Guomindang control. However, the China International Famine Relief Commission, with American aid, provided considerable support for the construction between Xian and Lanzhou in the northwest of a five hundred-mile highway, which was necessary both for the transport of relief goods to an especially impoverished area and for the passage of military supplies. Generally, foreign capital did not participate directly in road building. Aside from relief work, which required movement of goods and personnel to communities beyond the regions that most interested foreign capital, there was little incentive for foreign investment in this area.

AIRLINES

In contrast to road construction, the development of aviation as a means of transportation was of great interest to both Chinese and foreigners precisely because aircraft could reach quickly parts of the country that were inaccessible by railroad or motor road. China is an early example of the way in which the provision of air transport in developing countries surpasses in importance the construction of railways and motor roads. Today, the airplane is the only means of access to large parts of developing countries (a condition that is becoming increasingly characteristic of North America as well).

In the years before the establishment of the Nanjing government, Chinese attempts to develop civil aviation were hindered by warlords who seized planes for their own purposes. Immediately after the establishment of the Nationalist government, however, airlines became a focus of great interest. In 1929, Sun Yat-sen's son, Sun Fo, who was railway minister, signed a contract with the Curtis group for air services, and, after some initial bureaucratic competition, the minister of communications in 1930 concluded a ten-year contract for the establishment of the China National Aviation Corporation (CNAC), of which American private interest owned forty-five percent and the Chinese government fifty-five percent. The Americans participated directly in the management of the corporation, appointing a vice-president, the manager of operations, and assistant managers for business and finance. In 1933, Pan American Airways took over the entire operation, which was losing money, and turned CNAC into a profitable enterprise. Americans continued to dominate both operations and management, and when Chinese pilots began to be trained they were American-born Chinese; native-born Chinese were largely restricted to service as ground personnel, mechanics, and radio operators. Chinese penetration into the upper levels of flight and management activity proceeded slowly.

American capital was not alone in the development of Chinese aviation. In 1931, the Chinese Ministry of Communications and the German Lufthansa established the Eurasia Aviation Corporation, with the Germans appointing one-third of the board of directors. Although Eurasia was intended to serve the international market, international political conditions made it a primarily internal airlines. In 1936, the Japanese forced the Chinese authorities in the northeast to agree to the establishment of the Huitung Air Navigation Company, which served Tianjin, Peking, Manchukuo, and Japan. However, Chinese passengers and businesses tended to boycott this completely Japanese owned and operated company.

The magnitude of foreign participation in the development of Chinese aviation led to a growing demand for nationalization of the companies, but the outbreak of the Sino-Japanese War forestalled this step, and complete Chinese control of the country's air transportation industry had to await the Communists' victory in 1949.

FOREIGN INVESTMENT

Although both Sun Yat-sen and Chiang Kaishek tried to avoid foreign political control of China and to recover China's sovereignty from the unequal treaty system, the record of foreign participation in the development of Chinese foreign trade, industry, and transportation shows the degree to which foreign capital not only aided but also managed and controlled China's development. Government policy insisted that China or its citizens own at least half of any enterprise in which foreign capital was invested and that a majority of the directors of such enterprises be Chinese. At least three major conditions modified that policy. First, it could not apply to those areas under the sanction of the treaty system, such as the treaty ports and foreign concessions, which were the primary centers of development in the modern sector of the economy. Second, formal ownership and formal membership on boards of directors, described in percentage or majority terms, did not insure that management and policymaking were in the hands of the Chinese owners or directors. Third, Chinese ownership or membership on boards of directors did not necessarily affect the conditions imposed on firms by foreign investors.

The China Consortium, organized in 1920 on the initiative of the Americans and composed of banking groups from Great Britain, France, the United States and Japan, was a major instrument for the penetration of China by Oikoumenical finance capital after the conclusion of World War I. Like previous consortia, this association sought to diminish national rivalries, to promote cooperation among the participating powers, and to prevent any particular nation's banks or any other banking group from obtaining advantages in China. Japan's participation occasioned special conditions. Although Tokyo was unsuccessful in its attempt to exclude Manchuria and Mongolia from the consortium's sphere of operations, the other powers agreed that the South Manchurian Railway and its subsidiary enterprises, such as mines, timber concessions, and certain branch or smaller railways, would not come within the scope of the consortium's activities. Moreover, the United States and Great Britain guaranteed that no operations would be undertaken that were "inimical to the vital interests of Japan."[16] The consortium had hoped that a Chinese counterpart would be established with which it could cooperate, but experience had taught the Chinese that the consortium was, in fact, a financial monopoly and that it might behave in China as had its predecessors and become one of the contending players in the Chinese political and economic game. Consequently, the consortium was unable to find a market for the loans it proposed, although it was able to prevent some other transactions from taking place.

The consortium remained in existence despite its inability to overcome Chinese opposition. When, for example, the U.S. government extended cotton and wheat credits to China in 1933, Japanese and British finance capitalists complained that the American action was contrary to the consortium's spirit and interests. By the mid-1930s, conditions in China had stabilized to the point that the consortium was the instrument of interpower negotiations over the extension of financial aid to China. At the time, the Nanjing government was thinking about issuing public loans; when, at the beginning of 1937, British finance capitalists were considering the construction of railroads in southeast China, the consortium's Japanese members indicated that Japan wanted to participate in the project. Obviously, in 1937 Japan's policies in China did not favor the extension of another power's interest in an area that Japan was likely to occupy. The Japanese government went so far as to discuss the matter with the Ministry of Railways in Nanjing and the provincial authorities in Canton. Not surprisingly, however, Japan's actions in Manchuria and the activities of its armed forces in North China foreclosed any Japanese participation in railway construction elsewhere in China. The Americans and the French also agreed to exclude themselves from the railway project, and the British alone signed an agreement for the loan in August 1937. The British now proposed the dissolution of the consortium, for two reasons. First, it had proved itself a vehicle for possible Japanese participation in investment projects, and the other powers, with their rising suspicions about Japanese intentions, did not want this. In the 1920s the consortium's goal had been to protect each power's interests by including all the powers, but this arrangement now was a danger, and the exclusion, not the inclusion, of Japanese financial interests had come to be preferred. Second, the British recognized that the consortium had become "an obstacle which stood in the way" of Chinese economic progress and that, therefore, it played into Japanese hands. The United States opposed the dissolution of the consortium, possibly because its own internal economic weakness at the time would have made it hard to maintain the American position in China outside the control of international cooperation.[17]

The China Development Finance Corporation (CDFC) grew out of T. V. Soong's hope to create an alternative to the consortium as a source of finance for China's development. Jean Monnet, who was later to be the architect of the European Common Market, visited China to help Soong plan the CDFC. The corporation came into existence in the middle of 1934, despite strong Japanese protests against the extension of non-Japanese aid, both financial and technical, to China. Early indications suggest that had the Sino-Japanese War and World War II not intervened, the CDFC would have been a major factor in bringing together Chinese and foreign capital under Chinese control. However, survival, not development, became the national objective once war broke out.

The national and geographical distribution of foreign investment in China prior to the outbreak of the Sino-Japanese War demonstrates clearly the way in which sino-foreign interaction served the interests of the capitalist Oikoumene. Business investment accounted for seventy-nine percent of the total foreign investment in the country; government obligations accounted for the remainder. The heaviest investment took place in transportation, followed by foreign trade, manufacturing, real estate, and banking. Geographically, foreign investments were located mainly in the treaty ports and the open ports, primarily Shanghai. Outside these areas, foreign capital dominated or occupied the leading position in coal and iron mining, electric power, and cigarette production. It is important to note that this does not mean that Chinese enterprises did not prosper. In 1933, for example, Chinese firms produced sixty-five percent of the gross value in manufacturing. What it does mean is that foreign capital dominated the field, both because of its concentration in a few firms and because of its greater fluidity. Of the total foreign investment in China, some thirty-seven percent was British, thirty-five percent Japanese, and six percent American; Russian investment, mostly in the Chinese Eastern Railway, accounted for eight percent, but this interest was liquidated when the railroad was sold to Japan in 1935. Although investment in China constituted a relatively small portion of the total foreign investment of the other major powers, it accounted for four-fifths of Japan's overseas investment, which is explained by Japan's concentration on Manchuria.[18]

FOREIGN CREDITS

While foreign investment in China may be defined as foreign ownership of a source of income and profit inside China, regardless of whether the foreigner lives in China or abroad, foreign credits can be understood as the provision of funds for the construction, modernization, or improvement of the country's transportation—particularly railway—and industrial infrastructure.[19] Obviously, foreign credits are a source of profit to the individual, institution, or government extending them, but they may be distinguished from other forms of foreign investment by virtue of their concentration in infrastructural growth and the relatively long term of return on them. By the mid-1930s, the largest private investment in railways, for example, came from Germany, and the British, French, Belgians, and Czechoslovaks followed closely behind. The Germans invested in raw materials, equipment, and railway construction. Their loan was secured, in the traditional fashion, with the revenues and assets of the Zhejiang-Jiangxi Railway. Germans also engaged in the construction of railway bridges and the provision of industrial and military supplies and equipment. Goods were delivered on terms of repayment that extended interest over a considerable period. The terms of repayment included barter arrangements whereby China provided Germany with raw materials, including tungsten, that were important for Hitler's rearmament of Germany. However, as Germany's alliance with Japan grew after 1936, German support of Chinese development, particularly military development, declined rapidly. British and other foreign investments continued to grow until the outbreak of the war blocked them.

In 1937, H. H. Kung, minister of finance after T. V. Soong, visited the United States and Europe to encourage the continuation and growth of investment at a time when China was beginning to be sorely pressed by Japan. In England to attend the coronation of King George VI, he tried to borrow British pounds in order to re-fund his government's internal indebtedness. On the one hand, this strategy implied an increased foreign participation in China's internal finances; on the other, London's interest rates were considerably lower than China's and Kung hoped to save considerable funds by this maneuver. The British were prepared to make a somewhat smaller loan than he requested, but they specified certain conditions, including continued foreign administration of the customs service and greater employment of foreign personnel in it; finally, consultation with a British advisor was required before the loan proceeds could be used. In the end, the outbreak of war prevented the loan from going through, and when, in the early 1940s, the British proposed similar conditions for a wartime loan, the Chinese claimed that the conditions were colonial in nature.

In the United States, minister Kung made arrangements with the American secretary of the treasury, Henry Morgenthau, for the purchase of large amounts of silver. He also made arrangements to draw upon gold owned by the Chinese but held in the United States. Action on his proposals for capital loans, however, was postponed because of the political and military situation in the Far East.

These and similar activities represented a remarkable shift of initiative in sino-foreign economic relations. Until the early 1930s, the Western powers and their bankers had pressed loans upon China or responded with alacrity to Chinese requests for loans, because control of China's financial structure was both a source of security and a promise of profits. After the early 1930s, however, as the Nanjing regime was overwhelmed by internal development problems in the face of its inability to raise revenues within the country and as the pressure of Japanese military action mounted toward a formal outbreak of hostilities, the Chinese government became aggressive in its search for foreign credits. At the same time, the major powers became more wary in their responses. However, this shift concerned only the source of initiative; the structure that gave the foreigners direct control over significant portions of the Chinese economy had not changed since the end of the nineteenth century.

RELIEF AND REHABILITATION

In 1931, the Changjiang flooded to such an extent that it may have been not only the greatest flood in Chinese history but "the greatest flood in historical record." Sixty-five thousand square miles were badly flooded, and another five thousand were flooded somewhat less seriously, leaving a damage area greater than England, or about the same size as New York, New Jersey, and Connecticut combined. Some twenty-five million people were affected by the flood, thousands drowned, and millions were forced to leave their home areas at least for the winter. Forty-five percent of farm buildings in the affected area were destroyed, and millions upon millions of dollars' worth of crops were lost.[20]

In the 1920s, relief work in China was dominated by private financial and technical aid, as embodied, for example, in the China International Famine Relief Commission. The establishment of the Nanjing government meant that a central authority would now concern itself with these matters, and with the 1931 disaster the government for the first time actively stepped into relief work on a major scale. This was also the first time that foreign government aid was a major factor in Chinese relief. The affected area needed medical aid and food both for immediate relief and for preventive measures. In addition, production needed to be restored as quickly as possible since the area was one of China's most important "rice bowls." In order to move expeditiously, the Chinese government established the National Flood Relief Commission on August 14, 1931, including both Chinese and foreign members, under the chairmanship of T. V. Soong. The British navy began an aerial survey to determine the full extent of the region's needs. In September 1931 the Lindberghs arrived with their seaplane from the United States and entered into the aerial survey activity, which brought considerable publicity in the United States. Other foreigners working in China joined in important activities either on their own initiative or at the suggestion of their companies. At the same time, the government began to negotiate with the United States for the wheat needed to alleviate the famine. Although the American minister to China recommended that Congress vote the wheat as a gift, arrangements were made for sale at current market prices with payment in three equal installments, to be completed by 1936, with four percent interest. The cost of distribution and administration of this "aid" was to be borne by the Chinese themselves. In order to pay for the wheat and related expenses, the government was forced to place a surtax on customs revenues, railway fares, and other forms of income. The Japanese attack on Manchuria in September 1931 seriously inhibited any Chinese government attempt to obtain supplies from Manchuria or to use Manchurian resources as security for relief loans. Private donations from both Chinese and foreigners helped considerably, as did, for example, an Italian government grant from Boxer indemnity funds for the purchase of tools in Italy.

At China's request, an Englishman took over the management of the immense and complicated relief program. The success of the reconstruction effort, manifested in 1932 by record rice production in the stricken area, had a strong impact, economically and politically, as well as socially, on the daily lives of the villagers who were affected. Against this background, China entered into new negotiations with the United States for the purchase of wheat and cotton on credit. Once again, however, the Americans insisted upon a high degree of control not only over the conditions of the loan, which was natural, but over the ancillary actions connected with it. For example, at least half the wheat and cotton was to be shipped on American bottoms, and at least half the insurance for the shipments was to be placed with American companies in the United States. Moreover, Washington reserved the right to veto the appointment of China's purchasing agents in the United States so that it could assure itself that the appointees would serve Washington's own political interests. This constituted a profound infringement of Chinese autonomy. Furthermore, accounting and other transactional procedures were to be placed under the control of the American firm of Price, Waterhouse, and Company. When the Chinese attempted to assert their independence in some of these matters, Washington balked.

These purchases, even if they were profitable for the United States, were intended for the relief of China at a moment when its economy was suffering the severe consequences of natural disaster. Nevertheless, the American aid quickly became an international issue. The Japanese complained that American relief to China was an unfriendly act to Japan because it helped support a government in China that was opposed to Japan. The Americans responded that the extension of credit to China for the purchase of wheat and cotton was a purely commercial transaction intended to help American farmers during the Depression; no doubt that was also true. Japan continued to oppose the transaction, however, and forbade its mills in China to purchase American cotton. Both the British and the Japanese complained that the relief loan violated the agreements of the consortium. This particular argument did not concern China, however, which from the beginning had refused to deal with the consortium. British, French, and Japanese financiers complained that Chinese measures to provide funds for the repayment of the relief loan, such as the surtaxes, infringed upon their own debt claims. In the end, the U.S. State Department concluded that the entire experience of extending government credit to China for relief purposes had been unpleasant and had complicated America's international position. From the Chinese point of view, the loan constituted a source of funds for constructive purposes that had been obtained at an interest rate considerably below what the government could have obtained inside China; the money had been used for purposes that were humanely, economically, and even politically important, particularly in the face of Japanese policy in China.

On the whole, it can be argued that foreign administrative, technical, and financial aid played an absolutely crucial role in the development of the modern sector of China's economy before World War II. Such assistance also affected the nonmodern economy. In immediate circumstances that included the establishment of a new central government, the need to recover from years of warfare among the constituent members of the polycentric system, and, beginning in the 1930s, the mounting and overt political and military activities of Japan on the mainland, the interests of the foreign finance capitalists and those of the Nanjing government and significant sectors of Chinese society coincided.

Foreigners in China

The role of foreigners as advisors, reformers, and channels of external influence within Chinese society and culture, so marked in the Empire from the Jesuits in the Ming dynasty to the Imperial Maritime Customs Service in the Qing dynasty, continued during the period of decentralization and international conflict and into the period of reconstruction of central power under the Guomindang. F. J. Goodnow, Yuan Shikai's advisor on constitutional government, and Arthur Young, financial advisor to the Nationalists' Republic of China from 1929 to 1947, are two foreigners—Americans in this case—who had a profound impact on the governments they served. As the institutions of central power disintegrated at the end of the Qing empire, the foreigners' roles also changed, and they began to serve local rulers just as they previously had served the imperial center. They now became advisors to the Chinese powers contending for primacy in China.

MILITARY ADVISORS

In the declining years of the Empire, attempts at modernization included the use of foreign specialists as advisors. For example, in the 1880s Li Hungzhang and Zhang Zhidong established military academies for the purpose of training officers in the Western fashion, and to this end they hired German instructors. As vain as these attempts were in the years before the Sino-Japanese War of 1894–1895, they formed a pattern. When he organized his famous Self-strengthening Army in 1895, Zhang Zhidong employed German officers to command and train three thousand carefully selected soldiers in the strategies, tactics, and equipment used by European armies. Yuan Shikai was named that same year by Li Hungzhang to organize another army, also German commanded and instructed, of some seven thousand men. With the Japanese victory over the Russians in 1905, imperial respect for Japanese accomplishments rose, and the government began both to employ Japanese instructors and to send Chinese officer candidates, Chiang Kaishek, for example, to Japanese military academies.

The principle of employing foreign advisors was sufficiently well established among the military by 1911 that it persisted after the disappearance of the Qing dynasty. Many of the warlords had military or political advisors. The great Manchurian warlord Zhang Zuolin (d. 1928) had risen to power under the aegis of the Japanese and in opposition to Russian expansion in the northeast; he had Japanese advisors. Wu Peifu (1871–1939) in central China had been trained by Japanese officers at the Chinese Paoting Military Academy; in the warlord period he was the recipient of British advice and, on occasion, also was advised by a Japanese officer. Feng Yuxiang (1882–1948), baptized by a YMCA official in 1913 and known as the "Christian General" for having attempted to convert his entire army, had at various times used both Russian and Japanese advisors. When in the mid-1920s the Guomindang, allied with the Communists, prepared to enter the military struggle in China, it established its own military academy at Whampoa, near Canton; Chiang Kaishek was superintendent and Zhou Enlai, the future Chinese Communist premier, was deputy director of political education. By 1925, the Soviet Union had about one thousand military advisors in China, mostly working with the Nationalist army, which was officered by Chinese who had been trained by Chinese who, by and large, had been trained by Japanese. Although Soviet advisors were also responsible, ultimately, for the political education of the Chinese Nationalist armies, the regular political education of the troops was in the hands of the Chinese Communists. The lessons and traditions introduced by foreign advisors were gradually becoming sinified.

After the KMT's break with the Communists and the Soviet Union in 1927, Chiang Kaishek's Soviet military and political advisors left the country and he shifted to Germany as a primary source of advice, partly because in their military thinking, administration, and structure the Germans so resembled the Japanese, who had been Chiang's own tutors and who themselves had learned from the Germans. In 1931, when Chiang launched his anticommunist campaigns, German advisors already were prominent in his organization, and by the mid-1930s, German military advisors in the Nationalist armies numbered up to seventy at any one time.

German tutelage was responsible for the development of a modern and efficient army of 300,000 men, who were trained in the use of German-type weapons produced in German-designed arsenals. Special attention was paid to the training of the officer corps, and by 1937 some two thousand German-trained officers had graduated from the Chinese Army Staff College. German generals also were influential in administrative reforms within the military and urged the inclusion of armaments production in industrialization projects. After Hitler came to power, German industrialists were particularly interested in expansion of their armaments trade with China, and the German government itself, after some initial doubt, realized that the officers' advising experience in China was contributing to the Nazi rearmament program. Many of Germany's top military leaders, including Ludendorff and Goering, took a direct interest in the China program. By 1937, about eighty thousand Chinese troops were completely armed with German-made weapons. The Tokyo-Berlin alliance of 1936, however, changed the context within which the German advisory program operated, since Germany could not continue to aid a China that was at war with its new ally, Japan. Nonetheless, the Germans remained in China, working for the Chinese against the Japanese, for a year after the outbreak of the Sino-Japanese War, when Hitler finally ordered them home. With the advent of the Pacific war, the United States replaced Germany as China's chief source of military advice and supplies.

Even before the outbreak of the Pacific war, Americans contributed to the development of a Chinese air force. In 1932, Japanese planes, in complete control of the air, wreaked havoc on Shanghai, which was practically defenseless. An American volunteer pilot, Robert Short, was killed in the fighting and became something of a hero. The China Aviation League began a campaign for funds to purchase military aircraft, and it had limited success. Shortly after the end of the fighting, the Chinese government approached the United States with a request for aid, but the neutralist climate in the United States and American fear of giving offense to the Japanese led the State and War departments to reject the appeal. Curiously, the Department of Commerce came to China's aid. A former air force major who belonged to the department's staff in Shanghai proposed the employment of a group of American civilian specialists to retrain experienced pilots, train new pilots, and contribute to the reorganization of China's aviation. This group would order needed equipment from America for use in China but would be prohibited from taking part in military engagements. In 1932, against the wishes of the State Department, a former American air force colonel arrived in China with a staff of nine pilots, four mechanics, and a secretary; they set up shop, under remarkably primitive conditions, in the city of Hanchow. Within months they had succeeded in turning almost useless facilities into the Central Aviation School, which trained pilots and developed its own corps of Chinese flying instructors, mechanics, and aviation doctors. The school's accomplishments were particularly remarkable in light of linguistic difficulties, bureaucratic interference, Chinese jealousies, and conflicts of authority.

The work of the unofficial American aviation mission was complicated by the arrival of an Italian aviation mission toward the end of 1933. H. H. Kung visited Italy in 1933 and was impressed by Mussolini, who told him that "since the time of Marco Polo, China and Italy have had cultural affinity."[21] Moreover, Italy was prepared to return some of its Boxer indemnity funds to China for the purchase of Italian planes. The official Italian mission, headed by an Italian general on active service, had strong support in the Italian government and from a consortium of Italian airplane manufacturers. The Italians proposed to build a factory for the production of airplanes in China and provided approximately $1.5 million for materials and machinery. Moreover, Mussolini presented Chiang Kaishek with the gift of an airplane. In the end, the Italians left China as a consequence of the outbreak of the Sino-Japanese War and Mussolini's participation in the Berlin-Tokyo axis.

The arrival of the American Colonel (later General) Claire Chennault in China just before the beginning of the hostilities initiated a new period in the history of American participation in the development of Chinese military aviation. Chennault had retired from the army in the spring of 1937 and had gone to China at the invitation of the Chinese government to survey its needs in the field of aviation. He was an advocate of pursuit aviation, but his ideas were unpopular in the American air force. While in China he was free to develop this approach, which proved valid in the course of World War II.

ADVISORS AS REFORMERS

Jesuit activities in the Empire fell for the most part into two categories: either they were supportive of the dynasty, as when the Jesuits cast cannon or made maps, or they served to introduce novelties, such as European styles in art, architecture, and amusements or refinements in Chinese astronomical instruments and knowledge. The generation of late imperial foreign advisors, like Sir Robert Hart, exhibited reformist tendencies, but their primary objective was the maintenance of the dynasty, and the reforms they recommended or undertook were intended to strengthen the dynasty, not to reform society. Nonetheless, foreign tutelage and advice

often had potential or real repercussions that went beyond the advisors'
intentions. In 1907 one Shen Jiaben, for example, under the influence of
Japanese and German legal theory, proposed a new criminal code for the
Empire that constituted a direct attack on traditional legal concepts and
social structures. It is likely that Shen was unaware of the profound implications of the proposal he was making; in any event, his ideas were unacceptable. In the same way, Goodnow's constitutional recommendations to
Yuan Shikai after the fall of the Qing dynasty were perfectly reasonable,
but within the reality of Chinese politics they contributed significantly to
Yuan's own demise. During the period of decentralization, the influence of
civil advisors was particularly marked in areas like education, philosophy,
and law. Americans such as John Dewey in education and philosophy and
Roscoe Pound in law and Englishmen like the philosopher Bertrand Rus-
sell visited China to lecture or work in their fields of specialization, and
they had a profound effect. The ground had been well prepared for them.

The West had an especially strong impact on education in general and,
most significantly, on the education of China's future leaders. By the end
of the Qing dynasty, foreigners, particularly Americans, had laid the
groundwork in the country for an essentially non-Chinese system of education that had a profound impact upon indigenous institutions. Even before the traditional examination system was abolished in 1905, foreign missions had established 2,200 lower schools and 389 middle schools, high
schools, and colleges. Christian colleges like St. John's in Shanghai already
had several decades of work behind them. In the early years of the twentieth century, the United States and other Oikoumenical powers began to
take a direct role in the field of education. In 1908, for example, the
United States returned about two-thirds of its share of the Boxer indemnity
for the establishment of a foreign-style college in Peking and for scholar-
ships for Chinese students to study in the United States. In France,
Chinese took the initiative in establishing a work-study program, and during World War I the presence of about 140,000 Chinese workers in France
magnified the impact of the West on significant groups of Chinese intellectuals. Translation of Western works, including, for example, anarchist and,
later, Marxist writings, was another form of influence. Chinese who maintained ties with their foreign teachers constituted with them a bridge
whereby Western ideas were transported into China and let loose upon
the society. The depth of the penetration of foreign education in China can
be briefly indicated by a family history: Chiang Kaishek studied in Japan;
his wife, Soong Mei-ling, whom he married in 1927, graduated from
Wellesley College; her brother, T. V. Soong, was a Harvard graduate; and
her brother-in-law, H. H. Kung, graduated from Oberlin. (Chiang himself
became a Methodist, the first Christian to reach such political heights in
China since the end of the Ming dynasty.) Foreign influence was also felt
strongly in literature: writers like Lu Xun and Mao Dun both adopted

Western literary forms and looked at China from new perspectives suggested by the West. The great Lao She, best known in the West for his novel *Rickshaw Boy*, spent considerable time in England, and another great writer, Ba Jin, took his pen name from the Chinese transliteration of the first syllable of "Bakunin" and the last syllable of "Kropotkin," the names of two great Russian anarchists. By the 1930s foreigners and their Chinese students, particularly Americans and American-trained Chinese, dominated the major universities and research institutions in the country.[22]

In the 1920s, foreigners became active in many new areas. In that decade, J. Lossing Buck, together with Chinese and American colleagues at Nanjing University, began the serious study of Chinese agriculture and agricultural society and economy at the village level. They were concerned with both the improvement of agricultural production and the reform of rural society. Cornell University and the Rockefeller Foundation initiated programs in research and instruction at Nanjing in 1920. By 1932, a National Agricultural Research Bureau, drawing on staff and students trained by Americans at Nanjing University and at the College of Agriculture of Southeastern University, was established; the bureau provided the first comprehensive reporting on Chinese agricultural production in history.

By 1928, the putative national government at Peking had over four hundred foreign advisors, of whom well over two hundred worked in the maritime customs service, one hundred in the postal system, and fifty in the salt service. The Nationalists continued to employ foreigners, although mostly in advisory roles. For example, in the first decade of the Nanjing government the number of foreign employees in the customs service, the salt service, and the post was cut approximately in half; over time the government tended to rely more heavily on advisors appointed by the League of Nations and other foreign or international institutions.

The Nanjing government used foreign advisors in a broad spectrum of activities. In 1928, for example, Sun Fo established a commission of financial experts, based in the United States possibly for the very reason that American financial interests in China were less than those of the European powers. The commission arrived in China in 1929, studied the country's financial situation, and made proposals in fields such as currency reform, the banking structure, budgeting, fiscal reform, and taxation. Edwin Kemmerer, who headed the commission, was a professor at Princeton University. He had led previous commissions to various countries in Latin America that had succeeded in obtaining loans from the U.S. government and American banking institutions. This may well have been in Sun Fo's mind. The Kemmerer Commission was the first in a series of advising groups, of which some came from England or were dispatched by the League of Nations.

Almost from its inception, the League of Nations was involved in aiding and advising China, but it was particularly active between 1931 and 1935.

Health was one of its major concerns, and the director of the League's health section, Ludwig Rajchman of Poland, spent considerable time in China and even involved himself in the support of China's case against Japanese aggression in Manchuria in 1931. He also brought in Sir Arthur Salter, an Englishman who directed the League of Nations' economic and financial organization, and Robert Haas, a Frenchman who directed the League's transit and communications organization, to consult with the government.

Against the background of these activities, the Nanjing government established the National Economic Council (NEC), headed by Chiang Kaishek and directed by T. V. Soong. The NEC immediately sought the direct collaboration of the League of Nations in the provision of reform proposals, advice, and training for economic development. The Japanese invasion of Manchuria and the 1931 flood delayed the real beginning of the NEC's activities. Moreover, Rajchman's political concerns led to a certain reluctance on the part of the League to move ahead with the project. Nonetheless, the League made important contributions. In 1931–1932, it sent a mission to China to study the improvement of China's intellectual and educational relationships with foreign countries, and three months of research produced a proposal for educational improvement that warned against the "remarkable, not to say alarming consequences of the excessive influence of the American model on Chinese education." The proposal argued that the objective of any kind of education ought to be "to prepare students for a life of useful work in China," not for life in the United States. (The United States, of course, was not a member of the League of Nations, and European intellectuals were suspicious of American cultural influences.)[23]

The League of Nations, often in connection with the National Economic Council, provided China with aid and advice in a broad range of other activities, including the teaching of geology, geography, and English literature; the organization of labor; the development of public works projects; flood relief; civil service reform; cotton and silk production; public health; irrigation; animal husbandry; veterinary medicine; and the organization of agricultural cooperatives. But the League was not the only source of foreign aid. The Chinese Ministry of Railways improved its administrative activities with American advice on accounting and financial administration; the British provided assistance in survey work. The American Paul Linebarger became legal advisor to the Chinese government, which employed other foreign advisors in the Industry and Foreign Affairs ministries. An Italian legal expert was invited to give advice on penal code reform in 1933. On the subnational level, the Australian William Donald was advisor to Zhang Xueliang (the "Young Marshal"), who was the son of the Manchurian warlord Zhang Zuolin; and for several years the city of Nanjing employed a group of Americans to advise it on urban planning and administration.

Foreigners also were active in social and economic reform and rehabilitation on the village level through such organizations as the China International Famine Relief Commission, which by 1936, to cite but one of its efforts, had organized 200,000 people in North China into rural credit cooperatives. One of the most striking examples of foreign activity in rural reconstruction was the "mass education movement," developed and led by James ("Jimmy") Y. C. Yen, who had graduated from Yale University and had worked for the YMCA. The movement, which began in 1926 with a model village experiment at Ding-xian, near Peking, enjoyed considerable financial support from the Rockefeller Foundation. Yen's efforts had many ramifications, including the use of a one thousand-character writing system to overcome illiteracy, the development of basic agricultural education along with elementary literacy, the establishment of cooperatives and peasant associations, and the development of agricultural credit.

On the eve of the Sino-Japanese War in 1937, the Rockefeller Foundation was involved in plans for putting Yen's experience to use in other areas of North China. The Rockefeller Foundation's main contribution to China, however, was undoubtedly the Peking Union Medical College, in which, by 1934, it had invested almost $37 million. This institution, the leading medical college in China, belonged to the best tradition of medical education in the world.

The history of foreign aid to China in the period of decentralization and reformation under the Nationalist regime demonstrates that American foreign aid programs all over the world after World War II did not spring full-blown from the head of Washington but were rooted in experience.

From Empire to China

Changing relationships between China Proper and the Empire's frontier regions accompanied the decline of central power and authority consequent upon the end of the Qing dynasty. Manchuria, Mongolia, Xinjiang, and Tibet each had a special relationship with the dynasty. The new government in Peking claimed to be the dynasty's legitimate successor and therefore heir to its relationships with the frontier regions. The second half of the nineteenth century, however, had already witnessed profound changes as Russian and British power grew in all these areas. The disappearance of the dynasty only shifted the direction and increased the speed of change; it did not alter the fact of it.

By 1911, all the powers, including Japan and the Empire, had recognized Russia's dominant position in Manchuria and commercial and even political penetration of Mongolia and Xinjiang. Japan's victory over Russia in 1905 had limited Russian imperialism in the Far East but not in Mongolia, and the net effect of the Qing assertion of its power in Xinjiang in the 1870s and 1880s had been a delay, but only a delay, in the advance of

Russian influence. Russian settlement in the vast Siberian lands increased markedly, and it was not surprising that the civil war that followed upon the October Revolution in Russia should spill over into the Empire. By the mid-1920s, however, Soviet power had been established throughout the former Russian empire, and the new state was becoming a Far Eastern power as well. In 1924, a Sino-Soviet treaty reestablished joint administration of the Chinese Eastern Railway, and in 1925 Japan finally concluded a treaty with the Soviets and withdrew its forces from the last vestiges of the Soviet territory it had occupied during the intervention. The stabilization of Soviet political control in Siberia was paralleled by considerable internal economic growth and the concerted integration of the region into the Soviet economy, which remained centered in European Russia. This brought an ethnically European population and European political interests directly to the Empire's land frontiers in a fashion that impinged far more directly than ever before on the relations between metropolitan China and the frontier regions, on the one hand, and on the internal affairs of each frontier area, on the other. Moreover, Russian Central Asia and Siberia underwent profound internal changes as Soviet socialist ideas and institutions propelled the local populations into modernization.

The developments that were taking place in Soviet Central Asia and Siberia could not but influence the regions across the frontier from them. A certain non-Russian ethnic continuity transcended the border between Xinjiang (Chinese Turkestan) and Soviet Central Asia (Russian Turkestan) and between Outer Mongolia and Buriatia (the part of Siberia inhabited by ethnic Mongols called Buriats); in the Far East a large Russian population lived in Northern Manchuria and a Chinese population lived in Eastern Siberia and the Maritime province of the Soviet Far East. Consequently, the population on the Empire's side of its frontier with the Soviet Union increasingly felt the impact of the changes wrought on the Soviet side; these forces gradually modified, and in some cases even appeared to supplant, the previously dominant Chinese influence.

MANCHURIA

Manchuria, as the ancient homeland of the Manchus, fulfilled a dual function for the Qing dynasty. Realistically in the dynasty's early years, and more symbolically as the dynasty became increasingly sinified, Manchuria combined the virtues of the geographical embodiment of traditional Manchu life with the potential for serving as a refuge should China Proper become inhospitable to the Manchus. Therefore, the establishment of stability in the region through the Treaty of Kyakhta of 1728 was of particular importance to the Qing. However, the improvement of Russia's position throughout Siberia, especially in its eastern reaches, from the middle of the nineteenth century led to the collapse of almost a century and a half of stability along the Empire's northern borders and in the institutional structure of its continental relations with the Oikoumene.

The fall of the dynasty and the consequences of the Russo-Japanese War of 1904–1905 made Manchuria's relationship to China Proper somewhat ambiguous, an ambiguity increased by the Empire's last attempt to control foreign penetration into the area. In 1907 the empire converted its traditional administration in Manchuria into regular provincial governments; it also permitted previously prohibited Chinese immigration into the area. Both the industrial growth of Manchuria and the development of the transportation network—which together made Chinese immigration necessary and possible—were the direct consequence of the presence of foreign power and finance, however, so immigration of Han Chinese into the region was attractive to the imperial government as a means to build up a population basis for its own claims against those of Russia and Japan.

By the end of the first decade of the twentieth-century, Northern Manchuria was widely recognized as little more than a Russian colony in fact, if not in law. The city of Harbin, for example, was, to all intents and purposes, a primarily Russian urban center, economically based upon the railroad but culturally and even administratively an extension of Russia. Russian courts and civil administration and Russian management of the economy expanded throughout the region, coming to supplant the administrative and juridical institutions of the Empire. Russia's predominance was recognized in a secret Russo-Japanese convention in July 1907, which drew a demarcation line between the Russian and the Japanese sector and recognized the rights and privileges of each power in its own territory. The Empire was not even a party to this convention, which testifies to the Empire's growing inability to manage its external relations, even when they concerned imperial territory. Both before and after the collapse of the dynasty in 1911 Peking continued to assert its juridical claims over Manchuria but was too weak to develop a policy to reassert its rights upon the ground. In fact, the collapse of the imperial center created a vacuum of legitimacy to the south and west of Southern Siberia and Northern Manchuria that invited the further extension of Russian power.

Northern Manchuria, as a *de facto* Russian colony, provided one of the primary arenas in which the political, diplomatic, and military battles of the revolution and civil war were fought. From March 1917 to March 1920 it was ruled as a "railroad state" by General Dmitrii Leonidovich Horvath, general manager of the Russian railway system in Manchuria since 1902 and a member of the Russian royal family. Almost immediately after the revolution that overthrew the tsar, Horvath declared the railway's own administration a "provisional Russian republic," independent of Petrograd (St. Petersburg); he assumed control, called a "national assembly," conducted a "general election," and named himself the "director-general of the all-Russian provisional government." All these actions were taken despite protests from the government in Peking, which continued to assert its suzerainty over a territory technically its own, the governance of which, however, lay completely beyond China's reach. To complicate matters, Horvath was not unopposed in Northern Manchuria itself. A council of soldiers' and workers' delegates was organized in Harbin on the model of the Petrograd soviet, and in December 1917 Lenin telegraphed the council to take revolutionary action. Faced with a mutiny among his own troops, Horvath enlisted the aid of the Chinese authorities. By the end of 1917, the leaders of the soviet were expelled from the territory. Horvath, with Chinese support, retained his position until 1920, allied to counter-revolutionary forces operating in Siberia.

The extension of the Russian Revolution and civil war into Northern Manchuria and the Allied intervention in Siberia placed the governance of Northern Manchuria on the agenda of all the major Allied powers. The status of the Chinese Eastern Railway was linked to the future of the Trans-Siberian Railway by virtue of Russian ownership of both and by the Allied intervention; the United States proposed that an inter-Allied commission take charge of both systems. Neither the Japanese nor the Chinese—each for their own reasons—were happy with the proposal, but in January 1919 the powers participating in the Siberian intervention signed an agreement placing the Trans-Siberian under an inter-Allied committee. A special technical board, under the committee, was given responsibility for the management of both the Trans-Siberian and the Chinese Eastern railways. Allied supervision of the Chinese Eastern ended only in October 1922, after the departure of the last, Japanese, interventionist troops from Siberia. The defeat of the anti-Soviet counterrevolutionary forces in Siberia and the withdrawal of the Allied armies made it possible for Peking to begin to assert its authority as well as its suzerainty. In September 1920, the Chinese government ended its recognition of the prerevolutionary, tsarist minister in Peking and of the Russian consuls in China and insisted upon its rightful jurisdiction over the Chinese Eastern Railway. The break with the representatives of the Russian *ancien régime*, a consequence of Soviet diplomacy, was for China a necessary recognition of reality. The new Soviet regime proclaimed itself the world's first socialist state. As such, it was a new phenomenon in world history and not simply a governmental successor to the tsars. The internal revolution, the argument continued, was also an international revolution; therefore, the new state's foreign policy inevitably broke with the pattern of international relations characteristic of the now defunct Russian government. This change seemed to manifest itself quickly in the Far East. As early as July 1918, Grigori Chicherin, Soviet Commissar for Foreign Affairs, announced: "We notified China that we renounced the conquest of the Tsarist Government in Manchuria and we restore the sovereign rights of China in this territory, in which lies the principal trade artery—the Chinese Eastern Railway, property of the Chinese and Russian people."[24] While it is tempting to see no small degree of cynicism in this statement, since Chicherin insisted upon Russian rights of property in the railroad, Marxist theory supported the Soviet position: the railway had been built with Russian capital, which was, by definition, produced by Russian labor. Therefore, the Soviet state could not alienate the property of the Russian people.

The negative Chinese reaction to the Treaty of Versailles led to a further Soviet statement. The vice-commissar for foreign affairs, Leo Karakhan, declared in July 1919 that the Soviet government undertook "to start negotiations for the annulment of the Treaty of 1896, the Peking protocol of 1901, and all of the agreements with Japan from 1906 to 1916." This thorough repudiation of pre-Soviet Russian foreign policy in the Far East was supported by a broad statement that the new regime was prepared to return to the Chinese people "all the power and authority which were obtained by the Government of the Tsar by tricks or by entering into understandings with Japan and the Allies." Moreover,

> The Soviet Government returns to the Chinese people without demanding any kind of compensation, the Chinese Eastern Railway, as well as all the mining, lumber, gold, and other concessions which were seized from them by the government of the Tsars, that of Kerensky, and the brigands Horvath, Semenov, Kolchak, the Russian ex-generals, merchants, and capitalists.[25]

This statement went far beyond Chicherin's announcement in July 1918, but it, too, was based in the Marxist theory of the international unity of the working class. In this perspective, the Soviet renunciation of the railway was an act of proletarian internationalism. The Karakhan declaration was, in effect, a diplomatic Magna Carta that placed the new Soviet regime outside, and opposed to, the Oikoumene. Issued before Soviet victory in the civil war, the declaration was intended as a basis for the inclusion of the Soviet government in Far Eastern affairs and for future negotiations with China about the status of the Russian possessions in territories over which China claimed suzerainty; it was intended also to arouse support in China for the Soviet cause.

Despite its skepticism when the declaration finally reached Peking in March 1920, the Chinese government dispatched to Moscow a special military-diplomatic mission that negotiated with the Soviets between September and December 1920. In December 1920, the Asian avatar of Soviet power, the Far Eastern Republic, sent a delegation to Peking for commercial negotiations. These exchanges prepared the way for further interaction, and in September 1923 Leo Karakhan himself led an extraordinary mission to China to win formal diplomatic recognition from Peking and to improve the Soviet position in Manchuria. The conversations were concluded successfully at the end of May 1924, and the resulting agreement provided for joint Sino-Soviet management of the Chinese Eastern Railway and for the regularization of the Soviets' status in Northern Manchuria. These agreements were a major victory for Moscow because they were the first extension of Soviet power beyond Russian frontiers by means of an international treaty. In return, the Soviets recognized Chinese sovereignty unreservedly and agreed to equal Soviet and Chinese representation on the board governing the railroad; moreover, mutual consent was required for all the railroad's activities. For China, then, the agreements with Moscow also represented a victory; they were the first, if only tentative, post-dynastic recognition of the Empire's legitimacy and power in its own frontier regions. To insure the viability of the accords, Karakhan also signed, in September 1924, a separate agreement with the warlord Zhang Zuolin, the official military governor of Manchuria since 1911.

The efficacy of the Sino-Soviet agreements of 1924 was vitiated, however, by continuing chaos and growing nationalism inside China and by a profound conflict of interests between the two powers that no formal documents could mask. By 1929 the relationship had deteriorated into a state of undeclared war. In the second half of that year Soviet troops reportedly attacked Chinese border positions and a general mobilization was ordered in Siberia. The escalation of the military conflict was halted only by the intervention of other powers. This situation continued until March 23, 1935, when the Soviet government sold the Chinese Eastern Railway to Japan through Tokyo's client state of Manchukuo. The sale was tantamount to recognition of Japan's dominant position in East Asia and, at the same time, to liquidation of what was, for Moscow, a distant, relatively indefensible, exposed position.

Japan's interest in Southern Manchuria after 1905 complemented the Russian position in the north. Japanese defeat of Russia, annexation of Korea in 1910, and expansion of economic interests in Southern Manchuria, along with a certain sentimental attachment to the region because of the blood spilt in the first Asian victory over a European power, all combined to make Manchuria a primary object of Japanese attention. The presence of one million Korean subjects of Japan in Manchuria and the fact that seventy-five percent of all foreign investment in Manchuria was Japanese, not to mention Japanese ownership of the South Manchurian Railway Company, gave Japanese interest in the region considerable substance. These interests were served by two agencies, the Japanese Kwantung army, which tended to pursue policies somewhat independently of Tokyo, and the Manchurian warlord Zhang Zuolin, whose own position depended upon his recognition of Japan's paramountcy. The Kwantung army and Zhang did not always cooperate, however, and as the Guomindang began to unify China Proper in the 1920s, Zhang exhibited nationalistic tendencies that disturbed the Japanese; in 1928 the officers of the Kwantung army assassinated him in the belief that his son and successor would be more pliant. The formal establishment of the Nanjing regime in 1928 deepened fears of a resurgent China, and, anxious to strengthen Japanese control over Manchurian affairs, the Kwantung army, acting largely on its own initiative, ordered a full-scale attack against Chinese forces at Mukden and elsewhere, using as pretext a bomb explosion on the South Manchurian Railway on September 18, 1931. The Japanese undoubtedly had planted the bomb. On September 24, Tokyo announced that Japan was acting in self-defense, and on October 8 the Japanese army attacked the headquarters of Zhang Zuolin's son and successor, Zhang Xueliang, "Young Marshal."

Japan's conquest of Southern Manchuria was completed during the first part of 1932. The Japanese proceeded to set up a puppet government, inaugurating the independent state of Manchukuo ("Manchu country") at Mukden on March 1, 1932, and installing the last emperor of the Qing dynasty, Henry Puyi, who had been a child when the dynasty had abdicated in 1912. In the entire world, only El Salvador joined Tokyo in recognizing Manchukuo. This entire episode became known as the "Manchurian incident," and neither Chiang Kaishek's government in China Proper nor the League of Nations, which investigated the situation, could alter Japan's policies and their consequences. To consolidate its position, Japan elevated Henry Puyi to the restored Manchu throne in 1934 as the Kangde Emperor and made the Japanese ambassador to Manchukuo the governor of Kwantung Peninsula and the commander-in-chief of the Kwantung army, that is, the primary military and political figure in the country.

In China Proper, an undeclared war broke out between Chinese and Japanese forces in Shanghai between January 28 and March 3, 1932; although an armistice was signed, this episode signaled the beginning of a nationalist Chinese resistance to Japanese aggression. The Chinese effort was not sufficient, however, to deter Tokyo, which withdrew from the League of Nations in March 1933, by which time Japanese forces had tentatively occupied a small portion of Jehol province in China Proper itself. No other power, including the League, was able to curtail Japanese aggression. The United States limited itself to refusing to recognize the legitimacy of Japan's actions. The Soviet Union was deeply concerned by Japanese expansion in territory contiguous to Siberia, but it was preoccupied by the rise of fascism in Europe and by its own program for economic development, so Stalin decided to diminish the Japanese challenge to the Soviet position in the Far East by selling Moscow's interest in the Chinese Eastern Railway in 1935. This left Japan a free hand to use Manchuria as a military and industrial base for further anti-Chinese aggression, which entered a new and far more active phase in 1937.

OUTER MONGOLIA

The Qing dynasty's relationship with the Khalkha Mongols of Outer Mongolia was a complex structure of interactions that included diplomatic, military, religious, familial, and economic ties. Prior to their invasion of

China the Manchus had concluded a diplomatic and military alliance with the Khalkhas that both secured their western flank and gained participatory support. This alliance was bolstered by the fact that, also prior to their invasion of China, the Manchus had entered into good relations with the Dalai Lama and the Tibetan Buddhist church, among whose strongest adherents were the Mongols. The alliance was also intensified by the limited integration of the Mongol sociomilitary structure with that of the Manchus, the assignment of individual Mongols to important military and even civil bureaucratic positions, and the use of more traditional tribute system instruments. The Mongols were further integrated into the Empire by marriages between imperial daughters and Mongol princes, by the appointment, after the middle of the eighteenth century, of imperial residents, military governors, and agents in Mongolia, and by Peking's control of the postal routes.

In order to maintain its authority within Mongol society, the Qing dynasty forbade Han Chinese emigration to the region, but with the growing sinification of the Manchus, vigilance of control over the details of daily life and policy relaxed somewhat, and Han merchants, organized in companies based upon provincial centers in China Proper, began to penetrate the Mongolian market. As noted in Chapter V, these merchants, offering many luxuries and manufactured goods that were previously hard to come by, found eager customers in spendthrift Mongol princes, to whom they extended large amounts of credit at highly unfavorable terms. One observer estimated, perhaps with some exaggeration, that at the end of the nineteenth century there may have been over 100,000 Han merchants circulating in Mongolia among a population that numbered about 750,000. In the 1920s the Mongols owed one Han Chinese company alone—and there were many companies—more than $1 million. All this had an immediate effect on the rest of the Mongol population, since the debt was passed on to the lower orders of society in the form of increased taxes and other collections. The burdens of the lower orders were further increased by imperial taxation.[26]

By the turn of the twentieth century the Manchus were increasingly fearful of the growth of Russian settlements and power along Siberia's frontier with Mongolia, upon which also abutted the Russian sphere of influence in Manchuria. Therefore, in 1902 they decided to open Mongolia to Han Chinese colonization in order to build a countervailing population base on the Qing side of the Empire's border with the Russians. The Chinese began to enter Mongolia both as merchants and as agriculturalists, in Inner and, increasingly, in Outer Mongolia, and Mongol-Chinese relations began to reach the boiling point. Not only were the upper classes, and therefore the lower orders, of Mongolian society indebted to Chinese merchants but now Mongols, with their distinctive culture and nomadic way of life, began to come into contact and conflict with sedentary, agriculturalist Han Chinese who were colonizing Mongol lands. After 1909 the operation of the new Chinese-built and -owned Peking-Kalgan-Suiyuan Railroad further encouraged this movement.

Russian expansion in Central Asia and, particularly, the growth of the Russian population in Siberia made Mongolia a natural object of St. Petersburg's interest. Mongolia and China were closer than Russia to Southern Siberia and were more convenient and cheaper sources of supplies. In a process similar to the opening of the Empire by the maritime powers of the Oikoumene, Russia negotiated a series of treaties and agreements with Peking (ranging from the Treaty of Kuldja in 1851 to the negotiated understandings of 1881) that opened Mongolia and Xinjiang to trade and gave the Russians the right to establish permanent representation in key centers. By 1911, St. Petersburg had official representation at Urga, Kuldja, Chuguchak, Kashgar, Turfan, Kobdo, Uliasutai, Hami, and Urumchi, all in Mongolia and Xinjiang, and Russian agriculturalists were permanently settled in the region now called Tuva in northwestern Mongolia.

Russia's commerce before 1911 was much less significant than that of the Han Chinese: while Chinese merchants in Mongolia had their commercial bases in China Proper, within a reasonable distance from the markets they sought to penetrate, Russian merchants, even if based in Siberia, had to import goods from distant European Russia at a price that did not appeal to the Mongols; also, neither modern Russian business methods nor Russian goods seemed to please the Mongols. Centuries of cultural and social interaction had created among the Mongol upper classes a taste for the luxury goods of China; they also had acquired the tea habit. The traditional Mongol upper classes—the princes and monastic abbots—had little or no use for the products of advanced industrial civilization as represented by Russian commerce. Russian reports of the period complain about Russian inability to compete successfully with China for control of the Mongolian market. At the same time, the Russians had a powerful cultural and political impact on the country, primarily through the Buriat Mongols. A sedentary rather than a nomadic people, but Mongolian in culture and language and Lamaist in religion, the Buriats had been Russian subjects since the second half of the seventeenth century. They had been subjected to russification and were therefore natural intermediaries between the European Russians and the Central Asian Mongols, providing a conduit for new institutions, new ideas, and general modernization. Events outside Mongolia, such as the Russian Revolution of 1905, reverberated, however faintly, in Urga through the Buriats and Russians resident there.

The Russo-Japanese agreement of 1907 that assigned Northern Manchuria to Russia and Southern Manchuria to Japan also assigned Outer Mongolia and Inner Mongolia to them, respectively. Britain and China recognized the agreement in 1911. This enabled the Mongol ruling classes to consider a political solution to their intolerable indebtedness to the Han

Chinese merchants and to the growing Manchu and Han Chinese administrative and economic penetration of the Mongol lands. The Mongol leaders became more conscious of alternatives to Qing control when the Japanese tentatively expressed interest in establishing direct relations with them (which the Russians read, of course, as an attempt to outflank their influence in Northern Manchuria despite the 1907 agreement). And months before the outbreak of the Chinese Revolution on October 10, 1911, the Living Buddha of Urga sent a mission to St. Petersburg to seek aid against the importunities of the Empire's officials and merchants.

The Mongols took advantage of the Chinese Revolution to declare their independence in December, and the Living Buddha, assuming the title of king, began to rule with the advice of a council of notables. Not unexpectedly, one of the new government's first acts was the cancellation of the debts owed by Mongols to Chinese. This step was accompanied by widespread violence against Chinese merchants and other Chinese who were living in Outer Mongolia's urban centers.

St. Petersburg, mindful of the broader implications in the Far East of its actions in Central Asia, did not rush to the support of the new Mongol government. Instead, it promoted an agreement with Urga and Peking that recognized a Russian protectorate over Outer Mongolia within the context of continued formal Chinese suzerainty. This arrangement particularly advantaged Russia by giving it a free hand in the country while denying the Japanese any access on the pretext that Mongolia was part of China. In January 1912, St. Petersburg defined the formula more precisely, suggesting that Peking withdraw its troops and stop colonization while Russia, still recognizing Chinese suzerainty, prepared to train and arm a Mongol army. In November 1912, St. Petersburg and Urga signed a treaty that established Mongolia's autonomy, but not her independence, and granted Russia special trading privileges. One year later Peking accepted the Russian formula, and a tripartite Russian-Chinese-Mongolian agreement confirmed it in June 1915. Meanwhile, with the outbreak of World War I in Europe, Russian demand for the products of Mongolia's animal-husbandry economy increased markedly, and a special Russian trade mission with broad commercial and quasi-diplomatic powers entered the country. However, China still dominated the market.

The Living Buddha's government never succeeded in establishing firm control over the country, and the intrusion of both Russian and Chinese military forces exacerbated the situation. In 1918, a Chinese warlord army, led by General Xu Shuzeng ("Little Xu") invaded Mongolia and occupied Urga. Xu then attempted to establish Chinese control over the country by means of frontal attacks upon the population, attacks that were tantamount to massacres. Xu took this action at the behest of the Japanese, who had intervened in the Russian civil war. At the same time, Mongolia provided an attractive refuge for Russian counterrevolutionaries, and in 1920 an army of anticommunist Russians, led by Baron Ungern von Sternberg (the "Mad Baron"), who was also encouraged by the Japanese, invaded Mongolia and expelled the Chinese, instituting a reign of terror of no meaner proportions than Xu's. Victimized both by Chinese and by anticommunist Russian forces, the Mongols responded by building a partisan resistence movement at home and seeking Soviet support against Mongolia's three enemies, the anticommunist Russians, the Japanese, and the Chinese.

Two remarkable men led the Mongolian resistance. Sukhebator (1893–1923), who had been trained by Russian officers in the new Mongol army between 1912 and 1919, provided political and military leadership. Choibalsan (1895–1952), whose education combined traditional monastic training and modern Russian schooling, contributed a knowledge of Marxist ideology, Russian affairs, and the outside world. Each was the leader of a partisan resistance group, and they joined forces in 1919–1920 to establish the Mongolian People's Revolutionary Party, which, with Soviet aid, succeeded in expelling the anticommunist Russian forces from Mongolia. In 1921 they established a new government, secular in nature and oriented toward Soviet Russia; continuity and legitimacy were provided by the Living Buddha, who continued to reign, nominally, as king. In November 1921 Sukhebator led a Mongolian delegation to Moscow, where the mission had an audience with Lenin. At home, the new government moved to restructure Mongol society, and when the Living Buddha died in 1924 it sought no reincarnation but, rather, declared Mongolia a republic.

By 1924, therefore, this part of the former Qing empire had effectively gained its independence or, rather, its semi-independence; Mongolia was, in effect, the first Soviet satellite. In the late 1920s and during the 1930s, Mongolia attracted Japan's attention as a prize in that country's drive for continental dominance: it appeared to provide both a path into the heartland of Asia and a way to threaten the Soviet Union along the length of Siberia. The threat from Japan drove Mongolia into even greater reliance on the Soviet Union and into even more rapid social change in order to develop the internal strength necessary to resist the new danger. In 1936 reliance on the Soviet Union and recognition of the role of the Soviet Union inside Mongolia was formalized in a mutual aid treaty between the two governments, which included provisions for the presence of Soviet troops. Fears about Japan's intentions were confirmed between July 1938 and September 1939, when, in a series of incidents first along the border between Manchuria and Mongolia and later along the border between Manchuria and Korea, the Japanese probed Soviet defences and tested Soviet resolution. As a consequence of the lessons she learned at the time, Tokyo excluded Siberia from its sphere of military activity as Japan turned its attention to China, Southeast Asia, and the Pacific.

Throughout the growth of the Mongol-Soviet relationship and the development of the Japanese threat in Inner Asia, the Chinese Nationalist government continued to maintain that Mongolia was part of China. In fact, the Chinese recognized Mongolia's independence only on January 5, 1946, after a plebiscite in which the Mongolian people ritually expressed themselves in favor of what had been a reality for at least a quarter of a century, the fact that Mongolia was no longer part of the Empire, regardless of who governed in China Proper. Moreover, with Mongolia firmly under Soviet protection and tutelage, no Chinese government, whatever its strength, could reasonably hope to reassert China's primacy over that territory.

INNER MONGOLIA

Outer Mongolia's example of *de facto* independence and internal social change and development encouraged Inner Mongolian nationalism and demands for local autonomy from Chinese rule. The Nanjing regime divided the region into two provinces and placed them under the control of a special commission that was to serve as intermediary between local government and interests groups and the central government. In response, local leaders sought support from Japan, whose armed forces invaded in 1936–1937 and established a puppet regime, the Mongolian Autonomous Nation. Japan's defeat in World War II meant the collapse of any realistic prospect for an independent Inner Mongolian polity and the reversion of the region to Chinese control as the Japanese surrendered and withdrew. Neither the Soviet Union nor Outer Mongolia was prepared to assume the risks that the expansion of Outer Mongolian nationalism into Inner Mongolia would have entailed.

XINJIANG

In 1911 Xinjiang's population was ethnically far more complex than Mongolia's but no less linked to groups on the Russian side of the frontier. In a population of perhaps three million, ninety percent of the agricultural and eighty percent of the total population were Kazakh and Kirghiz Turks whose cultural kinsmen inhabited Russian Turkestan. There was also a small community, the Dungans, who were Han in race and Chinese-speaking but Moslem in culture; it hewed more closely to its Moslem co-religionists than to the non-Moslem Hans of Xinjiang or to China Proper. The picture was further complicated by remnants of Mongol and other tribes that had passed through the region's history. Far from Peking, the province was more often than not administered in the interests of the local officials whom Peking appointed but could not control closely, and sociopolitical hierarchical relationships reflected ethnic identity, with the Han occupying the higher positions and governing the indigenous non-Han population, which constituted the overwhelming majority of the lower social and economic orders.

The end of the dynasty and the disintegration of the imperial center, togther with Mongolia's growing autonomy, encouraged local political processes to operate without reference to the interests of the contenders for power within China Proper. In 1912, for example, a new governor, Yang Zengxin (1859–1928), was appointed not by Peking but by the previous governor. Although he was a Han Chinese administrator in the imperial tradition, Yang had spent his career in, and had become identified with, the non-Han frontier region. His policy's primary focus was the maintenance of his personal rule and of Chinese suzerainty in an ethnically complex community characterized by low-level political violence and social disruption. Yang combined traditional and modern techniques in pursuit of this goal. For example, all the district magistrates in the south of the province were either his direct kin or his relatives by marriage. On the other hand, he was fully aware of the importance of modern information. He forbade the publication of Turkish-language newspapers and censored the press; to insure his direct control in this vital area, he himself possessed the only key to the provincial telegraph office, for which he assumed personal responsibility.

Yang's skillful diplomacy limited Xinjiang's involvement in the Russian civil war. In 1920 and 1921 two groups of counterrevolutionaries, numbering perhaps thirty to forty thousand, crossed into Xinjiang, ostensibly to join the "Mad Baron" in Mongolia or to reach China or India. The governor carefully negotiated the disarmament of these Russians and an amnesty for those who wished to return to the Soviet side of the frontier and invited Moscow's help in dislodging recalcitrant groups from outposts along the province's frontier with Russian Central Asia.

If the Chinese Revolution of 1911 had allowed the local administration a great degree of autonomy, the Russian Revolution of 1917 challenged Han domination of the province as the new Soviet regime conquered the ethnically related regions of Central Asia and initiated policies of social and cultural transformation among their populations. Yang was not unaware of the significance of these developments, and in 1925 he proposed the establishment in Xinjiang of an ethnic federation to diminish cultural antagonisms. Moreover, he realized that growing Soviet power was more likely to affect his domains than was a central government in China; consequently, he undertook to strengthen his position by initiating a cautious policy of modernization that included reform of the taxation system, control of the currency, and development of foreign trade, particularly with Soviet Central Asia.

In confronting the immediate consequences of the Russian Revolution and civil war and therefore in handling the Soviet authorities, Yang functioned essentially as had Qing officials along the China coast in the last decades of the nineteenth century: with the disintegration of central authority, the provincial authorities assumed more and more responsibility for the conduct of foreign relations. When, for example, formal diplomatic relations were reestablished between China and Russia in May 1924, Russian consulates were opened in Xinjiang and Chinese consulates in Soviet Central Asia, but when Chiang Kaishek broke off diplomatic relations in 1927, Yang believed that Xinjiang's interests would be better served by ignoring the move and continuing formal relations with the Soviets. He also continued to seek Soviet support for Xinjiang's development; indeed, Russian was the primary foreign language taught in such schools as existed in the province. Yang was assassinated in July 1928 in a local *coup d'etat* and was succeeded by the chief of the province's political department.

Xinjiang's ethnic diversity and its distance from both Chinese and Soviet centers of power, which had contributed to the province's autonomy, made it particularly vulnerable to Japanese expansionism in the 1930s. Tokyo was interested in interposing Japanese forces in the region between China and the Soviet Union. Xinjiang was also potentially useful as a springboard for a Japanese presence in Tibet and, no less important, as a basis for the development of Japanese influence among the Turkish-speaking Moslems throughout China Proper and in both Chinese and Soviet Central Asia. After making preliminary contact with Moslem communities in Xinjiang and China Proper, the Japanese sponsored an invasion of Xinjiang from China's northwest province of Gansu. The invasion was led by Ma Chongying, a Han Moslem adventurer who had important international ties. In addition to two Japanese advisors, his chief military advisor was a Turk from Istanbul named Kamal, who had studied in Germany and France before World War I, been captured by the Russians, and found his way to Manchuria, where he taught Turkish in a local school and probably became a Japanese agent. Kamal provided Ma, and the Japanese, with links to pan-Turkish interests. Rumors at the time insisted that Ma also had Chinese Nationalist support; in fact, the Guomindang, seeing him as a threat in Gansu, welcomed his removal to more distant Xinjiang. Ethnic and religious animosities throughout the Moslem regions of Northwest China fed the revolt, and Han Chinese civilians and a division of troops nominally loyal to the Guomindang joined Ma. It was also rumored that the British in India were extending him aid in the hope that a Turkish and Moslem nationalist movement in Central Asia would serve as a buffer between British and Soviet interests. Be all that as it may, Ma's forces penetrated Xinjiang in 1931–1932 and attacked Urumchi in the winter of 1932; in November 1933 he established the Eastern Turkestan Republic at Kashgar, an important trade center in western Xinjiang near the Soviet border.

Ma's revolt was defeated by the middle of 1934 (some pockets of resistance held out at least until 1937) by a Manchurian officer, Sheng Shicai, who commanded over a thousand troops. This army had fought the Japanese in Manchuria and had retreated into Siberia. Now the Soviets were repatriating them to China through Xinjiang. By this means the Soviets could aid the provincial government without appearing to interfere in internal Chinese affairs. Moscow was not eager to see a Moslem nationalist regime in Xinjiang. The potential effects of such a development on Russia's own Central Asian population would not have been positive. Moreover, the completion in 1930 of a railway that passed near the Xinjiang frontier and linked Soviet Central Asia with the Trans-Siberian Railroad increased Soviet strategic concerns in the area and the potential for mutually beneficial trade. Moscow wanted a pliant regime in Urumchi, Xinjiang's capital, not a government of militant nationalists. Sheng's defeat of Ma meant that the province was now ruled by someone beholden to, and dependent upon, Soviet power and authority; the Soviet position was further strengthened by the fact that Ma himself took refuge from Sheng in Russian territory as a Soviet guest. This gave Moscow leverage with both the non-Moslem Han ruler of Xinjiang and the Moslem, both Han and non-Han, population.

Sheng skillfully bartered Soviet primacy in Xinjiang for support of his regime. He obtained Soviet loans, war materiel, planes for bombing the rebels, advisors, and even contingents of troops. He gave the Soviets significant trade advantages and security for the Central Asian frontier. At the same time, he built his own power base within the province by making significant concessions to the Uighur Turkish and other non-Han ethnic groups, fostering a strictly local nationalist movement that was anti-Han but pro-Sheng, developing cultural associations for the ethnic groups, publishing a local newspaper in no less than seven languages, and developing a school system that included adult education. He recruited to his administration a vital group of Han experts and advisors who, as liberals and leftists, were uncomfortable in Guomindang China. These Han Chinese were loyal to China, not Sheng, but they saw in him a leader, even in remote Xinjiang, who was not afraid of reform. Sheng even invited Chinese Communists to work in popular organization and economic and financial planning. All these activities were supported by a loyal and efficient secret police. Sheng developed, in short, a creative amalgam of autocratic style and reformist policies.

The Sino-Japanese War and World War II found Sheng firmly entrenched in Xinjiang, therefore. However, as the Soviet Union became utterly absorbed in the European conflict, Sheng was unable to continue to rely on Russian material and economic aid. In 1940–1941 he began to shift his attention toward Nationalist China, and in 1943 he met with Chiang Kaishek. Sheng recognized that his and his government's survival depended upon his ability to walk a tightrope between Soviet and Chinese interests. Consequently, by 1944 he was trying to move away from the Chinese Nationalist regime and back toward a satellite relationship with the Soviet Union. He understood that the ability of those two regimes to effect policy developments in Central Asia defined his own independence. (In this respect his position and problem strongly resembled those faced by the leaders of satellite governments caught after 1960 in the Sino-Soviet conflict.) However, this attempt effectively ended his role in Central Asia. Chiang Kaishek, in what has been described as a delicate surgical procedure, removed Sheng by persuading him to accept appointment as minister of agriculture and forestry in the Chinese Nationalist government in Chongqing, and in September 1944 he left Xinjiang for China Proper. Chiang's move derived directly from the imperial tradition: he was co-opting a local ruler into the central bureaucracy, thereby neutralizing the threat to central authority.

With the removal of Sheng Shicai from the scene, and with the Chinese Nationalist pursuit of ethnocentric policies in the region, the social, ethnic, and economic conflicts in the province revived. In July 1947 a new rebellion broke out, adopting the name East Turkestan Republic as a direct reference to the Moslem nationalist movement of the 1930s. The rebel and Chinese forces remained deadlocked until December 1948, when feeble attempts at reform held out some hope for internal change. By this time, however, conditions in China Proper had dissolved to the point that no Nationalist solution for Xinjiang's problems was attractive. As the Chinese Communist victory approached, the Soviets and the Nationalists entered into negotiations for a new economic arrangement in the province that would favor Soviet interests no matter who won the conflict in China and that, the Nationalists hoped, would encourage the Soviets to find that their interests lay more with the Guomindang than with the Communists. In the end, however, the Nationalist defeat came so swiftly that the treaty was never concluded, although the Russians did retain certain rights in Xinjiang during the early years of the Chinese Communist regime. The reestablishment of a strong central government in China, in other words, the reintegration of the East Asian empire, meant the reassertion of imperial control over Xinjiang.

Xinjiang's reinclusion in the Empire stands in sharp contrast to Mongolia's removal from the Empire into the Soviet orbit as an ostensibly independent nation. Two factors can explain this divergence. First, ethnic diversity in Xinjiang prevented the development of a nationalist movement or even of nationalist sentiment that could unite the population in the face of the Han Chinese presence. Second, Mongolia's relationship with the Qing dynasty had been that of an administered ally; the dynasty was present in the country in the person of imperial residents and small military units. Xinjiang, largely because of the Ili crisis in the latter part of the nineteenth century, had been recently subjected by conquest to direct imperial administration, and while the region developed a *de facto* autonomy from central Chinese authority after 1911, the local governors and their bureaucrats were outlanders with no real ties to the country or its future. They played China and the Soviet Union off against each other not for

Xinjiang's future but for their own future in Xinjiang. Therefore, the re-establishment of central authority in the Empire logically led to the reintegration of Xinjiang into the Empire.

TIBET

The dissolution of the imperial center in 1911 found Tibetan affairs already in a high degree of disarray. When the dynasty reimposed its control over Tibet in 1910, the Dalai Lama fled to India, where he remained at the hill station of Darjeeling as the guest of the government of India until 1912. In the immediate aftermath of the revolution, the Manchu resident (*amban*) at Lhasa was replaced by a Chinese general. But as in Mongolia, so in Tibet: long years of friction and exploitation had led the local populace to take advantage of the weakness of the Chinese presence, and in Lhasa, Shigatse, and other settlements fighting broke out between the Tibetans and the Chinese garrisons. The Nepalese government intervened to negotiate an agreement whereby the Chinese troops remaining in Tibet were repatriated to China via India by the end of 1912. In the middle of 1912 the Dalai Lama returned to Tibet, but he did not enter his capital of Lhasa until January 1913, after the departure of the last Chinese.

In April 1912 Yuan Shikai insisted on the republic's right to assume the Empire's traditional relationship with all parts of the Empire, including Tibet. He opened up the very question he sought to foreclose. The president of the republic tried to assume the role of patron of Tibet's senior ecclesiastical-secular official, just as the Qing emperor had done previously. This was a particularly imperial concept. Great Britain, the Western state primarily concerned with Tibetan affairs, continued even after 1911 to describe the relationship between Tibet and China as one in which China possessed suzerainty over Tibet. This allowed London and New Delhi to talk about the possibility of Tibetan autonomy under Chinese suzerainty much as the Russians talked about Mongolian autonomy under Chinese suzerainty. In Western diplomatic language, the terms "suzerainty" and "autonomy" were as imprecise as the relationship between China and Tibet appeared to be in Western eyes. China and Great Britain each had its own concepts and terms to define the relationship, but these were different.

Peking's need to assert a superior-inferior relationship with Tibet was partly, but only partly, a consequence of tradition. China was well aware of both Russian and British interests along the Central Asian frontiers of the Empire and was anxious to establish Chinese priorities first. In August 1912, therefore, Yuan Shikai notified the British that he was restoring the Dalai Lama's titles and permitting him to return to Tibet. The Dalai Lama, of course, did not need Chinese acquiescence to his titles at this time, and he was already back in Tibetan territory. This situation was not clarified when the Dalai Lama, responding to Yuan's cable announcing the restoration of his titles, informed the Chinese president that he was now fully in control of the temporal and spiritual government of the country. Tibetans and others later took this statement to be a Tibetan declaration of independence.

Great Britain, for its part, wanted to define Tibet in a way that would protect the British position in India, and London called for a tripartite Chinese-Tibetan-British conference to be held in the Himalayan hill station of Simla in the fall of 1913. Each party approached the conference from its own perspective. The Chinese, reluctant to attend in the first place, claimed Tibet as an integral part of China, basing this claim on imperial tradition. The Tibetans, who were advised by Sir Charles Bell, a British Indian civil servant long interested in Tibet, insisted on Tibet's independence and had specific materials to support this claim. The British wanted to protect China's suzerainty over Tibet in order to insure sufficient Tibetan autonomy to safeguard Britain's Himalayan interests while not provoking a conflict with China. The British were disinclined, therefore, to support Tibet's claims to independence. The Simla conference lasted for six months and ended with a convention that recognized both Chinese suzerainty over Tibet and the autonomy of Outer Tibet, that is, the part of the country under the Dalai Lama's authority. China was permitted to maintain a resident and an escort of three hundred men in Lhasa, and the British could send to the country trade agents who were granted "most favored nation" treatment in Tibetan commerce. In July 1914 the British and the Tibetans signed the convention; the Chinese refused. In China's opinion, therefore, Tibet's status remained unresolved. Britain, on the other hand, considered that China's refusal to sign freed it to negotiate directly with the Tibetans, thus establishing Tibetan independence *de facto* and giving Britain primacy of position in Tibet. The British and the Tibetans now proceeded to negotiate a definition of the frontier. This frontier, the so-called McMahon line, was to become an issue in Sino-Indian relations half a century later.

The continuing chaos inside China, together with the Russian Revolution, which aroused British fears of a renewal of Russian interest in Central Asian affairs, prompted the British to put flesh on the bones, as it were, of their primacy in Tibet. In November 1920 Sir Charles Bell arrived in Lhasa as advisor to the Dalai Lama. In the next few years the British offered the Tibetans arms and ammunition for self-defense, provided military training in India for Tibetan officers and men, constructed a telegraph line to Lhasa, surveyed central Tibet, built a small hydroelectric plant at Lhasa, organized a police force for the city, and opened a small English-language school at Gyantse for the children of the Tibetan upper class. The Dalai Lama, perhaps because of his years in British India, favored, within the limits of Tibetan tradition and politics, progressive change. The Panchen Lama, the Dalai's rival for authority within Tibet, opposed these developments and fled to China in 1923, where he remained until his death in 1937. Both Britain and China, therefore, had their parties in Tibetan politics. Not to be outdone, the Soviets dispatched a group of russified Mongols to Lhasa in 1927, but the Tibetans immediately informed the British of their presence. The Mongols were followed by a Soviet officer, sent from Mongolia, who remained in Lhasa for a full year, but to no avail. The Dalai Lama carefully pursued a policy of balancing China and Britain off against each other in order to maintain as much independence for Tibet as possible. Disputes between Tibet and its Himalayan neighbors or conflicts with the Chinese were never allowed to reach proportions that would provoke either of the two great powers in the area to intervene. Repeated attempts by the Guomindang regime to bring Tibet under its control met with frustration. The thirteenth Dalai Lama died in December 1933, and when his successor, a child, was installed in February 1940 both British and Chinese representatives were present. The Chinese, eager to preserve their claims, recognized the new Dalai Lama, but this was already after the fact of his acceptance by the Tibetans themselves. The Chinese were behaving toward the Tibetans much as the Qing had behaved toward the West throughout the eighteenth and nineteenth centuries: the relationship was defined and redefined in ways that allowed it to fit traditional patterns of behavior and perception, which often varied greatly from political reality.

In World War II Tibet adopted a policy of neutrality that in both theory and practice denied China's claims to suzerainty. In 1942 the government opened a Bureau of Foreign Affairs as a statement of its *de facto* independence. The British recognized this office; the Chinese did not. China repeatedly sought to build roads through Tibet, which the Tibetans refused to allow. Moreover, the Tibetans were careful to make sure that British representives were present whenever they met with Chinese officials. In 1947, at an Asian relations conference sponsored by the Congress Party of India before Indian independence, a Tibetan delegation attended, under its own flag, as a representative of an independent country.

Tibet at no time succeeded, however, in winning any international recognition of its independent status. Neither the British nor the independent Indian government that came into existence in 1947 wanted anything more from Tibet than security in the Himalayas, and that goal was best achieved, they thought, by participating in Tibetan affairs only to the extent that China was not permitted to exercise real power in the region. The United States, never seriously interested in Tibetan affairs, was led by its support for the Guomindang regime in China, and later on Taiwan, to support Nationalist claims to suzerainty over Tibet.

In the late 1940s, as the Communists approached power in China,

unease over the ambiguity of Tibet's position mounted in Lhasa. All signs
pointed to trouble. Although it had not rained, a gilded dragon on one of
the roofs of the great temple in Lhasa daily dripped water from its mouth.
A great comet lit the night sky for weeks. Deformed children and animals
were born throughout the country. Some stones at the foot of the Dalai
Lama's palace fell to the ground one night. The government decided to
send a trade mission to India, Great Britain, China, and the United States
to seek support. All the powers except China accepted the Tibetan pass-
ports on which the mission traveled. Lhasa even permitted Lowell
Thomas, a well-known American radio personality, to visit the country to
develop its public relations. All this failed, however, and the reestablishment of a strong imperial center under the Chinese Communists brought
Tibet back into the fold.

Between 1912 and 1949, the record of China's relations with the periphery of the Empire suggests a continual attempt, by both Westerners
and Han Chinese, to define China as a modern nation-state. The resur-
gence of the Empire after 1949 led to relationships between the periphery
and the imperial center that were conducted on terms different from those
of the polycentric period. Although Mongolia was never regained, Manchuria, Xinjiang, and Tibet were, by one means or another, eventually
brought under direct Chinese control and removed from the arena of international relations.

Domestic and Foreign Conflict

An analysis of China's foreign relations between 1912 and 1949 must be
based on the assumption that China, in the political sense of the term as it
may have been understood before 1911, simply did not exist between 1912
and 1949. Indeed, Chinese reality suggests that it is impossible to speak of
China's foreign relations during this period, unless in the broadest terms,
that is, if by China we only mean a cultural ensemble that had no real
unified political superstructure except for a very brief period of time, particularly between 1928 and 1936. In those years the Nanjing government
of the Guomindang, under the leadership of Chiang Kaishek, held a promise of coherence and of national purpose. Even that period presented only
the semblance of unity, however, since the Nanjing government depended
for its existence upon a series of agreements with various warlords and
political groups, agreements that did not unify the country but resembled,
rather, arrangements for a confederal coexistence. None of this is to suggest that there were not striking attempts at unification and, equally important, at social, economic, cultural, and even political reform. However,
from the viewpoint of international relations it is difficult to justify a dis-

tinction between China, as a single entity on the international scene, and the rest of the world. It is more accurate to understand this period as one in which the powers external to China were participants in the internal politics of the Chinese culture area. Before 1927–1928, the powers were elements in the interaction among the warlords, the various governments that claimed to be legitimate, political parties, etc. After 1936–1937, as the Communists began to establish their primacy in an area that they proceeded to enlarge in the face of both Japanese and Guomindang opposition, China could be considered two societies. If Xinjiang and Tibet and, eventually, the puppet regime established by the Japanese at Nanjing, not to mention the putatively independent Manchukuo, were all included, the number of Chinas would increase to the point that it would be no more than a conceit of tradition to speak of China and its foreign relations.

World War I was to all intents and purposes a European war. The United States, which certainly did not consider itself a European power, much less a world power, tried to remain out of the war until German activities made American neutrality increasingly difficult to maintain. Japan joined the war not because of any direct interest in European affairs but because of a keen sense that such participation was the necessary next step in Japan's becoming a true world power and a player in the postwar settlement games, which Japan correctly perceived would have global implications. Indeed, Tokyo understood that its participation in an essentially European war was the essential precondition to the expansion of Japanese interests on the Asian continent. Thus, when the putative government of China declared China's neutrality in August 1914, the Japanese joined the Allies, declared war on Germany, and proceeded to occupy the German port of Qingdao in China's Shandong province. It is by no means clear that Germany's semicolonies along the China coast would have participated in the European struggle in any way, much less in any meaningful way; Japan joined the war for Asian, not European, reasons. On January 18, 1915, Japan presented Yuan Shikai with the famous Twenty-one demands. China was becoming a victim of a war in which it was not a participant.

Domestic, not international, considerations propelled China finally to declare war on Germany. The warlords of the "northern clique" saw the international conflict as a means both to increase their financial resources and to improve their political positions. They ordered mass demonstrations in May 1917, intending to persuade the Chinese Parliament to declare war, but the demonstrations failed and the Parliament and president combined to force the premier, himself a prominent warlord, out of office. China's entry into the war became one among many issues in the military and political struggles of the competing groups within geographical China. For example, Premier Duan Qirui, arguing that he had to prepare China for war with Germany, borrowed heavily from Japan (the so-called Nishihara loans), which financed his military struggle against other warlords. Nonetheless, China simply by its declaration of war against Germany earned a seat at the peace conference, and the fact that some kind of unitary representation was necessary at Versailles contributed to the pressure for the negotiation of an internal peace.

China was represented ably at the Versailles peace conference by a delegation that included individuals who were later to figure prominently in Chinese foreign and domestic politics. The delegation was not noted for its cohesion. As a representation of China, however, the delegation reflected the conflicts that plagued that region. Moreover, the chief of the delegation was the foreign minister, Lu Zhengxiang, who on behalf of Yuan Shikai had capitulated to Japan's twenty-one demands in 1915.

When the discussion of the disposition of German territories and interests in the Far East began in January 1919, the issue between Japan and China was joined. Japan, basing its case on secret agreements with Britain, France, and Italy, as well as on secret agreements with the Peking government, argued strongly for Japanese assumption of German interests in Shandong province. The issue was brought before the Council of Foreign Ministers, which included Japan but not China, and on April 30 the Japanese position was adopted. In China, meanwhile, students in Peking set aside May 7 as a "national humiliation day" for a demonstration commemorating Japan's twenty-one demands ultimatum of 1915. When news of the Paris decision reached Peking on May 3, the students decided to move the demonstration ahead to the next day, May 4, to protest the disposition of Chinese territories that was being imposed upon the nation by the big powers in Paris. Within China itself, this demonstration on May 4, 1919 gave its name to the intellectual modernization movement that had its roots in various political and economic changes that dated as far back at least as 1917. Internationally, China had no strength to resist the Versailles decisions, but the May 4 demonstration resulted in a manifesto that declared: "China's territory may be conquered, but it cannot be given away. The Chinese people may be massacred, but they will not surrender. Our country is about to be annihilated. Up, brethren!"[27] Unable to frame a national foreign policy and faced with growing popular anger that was sparked by the students' demonstrations on May 4, Peking left the Chinese delegation in Paris uninstructed. When the Treaty of Versailles was signed on June 28, the Chinese did not appear, indicating their inability to sign the peace treaty. Emblematic of China's lack of a foreign policy was the fact that the Peking government authorized the Chinese delegation in Paris not to sign the Versailles treaty on July 10, a full two weeks after the event. (China's failure to sign the peace treaty was interpreted by the American opponents of the treaty as a refusal, and the China question became one of the instruments with which President Wilson's opponents fought his international policies.)

The Soviet Special Case

Between the Versailles peace conference in 1919 and the outbreak of World War II in the Far East, China's foreign relations were preoccupied with the Oikoumene's continuing encroachment on China's socioeconomy, as they had been in the last decades of the Qing imperial system and the first years of polycentrism. The Soviet Union, however, undergoing its own systemic change and adopting a new posture in international affairs, represented a special case in China's foreign relations during the multistate period.

SOVIET RUSSIA AND THE CHINESE REVOLUTION

In the perspective of the Oikoumene's traditional bourgeois establishment, the Chinese and Russian revolutions were questionable. The Chinese Revolution of 1911 was a puzzle to be solved, and that puzzle contained many of the same elements with which the Oikoumene had wrestled in China previously: how could a non-Christian and nonmodern society be guided in directions that the Oikoumene would find compatible with its own objectives in that society, to wit, the maintenance of its privileged political, economic, and social position? The collapse of central power compounded the puzzle but did not change its essential structure. That the apparent guiding light of the revolution, Sun Yat-sen, was a Chinese Christian who had some experience with the West and spoke a familiar language of sociopolitical discourse was a complicating, and sometimes encouraging, element, but from the viewpoint of the West's primary concerns it was no more than that.

The Russian Revolution, on the other hand, was no puzzle for the West. It was a blatant challenge to the power of the bourgeois class, the structure of the society over which it ruled, and the philosophical—in the broadest sense of the term—and cultural foundations upon which that class depended. The leader of the Soviet revolution was no Asiatic who exhibited Western influences; he was a Westerner who rejected the West in its current condition in all its aspects. The West's problem with the Chinese Revolution was how to manage it. In Russia, the West's problem was how to defeat the Russian Revolution and, failing that, how to prevent it and its influence from spreading beyond Russia's frontiers. The Oikoumene did not yet perceive that these two revolutions might be linked in their immediate political and long-range historical significance. Ironically, as we shall see, it was the newest and most Asian member of the Oikoumene, Japan, that drew the correct inferences from these parallel events, even if

Japan also came to policy conclusions that ultimately would end in war and disaster for it.

Russia and China viewed each other's revolutions from perspectives wholly different from the Oikoumene's. The objectives of the Chinese Revolution of 1911—they were never spelled out very clearly—included the end of Qing control over China, the transformation of the Empire from a Manchu imperial domain into an imperial republic dominated by the Han Chinese, the reassertion of China's independence, the recapture of its economic freedom, the modernization of China's society and culture, and the equalization of its status, generally, with the Oikoumene. The Russian Revolution did not take place until six years later. Meanwhile, Russia's tsarist government, an integral part of the Oikoumene even if an element in its exploited periphery, not unnaturally took advantage of China's polycentric chaos to advance tsarist interests in China, most particularly in Manchuria, Mongolia, and Xinjiang.

While St. Petersburg was pursuing its own, and therefore the Oikoumene's, interests in China, Lenin was developing a revolutionary thesis about the function of China in a broader global perspective. He clearly saw China as the victim of oikoumenical capitalism and imperialism and believed that the national, or "native," bourgeoisie was the only class capable of leading revolutionary action in the colonial and semicolonial countries. Moreover, revolution in these areas would contribute to revolution within the Oikoumene because it would constitute an attack on the sources of capitalist strength, which lay, in part, in the cheap labor and raw materials, as well as the markets, of the colonial and semicolonial regions. Thus, the Chinese revolution was, in Lenin's analysis, a progressive factor in history and in the struggle against capitalism. Consequently, the revolution in the more advanced industrial capitalist societies had to support revolutions in the colonial and semicolonial regions such as China, even though, in the latter case, the Chinese revolution was reformist and bourgeois.

Russia's interest in China in the years immediately after the October Revolution was rooted in more than Lenin's theoretical musings about China. The Soviet revolution's forward momentum resulted from the combined effects of Soviet ideology and internal crisis in Central Europe (particularly in Germany and in Hungary) in 1918. This impetus was blunted, however, by the internal collapse of the revolutions in Hungary and Germany and the growing opposition, leading to intervention, of tsarist Russia's former Western allies, Britain, France, and the United States, joined in the Far East by Japan. The Soviets could make significant progress in areas of the world that were the object of the capitalist Oikoumene's attention by relinquishing tsarist Russia's interest in regions over which the new revolutionary government had no immediate control. This happened, as we have already seen, in Manchuria. Meanwhile, Moscow also pursued its revolutionary interests in those areas that could serve as bases for counterrevolutionary forces, like Mongolia. Here, Soviet intervention, countering Russian counterrevolutionary activity, was itself a progressive act within the context of such regions' political, social, and economic history.

The growth of Soviet power, leading to final victory over the counter-revolution and, consequently, the withdrawal of the interventionists from Soviet territory, meant that the new Soviet regime almost immediately had to face the problem of developing foreign alliances as a means of both insuring its self-defense and establishing of its international legitimacy. China, still in the throes of its own bourgeois revolution, presented Soviet Russia with potentially a most fertile field for diplomatic and even revolutionary activity. Moreover, the development of a positive relationship with China was a *prerequisite* for the pursuit of other Soviet interests in Asia: the final extinction of counterrevolutionary forces operating in those regions of the Empire that marched with Siberia and Russian Central Asia and the securing for Moscow of those tsarist Russian interests, however defined, that would serve the purposes of the new Soviet regime. In this connection, the Soviet Union's interests in Northern Manchuria and Mongolia were direct and immediate.

If China constituted a significant object of Soviet interest, the Soviet revolution also had a potential role in China. Chinese of various political orientations and real degrees of legitimate or revolutionary power saw the Soviet revolution as evidence that it was possible not only to withstand but even to expel imperialist power and influence from one's own territory. For China—pressed by foreign public and private power, nakedly by Japan and perhaps only slightly less blatantly by the Western powers and private economic interests—the Russian Revolution had significant psychological impact. Moreover, the Soviet victory in the civil war could not but have a heavy impact upon those frontier regions that the Chinese government claimed to be an integral part of the new republic. Finally, within the context of the polycentric chaos inside China, some of those seeking power, particularly Sun Yat-sen and his followers, saw in the new Soviet state a possible source of support in the face of the reluctance and even the refusal of the Western powers to support movements that had as their objective the overthrow of the "legitimate" regime in Peking. The Western powers needed that regime to legitimate their own positions and role inside China, and they were not about to aid its overthrow. The special interest that China and the new Soviet government held for each other was deeply rooted, therefore, in the internal and international conditions of each country, as well as in those particular areas wherein their separate interests converged directly, such as Manchuria, Mongolia, and Central Asia.

The structural confusion of China's internal politics was matched only by the structural complexity of the instruments available to the new Soviet regime for making and executing foreign policy. On China's side, the government in Peking represented the Chinese state and its legitimacy. Therefore, control of that government became the objective of each of the many competing personal and political groupings that constituted the maze of Chinese politics at the time. A warlord's capture of Peking and victory over his opponents meant the establishment of his legitimacy as the state power. The frequency with which control of Peking and the government changed hands only reflected the inability of any given warlord to establish his own power once and for all. Within this structure of Chinese political processes, Sun Yat-sen and his Nationalist forces were but one element, claiming for themselves a certain historical legitimacy but lacking power to establish that legitimacy on the field of military or political struggle. Inside Soviet Russia, the new state represented political power within the context of the traditional discourse about political power that was always held in the West. Internationally, the revolution in its social and historical guise found institutional existence in the establishment of the Communist International (Comintern) and various other international communist organizations. From the very beginning, therefore, the field of Soviet interests in China was much broader than state-to-state diplomatic interaction, and the institutional mechanisms available to the Soviets for the pursuit of their interests in China were almost as varied as those interests. Consequently, both theoretically (ideologically) and institutionally, Soviet policy toward China could take advantage of a rather remarkable degree of flexibility, which was maintained until the middle 1920s. That flexibility diminished to the extent that, in the Soviet Union, Stalin brought both state and party under his own unitary control and, in China, Chiang Kaishek and the Guomindang established at least a putative unity in China Proper and in some of the frontier regions.

In the early months following the October Revolution, those issues that were the daily bread of international diplomacy between Russia and China—control over the Chinese Eastern Railway, customs regulations, etc.—continued to occupy the diplomats. At the same time, however, Russian revolutionary optimism (and perhaps romanticism) found clear expression in Moscow's China policy in the Chicherin declaration. This duality of diplomacy and revolution was perfectly consonant with the Soviet government's dual persona of Russian government and socialist state. A month after the declaration, in August 1918, Chicherin expanded the range of this dualism when he wrote Sun Yat-sen, defining their common interests in revolutionary terms and stressing their revolutionary brotherhood and commonality: "Our success is your success. Our ruin is your ruin."[28]

It may seem, from hindsight born of more than half a century of international political, military, and ideological conflict, that the multifaceted Soviet approach to China in the early years of the revolution was duplicitous. Quite the contrary, Soviet policy displayed the complexity of the wide range of responsibilities that properly belonged to the new Soviet state and indicated that the first socialist state in the world did not consider itself bound by the diplomatic structures, niceties, procedures, and traditions of bourgeois establishmentarian diplomacy. In the realm of diplomatic practice and style, the Soviet revolution was assumed to have canceled the Congress of Vienna. Moreover, the institutional range of Soviet diplomacy responded more accurately to the realities of the Chinese political scene than did the traditional state-to-state and government-to-government relationships that the other Western powers continued to maintain. For its part, the Oikoumene presumably could turn the nonideological and self-interested warlords who sought control over the government at Peking more to its own purposes than it could Sun Yat-sen and his Guomindang, which was ideologically flabby but fervently nationalist.

The situation was not without irony, of course. As Soviet power proceeded to triumph over the counterrevolutionaries and the interventionists, and as the revolution inevitably had to transform itself into administration, more particularly into the administration of a well-defined geographical territory, traditional state interests proportionately increased in importance. The Soviets found that these interests were better served by traditional diplomatic structures, strategies, and tactics. Stalin's victory in the Soviet internal struggle for power in 1927 simply put the cap on a process that was already under way. The establishment in China, a year later, of a national government with pretensions to unity under the leadership of Chiang Kaishek was a parallel development that reinforced the return to traditional diplomacy on both sides.

Negotiations over the disposition of tsarist Russia's interests in China were surrounded from the beginning by considerable confusion, despite the apparent clarity of Chicherin's statements and of the Karakhan proposal. Soviet and Chinese official objectives were by no means commensurate, and Soviet spokesmen often denied Chinese interpretations of Moscow's statements. The Chinese government—whatever Chinese government—sought a reversal of the trend toward surrender of sovereign rights to foreign powers. Some progress in this area was almost necessary for the legitimation of any government in China in this era. Therefore, whoever its negotiating partners—tsarist authorities in Northern Manchuria, representatives of the Far Eastern Republic, or Soviet representatives in Moscow or China—Peking always sought the recapture, to the extent possible, of China's sovereign rights both in theory and in practice along the Chinese Eastern Railway and in Northern Manchuria and the recognition of China's sovereignty in Outer Mongolia. The Soviet Union's objectives were contrary: the preservation of Soviet Russia's legitimate, and controlling, position in Northern Manchuria; Peking's recognition of Russia's privileged status in Outer Mongolia and of Mongolian autonomy; Chinese recognition of the Soviet government, both as a form of international legitimation and as a means of denying Chinese sanctuary to counterrevolutionary forces; and the conclusion of a commercial arrangement with China that would secure for Siberia's population access to needed Chinese sources of food and materiel.

Toward these ends a series of missions were exchanged between China, on the one hand, and Russia and the Far Eastern Republic, on the other. Most of the important negotiations took place in Peking; as negotiations progressed, the status of Soviet representation rose by virtue of the appearance on the scene of officials with higher and higher rank, including Adolph Joffe, one of the Soviet Union's most accomplished diplomats. Finally, Leo Karakhan himself arrived in August 1923. The dispatch of the vice-commissar for foreign affairs to conclude negotiations with the Peking government signaled the importance Moscow attached to the talks. The protracted Sino-Soviet diplomatic exchanges began to reach a conclusion when Great Britain granted Moscow *de jure* recognition at the beginning of February 1924, which made it possible for Peking to proceed with its own acts of recognition without appearing to be transgressing behavioral limits established by the imperialist powers. Moreover, during the five years in which the negotiations had taken place, Russia's immediate postrevolutionary weakness had been transformed into strength through victory in the civil war and the achievement of at least a measure of international recognition. On the other hand, Peking's apparent strength had been exposed as weakness in the face of the mounting force of the Nationalists' movement in the south, which was soon to launch a drive for national unity under the aegis of the Guomindang. Therefore, despite the protests of some foreign powers, particularly France, the Russians and the Chinese signed an agreement on March 14, 1924, laying down the principles for the resolution of particular questions at a future conference.

On the basis of Moscow's increasing strength and Peking's growing weakness, Karakhan won an almost complete victory. Peking granted Moscow *de jure* recognition and attained nothing of importance in return. Soviet Russia's privileged position in Outer Mongolia was recognized, the People's Revolutionary Government was left in place in Urga, and China retained formal recognition of its sovereignty over Mongolia but no ability wherewith to exercise it. While encompassing the essence of the Soviet declaration renouncing Russian interests in China, the treaty left the Russian position essentially unchanged vis-à-vis the Chinese Eastern Railway and Manchuria. China reserved the right to acquire the railway, but the conditions of acquisition were unspecified. The future of the railway was a subject for determination by *both* China and Soviet Russia, and until a final disposition of the entire matter could be made, the stipulations of the Sino-Russian agreements of 1896 remained in force. (In the end, as we have seen, Russia sold the railway to Japan without reference to China's interests, thereby demonstrating utter contempt for Chinese sovereignty in the region.)

For China, the 1924 Sino-Soviet agreement represented a continuation of the Oikoumene's traditional diplomacy toward the Empire, and this despite the anti-imperialist Soviet revolution. What little China gained in Russian recognition of Chinese sovereignty over Mongolia and China's right to purchase (under unspecified conditions) the Chinese Eastern Railway could not offset the fact that the treaty actually did nothing for China, not even strengthening the Peking government in its struggle for primacy in China. At the time it was not yet understood that an anticapitalist socialist revolution in one part of the Oikoumene did not necessarily change either the Oikoumene's or that part's relationship with the Empire (or, for that matter, with any other part of the world). In the end, the new Soviet socialist state asserted its prerogatives in China in terms so similar to the tsarist position within the Empire as to be fundamentally indistinguishable.

RUSSIA AND THE SECOND CHINESE REVOLUTION

Soviet interest in the Chinese Revolution was already marked at the first congress of the Communist International in 1919. An appropriate Communist policy toward revolution in the regions of the globe we now call the Third World became a subject of debate between Lenin and the Indian Communist M. N. Roy. While Roy argued for a communist policy that would be based upon class struggle and the proletariat (even though a proletariat substantially did not exist in most of the Third World), Lenin insisted that national revolution under the aegis of the national bourgeoisie with communist support was a necessary step in the direction of the socialization of the nonindustrial regions of the world. Much of this debate was carried on in terms of the Chinese Revolution and the sociopolitical conditions of China, just as a few years later the rhetoric of the Stalin-Trotsky struggle for power was, to a certain extent, derived from conflicting analyses of the Chinese situation.

The establishment in 1921 of the Chinese Communist Party, together with the appearance of Communist influence among Chinese in France (including Zhou Enlai), provided the opportunity for the Comintern to enter directly into the maelstrom of the Chinese revolutionary chaos. Several foreign representatives of the Comintern appeared from time to time in China. For example, G. Maring traveled in China in 1921, met Sun Yatsen, attended the opening session of the Chinese Communist Party, and generally surveyed the situation with regard to prospects for the growth of a Marxist movement. As the party grew slowly but surely, the question of its relationship to the Guomindang also developed, and Maring, as the Comintern's representative, called at a special plenum of the Central Committee of the Chinese Communist Party in August 1922 for a "united front," by which Maring meant that individual Communist Party members would join the Guomindang while maintaining their own party membership and discipline. As its negotiators ran into increasing difficulties with the Peking government in 1922, the Soviet government began to shift its focus from the Peking government to Sun Yat-sen's movement in the south, centered at Canton. Previously, the Soviet government, as separate from the Comintern, had been correct, in traditional terms, in its relations with the Peking regime. However, Adolph Joffe, Soviet Russia's negotiator in Peking, had suggested in articles published in *Izvestiya* that the Guomindang, as a revolutionary movement centered in the south, deserved attention: "Dictators come and go, but the masses remain, and just as in China there has already been born a mass, national revolutionary movement, so, on it depends the fate of China."[29] Joffe left Peking in January 1923 and met Sun Yat-sen in Shanghai later that month; this was the beginning of an extraordinary collaboration between Chinese and Russian revolutionaries whose final outcome is yet to be seen.

The possibility of a relationship between Moscow and Canton had been suggested, however fleetingly, as early as 1920, when Sun wrote Chicherin to express his admiration for Soviet revolutionary and organizational techniques and to seek his counsel:

> I am extraordinarily interested in your work and in particular in the organization of your Soviets, your army, and education. I would like to know all that you others can tell me of these matters, particularly about education. Like Moscow I would like to lay the foundation of the Chinese Revolution deeply in the minds of the younger generation—the workers of tomorrow.[30]

The Sun-Joffe meeting in Shanghai was not a chance encounter, therefore, although prior to that time there had been no firm commitment on the part of the Soviet government (as distinct from the Comintern) to support the Chinese Revolution. The meeting produced an agreement that served as the basis for an alliance between the Guomindang and the Chinese Communist Party and for participation (to a limited extent) by the Guomindang in the Communist International. The agreement consisted of four basic points. First, both sides recognized that neither communism in general nor the Soviet system in particular was appropriate to China under current conditions. Second, Joffe declared his willingness to negotiate with China—any China in this case—on the basis of the Karakhan declaration of 1919. Third, Sun implicitly and explicitly accepted the primacy of Russian interests in Northern Manchuria and along the Chinese Eastern Railway, in terms similar to those that eventually were used in the 1924 Sino-Soviet agreement. Finally, both sides recognized that the Soviet Union had no imperialistic interests in Outer Mongolia and that immediate withdrawal of Soviet forces from Outer Mongolia was not a necessary goal of Chinese policy. This declaration accomplished two things: first, it laid the groundwork for cooperation on an interparty basis; second, it established the principles for intergovernmental relations should Sun and his party come to power and be in a position to negotiate a treaty with Soviet Russia. It must not be thought that Joffe's meeting with Sun was purely a matter of Soviet self-interest or that it smacked of cynicism. The Soviet leadership at the time considered the interests of the Soviet state and of the Communist movement to be identical, or close to identical. To Sun, Soviet Russia represented an example for China to follow in particular strategic or tactical situations, not to mention the Soviet Union's potential role as China's ally in the continuing Chinese struggle with the Oikoumene.

The Sun-Joffe agreement had immediate consequences. In the middle of 1923, Sun sent Chiang Kaishek, then a promising military leader in the Guomindang, to Moscow to carry the discussion further. Chiang's reception in the Soviet capital convinced Sun that a Soviet connection would be valuable. Leo Karakhan, arriving in Peking to negotiate with the Chinese government, sent Sun Yat-sen greetings, in response to which Sun wrote him reasserting his desire to obtain Soviet aid through the agency of Chiang Kaishek. On September 23, 1923, Karakhan again wrote Sun, this time establishing, in the person of Mikhail Borodin, official representation to Sun and his movement at Canton. All the while, of course, Karakhan was negotiating in Peking.

Borodin and Sun met daily during the winter of 1923–1924; the consequences of this collaboration were not long in coming. By the middle of 1924, Soviet influence over the Chinese Revolution was paramount, beginning with the establishment of the Guomindang-Communist alliance at the first Guomindang congress in January 1924, the founding of a military college, and the development of strategies and tactics for the unification of China under the banner of radical nationalism. Thus, the existence of competing political groups inside China and the variety of diplomatic and political instruments available to the Soviet Union resulted, by the middle of 1924, in an extraordinary situation in Chinese foreign relations. The Peking government had concluded, despite the protests of many Western powers, a treaty with the Soviet government that to all intents and purposes represented a total diplomatic victory for the Soviet Union while, at the same time, the Chinese Revolution, in its nationalist phase under the leadership of Sun Yat-sen and Chiang Kaishek, had come almost completely under Russian influence and guidance. Lenin died on January 21, 1924, and the remarkable relationship that seemed to be developing between China and Soviet Russia was wrecked in the struggle for power in the Soviet Union that ensued upon the leader's death. Stalin's victory over Trotsky entailed Soviet Russia's defeat in China.

Sun Yat-sen tried to use the alliance between the Guomindang and the Comintern to transform one of the many movements that were vying for political power into a movement that was truly national by virtue of its international status. He tried to accomplish this in 1923 when he sought access to the surplus produced by the local Maritime Customs. The treaty powers rejected his request, however, and fifteen foreign warships were brought into Canton harbor in order to prevent any attempt by Sun to seize the customs. The meeting with Joffe, the dispatch by Sun of his assistant to accompany Joffe to Japan, and the appointment of Borodin to be his advisor, all gave substance to Sun's claim to be China's national leader. From 1924 to 1927 the Russian connection grew considerably. In fact, the Soviets launched the first full-scale foreign aid project in China, the forerunner of various projects in the 1930s and, more particularly, of massive American aid during and after World War II. By the end of 1924, significant shipments of Russian arms and ammunition began to arrive in China to provide the weaponry for the Nationalist military forces. By 1925, several thousand Russian military advisors in China were in charge of training Chinese and of distributing military materiel. This international alliance with Soviet Russia and the Comintern and the internal alliance with the Chinese Communists catapulted the Guomindang into the position of major contender for political power inside China. Because of the institutional structure of the alliance itself, this position survived Sun's death in March 1925 and developed further.

The revolutionary struggle for power within China always had an international dimension by virtue of the position the foreign powers occupied in China. Despite Wilson, despite the high hopes of the Versailles conference (which, as we have seen, were irrelevant for China), and despite the Washington conference, with its declaration of intentions regarding Chinese sovereignty, the powers continued to dominate China's economy to their own advantage. Japan in Manchuria; the British in China (especially in the mining industry); the extraterritorial rights pertaining to foreign diplomats, citizens, and possessions (including real estate); the alienation of part of the great city of Shanghai and the other treaty ports; the presence of foreigners in positions of command in such internal Chinese bureaucratic structures as the maritime customs, the salt administration, and the post office; the continuing foreign access to Chinese revenues; the heavy foreign investment in, and extensive control of, Chinese industries; and the freedom with which foreigners traveled in China and foreign ships plied Chinese waters, including the internal waterways—all perpetuated the semicolonial status of China.

Occasionally the constant antiforeign reaction engendered by imperialism and the exploitive and foul working conditions imposed upon Chinese by foreign interests erupted in "incidents" and "movements," which punctuated the flow of events. For example, on May 30, 1925, Chinese police under British officers killed thirteen antiforeign labor union demonstrators on Nanjing Road in Shanghai; almost immediately protests, strikes, demonstrations, boycotts, and other antiforeign acts spread throughout the country, involving people from all classes of Chinese society. This was the so-called May Thirtieth movement, the greatest antiforeign manifestation in China to that date. Toward the end of June, fighting started at Canton between the cadets of the Chinese Nationalist army from Whampoa and English and French troops. As many as fifty-two Chinese were killed, and this led directly to a fifteen-month strike and boycott directed against the British Crown colony of Hong Kong. British commerce in South China suffered significantly from this nationalist, anti-imperialist activity.

The May Thirtieth movement and other popular actions against the foreigners (particularly the British) provided the context within which the Guomindang, with Soviet support and in alliance with the Chinese Communists, began the northern expedition. While the powers of the Oikoumene looked on with suspicion, the Guomindang armies moved north during the second part of 1926 and 1927. The Nationalists won victory by a combination of military conquest, diplomatic agreements with warlords, and popular organization. By April 1927, Chiang Kaishek had established his government at Nanjing in the Changjiang valley; having demonstrated his strength, Chiang was able to proceed with the unification of the country.

The Sino-Soviet, or Guomindang-Comintern (Chinese Communist), alliance did not survive the success of the northern expedition. Chiang Kaishek, a member of the landlord class who had based the personnel infrastructure of the Guomindang's officer corps on that class, found the alliance with Soviet Russia and the Communists politically inconvenient. His natural class allies in Chinese society were the landlords, the merchants, and the modern commercial elements, not the leaders of the nascent working class and labor movement or the leaders of antilandlord peasant rebellions. A primary object of his political attention was the group of warlords who had to be won over to Nationalist rule either by military force or by political intervention and agreement. These social, economic, and political considerations undoubtedly would have led sooner or later to conflict with Chiang's political allies but class enemies, the Communists. In Soviet Russia, however, the growing struggle between Stalin and Trotsky found in China a convenient focus for argument. This is not to say that China was the cause, or even provided the primary substance, of the conflict between the two Soviet leaders; rather, the nature and direction of the Chinese Revolution gave both Stalin and Trotsky a vehicle with which to argue about power for themselves and their followers. To be sure, each had his own ideological analysis and political description of China. Stalin wanted to continue collaboration with Chiang Kaishek and the Guomindang even in the face of increasing antagonism between the Nationalists and the Communists and direct attacks by Chiang on the Communists. Stalin's instrument in China was the government established at Wuhan, in the Changjiang valley, by the left wing of the Guomindang and the Communists in opposition to Chiang Kaishek's growing anticommunism. He sought an alliance between Wuhan and Nanjing. Even if Chiang became the enemy in China, Stalin was prepared to proceed with a nationalist, anti-imperialist, but not necessarily social revolutionary strategy. The Trotskyites, for their part, believed in a radical, rural based revolution that sought conquest of the urban centers and was prepared to carry out a social revolution.

Chiang's military and political victory over the Wuhan government, the Communists' failure in an armed uprising at Nanchang, and their subsequent withdrawal and continued persecution at the hands of Chiang Kaishek and his followers, together with particular incidents of conflict and mismanagement, effectively ended the alliance. By the end of 1927, the Soviet advisors were on their way back to Russia and the Nationalist government's anticommunist policy was clear for all to see. By the middle of 1928, the Communists who had survived the persecutions were in retreat in the mountainous border region between the provinces of Hunan and Kiangsi.

Chiang Kaishek's anticommunism had direct diplomatic consequences beyond the break in interparty relationships within China. The new Nationalist government, which came into formal existence in October 1928 at Nanjing, maintained diplomatic relations with the United States and those other powers in the Oikoumene that traditionally had preyed on China from the sea. Chiang also recognized Japan and its "legitimate" rights in Manchuria, even though Japan had been a primary target of the Nationalists' anti-imperialism (or, to put it another way, of anti-imperialist nationalism).

While the Nanjing government established diplomatic relations with the Oikoumene's Western powers, it refused to do so with Soviet Russia. In fact, by the end of 1928 there were indications that China was spoiling for conflict with its northern neighbor. In Manchuria, the "Young Marshal" declared that Soviet citizens would be loyal to China or face action from the government. He also declared that the Chinese Eastern Railway's Soviet administration had to introduce complete parity between Russians and Chinese in employment and management or face action on the part of the Chinese government, perhaps including a takeover. In January 1929, the first overt move against the Soviet authorities was made when the Chinese authorities confiscated, without compensation, the telephone system installed by the Chinese Eastern Railway in Harbin. Matters worsened, and on May 27, 1929, a Chinese force besieged the Soviet consulate at Harbin and arrested the entire staff, including the Soviet consul in Harbin and the Soviet consul-general from Mukden. The Chinese claimed that the raid was occasioned by a meeting at the consulate for the plotting of unrest in North China. Leo Karakhan, now acting commissar for foreign affairs, protested in vain. The Chinese released the consul and the consul-general, but thirty-eight other Soviet citizens remained under arrest.

The raid on the Soviet consulate was followed within a month by Chinese seizure of the railway and various of its properties (including the telegraph system) and the dismissal of the Soviet management and many Russian workers, some of whom were deported to the Soviet Union while others were placed under arrest. Soviet commercial offices in Manchuria were closed and Soviet organizations dissolved. Zhang Xueliang, claiming to act on orders from Nanjing, stationed about sixty thousand troops along the Soviet frontier.

The Chinese Nationalist action against Soviet interests in Manchuria probably had two purposes. First, such moves may have appeared to be a relatively inexpensive way of establishing the anti-imperialist character of the new Nanjing government, particularly in light of the obvious failure of Soviet policies in China in the middle and latter part of 1927. The world at large was anticommunist, and Chiang could win support at home by transforming anticommunism into anti-imperialism. Second, aware that his government commanded more apparent than real support in China, Chiang undoubtedly thought that he would benefit from denying the Soviets a base in North Manchuria from which they could support or carry out antigovernmental activities in China Proper. Zhang Xueliang, newly allied with Chiang Kaishek and the Nanjing government, probably saw in this move a means of establishing his own political position in Manchuria on a more popular basis and of demonstrating his allegiance to the Nanjing regime. However, the Soviet government responded to the original incident and to the replies made by Nanjing to its protests more resolutely than the Chinese had expected. Moscow canceled all its relationships with China, withdrew all its officials from China, and declared that it reserved all the rights it had obtained in March 1924, including, therefore, the right to intervene militarily. Finally, it announced that Germany would take over the protection of Soviet interests.

The Chinese authorities should have expected nothing less than the response they got. What they certainly did not expect was the lack of support their position received from the Oikoumene's Western powers. In the middle of July 1929, Nanjing published an extensive statement on its relations with the Soviet Union in Northern Manchuria, together with what it claimed to be evidence of Soviet subversive activities. China erroneously thought it would elicit the sympathy of the Western powers. The Western powers were well aware that an attack on "legitimate" and treaty-based Soviet interests in China—a matter quite separate from their own antipathy to the Soviet regime—carried the implication of a threat against all foreign "legitimate" and treaty-based interests in the territories under the real or theoretical control of the Nanjing government. The United States, for example, told China that its actions in Manchuria seemed to be a violation of the 1924 Sino-Soviet agreement and, therefore, could be taken as a direct attack on the Soviet Union. The foreign press echoed these sentiments, and it quickly became obvious that Britain and France shared the

American view. Even the Japanese, from whom the Chinese government probably expected support because of Tokyo's own interest in Manchuria, decided to remain neutral in the conflict, which was tantamount to a declaration of opposition to the Chinese position.

Fearful of Soviet action and lacking support among the Oikoumene's Western imperialist powers, the Chinese foreign minister now sought a mediator among the powers. The United States refused to play this role, even though both China and the Soviet Union requested it to do so. The French also expressed reluctance to serve as mediator since they well understood that the Chinese accusations against the Soviet Union were only a pretext for antiforeign action. Nevertheless, the Kellogg-Briand Pact renouncing war was about to be signed in Paris. The French approached Moscow to suggest that a peaceful solution be found to the Sino-Soviet conflict. In July, Karakhan demanded that China restore the Soviet Union's legal rights in Manchuria before negotiations could take place.

By the middle of August 1929, a Sino-Russian military conflict was beginning. On the last day of July, Sun Yat-sen's son, Sun Fo, the minister of railways, gave a press conference in Peking in which he declared that the Soviet Union was too isolated internationally and too strained internally to enter into armed conflict with China. While Sun Fo was declaring China's invulnerability to Russian attack, Chinese local officials in Manchuria were trying to negotiate with their Soviet counterparts. The Soviets, however, charged that Chinese and White Russian military units based in Manchuria were making attacks on Soviet territory. On August 6, Moscow appointed Vasili Blükher, who had been the chief military advisor to the Guomindang during the years of the alliance with the Communists, commander of a special army in the Far East whose obvious focus of attention was Manchuria and defense against the Chinese. Border clashes between Chinese and Soviet military forces continued, and by the middle of the month Nanjing was worried. It sought more actively to engage the Western powers in mediation with the Soviet Union; the German government, although unsympathetic to China, agreed to use its good offices to prevent further conflict.

Nanjing now attempted to use German willingness to mediate as a means of delaying diplomatic action on its own part so as to maximize China's political and military advantages, and it continued its hostile actions. For example, on October 15, after keeping them in prison in extremely bad conditions for five months, the government tried the Soviet citizens arrested at Harbin and gave them sentences ranging from two to nine years at hard labor. This was not an action intended to mollify Moscow. On September 7, the Soviets bombed a Chinese railway town on the frontier. Moscow accused Nanjing of interfering with Soviet shipping on the Amur River and of supporting White Russian forces that were making raids into the Soviet Union. Early in October, the Chinese mined part of the Amur and fired on Soviet military posts along the river. In retaliation, the Soviets attacked a Chinese garrison forcing it to retreat. Throughout this border conflict, Soviet military action was clearly intended to be punishing, not aggressive, and Soviet troops raided Chinese territory only in response to attack. They consistently withdrew once their missions were accomplished. By November the conflict had spread along almost the entire length of the Sino-Soviet border between Siberia and Manchuria. The Soviets had soundly defeated Chinese military units and had taken at least eight thousand prisoners. By the end of November, the Soviets had moved to the offensive and now occupied the Hailar region of Western Manchuria, destroying a significant Chinese force. Zhang Xueliang declared himself ready to settle the conflict on the basis of terms that Karakhan had originally set forth in the middle of July.

Failing at the last moment to enlist the support and sympathy of the Western powers, the Chinese signed an agreement with Moscow on December 3 in which Nanjing acknowledged that the terms set in 1924 still governed the Chinese Eastern Railway. Nanjing's appointees to management positions in the railway were dismissed, to be replaced by Russian appointees. Finally, on December 22, a Chinese representative, fully empowered by both the Nanjing and the Mukden authorities, signed a definitive treaty with the Soviet Union: the Khabarovsk Protocol essentially restored the *status quo ante*, with the exception that China now agreed to disarm the White Russian military units in Manchuria and to deport them from that region, as well as to insure the "full inviolability and all privileges" of Soviet institutions in Manchuria. The two powers further agreed to meet in Moscow on January 25, 1930, to resolve all other outstanding issues.[31]

Chiang Kaishek's Nationalist government at Nanjing claimed to be a truly national government, but with regard to policy toward the Soviet Union the new administration continued to pursue narrow objectives by often illegitimate means, which was more characteristic of a regime in a period of polycentrism than of a government truly representative of the Empire. Moreover, in doing so the Nationalists displayed their own misperceptions of the international scene and of China's role in it.

Cataclysm: China and World War II

CHINA'S INTERNATIONAL STATUS as a semicolony was clearly demonstrated during the years leading up to, and including, World War II. Like World War I, this was a conflict among the primary capitalist and imperialist powers. The full participation of the Soviet Union in the war as a consequence of the German attack of June 1941 did not change the nature of the war. This war differed from World War I, however, because China, neither a capitalist nor an imperialist power, became a major battlefield and a potential spoil of victory. The period of polycentrism in China ended in the crucible of war with the emergence of a new centralizing force, the Chinese Communist Party, which succeeded in reestablishing a single center of power and authority in and for the Empire.

China in the World on the Eve of World War II

China's semicolonial status meant that the Oikoumene's powers participated in Chinese politics, responded to changes in China and protected their own interests but did not control China in the radical sense of that term. For example, foreigners, including missionaries, withdrew from the interior of the country in the mid-1920s in the face of the rising tide of popular xenophobia, but the powers sent forty thousand troops to defend Shanghai against possible incursions by Guomindang revolutionary forces. In the aftermath of the May Thirtieth movement, the powers liberalized the political and social regime of Shanghai and even admitted Chinese to the municipal council. A Chinese district court replaced the Shanghai mixed court in 1927 and had jurisdiction over Chinese subjects. The Oikoumenical powers further recognized Chinese sovereignty in 1926 and

1927 by returning the right to collect customs duties at Canton, and the British negotiated the return of some small concessions in minor cities. Nonetheless, the oikoumenical powers continued to arrogate to themselves the right to intrude into China's internal affairs. On March 24, 1927, to cite one instance, American and British gunboats on the Changjiang bombarded Nanjing when six foreigners were killed during the Nationalists' attack on that city.

With the Guomindang government established at Nanjing, the foreign powers began to recognize the new regime and to conclude those international agreements that were necessary to regulate their intercourse with China. While the Nanjing decade (1928–1937) saw the gradual development of the symbolic and legal forms of political and economic autonomy from the Oikoumene, the Oikoumene's real economic penetration of China continued apace. This was paralleled by the extraordinary growth of the influence of Western, particularly Anglo-American, culture on Han Chinese culture. Han students studying abroad and foreigners in China, especially American missionaries working in both religious and secular fields, were vehicles for Western influence on Han Chinese literature, religion, education, and law, but the reach of this influence was restricted mainly to small groups within the Chinese population, such as intellectuals and middle- and upper-class residents of major urban centers along the coast and in the principal river valleys, and to the adminstrative bureaucracy and political activists in the public arena. The vast majority of the Chinese people were barely touched by the Western cultural impact on China in the 1920s and 1930s.

THE SCENE IS SET FOR WAR

World War II did not suddenly break out in China. Japan, along with the other members of the Oikoumene, functioned in China as an element in the Chinese political scene, where the military and the political were hardly distinguishable. (Indeed, it may be argued that the sharp distinction Western theorists like to make between military and civilian politics is more a function of Western culture than a reflection of reality.) The Japanese invasion of Manchuria in 1931, therefore, did not occur in a political vacuum; it was, in fact, an action taken by a full participant in Chinese politics. While this aggressive step exacerbated the Chinese conflict, it did not change the nature of that conflict. When Zhang Xueliang withdrew into North China, he was engaging in a maneuver in the warlord tradition.

Chiang Kaishek and the Guomindang regime sought to avoid a direct military confrontation with the Japanese. This policy rested on three distinct considerations. First, politically, organizationally, and materially, the Chinese forces were in no condition to oppose the Japanese in battle. Although Chiang was in the process of strengthening his military forces with the aid of German advisors, he was convinced he was not yet in a position to confront the Japanese without weakening his political position inside the country. Second, as time was to show, Chiang apparently had an agenda for China that set a higher priority on the development of internal political control than on resistance to the Japanese, whom he tended to treat, not incorrectly, as a longtime party to Chinese politics rather than as a foreign invader. Third, legitimacy has always been a major concern in Chinese political culture, and Chiang wanted to establish his own and his regime's legitimacy by vanquishing once and for all the only political group in China capable of challenging that legitimacy, the Communists. The historical lesson of the warlord period was not lost upon him: without legitimacy, military power is only military power. This interpretation ascribes almost altruistic motives to Chiang Kaishek. The achievement of legitimacy could also serve baser motives: it was essential to Chiang Kaishek as an instrument in his exploitation of the country for the aggrandizement of his class allies, his friends, and his family. That Chiang was prepared to amass great forces in this search for power and legitimacy was clearly demonstrated in 1934 by his mobilization of 700,000 troops for the fifth anticommunist "bandit suppression campaign," which led to the Long March.

For these reasons, Chiang instructed the "Young Marshal," Zhang Xueliang, to "resolutely maintain the principle of non-resistance"[1] to the Japanese and announced on September 23, 1931, that he was submitting the case to the League of Nations. Perhaps he believed that the powers of the Oikoumene would prevent their Japanese colleague from becoming too strong in East Asia and, therefore, a threat to Western interests. The Japanese, therefore, met with relatively little resistance; actual opposition was more a spontaneous display by isolated commanders or popular groups than an expression of national policy. By the end of March the Japanese also controlled the province of Jehol in northeastern China Proper.

THE LEAGUE OF NATIONS

If anyone doubted the League's impotence in the face of international crisis, the Manchurian incident exposed it once and for all and ended any hope that the League could serve as an instrument for the prevention of aggression. The League twice established deadlines for the Japanese to withdraw and twice Tokyo ignored them. The League considered imposing sanctions on Japan, but they would have been useless without the cooperation of the United States, Japan's chief competitor, and the United States was not a member of the League. Indeed, Washington refused to join in collective action against Japanese aggression. In December 1931, the League appointed the Lytton commission to go to the scene to investigate and recommend a solution. The commission undertook extensive investigations and held long hearings, but the Japanese refused to cooperate; in any event, the commission's report was not published until October 2, 1932, by which time the Japanese position in Manchuria was secure. The commission's report finally came up for discussion in the League of Nations at the beginning of 1933; its findings were ambiguous. Declaring both China and Japan guilty of acts of aggression that were threats to international peace, the commission proposed a compromise that both sides rejected, China because it did not see any need to compromise and Japan because, it saw compromise as a threat to national security. Japan withdrew from the League of Nations in March 1933. Two years later, the Soviet Union, whose own priorities did not include conflict with Japan, avoided confrontation by selling the Chinese Eastern Railway to Tokyo.

Chiang Kaishek, unable to depend upon the League, the Soviet Union or the Western powers of the Oikoumene for aid against Japan, now sought to translate his policy of nonresistance into a policy of positive accommodation, but Japan's price was too high. In effect, Tokyo told Nanjing it could purchase such an accommodation by becoming a cooperative satellite. The Guomindang government was in a precarious diplomatic position and was unable to muster the necessary resources to provide for its own military, political, and economic defense. The arrival in late 1935 of Chinese Communists in the northwest, at the end of their Long March from the region from which Chiang Kaishek had driven them earlier, made Nationalist China's propsects look even dimmer.

WORLD WAR II

By the mid-1930s the world's significant powers and forces were preparing for war. Whatever the liberal democracies may have thought or wished, negotiations, pronunciamentos, and compromises were not going to hold off the apocalypse. The rise of fascism and Nazism in Europe, the rearmament of Germany, Italian expansionism in Africa, and the failure of the democracies to come to the aid of the Spanish republicans in their vain struggle for survival against the Spanish fascists and their German and Italian supporters exposed the weaknesses of the international system established at Versailles and the irresponsible self-interest of the bourgeois governments throughout Western Europe and North America. On November 25, 1936, Berlin, Rome, and Tokyo signed the Anti-Comintern Pact, a treaty ostensibly intended as a defense against communism but actually an alliance of assistance and collaboration among mutually sympathetic fascist regimes. Embarrassing as it may be to recall now, almost the only voices calling for collective security in the face of German, Italian, and Japanese expansionism were the Soviet Union and the Comintern (effectively the same voice). The "great democracies" failed to respond creatively to this initiative, and the world moved closer and closer to war.

In the Far East, Japan steadily refined its position. At the end of 1934, for example, Japan denounced the five-power Pacific naval treaty, one of the agreements that issued from the Washington conference of 1922; this was tantamount to admitting that Japan had been strengthening its naval forces beyond the prescribed limits for some time (an action that paralleled, in the Far East, Hitler's rearmament of Germany in Europe, just as Japan's aggression in China prior to 1937 was later paralleled in Europe by Hitler's moves into Czechoslovakia and Austria). The conclusion of the Anti-Comintern Pact simply put the international capstone on an edifice of aggression that Tokyo had been busily constructing. Japan continued to move steadily on the ground too.

THE FOREIGN POLICY DEBATE

The Nanjing government's response to Japanese aggression was as ineffective politically as it was militarily. When Japan occupied Jehol province in China Proper in March 1933 and declared eastern Inner Mongolia a new political unit and an autonomous division of Manchukuo, the Guomindang responded by establishing, in August 1934, the Autonomous Mongolian Political Council, which included some Inner Mongol leaders. This weak answer to Japanese strength created severe doubts in Inner Mongolia about Nanjing's willingness to oppose Japan. In contrast, the Soviets and Outer Mongols signed a defense agreement in November 1934, and a series of military clashes confirmed the resolve of both Moscow and Ulan Bator to prevent further Japanese incursions into their spheres.

The Nanjing policy of accommodation and nonresistance continued until almost the end of 1936. Indeed, the Guomindang confirmed its view of Japan as a characteristic participant in internal Chinese politics by making clear Nanjing's readinesss to recognize Japan's special position in North China if Tokyo were willing to confirm China's (that is, the Nanjing regime's) suzerainty over the area. The Guomindang's view that Japan was only one among many contenders for power was demonstrated when, in the face of Japanese aggression, Nanjing began preparations for the sixth in a series of anticommunist campaigns just one day after the utter failure of conversations between its foreign minister and the Japanese ambassador.

Only a breakdown in the polycentric political system dominated, but not controlled, by the Guomindang succeeded in deflecting Chiang Kaishek from his chosen course. This course became, even earlier than 1936, the focus of what was the greatest public debate about foreign policy that China had ever witnessed. Not a debate in the contemporary Western sense of the term, this episode consisted in the enunciation of various and often conflicting demands by one group or another. The growth of a populist response to the Japanese provided the background for the debate and for the appearance of organizations that attempted to force the regime to change policy. For example, in May 1936 a so-called National Salvation League organized to demand an end to the civil war and a united front against Japan. The Communists strongly supported these initiatives and movements, and in May 1936 Zhou Enlai and a Comintern representative met Guomindang officials in Shanghai to discuss the issues; similar meetings were held at Nanjing.

The "Sian incident" provided the focal point of change. Zhang Xueliang and his Manchurian forces in Northern China were the most cohesive center of discontent with Chiang's policy toward the Japanese, both because they had been forced out of their homeland by the Japanese and because close communications were developing between Zhang and the Communists, who now had their headquarters in the Northwest. In fact, in the summer of 1936 the Communists appointed permanent representatives to Zhang's headquarters at Xian (Sian). It was also clear that Chiang's sixth bandit suppression campaign was aimed at Zhang Xueliang, as well as at the Communists in the Northwest, and that this campaign, together with the Japanese forces that were engaging in flanking maneuvers in North China and Inner Mongolia, could eliminate Zhang from the scene. Chiang had visited the "Young Marshal" in Xian in October to discuss the anticommunist campaign and had rejected at that time Zhang's proposals for a united anti-Japanese front. Subsequently, Chiang ordered the arrest in Shanghai of seven prominent leaders of the National Salvation League, which was a clear indication of his immovability. Apparently monomaniacal in thought and deed and blind to the depth of commitment on the part of some Chinese to the struggle against Japan, Chiang returned to Xian on December 7, 1936, to inform Zhang that the campaign against the Communists was to begin on December 12. Zhang, unable to tolerate Chiang's policies any further, arrested Chiang Kaishek on December 12. Although the radicals at Xian wanted to execute Chiang for treason immediately, delegations from Nanjing, including Madame Chiang Kaishek, and from the Communists, led by Zhou Enlai, and a message from Stalin dissuaded his captors; Zhang's and Chiang's camps negotiated a compromise eight-point plan for opposition to the Japanese. The "Young Marshal" released Chiang on Christmas Day 1936. Everyone recognized that in China Chiang alone could serve as the national leader of a united anti-Japanese front.

The agreements reached at Xian constituted an apparently complete about-face in the Nanjing regime's foreign policy. Chiang agreed to reorganize his government, to replace pro-Japanese party and government officials with men committed to national defense, to end the anticommunist campaigns, to organize joint resistance against the Japanese, to hold a national conference for the development of a broad national program, and to develop constructive relations with other antifascist powers (which meant, primarily, the Soviet Union, since it was the only active antifascist power at the time). The Japanese informed Nanjing that Tokyo considered the agreement an unfriendly act. Chiang himself immediately began to temporize. Back in Nanjing he declared the Xian agreements null and void and placed Zhang Xueliang under house arrest, dispersing his forces. It must be recorded, however, that Chiang also replaced some government personnel, canceled the sixth anticommunist campaign, and, for a time at least, brought an end to the civil war. Gradually the foundations were laid for an active Chinese foreign policy in defense of the nation's interests against manifest Japanese aggression and the apparent neutrality of the other powers of the Oikoumene.

THE WAR CONTINUES

What is popularly considered the second world war in Asia began with a whimper, not a bang. On the evening of July 7, 1937, a group of Japanese troops, ostensibly searching for a missing comrade, tried to enter the walled town of Wanping, not far from the Marco Polo Bridge, near the walls of Peking. The Chinese officer in charge refused them entry. The Japanese attacked the Chinese troops, and the Chinese returned fire. At first the Chinese authorities treated the event, which became known as the "Marco Polo Bridge incident," as just another moment in the ongoing Sino-Japanese conflict and assumed that the matter could be settled by local negotiations, as similar incidents had been. The local negotiations involved Chinese concessions to the Japanese. This time, however, Chiang and the Nanjing government declared, on July 19, that they would not be bound by local agreements made without their sanction, and Chiang declared his and the government's intention to resist all further Japanese pressure and aggression. The Sian incident had not been without effect. The conflict spread. Japanese troops moved up to the Tianjin-Peking Railway, and the Chinese forces evacuated Peking on August 8. On August 13, the Japanese attacked Chinese forces at Shanghai but met strong resistance. Nanjing had decided to act. In September, Chiang Kaishek and Zhou Enlai concluded negotiations for the creation of a united anti-Japanese front, the second KMT-CCP alliance. Mao Zedong declared that the war against the Japanese would be rooted in the people.

The Oikoumenical powers responded to the heightened level of hostilities each in light of its own interests. On July 16, 1937, the Americans spoke about principles that should guide international behavior and emphasized Washington's traditional interest in maintaining maximum opportunities for American commerce. In August the American secretary of state informed the Japanese that he was prepared to use his good offices to mediate the conflict, but Tokyo did not respond. The American declarations continued. In October the U.S. State Department observed that Japanese behavior in China contravened both the Washington Treaty of 1922 and the Kellogg-Briand Pact of 1928, and President Franklin Roosevelt delivered his famous "quarantine speech" against the "epidemic of world lawlessness." No one took these statements seriously, and for good reason. The United States itself had rejected the idea of intervention against Japanese aggression in Manchuria in 1931, and now, despite official condemnation of Japanese actions, the United States continued to sell significant quantities of scrap metal to Japan while offering China no aid. Washington also continued to declare itself bound by the Neutrality Acts of 1935 and 1937. The British were more active than the Americans in trying to mediate the conflict, but London was as irresolute as Washington in taking concrete political or economic actions to force the two sides to a resolution of their differences.

Germany found itself in a most ambiguous position. Berlin and Tokyo were linked in the tripartite axis. On the other hand, Germany was the primary source of military advice and aid to China at the time the conflict began to accelerate. Furthermore, Berlin believed that while a full-scale Sino-Japanese war would only weaken Japan to the benefit of the Soviet Union in the Far East, a Japanese victory would represent a threat to German Far Eastern interests. Finally, although some important Germans favored Japan, other prominent military and political figures, including Goering, favored China, which they saw as a potential center for German influence and power in Asia. This camp considered Japan an ally, not a friend. Japan recognized Germany's ambiguity in the conflict and, in August 1937, urged Berlin to withdraw both from mediation and from China. In the end, Germany, whose immediate ambitions lay in Europe, not Asia, acquiesced to Japan's request. On November 5, Germany conveyed Japanese demands to China, which were rejected, leaving the Germans no choice. By March 1938 Germany had practically ended all aid to China.

The more China sought aid from the non-Axis members of the Oikoumene, the more isolated the Chinese position became. China's appeals to the League of Nations between July and November 1937 were met with pious expressions of concern but no recommendations for action. Having exhausted that avenue of approach, China turned to the United States, Britain, and France for a loan to purchase war materiel. Hewing to tradition, Nanjing was prepared to offer customs and salt monopoly revenues as security for the loan; this time China also offered a more modern form of security, oil concessions. The request was largely ignored. The United States agreed to purchase Chinese silver for American dollars so that China could obtain hard currency; this facilitated Chinese military purchases but did not increase China's purchasing capacity. Abandoned by Germany and unable to obtain aid from the liberal democracies, China stood alone. By the end of December 1937, Chiang Kaishek had rejected a Japanese proposal for a negotiated settlement that was tantamount to an ultimatum for surrender. On January 14, 1938, the Japanese government decided to pursue its "special undeclared war" against China until it conquered the Empire.

RUSSIA COMES TO CHINA'S AID

As the Sino-Japanese conflict intensified, China and Russia once again found that their mutual interests overrode their mutual suspicions. Soviet inability to arouse the capitalist members of the Oikoumene to collective action against the growing aggressivity of the fascist states aided this understanding. As Japanese intentions became clearer, Moscow's self-interest required a China prepared to absorb Japanese activity, thereby deflecting Japan from Siberia and limiting Japan's capacity to threaten the Soviet Union. Moreover, with war approaching in Europe, Moscow did not want to fight on two widely separated fronts.

China signaled its need for an understanding with Russia as early as November 1936 by appointing T. F. Tsiang, a well-known proponent of Sino-Russian amity, as ambassador to Russia. Tsiang was instructed to obtain guarantees that Moscow would support China with both men and materiel if war with Japan broke out.

The Soviet Union, in turn, signaled its interest in contributing to China's capacity to resist Japan when Stalin intervened on Chiang Kai-shek's behalf during the Sian incident. Subsequently, in April 1937 Moscow proposed that Russia and China conclude a nonaggression pact and a treaty of mutual assistance. Nanjing was prepared to accede to a nonaggression pact but feared that Tokyo would interpret a treaty of mutual assistance as a military threat to Japan. Furthermore, Nanjing did not want to damage its relations with Germany, which was supplying military aid, advice, and some commercial support. As Sino-Soviet discussions continued through the spring and summer, some Chinese diplomats—not including the ambassador in Moscow—concluded that China would receive active Soviet military support in addition to material aid if Nanjing actively resisted Japan.

Two conditions militated against this conclusion. First, prior to offering active support for China, Moscow needed security in its own frontier regions in Central Asia and Siberia, but Stalin was in the midst of the great purges that were rocking the Soviet establishment, both military and party, to its very foundations. Moreover, the Soviet Union was anxious to protect its own and Outer Mongolia's frontier with Japan's Manchukuo from incursion by Japanese or puppet Manchukuo forces. Tokyo knew that it could use to its own advantage the decimation of the Soviet officer corps, which process reached to the very top with the execution in June 1937 of Marshal Tukhachevskii and many others. Indeed, Tokyo tested Soviet resolve by demanding Russian withdrawal from some strategic islands in the Amur River. The Soviets did withdraw, and when the Japanese landed their own troops on the islands the Soviets only protested verbally. Japan's military leaders were reassured by this incident. The second reason why Nanjing might have thought that Russia was unwilling to lend China active military support required no great act of perception. In the latter part of July 1937, German and Italian diplomats in Moscow informed the Chinese ambassador that Russian intervention on China's behalf against Japan would require German and Italian intervention on Japan's behalf against China. Anyone in Nanjing with the slightest knowledge of the world situation at the time would have understood this rather simple message.

Despite these contraindications, the Soviet Union and China signed a nonaggression pact on August 21, 1937, which strongly encouraged China's resolve to refuse to capitulate to Japan's demands for China's surrender. No doubt the development of a KMT-CCP détente inside China, however temporary, facilitated the construction of a potentially productive *modus vivendi* between Nanjing and Moscow, as did Moscow's need for strategic security in the Far East in the light of potential conflict in Europe.

China began to receive aid from the Soviet Union almost immediately after the pact was concluded. American historians' concentration on the role of the United States in World War II in the Pacific and the distortions introduced into the historical record by the Cold War have tended to belittle, if not obscure, the role Soviet men and materiel played in defending China against the Japanese during the first years of the war. While all the other world powers equivocated, the Soviet Union alone invested significantly in the defense of China.

By the end of 1937, the Soviet advisors in China included personalities already prominent, or soon to become prominent, in military affairs. Marshal Klimenti Voroshilov took direct responsibility for Soviet programs in China. In order to assure Moscow efficient and direct access to the Chinese government, Voroshilov's immediate adjutant became Soviet ambassador to China. His embassy included General Georgi Zhukov, later one of the Soviet Union's principal military strategists. Another advisor, General Vassili Chuikov, was to organize and lead the defense of Stalingrad against the Germans at the end of 1942 and the beginning of 1943. The Soviet advisory mission also included approximately five hundred officers who served as tank and artillery technical advisors.

The Soviet Union in 1938 facilitated the development of a Chinese air defense against the Japanese, however limited. Russian personnel who "volunteered" to help China flew Russian planes. More than two hundred such volunteers, dressed in civilian clothes, flew against the Japanese from a temporary Soviet air base in Northwest China. On April 29, 1938, the greatest air battle before World War II was fought near Hankou. The Russians played an important part on the Chinese side but were unable to prevent a Japanese victory. Russian planes and pilots also flew in defense of other Chinese cities, including Chongqing and Xian, and participated in the strafing of Japanese ships on the Changjiang and in the bombing of Formosa. Over one hundred Soviet pilots were killed in China. Relationships between the Soviet advisors, pilots, and other personnel in China and their Chinese colleagues exhibited the same problems that later were to plague American-Chinese relations in the same context. Each side accused the other of lack of cooperation, lack of respect, misbehavior, failure to plan jointly, and general rowdiness. On the other hand, an observer as prejudiced as the chief American air force advisor in China, General Claire Chennault, the founder in 1940 of the Flying Tigers, remarked on the discipline that characterized the Soviet military command both in battle and behind the lines.

The Soviet Union also aided China with money and materiel. Moscow extended credit to the value of approximately $30 million in August 1937, when the nonaggression pact was signed. The loan was quickly exhausted, and Sun Fo went to Moscow in 1938 to ask for more money. In May, the Russians extended a new credit, valued at $100 million, specifically for the purchase of military supplies.

Soviet supplies began to arrive in China through Xinjiang. With its maritime access to the world cut off by Japanese occupation of the coast and access to India and Southeast Asia (itself soon to be occupied by the Japanese) made difficult by high mountains and thick jungles, China could receive Soviet aid only across the Sino-Soviet frontier. Consequently, toward the end of 1937 the Chinese began to construct a highway from the Soviet frontier across Xinjiang to the city of Lanzhou in Gansu province; there the road turned south to the wartime capital of Chongqing. This highway, stretching fifty-two hundred kilometers, was completed by a vast number of workers, in approximately one year. The road greatly improved the efficiency of communications between China and the Soviet Union and increased the importance the Soviet Union attached to Xinjiang.

As Soviet aid to China mounted, so did the possibility of a Soviet-Japanese conflict. In early July 1938, a small Soviet military unit occupied a relatively unimportant height to the west of Lake Khansan near the intersection of the Soviet, Manchurian, and Korean borders. The Japanese claimed the hill was Manchukuo territory and insisted upon the withdrawal of the Soviet troops. Moscow refused, and the Japanese attacked on July 29 and forced the Soviets out. Both the Soviets and the Japanese then increased their strength in the region. Soviet forces grew to approximately twenty-seven infantry battalions, artillery regiments, and tank units. With the Japanese deeply involved in military campaigns in China Proper, particularly in the Changjiang Valley, the Soviets held a distinct advantage in the region. The Germans urged moderation on Tokyo, announcing they would render Japan no aid in the event of conflict between the Soviet Union and Japan. In the face of Soviet military superiority and German warnings, Japan decided to moderate its position and in the middle of August 1938 signed a truce that left the Soviets in command of the field but saved Japanese face. The incident cost the Japanese at least five hundred soldiers; the Soviets may have lost half that number.

The Soviet aid program was problematic for both the Soviet Union and China. On the Soviet side, internal party politics, specifically the Great Purge, deprived China of Soviet advisors with considerable field experience. On the Chinese side, Soviet aid cost the Nationalist regime its German support. The German advisors, who left China by the middle of 1938, had been largely committed to the Chinese cause and departed reluctantly, careful not to lend aid to the Japanese. Finally, Soviet aid in men, materiel, and credit went almost completely to the Guomindang regime; there is no record to suggest that the Chinese Communists received significant Soviet help during the entire course of World War II. In the 1930s, as in the 1920s, Stalin judged that only Chiang Kaishek was capable of providing the kind of leadership in China that Russia needed.

With tensions growing in Europe, the Soviet Union continued in 1939 to seek security in the Far East. Sun Fo again visited Moscow and on June 16, 1939, signed a new Sino-Soviet commercial agreement that vastly improved the conditions of trade between the two countries. This made possible the negotiation of further Soviet credits to China to the value of $150 million. In the Far East itself, with the situation along the Soviet-Manchukuo border in the east at least contained by the truce of August 1938, tension began to build along the frontier between the Soviet Union's Mongolian satellite and Manchukuo. The Soviet position inside Mongolia was strengthened not only by the presence of Soviet troops but also by a purge carried out by Choibalsan, who had been Sukhebator's comrade. Removed from power or liquidated were all those who might have had sympathies for the Japanese or for those Inner Mongols who were increasingly collaborating with the Japanese against the Nanjing government. By 1939 Choibalsan was premier and Mongolia was thoroughly a Soviet ally.

Japanese fear of an improvement in the Soviet strategic position in Central Asia led Tokyo to prepare an attack on Mongolia. On May 11, 1939, Japanese soldiers assaulted Mongolian border guards near Nomonhan, a small hill in the region of the Khalkhin River. The Soviets believed the Japanese intended to thrust north and cut the Trans-Siberian Railway. Soviet-Mongol and Japanese-Manchukuo troops fought along the river on May 28 and 29. The Japanese reinforced their troops, and in mid-June Moscow sent General Zhukov to take command of all forces in the Mongolian People's Republic, which were also reinforced. Zhukov built up an infantry and cavalry force of some strength and brought in about five hundred tanks and an equal number of planes, together with armored vehicles. The Japanese opened what they thought would be a decisive campaign on August 17, scheduling their main attack for August 24. Zhukov, however, commanding superior firepower and the best tank force ever assembled in the Far East, counterattacked on August 20. By August 30 the main Japanese forces had been surrounded and destroyed. Japan may have suffered as many as fifty-five thousand casualties in the Nomonhan battle, while the Mongols and the Soviets together suffered about ten thousand. The Nomonhan battle was the most important Russian-Japanese conflict since the Russo-Japanese War of 1904–1905. Much more significant, it was a major experiment in the use of tanks: Zhukov later applied in European Russia the lessons he had learned in Mongolia.

Events in Europe now overtook the Far East. In the midst of the Nomonhan battle, the Japanese learned, to their surprise, that on August 23 their chief European ally, Germany, had signed a nonaggression treaty with their chief Asian enemy, the Soviet Union. According to American sources, the Soviet Union in turn proposed a nonaggression treaty with Japan, but the Japanese were not prepared to respond. On September 1, 1939, Germany began the war in Europe by invading Poland. Japan, defeated at Nomonhan and recognizing that Germany was going its own way, decided to resolve Tokyo's conflict with Moscow. On September 16, the Soviet commissar for foreign affairs, Vyacheslav Molotov, and the Japanese ambassador in Moscow signed an agreement terminating the conflict and leaving each side in control of the positions it occupied at the moment. This settlement, which implicitly recognized the Soviet-Mongolian victory, was reconfirmed by a Japanese-Soviet border protocol at the beginning of June 1940.

The stabilization of Soviet-Japanese relations was fraught with implications for China. As war spread across Europe, the Soviet Union had to concentrate more and more of its resources in areas and activities that diminished the Russian capacity to extend aid to China; the stabilization also diminished Moscow's interest in extending aid. Stabilization permitted Tokyo to concentrate more and more of Japan's attention on China and, eventually, on the Pacific theater. That both parties' interests were thus served was recognized by the conclusion on April 13, 1941, of a nonaggression treaty between Moscow and Tokyo. Consequently, when Germany attacked Russia two months later, Japan was no longer prepared to engage in diversionary activities in the Soviet Far East. Japan itself was free to continue its conquest of China and to prepare for Pearl Harbor.

THE COURSE OF THE WAR

From the middle of 1937 to the end of 1941 China fought Japan alone. The democracies maintained a policy of political inaction and commercial action that favored Japan. Ahead of the Japanese advance, the Chinese government, whole factories, arsenals, schools, and universities, with their workers, students, managers, and faculties, moved beyond Tokyo's military reach to remoter, but safer, regions in the southwest and west, where they could establish bases for the long struggle. No little heroism was demonstrated throughout Chinese society during those epic times. By the end of 1938, the Japanese had completed their occupation of almost all of east and southeastern China, controlling some 1.5 million square kilometers of territory and a population of over 170 million. Tokyo set up a puppet regime in Peking and, later, Nanjing, and in October 1938 announced the establishment of "the new order in East Asia," in which all Asia would be ranged in hierarchical relationships around Japan at the center and pinnacle. By the beginning of 1939, however, the war had reached a stalemate; Japan found itself deeply mired in a static situation in which its China conquests were becoming increasingly costly in men and materiel as popular resistance grew.

Japan's only way out of immobility in China was expansion of Japanese horizons of conquest to more distant territories in search of necessary raw materials and a sense of forward motion in the war. In September 1940, after the fall of France, Japan occupied northern Indochina and, in the middle of 1941, southern Indochina. On July 2, 1941, Tokyo decided to establish the Greater East Asia Co-prosperity Sphere, which was intended to provide a political structure for the integration of China and the other conquered territories into the new order. On July 26, the United States froze Japan's assets and placed an embargo on the export of petroleum to Japan.

An American-Japanese crisis was in the making, and by November 1941 the two powers were frantically seeking to avoid war. In the midst of negotiations, however, Japan attacked the Americans in Hawaii; soon after December 7, 1941, the Japanese invaded and occupied Dutch and British, as well as American, possessions in the Pacific and Southeast Asia. The U.S. Congress declared war on Japan on December 8, and China declared war on Japan, as well as on Italy and Germany, the same day. The Soviet Union, deeply embroiled in Europe, carefully avoided becoming involved in the Far Eastern war. This war continued until, after years of hard fighting and two atomic bombs, General Douglas MacArthur accepted Japan's unconditional surrender on September 2, 1945.

Chiang Kaishek's conduct of the war inside China was as much a matter of continual contention as his policy of accommodation had been before 1937. Essentially, his government held the war in abeyance from 1941 to 1944 while, contrary to its own declarations, it continued the civil war against the Communists by attempting to close a military ring around their base in the Northwest. Moreover, although China was officially at war with Japan, trade flourished between the Japanese-occupied part of the country and so-called Free China, with high government officials often reaping great profits. Chiang simply refused to fight the Japanese or the corruption within his own ranks, with often disastrous results; for example, a 1943 campaign in Burma had to be aborted because of his inaction.

Throughout the war, Chiang literally blackmailed Washington into granting greater and greater concessions to prevent the Guomindang's withdrawal from the war against Japan, thereby releasing large numbers of troops for battle against the Allies in the Pacific. Sometimes these demands were diplomatic, as at the Cairo conference, where Chiang demanded, and obtained, an Allied promise to return to China the Japanese occupied territories of Manchuria, Formosa, and the Pescadore Islands. Sometimes Chiang's demands were economic, as when, toward the end of 1943, he insisted that Washington extend him a $1 billion loan. By the end of 1943 the Nationalist government's relations with its allies were strained to the extreme, but its policies did not change. Only the Communists engaged in serious fighting and inflicted telling defeats on the Japanese, liberating significant territories from occupation. The Japanese surrender in September 1945 found Japanese troops in China in approximately the same position they had held at the height of their advance, with the exception of the areas liberated by the Communists and that part of Manchuria the Soviets occupied in the war's last days.

World War II: China in the World

The titanic international struggle the West calls World War II was for China only one episode—albeit a major one—in many decades of conflict and chaos. However, the war wrought profound changes within China and without, changes so sweeping that speculators futurizing before the outbreak of the Sino-Japanese War in 1937 could not have imagined them in their depth or speed. By the end of the armed conflict in 1945, China had been given the title and trappings of world power, but with little or no regard for the reality of Chinese power. The stage was set for an internal transformation that, within forty-nine months, would end the period of polycentrism, reunify the Empire, and begin China's restoration to a position of real influence and power in the world. All of this was in the future, however, and the observer searches in vain for its prefiguration in the objectives and behavior of the parties to the conflict between 1937 and 1945.

The entry of the United States into the war changed the structure of each participant's strategy and expectations. China was now able to replace the Soviet Union with the United States as a source of aid. Undoubtedly China entertained this move with high hopes and much wishful thinking. The Soviet Union, battling the German juggernaut mightily, could be assured now that the Russians would not face the danger of a second front in the Far East. The United States suddenly found itself roughly shaken loose from its increasingly uncomfortable isolation; it was forced to take on international responsibilities with scarcely sufficient experience and information to make reasoned and intelligent choices among possible strategies and tactics. And Japan, bogged down by the immensity of China, now turned its attention to a war more easily conceived and fought because the territory and population—the islands of the Pacific—were more readily defined and administered and because they could offer, once occupied, little internal resistance to Japanese power.

World War II, because of its confusion and violence, raised more distinctly than any other episode after 1911 the question of the nature of Chinese foreign policy during the era of polycentrism between the Qing and the Communist avatars of the Empire. The extraordinary confusion of those times forces the observer to occupy a position of such distance that the broader outlines of policy become more immediately discernible; the rawness of the years of conflict makes the motives of the participants more obvious in retrospect than they were at the time. Certain traditional patterns of Chinese behavior asserted themselves in that period. This is not to say that they reasserted themselves, but only that they were more clearly observable. Three trends in particular stand out.

First, Chiang Kaishek provided a traditional, personalistic form of leadership, not a Western style of national leadership. He identified China with his chosen political instrument, the Guomindang, and more especially with his own person, so that China's destiny was subsumed in his own and that of his close relatives and followers. Patriotism became loyalty to Chiang's person. Corruption and the narrow politics of cliques lost any negative significance and became another, and normal, way of doing business. This style of leadership had roots deep in the traditional political culture, with its linkages between the emperor's leadership and the Empire's well-being, linkages that became obvious only when they were weakened, because disruption in the Empire or its environment represented error on the part of the emperor. The fate of the emperor at the apex of human society was practically synonymous with the fate of Chinese society; the emperor as the son of heaven nourished society. This contrasts strikingly, if subtly, with Western (or modern) styles of leadership in which successful statesmen give voice to society's needs or provide a means for transcending societal contradictions that would otherwise injure society. In China, moreover, polycentric politics frequently emphasized a narrow personalism in leadership, as the phenomenon of warlordism indicates. Chiang Kaishek exhibited imperial pretensions in republican form but was primarily a warlord in style. Western leaders, like Franklin Roosevelt, mistook this traditional style for national leadership in their own terms largely because Chiang successfully clothed his traditional political persona in the rhetoric of the Western political world; he was also a Christian. Wishful thinking by Westerners also played a role. Stalin, it must not be forgotten, also supported Chiang and his regime. In this case, however, support was the consequence of Stalin's recognition of the need for a unified China based upon class alliances, not of confusion concerning Chiang Kaishek's historical identity. It is doubtful that anyone in the Soviet Union seriously mistook Chiang for a progressive.

A second traditional characteristic whose visibility, retrospectively, was heightened during the war years was the use of foreign (non-Han) personnel in significant positions in the indigenous bureaucracy, in this case, the military establishment. This practice was not unknown in the prior history of the Empire's administrative culture, and the appointment of the American General Joseph Stilwell as chief of staff of the Chinese armed forces was only a modern instance of the tradition. The Americans may have insisted upon the appointment, but the ability of Chinese political culture to absorb the foreigner in command positions and by virtue of that very absorption to limit the foreigner's influence, if not to eliminate it altogether, was as apparent in World War II as it was during the Twenty-one Years' War in the nineteenth century. Inevitably this process of limitation by absorption led to profound misunderstandings between China and its external supporters, particularly the United States. For Washington, Stilwell's appointment was a means to increase efficiency and cooperation in the war effort; for Chongqing it was a consequence of imperialist pressure that required a traditional Chinese response. This occasion also gave the Chinese government the opportunity to employ a traditional strategy, "using the barbarian to control the barbarian."

Third, China and the West differed profoundly not only in their respective degrees of industrialization and standards of living, measured either impressionistically or statistically, but also in the nature of their societies. The society of the United States, China's chief wartime oikoumenical ally, was based upon small family units with social loyalties focused on public institutions in a social structure highly integrated by virtue of both communications and the remarkable division of labor typical of a highly industrialized society. China's society, even along the more advanced east coast, was remarkably feudal; individual and familial relationships were augmented by strongly personalized hierarchical loyalties focused on individuals rather than institutions within a society that lacked coherence beyond local regions. Army units and armies tended to be loyal to their leaders, not to the state, and one's attachment to one's locale was, inevitably within this structure, more powerful than one's attachment to one's homeland.

The personalistic and hierarchical nature of Chinese political relationships was as clear at the top of the government as it was at the village level among the peasants. Individuals were loyal to those who were their leaders because of provincial origins, ability to deliver advantages, and kinship ties. Those individuals who truly put the interests of the nation above their own or those of family and friends stand out as remarkable by virtue of their scarcity. As Chinese policy toward Japanese aggression before the

Sian incident shows, the movement to resist Japan actively was far more a popular movement (in both senses of the term "popular") than projection of vision by a national leadership. The same statement can be made with equal force about the years 1937–1945. Before 1949 China had no societal basis for national leadership.

The Guomindang regime's objectives during World War II were relatively straightforward and ordinary. First, Chiang Kaishek tried to fight the Japanese as little as possible. Although this decision led to extraordinary friction with the United States, it was no more than a continuation of the policy Chiang had pursued since the Japanese conquest of Manchuria in 1931. The reason behind this policy also remained the same: Chiang did not wish to expend treasure and materiel in a fight that was of only secondary importance to him. The primary struggle continued to be against the Communists. In 1941 he summarized his views: "The Japanese are a disease of the skin. The Communists are a disease of the heart."[2] For Washington, defeat of Japan was the Pacific war's main objective, but the United States often interpreted its problems with China not as a difference in priorities but as either a failure of Chinese command, will power, or planning or a consequence of corruption.

Chiang's reluctance to fight the Japanese was not a reluctance to fight *per se*; he was more than ready to fight the Communists whenever and wherever possible and often used aid intended by Washington for the struggle against the Japanese to bolster his anticommunist campaigns. Reluctance to fight the Japanese and insistence upon pursuing the struggle with the Communists were two facets of Chiang's, and therefore his government's, overarching purpose, which was the maintenance in power of the Guomindang and of Chiang Kaishek himself. Perhaps the Guomindang's survival was identified in the generalissimo's mind with the very existence of China. Much evidence supports the conclusion that for him the Guomindang's future encompassed China's. Even after the Sian incident, Chiang Kaishek was reluctant to enter into real cooperation with the Communists. His frequent betrayals of promises made to potential supporters, both military and political, his unwillingness to cooperate fully with his chief ally and almost sole source of foreign aid, the United States, and his continual use of political blackmail to increase American contributions to his government and its policies all formed part of the larger picture. Evidence also suggests that one of Chiang's wartime aims was the aggrandizement of himself, his family, and his friends in both political and financial terms. The corruption of wartime China was so much greater than that traditionally associated with Chinese governments as to be tantamount to corruption of a different kind. Although there were many honest civil and military servants of the nation, some even in the upper echelons of the civil and military bureaucracy, the cupidity of Chiang's immediate entourage was such that one can conclude only that the war provided wonderful opportunities for the private pursuit of public wealth by those who in the West would have been charged with responsibility for guiding the nation by setting the very best examples. During and after the war, foodstuffs intended for public relief were often diverted to high government officials or members of Chiang's entourage, who sold them on the market for private profit. Military aid was sometimes distributed to fictitious units so that members of the officer corps close to the generalissimo could realize private gain from the sale of arms and munitions. Taxes and other monies intended for public use would end up in private accounts. American officials in China during and after the war expressed great frustration at the behavior of Nationalist bureaucrats in the face of national need and impending disaster.

Chiang Kaishek and his supporters, in the best warlord tradition, constituted the national government. The Guomindang was their personal possession, to be used and exploited for their own purposes. The record of those years allows for very little other interpretation. China's Nationalist leaders did not adopt any real moral posture; they possessed no genuine national vision, either as nationalists or as internationalists. For them, World War II was really an extension of the multistate wars in which they were seasoned participants; now those wars were larger, had more participants, and presented greater opportunities for the acquisition of power and wealth.

A WARTIME FOREIGN POLICY?

The Chongqing government's primary foreign policy problem throughout World War II was its relationship with the United States. Indeed, this multifaceted and problematic relationship overshadowed every other foreign policy question and constituted one of the primary factors informing the Chiang regime's policies toward the Chinese Communists.

American strategy in the Pacific required a China capable of maintaining its struggle with Japan at a level of intensity that would lessen the pressure of Japanese men and materiel on the United States. During the European war this would leave the Americans free to concentrate most of their energies on the defeat of Nazi Germany and fascist Italy. After victory in Europe, when the Allies would turn their attention to the Pacific, this strategy would keep the Japanese fighting on two fronts, thereby holding down American losses. For some time, in fact, Washington assumed that victory over Japan would require major campaigns on the Asian mainland, a further reason for maintaining China's ability to fight.

American strategy took concrete form with the establishment in January 1942 of the China-Burma-India (CBI) theater of war. To link American and Chinese military activities and war objectives, Chiang Kaishek was named commander-in-chief of the China theater and Lieutenant General

Joseph Stilwell was appointed the American commander of the CBI theater and chief-of-staff of Chiang Kaishek's forces in the China theater, a position he shared with General He Yingqin, who was extraordinarily active in the KMT and in Chiang's personal entourage.

Stilwell was no newcomer to China; he combined a knowledge of the country and its culture with real faith in the fighting qualities of the Chinese peasant-soldier. This faith, however, was a weakness in the Sino-American command relationship. Within the context of massive public and private corruption in Nationalist China, any expectation that Chiang Kaishek's forces would be properly trained, led, and equipped was doomed to disappointment. Another weakness was the assumption that Chiang and the Chinese government had the same objectives in the war that Franklin Roosevelt and the American government espoused and that, therefore, anyone serving one entity was also serving the other—in short, that the war overrode all other considerations. Patently, this view was not true of Chiang Kaishek. Consequently, Stilwell immediately found himself serving two masters with different objectives; moreover, the two masters, one of whom was Roosevelt, may have had a less than adequate understanding of each other's aims and *modus operandi*. From the beginning, therefore, Stilwell's attempts to get the Chinese to wage an active war were frustrated. As the Japanese advanced through Burma in early 1942, he led a Chinese force into the region to support the British and to give battle to the enemy. The British and Chinese suffered a major defeat, and no little responsibility belonged to the ill-equipped and badly trained Chinese forces and their officers. Stilwell proposed a second Burma campaign for spring 1943, for which he tried to train some thirty Chinese divisions, but Chiang rejected any attempt on Stilwell's part to reorganize the Chinese army and command structure.

The presence in China of Claire Chennault, a retired U.S. army general who was an enthusiastic advocate of pursuing victory through air power, further complicated Stilwell's tasks and the Sino-American relationship. As we have seen, Chennault had established the Flying Tigers, or, more properly, the American Volunteer Corps, in China in 1940, when the United States was still maintaining neutrality and selling potential war materiel to Japan. After Pearl Harbor, Chennault was appointed commander of the China air task force of the U.S. army air corps. As an early recruit to the Chinese and, therefore, the Nationalist cause, Chennault had Chiang Kaishek's ear, an advantage he used to persuade Chiang that the war would be won by air, not ground, forces. Chennault and his argument played directly into Chiang's hands. Although Stilwell was technically Chennault's commander, Chennault had privileged access to the generalissimo, which allowed Chiang to play the two men off against each other to his own advantage. Moreover, the theory of the supremacy of air power that Chennault advocated gave the generalissimo arguments to use against Stilwell's demands for the reorganization and strengthening of China's ground forces. Again, Chiang could employ the classic stratagem of "using the barbarian to control the barbarian."

Pearl Harbor strengthened Chiang's position. Japan now was fighting the United States, Great Britain, and their allies, as well as China, and Japanese expansionism was finding more fertile fields in the South Pacific and Southeast Asia than in China. This permitted Chiang to conceive of the game of barbarian versus barbarian not just in the narrow sense of pitting one American officer against another but in the broadest possible terms, allowing the Japanese barbarian on one side and the American and English barbarians on the other to engage each other; his own forces, meanwhile, could avoid engaging the foreign enemy and, instead, concentrate on fighting the Communist internal enemy. The enlargement of the war brought allies to China's side but, ironically, permitted Chiang to pursue more energetically his own narrow interests rather than those of the anti-Japanese wartime alliance. Consequently, from 1941 to 1944 the struggle against the Japanese in China came largely to a standstill not because the opposing sides were equally matched but because one side was actively engaged elsewhere and the other did not care to do battle with it.

As we have seen, Chiang used both potential participation and potential capitulation as a means to obtain and to maximize financial and material advantages from the United States. On the one hand, he argued that without such aid he could not fight the Japanese; on the other, he threatened withdrawal from the war if his demands were not met. The first argument encouraged Washington's hope for action in the China theater; the second fed Washington's fear of a separate peace in China, which would release significant numbers of Japanese soldiers for battle against American troops in the Pacific. The blackmail inherent in Chiang's continuing stream of demands was obvious from the beginning. On December 30, 1941, Chiang informed the American ambassador in Chongqing that he wanted to borrow $1 billion, half from the United States and half from Great Britain. The Chinese told the Americans that they needed this loan to demonstrate Washington's faith in China at a time when China's morale was at low tide. It was clearly a political loan: although it was theoretically intended to facilitate currency control inside China, no measures were proposed to control inflation. Without doubt, the Americans in both Washington and Chongqing were well aware that this initial demand had little to do with any immediate or future reality. Chiang had the ability to promise and to threaten at the same time, and Washington concluded that it had no choice but to accede.

American attempts to placate the generalissimo—to buy him off, in effect—did not encourage him to engage Japan. The proposed Allied campaign in Burma in 1943 never started. In fact, Chiang successfully applied the same technique to the political domain. In December 1943, President

Roosevelt, Prime Minister Churchill, and Chiang met in Cairo to discuss the future course of the war. Chiang promised more active participation in return for a guarantee that, at war's end, China would be given back Manchuria, Formosa, and the Pescadore Islands. He also obtained agreement for Operation Buccaneer, an Allied amphibious action in the Bay of Bengal to parallel a land campaign in China. Chiang claimed this campaign was necessary in order to insure a continued flow of money and materiel into China, which, he argued, was the primary base for operations against Japan and therefore needed better supply routes from outside. He feared that the Allied strategy would shift from China to the Pacific, which would deprive him of certain obvious advantages. At the same time, Chiang's demand for an amphibious operation was intended to limit the commitment of Chinese men and materiel on the field of battle.

Nationalist China's international position began to weaken immediately after the Cairo conference, when Roosevelt, Churchill, and Stalin met at Teheran. Stalin was to have attended the conference in Cairo, but evidently he refused to sit down with Chiang Kaishek. Therefore, the original Cairo meeting was divided, and the second half, with Stalin participating, took place at Teheran immediately following the Cairo session. For several reasons, the Teheran conference marked a watershed in the Chinese government's relations with the outside world. First, by that time it was evident that the China front was not central to the war; at best, it was a holding operation, preventing Japan from transferring significant forces from the continent to the Pacific. In this perspective, China's war needs were minimal. Second, it had become obvious that the tide in the Pacific had turned and that a Pacific based strategy better suited both the immediate and the long-range war aims of the United States than did an attempt to revitalize the China theater; this was especially true in view of the intense frustration American military and civilian leaders were beginning to experience with Chongqing. Third, the Allied leaders decided to lay greater emphasis on the invasion of Europe through Normandy than on any other immediate strategy. Fourth, the end of the war in Europe would open the way for the Soviet Union's entrance into the Pacific war; at the time everyone thought this factor would contribute significantly to shortening the war. All this diminished the importance of China in Allied strategy and, therefore, weakened Chiang Kaishek's bargaining position with the United States. At Churchill's insistence, the amphibious part of the Burma operation was dropped: all resources were needed in Europe; moreover, the operation had been of doubtful significance in the first place. Chiang was furious.

The generalissimo again attempted to maximize his financial advantage by demanding that the United States extend him a $1 billion loan and give Chongqing planes as well as greatly increased supplies. China still had not spent $460 million of the $500 million loaned to it in 1942, and Chongqing was receiving $20 million monthly for military expenses. Chiang's protestations and threats damaged his relations with the United States.

Inside China, Communist-Nationalist relationships had not improved as a result of the war. Quite the contrary, a Nationalist attack on Communist forces in January 1941, unprovoked and necessary only within the context of Chiang's anticommunist policy, created an atmosphere of such deep suspicion that his patriotic protestations rang more hollow than ever. By February 1944, he had deployed more than half a million Nationalist troops in positions to fight the Communists in the northwest, not the Japanese in the east. Moreover, his government sought Washington's approval for the use of American materiel against the Communists rather than the Japanese. Tokyo was aware of these difficulties and of the conflict between Chennault and Stilwell, in which Chiang sided with Chennault, and concluded that this situation weakened the Chinese. The Japanese launched a major campaign in east and central China in April 1944. Although the Nationalist troops vastly outnumbered them, the Japanese won a resounding victory against the ill-equipped and badly led Chinese forces.

By mid-September, the Japanese had achieved most of their objectives. Roosevelt, whose frustration with the Chinese was increasing by leaps and bounds, now proposed that Stilwell be appointed field commander of the Chinese army. China had received more aid from the United States than it could absorb and still had suffered a major defeat at the hands of the Japanese, for which the Chinese leadership was to blame. Nevertheless, Chiang strongly pressured Washington to replace Stilwell with somebody more acceptable, that is, someone whom he could manage. Stilwell was recalled, and as the U.S. Department of the Army's official war history states, "It was the last diplomatic victory [Chiang Kaishek] was to win for many years."[3] The victory was symbolic only of Chiang's self-seeking, not of any wisdom or purpose in Chinese policy.

The Japanese sweep in the spring and summer of 1944 did not galvanize the Chinese Nationalists into action against them. Quite the contrary, the conflict with the Communists continued to preoccupy Chiang. Therefore, as the war in Europe moved toward victory and Allied attention began to shift to the Pacific, Washington had to concern itself more directly with preventing the outbreak in China of an all-consuming civil war.

SOVIET POLICY TO THE YALTA CONFERENCE

The German invasion of the Soviet Union practically ended Moscow's ability to aid China, and Chongqing perforce turned to the United States as its primary source of foreign support. At the same time, however, Chiang tried to wring every advantage out of the difficulties the Soviet Union was facing. The Soviets' primary objective in the Far East, however, was noninvolvement so that all Moscow's resources could be concentrated on the war with Germany. Soviet relations with Japan were based on the neutrality agreement of April 13, 1941. So wedded was the Soviet Union to this neutrality that when the United States inquired on December 8, 1941 about the possibility of obtaining bases in the Soviet Far East, Moscow replied within three days that it could do nothing that might endanger Soviet neutrality vis-à-vis Japan.

Although they rejected the American request for Siberian bases, the Soviets informed their new allies that they considered Japan an enemy and looked to its defeat. Washington continued to press its case, however, and in October 1943 Stalin told the American secretary of state that the U.S.S.R. would enter the Pacific war as soon as the European war ended. Later that year, at Teheran, Stalin informed Roosevelt and Churchill that after the end of the war with Germany he would be able to expand Soviet forces in the Far East sufficiently to permit Soviet entry into the war with Japan. He also made it clear that he disagreed with Roosevelt's perception of China as an actual or potential major participant in postwar international affairs. In fact, Stalin's position on China's future international role rested on a much more realistic appreciation of Nationalist China's politics and resources than did the American position. Stalin's declaration of intent at Teheran itself contributed to the diminution of China's importance to the war effort, since foreseeable Soviet participation in the Pacific war gave better assurance for victory than did present troubles with Chiang Kaishek. Undoubtedly, this kind of reasoning helped Roosevelt and Churchill decide on December 6 to abandon Operation Buccaneer in the Bay of Bengal in favor of concentration on the invasion of the European continent.

As the war in Europe progressed, Soviet interest in the Far East rapidly developed. When Churchill visited Moscow in October 1944 Stalin not only discussed further the possibility of American bases in the Soviet Far East but undertook to enter the Pacific war within three months following the defeat of Germany, upon condition that the United States help supply the Soviet Union's military needs for an Asian campaign. Stalin added one more condition: clarification of the political implications of such a move. Although he refused to put anything in writing, he presumably was referring not only to American and British but also to Chinese acceptance of Soviet terms. The United States began to supply Soviet needs but never obtained the air bases it sought.

China's agreement to Soviet political and territorial objectives in the Far East undoubtedly was necessary to Soviet plans for at least two reasons. First, an international agreement as a condition for Soviet entry into the war against Japan would legitimate those objectives. Second, Moscow obviously did not want to go to war in or with China to obtain Soviet objectives. Soviet analysts must have been aware that the presence in China of millions of Japanese troops, with their materiel, could present difficulties for the Soviet Union if, upon Japan's defeat, the Chiang Kaishek government were to invite the Japanese forces to join it in resistance to the U.S.S.R. in precisely those areas where the Soviet Union would be weakest, Siberia and the Far East. At the same time, recognizing how low were Sino-Soviet relations and probably wishing to give some indication of its disdain toward Chiang and his government, Moscow wanted to use the United States to obtain China's agreement to its *quid pro quo* demands. This, in turn, meant convincing Washington that it was in everyone's interest that the Soviet demands be met and, moreover, that these demands were both politically and historically legitimate. Thus, for example, when Major General Patrick Hurley visited Moscow to discuss American-Chinese relations, the Soviet foreign minister, Vyacheslav Molotov, instructed him in the history of Sino-Soviet relations. The Soviet Union had saved Chiang Kaishek at Xian in December 1936, Molotov claimed, hoping that this would improve the Chinese leader's attitude, but these hopes had not been fulfilled. Molotov disavowed any Soviet interest in participation in Chinese affairs or any serious concern for the Chinese Communists.

In China, Hurley, who had accepted Molotov's disclaimers, tried to persuade Chiang that the Soviet Union's interest in China was benign. Hurley's naivete in Moscow was equaled only by his naivete in China. At that very time, the Soviet press was growing exceedingly critical of the Chongqing regime; while refraining from direct attacks upon the generalissimo, the press went to great lengths to describe his regime as reactionary and corrupt. Chiang certainly was not about to believe that the Soviet Union was disinterested in regard to either the Chinese Communists or his own demise. There is little doubt that Soviet attitudes toward the Chinese Communists were neither highly developed nor overly enthusiastic. Moscow's attention was riveted on Europe; in the Far East, the maximization of their own potential advantages as a direct consequence of participation in the Japanese war was far more important to the Soviets than any potential the Chinese Communists might have had. Moreover, the nature of the Chinese Revolution and, more particularly, of the Chinese Communist Party continued to elude Stalin's grasp.

Only in December 1944 were Russia's desiderata in the Far East clearly made known to the United States. Ambassador Averell Harriman reported from Moscow that the Soviet Union expected to reestablish the position Russia had occupied prior to the Russo-Japanese War of 1904–1905. This position Stalin described as follows. (1) The Kurile Islands and the lower half of Sakhalin Island north of Japan should be returned to the Soviet Union as a protection for Russia's Pacific ports. (2) Russia would lease the ports of Dairen and Port Arthur and the railways in Manchuria that had previously been part of the Soviet domain, namely, the Chinese Eastern Railway. This would provide a direct link between the Trans-Siberian Railway and Vladivostok on the Pacific. Russia would also lease the South Manchurian Railway, connecting the Trans-Siberian with Dairen. (3) Russia was prepared to recognize Chinese sovereignty over Manchuria and expected Chinese recognition of the status quo in Outer Mongolia. These desiderata did not completely match American expectations. For example, at Teheran the powers had agreed that Dairen would be internationalized, not leased to the Soviet Union.

The Yalta conference was held in the first part of February 1945. Although the famed agreements were signed by the Soviet Union, the United States, and Great Britain on August 11, they were kept secret for a year. The Soviet Union agreed that within two to three months after German surrender in Europe it would enter the war against Japan. The conditions for entry were almost the same as those Stalin had presented to Harriman in December 1944, with the exception that Dairen's commercial port was to be internationalized, with due recognition given to the "preeminent interests" of the Soviet Union, and Port Arthur was specifically defined as a Soviet naval base; the Chinese Eastern Railway and the South Manchurian Railway were to be "jointly operated by the establishment of a joint Soviet-Chinese company, it being understood that the preeminent interests of the Soviet Union shall be safeguarded"; and finally, "the agreements concerning Outer Mongolia and the ports and railroads referred to above will require concurrence of Generalissimo Chiang Kaishek. The President [Roosevelt] will take measures in order to obtain this concurrence on advice from Marshal Stalin." At the end of the agreement, the Soviet Union expressed "its readiness to conclude with the National Government of China a pact of friendship and alliance between the U.S.S.R. and China in order to render assistance to China with its armed forces for the purpose of liberating China from the Japanese yoke."[4]

The Yalta conference marked the nadir of Chinese foreign policy. The international status of the government was as low as it could get, short of loss of recognition from other governments. The surrender of the Oikoumenical powers' extraterritorial privileges in China at the beginning of 1943 had been a legalistic but hollow victory for China; the rights in question pertained largely to areas under Japanese occupation. Now, at Yalta, the United States, Great Britain, and the Soviet Union agreed, to all intents and purposes, upon a redistribution of political and military power in the Far East without China's presence or participation; in fact, China was not taken into account as a power in its own right. The fact that the United States was asked to undertake to obtain Chiang Kaishek's concurrence shows clearly that he was considered a problem, not a participant or a power.

Exactly how the United States expected to secure Chinese acquiescence to the Soviet conditions is not clear. Certainly Chongqing wanted, and expected, the United States to act as advisor to China in its relations with the Soviet Union and, if possible, to represent China's interests to

Stalin. In the middle of 1944, when American Vice President Henry Wallace visited Chongqing, Chiang Kaishek asked America to play this role. Wallace reported that "if the United States can bring about better relations between the U.S.S.R. and China, and can bring about a meeting between Chinese and Soviet representatives, President Chiang would very much welcome such friendly assistance."[5] The vice president rejected the role of middleman for the United States, but General Hurley played that role perhaps without really understanding he was doing so. In February 1945, in the midst of the Yalta conference, Chiang considered sending T. V. Soong as his personal representative to Moscow for a meeting with Stalin; through Hurley the Chinese government transmitted a proposed agenda for that conference to Washington, but the U.S. State Department, full of frustration and resentment over its relations with the generalissimo, refused the role of advisor and Soong did not make the trip. Ironically, at the very time the State Department was refusing to play the role of advisor to China in its relations with the Soviet Union, the American president in Yalta was agreeing to act as intermediary between the signatory powers and Chiang Kaishek. Clearly the United States lacked a well-defined policy in China.

The reestablishment of Moscow's traditional (prerevolutionary) Far Eastern sphere of influence through coordinating cooperation among the Oikoumenical powers was the ultimate objective of the Soviet Union's China policy. This goal became clear when Stalin met President Roosevelt's close friend and advisor, Harry Hopkins, in Moscow on May 28, 1945. The Soviet leader informed Hopkins that the Soviet Union would be ready to move against Japan by August 8 and that he wanted to meet T. V. Soong in Moscow before July 1 in order to discuss China's acceptance of the Yalta agreements. The Soviet Union was using the United States to obtain its own objectives in China. Stalin also told Hopkins that he was prepared to encourage the unification of China under Chiang's leadership. This was a recurrent theme in Soviet communications with the United States throughout the first half of 1945. George Kennan, who was serving in Moscow at the time, understood that the Soviet Union really wanted "the maximum possible exclusion of penetration in that area (of China of interest to the Soviet Union) by outside Powers including America and Britain."[6] Moscow, according to Kennan's description of its policy objective, was seeking a sphere of influence in the tradition of late nineteenth century oikoumenical imperialism in China.

Soong learned of Stalin's invitation at the beginning of June. On June 14 he met with President Harry Truman, who told him about Stalin's conversation with Hopkins. The next day in Chongqing, Hurley gave Chiang Kaishek the details of the Yalta agreements; evidently Chiang had already received them from Moscow. Chiang immediately proposed that both the United States and Great Britain join in any Sino-Soviet accord implementing the Yalta understanding. Washington rejected this proposal, and China had to go to Moscow alone. Soong, heading the Chinese delegation, arrived on June 30 ostensibly to negotiate a new Sino-Soviet friendship agreement. He was accompanied by Chiang Kaishek's son, Chiang Chingkuo, who, having spent many years in the Soviet Union, had returned to China in April 1937 with a Soviet wife, spoke Russian, and was well acquainted with the Soviet scene. Although he was nominally an aide to the head of the delegation, the younger Chiang actually functioned as the generalissimo's personal representative. The minister-counselor of the Chinese embassy in Washington also accompanied the delegation, thereby underscoring China's desire for American participation even though such participation was not forthcoming.

The Chinese delegation was not in a strong bargaining position because at Yalta the United States and Great Britain had already endorsed the Soviet Union's demands. China had little to offer the Soviet Union in return for compromise. Moreover, with Soviet entry into the Pacific in the offing, Chongqing had to conclude an accord with Moscow before August 8 if it hoped to limit Soviet demands by international agreement. The Soviet Union began the negotiating process by stating demands that exceeded those agreed upon among the powers at Yalta: (1) the Soviet Union should have full ownership of the Chinese Eastern and South Manchurian railways, together with the coal mines and other enterprises associated with them; (2) the geographical definition of the leases in the Liaodong Peninsula should be restored to their 1898 boundaries; and (3) China should recognize the complete independence of Outer Mongolia. Not only did these demands exceed those agreed upon at Yalta, but Soong did not have the authority to grant them. Moreover, Chongqing wanted Soviet recognition of Chinese sovereignty over Outer Mongolia, not its independence. The negotiations were protracted. On July 13 they were adjourned so that Stalin and Molotov could attend the Potsdam conference, and on July 14 Soong left Moscow for consultations in Chongqing. Chiang Chingkuo, acting on his father's instructions, had met with Stalin privately and had found room for negotiation over Manchuria but not over Mongolia. He told Stalin that with the end of the war in the Pacific, Japan would be forever removed as a major power; only China, prepared to conclude a thirty-year agreement with the Soviet Union, would remain a power in the Far East. Stalin rejected this reasoning, arguing that Japan would regain its importance and that a strong China would be inclined to pursue its own interests. In any event, he said, treaties were "unreliable."[7] Of course, Stalin was correct on all counts.

At Potsdam Truman expressed concern to Stalin over the degree to which Soviet demands on China had exceeded expectations. Stalin tried to reassure Truman about the preservation of American interests in those areas under Russian influence. Historically, the parallel to the spheres of influence had been the Open Door, and Stalin was fully aware of the significance of this for the Americans. T. V. Soong, in Chongqing, did not find America's reassurances comforting; in protest against what he perceived to be Soviet victimization of China with American acquiescence, he resigned as foreign minister. The Chinese delegation returned to Moscow on August 7, headed by the new foreign minister, Wang Shijie, but including Soong as a member. Now events moved rapidly. The day before, August 6, 1945, the United States had dropped the first atom bomb on Hiroshima; the day after, August 8, Moscow declared war on Japan, and the Soviet Union attacked the Japanese in Manchuria ten minutes after midnight, on August 9. That same day the Americans dropped the second atom bomb, this time on Nagasaki. On August 10, the Japanese announced that they were ready to surrender, which they did on August 14. Only in Manchuria did the cease fire not take effect immediately: Soviet forces continued to drive ahead in order to maximize Moscow's advantage in any future negotiations.

With events unfolding so quickly, Stalin told Soong on August 10 that it was in China's interest to conclude an agreement with Moscow sooner rather than later, and Soong well understood that failure to reach an accord would only benefit the Russians. Moreover, lack of an agreement would leave open the possibility of expansion of Chinese Communist influence in those areas whose disposition had not been settled between Chongqing and Moscow.

The Chinese had to take what they could get. On August 14, the day Japan surrendered, the Russians and Chinese signed a series of agreements. A thirty-year treaty of friendship and alliance focused on prevention of renewed aggression by Japan. The treaty was overshadowed in importance by its accompanying notes and other agreements. In them the U.S.S.R. bound itself to the moral, military, and material support of the Nationalist government to the exclusion of its rivals and reaffirmed its respect for China's full sovereignty over Manchuria. Moscow also denied any intention of interfering in Xinjiang. In another note, China agreed that if a plebiscite in Outer Mongolia confirmed that region's desire for independence, "the Chinese government will recognize the independence of Outer Mongolia with the existing boundary as its boundary."[8] In effect, China, with no influence in Mongolia at all, accepted Soviet demands. Moscow and Chongqing also agreed to combine the two major rail systems in Manchuria—the Chinese Eastern Railway and the South Manchurian Railway— into one system to be jointly owned and operated by a ten-man board of directors, five Chinese and five Soviets. The Chinese would appoint the chairman; the Soviets, the vice-chairman. One of the Soviet board members would be manager, and his deputy would be Chinese. These agreements were also valid for thirty years, at the end of which time the railway and all its properties (subsidiary lines, coal mines, factories, and lands) would be turned over to China with no compensation to the

Soviet Union. Finally, China and the Soviet Union would share use of the naval base at Port Arthur, but the military commission governing that area would contain a Russian majority. On the other hand, the Chinese were given the civil administration of the Port Arthur area, but they would have to carry out Soviet recommendations in matters of defense. Although Dairen was declared a free commercial port, the Soviet lease of the port facilities established Moscow's privileged position there, as did the requirement that the harbor master be a Soviet citizen. These were also thirty-year agreements.

Both the Soviets and the Chinese expressed satisfaction with the results of their negotiations. Moscow had gained its primary objectives. Chiang Kaishek and his followers were also pleased, not necessarily with the particular terms but with the fact that the treaty and its accompanying agreements had been concluded between the Nationalist government of China and the Soviet Union. The Chinese Communists had played no role in the negotiations, and the Soviet Union had undertaken to bind itself to support the Chiang regime. Once again, the survival of Chiang Kaishek and his regime took precedence over national interests, and, as in the last years of the Qing dynasty and the early years of polycentrism, the survival of the Chinese government depended upon the support of a foreign power purchased by acquiescence to that power's demands inside China.

Both parties ratified the agreements on August 24, the same day that hostilities ended in Manchuria, and the ratifications were exchanged in Chongqing on December 5. Implementation began almost immediately. As early as August 24, Chiang Kaishek gave a speech in which he personally recognized Outer Mongolian independence; that reality was confirmed in formal terms when, on October 20, the Mongols held a plebiscite in which they voted unanimously in favor of independence. China accepted the results and formally recognized the Mongolian People's Republic on January 5, 1946. This recognition was more than a simple diplomatic act: it formalized the further disintegration of an imperial relationship that had spanned social and ethnic differences for more than two and a half centuries; it symbolized the Empire's contraction to China.

The Sino-Soviet agreements of 1945 seemed to provide the basis for a stable Far Eastern political settlement if only because they satisfied the Soviet Union's major demands. However, they created problems that were to bedevil Sino-Soviet relations for many years, problems that were to become more acute as the Empire reconstituted itself under Chinese Communist leadership.

AMERICAN WARTIME AID TO CHINA

Military and political self-interest was not the only motive for American aid in World War II. Both public and private concern for China arose from deep sources in American history and culture. For decades in the nineteenth century, American churches and missionaries had taken China as their primary, perhaps their most important, field of activity, as mid western towns with such names as Canton and Pekin attest. Moreover, once the Pacific war began, sympathy for China was supported by a certain sense of guilt that the United States had continued to trade with Japan throughout the 1930s and to send it war materiel despite China's agony. Washington certainly did not help—in fact, it did its best to hinder—private individuals who sought to help China before 1941.

Some American government officials were not without sympathy for China, however. Henry Morgenthau, Franklin Roosevelt's secretary of the treasury, was responsible for the policy of facilitating purchases of Chinese precious metals in order to provide China with foreign exchange to purchase strategic goods on the world market. In 1937, Chinese currency and credit commanded more international respect than at any previous time in the twentieth century, so Morgenthau's maneuvers on China's behalf were creditable.

The acquisition of financial resources for the purchase of war materiel abroad was not China's only problem in developing its defenses. Purchases made overseas had to be brought into the country, and with the Japanese blockading or occupying the China coast, other routes had to be found. Until the Japanese capture of Canton in October 1938, the Hong Kong-Canton route provided the main access into the country. The French railway from Haiphong in French Indochina to the Chinese border and on to Kunming in Yunnan province was badly managed and inefficient, and the Japanese capture of Nanning in Guangxi province ended its limited usefulness. Moreover, the French had already bowed to Japanese threats in the fall of 1937, embargoing shipments of arms and munitions to China through their Indochinese colony. The old silk route through Xinjiang, connecting Russian Central Asia with China Proper, was heavily used, although in the early months of the war a considerable amount of Russian materiel entered China through the Hong Kong-Canton route. Finally, once the war began, considerable effort was made to develop the old trade route between Burma and Kunming; in the beginning of December 1938 the Chinese government announced the completion of the Burma Road. By the beginning of 1939, some materiel was coming into the country this way.

The war quickly affected air transport, too. By August 1938, the Japanese were attacking Chinese civil aviation. Until the war, Hong Kong was the main point of air access into China from the outside, but after the fall of Canton flights became more problematic because they had to take place over enemy territory. Nonetheless, the China National Aviation Corporation (CNAC) continued flying, connecting Chongqing with Hong Kong, Burma, and India.

China's increasing difficulties during 1938 had severe economic repercussions that ranged far beyond the problems of purchase of war materiel abroad and its transport into the country. Economic disruption could only favor the Japanese cause. China badly needed foreign loans to stabilize its currency. Great Britain, not without American encouragement, was prepared to make significant credits available to Chongqing, but on condition that Chiang Kaishek reform the Nationalist administration, organize his friends and kin into "a solid front to Japan," and give T. V. Soong, whom the British respected, responsibility for managing the use of the credits. Chiang rejected conditional assistance of any kind. Whether his reasons derived from the experience of foreign interference in Chinese affairs or from cupidity, he displayed even at this early date an obstinate independence that more often than not stood in the way of efficient prosecution of the war in China.[9]

By the middle of 1938, pressure had begun to mount in Washington for direct financial aid to China. Joseph Stilwell, who was then military attaché at the American embassy, recommended the extension of military as well as commercial credits. At the same time, however, there was equally strong pressure to maintain an even hand in the Far East and to offer Japan the equivalent of any offer made to China. This was not the first time in the history of American foreign policy that equity would be used to mask a dubious morality. The Roosevelt administration decided, however, that because China and Japan had not declared war on each other formally, the United States could act outside the constraints that the Neutrality Acts otherwise would have imposed. Therefore, in December 1938, Washington made a $25 million credit available to China for the purchase of agricultural goods and manufactured products. At the same time, the American ambassador in Tokyo was instructed to inform the Japanese that this was "a genuine and legitimate commercial transaction" unrelated to the war.[10]

The war threatened important Western economic interests in China. For the United States this meant trade, but Great Britain was concerned about safeguarding the maritime customs, which were essential to the servicing of China's debt. By 1938, Japan was inhibiting remittances from China's ports for debt servicing; moreover, Japan was violating the Open Door agreements that were so crucial to the whole structure of the Oikoumene's economic activities in China. The British, therefore, entered into negotiations with the Japanese, much to the dismay of the Chinese government, although the latter was consulted. By May, Great Britain, the United States, and France, the primary foreign beneficiaries of the customs remittances, had agreed to a complex but workable arrangement whereby Japan's Yokohama Specie Bank would serve as intermediary between the Chinese maritime customs, now under Japanese control, and the foreign financial interests. While this arrangement prevented the immediate Japanese takeover of the customs service, it also signaled the end of the Oikoumene's privileged position.

As Japanese aggression in China turned into a stalemated war, expansion of communications between China and the outside world, that is to say, between China and its potential but not yet actual allies, acquired increasing importance. Existing land and air routes were expanded, and private American sources provided considerable private aid and support. When Japan's forces cut the Burma Road into China, air transport became especially significant. Only two weeks before Pearl Harbor, the British gave permission for the survey of an air route from India over the mountains into China; this route eventually was known as the Hump. In general, however, Pearl Harbor found China not only wanting considerable materiel but also facing difficulties in bringing that aid into the country. Chinese currency was still passably strong, and it was not evident that China required great credits from abroad to wage the kind of war the United States now wanted Chongqing to conduct.

The key to the transport of war materiel seemed to be air power, and extensive Japanese bombing of civilian, as well as military, targets made Chongqing feel acutely the need to acquire an air defense capability. However, a variety of circumstances, including ignorance and laziness on the part of the responsible officials, the complete faith they placed in a Chinese airplane assembly plant in the far west that would be long in producing even out-of-date planes, and rivalry among various airplane companies and their partisans within the Chinese government, prevented any serious progress in this area. Japanese bombing of Chongqing in 1939 finally galvanized the government into action, but by the time T. V. Soong arrived in Washington in mid-1940 to obtain credits to purchase planes, the crisis in Europe had diverted all available production in that direction. Claire Chennault went from China to Washington in October 1940 to lobby for China's cause, but only in early 1941 did China begin to receive airplanes from the United States and then solely because Great Britain was prepared to forego deliveries at that time in exchange for increased deliveries later. These planes made it possible for Chennault to organize the Flying Tigers, which became the backbone of Chinese air resistance to the Japanese and the basis of the only really successful anti-Japanese air action in China even after Pearl Harbor.

The enactment of the Lend-Lease Act in March 1941 was the first major break in American isolationism. This legislation made it possible for China to acquire badly needed military goods with American credits. Chinese demands were often unreasonable, as to both quantity and suitability of goods, but during 1941 China received from the United States almost $26 million in lend-lease aid, which accounted for only 1.7 percent of the total lend-lease assistance to all countries fighting the fascists. In part, this was a consequence of the priority given in American strategic thinking to Great Britain and the Soviet Union; more deeply, it was a consequence of the extreme Eurocentric orientation of U.S. political and military leaders, a pattern that dominated postwar American diplomacy for at least three or four decades.

American aid to China before December 7, 1941, was too halting to support a major Chinese war effort against Japan. Even American attempts to back China's currency and to facilitate the conversion of its precious metal reserves into foreign currencies did not represent a significant contribution to China's self-defense. At the same time, the Guomindang government failed to convince the United States that it was pursuing the anti-Japanese war with single-minded purposefulness. Obviously it was not. The Chinese people were suffering greatly from the effects of the war, particularly in the eastern part of the country, and they often demonstrated great personal and group heroism. But their government's military record and the attitudes and policies of China's civilian and military leaders simply did not support the endless demands for increased foreign military, financial, and commercial aid.

AFTER PEARL HARBOR

The initial Japanese victories in the Pacific, together with the priority granted the continuing struggle against Hitler in Europe and North Africa, meant that in the years immediately after Pearl Harbor financial rather than military aid was all that the Allies, most particularly the United States, could supply China. Furthermore, Pearl Harbor was an American-Japanese event. It did not change the military situation on the ground in China. Consequently, China's ability to absorb military aid was never put to the test and remains a question for speculation.

Throughout the war, Chiang Kaishek's regime and entourage stood as filters or buffers between American aid and those for whom it was intended, whether military units or civilians. Moreover, they carefully made sure that American aid did not impinge upon the prerogatives of the ruling classes. For example, the wealthier strata of the population, upon whom Chiang greatly depended for internal support, at no time were pressured or encouraged to support the government's financial and economic efforts or to cooperate with American activities on behalf of the Chinese government. The only modifications of upper-class consumption were created by wartime scarcities, not by conscientious and consistent government policy. Undoubtedly there were patriots among these classes, but for most the war and American aid provided great opportunities to be exploited for the benefit of self, family, and friends. This trend did not go unnoticed in Washington. As early as the beginning of 1941, the American government tried to attach strings to its aid to insure its efficacy, but the Chinese government won a major diplomatic victory when Chongqing refused to agree to consult the United States about the use of the initial $500 million credit granted it.

A pattern soon emerged in Sino-American wartime relations. American fear of Chinese withdrawal from the war was greater than U.S. anxiety over the uses to which the Chinese put American aid. Consequently,

American aid functioned by and large as a continuing bribe to keep Nationalist China in the war. There was ample precedent in Chinese political culture for the development of policies of strength that derived from real or feigned weakness. Recognition of America's need to keep China in the war at all costs gave Chiang an effective tool for exploitation of Washington; by raising the level of his threats to leave the war because of China's inability to carry on, Chiang could up the ante whenever he felt called upon to do so. Between Pearl Harbor and mid-1945, the United States gave China financial support in the amount of almost $1 billion in one form or another. Even American payments to sustain Chinese military operations in the field provided opportunities for exploitation and therefore became a source of contention when China insisted upon receiving transfer payments at an artificially low rate of exchange. Cheap American dollars could be sold on the black market at great profit or deposited abroad against an uncertain future.

Some effort was made to provide China with military as well as financial aid. The Flying Tigers, Merrill's Marauders, and the pilots who flew over the Hump, for example, all contributed to the conduct of the war both by their actions and by their commitment to China's cause against Japan. However, the lack of a land route for the transport of men and materiel inhibited any large-scale effort. The loss of Burma in 1941–1942 was a major blow, and so fierce was the Japanese will to hold Burma and so unwilling was Chiang Kaishek to contribute significantly and cooperatively to Allied efforts to free Burma that the Burma route to China could be reopened only in 1944. It was not until January 1945 that the final link was completed. (Chinese forces fighting with the Allies in Burma were far better trained and led than Chinese armies inside China; however, they could not return to China until the Burma Road was available, and China was thus deprived of some of her best military resources. The quality of the Chinese forces in Burma was protected and promoted by their distance from Chinese Nationalist supply and command practices.)

The deterioration of the Chinese Nationalists' will to fight and of their fighting power became more and more evident as the war dragged on. Apologists for the Chiang regime insisted, and decades later sometimes continue to insist, that blame for this situation rested with the Allies, specifically the United States, for failing to provide sufficient aid early enough in the war. They also blamed the Allies for the decisions concerning the conduct of the war that were made at the Cairo conference. These factors may have contributed to the regime's inability or unwillingness to wage war in close cooperation and coordination with the Allies, but China's internal social and economic conditions and the class structure of exploitation, together with the politics of self-interest that characterized the regime, were the primary factors.

THE UNITED STATES AND CHINA
DURING THE WAR

Washington's China policy between 1941 and 1945 had two main objectives, according to Cordell Hull, then American secretary of state. First was the "effective joint prosecution of the war." Second was "the recognition and building up of China as a major power entitled to equal rank with the three big Western Allies, Russia, Britain, and the United States, during and after the war, both for the preparation of a postwar organization and for the establishment of stability and prosperity in the Orient." U.S. wartime policy in general may have had the broad political objective of preventing the Soviet Union from benefiting from the conditions that would follow from the defeat of Germany, Japan, and Italy, but this objective was formulated more clearly and earlier in the Far East than in Europe. However, American leaders by and large, or at least President Roosevelt, expected a greater degree of postwar cooperation from the Soviet Union in the Far East than they actually obtained.[11]

American policy objectives derived from at least two different perspectives on the world. The first was a sense of responsibility Americans felt for the world, most particularly for China. This sense of responsibility was more than slightly tinged with that romanticism that had sent missionaries and dollars to China for over a century. It was more than just romanticism, however, because it entailed a feeling of intrinsic superiority toward those whom the United States proposed to take under its wing, a sense of superiority that arose from Protestantism (as opposed to all other religions), capitalism (as opposed to all other socioeconomic systems), democracy (as opposed to all other political systems), and racism (Northwest European as opposed to everyone else). Ironically for China and the rest of the world, this American perspective took the form of a profound affection for those whom Americans wanted to raise to the American level, a level most Americans knew for a fact everyone in the world wanted to reach. The second U.S. perspective on the world derived from a political analysis of present reality that assumed that Japan's defeat would create a power vacuum in the Far East and the Western Pacific. Only China would be able to fill that vacuum because China was a potentially powerful nation that, in light of the first perspective, was America's natural friend and ally. The combination of these two perspectives—American global responsibility and political analysis—seemed to reassure American statesmen that a policy seeking to actualize the promise implicit in these perspectives would insure continued access to the China market for the U.S. economy after the war. That market always held out great potential although the potential was never quite realized.

The problems this policy entailed constitute the very history of American-Chinese relations through a good part of the twentieth century. In a history of Chinese foreign policy, it suffices to summarize them. First, China was *not* a great power during the period in question, nor had it been since the middle of the nineteenth century, when China suffered its first defeat at the hands of a small group of British soldiers in the Twenty-one Years' War. That one or another member of the Oikoumene, or all of them together, may have found the great power fiction useful to the Oikoumene's purposes did not make China a great power. China was least a great power during the years of polycentrism. Second, the assumption that China actually was, or potentially could be, a great power directly implied that its government was capable of behaving both within and without Chinese borders as the government of a great power. It is axiomatic in international relations that a country that is *potentially* strong because of its economy, natural resources, population, or some other set of circumstances is *actually* weak if its government is incapable of acting resolutely on the national and international scenes and of marshaling the nation's resources and utilizing them for the achievement of national objectives. By no stretch of the imagination could Chiang Kaishek's regime have been thought to possess the characteristics of the government of a great power; yet the logic of American political objectives in the Far East required that the United States treat that government as if it were indeed a great power government. The fact that the Chiang regime could not, and perhaps did not even want to, act politically, militarily, or economically as a great power government further complicated the matter. The simple truth was that U.S. political objectives in the Far East were hamstrung at the very outset by Chinese reality.

Other factors contributed to the inappropriateness of American policy. America's own wartime military policies gave priority to Europe over the China and Pacific theaters of war; Washington's stated Far Eastern political objectives were undercut by U.S. military policies. This had the added consequence that the prosecution of the war in Europe severely limited the resources the Allies could contribute to China, more particularly to the China-Burma-India theater of war, so that even those forms of aid that might have been used to support U.S. political objectives were lacking. China's paltry portion of American lend-lease aid during the war did not demonstrate a profound U.S. commitment to China as a great power. Finally, the early American and Allied insistence on Japan's unconditional surrender gave China a diplomatic advantage because any move that suggested either a separate or a negotiated peace with Japan constituted a profound threat to Allied war objectives. Washington's assumptions and wishes concerning China, combined with Chongqing's potential ability to prevent the achievement of the primary war objective, the unconditional defeat of the Axis powers, gave Chiang Kaishek the means to negotiate from strength in spite of his very real weakness.

The conditions had to be created for China to behave as the great power that American policy assumed it was. First, China had to be a great military and political power in the anti-Japanese struggle. Second, China had to be united internally so that its resources, in both men and materiel, could be enlisted in support of the status to which both the United States and Chiang Kaishek aspired for China. A major objective of American diplomacy, therefore, had to be the creation of the conditions of that status. The cancellation of extraterritorial and other privileges in January 1943 removed from China a condition of inferiority that no great power would have tolerated in the first place. China was also invited to participate in various international conferences. From the beginning the United States insisted that China be included integrally in all Allied activities and decisions. For example, Secretary Hull criticized Prime Minister Churchill for failing to include China among the great powers in a speech he made, and Hull successfully rejected Russian objections to the inclusion of China in the Four-Nation Declaration on General Security that the United States, Great Britain, the Soviet Union and China signed in Moscow on October 30, 1943.

Chiang Kaishek's participation in the Cairo conference was another step in the creation of a great power image for China. China also attended the Dumbarton Oaks conference in 1944 and became one of the five permanent members of the Security Council of the United Nations, which constituted the seal of international political and institutional recognition of China's great power identity. The irony was that as American diplomacy successfully achieved this status for China, more particularly for the Chiang regime, reality increasingly belied the image.

The second condition of great powerhood, the internal unity necessary for the achievement of national objectives, had to concern Washington if its image of China were to have substance. Diplomatic recognition of great power status for China without Chinese ability to sustain that status would have been a charade. Thus, Washington had to focus on the Guomindang–Chinese Communist relationship because it affected both Chongqing's prosecution of the war and American political objectives in the Far East. Washington's sole alternative in this context was defined by real conditions inside China. Civil strife harmed both China's war effort and Washington's diplomacy. Any concerted Guomindang attempt to conquer the Communists during the war would deflect attention, men, and materiel from the anti-Japanese fight, even if Chiang could have won such a contest, which was increasingly unlikely. The only alternative was a rapprochement between the Nationalists and the Communists, and diplomatic means alone could bring that about. Consequently, American diplomacy had to act upon the official Chinese government and between the official government and the governments of the other powers; the United States also had to become a party to the internal political struggle in China. In short, America was forced by circumstances to become a participant in Chinese politics much as other foreigners had been in the past.

U.S. diplomacy in China contained a triple irony. First, it reflected, by virtue of America's own self-defined objectives, the interests of the united front policy that the Comintern had adopted in the face of the growing fascist threat throughout the world in the 1930s. This evolution in American policy, which earlier had stood opposed to the collective security measures the Soviet Union had urged on the world through the League of Nations, was an application of the American-Soviet wartime alliance to a real political situation. Whether the Soviet Union desired a united front in China or was able to bring it about, the United States had to adopt that objective as its own. The second irony was that the United States, which historically had insisted on a policy of noninterference in the internal affairs of other countries, now found itself not only interfering but becoming an actual participant in another country's internal politics. Washington had both to assume a role in China for which it was ill prepared and to become a participant in a political culture that it understood but dimly if at all. (This irony would be lost in the postwar decades as the United States increasingly involved itself in many nations' internal affairs while denying it was doing so.) Third, the logic of American diplomacy thrust the United States into a role that Chinese political culture readily accepted; the Chinese found American participation in their politics neither unacceptable nor uncomfortable. This very fact confounded the Americans, who could not understand why the Chinese Communists directed their attention as much to the United States as to the Guomindang.

Chiang Kaishek had agreed to a united front with the Chinese Communists at Xian in December 1936, and the Communists' Central Committee had adopted a resolution in September 1937 that made strides toward implementing the united front policy. But the relationship between the two parties was uneasy; this was clear from the continuing political and military pressures to which Chiang subjected the Communists and from such significant statements by Mao Zedong as his "New Democracy" essay of 1940. In the years immediately after Pearl Harbor, however, American diplomacy encouraged the unification of all military forces in China against Japan and the development of "a free, unified, democratic government." Essentially, this was a holding operation to promote the development of those conditions that would permit major anti-Japanese action after the European war had ended. At the very least, the Nationalists and the Communists had to come together in a coalition government of national unity.[12]

Here the dilemma of America's position in China became painfully obvious. The United States could demand, urge, and entreat, but when all was said and done American theories of international relations dictated that the United States' primary responsibility had to be to treat with the duly established government of the country, however that government was con-

stituted. Even if the policymakers in Washington and the American representatives in China had not been ideologically inclined to support the
established government, whose policies or behavior they did not necessarily approve, the accepted principles of international behavior would have
required such action. In the Chinese perspective, the United States was a
participant in a political process *along with* the Nationalists and the Communists, and therefore American behavior toward one was always analyzed
in reactive terms by the other. There was no way in which the United
States could play the role of honest broker between two contending forces
within the structure of Chinese political culture when Washington itself
was a third force in contention. Nonetheless, almost all American actions
in China after Pearl Harbor were based upon the sequential policies of
unifying China democratically so that it could effectively fight Japan *and*
after the war fulfill the great power role assigned to it by American policy
planners.

During the summer of 1943, tensions between the Nationalists and the
Communists sharply increased. To a large extent, this was a consequence
of an impasse in negotiations between the two parties over questions of
integration. Demanding more than the Communists were willing to give,
Chiang was prepared to use force to gain his objectives against them.
Washington went to great pains to make it clear that such action would not
contribute to Sino-American cooperation. However, the area and scope of
Communist influence was increasing rapidly, in the face of which any
American position was by definition a picking of sides.

The record of Chiang Kaishek's behavior and the attitudes he expressed
about the Chinese Communists to the Americans severely restricted the
value of his promises and expressions of willingness to cooperate. The Wallace mission in 1944 succeeded in clarifying the issues but not in resolving
them. The success of the Japanese offensive in East China further diminished Washington's faith in Chiang's word and in the ability of his forces
to operate on the ground. The recall of General Stilwell, upon which
Chiang insisted, symbolized Washington's inability to exert political pressure on the Chongqing government. General Hurley, Roosevelt's first personal representative to Chiang Kaishek, later American ambassador to
China, continued the same policy. He even visited Yan'an, the Communist
capital, in pursuit of a mediated relationship between the Communists and
the Nationalists. Hurley, however, greatly underestimated the strength of
the Communists and misunderstood the quality of their vision for China
and the nature of their *modus operandi*. He was not alone in these misperceptions, of course. American China experts in and out of the Department of State also disagreed sharply among themselves about the Chinese
Communist phenomenon. Thus, although it was a full participant in the
Chinese political process, the United States operated in essential ignorance—circumstantial or willful—of the nature of its co-participants.

Hurley believed that the Chinese Communists were agrarian reformers and that the key to a resolution of the Nationalist-Communist conflict lay in the improvement of the relationship between Chongqing and Moscow; the U.S.S.R. would then use its influence over the Chinese Communists to bring them to accept a program of national unification on largely Nationalist terms. The Yalta agreements, which provided for Soviet support of Chiang Kaishek in return, of course, for the considerations discussed earlier, seemed a positive and logical step in the direction of the achievement of America's policy objectives. But American diplomacy as embodied in Hurley's activities foundered on three rocks. First, no real political or military settlement was achieved between the opposing sides, nor is it clear that Stalin was in a position to influence the Chinese Communists in the way and to the degree that American policy required. Second, at the same time that Hurley tried to implement his policy inside China—an implementation that required intense support from the Guomindang regime—Washington began to experience deepening frustrations with the regime. Finally, the Soviet Union continued to suggest that the Communists were a force to be reckoned with; they had to be allowed to play their natural and rightful role against Japan and to assume an appropriate position inside China. As time passed, the Soviets implemented this approach by gradually increasing cooperation with the Communists, particularly in Manchuria after the defeat of Japan.

By the end of the war in August 1945, American policy had broken down completely, and the Nationalists and the Communists were embarked upon a race to see who could occupy more territory after the Japanese surrender in order to gain the advantage in the immediate postwar period. Indeed, the Soviet Union went so far in Manchuria as to hinder Nationalist access to the surrendering Japanese armies. The Russians tried to give the advantage to the Communists, and the United States had to fly Chinese Nationalist troops into Mukden to accept the Japanese surrender there. The war ended, therefore, with the United States having failed to bring about unity by democratic or other means and with China far from being able to play its U.S. assigned role.

8

Polycentrism's End

THE ALLIES' VICTORY in World War II removed the Japanese as an immediate player in the game of Chinese politics, but the game continued as before. The four primary players—the Guomindang, the Chinese Communists, the United States, and the Soviet Union—had no choice but to play it out to the end.

Civil War or Revolution

The primary consequence of the war's end for China was a change in the relative strength of the participants in the country's political struggle. The Communists in 1936 had had perhaps 80,000 troops; they now claimed a party membership of 1.2 million, a military force of 915,000, and a popular militia of 2.2 million. They controlled a huge region they had "liberated" from the Japanese or from "feudalism" or "semifeudalism," and a population of perhaps more than ninety-five million. Thus, the Chinese Communists had become one of the world's major powers in population and traditional military strength. Moreover, their anti-Japanese struggle and socially democratic policies had won them broad support among both the people and the intellectuals, even outside the areas they ruled directly. Ranged against them were three million Nationalist troops, often poorly equipped and even more poorly trained and officered, and a government that, though superior to the Communists in population, weapons, communications, and air power (the Communists had none), was so disaffected from its people and so corrupt that it was practically incapable of mounting the serious anticommunist campaigns of which Chiang Kaishek still dreamed.

The Guomindang's position was further weakened by the country's internal condition. The Japanese invasion and occupation had been ruinous, and the government's economic policies had been even more disastrous. A slight revival when the government's currency began to flood back into formerly Japanese occupied territories was negated when Chongqing began to print money again. Between January 1946 and August 1948, prices increased 6,700 percent and in the next six months 8.5 million percent, which is to say that in less than four years from the end of World War II the Chinese economy under Guomindang management, or rather mismanagement, simply collapsed.

The history books may call the war in China a civil war. In reality, it was a revolution in which one of the parties was a foreign power, the United States, that participated in the Chinese political scene as the Oikoumene's primary representative. Calling the conflict a civil war or a continuation of the international conflict depends completely upon one's analytical framework. Be that as it may, the conditions for the perpetuation of the conflict were set toward the end of the formal phase of World War II. It quickly became apparent that whatever their specific policies, both the United States and the Soviet Union, each in its own way, were participants. On August 10, 1945, Washington instructed General Albert Wedemeyer, who was then commander of the American forces in the China theater and chief-of-staff of the Chinese forces under Chiang Kaishek, to help the Nationalists accept the surrender of the Japanese forces and reoccupy those parts of China that had been in Japanese hands. The United States firmly maintained that its support of a government that it defined in Western terms as legitimate did not involve it in the internal political processes of China, and Washington clung to this belief although in the Chinese perspective America was already involved. Because of this belief, Wedemeyer was also instructed to make it clear to the Guomindang regime that Washington would not extend support to the government in the "civil" conflict. Washington's ideological assumptions masked the fact that facilitation of the Guomindang government's return to territories it claimed actually constituted participation in the civil war. On August 11, Chiang ordered the Chinese Communists to keep their positions, to await orders, and not to accept the surrender of Japanese forces in areas under their control or to which they had access. Chiang clearly understood that what Washington perceived as acts on the international scene attendant upon Japan's surrender were, in China, domestic political acts. He drew a sharp distinction, not for the first time, between the Nationalist and the Communist forces and made the act of accepting surrender a domestic political question.

What was becoming an American alliance with Chiang Kaishek gained further substance when General Douglas MacArthur, the supreme commander of the Allied forces in the Pacific issued his famous order in which, among other things, he explicitly designated Chiang to accept the Japanese surrender in China (but not in Manchuria, which was under Russian control—the Allies wanted to avoid an immediate conflict with the Soviets), Formosa, and Indochina north of the sixteenth parallel. The United States moved quickly to provide the Nationalist government with the transport and support necessary to accept the Japanese surrender in the designated regions. Three Nationalist armies were airlifted to strategic locations in North and East China, while American ships transported Nationalist troops north along the coast. Altogether, some 500,000 Guomindang troops were moved into the eastern, northeastern, and southeastern areas of China Proper by American transport. Obviously, every area occupied by the Chinese Nationalists was denied the Chinese Communists; therefore, this reoccupation was a straightforward internal political operation. Moreover, the United States landed fifty-three thousand marines in North China for the occupation of Peking and Tianjin, the Kailan coal mines, and the Peking-Shanhaiguan Railroad, which connected Peking with the ocean. This went beyond support of the Guomindang; it was immediate and direct political action.

The Soviet Union, through the new Sino-Soviet treaty, also helped establish the legitimacy of the Chiang regime. Moreover, as with the United States in China Proper, the Soviet Union directly entered Chinese politics by its military activities in Manchuria. The Soviet campaign against Japan in Manchuria began on August 9; the Soviet Union ranged some seventy divisions against thirty or forty Japanese divisions. Although the Soviet Union had been badly injured in its war against the Germans and faced very difficult problems of supply and transport between European Russia and the Far East, it attacked the Japanese on three fronts and advanced quickly, using both naval and air support, which included intensive bombing activity. On August 11, Russian marines captured the main Japanese naval base in North Korea; by the time the Japanese surrendered on August 14, Soviet forces had penetrated deep into Manchuria.

The United States, Britain, and China understood the Japanese unconditional surrender on August 14 as the beginning of a cease-fire and the final end of hostilities. The Soviet Union, however, continued to advance in Manchuria and announced that it would carry on the war as long as Japanese troops kept fighting; furthermore, Moscow announced that it did not accept the Chinese and Western interpretation of Japan's unconditional surrender. Consequently, Soviet-Japanese hostilities ended only on August 24, although the Japanese Kwangtung army already had surrendered by August 20. By the end of the Soviet phase of the Pacific war, Russian troops had succeeded in occupying Manchuria's major urban centers: Harbin, Mukden, and Changchun. The conditions for immediate Soviet participation in Chinese politics now existed.

The disposition of Japan's forces in Manchuria became a major issue in the Far East. By September 17, the Japanese Kwantung army had been dissolved. The United States was beginning the occupation of Japan and had sent more than 100,000 troops to China to aid the Guomindang regime in reoccupying Chinese territory. A Soviet-American agreement divided Korea for purposes of occupation into a Soviet northern and American southern zone. Manchuria, however, was occupied only by the Soviet Union, with some 300,000 ground troops. During the negotiations leading up to the new Sino-Soviet treaty, Stalin had promised the Chinese that within ninety days of the end of hostilities with Japan, Soviet forces would leave Manchuria. Consequently, the Nationalist government began to prepare to occupy a region it had never directly controlled. On August 31, 1945, the government declared that it would establish a northeast headquarters of the Military Affairs Commission, which would have responsibility for the provincial administration of Manchuria and for liaison with Soviet headquarters. The director of the new northeast headquarters was to be assisted by a special foreign affairs commissioner, Chiang Chingkuo, Chiang Kaishek's son. This appointment signaled the importance Chiang attached to the move, and the new appointees proceeded to Changchun in the middle of October.

The fundamentally international character of China's internal conflict now was abundantly obvious. Soviet forces occupied territory that both Chinese parties claimed, and Chiang Kaishek tried to apply the traditional ploy of "using the barbarian to control the barbarian" by informing the Soviets that the United States was transporting thirteen divisions of Nationalist troops to Manchuria and that they would land at Dairen. This apparently straightforward declaration injected the United States into the situation as a Guomindang ally. The Soviets responded in a predictable fashion: Dairen, they argued, was a commercial port by virtue of the new Sino-Soviet treaty, and only Soviet and Chinese military forces could have access to its facilities. The United States, in other words, could not land troops of any nationality at Dairen since that would be equivalent to the introduction of a third military power into the area. The U.S. commander tried to land the Nationalist troops at two other points on the coast, but they were already in the hands of the Chinese Communists. Eventually a safe point of disembarkation was found.

This incident clarified the primary issue in Manchuria: with the Soviet Union in occupation on the ground, which Chinese party was to take over the formerly Japanese held territory and use it as a base against the other side? To no small extent, the Soviet Union helped answer this question. The Chinese Nationalists also contributed to the outcome by their immediate postwar reliance upon the United States. However reluctant Washington may have been to play the role Chiang Kaishek assigned it, his reliance on the United States transformed China into a Cold War arena whether or not the Soviets intended that result.

The Manchurian situation raised a second and broader question: was the legitimacy conferred upon the Guomindang regime by both the United States and the Soviet Union translatable into real power within the Chinese political process, whether that process was peaceful or violent? The ambiguities of Chinese politics—ambiguities that the Western powers did not understand—were the consequence not so much of chaos inside China, where the lines were fairly clearly drawn, but of the fact that the political discourse of the Oikoumene and of the Empire differed; the relationship between legitimacy and real power in the one was not the same as in the other. This difference permitted the United States to declare its unswerving support of the "legitimate" Nationalist government all the while it sought to bring the Communists into the Guomindang regime; this same difference permitted the Soviet Union clearly and unequivocably to recognize the Nationalist regime as the national government while in Manchuria it did not facilitate that regime's occupation of the position vacated by the Japanese. That this was not widely understood can be seen from the proposal made by General Wedemeyer on November 14, 1945, while he was still Chiang Kaishek's chief-of-staff: he suggested that an American-British-Soviet trusteeship be set up over Manchuria until such time as the national government could exercise control over the territory. For Wedemeyer, as for most other American observers or participants in the Chinese political scene at the time, the issue was not the government's legitimacy but its ability to exercise the power that belonged to it legitimately. Within the context of Chinese political discourse, weakness and legitimacy were closely related and contradictory concepts, while for the Oikoumene they were, to all intents and purposes, unrelated.

Fully cognizant of the terms within which he himself had to operate, Chiang sought to demonstrate his regime's legitimacy by exercising force, and on November 15 Chinese troops began to move overland into Manchuria from North China. This could only exacerbate the situation. Throughout the territory, local government was in the hands either of Soviet officials or of local groups that were Communist or well disposed toward the Communists, so Chinese occupation of Manchuria in reality had, by that time, little to do with the surrender of the Japanese. In order to avoid a direct Sino-Soviet conflict, the date for Soviet withdrawal from Manchuria, which originally had been set for ninety days after the end of hostilities, was now moved to January 3, 1946.

The Nationalists' continuing inability to develop sufficient authority in Manchuria to effect the withdrawal of the Soviet Union without allowing the territory to fall into the hands of the Communists led to further delays and contributed to international conflict over the disposition of the area. Stalin invited the generalissimo's son, Chiang Chingkuo, to visit Moscow. Stalin met him twice and, according to Chiang Chingkuo's account, offered China a close alliance and considerable aid if it would eschew reliance on any third power, meaning the United States. Stalin's offer carried the implication that it was conditional upon Guomindang-Chinese Communist cooperation, but he never made this situation explicit. Stalin also offered to meet Chiang Kaishek personally, but the latter refused. Stalin's explicit position, as expressed in his conversations with Chiang Chingkuo, had been stated more formally in the conference of Russian, British, and American foreign ministers held earlier in Moscow, December 14–26, 1945. At that meeting Soviet Foreign Minister Molotov had insisted that the bilateral Sino-Soviet treaty governed the relationship between the Soviet Union and the national government of China in Manchuria; American Secretary of State James Byrnes had insisted, in turn, that American troops were in China on the basis of a similar Sino-American agreement. A potential Soviet-American conflict was quickly becoming part of Chinese politics.

Soviet forces finally withdrew from Manchuria in March and April 1946, and on May 3 Moscow declared the evacuation complete. In the meantime, two other developments had begun to influence sharply the short- and long-range course of events inside China.

First, immediately upon the surrender of the Japanese, the Chinese Communists started to march into Manchuria and associated territories. On August 11, for example, four Communist military groups entered the provinces of Kirin and Liaoning, as well as Chahar in Inner Mongolia and Jehol north of the Great Wall. They closed off the main roads, which would have given the Nationalists land access to Manchuria. Before the end of the year, Chinese Communist forces controlled large areas of Western Manchuria, and by the time the Soviet Union completed its withdrawal at the beginning of May 1946 the Communists controlled almost all of Northern Manchuria and a good deal of the central portion of the region as well. So firmly were the Communists entrenched that Nationalist officials in the region withdrew with the Soviet forces and returned to Nationalist China via the Soviet Union.

A direct consequence of the prolonged Soviet occupation of Manchuria, whether intended or not, was the creation in Manchuria of a strong Chinese Communist base. The Communists were frequently well equipped with weapons, ammunition, and transport surrendered by the Japanese. Moreover, Soviet troops withdrew in such a way that a vacuum was left for a period, during which the Chinese Communists entered the region. For example, on October 29, 1945, the Soviets agreed that American transport ships could land Nationalist troops at Yingkow on November 10, when the Soviet troops expected to evacuate that port. On November 6, however, the Americans learned that the Soviets had evacuated the port a full five days ahead of schedule and that it quickly had been occupied by the Communists, who prevented the landing of the Nationalist troops. Often the Soviets simply turned over control of towns, cities, and regions directly to the Chinese Communist authorities. The real degree of Soviet aid to the Chinese Communists has never been determined. Nevertheless, as great as that aid may have been, Communist successes in Manchuria at that time undoubtedly resulted as much, if not more, from their own organization and training as from Soviet support.

The second important development was the dismantling of a very large part of the Manchurian industrial economy (much of which had been created under the Japanese) and its dispatch to the Soviet Union. As early as November 1945, Moscow suggested to the Nationalist government's economic representatives in Manchuria that fully eighty percent of the territory's heavy industry should come under some form of Sino-Soviet management. When the Chinese objected, the Soviets declared that, from their point of view, all Manchurian industry fell into the category of war booty and therefore was at the disposal of the victor as reparations. This meant that the Soviet Union assumed full authority over Manchuria's industrial infrastructure. The need for a decision concerning the disposal of Manchurian industry became one of the excuses for the delay of Soviet withdrawal from the region.

The Soviet government now began to dismantle and ship whole plants to Russia and, at the same time, to insist that joint Sino-Soviet companies be established, under a Chinese chairman and Soviet vice-chairman with Soviet managers and Chinese deputy managers, to control the main industrial and mining activities and the principal air fields in Manchuria. These "joint-stock companies" were to exist for thirty years, after which their properties would be returned to the Chinese without compensation. In any event, the dismantling of Manchurian industries by the Soviet authorities and the increasing power of the Chinese Communists in Manchuria, coupled with Chiang Kaishek's refusal to discuss anything before the withdrawal of the Soviet forces, made this a moot issue.

In May and June 1946, an American reparations commission, chaired by Edwin Pauley, visited Manchuria to examine the country's industrial conditions. The commission reported: "Upon their arrival, the Soviets began a systematic confiscation of food and stock piles and in early September started the selective removal of industrial machinery." In the end, according to the Pauley report, the Soviets had removed $858 million worth of property, the replacement of which would cost $2 billion. Property removed by the Russians ranged from complete industrial plants to machine tools and stockpiles of raw materials. In addition, they confiscated some $3 million in gold and $500 million in local currency. The economy was also hurt by the Soviet circulation of some ten billion Chinese dollars in occupation currency, almost twice the amount of currency in circulation at the time of the Japanese surrender. Industrial plants and goods that were not removed, as well as mines and other economic enterprises, were damaged. This systematic despoliation of the Manchurian economy, however justified it may have been in Soviet eyes, inflicted severe harm on the population and its immediate prospects. Moreover, it constituted a serious impediment to the recovery and development of the Chinese economy after the Communist victory at the end of 1949.[1]

The end of the war against Japan in China did not change the nature of the internal conflict that characterized the period of polycentrism, and Manchuria now became a major battleground. Not even Chongqing's partial diplomatic victories and the Nationalists' occupation of some key positions, such as Mukden, changed the dynamics of the struggle. By mid-1946, it was abundantly clear that any final resolution of the long-term political crisis in the Chinese world depended on military confrontation rather than on negotiation. Not everyone recognized this point, but it was apparent for all who would see. Two days after the Nationalists occupied Mukden, the Communists attacked a key railway junction between Mukden and Changchun, which they captured the following day. This incident exemplified the sporadic but widespread fighting between the Communists and the Nationalists, in which increasingly large numbers of troops were being committed on both sides. Fighting was often interspersed with negotiations and agreements that always proved temporary. Each side insisted upon its desire for peace and stability, and each felt itself forced to resort to military action to protect its interests.

This unending struggle took place within a context of worsening economic and social conditions. The Japanese had improved and expanded production in many key areas under their control and had left the economy in potentially better condition than they had found it. But China was now in dire need of aid to alleviate human suffering. The United Nations Relief and Rehabilitation Administration (UNRRA) tried to help China's recovery by immediately contributing over $658 million and, by the end of 1945, some 300,000 tons of supplies. But Nationalist China's resumption of power in the formerly Japanese occupied territories was accompanied by such corruption, and by such opportunistic and ruinous economic policies, that the economic infrastructural advantages inherited from the Japanese were quickly lost and a great proportion of the population at all social levels quickly became disaffected. What the Russians had done in Manchuria the Nationalists were doing elsewhere in reoccupied China. Many intellectuals and professionals had hoped for better policies and conditions, but they now began to desert the Nationalists for the only political organization that held out hope for a better future, the Communists. Furthermore, as the military conflict increased in intensity and socioeconomic conditions worsened, more and more units of the Nationalists' armed forces began to switch sides.

The end of the Nationalist regime came into sight with the rapid military deterioration of the Guomindang's position in North China and Manchuria in the second part of 1948. Throughout the area, and particularly in

Manchuria, Nationalist armies had been defecting to the Communists. The greatest battle of the war up to that date took place around Mukden, which surrendered on November 1. In that confrontation, the Nationalists lost by death or desertion over 400,000 troops, together with their armaments and supplies, which were mostly American.

The final stage of the military, and therefore of the political, conflict began with the battle of the Huai-hai in central China, which has been called one of the great battles of modern history. The Nationalists, with only two hundred divisions left, committed fifty to the battle, while the Communists controlled the countryside and the transportation system in the region and had the support of the population. The battle lasted sixty-five days, and when it ended on January 12, 1949, the Nationalists had lost some 550,000 men; the Communists claimed that of these 327,000 had surrendered to them. In January 1949 Tianjin and Peking surrendered, and by April the Communists were crossing the Changjiang.

As Communist victory approached, the country's economic structure collapsed, driving more people to the support of the Communists if only to bring about an end to the chaos. By August 1948, the wholesale commodity price index in Shanghai was over three million times higher than it had been on the eve of the Sino-Japanese War in 1937. From January to August, prices increased 4,500 percent and the black market rate for the U.S. dollar 50,000 percent.

In January 1949, Chiang Kaishek's government asked the Americans, British, French, and Soviets to negotiate a settlement with the Communists. It was too late. Nanjing and Shanghai fell to the Communists in the spring; by October the Communists were in Canton and by November in Chongqing. Meanwhile, on October 1, 1949, Mao Zedong formally announced the establishment of the Chinese People's Republic. Chiang Kaishek and the Nationalist government fled to Taiwan.

The U.S.S.R. and the Revolution

The functional cooperation and alliance between the Americans and the Guomindang regime within the context of Chinese political culture enabled the Chinese Communists easily to identify the United States as a primary element in the opposition, that is, as one of the domestic enemies that had to be overcome either politically or militarily. Within the same context, however, the definition of the Soviet Union's role in post-war Chinese politics was somewhat more difficult. After all, ideologically the Soviets appeared to be aligned with the Chinese Communists, and yet the Russians were not forthcoming with support. In fact, historical evidence suggests that the ambiguity that characterized Soviet policy toward China in the first fifteen months after the formal end of World War II—an ambiguity that permitted relations with the Nationalist regime at the same time that the Chinese Communists were benefiting from Soviet policies in Manchuria—continued to characterize Soviet policy in China almost to the end of the period of polycentrism. Furthermore, knowledgeable American observers at the time, including the American proconsul in China, General George Marshall, agreed that the Soviet Union gave no material aid to the Chinese Communists outside Manchuria or, if they did, it had relatively minor importance. (It is important to keep this in mind, given the rapid change in the American public's appreciation of the Chinese situation that developed in the wake of the so-called loss of China between the end of the war and 1949.)

In the absence of any clear distinction in Chinese political culture between internal and international politics, and confronted as early as the 1930s with the ambiguities inherent in the Soviet Union's China policy, the Chinese Communists, at least by 1940, began to try to develop a theory of international politics that would guide them. In his famous "New Democracy" essay in January 1940, Mao Zedong outlined a theory of a world divided into two camps, one headed by the Soviet Union and one by "imperialist Great Britain and the United States." The conflict between the two, he wrote, would intensify. In such a conflict, "it is inevitable that China must stand either on one side or on the other." "Is it possible to incline to neither side?" Mao continued. "No, this is an illusion." This was an implicit acknowledgment that the same structures that ruled international politics ruled China's internal politics as well.[2]

The theme was picked up again in January 1947 in an essay by Lu Dingyi, then chief of the Communists' information department. Lu defined the two camps as democracy and antidemocracy and predicted that the struggle between them "will cover a greater part of the world." Interestingly, he suggested that the primary contradiction between the two lay not between the U.S.S.R. and the United States but, rather, within the capitalist world itself (that is, within one part of the Oikoumene). In this view, the revolution within China was part and parcel of the global struggle; indeed, the two were not clearly distinguishable. Moreover, the internal and the international were linked in a "united front" of democratic forces ranged against the antidemocratic forces. The internal revolution was by definition an instance of international solidarity.[3]

Mao explored the problem further in "On the People's Democratic Dictatorship" in July 1949, when Communist victory, without significant Soviet aid, was in sight. He repeatedly argued that the Chinese Revolution was only part of the international struggle: "Victory is also possible without international assistance—this is an erroneous conception." China's foreign policy would be guided by such slogans as "You lean to one side" and "We want to do business," which meant that the only factor excluding some cooperation with the Oikoumene was the Anglo-American imperialist policy of anticommunism. There was nothing in the Chinese Communist view of the world that inhibited constructive relations with the West; it was the West's policies toward the Chinese Revolution that provided the inhibition.[4]

The theoretical foundations for an alliance between the Chinese Revolution and the Soviet Union and for the analysis of the Chinese Revolution as an integral component of international politics (and *vice versa*) were, therefore, laid between 1940 and 1949. But they did not provide a basis for the resolution of contradictions created by the Soviet Union's pursuit of its own interests in China when those interests did not coincide with the Chinese Communist Party's. This became abundantly clear on February 1, 1947, when the finality of the break between the Nationalists and the Communists began to affect foreign policy. The Communists announced on that date that they would not recognize any international agreement concluded by the Nationalist government after January 10, 1947. While this action was primarily a protest against American support for the Guomindang regime, it necessarily encompassed all Soviet agreements with the Guomindang government as well.

The outcome in China clearly interested the Soviet Union. The Russian press printed long and frequent reports about the deterioration of the Chinese situation, and the United States was often a target of criticism for its aid to the Nationalists. In March 1947, at the Moscow conference of foreign ministers, Molotov wanted to include China on the meeting's agenda, but despite Chinese Communist support for the move American and Nationalist opposition prevented discussions within or without the conference. Both sides agreed, however, to exchange notes about their fulfillment of the original Moscow agreement concerning the withdrawal of foreign troops from Chinese soil. On March 31, 1947, General Marshall gave Moscow a note in which he insisted that American forces in China had the sole mission of aiding the surrender of the Japanese, adding that they would be reduced to some six thousand men by June. Marshall also noted the lack of information concerning 200,000 Japanese captured by the Russians in Manchuria. The Soviet note stated that Moscow's withdrawal of Soviet forces from Manchuria in May 1946 had proved its determination to abide by the Moscow agreement.

During the rest of 1947, the Soviet Union contented itself with official and press comments on American efforts to mediate the Chinese conflict and on the unfolding social, economic, and political situation inside China. As the Communists made military headway, military events began to be reported more widely in the Soviet press. In December the possibility that the Soviets might try to mediate between the Nationalists and the Communists excited a flurry of interest in Nanjing: a Chinese general, Zhang Zhizhong, who had been active in the negotiations with the Americans, held brief conversations with the Soviet embassy. It is not clear, however, whether the initiative came from the Soviet or the Chinese side; in any event, the matter evidently went no further.

Throughout 1948, as Communist military activity rolled toward the climactic Mukden victory at the end of the year, the Soviet government continued to maintain correct relations with the Nationalist regime. In February, the Soviet ambassador to Nanjing returned home, which would have given the Soviets an opportunity to discontinue relations with the Guomindang, but instead a new ambassador was dispatched. In the same month, *Pravda* noted that the Sino-Soviet Nonaggression Treaty of 1937 was now automatically prolonged for two more years since it had not been denounced. In April, when a member of the Chinese National Assembly called upon the government to renounce the Sino-Soviet Treaty of Friendship of 1945, *Pravda* objected strongly, stating that the treaty was very important to both countries as a protection against renewed Japanese aggression.

As 1948 ended, the Soviet Union apparently grew increasingly circumspect with regard to developments in China. The fall of Mukden and the great Communist victory in Manchuria were considerably underreported in the Russian press, and Molotov, making a speech on the anniversary of the Russian Revolution, talked about the development of liberation movements in Asia but did not even mention the Chinese Communists. This Soviet reticence led to a curious development in the ranks of the Guomindang, in which the outlines of a policy change began to take shape. Some officials, including Sun Yat-sen's son, Sun Fo, began to argue that the Americans would be unwilling or unable to contribute the amount of aid to China that would be necessary for a victory against the Communists; therefore, the government had to find other solutions to its problem. In December 1948, Sun Fo was named premier; rumors began to spread about support within his cabinet for Soviet mediation of a compromise with the Communists. On January 4, 1949, the Soviet press took note of these rumors and suggested that there was some substance to them; on January 8 the Guomindang foreign minister sent a request to the four powers—the United States, the Soviet Union, Great Britain and France—for mediation. The United States and the Soviet Union—the only two powers in a position actually to engage in effective mediation—rejected the request.

Throughout January 1949 the issue of Soviet mediation percolated on the surface of events but to no effect. For its part, the Soviet government continued to maintain correct diplomatic relations with the Nationalist regime. When the KMT government, fleeing before the Communists, reached Canton, the Soviet Union alone sent its ambassador along. At the same time, as the Communists occupied cities, the Soviets formally closed their consulates in them, further supporting the contention that they were continuing to recognize only the so-called legitimate government of the country and to deal with it alone. Indeed, throughout this period Moscow did pursue negotiations with the KMT regime, particularly regarding Xinjiang. Perhaps it was only preparing the ground for its position in China after the Communists came to power, or perhaps even at this late date the Soviet leaders remained to be convinced that a Communist victory was possible.

Soviet policy finally began to exhibit some awareness of a potential Communist victory in April 1949, when *Pravda* printed a Chinese Communist statement declaring that the party would support the Soviet Union if another world war occurred. Later that month, *Pravda* hailed the "liberation of Nanjing" as the end of the KMT government. Thereafter, Li Zongren, who had officially become president of China after Chiang Kaishek's resignation on January 21, 1949—a resignation that was more apparent than real—was referred to as the "so-called acting president." The Russians continued to work with the Nationalist government despite these remarks, and in May 1949 the KMT regime and Moscow agreed to renew an aviation agreement for five more years; negotiations about Xinjiang also went on. When the KMT finally rejected some Soviet requests, the Soviet ambassador returned to Moscow for consultations, never to return.[5]

By summer, the Soviets had obviously decided that the Communists would win and that it was now necessary to shift the thrust of their diplomatic efforts in China. During the summer, Soviet consulates in Communist occupied cities reopened. The Chinese Communist Party also began to appear at international meetings, which further signified Moscow's shift since any Chinese Communist delegation had to travel through or over Soviet territory to reach its destination (the Communists did not have access to the ocean, and the Soviet Union was their only avenue to the outside world, whether by land or by air). *Pravda* increasingly reported news from Communist held areas and the statements of Communist leaders; the Chinese Communists, in their turn, more and more aligned their positions with Soviet policies. On October 1, the very day the government of the Chinese People's Republic declared itself the only legal government of China, the Soviet consul-general in Peking was given a note from Zhou Enlai, the new foreign minister, calling for the establishment of normal diplomatic relations between the Soviet Union and the Chinese People's Republic. On October 2, Moscow withdrew its recognition of the KMT regime and established formal relations with the new government in Peking. Relations were quickly established between Peking and the other members of the communist bloc as well, and on October 10 the last Soviet ambassador to the KMT regime was received in Peking by Chairman Mao as the first Soviet ambassador to the new government; on October 30, the first Chinese Communist ambassador presented his credentials in Moscow. The end, however, was only the beginning. Events were to prove that the presence in Peking and Moscow of governments using similar words about the world did not mean that the nature of the interaction between the Empire, now in the process of reestablishment, and the Soviet Union, fundamentally (even if not ideologically) still a member of the Oikoumene, had changed.

The United States and the End of the Chinese Revolution

The end of the Pacific war caught the United States without a coherent policy toward, or in, China. To a certain extent, this situation existed because the war had ended more precipitously than Washington had expected. America's political and military chiefs had thought a major invasion of the Japanese home islands would be necessary to conclude the war, and while they were fully aware of the power of the atom bomb, they could not predict its psychological and political impact on the Japanese and their will to continue fighting. As badly as Japan had been hit by American bombs, the very heavy and costly fighting in the Ryukyu Islands, particularly the great battle for Iwo Jima, had not encouraged the Americans to think that the war would come to an end rapidly.

The relief with which the conclusion of the war was greeted by the American people forced Washington, sooner than it was prepared, to begin thinking about conversion to peacetime conditions. This revealed the self-defeating contradiction inherent in the military approach to a solution of East Asian problems. On the one hand, the occupation of Japan set certain minimal requirements in men and materiel that had to be met. On the other, there was an overwhelming desire in the United States to demobilize the armed forces to the extent that the occupation of Japan and Germany permitted. This left no room for a military surplus to meet contingencies that might develop outside occupation responsibilities. The Cold War and its military requirements were still in the future, even if only some months away. At war's end, the United States had some sixty thousand men in China, and an additional fifty thousand marines were landed on the China mainland in 1946. Sixteen thousand men were brought home in September, however, and November 15 was set as the date for the withdrawal of the marines. Thereafter, the China theater of war was to be deactivated, at least as far as the United States was concerned.

Another source of Washington's unreadiness to respond actively and constructively to events in China was a set of three political assumptions that guided the immediate development of U.S. China policy. First, Soviet support of the Guomindang regime would lead to Communist cooperation with, and integration into, the Nationalist government. Second, Soviet support for the Guomindang regime excluded the likelihood, if not the possibility, of Soviet aid to the Chinese Communists. Third, the Soviets agreed with the thrust of American policy, which sought the peaceful unification of China. These three assumptions provided the point of departure for Ambassador Patrick Hurley's diplomatic mission, but by the end of November 1945 the first two were found to be false. Relations between the Communists and the Nationalists did not improve with the war's end, and the Soviet Union did nothing to encourage their improvement. Soviet policies in Manchuria aided the Chinese Communists, directly or indirectly, quite independently of Moscow's relations with, and support of, the Chiang Kaishek regime. The only evidence supporting the third assumption came from statements that Stalin and Molotov were wont to make to various Americans who passed through Moscow or came there for conferences.

Developments in the Far East immediately after the war clearly demonstrated that, Washington's posture and diplomatic assumptions aside, the planned deactivation of the China theater of war did not mean that the United States could absent itself from China and still hope to see American wartime objectives in the region achieved. The Manchurian situation alone demonstrated that without American support far beyond the aid the KMT regime needed to reestablish its presence and authority over the formerly Japanese occupied area of China Proper, the National government's writ would not extend to Manchuria. Indeed, General Wedemeyer thought that even North China would remain for a while, perhaps a long while, outside the reach of the government. At the same time, it also quickly became apparent that the regime was not about to accept American advice after the war any more than it had prior to August 1945.

A turning point in American policy was reached, even if it was not then recognized, at the end of November 1945, when the United States decided to postpone the departure of the marines and to facilitate the Guomindang's occupation of Manchuria. The United States thereby demonstrated that it was prepared to go beyond the actions necessary to tidy up after World War II, that is, to demobilize the Japanese armed forces and to return Japanese personnel to Japan; now it was ready to contribute actively to Chiang Kaishek's survival. But, how far was the United States prepared to invest in the KMT regime? Washington was ready to support the regime and to contribute to the reequipment and retraining of its armed forces, but the United States began to impose conditions on that support, which were intended both to force Chiang Kaishek to make necessary reforms in the government and to bring about a negotiated agreement with the Communists that would put an end to the "fratricidal war." No longer was the United States prepared to support Chiang unreservedly, as it had felt compelled to do in wartime. Faced with this change in policy, Ambassador Hurley resigned on November 27. In his resignation statement he more than suggested that there was too much sympathy for the Chinese Communist position among American diplomats. Curiously, however, he remained convinced that the Soviet Union fully supported Chiang Kaishek. Hurley simply did not understand that the end of the war had changed everything.

THE SELF-DENYING POLICY

Hurley's resignation symbolized both the failure of the Rooseveltian policy of transforming China into a great power and the ambiguities of American policy in the immediate aftermath of the war. President Truman's appointment of General George Marshall as his special representative in China, with the personal rank of ambassador, marked the beginning of a new China policy based upon what were now perceived to be the realities in China and in the broader world. The United States had to choose among a variety of strategies ranging from direct armed intervention to total withdrawal from the conflict. The choice of particular policies and strategies by Marshall and other American representatives in China rested upon the a priori assumption that China was not sufficiently important to the United States to warrant America's going to war in China. This put an immediate limit on the potential range of American activities, both military and political, and to no small extent prejudged the conflict's outcome. In short, the United States was still committed to bringing about a peaceful unification of the country under the aegis of the Guomindang regime, within the parameters of the traditional American Open Door policy, but Washington was not prepared to make the heavy investments in men and treasure that would insure the success of that policy.

If nothing else, this approach was based upon a fairly correct assessment of the temper of the American public. It also reflected the reappraisal of Chiang Kaishek and his regime that had started toward the end of the Roosevelt administration and continued under Truman. The generalissimo's unreliability was amply demonstrated by the nature of the regime that now was reasserting itself in East and North China, and Washington suspected that the provision of significant military support to the Guomindang would only enhance its propensity to seek a military, rather than a negotiated, solution to the conflict with the Communists. None of this vitiated the fundamental American objective of preserving the national government and enabling it to extend its control over the entire country; rather, American policy represented an effort to operate within the limits of what the United States understood to be the reality governing its freedom of maneuver. The decision that armed intervention was not a possibility within those limits had paramount importance. Other factors also helped set the parameters of maneuverability, such as misjudgments about the immediate and long-range intentions and the political and military capabilities of the Chinese Communists; the corruption and incompetence of the Nationalists' regime; and the changing patterns of world power that were revealed by the Cold War. The relative importance of each component in the mix changed over time, but the impact of the whole on policy did not.

The decision against armed intervention deserves examination. Armed intervention, other than in a situation in which the intervention takes place on the side of a preponderant power, always risks intervention by a third party. It also requires, as does any military conflict, an expenditure of men and treasure that, without a real preponderance of power on the side of the intervenor, contains no guarantee of the desired outcome. Intervention must be motivated by the conviction that the advantages to be gained thereby outweigh the potential disadvantages arising from a failure to intervene.

The assumption that the United States had no overriding interest in China that required American intervention in China's revolutionary warfare derived from several sources. First, the occupation of Japan and Germany and military demobilization and economic reconversion at home took priority over a possible military intervention in China. No nation's resources ever allow it to pursue all its national objectives simultaneously, and it must make conscious choices. Second, the Guomindang regime had failed to fulfill American hopes for it, but doubts about the Communist alternative were strong enough, particularly as the Cold War developed, to inhibit complete abandonment of Chiang Kaishek. The result was a frozen attitude of unenthusiastic toleration. Finally, the growing polarization of world politics, with the United States and the Soviet Union each at the center of a power bloc, increased the risk that intervention by one in a third area would lead to intervention by the other, and this risk was heightened as the United States lost the power that had derived from its sole possession of the nuclear weapon.

These considerations led to certain conclusions. First, it became a matter of military doctrine that American ground forces should never be committed to action on the Asian continent. The experience of Japan in China had demonstrated the futility of fighting in an arena of war that differed so markedly from the West and that was so vast. (Disaster followed from the violation of this doctrine in the 1960s in Southeast Asia.) Second, U.S. domestic objectives severely limited the pursuit of American foreign objectives and restricted the availability of American military personnel and materiel abroad. (When this principle was transgressed in the 1960s in Southeast Asia it brought political disaster for the incumbent administration.) Third, the United States recognized that international politics were now structured in a bipolar fashion and that America was no longer free to pursue its own interests at will. In the case of China, the unlikelihood of Soviet intervention made American intervention less desirable. Had the Soviet Union's intervention been considered probable, American intervention might have been necessary either to preempt the Russians or to maintain the balance of power. In the face of these assumptions and conclusions, American policymakers had only one alternative: to seek a solution to the internal Chinese conflict by negotiation, which meant, essentially, the formation of a coalition government.

In its turn, the coalition government policy suffered from a fatal flaw. Given the nature of the KMT regime and the wide popularity and coherent strength enjoyed by the Chinese Communists, any coalition between the two would almost inevitably benefit the Communists more than the Nationalists, except in the remote event that the Communists were to agree abjectly to all the Nationalists' terms and to obey them. Nonetheless, the hope was sustained by an equally improbable assumption, namely, that the Nationalist government could turn itself around and respond creatively to the needs of China and its people. The logic of the American position, therefore, led the United States further into the Chinese quagmire: reform of the Nationalist government became essential to the American vision of a resolution in China if American armed intervention were to be avoided and a Communist takeover prevented. The United States, however, had to become a party to that reform, involving itself still more deeply in China's internal politics.

Marshall, in his search for a negotiated solution along the lines outlined above, had to identify, seek out, and encourage responsible elements across the political spectrum while at the same time avoiding a show of partiality toward any one of them. Various political cliques and groups within the Guomindang itself, as well as the liberal "third force," were all parties to the complex game of Chinese politics, and the United States had insufficient leverage to disestablish the reactionary groups in the Guomindang in favor of the liberals. Moreover, the institutional reforms Washington wanted to introduce into China did not take into account the complexities of a society quite different from that of the United States. In the end, neither the personalistic nor the institutional approach sufficed. No matter which way Marshall turned, the negotiated solutions he sought slipped through his fingers.

Marshall arrived in China on December 20, 1945, and China remained his primary concern until January 1947. Despite all his efforts, the general was unable to bring about a permanent cease-fire and political solution, and the internal Chinese situation deteriorated rapidly throughout 1946. By the beginning of 1947, frustration and hopelessness had reached such a point that withdrawal seemed the only course. Marshall's experience in China was to contribute mightily to the denouement of America's China policy because he left China in 1947 to become the American secretary of state.

As early as July 1946, Marshall was convinced that a breakdown in efforts to achieve a negotiated settlement in China would result in a period of partial withdrawal, during which an "agonizing reappraisal" of China policy would be undertaken.⁶ When Marshall became secretary of state on January 21, 1947, he put his own ideas into practice, and seven days later Washington announced plans for limited disengagement and continuation of an embargo on military goods for China. Logically, reevaluation implied only two possible alternatives. First, withdrawal from China should be as complete as possible in order to exert maximum pressure on the KMT regime to make the institutional reforms and personnel changes that would equip it to provide leadership in China; failing that condition, complete withdrawal would serve the purpose of disengaging the United States from the political and even financial and military losses that the collapse of the regime inevitably would entail. Second, Washington should be willing, in the event the withdrawal achieved its hoped for positive result, to return to China with the massive aid that would be necessary. In any event, however, the withdrawal was only partial and Washington was not willing. Marshall, as secretary of state, did not possess the tools needed to accomplish the purpose his policy envisaged.

Conditions in China worsened throughout 1947. As the Democratic administration came under increasing Republican criticism, Truman was moved to take limited measures that only prolonged indecisiveness and ambiguity. Toward the end of May, the arms embargo was lifted, which in effect decreased the degree of withdrawal. In June, great amounts of ammunition were sold to China at a price that constituted significant aid. In July, Wedemeyer was sent back to China on a fact-finding mission, which led him while still in China publicly to criticize Chiang Kaishek and his regime. The generalissimo responded by asserting in no uncertain terms his government's rejection of Wedemeyer's criticisms and suggestions, thus perpetuating a policy that had failed continuously and was dooming the Nationalists' cause. Insistence upon American aid unaccompanied by any requirements for change did nothing to ameliorate the regime's diseases and contributed only to the deterioration of the regime's support in Washington.

The Americans' errors in China must be, in hindsight, an object of wonder. The United States had specialists, both in and out of government, who were profoundly experienced in Chinese affairs, and it was often well served by its diplomatic and consular personnel in China, but the policymakers would not heed their advice or accept their often correct analyses of the relative strengths and weaknesses of one or another party. As the 1948 presidential election approached, the Democratic administration's China policy became the object of still more vociferous Republican criticism. The Guomindang regime sought to use the quadrennial American political contest for its own purposes, and toward the end of December 1947 requested $1.5 billion in aid, of which a significant proportion was to be used for economic and military purposes during the first year of the aid program. Truman, not wanting to appear weak in his policy toward China at a moment when the Republicans were attacking him mercilessly, in February 1948 proposed to Congress a China aid program amounting to $570 million over fifteen months. While the package did not include any specifically military appropriations, the program was structured in such a way that the Guomindang could use its own reserves to purchase military supplies abroad without suffering significant losses in its foreign exchange holdings. Both President Truman and Secretary of State Marshall made it clear that this proposal was a response to demands that were historical, emotional, and political in nature; they did not pretend that the aid plan would enable the rapidly degenerating regime to rehabilitate itself. Congress passed the China Aid Act in April 1948 and approved the necessary appropriations in June. This was a compromise between the equally unacceptable alternatives of armed intervention and complete withdrawal, alternatives that were unacceptable primarily because of domestic political considerations in the United States.

In China, the Aid Act was widely interpreted as a sign of American support for a government whose unpopularity was growing and whose end was in sight. Anti-American demonstrations occurred throughout the country. The implementation of the act, which began, albeit hesitantly, in the latter part of 1948 (just as the Communists were preparing for their major campaign in Manchuria and North China), did not contribute either to American popularity among the Chinese population or to the growth of responsibility and a sense of cooperation within the dying KMT regime. By October, Washington was prepared to write off both China and Taiwan, and Marshall's policy of no military intervention was extended to exclude the possibility of the defense of Formosa as a Nationalist refuge. By the time Dean Acheson became secretary of state on January 21, 1949, the Communists had won the Huai-hai campaign and their victory throughout China was assured. As early as December 1948, Chiang explicitly had recognized his defeat when he requested the United States to ship future aid to Formosa rather than to the mainland, and before his retirement from office on January 21, 1949, he made sure that the government's foreign exchange and bullion reserves were sent to Taipei, the capital of Formosa. His resignation was, after all, only one more maneuver.

The bankruptcy and death of the Guomindang regime and the failure of American policy in China to prevent a sweeping Communist political and military victory now transformed the entire problem of America's China policy. The establishment of the new regime meant that the United States would thereafter be excluded as a participant in the Chinese political system. For Washington, the problem became one of containing the new regime. Although it did not so recognize at the time, the United States in China had to suffer the same fate as the Guomindang regime, for both had been participants in the same game and both had lost.

FORMOSA

The American decision not to use military force to support the Guomindang regime encompassed Formosa as well as China Proper. This did not mean that Formosa inevitably would fall to the Chinese Communists. The Communists were a continental power without naval capabilities, and Formosa was an island separated from the mainland by rough waters. The disposition of Formosa would depend not just upon American policy but also upon the new Chinese government's ability to mount the military effort necessary to attack, conquer, and hold the island. However, Formosa's geographical location and historical traditions fitted it well to serve as a relatively safe refuge for the defeated Guomindang regime.

Formosa and the Pescadore Islands had been peripheral possessions of the Empire until late in the nineteenth century. When various powers of the Oikoumene, including Japan, expressed interest in Formosa's potential uses or concern about its residents' inhospitality toward strangers, the Qing court disclaimed all responsibility for the island's administration beyond the coastal region. Although two progressive governors had transformed the island into perhaps the most modernized region of the Empire, Formosa was still marginal to imperial concerns when, on April 17, 1895, the Treaty of Shimonoseki, which ended the Sino-Japanese War of 1894–1895, assigned both Formosa and the Pescadores to Japan.

Tokyo inherited an island whose people were already conditioned to the process of rapid economic, social, and cultural change. Japan itself had embarked upon profound and far-reaching policies of development, and it found Formosa ready for modernization. The Japanese administration consciously and directly pursued policies intended to introduce and develop modern education, social structure, and agricultural and industrial techniques. As a modernizing personnel and economic infrastructure developed, the island became an increasingly important source of agricultural produce for Japan. In turn, the population improved its level of education and standard of living; by the time the Japanese war with China began in 1931, Formosa was making vital contributions to the maintenance of Japan and the furtherance of Japanese ambitions, contributions that, as the conflict accelerated after 1937, became increasingly vital to Tokyo's war effort. At the beginning of the Pacific war, Formosa was the primary base for the Japanese attack on the Philippines and supported the Japanese moves into Hong Kong and Singapore and along the China coast. Island institutions, such as the Bank of Taiwan, played active roles in Japan's expansion. The entire economy was geared to the war effort, with the result that Formosan production expanded prodigiously.

Neither the Chinese government nor the Allied powers ignored the island's importance in the Japanese war effort. In his book *China's Destiny*, published in March 1943, Chiang Kaishek described his plans for China's future, which included the reincorporation of Formosa into China. Roosevelt and Churchill agreed to this goal at the Cairo conference for two main reasons. First, the Americans considered Formosa important in their planning for a naval campaign across the Pacific to the China coast. In Japanese hands the island would be a major hurdle; in Allied hands it would be a staging base for a landing on the mainland. Second, the promise to return Formosa to China was intended to stimulate opposition to the Japanese in a region of great economic importance to Tokyo's war effort. In fact, by the time the Cairo Declaration was published on December 1, 1943, Tokyo had upgraded the Formosans' status by changing the island from a colony into an integral part of the Japanese empire. The Japanese hoped this move would counter Allied propaganda and better establish their ultimate claim to the island.

In 1944, with the war going in the Allies' favor, Formosan waters became an area of submarine activity and, with increasing economic hardship, the island began to feel the negative effects of the war. The first Allied bombing occurred on Thanksgiving Day 1943, and the provincial government began to plan for the possibility of an Allied invasion. In October 1944, Washington abandoned plans to invade Formosa, the better to concentrate on the reconquest of the Philippines, but bombing increased considerably. By and large, however, the island avoided the worst consequences of the approaching Japanese defeat. Formosa never became a direct theater of action. The Cairo Declaration was fulfilled when, on October 5, 1945, American planes brought in the first Chinese administrators and troops, followed by an entire army and provincial administration transported on American aircraft and naval vessels. About three weeks later, the Japanese commander on Formosa officially turned the island over to the Chinese Nationalists.

Formosa now became part of the same historical process that was developing on the mainland. As on the continent, only American transport enabled the Nationalist administrators and armed forces to occupy the formerly Japanese held territory. The Guomindang administration on the island, as on the mainland, quickly demonstrated a corruption and venality that, at least in Formosa, had been unknown during the fifty years of Japanese rule. The economy was despoiled in the interest of the private fortunes of high Guomindang officials. Moreover, Formosa, which had ended the war relatively better off than the mainland coastal regions, began to be exploited in the interests of territories from which it had been separated for half a century. The Chinese "liberators" and "brothers" quickly were transformed into enemies. At the end of February 1947 an islandwide revolt of major proportions took place; the uprising was suppressed only with the help, once again, of American transport and supplies. While on the mainland the United States was becoming firmly identified with one party in the conflict, the Nationalist regime, on the island the United States was identified with the Chinese, who were increasingly perceived by the local population to be outsiders who had come to exploit, not to liberate, their home.

Faced with a disaster of growing proportions, Chiang Kaishek began in 1947 to prepare Formosa as a refuge and bastion for his regime. The island also became a place of refuge for civilians and military personnel fleeing the Communists. The generalissimo retired from office on January 21, 1949, although he did not actually relinquish the reins of power. He himself soon arrived on Formosa and proceeded to establish his government there and to use the island as a territorial base from which not only to continue the fight with the Communists but also to perpetuate the international status of his government as the legitimate China. On the mainland, the end of 1949 saw the final collapse of the national government with the Communists' capture of a succession of temporary Nationalist capitals in the southwest. Taipei, beyond the reach of the Communists, now became the final "temporary capital."

The impending collapse of the Guomindang regime on the mainland raised a serious question in Washington about American intentions toward Formosa. As long as the island remained outside Communist control, it could be argued that the Communist regime lacked legitimacy in terms of international law and politics. At the same time, as early as October 1948 the State Department rejected the possibility of using American armed forces for the defense of the island. In August 1949, Secretary of State Acheson informed the National Security Council that with the impending fall of the national government, the fall of Formosa was probable: political and economic measures would not suffice to prevent the island's capture. In reply, the joint chiefs of staff affirmed their position that American military forces should not be used to protect Formosa. At the same time, Republicans in Congress insisted that the United States adopt a strong position on the island's future, including a commitment to its defense if necessary. That defense was intended, as Senator Alexander Smith of New Jersey declared quite publicly, to place American forces in such a position that a Communist attack on Formosa would be an attack upon the United States. The issue became more pressing when, on December 8, the Nationalist government moved to Taipei. The debate raged on, with various members of Congress making proposals that ranged from the stationing of an American military advisory group on the island to direct military action for its defense. On January 5, 1950, President Truman declared:

> The United States has no desire to obtain special rights or privileges or to establish military bases on Formosa at this time. Nor does it have any intention of utilizing its armed forces to interfere in the present situation. The United States will not pursue a course which will lead to involvement in the civil

conflict in China. Similarly, the United States Government will not provide
military aid or advice to Chinese forces on Formosa.[7]

In support of this position, Truman cited the Cairo Declaration, which,
he said, intended the restoration of the island to Chinese authority; he also
pointed out that the Allies had accepted the exercise of Chinese authority
over the island since the end of the war. What he did not say, but what
appeared to be part of his argument, was that the Cairo Declaration had
not defined China; it had only referred to the exercise of China's authority
over the island. China's dominion over Formosa was a question distinct
from that of American participation in the island's defense, but refusal to
aid the government on Formosa in no way vitiated its claim.

Truman's declaration did not end the debate; on the contrary, it continued at full tilt. Meanwhile, the new Chinese government, the Soviet
Union, and the United States were all engaged in defining their positions
in the Far East in the wake of the Communist victory. On December 16,
Mao Zedong arrived in Moscow for negotiations with Stalin, the consequences of which profoundly influenced the development of Chinese foreign policy. In a speech on January 12, 1950, the American secretary of
state, Dean Acheson, defined what Washington considered to be its defense perimeter in the Western Pacific, which included the Aleutian Islands, Japan, the Ryukyu Islands, and the Philippines. Formosa and South
Korea were not included. The Truman administration, despite the raging
domestic political debate, was seeking to avoid defining Washington's future policy in the Far East by distancing itself, to the extent possible, from
the Chiang Kaishek regime and avoiding, as long as possible, recognition
of the Communists.

The survival of the Guomindang regime on Formosa provided the substance of the last scene in the last act of the polycentric era. The Taipei
regime asserted its claim to be the government of more than the island
province by its continued occupation of small offshore islands that technically were part of the mainland provinces of Fujien and Zhejiang. In Taipei
itself, this claim was manifested in the maintenance of a full complement
of national institutions, including a legislative body with "representatives"
from all of China's provinces. However the Nationalist government described its situation and status, Chiang's regime now found itself engaged
in a diplomatic conflict to assert its legitimacy on the international scene
against the claims of the Communist government. The Communist government, for its part, embarked upon two not completely unrelated processes:
the renovation of China and the reconstitution of the Empire.

Imperium Revividum

THE ESTABLISHMENT of the government of the Chinese People's Republic at Peking on October 1, 1949, in effect brought the Empire back into existence after the long chaos of the interregnum. The Chinese Communist state displayed all the characteristics of the Empire: a highly centralized, hierarchically organized bureaucracy with a coherent view of the world; a socio-administrative structure into which all parts of the population fitted and which fitted all parts of the population; and an ideology that provided a basis for the conceptual unification of the entire society. The new Chinese state's ideology and vocabulary were not the same as those of the old dynastic state. But the structure and perceptions of relationships, the language, the imperative toward centralization and an ordering of the whole society, the primacy given to ideology—all those facets of a culture that change much more slowly than the events of history occur—once again found their natural refraction in the new Chinese Communist state.

The old dynastic state had had a foreign policy, which is to say, a conceptual map of the world. The philosophical foundation for that map was a set of assumptions about the world and a range of possible actions in that world. The concepts and possible actions combined in a matrixlike structure through which the state perceived the outside world and interpreted the latter's actions toward it; through this matrix, or structure, the state acted upon the outside world and attemped to project imperial intentions on it.

During the interregnum, the state, in various definitions, ceased to exist. Instead, the Chinese world reverted to that condition to which it perennially returned and which can be best described as an international system. It may be argued that none of the competing parties within the Chinese interregnal political process can be characterized as a state in the broad administrative-bureaucratic and intentional sense of the term. In fact, even those foreign powers (including the Soviet Union and the United States) that became participants in the process can be said to have lacked the characteristics of a state, at least to the extent that their representatives who participated in the Chinese political process did so on the same basis as the Chinese participants themselves. Whatever the foreigners participating in Chinese politics may have been in and of themselves, their projection inside China must be analyzed in terms of membership in the Chinese world, as competing parties seeking, in one or another combination, the same prize as the Han combatants sought. In this situation, foreign policy as I have used the term could not exist. Instead, intergovernmental or intergroup relationships took on an international quality, partaking of a dialectic of action but without exhibiting the traits of a foreign policy.

With the revival of the Empire, however, China once again possessed a foreign policy. As one would expect, this policy used the assumptions and the vocabulary of the new state, but it rested upon the same philosophical foundations that had supported the dynastic Empire's foreign policy and it exhibited deep structures that derived from the same sources as the structures that had characterized the dynastic Empire's foreign policy. Therefore, the renewed Empire's foreign policy resembled the foreign policy of the dynastic Empire. This is a particularly difficult point for Westerners in general, and Americans in particular, to understand. The citizens of the Oikoumene's Western democracies, especially the United States, are accustomed to interpreting the new China's foreign policy through the lens of the Cold War. Moreover, they are accustomed to mistake policies for policy; that is, specific tactical positions are confused with long-range (historically, socially, culturally, and geographically founded) strategic political policy. Thus, for example, shifts in policies after the death of Mao Zedong, often understood as profound policy changes, would be better interpreted as changes in the tactics chosen to serve the Empire's long-term historical policy objectives. It is important to try to comprehend the world as China sees it if the wellsprings of Chinese foreign policy and specific policies are to be understood.

The world into which the Chinese state reemerged differed from the world in which its earlier avatar had declined and fallen. While China had been floundering between Empire and Empire, between the traditional sinocentric world system and the establishment, or reestablishment, of a coherent *Chinese* world view, the Oikoumene had changed. Within the latter a new subsystem had been born and had come to maturity, the Soviet system, which included the Soviet Union, a kind of world empire in itself, and, after 1921, Mongolia and the Comintern's extensions, the loyal Stalinist parties, throughout the world; after 1945, this system also included the new satellites in Eastern Europe. The Soviet system constituted one pole within the Oikoumene; the other pole was the United

States. The existence within the Oikoumene of two poles, around which clustered satellites or clients, was not a new development; for example, long stretches of the nineteenth century had witnessed a similar structure, with Great Britain and tsarist Russia constituting opposed poles within the Oikoumene. From the perspective of China, the United States and the Soviet system were poles of the Oikoumene by virtue of their relationships with China and the rest of the world.

The United States and the Soviet Union were structured internally, and functioned, quite differently from each other, and conflict developed between them almost from the very beginning. The post-World War II Cold War was one form of that conflict. The new Chinese state had to find its way in this now multipolar world. The nature of the revolution that had brought the People's Republic into existence and reconstituted the Empire, as well as the legacy of the dynastic imperial tradition, already set the new state apart as a third system, a world outside the bipolar world of the Oikoumene. The history of Chinese Communist attitudes and policies toward the Soviet Union and the United States suggests that at its inception the new empire was already aware of the multivalent and multipolar world into which it was (re)emerging.

Though born officially on October 1, 1949, the new state, as well as its foreign policy, had been germinating within the dialectic of Chinese political culture since the establishment of the Chinese Communist Party in 1921. Likewise, the new state's foreign policy did not spring fully formulated from the minds of China's leaders at the beginning of October 1949. Both logically and historically, such policy was an integral part of the germination of the new state itself. Comprehension of Communist China's foreign policy, therefore, must rest upon a review of Chinese Communist foreign policy thinking before the state came into existence.

The precise form and thrust of Chinese foreign policy has to be interpreted against the background of both Chinese tradition and the Cold War. The history of the Cold War, after all, is the history of the relationship between the two poles of the Oikoumene, the American and the Russian, and China itself became for a while (1946–1949) one of the major battlegrounds in the conflict between them. In 1949, in light of the Communist character of the Chinese Revolution and the failure of American policy in China, the United States assigned China, both analytically and politically, to the Soviet bloc. This was a major error because the United States had confused intrasystemic conflict with intersystemic conflict. By automatically including China in the Soviet bloc, the United States inevitably was led to the perception that any conflict between China and the Soviet Union was intrasystemic rather than intersystemic, and this view unintentionally masked the profound differences between Moscow and Peking, which at a later date were to surprise the anticommunist West. A broader understanding of the nature of the Empire and its foreign policy might have avoided the mistake.

The Party's Foreign Policy

Before 1949, Chinese communism, together with its institutional expression, the Chinese Communist Party, was one response to the despoliation of China by the imperialism of the Oikoumene. Each earlier response, ranging from the nativistic reaction of the conservatives of the second half of the nineteenth century through the self-strengthening movement to the modernizing republicanism of Sun Yat-sen, had been the product of the interaction between the Empire of a particular moment in history and imperialism *in* China. The Empire and the Oikoumene had evolved according to the imperatives of both their separate histories and their interactions. This complex dialectical process meant that the particular forms that imperialism took over time, and the Empire's response to it, reflected the separate development of the Oikoumene and the Empire and the changing modes of their interaction. Moreover, developing technology, evolving business practices, and the psychological and social implications of the experience of success and failure all contributed to the definition of imperialism and anti-imperialism at any given moment. In this view, Chinese communism and the Chinese Communist Party were not consequences of Soviet interference in Chinese internal affairs, as some would have it, or a development *sui generis*, as others would maintain. Rather, they were the result of the forces active in a particular historical conjuncture and became, in turn, one of the forces determining subsequent conjunctures.

The internal development of Chinese communism and the party obeyed, and obeys, the same laws used to describe their appearance as phenomena in the interstices of the relationship between China and the Oikoumene. The transformations that occurred, and continue to occur, in Chinese Communist ideology, strategy, and tactics and in the institutions of Chinese communism, from the party itself to the rural soviets of the late 1920s and early 1930s to the military formations of the soviets, the Long March, and the Yan'an period, as well as the institutions and politics of the Sino-Japanese War and the post–World War II era, all were, by definition, a localization or realization within China of broad historical movements and particular political forces; at the same time, they were independent and indigenous phenomena. This kind of thick description insists upon continuity, both in the relevance of different elements at play in international relations and in cause-and-effect relationships, between the structures of foreign policy and the thought that accompanies it on the one hand, and "internal" social structures and political culture, on the other. There is no real or apparent contradiction in the duality of foreign and internal in the nature of the Chinese Communist experience, and the complexities of the phenomenon cannot, and should not, be simplified for the sake of analysis. What may seem curious or unexpected in the history of the party's foreign policy is so only if sight of Chinese communism's complex nature is lost.

EARLY DEFINITIONS

China's evolution toward economic, political, and commercial modernity differed significantly from the pattern of modernization found among the great powers of the Oikoumene. Two factors explain this difference. First, from the latter part of the eighteenth century on, Western technology changed rapidly in directions that the Empire's technology could not match. This technology enabled the Oikoumene's geographical, military, social, political, and economic domains to extend into the very heart of the Empire. Western presence and activity *inside* the Empire stimulated the development of a sector of the national economy that was modern or modernizing, but—and this is the second factor—the economically most significant elements in the modernizing sector of the economy were owned directly, or at least controlled, by the foreigners. The profound structural change that was taking place in the Oikoumene (actually, the transformation of the Holy Roman Empire and Western Christendom into the Oikoumene from the middle of the sixteenth century on) was made possible partly by the accumulation of capital and led to the further accumulation of capital, first for internal investment and later for foreign investment. The availability of capital for investment outside the Oikoumene was a factor in the Oikoumene's transformation into a world system that came into conflict with the world system of the Empire.

A direct consequence of the penetration of the Empire by capital from the Oikoumene was that foreign, not Chinese, preference largely determined the development of the Chinese economy, particularly in the spatial distribution of productive and commercial activities, in the choice of commodities to be produced or, in certain areas, imported, in the focus of investment, and in the direction of government policy. For example, Shanghai became China's most modern metropolis and most important commercial entrepôt not only because of primary causative factors that arose within the fabric of Chinese social development but also because of the West's need for an urban *pied-à-terre* within the Empire. The British crown colony of Hong Kong developed within the social and geographical fabric of the Empire, but beyond the reach of its political writ, for exactly the same reason. By the time of the Versailles peace conference in 1919, the more modernized sectors of the Chinese population were well aware of the quality of imperialism's impact on China. The gradual spread of Marxist theory and terminology, greatly accelerated by the example of the Russian Revolution of 1917, provided many Chinese with the tools of a cogent analysis of imperialism and its effects on China. Bourgeois theory could supply no analogous instruments for analysis and policy formulation.

(It can be argued persuasively that the attractiveness and the political influence of Marxism in the world outside the West throughout the twentieth century, particularly after 1917, is a consequence of the power of its analytical tools, which enable those who use them to grasp both intellectually and psychologically the reality they are experiencing and to develop responses to it. Close analysis demonstrates, moreover, that the power and reach of Marxism in this regard was not, and is not, related directly to the political influence of groups that officially espouse Marxism; nor does it relate directly to the political commitments of those wielding Marxism's tools. There are many throughout Asia, Africa, and Latin America who use Marxism for analytical activities and policy formulation but who are not communists in the sense that term is used in Western scholarship and journalism. The discontinuity between the analytical power of Marxism and the political commitments of those who use it accounts for the lack of isomorphism between the spheres of Soviet and Chinese influence, on the one hand, and the world that thinks in terms of socialism and opposes imperialism, on the other. Failure to perceive these distinctions often leads American policymakers into grave mistakes of judgment about the nature or political direction of one or another regime. Furthermore, political alliances as often as not develop out of shared analyses. For example, the Nicaraguan revolutionaries' analysis of Western capitalism and its imperialism in the late 1970s and early 1980s developed on a Marxist basis; this Marxist analysis led Washington to assume they were communists— Washington often looks for communists in many places in the world that have only Marxists—and this assumption inhibited the development of an American policy supportive of the Nicaraguan revolution, which, in turn, forced the Nicaraguans more and more to seek support from Cuba and the Soviet Union. Conversely, in the late 1940s, Yugoslavia shared the Marxist analysis with the Soviet Union but was forced, by Stalin's aggressivity, to break its alliance with Moscow and seek ties with the West. Similarly, China after the mid-1970s developed great interaction with the United States without necessarily abandoning Marxist analysis, although the United States, to accept the growing alliance with China, had to interpret tactical changes as ideological changes. The Marxist world seems more flexible politically and less bound by ideological strictures than does the United States.)

As early as 1922, the Chinese Communist Party began to develop, within the framework of Marxist analysis, a phenomenological approach to the description and analysis of imperialism in China. In fact, at that time the party issued a manifesto that vividly described imperialism in China. In this approach, imperialism was more than just a statistical indication of the relative weight of one or more foreign powers in the country's internal economy. It was a force that affected the daily life of the people as groups and as individuals; this departure in description and analysis gave a special direction to the foreign policy thought of the Communist Party. The departure rested on a distinction between formal structures and substantive relationships. For example, the Oikoumene did not oppose the movements for tariff autonomy and treaty reform in the 1920s, but the Communists understood that the solutions these movements sought were formalistic and not substantive. The dismantling of the legal structure of imperialism (which actually was not accomplished until the end of extraterritoriality in 1943) would not change the substance of imperialism in China, which rested upon political, social, and economic relationships of power, not upon legal formulations, and these real power relationships directly affected the daily lives of millions of Chinese workers or peasants in such different ways as, for example, determining what they produced or what they could purchase. The issue at hand for the Chinese Communists was not the legal description of a relationship but the actual locus of power to make decisions and the actual relationships that derived from that power.

The Chinese Communists also were aware that the development of capitalism in China was, in Marxist theory, a progressive historical development. In this view, capitalism was a necessary step in the improvement of the daily life of the Chinese people because it involved the growth and expansion of the means of production, which would both improve the quality of life and give China the capital and means to defend itself from the Oikoumene. At the same time, however, the Communists considered the deformations of Chinese society produced by the particular form of capitalism developing in China, a capitalism that was under imperialist direction and domination, a pathological condition. A capitalism domestically fueled and therefore more amenable to domestic pressures was a very different thing from a capitalism whose command posts lay abroad, far beyond the influence of China's internal political forces.

This phenomenological analysis of international relations gave the Chinese Communists a view of the world that necessarily differed from the Soviet Union's. The Soviets were not more doctrinaire than the Chinese Communists, although from the Chinese point of view Stalin appeared quite doctrinaire in the mid-1920s; rather, what seemed doctrinaire in the Soviet Union's policy toward China at that time was, in fact, a misguided attempt to impose Soviet experience on a non-Soviet society and the reality within which it functioned. This was an error often repeated by the Stalinists, and it usually led either to disaster, as in China in the mid-1920s, or to the need to impose Soviet analysis and Soviet policy on another society by *force majeur*, as in Czechoslovakia in 1968.

The collapse of Stalin's strategy in China in the mid-1920s forced a significant part of the small Communist Party to seek refuge in the mountains along the Hunan-Kiangsi provincial border. Mao Zedong used the opportunity to reflect further on China's position in the world. By defining China as a semicolony Mao indicated that China was not, in the classical sense of the word, a colony or the possession of a single foreign power; rather, China retained the legal fiction of independence while phenomenologically it was a colony of the congeries of foreign powers here called the Oikoumene, at least of those oikoumenical powers directly interested in East Asia. Moreover, these powers were contending among themselves for dominance in China, and they had their agents inside China. For example, the Chiang Kaishek regime was such an agent: its anticommunist policies, use of the foreigners' legal language to analyze China's condition, and reliance upon foreign support to pursue its own internal policies demonstrated that the Guomindang was the agent of the Oikoumene. This observation, based upon phenomenological analysis within the Marxist framework that characterized the party's 1922 manifesto, had direct implications for the development of the party's political strategy because it meant that the Chinese Revolution, by virtue of the nature of Chinese reality, could not assume the character of a proletarian revolution against a dominant bourgeois class; nor could it assume the character of a peasant revolution against a landlord class since the landlord class did not stand alone in Chinese society. The revolution had to be a national revolution against the imperialists *and* their agents within Chinese society.

This analysis is fraught with implications that are important in understanding Chinese Communist foreign policy down to this very day. First, imperialism is considered a relationship of dominance and exploitation; those who dominate and exploit China, or try to do so, are imperialists, and those who serve the interests of the imperialists are their agents. To serve the interests of the imperialists means much more than to act as the direct agent of an imperialist power; this notion encompasses the rationalization and justification of the imperialists' policies and behaviors, the attempt to explain away the imperialist relationship, and the use of the discourse of the imperialists, their terminology and logic, to analyze China's internal and external situation. In other words, to act as an agent of the imperialists means to place oneself in the same relationship to China and its society, economy, and culture that the foreigner occupies, to internalize the foreigners' values and mental structures, as well as to behave like a foreigner in the world of economics and politics.

The concept of imperialism thus took on, in the thought of the Chinese Communist Party, a much deeper and richer significance than it had enjoyed in the thought of Western Marxist and non-Marxist theoreticians and analysts. It followed from the Chinese content of the term that one could cease to be an imperialist by eschewing the relationship of dominance and exploitation that the term denoted; similarly, one ceased to be an agent of imperialism by opposing imperialism and fighting against it politically, economically, intellectually, psychologically, and socially. In other words, no one was intrinsically an imperialist or an agent of imperialism; one defined oneself actively by assuming a particular relationship to society. This was no abstract train of thought. The united front policy of the 1930s and the continuous Chinese Communist attempt to persuade Chiang Kaishek to take the field against the Japanese in concert with the party and the party's armies were predicated upon this philosophical position; had Chiang and the Guomindang regime taken the leadership the Communists urged them to assume, they would have defined themselves as anti-imperialists. Chinese Communist proposals for a united front were both strategic and tactical, to be sure, but they grew directly out of a fundamental analysis of the world, not out of opportunism.

Second, Mao recognized that the internecine struggle that character-ized China's own internal political condition was complementary to the struggle among the powers for a dominant position within China. This cre-ated the space within which the Chinese Communist Party could survive, and it required the party, as a political actor inside China, to have a foreign policy and constantly to take into account in the planning of its own actions the problems presented by the foreign powers. Moreover, China's local agricultural economy, rather than a (nonexistent) capitalist economy, pro-vided the economic infrastructure for the political fragmentation that was characteristic of the period; therefore, the Communist Party had to wage war within that agricultural economy. Unless the party fought where the fight was going on, so to speak, it would be irrelevant. A peasant based revolutionary strategy was not a matter of choice; it was dictated by Chinese reality. Nevertheless, the fight had to be led by the workers, that is to say, the party, even if the revolution were based on the peasants. Within the context of the revolution, individuals and groups were defined by the relationship of dominance and exploitation they maintained with other groups in the society, and the landlords who abandoned that partic-ular relationship could ally themselves with the peasants. This was the basis of the Yan'an policy that led so many foreigners to think that the Chinese Communists were merely agrarian reformers.

In Mao Zedong's perspective, the revolutionary struggle inside China was not an isolated process or historical event. Given China's condition, the revolution had to be an integral part of international political pro-cesses. After 1949, this view would have implications for the strategy rec-ommended to other nations struggling against imperialism, and it would allow Peking a latitude in policy development that the West, which gen-erally failed to understand the implications of Mao's thought, saw as cyni-cal opportunism.

THE UNITED FRONT AND FOREIGN POLICY

By the end of 1935, the Communists understood the Japanese war as a means whereby China was to be transformed from "a semi-colony of all the imperialisms to Japan's own colony." In other words, the war was the means whereby China would undergo a transformation in which it would lose the legal fiction of independence and would become one foreign power's possession, no longer the possession of the Oikoumene in general. This analysis, in turn, meant that the struggle against Japan would be transformed into a national revolution; it would no longer be a national war. In this light, the Japanese were clearly the primary enemy, distinguished from the other foreign powers, which, had they been allied with China *against* Japan, would have belonged to a different category and required a different response. As Mao said in 1937, "Our united front is anti-Japanese, not anti–all imperialists." The contradictions among the imperialist powers themselves, in other words, had to be exploited to China's benefit. Mao continued:

> The strengthening of British influence in China is a contradictory phenomenon of today. In the fight against Japan, because of China's colonial position, it is possible for a third power to strengthen its position in China. Can it then be said that this is pushing the tiger out the front door and letting the wolf in the back door? No, that would not be correct.

If the Chinese were to oppose the British, for example, they would be driven into the arms of the Japanese. Mao concluded that this result would not be in China's interest. "Consequently, the contradictions between China and certain other imperialist powers have been relegated to a secondary position, while the rift between these powers and Japan has been widened." This widened the scope of the United Front concept to include those imperialist powers that could become China's allies as a consequence of the contradictions within the imperialist camp itself. The choice of ally depended upon the need to maximize the advantages of the Chinese Revolution. Any realistic analysis of the world situation at the end of the 1930s and the beginning of the 1940s would have indicated that those powers arrayed against Japan were, even if imperialist, potential allies for China. The same analytical structure applied in the late 1950s and the 1960s led to conclusions that startled the world. Still, the analysis was consistent and coherent.[1]

The united front policy and the Maoist analysis of imperialism had direct implications for the party's foreign policy strategy and tactics. In 1936, an American journalist, Edgar Snow, went to Yan'an to interview Mao and write about the society the Chinese Communist Party was fashioning in that region. Mao, speaking through Snow, tried to obtain the neutrality of the major oikoumenical powers and even their active financial and military supply support. Moreover, he declared that a successful war would strengthen China and that a strong China would welcome foreign support of its development. He applied his analysis to make a distinction between legitimate and illegitimate foreign rights and activities in China; the former, he said, would be respected after the end of the war.

The failure of the West to move more actively against the Japanese, particularly after the Marco Polo Bridge incident, indicated to Mao that perhaps he had overestimated the degree to which contradictions among the imperialist powers had developed and that, therefore, China could not depend upon foreign aid but would have to become self-reliant. That same year he clearly stated that, in the broader scene, the rise of fascism in Europe and the necessity to combat it took primacy over the Sino-Japanese conflict in East Asia. Therefore, reality itself suggested that the Soviet Union would not be a major source of support in China's conflict with Japan.

Several features of Mao's early thinking concerning international relations deserve emphasis because of their fundamental role in the later development of Chinese foreign policy. First, Mao favored cooperation with foreign powers if that cooperation were beneficial to China's interests. He did not adopt a doctrinaire position opposing all foreign involvement. Second, he insisted upon a realistic analysis of international realtionships, using the concept of contradiction as an analytical tool. China could use contradictions among the outside powers, that is to say, among the members of the Oikoumene, to its own advantage. Third, war was, of course, a human misfortune, but it could contribute to historical progress; indeed, war made China's revolution part of the international historical struggle. War, therefore, should not necessarily be avoided.

HEIGHTENED CONTRADICTIONS

The formal outbreak of World War II in Europe in 1939 confirmed Mao's analysis of the international scene. The Hitler-Stalin pact of August 1939 was a tactical maneuver: on the one hand, it was a consequence of the heightened contradictions among the imperialist powers in the context of which the Nazis would do battle against the British and the French while the Soviets conserved their power. Indeed, Mao seemed to think that the entire European war and the Hitler-Stalin pact was a question of protecting socialism against imperialism. The possibility of a similar pact between the Soviet Union and Japan was also seen by Mao as a perhaps necessary tactical maneuver; for China, this possibility only emphasized the importance he placed upon self-reliance.

The United States, however, presented a different picture. Japanese-American negotiations over those issues that might lead the two Pacific powers to war was, on more than one occasion, referred to in Communist documents and publications as the Pacific equivalent of the Munich appeasement in Europe. Here, too, however, Mao's structural and pragmatic analysis of the world allowed great latitude in response to changing reality. If history were to bring the United States into armed conflict against Japan and, therefore, transform America into a potential ally of China's the Communists would welcome American aid and military cooperation. This type of analysis meant that Germany's invasion of the Soviet Union on June 22, 1941, and Japan's attack on Pearl Harbor on December 7, 1941, radicalized the contradictions among the imperialists and made one of the two impe-

rialist camps a potential ally of the Chinese. Yan'an now became actively
interested in cooperation with the United States, which held out a more
realistic possibility of aid for China than did the Soviet Union, which was
deeply embroiled in a difficult war with the fascists. None of this, however, changed the progressive nature of the war in the Communists' view
of history.

THE PACIFIC WAR

Mao Zedong saw the Chinese revolution as central to the movement of
the world toward socialism. At the same time, he understood this revolution to be quite independent of Soviet policy or of the particular policies
of particular institutions of the international communist movement, such
as the Comintern. Soviet foreign policy and the progressive movement of
the world in the direction of socialism were not the same thing. Among
the factors that contributed to Mao's thinking in this regard were the profound involvement of the Soviet Union in the war against the Germans,
Moscow's neutrality pact with Japan, the dissolution of the Comintern in
1943, and the delivery of Soviet aid to the Guomindang regime but not to
Yan'an. Indeed, throughout the Pacific war the Soviet Union paid little
attention to the Chinese Communists, either as communists or as Chinese
who were potential allies; for their part, the Chinese Communists paid the
Soviet Union only symbolic attention, citing Russian statements in various
declarations and manifestos and paying lip service to Soviet leadership in
the anti-imperialist struggle. After all, the Soviet Union *per se* was not
crucial to historical development. The U.S.S.R. was important only because it was in a position to provide leadership during a particular period
of history; if it failed to provide that leadership, its importance accordingly
would diminish. The structure of history, not the immediate importance of
Joseph Stalin or the Soviet Union, mattered.

The United States was altogether a different question. As the major
foreign power fighting the Japanese and as the primary source of aid for
China, America had great potential for intervention in Chinese affairs;
therefore, the United States preoccupied the Communists. The war posed
two problems in this respect: first, the Communists needed material aid,
but for its own reasons the United States was channeling almost all its aid
to Chiang Kaishek; second, American policy toward China after the war
had to be a matter of present, not future, concern. Economic cooperation,
Mao thought, would be beneficial to China as well as to the United States.

As the war dragged on, the Communists tried to make contact with
Americans stationed in or visiting Chongqing. Eventually they succeeded.
They wanted to impress the Americans both with Yan'an's need for material support and with the advantages of American–Chinese Communist cooperation. In 1943, Zhou Enlai on more than one occasion invited the

Americans to send observers to the Communist held areas, and in July 1944 a U.S. army observer group was established in Yan'an. The group was greeted personally by Mao Zedong and many members of the Politburo. One of the liaison officers assigned to the Americans was Huang Hua, later to become the first Chinese Communist ambassador to the United Nations and, eventually, foreign minister. Through the agency of the Dixie mission, as the observer group came to be called, knowledge of the Chinese Communists reached the United States directly rather than indirectly through the filter of the Guomindang. Communist popularity among the people and willingness to fight the Japanese contrasted sharply with conditions in Nationalist China. But while the United States wanted to mediate between the Communists and the Nationalists in order to bring about a united front, in the end Washington rejected Communist attempts to create a relationship that would mutually benefit both the Americans and the Communists. Whatever the merits of the case, Patrick Hurley, who came to China in September 1944 as President Roosevelt's personal representative to Chiang Kaishek, and others in similar positions were too ignorant about Chinese reality not to be beguiled by Chiang's propaganda. Those, like Stilwell, who had a keener appreciation of the situation, were removed at the instigation of the Nationalists.

American policies seemed contradictory to the Chinese Communists, and they began to make a distinction between the American people and friends in the American government, on the one hand, and the American imperialists, on the other. This distinction, as "theological" and pointless as it may seem, was an important instrument for keeping open the possibility of present and future cooperation between the United States and the Chinese Communists. After all, the war against Japan remained the primary concern of both, and Yan'an did not want to foreclose future opportunities for cooperation with the Americans. The Communists never stopped making this distinction, so they always had more latitude in their response to American initiatives than Washington believed.

AMERICAN MEDIATION

The implications of differences in world view for international relations could have been no clearer than they were in the immediate post–World War II era. American actions in China that Washington perceived as normal operations attendant upon the surrender of Japan (such as American aid in the transportation of Nationalist forces to reoccupy Japanese held portions of China) were, in Communist eyes, direct American intervention to inhibit the Chinese Revolution. Had the United States not appeared on the scene with planes and ships, the Communists would have succeeded in occupying more territory than they actually did. The situation was aptly described by the famous American journalist Theodore H. White:

The United States Marines, the Kuomintang, the former puppets, and the Japanese army, in one of the most curious alliances ever fashioned, jointly guarded the railways against the Chinese partisans. By a bitter irony the very area where the situation was most tense—about Peking and Tientsin—was one in which Communist partisans had risked their lives time and again to rescue American flyers from the Japanese; crews of B-29's bailing out on their return from bombing Japan had been smuggled to safety by villagers who were now held to be enemies. In this area Communists now sniped at marine trains; marines shelled a village in retaliation.[2]

Communist protests to General Wedemeyer were to no avail, although Wedemeyer himself recognized the contradiction in the situation.

While the Americans argued that the U.S. presence in China was necessary to facilitate Japanese surrender and repatriation, in the eyes of the Communists the objective purpose of the United States was the survival of the Chiang regime. American diplomatic efforts to bring about some kind of coalition between the Communists and the Nationalists led to the same conclusion. As the behavior of the Nationalist government led only to growing disaffection in the reoccupied areas and to an increasingly chaotic economy, and as Communist popularity increased, American attempts to mediate between the two parties seemed a way to insure the survival of the Chiang Kaishek regime in the face of what would otherwise quickly be a Communist victory. Withdrawal of the American marines at the end of 1946 did not change this analysis: at Chiang's request an American military advisory group was established at the generalissimo's headquarters and it functioned from February 1946 through 1948; although the group numbered only about one thousand men, and although its contribution to Chiang's survival was limited, this body stood as a constant reminder of American participation and partisanship in the Chinese Revolution.

The Communists initially adopted a posture of forebearance toward American participation in China's postwar politics. On the one hand, they recognized American activities for what they were; on the other, they hoped that internal American considerations would encourage President Truman to limit the American presence in China or to cease interference altogether. By the middle of 1946, however, the Communists realized that U.S. policy was not about to change and that, on the contrary, America seemed to be increasingly involved in China. The glaring contradiction between American support for Chiang and American insistence upon playing a mediating role in Chinese politics undercut not only the Marshall mission (see Chapter 8) but all other American efforts to resolve China's internal crisis. This, together with the Soviet Union's apparent lack of interest in the Communists, led to the growth of Communist cynicism about the intentions of the foreign powers and reinforced their propensity to rely wholly upon their own resources. They did not isolate themselves; they were isolated by both Washington and Moscow. This experience of isolation and self-reliance, which the Communists' victory in the revolution validated, strongly influenced Chinese foreign policy in the decades after 1949.

THE PROBLEM OF THE SOVIET UNION

The circumstances under which the war ended, combined with Soviet support for the Guomindang regime during the years of conflict, forced the Chinese Communists to develop a policy toward the Soviet Union. Moscow's participation in the very last days of the war against Japan and its consequent dominant position in Manchuria made the U.S.S.R. what it really had not been during the war itself, an immediate factor in the Chinese internal political scene. Moreover, Stalin believed in 1945–1946, just as he had in 1925–1926, that China's, and presumably the Soviet Union's, interests were best served by some form of an alliance between Moscow and the Guomindang. American support for Chiang Kaishek made Soviet policy a particularly difficult problem for the Chinese Communists. Although they were on the same ideological side as the Soviet Union, they had to confront Moscow's historical failure to develop, at almost any time since 1921, a constructive policy toward the Chinese Communist Party. Moreover, this problem was now compounded by the fact the Soviet Union and the United States, who were increasingly inimicable to each other on the broader international scene, were both supporting the Communists' enemy, the Guomindang, whose primary ally within Chinese politics was the United States.

From the outset, Mao Zedong began to develop a policy that was remarkably prescient in its appreciation of the relationship between the two great powers. As early as April 1946, he declared that armed struggles outside the two powers' metropolitan domains were, at best, only tangential to the interests of the two powers; they would seek their compromises regardless of their conflicts in third areas or through third powers. This came close to a direct refutation of the Soviet position that civil war in China would be a threat to world peace. It was also a piece of forward-looking analysis that history was to verify: once the United States and the U.S.S.R. embarked upon détente, events such as the Vietnam War, the pro-Soviet coup in Afghanistan in 1978, and various conflicts in Africa did not seem to damage the foundations of Soviet-American understanding. Even Washington's reaction to the Soviets' invasion of Afghanistan in 1980 did not result in a real breakdown in Soviet-American relations; at most it led to a temporary hiatus in progress toward accommodation. Mao's analysis did not define the parameters of the great powers' metropolitan authority; those limits would be defined by historical circumstance, as when the United States refrained from interfering in the Soviet invasion of Hungary in 1956. But the principle, as Mao enuciated it, was sound.

In Mao's view, the world consisted of three zones: the United States and its sphere of influence, the Soviet Union and its sphere of influence, and an intermediate area that included China and belonged to neither power's sphere. The struggle against imperialism and for democracy would be waged in the third zone. This three-zone theory, clearly stated as early as 1946, was an accurate projection of international reality at the time and, for that matter, for the years to come. On the one hand, it prefigured the concept of a First, a Second and a Third World; on the other, the theory reflected China's position in the world and remained a major point of departure for all Chinese foreign policy thinking down to the present. It must be emphasized that the significant part of Mao's analysis was not the immediate political statements to which it gave rise but the structure of relationships that it refracted. Thus, for example, what was important was not which country or society belonged in which zone but, rather, that the concept of zones refracted real relationships; any particular country or society or government could move from one zone to another depending upon the immediate historical conjuncture that defined its politics, its international relationships. Furthermore, the three-zone theory made it possible for the Chinese to redefine the Soviets as "social imperialists" in the 1960s and afterward without violating the integrity of the concept of a socialist camp. Politics, or real relationships of power, defined zone membership; zone membership did not define any member's politics. Finally, this theory enabled Mao to perceive the possibility of Soviet-American détente along with armed conflict between the imperialists and the anti-imperialists in the intermediate zone. Direct bilateral relations between the powers of the first and second zones were one matter; their relationships with the members of the third zone or their mutual relationships *in* the third zone were conceptually and practically quite a different matter. (In the analytical perspective adopted in this book, the first and second zones are the poles of the Oikoumene, the relations among the members of which are distinct from their internal socioeconomic structures.)

The three-zone theory did not mask the possibility that the first or second zone could be riddled by internal contradictions. Indeed, since Mao's definition of the zones seemed to rest more upon relationships of power than upon ideology, contradictions within any single zone as a consequence of the tensions inherent in the domination of one state by another were predictable. Thus, for example, he suggested that the primary contradiction at the end of the war was between democratic and antidemocratic forces within the first (capitalist) zone, not between the United States and the Soviet Union. Therefore, the thrust of American policy in the immediate future would be the attempt to gain dominance over other first-zone powers. In fact, Mao did not miss the mark by far: the campaign against the Italian Communists in the 1948 Italian elections, Franco-American relations during the De Gaulle era, and American-German relations in the 1970s and 1980s all fall into the category of contradictions within the first zone; American relations with U.S. clients in Latin America, Asia, and Africa also belong in this category. Similarly, though Mao did not specify this example, contradictions would develop within the second, or Soviet, zone. Cases in point are the Soviet-Rumanian relationship, in which Bucharest has pursued an independent foreign policy with anti-Soviet implications although Rumania has not changed its internal structure and remains quite Stalinist; the anti-Soviet thrust of the Hungarian revolt of 1956 is another example, as is the Soviet need to dominate Czechoslovakia by crushing the "Prague spring" of 1968. The Polish workers' peaceful uprising in the middle of 1980 illustrates a contradiction internal to Polish society that, because of the power structure within the second zone, also became an issue in Soviet-Polish relations. (Each zone has its own structure of relationships that gives form to any particular historical conjuncture within it. Thus, for example, the workers' strikes in Poland were an issue in Soviet-Polish relations in 1980 because of the structure of the relationships within the second zone. However, a strike in France or Germany or England or Mexico would not necessarily become an issue in Washington's relationship with any of those countries; in fact, more than likely it would be defined as a strictly "internal" affair, and Washington would be extraordinarily careful to maintain its distance from the event.)

The three-zone analytical structure and the consequent assumption that the primary international contradiction at the time was between the United States and the other powers of the first zone had immediate implications for Chinese foreign policy. In fact, the analysis led directly to the logical conclusion that China's interests were best served not by a bilateral alliance with the Soviet Union (which, in any event, was then impossible) but by an alliance of all anti-imperialist forces in all three zones against the United States. This would give the Chinese Communists two advantages. First, it redefined the Chinese Revolution, within the political discourse of the postwar world, as belonging to the same category of events as the anticolonial and anti-imperialist movements and wars occurring, or soon to occur, in such geographically, culturally, and politically disparate places as Greece and French Indochina. If the United States were the enemy, then the civil war in Greece, in which the U.S. was deeply involved, or the anti-French struggle in Indo-China, which was being waged against America's French ally, contributed to the Chinese Communists' opportunity to wage war against the Guomindang, America's client inside China. Second, this theory allowed China to accept the leadership of the Soviet Union in the anti-imperialist struggle as long as the Soviet Union provided that leadership, but it did not require China to accept the Soviet Union either as the font of all truth or as the model for its own social, political, or economic development. In other words, the theory guaranteed the potential internal independence of China within an alliance led by the Soviet Union, a position the Soviet Union's East European satellites could not occupy both because of geographical proximity and relative weakness of power *vis-à-vis* the Soviet Union and because they lacked any theoretical foundation on the basis of which to pursue internal independence. At the same time, the theory contained the seeds of contradiction and conflict between China and the U.S.S.R.

Mao's analyses of international relations at the time that are relevant to the development of Chinese Communist foreign policy went beyond the three-zone theory. He fully recognized that the United Staes was militarily superior to any other force in the world; Washington was then the sole possessor of the atom bomb. American superiority was purely technological, however, not historical or political; China's own experience demonstrated that technological superiority did not always prevail over revolutionary enthusiasm. Consequently, the technological superiority of the United States and, within a short time, of the Soviet Union did not place the intermediate (third) zone at a disadvantage. Eventually the United States demonstrated the validity of Mao's thesis: in Vietnam, its overwhelming military superiority fell victim to a national-revolutionary enthusiasm that was little understood in the advanced industrial societies of the West. Mao's thesis that imperialism was a "paper tiger" was not a denial of the power of the atom bomb; rather, it was a statement that military power is not sufficient unto itself and that other forms of power, primarily political and spiritual, can equal and perhaps overcome technological superiority. More immediately, this theory explained that a Chinese peasant revolution could defeat a Guomindang allied to the world's most advanced technological power.

The apparent reluctance of the Soviet Union to countenance, much less actively to support, a Communist victory in China has already been discussed. Mao's locating China in the third, or intermediate, zone was a reflection upon Soviet policy more than it was an abstract meditation on international politics. As victory approached, the issue of the future Chinese state's relations with the Soviet Union grew in importance. Mao was fairly consistent in recognizing Soviet *leadership* in the anti-imperialist bloc, even if the Soviet Union's immediate attitude toward the Chinese Revolution did not satisfy him. Some inside the Chinese Communist Party raised questions about the structure and nature of an eventual alliance with the Soviet Union; Mao himself certainly did not want to rush into Moscow's close embrace. Nevertheless, circumstances required him to define his future government's foreign policy, which he did in a momentous declaration on July 1, 1949, entitled "On People's Democratic Dictatorship." China would ally itself, he said, "with the Soviet Union, . . . with all the New Democratic countries, and . . . with the proletariat and broad masses of the people in other countries, to form an international united front." However, he immediately defined this policy as an alliance rather than a petition for membership in the bloc. China's foreign policy would reflect its need for international alliances with other anti-imperialist forces under the leadership, to be sure, of the Soviet Union, but China would not accept domination. It is doubtful that Mao intended to close the door to relations with the United States, but Washington interpreted his policy statements in an atmosphere of despair as the Nationalist position in China dissolved.[3]

At the same time that Mao was providing theoretical and political indications of the future course of China's foreign policy, practical developments in the relations between Manchuria, where the Chinese Communists were already in command, and the Soviet Union began to give that policy objective existence. After their Manchurian victory in 1948, the Communists had requested technical aid from the Soviet Union, and in response Soviet engineers and technicians began to arrive in Manchuria to help reconstruct the economy and its technological infrastructure. In July 1949, Gao Gang, the primary Communist leader in Manchuria, led a delegation to Moscow; by the end of the month the Chinese had signed an agreement with the Soviet Union for the barter of goods. As limited a beginning as this was, Sino-Soviet cooperation had begun to take form even before the new regime officially assumed power on October 1, 1949 and was recognized by the Soviet Union.

THE NEW CHINA AND THE UNITED STATES

Mao's proposed policy of "leaning to one side" certainly did not foreclose the possibility of constructive relations with the United States, even if Washington sought to interpret his remarks in that vein. Quite the contrary, he left the door open for a positive, or at least neutral, American response to the new state. In November 1948, the Communists had declared that they sought good relations with all countries, including the United States, provided that the foreign powers respected China's territorial integrity and did not support Chiang Kaishek. Combined with the statement in early 1947 that the Communists would refuse to recognize any international agreement concluded by the Guomindang regime after January 1946, this assertion meant that the new regime would enter the web of international relations with the sole precondition that China and its partners in diplomacy begin their relationships anew and unencumbered by the restrictions imposed by the past. The new regime would respond to any constructive approaches made by foreign powers, regardless of their former role in Chinese affairs. From the American point of view, however, this position was tantamount to a repudiation of China's international obligations. America's political and legal culture laid great store on the concept of the inheritability of contractual agreements, and China's call for a new beginning both outraged American legalistic sensibilities and provided

Washington with a pretext to evade the political issue of both *de facto* and *de jure* recognition. From the outset, therefore, Washington's view of the new Chinese state was inimical to the development of anything approaching a reasonable relationship. Furthermore, the paranoia that characterized the American political mind during the Cold War (and which found one of its most important internal expressions in McCarthyism) required U.S. policymakers to view a Communist China as nothing more than a Soviet creature.

As early as May 1949, months before the establishment of the new regime in Peking, the American State Department initiated a policy of discouraging other noncommunist powers from recognizing a possible new Communist regime in China. The United States approached various foreign ministries around the world to suggest the inadvisability of any positive approach to China. At the same time, the Chinese Communists, through Huang Hua, tried to establish direct contact with the United States. Huang named three conditions for the establishment of Sino-American diplomatic relations after the Communist victory. First, all foreign forces had to be withdrawn from China. Second, relations had to be based on "equality, mutual benefit, and mutual respect of each other's independence and territorial integrity."[4] Third, recognition of the Nationalist regime must be withdrawn. Washington was deaf to this message and proceeded to organize its friends and allies against recognition. According to some reports, the United States expressed unwillingness to recognize a China that concluded an alliance of any kind with the Soviet Union. To the Chinese Communists, such a position, if it was actually taken, could have had only one meaning: the United States would recognize China only if the latter surrendered its foreign policy independence. Nevertheless, as late as June 1949 the Communists again expressed their willingness "to discuss with any foreign government the establishment of diplomatic relations."[5] The United States refused to see this as an opening wedge for the exploration of future Sino-American relations and rejected the implicit invitation on the basis that the policy of "leaning to one side" placed China squarely in the Soviet bloc.

The next American diplomatic move against China was the publication at the end of July 1949 of the famous white paper officially entitled *United States Relations with China*. This document, written inside the State Department to justify past American policy, laid the groundwork for a future policy of antagonism and defended the administration against its domestic critics within and without Congress. The State Department's claims that the United States had left nothing undone that could have affected the situation inside China and that the "ominous result of the Civil War in China was beyond the control of the government of the United States"[6] were evidence to the Communists that the United States intended to pursue its imperialist objectives and reject relationships of equality. Moreover, it seemed to them that American aid, if offered at all, would have a significant political price tag attached.

The United States did not limit itself to verbal and documentary antagonism toward China. In February 1949, Washington suggested to Great Britain that the Cold War restraints governing Western trade with the Soviet Union and its satellites be extended to China; in the middle of the year the United States tried to include other European countries in a broad embargo. Agreement was reached in September, and by November a policy was in place that inhibited trade with China for a quarter of a century. In the Chinese view, the United States, despite the defeat of the Guomindang regime, was now preparing to continue its intervention in Chinese affairs by other means.

Secretary of State Acheson clearly expressed the American view of the new China on July 30, 1949. China, he said, was coming under a "foreign yoke,"[7] which eventually it would throw off. The United States now perceived China as a direct threat to American interests in East Asia and began to build a ring of defenses around that part of China's perimeter that was exposed to possible American initiatives. For Japan, the United States prepared a peace treaty that would include neither China nor the Soviet Union and that would permit Japan to serve as a base for an American military presence in the Western Pacific. In an important speech on January 12, 1950, Acheson declared that the American defense perimeter extended from the Aleutian Islands to the Philippines through Japan and the Ryukyus. Although he did not include South Korea and its militantly anticommunist government within this zone, he declared that the United States had a responsibility there; this claim led Peking to conclude that the United States indeed considered Korea part of its defenses in the Far East. While disavowing any special American interest in Formosa, Chiang Kaishek's refuge, and declaring that the United States did not plan any military intervention in China, Acheson made it clear that the United States would not prevent Formosa from purchasing American military goods and that Washington would continue to provide economic assistance to the Nationalist regime. Whatever these statements may have meant in Washington, Peking understood them to signal a continuation of American intervention in the civil conflict whose prolongation Chiang's presence on Formosa made possible. Finally, by the middle of 1950 Washington indicated that the direct (through colonial regimes) or indirect (through controlled regimes) participation of the anticommunist West in the internal affairs of Indochina was a matter of some consequence to the United States. Accordingly, the United States supported indigenous nationalists so as to prevent the development of communist power in the region. This policy, already taking distinct form in 1949, culminated in the disaster of the Vietnam War in the 1970s. But as early as the first part of 1950, Zhou Enlai, the new Chinese state's foreign minister, remarked:

> I think I must tell Acheson on behalf of the biggest nation in Asia and of her people that these ridiculous threats are already an anachronism. Cool down and look at the map! The affairs of the Asian peoples must be settled by the Asian peoples themselves and must never be interfered with by such American imperialists as Acheson and company on the other side of the Pacific Ocean.[8]

The issue was joined. The Chinese Communists wanted to entertain the possibility of a constructive relationship with the United States and the other imperialist powers. The United States, however, defined its own interests in such a way as to exclude recognition of the new state and to lead Washington actively to oppose the development of relations between China and the other non-Soviet powers of the Oikoumene. The inherent logic of America's posture required it to maintain a military establishment in East Asia that Peking could interpret only as a direct threat to the new China's security. Within this dialectic of conflict each side began to behave toward the other in a hostile fashion. The Chinese placed the American consul-general in Mukden, Angus Ward, under house arrest and eventually expelled him from China. In Peking itself, the Military Control Commission, a primary organ of the new government, requisitioned a part of the American consular compound for its own use, thereby prompting the United States to protest against what it considered an infringement of its property rights. What the United States understood as private property (albeit government owned), which was sacred in the American consciousness, was, in the consciousness of the Chinese, an extraterritorial privilege. The Chinese responded to the American protest by claiming that all extraterritorial privileges had been relinquished by the foreign powers in 1943, at the same time that all other unequal aspects of China's relationship with the West had been abolished. In its turn, the United States seized upon the house arrest of Ward and the confiscation of the consular compound in Peking as indications of Chinese hostility. Washington initiated a series of actions intended to inflict direct harm on China's program for economic recovery. For example, Washington prevented the return to China of the civil aviation squadron that had been flown out to Hong Kong during the last days of the revolution, blocked West German steel exports to China, froze Chinese assets in the United States, and excluded the new state from participation in innumerable international agencies, commissions, and organizations. Nowhere could Peking find evidence for anything but enmity from Washington.

The New State

The establishment of the government of the Chinese People's Republic in Peking on October 1, 1949, marked the reorganization—indeed the reestablishment—of the East Asian imperial state in a revolutionary and mod-

ernizing form. In population China was, and remains, the largest state on
earth. It was, and remains, the third largest unified territory in the world,
following only the Soviet Union and Canada. China was, and remains, an
overwhelmingly agricultural land. When the state was reestablished, approximately seventy-five percent of the population was engaged in agriculture, which accounted for forty percent of the gross national product. Another ten percent of the population lived in the countryside and worked in
nonagricultural but related economic activities, including petty commerce.
However, only about one-seventh of China's land area is arable (or roughly
half the agricultural land available in the United States). In 1949 the new
state, with a population of 650–700 million, had to support one-quarter of
the world's entire population on only seven or eight percent of the world's
cultivated land; almost no opportunity for expansion of agricultural territory existed inside the country. China's density of population, calculated
on the basis of cultivated land, is among the highest in the world: 695–850
people per square kilometer (depending on the population estimate). Although contemporary China's natural resources, including energy, are in
quantities and qualities that are not unfavorable to economic development,
in 1949 the People's Republic was considered poor in resources. In 1974,
China became a major world oil producer, and by 1978 Peking contemplated the possibility of exporting oil to finance its economic modernization; but in 1949 the country depended heavily upon oil imports, particularly from the Soviet Union, a situation with grave implications for both
economic development and military policy. These indications, among others, suggest that even under relatively stable political, economic, and social conditions, the new state would have had to confront difficulties of a
high order if it were to maintain the living standards, however low they
may have been, of a growing population in an environment that was already strained to the limits of its productive capacity. Of course, there was
no such stability.

The new state came into existence amid social and political conditions
that were extreme in character. A century of turmoil, which saw some
twenty-five years of civil conflict, eighteen years of international warfare
on China's territory, and four years of so-called civil war, had resulted in
massive economic and social dislocations that exacerbated the already sub-
marginal conditions in which the masses of the population were trying to
survive. These dislocations were caused by, and contributed to, the disintegration of traditional patterns of life, a disintegration accentuated by
modernization processes, imperialism, natural disasters, and long years of
warfare. The new regime's problems were staggering.

However, the state was not without resources. An important strain of
the Great Tradition of Chinese civilization was the concept of a unified
state whose lines of power radiated from a central person and place (the
emperor and the capital) to all corners of the Empire, supported by and

administered through a coherent bureaucracy held together by shared patterns of ideology, education, and custom. For the new state, Mao Zedong, Peking, and the Communist Party provided contemporary satisfaction of the civilization's requirements. The anti-Japanese war had tempered both Mao and the party experientially, and the selection of Peking as the capital was a reassertion of the imperial tradition over against the discontinuities of the polycentric period, during which Nanjing had been the capital. The growth of a protomodern patriotism during the anti-Japanese war, which was enriched by an increasing anti-Americanism that was the consequence of Washington's support, real or apparent, of the Guomindang regime, was another resource upon which the new regime could draw. The personnel of the Communist government had gathered considerable practical administrative and political experience through the administration of a very sizable population in the liberated areas in the course of the anti-Japanese war. Finally, the new state had available a small but well-educated cadre of technical experts and people well trained in social and economic reform measures whose patriotism, regardless of their political orientation, impelled them to offer their services to Peking. These were the resources with which the Chinese Communists faced their immediate tasks.

The new state had to be politically organized and to spread its dominion throughout Chinese society. By May 1950 the Communists had completed their occupation of the entire country, including the island of Hainan in the South China Sea. Only Formosa, the Pescadores, and a very few coastal islands remained beyond Peking's reach. The country's size required the regime to approach the implantation of a new administrative apparatus and a new personnel resolutely but gradually. The party defined the people of the newly reconstituted Empire as consisting of four classes, the proletariat, the peasantry, the petty bourgeoisie, and the national bourgeoisie; therefore, both theoretically and technically, the new government had to be a democratic coalition that took the form of a dictatorship and whose primary internal mission was to crush the enemies of the people, that is to say, the reactionary classes and elements that opposed the new state or allied themselves with the imperialists. The state temporarily did not confiscate private property either in land or in business and industry, so that the society and economy could regain a measure of stability before revolutionary changes were introduced. The general aims of the new regime were embodied in the Common Program, a broad statement of objectives that had been validated by the People's Political Consultative Conference, held in Peking in September 1949. This conference also passed the Organic Law of the Central People's Government, a kind of national constitution that firmly defined the class and ideological character of the new state. In the first period of the government's existence, noncommunist intellectuals were given many roles to play and noncommunist parties symbolic posts to fill.

The new state consisted of numerous elements. Its primary components were the government, the Communist Party, and the People's Liberation Army (PLA); interacting and interpenetrating personnel unified the three as facets of a single object. The state penetrated the population through a congeries of organizations at different administrative levels down to the village, the factory, and the school. This provided a vertical and territorial structure for the exercise of power and the development of policy and popular support. A great variety of horizontal organizations also spread through the society, ranging from trade unions to women's organizations, youth movements, students' and children's organizations, and associations based upon specialized activities. This great structure of vertical and horizontal organizations was utilized to mobilize the population for education, for political support of the different campaigns by means of which the regime sought to reorient the culture's priorities, and for action in pursuit of one objective or another, ranging from the killing of flies and sparrows to increasing food production. The speed with which the new state brought order out of the chaos of polycentrism was truly impressive.

Another, but certainly no less important, immediate task was the reconstruction of the devastated economy. Industrial production and mining had fallen below prewar standards, and Soviet despoliation of the Manchurian economy in 1945–1946 had further weakened the country's real or potential economic health. The small industrial labor force was disorganized, railroads had been severely damaged in the civil war, great shortages of food and other essentials existed in the cities, the currency in circulation was next to useless, and inflation was rampant. The regime had to take immediate measures to control inflation, establish a taxation system, build a fiscal administration, and generally restore confidence in an economy that it also had to make function. Production had to be increased and consumption controlled if people were to survive and inflation were to be ended. Economic recovery moved ahead rapidly as the national transportation system was reorganized and expanded and good harvests were brought in. The reviving economy also had to be socialized, gradually but steadily. Private enterprise was permitted to survive but state control was increased. Land reform, which was political and social as well as economic in intent, was introduced in the middle of 1950 and completed by the beginning of 1953. Total collectivization followed. The whole process of economic revival was accompanied by a conscious intensification of class antagonisms and class consciousness through the organization of meetings and movements, particularly in the countryside, as a way of mobilizing the population for production.

Mobilization for production had to be paralleled by a program of social change aimed at the transformation of the structure of society and its values. The goal of socialism, albeit in its authoritarian or totalitarian rather than democratic form, had distinguished the Communist Party from all its rivals on the Chinese political scene from 1921 on, and the achievement of this objective was the party's, and the new regime's, *raison d'etre*. Consequently, from the very beginning the government introduced, again gradually, measures that ranged from new laws to popular movements, all intended to move China toward the social goals the party had set. In 1950, a new marriage law gave women full equality in marriage, divorce, and property, and a variety of popular campaigns encouraged the reorganization of the family structure and the traditional set of affectional relationships. Sociopolitical mobilization was encouraged through the "three self movement," which tried to remove the influence of "cultural imperialism" by encouraging "self-government, self-support, and self-propagation." This program was directed primarily at the Christian elements of the population, but other movements were more broadly defined. In the early 1950s, the "three anti movement" fought waste, corruption, and bureaucratism primarily in the official caste. The "five anti movement," aimed at the bourgeoisie, fought "bribery, tax evasion, theft of state property, cheating and the stealing of state economic intelligence." Most of these campaigns were intended to sharpen class differences and antagonisms as a means of heightening the consciousness of workers and peasants; specific measures ranging from public confessions and apologies to reform through the performance of labor tasks were used for the same purpose. The recalcitrant elements were sometimes consigned to labor camps; however, these camps apparently never reached the size or barbaric conditions that characterized similar institutions in the Soviet Union. Large groups of the population were also mobilized to complete public works projects, such as the construction of dams, and these, too, served the purpose of social change.

The total transformation of Chinese society required profound changes in culture. The party and Mao Zedong had demonstrated their awareness of the importance of cultural revolution during the Yan'an days, when everything from literature to work style was discussed. The very thought processes and behavior patterns of the Chinese culture and population had to undergo change. Thought reform and what is now called behavior modification were widely used, intensively on individuals and more broadly on larger groups. Literature, art, and music all developed new forms and were expected to play appropriate roles in the reborn China; scholarship in every field had to evaluate the implications of bourgeois science and knowledge and develop new socialist patterns of research and explanation.

Hindsight from a time in which China appears to the outside world to be an increasingly powerful and stable society must not blind us to the herculean proportions of the tasks that faced the new regime in the political, economic, social, and cultural domains. Not only did Peking have to restore stability to China; it also set for itself the task of the total transformation of Chinese society in all aspects, and not just Chinese society but the cultures and societies of the ethnic minorities that belonged to the new

People's Republic. Moreover, all this had to be undertaken in an international climate that, at best, seemed unfriendly and that, more realistically, could be judged downright hostile. The People's Liberation Army had to be transformed from a revolutionary organization that had functioned superbly inside China against both the Japanese and the Guomindang into an army capable of providing the regime with internal security and national defense against foreign enemies. However, the modernization and reorientation of Peking's military forces could not be accomplished with the financial and production means available to the new government if any of the other tasks were also to be performed. Foreign aid was not just an interesting possibility; it was a necessity. Moreover, the new regime had to find a way not only to protect itself from the hostility of the United States and its close allies but also to diminish, to the extent possible, the complications that an unfriendly international atmosphere would create for the accomplishment of China's internal tasks. The nation's domestic objectives, its defense requirements, and its need for an external environment that would permit China to go about its tasks of reconstruction and socialist construction were the primary factors that determined the thrust of the new state's foreign policy. Peking needed friends, a source of financial and economic aid, and a foreign policy posture and international arrangements that would diminish interference from the outside while China went about its internal business.

THE SOVIET ALLIANCE

The policy of "leaning to one side" was one of the two major rationales for the creation of the Soviet alliance as the mainstay of China's foreign policy in the years immediately after the reestablishment of the state. The hostility of the United States was the other. The United States seemed a major threat to China's security and furnished the new government with the necessary reason to seek a close alliance with the only other power in the world capable of providing China with both a security umbrella and economic and military aid. America's implacable attitude did not hold out even a hope that would temper the development of a relationship of dependence between China and the Soviet Union.

The party and the new government carefully prepared the ground for the construction of an involved relationship with the Soviet Union. Mao and other Chinese Communist leaders made appropriate expressions of loyalty to the Soviet Union from time to time before, during, and after World War II. All suggested an appreciation of the Soviet Union's role as leader of the socialist camp. However, the Chinese leadership was not sycophantic and did not contribute to the image of Stalin as the source of all light, power, and grace. Several factors militated against that. First, the Chinese were acutely aware both of Stalin's policy errors toward China

over the years and of continued Soviet support for the Guomindang regime. Second, the writ of the Soviet secret police forces and of the various
international communist agencies of the Soviet government did not extend
to China or at least not to the Chinese party. (During the Soviet occupation
of Manchuria after the war, the Soviet secret police had been very active
among the Russian population of Manchuria, but that is a different story.)
Finally, within the Chinese Communist ranks broader and more profound
doubts centered, by and large, on the recognition that the Chinese Revolution had not benefited from Soviet aid and that any intimate relationship
with the Soviet Union was likely to be to China's disadvantage. In the first
issue of a new Communist Party theoretical journal, which began publication after liberation, pains were taken to counter expressions of doubt such
as "Why is it only China which has got to lean to one side; why not the
Soviet Union as well?" and "Aren't these Soviet experts just like the old
American ones? They just want to control everything."[9]

Ideological considerations also played a role in dampening Chinese enthusiasm for a Soviet alliance. As late as December 1949, when negotiations toward an alliance were getting under way in Moscow, Chen Boda,
a party historian who often served as Mao Zedong's intellectual secretary,
wrote an article stressing the independent path by which Mao had arrived
at conclusions similar to Stalin's. This was a subtle declaration of equality
with Stalin, and it carried more than just an implication of intellectual and
ideological independence. So obvious was the message that when the article was published months later in the Soviet Union, statements conveying this message were excised. However esoteric the discussion of them
may have been, the issues were immediate. Soviet political and ideological
leaders had ignored the anti-imperialist and anticolonial struggle in China
and other parts of Asia for years, and the Chinese leaders did not intend
to serve Soviet political and ideological interests when China and those
areas most resembling it commanded such little concern in Moscow. Indeed, the Chinese Revolution, by its very success, constituted a direct
challenge to Soviet analysis of, and policy toward, the anti-imperialist
struggle in that vast area now called the Third World. Moscow could not
have welcomed a statement like the one made by Liu Shaoqi in 1946:
"There are similar conditions in other lands of Southeast Asia. The course
chosen by China will influence them all." As if to drive the point home, Liu
repeated his meaning at the first international meeting held in China after
the new state came into existence, a conference of Asian trade unions con-
vened in Peking on the very eve of the beginning of negotiations in Moscow. Liu said: "The path taken by the Chinese people in defeating imperialism and its lackeys and in founding the People's Republic of China is
the path that should be taken by the peoples of many colonial and semicolonial countries in their fight for national independence and people's democracy." This was more than a veiled suggestion that China, not the
Soviet Union, was the Third World's natural leader. The language used in

the early days of the developing Sino-Soviet relationship was, to be sure, esoteric and often indirect but, for those who could read it unblinded by anticommunist paranoia, it betrayed the fact that the relationship would be anything but easy.[10] In Moscow, too, steps were taken to lay the groundwork for an alliance with China. Throughout 1949, news of Chinese events occupied increasing space in *Pravda*, and this included reports of speeches by Chinese leaders at international conferences as well as inside China. Soviet publications paid particular attention to Chinese expressions of adherence to orthodox communist doctrine. The speed with which the Soviet Union recognized the new Chinese government, to be followed quickly by the other members of the bloc and, within the month, by the exchange of ambassadors between Moscow and Peking, was intended to prepare the ground for the bilateral negotiations that inevitably would take place. Nevertheless, the Soviets could not resist asserting their own primacy. "Now in the East there is not a single country where the banner of struggle does not gleam Red and where the toilers are not inspired by the example of the peoples of the Soviet Union,"[11] wrote a Central Asian poet, echoing a practically universal theme heard in the expressions of satisfaction at the Chinese Communist victory. In song as well as in politics, Moscow made clear the quality of the relationship it expected to emerge from Sino-Soviet negotiations.

MAO IN MOSCOW

Negotiations between China and the Soviet Union took place in Moscow, where Mao Zedong arrived on December 16, 1949, the first trip abroad by a Chinese head of state (with the exception of Chiang Kaishek's short visit to Cairo in 1943). At this crucial period inside China, so soon after the establishment of the new regime, Mao remained in Moscow for two full months. The length of his stay, as well its timing, indicates that his negotiations with Stalin were difficult at best. It was rumored in Peking that Mao had not made the trip willingly. Moreover, the hardening of American attitudes while he was in Moscow finally closed the door to any other alternative than an alliance with the Soviet Union. Innumerable small mysteries surrounded the visit, not the least of which was the reason for the absence of Zhou Enlai, China's foreign minister, until only a few days before the signing of the new Sino-Soviet treaty. As Mao himself later made clear, the negotiations took place in an atmosphere of struggle in which the Soviet Union inevitably had the upper hand:

> In 1950 I argued with Stalin in Moscow for two months. We argued about the Treaty of Mutual Assistance and Alliance, about the Chinese Changchun Railway, about the joint-stock companies, about the border questions. Our attitude was like this: "If I disagree with your proposal I shall struggle against it. But if you really insist, then I shall accept it." This was because we took into account the interests of socialism as a whole.[12]

Mao made public the Chinese *desiderata* in a New Year's interview with Tass, the Soviet news agency. First, he wanted to renegotiate the 1945 Sino-Soviet treaty, which embodied the Yalta agreements and gave the Soviet Union special privileges in Manchuria. Second, he sought Soviet economic aid for China in the form of credits. Third, he wanted to negotiate an agreement that would facilitate a mutually beneficial trade between the two countries. Fourth, he wanted to discuss "other questions," which remained unspecified at the time. Mao's successes, failures, and compromises must be read in the instruments to whose conclusion the negotiations led.

The Sino-Soviet alliance consisted of three agreements signed on February 14, 1950, the contents of which exhibited the strains of conflict. The first agreement, the Treaty of Friendship, Alliance, and Mutual Assistance between the People's Republic of China and the U.S.S.R., was modeled closely on the 1945 Soviet treaty with Chiang Kaishek. The treaty's stated objective was the prevention of a "repetition of aggression and violation of peace on the part of Japan or any other State which should unite in any form with Japan in acts of aggression"—clearly, this meant the United States. In language, the document resembled the treaties the Soviet Union had signed with its East European satellites. Each party agreed to extend military and other forms of aid to the other "by all means at its disposal" in the event of aggression. Each party also pledged to avoid any alliance directed against the other or any coalition or actions that might be inimical to the interests of the other. In the fourth article of the treaty the signatories agreed to "consult with each other in regard to all important international problems affecting the common interests of China and the Soviet Union." The 1950 treaty, like the 1945 agreement, was to remain in force for thirty years, after which it would be automatically renewed every five years unless one of the parties denounced it. All in all, the treaty contained no surprises, except for its close resemblance to the Soviet treaty with Chiang Kaishek and the Soviet treaties with the East European countries. These resemblances could not have escaped Chinese notice, of course, and raised the question of China's status *vis-à-vis* the U.S.S.R.[13]

The second agreement, which concerned the disposition of Soviet privileges in Manchuria, Port Arthur, and Dairen, implicitly raised the same question. Basically, the Soviet Union renounced its rights everywhere except Dairen, but the renunciation did not take effect immediately. Moscow agreed to relinquish its rights to the joint administration of the Chinese Changchun Railway, along with all the property belonging to the railway, when a peace treaty with Japan was signed, but not later than the end of 1952. The Soviet Union also agreed to withdraw its military forces from Port Arthur, although in the event of emergency, and on China's proposal, the two powers could agree to the reestablishment of joint use of the facilities. The agreement left the issue of Dairen in abeyance; it would be the subject of negotiations once a peace treaty with Japan was concluded. With relatively minor differences, this second agreement reiterated the conditions of the earlier Soviet agreement with the Guomindang regime. One new proviso, however, could not but have annoyed the Chinese in the economic condition in which they found themselves: China was to compensate the Soviet Union for the expenses it had incurred in restoring and constructing installations at Port Arthur after 1945.

The third agreement signed on February 14 concerned economic aid, and the long and difficult negotiations certainly resulted in less than the Chinese had hoped to obtain. The Soviets agreed to extend to China a fixed credit equivalent to $300 million, which would be delivered in five equal amounts over as many years, beginning January 1, 1950. Given China's need for aid in recovery and construction, this was a small sum indeed; moreover, the Soviets hedged it around with serious restrictions. The credit was not a grant but rather a loan at one percent interest per annum, to be repaid in ten annual installments between December 31, 1954, and December 31, 1963. The repayments were to consist of "raw materials, tea, gold, [and] American dollars"; the Chinese would use the credit to pay for the purchase and delivery of materials and equipment that the Soviet Union would supply for the "restoration and development of the national economy of China." Such terms at a time when China was in the throes of economic recovery must have been a source of disappointment and frustration to the Chinese. Moreover, they must have been aware that only a year before Poland, a considerably smaller country whose economic problems were on a very different scale, had obtained a larger loan of $450 million from Moscow.[14] (It is not clear what "other questions" Mao wanted to discuss, but presumably they included the status of Outer Mongolia, whose independence the new Communist government recognized, as had Chiang Kaishek.)

When Mao and the Chinese delegation left for Peking, a group of economists and other specialists remained in Moscow to negotiate the details of the economic agreements; they were joined by a special delegation from Xinjiang, whose practical semi-autonomy had not yet disappeared. Additional agreements were signed on March 27, 1950. Two, of thirty years' duration each, reaffirmed and extended the 1942 Soviet agreement with Xinjiang's governor, Sheng Shicai, under which Sino-Soviet joint-stock companies had developed petroleum and other raw materials in the province. A third agreement established a Sino-Soviet joint-stock company to operate three civilian airline routes between the two countries for ten years. Short-term trade agreements also were concluded whereby China would supply the Soviet Union with soya beans, tobacco, wolfram, and other items in return for textiles, chemicals, metal products, and technical equipment. These accords also identified tin, rice, and tea as potential exports from China to Russia. On April 19, 1950, as the Chinese were preparing to leave Moscow, three further agreements were signed. These governed the specific arrangements for trade and deliveries from 1950 through 1952. On April 25, the new Sino-Soviet company for the management of the Chinese Changchun Railway was established. The general manager was a Russian, and mixed commissions were to deal with the designation and transfer to China of various Soviet properties and of Japanese property acquired by Soviet agencies in Manchuria and in Peking.

By the end of April 1950, therefore, the Sino-Soviet alliance was functioning. Its terms did not satisfy Peking, however. Despite the various treaties and agreements, the alliance was an unequal relationship whose details differed from those of the unequal treaty system that the West had maintained with China but whose power relationship was almost the same. Disappointed and frustrated as Peking may have been, however, the alliance gave China Soviet protection against any attack by Japan or states allied with it, meaning the United States, of course, at a time when China felt vulnerable in the face of American hostility. Moreover, it guaranteed Soviet military and other assistance in the event of war. It also gave China the means, albeit minimal, to begin the process of economic recovery and, with Soviet protection guaranteed, to utilize its internal resources more effectively for that purpose. Whatever Stalin's ultimate motivations may have been, the agreements signed in February, March, and April 1950 allowed Moscow to bind China to the Soviet Union and, at the same time, to adopt a wait-and-see attitude until Peking's policies and intentions became clearer; Stalin did not have to commit Soviet resources to China as a wager on the future. This caution was represented by the two-year delay before most of their provisions would become operative that was written into some of the Sino-Soviet agreements.

Under the terms of the alliance, the Soviet Union now began to contribute to China's internal development, and Soviet advisors started arriving in China in small but increasing numbers. In February 1951, a Chinese delegation visited Moscow to negotiate new trade agreements, including the expansion of rail and even motor transportation between the two countries. Cultural exchanges developed, and Soviets were sent to China to teach Russian and other subjects in the universities. Chinese students began to go to the Soviet Union to study subjects ranging from communist ideology to highly technical disciplines. Cut off from the West, China now turned to the Soviet Union for the satisfaction for its requirements for modernization.

CHINESE ECONOMIC DEVELOPMENT
AND SOVIET AID

The disappointment of Chinese expectations in the 1950 negotiations in Moscow did not mean that Soviet involvement in Chinese economic development was not important or sought. On the contrary, the Soviet Union made contributions in one form or another during most of the period of the alliance. In September 1953, in support of China's first five-year plan, Moscow agreed to contribute to the construction of 141 industrial plants in diverse industries: machine building, automobile and other motor vehicle construction, petroleum processing, power, metallurgy, coal mining, and iron and steel. In their visit to Peking in the fall of 1954, the Soviet leaders Bulganin and Nikita Khrushchev agreed to loan China additional credits valued at $130 million and to deliver $100 million in supplies and equipment over and above previously pledged aid. At this time, Moscow also decided to sell Peking its shares in the Sino-Soviet joint-stock companies. An agreement was also reached to enlarge the Sino-Soviet transportation network by constructing a rail line linking China and the Soviet Union through Xinjiang. In 1956, Anastas Mikoyan, then the chief administrator of the Soviet economy, visited China and promised Soviet aid in fifty-five new projects, which called for deliveries of supplies and equipment valued at $625 million.

Soviet advisors and technical experts also contributed to Chinese development. The Chinese themselves later admitted that by the beginning of 1958 some seven thousand Soviet experts had participated in Chinese economic development at one time or another, and non-Chinese observers think the figure may have been as high as twenty thousand, not including military advisors.

Sino-Soviet trade increased in proportion to Soviet participation in Chinese development. By the end of 1959, the Soviet share of Chinese foreign trade had grown from a preliberation five percent to fifty percent, and Soviet exports to China equaled Soviet exports to the rest of the Third World. China received about one-sixth of all machinery exported from the Soviet Union and three-fourths of all the industrial plants it exported.

The Soviet role in Chinese economic development between 1950 and 1959 was significantly greater than dollar values would indicate. The Soviet Union fulfilled two exceedingly important functions for China. First, it embarked upon a program of plant construction and delivery that, had the alliance continued, would have given China a small but varied industrial system adequate as a basis for China's further economic development. Second, the availability of Soviet technology and experience meant that China could plan its economic development in such a way as to avoid many problems the Soviet Union had had to face in its early days: The Soviet Union had gone it alone, whereas China could rely upon an advanced industrial society for satisfaction of its own developmental needs. Soviet research, designs, and production systems were available to Peking, and the transfer of Soviet capital goods enabled China to intensify and reorient domestic investment, which grew at an average annual rate of twenty-seven percent.

The Sino-Soviet alliance and Soviet contributions to Chinese development, fraught though they may have been with problems and conflicts, differed radically from previous relationships between the Oikoumene and the Empire. As an advanced industrial state, at least when compared to China, the Soviet Union consciously contributed to China's development; it was not looking either for markets for its goods or for cheap labor to manufacture them. Moreover, the Soviet Union's economic relationships with China during the years of the alliance were part of a concerted economic plan that had political objectives as well; they were not the consequence of the power and profit interests of one or another privately owned industrial or financial giant, backed by the national government under which it operated, seeking to penetrate the China market to its own advantage. Therefore, as uneven and unequal as the relationship between China and the Soviet Union may have been during the 1950s, it was both structurally and intentionally different from anything that had gone before.

None of this is to suggest that the Soviet Union alone was responsible for China's economic development or that the policy of reliance upon the Soviet Union was in China's best interests. The mobilization of China's vast, hardworking population and its education and orientation to productive activities was one of the Communists' greatest achievements, without which the economic picture would have been bleak. The rational approach that the five-year plans represented allowed Peking's economic planners to make crucial decisions with far-reaching consequences. They could set priorities in terms of the national interest rather than in terms of the particular interests of one or another segment of the population.

Errors were also made, and on occasion they were serious. Soviet aid was sometimes ill suited to the place and purpose for which it was intended. Bad architecture and engineering made conditions in some Soviet designed buildings in South China intolerable, and errors occurred in hospital planning in Shanghai. Soviet advisors and their families created no little resentment by their self-imposed isolation and their overbearing attitudes. Chinese economic planners also made mistakes, so that, for example, the first five-year plan resulted in a distinct lag in agricultural production, a problem made the more serious by the growth of China's population and, by the end of the 1950s, the sharp decline in Soviet aid. Managerial problems began to develop out of a lack of personnel trained for the rapidly expanding industrial sector. Consequently, in the first part of 1958 the second five-year plan was scrapped in favor of the Great Leap Forward.

The Great Leap Forward was intended as a campaign for extraordinarily rapid economic expansion by means of the application to the economy of the intense political methods of mobilization of people and materiel that had characterized, in more narrowly political and cultural terms, the Long March and the Yan'an period. At the time, both Western and Soviet observers predicted that the Great Leap Forward would lead to economic disaster and they quickly congratulated themselves on the accuracy of their predictions. However, the economic consequences of forced-march industrialization and the application of guerrilla tactics to economic development may not have been quite as disastrous as the outsiders predicted and perhaps wanted them to be. In purely economic terms, China apparently doubled its oil reserves and by 1963 claimed to be self-sufficient in petroleum products. However, the growth rate dropped from what may have been a high of forty-five percent in 1958 to four percent in 1960. The economic difficulties attendant upon the Great Leap Forward were exacerbated by the Soviet withdrawal of its experts in July 1960.

The Great Leap Forward was very significant for Sino-Soviet relations. In essence, it was the means whereby China sharply broke its growing dependence upon Soviet support in the form of credits, technology, organization and modernization models, and personnel. The cost of the break may have been great, but China successfully asserted its ability to pursue economic development and sociopolitical modernization on the basis of China's own human and natural resources directed toward social and economic goals Peking itself set. Self-reliance, not dependence on another power, thereafter became the catchword in economic development, at least down to the late 1970s. This radical shift in development strategy had other advantages as well. The widespread, small-scale production of pig iron in backyard furnaces, which internationally became a symbol of the Great Leap Forward, may have been economically unproductive, but it and similar measures introduced large sections of China's peasant population to the nature of industrial processes and, therefore, had important educational implications. This effort also demonstrated that, in the long run, China's burgeoning population could become a productive asset, not just an economic burden.

The abandonment of the Great Leap Forward made a significant economic recovery possible by the mid-1960s. This was facilitated to no small extent by new economic support, in the form of credits, from the communist bloc countries. In 1961, China received $46 million in Soviet credits for the purchase of 500,000 tons of sugar from Cuba and, later, a long-term credit of $320 million to fund the large debt it had developed in its balance of payment.

In the perspective of history, the Great Leap Forward represents one of the landmark decisions made by the Empire's leaders in the historical saga of Chinese relations with the Oikoumene. They made the choice against broad economic development at the expense of dependence and, albeit limited, integration with the economies of the Oikoumene. That would have made China a structural dependency of the Oikoumene. The trend toward dependence was well marked in the history of China's relations with the West during the last dynasty and the era of polycentrism. Instead, Peking made the choice for independent economic development, even if that choice meant a slower growth rate than would otherwise have been the case. The years have shown that China is capable of development without uncontrolled reliance on foreign contributions. In a real sense, the lessons learned in the 1960s and the first half of the 1970s, the period of the Great Proletarian Cultural Revolution, when a xenophobic Chinese leadership turned the Empire's face away from the outside world, made it possible, in the late 1970s and 1980s, for Peking to explore various ways to increase foreign contributions to China's economic development without running the risk of becoming hopelessly dependent. Moreover, by that time the Chinese population was sufficiently disciplined—intellectually, politically, and organizationally—that an opening to the outside world did not carry the dangers of cultural and moral subversion that it had posed under polycentrism. The Soviet interlude confirmed the lessons China's leaders had learned from their own national and party history: the Empire could preserve its independence only by building barriers to the penetration of its economy and society by one or another oikoumenical power, whatever its ideology. The revived Chinese state's rejection of Soviet, and by implication other foreign, economic penetration paralleled late Qing attempts to inhibit foreign activities in China. The Communists were more successful than the Manchus had been and from this success they drew the security that made a new kind of economic relationship with the Oikoumene possible.

CHINA'S MILITARY INDEPENDENCE

The armed forces of any large-scale modern society, in which foreign policy and military policy are inextricably bound to each other and even approach synonymity, inevitably impinge upon the broad national economy and the economic planning that may accompany it. The tremendous costs of maintaining men and equipment in sufficient quantities to satisfy a society's needs as it defines them for itself account for this economic importance of the military sector, and a rapidly evolving technology magnifies the military's importance. Military goods and the training that use of them requires are not consumer goods in the ordinary sense of the term; their design, production, and replacement absorb tremendous amounts of an economy's potentially productive resources. This may have profound economic significance without a commensurate broad and progressive social value. In an advanced industrial country like the United States, direct and indirect military and defense spending constitutes the largest single component of the national budget. The defense establishment is the largest consumer in the society, the largest single distributor of government monies, and the largest single employer in the nation.

In an underdeveloped society that, for reasons of external defense or internal power, must give high priority to the defense establishment, the armed forces' economic (and social) significance may be even greater than in an advanced industrial society: the economic base that must sustain the less developed society's military activities is smaller and weaker relative to the priority the society assigns its military needs. The new Chinese state assigned very high priorities to its armed forces. This was a direct consequence of the historical and political experience and tradition of the party, developed through the long years of its struggle for power. The armed forces assumed more than a defense role; they exercised important responsibilities in economic production and played a key socioeconomic role in many nonmilitary domains, such as education, land settlement, and social mobilization and integration. Consequently, in China the military was given an economic and ideological significance that was relatively greater than in other societies, be they of the underdeveloped or of the advanced industrial type. Furthermore, while this tradition had its roots in the history of the party before 1949, after liberation the armed forces needed to be rearmed and retrained in order to shift from a guerrilla and revolutionary focus to service as the military sector of a recentralizing, state-dominated society.

The broad functions assigned to the military in the new China were reflected in important debates that developed around issues such as the relative importance of the political as opposed to the professional orientation of the People's Liberation Army, the relative importance of tasks associated with technical modernization and training as opposed to productive activities, the need for the acquisition of modern weapons even if they had to be purchased abroad, and the development of a military establishment based upon democratic principles as opposed to traditional hierarchy and discipline. By the mid-1950s, China's military commanders were aware of the armed forces' shortcomings in equipment and training. On the one hand, foreign policy planning required attention to the nation's defense, the state of which had to be taken into account in the planning and execution of any policy, even if that policy led to the adoption of a strictly defensive posture. On the other, inadequacies in the military sector themselves constituted a foreign policy problem because the country could not generate within itself the resources necessary for modernization. Thus, foreign policy influenced military development, and military development (or its inadequacy) placed restrictions on the development of foreign policy. The issue of military modernization paralleled, and was intimately related to, the entire problem of economic development strategy and foreign aid.

China's profound concern with its defenses in the face of American hostility in the years just after liberation, and the primacy China accorded to economic development and social change, meant that Peking's foreign policy concerns in the military domain fell primarily into two categories. First, if the Soviet alliance was intended as a form of military defense because it meant the spread of the Soviet strategic umbrella over China, Soviet strategic planning became a matter of keen interest to the Chinese leadership. Second, direct Soviet aid for Chinese military development became a matter of concern, given both the state of Chinese armaments at the end of the civil war and the diminishing availability of budgetary allotments for military expenditures in the face of increasing economic demands throughout the socioeconomy. That the limited availability of both internal funds and Soviet aid was a matter of some worry is seen in the fact that in 1950 41.5 percent of the regime's budget was devoted to defense expenditures while in 1952 only 26 percent was available for the same purpose (by 1960, this figure had fallen to 8.3 percent).

During the Soviet occupation of Manchuria, Communist military forces in the area benefited from the acquisition of Japanese arms either from the Soviet authorities or from the surrendering Japanese. Throughout the last years of the civil war, the Communists also acquired significant amounts of American equipment from Chinese Nationalist units that changed sides or surrendered. One of the "other questions" that Mao Zedong discussed in Moscow during the two months of negotiations was, undoubtedly, Soviet military aid to the Chinese armed forces, but there is no public evidence that he was successful in obtaining such help. Indeed, it has been pointed out that the Chinese armies fighting in the Korean War in October and November 1950 did not appear to have been trained in the use of Russian weapons; moreover, they apparently had only one type of Russian arms available, a particular species of submachine gun. The "volunteer" units fought with Japanese and American weapons they had acquired in 1945 and later. Once China entered the Korean War directly and significantly, the Soviet Union gave Peking considerable military aid and also made it possible for China to produce MIG-21s. On the whole, however, the Chinese apparently considered military aid from the Soviet Union insufficient for China's purposes, and this frustration was greatly magnified by the Soviet Union's refusal in the late 1950s to make available to China atomic bombs or the knowledge of how to produce them. In short, Soviet military aid to China outside the immediate context of the Korean War years was of an amount and type such that China had to continue to assume the primary economic burden of its own military defense. The complete cessation of Soviet military assistance in 1960 as a consequence of the general breakdown of the Sino-Soviet alliance was more a symptom than a problem to the Chinese. Like it or not, the People's Liberation Army had never become greatly dependent on the Soviet Union, although the independence consequent upon this status did not necessarily make for a militarily stronger China.

In the early 1950s, despite all the disappointments, frustrations, and problems that pertained to it, the alliance with the Soviet Union was the cornerstone of Chinese foreign policy and national defense. However, this arrangement contained within it the seeds of its own destruction, which was only a decade in coming. In the meantime, the international environment presented the Empire with other problems to solve.

THE RESPONSE TO HOSTILITY: KOREA, FORMOSA, AND SOUTHEAST ASIA

The defensive umbrella provided by the Soviet alliance affected Peking's foreign policy paradoxically. Instead of giving Peking such security that foreign policy could be removed from the state's agenda, the alliance heightened, in a sense, China's need to define its position in the world. This may have resulted in part from an innate Chinese distrust of Soviet intentions. Certainly Mao Zedong did not return from Moscow enthralled by the glorious prospects that an intimate relationship with the Soviet Union held for China. In part, however, the Soviet alliance simply provided the context within which the Chinese state had to define itself internationally in order to distinguish itself from the Soviet Union and in order to maintain its own historical and political integrity. At issue was China's status *vis-à-vis* the Soviet bloc: it could become a satellite, following the example of the East European members of the Soviet Union's sphere of influence, or it could define itself as a partner of the Soviet Union.

The new government in Peking was but the political expression of the Empire and the Chinese state that reemerged into the world after a hiatus of thirty-eight years. The Empire and its state had always defined themselves in the world as a distinct entity (at least in the minds of the ruling class and its institutions), demanding recognition of their centrality and world status. Two factors now made pursuit of this same identity inescapable. First, Chinese history and tradition, no matter how much the Communists may have wanted to escape and deny them (and in the field of foreign policy there is no evidence that they ever wanted to escape them), force the state as a state to pursue self-definition, regardless of who occupies the seats of power. Han Ming, Manchu Qing, or Han Communists all were forced to this task by the history whose phase they were. Second, the contemporary realities of China's existence moved it in that same direction. The new state-Empire encompassed vast territories and a quarter of all humanity; it was not a small East European country resting, however uneasily, in the shadow cast by Mother Russia. There is a difference between humility and humiliation, and China rejected humiliation at the hands of anyone, the imperialists or the Soviet Union: it was simply not an acceptable facet of the state-Empire's self-definition.

Once China's relations with the Soviet Union were settled, formally if not satisfactorily, the new Empire turned its attention to defining a relationship with the other great power, the United States. Washington's failure to find a *modus vivendi* with the Chinese Communists either before or after October 1, 1949, meant that there was neither an institutional nor a political framework within which the state-Empire could establish its international identity *vis-à-vis* the United States and pursue solutions to the problems American policy presented.

American hostility toward Communist China can be understood best as a result of the convergence of at lease three related tendencies. First, the Cold War with the Soviet Union had contributed to, and also resulted from, a general paranoia in the American mind, including the minds of the U.S. leaders. While this paranoia may not have been entirely groundless with regard to the Soviet Union (though it certainly developed from an exaggerated and very ideological view of Soviet behavior), it was extended to include the Chinese Communists on the basis of little or no evidence of a Chinese threat to American interests or, for that matter, of Chinese enmity toward the American people. The Chinese Communists consistently opposed American imperialism; they did not oppose the American government. This paranoia allowed the American secretary of state, Dean Acheson, unblinkingly to insert two contradictory propositions in his letter of transmittal for the 1949 white paper on American-Chinese relations. He asserted that the Chinese Revolution was primarily indigenous; he also maintained that China had become subservient to the Soviet Union. That China might have become, or could become, subservient to Moscow was a theoretical possibility; no empirical evidence supported this conclusion, however, as Acheson and his colleagues would have clearly recognized had not their vision been dimmed by paranoia.

The second tendency was Washington's need to defend U.S. foreign policy against domestic critics. Whatever the relationship between domestic and foreign policy may be in other countries, in the United States it can be quite close indeed if an administration's congressional colleagues of either or both parties choose to make it so. At the end of the 1940s and the beginning of the 1950s, men like Senator Joseph McCarthy of Wisconsin were using an assault upon American foreign policy for domestic reasons. The "loss" of China gave them a convenient issue with which to attack those whose power they wanted to conquer.

Third, for more than three-quarters of a century before World War II China had occupied a particular position in the American mind and heart; as we saw in Chapter 5, Americans had assumed an almost religious and political responsibility for China (whether China wanted them to assume it or not). During World War II, this American emotional attitude toward China had deepened for a variety of reasons, ranging from a visit by Madame Chiang Kaishek to the United States to a raft of motion pictures about the plight of the Chinese that stirred the hearts of all Americans possessing even a modicum of charity toward their fellow humans. Consequently, the indigenous quality and self-reliant course of the Chinese Communists' revolution and, after the end of the civil war, the independence expressed by the Chinese government were interpreted in America as a rejection as much in emotional as in political terms. Moreover, the image of a strong Chinese state differed sharply from the quaint but doddering behavior of the traditional Chinese state before 1911 and from the behavior of Chiang Kaishek (who, despite his orneriness, retained the respect of those who were often most frustrated with him). Consequently, the new government proved almost incomprehensible to those Americans concerned with Far Eastern policy.

The Chinese, for their part, were more than aware of Washington's implacable hostility toward their revolution, their new state, and their policies. Washington's actions did nothing to allay Peking's suspicions. When in January 1950 the United States defined its Western Pacific defense perimeter, the Chinese were well aware that America had declared that its first line of defense lay up against China itself, not in the middle of the Pacific Ocean. In case Peking had any doubts concerning the meaning of the exclusion of Formosa from America's defensive penumbra, these were laid to rest by a State Department declaration to the House of Representatives in February 1950 that the Chiang Kaishek regime on Formosa was politically secure from any attempts to unseat it. Washington may not have been able to go to the Guomindang regime's defense, but it defended Taiwan's right to exist.

The new regime in Peking did not want, and did not seek to provoke, a confrontation with the United States. The openings China had created for a rapprochement with the United States had been closed by Washington, as when the Americans had willfully misconstrued the policy of "leaning to one side." At the same time, China's failure to enunciate its own Far Eastern policy seemed to confirm the American assertion that Peking was nothing but Moscow's satellite. Three regions, all on China's frontiers—Korea, Formosa, and Indochina—now provided the issues that served as instruments for the definition and description of China's foreign policy in East Asia. In each case, the issue, together with the rhetoric and language it supplied, was local to the region concerned. But in each case, too, both the United States and China were closely interested and involved parties, and each was the true object of the other's concern. The consequences of the events in these three areas in the early 1950s set a pattern for Chinese-American relations that is still being dismantled.

THE KOREAN WAR

Japan had controlled Korea since 1895 and had ruled it directly since 1910. The Allied powers in World War II were concerned, therefore, with the disposition of the peninsula after Japan's defeat. The Crimean and Potsdam conferences reached decisions according to which the country would be divided into two parts at the thirty-eighth parallel, the Soviet

Union occupying the northern and the United States the southern part. However, the occupation immediately took on the character of the occupying powers. In the south, the United States relied heavily on advisors drawn from among the most conservative circles of Korean society, while in the north the Soviet Union depended upon Communist or procommunist Korean personnel, many of whom had spent long years in the Soviet Union or China. In December 1945 in Moscow, the United States, the Soviet Union, and Great Britain jointly called for the creation of a provisional Korean government, democratic in form and operating under a five-year trusteeship of the three powers and China. The United States and the Soviet Union could not agree on the definition of a democratic government, however, and an American-Soviet commission proved unable to put the Moscow agreement into effect. The two zones of occupation gradually evolved into two nations with distinct and rival governments, each claiming sovereignty over the entire country. In August 1948 the Republic of Korea was established in the American zone in the south, with its capital at Seoul, and in September of that same year the Korean People's Democratic Republic was established in the Soviet zone in the north, with its capital at Pyongyang. The United Nations failed to achieve a reunification of the country.

The Soviet Union provided the government of the People's Democratic Republic of Korea with economic aid and military support, the latter particularly after the establishment of the new Chinese Communist government and Mao Zedong's Moscow visit. The Soviet Union possibly intended its aid to North Korea to bind Pyongyang to Moscow rather than to Peking; more likely, increased Soviet activity in North Korea was a consequence not of the recentralization of China under the new regime but, rather, of Western success in overcoming the Berlin blockade and the resultant check on Soviet ambitions in Europe. Stopped in the West, Stalin sought an arena in which to continue a forward, and therefore vital, Soviet foreign policy; East Asia, in which Soviet geographical and military presence already loomed large, seemed most promising.

In the years after World War II, a succession of Soviet-American confrontations resulted consistently in limits upon the potential expansion of Soviet influence and power. In Iran in 1946, the United Nations, primarily at the instigation of the United States, prevented Soviet penetration of the Middle East. The anticommunist success in the Greek civil war (1947–1948) blocked direct Soviet access to the Mediterranean. In Central and Western Europe the failure of the Berlin blockade accomplished the same objective. In August 1949 the Soviets exploded their first atomic bomb. This capability gave them the potential to rival the United States militarily at the very moment that Moscow's foreign policy was losing momentum along the interbloc frontier that ran from Central Europe to the Middle East. With the military and communications technology available at the time, including air power and air transportation (it was still a pre-jet age), the only arena left for Soviet foreign policy activity was the Far East. The Chinese Communist victory and the new government in Peking did not necessarily provide Moscow with greater potential in the Far East but certainly removed a major preoccupation. The end of the confusion intrinsic to polycentric politics in China clarified the position of the political and military forces ranged against each other in East Asia. To the Soviet Union the importance and the potential threat of the American military forces in occupation of Japan and South Korea, which was a natural extension of the American sphere of interest onto the Asian continent, were very apparent. The exclusion of South Korea, along with Formosa, from the American defense perimeter in January 1950 did not change realities. Nonetheless, South Korea was not yet an area of major American military buildup or investment.

North Korea's attack on South Korea on June 25, 1950, exacerbated every real or potential tension in the region and radically altered the thrust of American policy in the Western Pacific from hostile disengagement to antagonistic intervention. In an immediate response to the attack, the United States, flying the United Nations flag, committed itself to a land war in Asia, directly reengaged itself with the Guomindang regime on Formosa, placed the American Seventh Fleet between that island and the Chinese mainland (ostensibly to protect American forces in Japan and Korea from the implied threat of a Chinese flanking movement toward Formosa), and set American diplomacy in Asia on a course that would continue the confrontation with China in one geographical region or another on either the military or the diplomatic level or both.

The immediate causes of the North Korean attack and the source of the original initiative have been the subject of much speculation and contention since 1950. South Korean President Syngman Rhee, who the Americans may have thought was their creature at the beginning but quickly showed a considerable tendency toward independent behavior, certainly did not cease to trumpet his intention to unify Korea, if necessary by military means. North Korea's Kim Il-sung displayed no more humility toward his southern competitor than the latter did toward him. Moscow may have thought that a quick North Korean campaign would both drive the Americans from the Asian continent and unify Korea under a government that would then be beholden to the Soviet Union; this would thwart any tendencies on the part of Peking to try to compete with Moscow for influence in Korea. Korea, after all, had been one of China's traditional tributaries, but it shared a common frontier with the Soviet Union in the proximity of Russia's major Pacific naval base, Vladivostok. The Soviets undoubtedly would have felt more secure with their own, not Chinese, power paramount on the peninsula. Stalin may have considered Korea a convenient test in the Pacific of that resolve America had shown in Europe and the

Middle East. Finally, the defeat of the United States and its South Korean client would have weakened severely the American position in Japan, both politically and militarily.

The attack immediately led to changes in the powers' relative military positions. American troops entered combat in South Korea. General Douglas MacArthur, acting as the United Nations' commander but still an American general (the highest ranking American general in the Far East and the supreme Allied commander in Japan), visited Taipei, the Guomindang capital, as the American Seventh Fleet moved into the Straits of Taiwan and important units of the People's Liberation Army took up new positions in Northeastern China and the Shandong Peninsula across from Korea. The American military buildup proceeded rapidly, and after absorbing the shock of the initial attack and suffering severe military reverses, the South Korean and U.N. forces crossed the thirty-eighth parallel and advanced into North Korea. India, acting at China's urging, had already warned the United States that the advance of American troops into North Korea would force the Chinese Communists to intervene. By the middle of October, Chinese "volunteers" crossed the Yalu River, the traditional border between the Empire proper and its Korean tributary, and began taking up defensive positions in North Korea. The Communists then opened a counteroffensive, forcing the United Nations into retreat again. The Korean War became a long military stalemate in which each side made advances or held positions at great cost in men and materiel while diplomatic maneuvering looked for solutions that evaded the powers on the field of battle.

Historical analysis no more dispels the uncertainties surrounding the Chinese decision at the end of 1950 to intervene directly in the Korean conflict than it explains the North Korean (and Soviet) attack on South Korea. China evidently was reluctant to take the step and tried to convey to the United States the message that an American approach to the Yalu River border would lead inevitably to intervention. The American decision—actually MacArthur's decision—to approach the Yalu implied an immediate and direct threat to China's Manchuria and the Soviet Union's Far East. Some response was required, and had China not acted the Soviet Union, flying whatever banner was convenient, would have been forced directly into the conflict, thereby engaging American and Soviet troops head-on and bringing the world many steps closer to a Soviet-American global confrontation and a third world war. From the point of view of *post hoc* analysis, China acted as the Soviets' proxy in order to prevent an expansion of a local war into a global conflict, which neither Moscow nor Washington wanted. For all that, the intervention was decidedly inconvenient for China, which was about to demobilize part of its army and launch the first five-year plan. No country preparing for a military involvement of the proportions of the Korean War would have contemplated either, much less both, of these processes. Peking took the decision to intervene only after Washington, or its Far Eastern agent, Douglas MacArthur, refused to understand China's messages about tolerable limits to the zone of conflict.

China's intervention made it the primary great power "on the other side" on the Asian continent and in the Pacific region. The Chinese, not the Soviets, undertook to "contain" the Americans. Indeed, as Chinese military action proceeded, the Soviet Union began to assume a more conciliatory tone toward the United States, proposing a four-power conference on Germany and informally letting the Americans know that Moscow's relations with Peking were not the best. The Soviets demonstrated their determination to maintain a conciliatory approach toward the United States in June 1951, when, on the morrow of the collapse of the conference on Germany, Moscow proposed to Washington a truce in Korea with an armistice line drawn along the thirty-eighth parallel. This proposal evidently came without Chinese approval or, probably, knowledge. At the same time, the Soviet Union's aid policy toward China inhibited Peking's pursuit of total victory after initial Chinese successes. Moscow certainly did not want China to emerge the military victor over the United States in Korea: such a victory would have raised Chinese political power and prestige to a point intolerable to the Soviet Union. Only in the fall of 1951 did Soviet aid become adequate to the war's requirements, and it appears that the Chinese may have had to pay for such help by accepting, at least tacitly, certain ideological strictures that the Soviet Union imposed as a means of containing greater political claims.

Peace talks opened in July 1951 at Panmunjom, on the thirty-eighth parallel, as a direct consequence of the Soviet initiative. They dragged on until June 1953, when the combatants agreed to sign a truce. The details of the long negotiations, which are amply documented both in the press and in scholarly analyses, demonstrate that at the outset the Chinese and North Koreans began to make those concessions they considered necessary to move the negotiations to a successful conclusion. The Americans insisted that the truce line be drawn along the actual battle line between the opposing forces, not at the thirty-eighth parallel. The Communists accepted the American position in November 1951, although it gave a distinct advantage to the United States. At this point, the Americans began to raise issues that, whether they were so intended or not, delayed the conclusion of the negotiations. Washington first addressed the issue of exchange or return of prisoners of war. By the end of 1951 a resolution of this problem appeared on the horizon, at which point the Americans raised a new aspect of the problem, preventing further progress. The prisoner-of-war agreement originally envisaged an arrangement whereby all the prisoners held by either side would be exchanged for all the prisoners held by the other side. In effect, this meant an exchange of some 150,000 American-held prisoners for about 10,000 North Korean and Chinese-held prisoners. The new issue the Americans introduced in December concerned voluntary repatriation, that is, the Americans insisted that each prisoner be allowed to decide whether he wanted to be repatriated. Arguing from humanitarian considerations, the United States gained a considerable propaganda victory at the expense of progress toward a conclusion to the negotiations.

The Panmunjom negotiations recessed in October 1952, at which time only the prisoners-of-war issue remained to be resolved. The United States had declared the issue nonnegotiable, and the Communists did not want to surrender. Regardless of the merits of the case, Washington had structured the negotiations in order to achieve at the conference table the total surrender of the Communists that had eluded the United States on the battlefield; this Peking and Pyongyang not unnaturally found unacceptable.

In addition to changes in the Americans' negotiating posture, three other factors apparently contributed to the protraction of the negotiations. First, it was not at all clear to the Chinese or the North Koreans that the United States was really committed to a negotiated settlement. In July 1952, with negotiations still in progress, the North Korean capital suffered an eleven-hour American bombing attack that dropped two thousand tons of bombs and twenty-three thousand gallons of napalm on the city. At the end of August, the North Koreans claimed that six thousand civilians had been killed in a single bombing raid. While the negotiations were in recess, the United States continued and even increased its bombing of North Korea, striking targets on the Korean bank of the Yalu River and thereby threatening the Chinese directly. The Chinese interpreted these moves both as a form of pressure to weaken their negotiating position and as a provocation. In their eyes, the United States would be satisfied either with surrender at the conference table or with a Chinese response on the field of battle that would allow Washington to escalate the war into China itself. (A decade and a half later, the United States pursued exactly the same strategy in Vietnam, and it resulted in defeat and rout.) Second, the American presidential campaign, which ended in November 1952 with the victory of Dwight D. Eisenhower, a Republican, placed American leadership in doubt and made the adoption of a hard line in Korea a political necessity for the Democrats. Eisenhower had vowed to bring peace to Korea, while Harry Truman, the incumbent president and a Democrat, was considered bellicose by the Chinese and North Koreans. Eisenhower's election somewhat changed the East Asian international political climate. Finally, protracted and difficult Chinese negotiations with the Soviet Union undoubtedly contributed to the delay at Panmunjom. The Chinese were seeking Soviet economic aid for the development program they were about to undertake but that the Korean War had delayed. The longer China held out against American demands, Peking hoped, the more inclined the Soviet

Union would be to encourage China's tractability by increasing the amount of aid it made available. Stalin was never comfortable with either the reality or the potential of Chinese power, however, and tried to keep the level of aid as low as possible.

Developments in the first part of 1953 profoundly changed the political climate in East Asia. Shortly after his inauguration in January 1953, Eisenhower "unleashed" Chiang Kaishek, which meant that the United States would no longer use its Seventh Fleet to prevent a Nationalist attack against the mainland. Neither Taipei nor Washington realistically contemplated such an attack, but the threat reminded Peking that the United States now supported, once again, China's primary antagonist in a civil war or revolution that neither Taipei nor Peking considered completed. Furthermore, quiet conversations began to take place in Washington and Taipei about the possible extension of the Korean War into China itself, including the use of atomic bombs. The Chinese apparently did not take the threats implied by these conversations seriously. Much more threatening were the American bombing attacks on dikes and reservoirs in North Korea; these were not only attacks on the civilian population but also portents of what the Americans might have in store for the Chinese. At the same time, Eisenhower had committed himself to a Korean peace, and his presence in the White House allowed for a new beginning at Panmunjom.

Stalin's death in 1953 contributed to the renewal of the negotiation process, if only because it improved the prospects for a successful conclusion to the Sino-Soviet aid negotiations. In May 1953, a Chinese mission that had been in Moscow for six or seven months departed with significantly improved Soviet commitments to China's five-year plan. This removed some of the pressure on the Chinese to remain intractable in their negotiations with the Americans.

The path to a Korean truce emerged in a proposal made in October 1952 by the Indian government. Seeking a compromise to the prisoner-of-war issue, New Delhi recommended that each prisoner of war be invited to declare his wishes concerning repatriation, after which he would be remanded to the custody of the side he chose. Each individual held by the Americans, for example, could, if Chinese, elect to return to China or to be sent to Taiwan; if Korean, he could choose to return to North Korea or to remain in South Korea. The Indian proposal led to complex arrangements, but finally, in June 1953, a Korean truce was signed. The truce established a stability in the peninsula that has continued until the present. No final peace agreement was ever concluded, and the two Koreas remain independent, and increasingly different, political entities.

The Korean War and the protracted peace negotiations helped shape the context within which the new Chinese state began to arrive at a definition of its international persona. The two great powers, the United States and the U.S.S.R., were forced to come to terms with China's magnitude.

The Soviet Union could not deny that China had proven itself to be an important ally. The United States recognized China as an important enemy, which, possessing significant power of its own, could not be intimidated. Washington continued to refuse to recognize Peking; it had no choice but to negotiate with it.

THE ISSUE OF FORMOSA AND
THE TAIWAN STRAITS

The Korean War provided the new Chinese state with one opportunity to define its international existence and personality. The issue of the disposition of Formosa provided a second.

Formosa presented Peking with two primary problems. First, as Chiang Kaishek's and the Guomindang's place of refuge, Taiwan represented, both symbolically and actually, the continuation of the ruinous war from which the Communists had emerged victorious on the mainland. Alone, the ·Guomindang regime on the island did not represent a real threat to Peking's security; in alliance with the United States, however, it became a potential threat. Most important, perhaps, the survival of the Chiang regime challenged the legitimacy of the Communists' claim to be the government of all China and to be the final victors in the revolution. The second problem derived from the first. Peking needed peace in order to concentrate on what it considered to be the most important issues of the moment, economic development and social change inside China. The United States, not Chiang Kaishek, was the major threat to that peace. Therefore, the menace from the United States had to be defused, and the Korean truce was only the first step toward that goal. In other words, while the United States was attempting to contain China, China had to contain the United States in order to free itself to attend to its economic, social, and political agenda. The closer the United States came to the inclusion of Formosa in its Western Pacific defense perimeter as a direct consequence of the Korean War, and therefore the greater the military and economic aid Washington granted Taipei, the more significant the threat from Formosa became to Peking and the more pressing the Chinese need to contain the United States became. The conclusion of a mutual defense treaty between Washington and Taipei in December 1954 confirmed Peking's fears by putting the capstone on a relationship that had been building since President Truman ordered the Seventh Fleet to patrol the Taiwan Straits in 1950. Formosa had become an American base aimed against China.

The Korean War taught Peking several important lessons. First, the way to decrease tension was to increase it. In Korea, long after the truce negotiations had begun, Washington sought to bomb the North Koreans and Chinese into an agreement at the peace table. This tactic had strong

support in Chinese tradition, too. Second, Peking was learning to be reactive; because China's primary concerns at the time were internal, Peking's foreign policy moves were less matters of initiative than they were
responses to the initiatives of others or attempts to communicate in a language often used by the other side. In Korea, for example, Chinese intervention was a reaction to an American initiative and the use of a language
of violence after verbal communications (through India) had failed. Peking's message had been clear: stay away from China! The United States
had ignored it. Third, the prolonged negotiations at Panmunjom had
ended not in a definitive resolution but in a truce that, even in its temporary character, could continue indefinitely into the future, as indeed it has.
Problems, China was learning, need not be ultimately resolved. Americans
are traditionally uncomfortable with open-ended situations, but both
Chinese history and Marxist dialectical theory made the Chinese no
strangers to such a state of affairs. Fourth—and this, too, was a lesson
learned from the United States in Korea—the only way to contain the
other side was to respond constantly to the other side's *individual* initiatives, or, to put it in the vernacular, to give tit for tat. The other side was
almost bound to misinterpret any failure to respond as a sign of weakness
or loss of will, an invitation to escalate the conflict.

Throughout 1954, perhaps in response to what Washington considered
a less than satisfactory conclusion to the Korean War, the United States
continued to strengthen the anticommunist ring around China. A primary
means to this end was a rapid and significant increase in American aid to
the Guomindang regime. Between 1951 and 1962, Washington gave more
than $2 billion for the support of the Nationalists' military forces; during
that same period American economic aid came to about $1.2 billion. It is
interesting that the lowest amount of annual aid granted Taipei was in
fiscal year 1952, the second year of the Korean War, when the United
States gave the regime on Formosa $81 million; the highest was in fiscal
year 1955, when Washington gave Taipei U.S. $138 million. It was obvious
that the Americans were becoming more and more deeply involved with
the Nationalist regime, and the stationing of U.S. military advisors and
personnel on the island only strengthened this impression. But that was
not all. As we have seen, the United States unleashed Chiang Kaishek
shortly after Eisenhower became president; the rapid increase in American
aid gave that unleashing some bite. The Nationalists now began to make
raids along the China coast. Each side contributed to the increasing tension in the Straits. The Chinese Communists had attempted to interfere
with American Seventh Fleet planes searching for survivors of a British
airliner that had been downed by Chinese anti-aircraft on Hainan Island,
and this incident resulted in an exchange of sharp words.

American aid to Formosa was only one part of American activity in the
region, however. The United States called for the establishment of a de-

fensive organization in Southeast Asia that had only one possible target, the Chinese, and in the first week of September 1954 a conference opened in Manila for the purpose of creating the Southeast Asia Treaty Organization (SEATO). SEATO united the anticommunist states of Southeast Asia, the United States, Britain, and France in an obviously anti-Chinese alliance and defensive arrangement; its first concern was the containment of communism in Indochina. The Chinese Communists, in other words, had reasons for suspecting American intentions. The lessons of Korea had to be applied if the United States, too, were to be contained and a greater explosion avoided.

In the middle of 1954, Peking began a domestic propaganda campaign to inform the population about developments in East and Southeast Asia, the growing cooperation between the United States and Chiang Kaishek, and the need to take such action as would serve the new state's best interests. One focus of the campaign was the liberation of Formosa. In view of China's lack of a real capability for invading the island, this was a rhetorical form used to reinforce the lesson that the Chiang regime was outside the pale of Chinese politics, not the least reason for that being Taiwan's closeness to the United States. From time to time Peking took action, however, if only to give substance to its words. On September 3, 1954, for example, Communist artillery began the systematic shelling of Quemoy Island in Xiamen harbor and other points off the China coast held by the Nationalists. In their turn, the Nationalists, both before and after the beginning of the shelling, made air and sea raids on mainland positions. The American secretary of state, John Foster Dulles, declared that the United States would defend Quemoy if such a measure were necessary for the protection of Formosa. Early in January 1955, the Chinese captured another Nationalist held island and seemed about to attack a third. President Eisenhower obtained the Senate's authorization to use American armed forces to protect Formosa, and air and sea reinforcements were sent to the area.

Now another lesson the Chinese had learned in Korea was reinforced: the Soviet Union consistently defined its own interests with no necessary reference to China's. The Soviet duumvirate, Khrushchev and Bulganin, arrived in Peking ostensibly to attend the celebrations of the fifth anniversary (October 1, 1954) of the establishment of the Chinese government. In the spirit of the post-Stalin age, they appeared to want to rectify the structure of Sino-Soviet relations, placing Peking and Moscow on a more equal footing. The United States viewed the visit apprehensively because it thought that the Soviet Union was prepared to give China direct support in its confrontation with the United States in the straits of Formosa. American perceptions of China's relationship with the Soviet Union or, for that matter, of the intentions of the Chinese Communists themselves were no more accurate in the mid-1950s than they had been five years earlier. In fact, Khrushchev had other objectives in mind. First, he and Bulganin evidently sought Chinese support for moves they planned to make to remove Stalin's immediate successor, Georgi Malenkov, from the premiership. What role this motive played in various agreements made at Peking is not clear. The results of the negotiations, announced on October 11, 1954, were far less than the Chinese would have liked, however; the agreements contained no indication that the Soviet Union interpreted its treaty with China in any way that might be construed to require Moscow to lend Peking support in the Formosan crisis.

The new Sino-Soviet agreements did not appreciably improve the two powers' relationship. The Soviet Union extended China another $130 million credit. Soviet forces would be withdrawn from Port Arthur in the spring of 1955. The Sino-Soviet joint-stock companies would be liquidated in China's favor beginning in 1955, and China would pay due compensation to the Soviet Union. The Soviet Union would extend scientific and technical aid to the Chinese in a variety of areas, including further railroad construction through Xinjiang and Mongolia and perhaps in some fundamental nuclear research. Significantly, the political content of the agreements displayed, once again, the Soviet Union's profound reluctance to support China's foreign policy objectives or to lend China the kind of political or military support it needed in its international situation. While the joint declaration contained ritualistic condemnations of the American occupation of Formosa, it made no reference to the offshore islands, which were, after all, the immediate focus of the problem; indeed, it included specific statements that must have been intended as a signal from Moscow to Washington that the Russians were not only not supporting the Chinese but also were prepared to try to inhibit Chinese independence of action. The joint declaration stated that negotiations were preferable to war in the settlement of international disputes, particularly in the Far East; on the surface, this expressed a sentiment that could not be faulted, but the declaration also stated that the two powers were willing to normalize their relations with Japan, even though the Japanese government was quite conservative and pro-American and Japan was the primary American military base in the Far East. While Peking wanted to minimize the American presence in the Western Pacific, the Soviet Union seemed to be willing to accept that presence, perhaps hoping that it would serve as a countervailing force to keep the Chinese occupied and in line. The Soviet delegation apparently persuaded the Chinese to join in a statement that essentially recognized the international *status quo* in the Far East. If any doubts about Soviet intentions persisted, the Sino-Soviet agreements of 1954 provided for consultation between the two countries on matters affecting their security so that they could develop joint policies and actions.

China was quickly learning, long before the rest of the world acknowledged that it was, that in foreign affairs the People's Republic would have to go it alone, without significant Soviet support or aid. In their public exchanges at that time and in the following months, Moscow and Peking made their differences clear. Soviet statements stressed the advisability of China's following Soviet leadership in a broad variety of policy questions, ranging from internal development to foreign policy, while the Chinese emphasized the need for cooperation in "smashing" imperialism. Their respective responses to the signing of a mutual security treaty between the United States and Formosa also reflected this divergence of views. The Soviets made it obvious that they would not support China if this led to a new crisis, while the Chinese argued that appeasement was no way to obtain peace: "[Some people] hold the mistaken view that the Chinese people's just struggle to liberate Tawian will create tension. . . .Peace should not be threatened or undermined by tacit understandings and indifference to U.S. aggression. To defend peace, aggression must be stopped."[15] At the end of January 1955 the Sino-Soviet disagreement was aired in the United Nations. A Soviet resolution called upon both China and the United States to avoid hostilities in the area of Formosa. In the face of China's insistence that Formosa was part of China and, therefore, that the waters around Taiwan were part of China's territorial waters, this resolution in effect called upon Peking to relinquish its right to use force in territory it considered its own. Although the Chinese, not yet members of the United Nations, supported the Soviet resolution, they did so only in emphasizing those parts of it that were directed at the United States. Furthermore, the Chinese rejected a Soviet sponsored invitation to send a representative to the Security Council for discussions of the issue. Additional differences surfaced when the Soviet Union suggested the convening of an international conference to discuss the Formosan issue. China agreed but called for particpation by ten countries: five Asian states, the Soviet Union, Great Britain, France, China, and the United States. The Guomindang regime was not included, and the United States used this as an excuse to reject the proposal. But the real issue was that China wanted the conference to consider the broad and general problems of the maintenance of peace in the Far East, which primarily meant the American presence; the United States, considering itself an integral part of all Far Eastern security arrangements, wanted to limit the conference to a discussion of the Formosa issue. The two chief parties to the dispute could not agree on its definition. Meanwhile, Soviet leaders had begun making rather obvious, and certainly indiscreet, remarks to their Western colleagues concerning Chinese intractability and Moscow's fears of growing Chinese power.

The Formosan crisis began to subside when, in the spring of 1955, both Washington and Peking moved to control the risk of open conflict. In a speech in Bandung, Indonesia, at a conference of Asian and African nations, Premier Zhou Enlai suggested that Peking and Washington engage in bilateral discussions, and the Chinese eased their pressure on the offshore islands of Quemoy and Matsu. The United States rejected the Chinese proposal but did try, without success, to get the Nationalists to evacuate the offshore islands voluntarily. With the exchange of these signals, the crisis in the Formosan Straits diminished to the level of occasional Nationalist raids on Chinese mainland positions, occasional Chinese shellings of the offshore islands, mostly with rockets containing propaganda leaflets, and a continuous barrage of propaganda statements between Peking and Taipei. In 1957, the United States agreed to provide the Nationalists with surface-to-air missiles on Formosa itself, which reinforced the Nationalist government but reduced the military significance of the offshore islands.

This de facto continuation of the *status quo ante* resembled the conclusion of the Korean conflict; like the Korean conflict, it contributed greatly to China's knowledge of American international behavior, to Peking's definition of its own foreign policies, and to a clarification of Chinese expectations concerning the Soviet Union. Finally, it taught China that American policy in the Far East did not command serious support from America's allies. Great Britain and France had remained distinctly apart, participating in general discussions at the United Nations and elsewhere but withholding direct support of the United States. SEATO, newly formed and perceived by Peking as part of the American threat, had not contributed significantly to the American position.

This first inning of the Formosan Straits crisis taught Peking's leaders that a combination of military strength and diplomatic interaction was necessary in their dealings with the United States. Mao Zedong summarized this in declaring, "We must look down upon America because she is a paper tiger and entirely vulnerable to defeat."[16] According to Mao in 1956, "We must do as Mencius says: 'When speaking to the mighty, look on them with contempt.' We must develop the spirit which we had during the 'Resist America Aid Korea' campaign of looking with contempt on imperialists."[17] It is within the context of this analysis of the appropriate approach to dealing with the United States that China's statements about its ability to survive American nuclear action must be understood. Chinese foreign policy analysts were not really in a position to judge whether American threats to escalate military action in the Far East were to be taken seriously and, if so, how far. On the other hand, they were keenly aware that the Soviet Union's support of China was not exactly unalloyed, and they were also keenly aware of China's own military weakness. Peking had no choice, therefore, but to keep up its guard while continuing to engage in low- and middle-level negotiations.

Direct talks between Washington and Peking started in Geneva on August 1, 1955. The Chinese and American ambassadors began conversations that would continue, later in Warsaw, until 1971, when contact was established between high-level officials on both sides. These ambassadorial conversations provided a structure for interaction through which negotiations could take place at a level that did not commit either side to major policy changes or to agreements that challenged their perceptions of the world. The ambassadors could only explore and exchange ideas; they could make no commitments. Although fitful starts and accusatory delays characterized the discussions, they served their purpose.

The ambassadorial talks gave the United States and China an opportunity to resolve some minor problems. At the beginning, for example, each agreed that Chinese citizens residing in the United States and Americans in China could return home; as time went on, however, each accused the other of failing to abide by the agreement. The ambassadorial structure also gave each side the opportunity to learn how to negotiate with the other. At the same time, the talks served to clarify the issues dividing the two, and Formosa remained the chief one. The United States continued to insist that Peking renounce the use of force in the Formosan Straits (it never demanded the same of Chiang Kaishek). China could never agree, because to do so would have been to question Peking's sovereignty in areas it claimed to be Chinese. But Peking continually stressed its disinclination to use military means to resolve disputes. In 1956, Zhou Enlai even invited Chiang Kaishek's representatives to enter into specific negotiations over the disposition of Taiwan; although the invitation was rejected, it served to emphasize Peking's peaceful intentions. The United States continued to insist that any progress in U.S.-Chinese relations depended upon Peking's renunciation of force; Peking expressed its willingness to do so in terms of U.S.-Chinese relations, but the Chinese could not make a general declaration, which would have been tantamount to assuming to an inferior status by allowing the United States to dictate Chinese foreign policy. Obviously, the United States did not intend to make a similar declaration.

China also learned in the course of these conversations that American intransigence extended to areas that might have been utilized to alleviate tensions. China proposed discussions about the American embargo on trade with China and possible exchanges of journalists. The United States rejected the embargo discussions and prohibited American journalists from visiting China. When the United States eventually lifted the prohibition, it did so only to permit visits by American journalists to China; it did not allow Chinese journalists into the United States, in effect making the American move unacceptable to the Chinese. By the time the first series of ambassadorial conferences ended in December 1957, after fifty-nine separate meetings, the two powers had realized that they would simply have to bide their time until the United States was prepared to change its attitudes. A Chinese proposal for judicial aid to the citizens of each side involved in disputes in the courts of the other brought no response from the Americans; instead, the American ambassador in Geneva was transferred and no successor was appointed. The Chinese had continuously probed the American position with constructive suggestions, and they had been consistently rejected.

Ambassadorial conversations having come to no conclusions, Peking returned to the propaganda offensive in the summer of 1958, and on August 23 it resumed the bombardment of Quemoy and Matsu. Chinese radio stations began broadcasting threats of an attack on Formosa. The United States sent military reinforcements to the area, and Secretary of State Dulles issued stern warnings. Once again, the United States had responded to propaganda by dispatching the hardware of war. The Chinese proposed renewed ambassadorial talks, and they opened in Warsaw on September 15, 1958. Peking, making clear that its bombardment of the offshore islands was a propagandistic move and not a prelude to invasion, unilaterally ceased fire on October 6 for two weeks; it then resumed firing on odd-numbered days. This second inning ended no more conclusively than the first. Taipei continued in control of the offshore islands but had to abandon plans for an invasion of Communist China, and the United States brought the islands of Quemoy and Matsu under its defensive umbrella. Peking had tested the American position, which had not changed.

A third inning in the Formosan crisis took place in the summer of 1962. In response to Communist allegations that Chiang Kaishek was preparing to invade the mainland, the United States increased its military aid to Formosa by $90 million and sent, for emplacement on Quemoy, guns that could be used as tactical nuclear weapons. These moves took place within a context of mounting tensions in Asia. Revolutionary disturbances in Southeast Asia had provoked an American decision to send troops to Thailand. A Sino-Indian conflict appeared to be developing. And rumor had it that Soviet activities in Central Asia were not contributing to civil peace in Xinjiang. In response to Chiang Kaishek's threatened invasion of the mainland, the Chinese reinforced their land and air forces along the coast of Fujian province. The pattern was repeating itself. The United States responded to propaganda or crisis rumors with real acts or threats to act. As the crisis grew, President John Kennedy announced that, on the one hand, the United States would not support a Guomindang invasion of China; on the other, Washington would not permit the Chinese Communists to attack either the offshore islands or Formosa. The Chinese interpreted this to mean that the United States would not stop a Nationalist attack on the mainland but would prevent an aggressive Chinese response. As artillery duels took place between Quemoy and the batteries on the mainland opposite it, Peking accused the United States of intruding into Chinese air and sea space, and Premier Khrushchev announced that an attack on China would be considered an attack on the Soviet Union. Minor artillery and air skirmishes took place intermittently through October, but this crisis, like the two before it, ended with no change. Once again, the Chinese perceived no evidence of evolution in American policy or behavior.

Chinese policy had established the limits of possible activity in the Formosan Straits. Until some profound change occurred in American attitudes, no further developments could be expected. Meanwhile, a crisis of major proportions was brewing in a third area, Southeast Asia, which required a refocusing of Chinese policy attention.

THE INDOCHINA WARS

The third arena that provided the new China with the opportunity, and the necessity, to learn about the ways in which the international world functioned and to define its own role in the world was Indochina, whose post-World War II history had focused upon the continual struggle against colonialism. Indochina, particularly Vietnam, exhibited certain parallels to China. The representatives of France's collaborationist Vichy government had cooperated closely with the Japanese until the Japanese had dispossessed them of their authority and their position in Indochina (as the Germans had done with Vichy itself in France). The anti-Japanese struggle was carried on mainly by guerrilla forces built upon the basis of an indigenous Communist Party led by Ho Chi Minh. Ho had participated in the Chinese Communist Party, had been a member of the Comintern in Moscow, and, finally, had returned to Indochina to organize the national liberation struggle. The recipient of some Allied aid against the Japanese, he and his followers liberated significant territories from the Japanese and demonstrated both great combat prowess and a considerable degree of popular support.

At the war's end, the French insisted on returning to their former colonial position in Indochina, a project resolutely resisted by Ho Chi Minh and his people; they had declared Vietnam's independence after the Japanese surrender. The United States provided the French with the transport necessary for their return, and as the French began military operations to reestablish their authority and defeat the independence movement, American aid to the French was not insignificant. The French tried to use a variety of local puppets as a means to legitimate their attempt to maintain their colonial authority, but to little avail.

Whatever Peking's intentions and interests elsewhere may have been, the new China, with a proprietary interest in Vietnam that had ancient roots and reflected a contemporary political concern for the revolution in Indochina, could not help but extend aid to Ho Chi Minh. As the struggle intensified, Chinese aid increased. Consequently, China became, as in Korea, a party to a conflict on its own frontier in a world in which Chinese behavior, which the West may have interpreted as aggressive, was rooted in Peking's traditional and contemporary interests in the area in question.

As elsewhere along the rim of China, in Vietnam Chinese activity was countered by an increase in American military and diplomatic support, in this case support of the French colonists. As in Korea, the Americans eventually were to intervene, but at a later date. In Southeast Asia, the Chinese had the opportunity to learn about the national liberation struggle in regions that differed significantly from China insofar as they were colonial, not semicolonial, societies in which a single major Western power was the real or putative ruler; in China the entire Oikoumene had fastened upon the body politic and social. Peking also was to learn about the range of policy alternatives available to China in such regions.

The Chinese began to define their policy toward the anticolonial effort in September 1953. After eight years of struggle against the French, Ho Chi Minh claimed that peace could come only with complete victory. China, on the other hand, argued at the time that "France can only extract herself from the bog of the Vietnam War by the principle of settling international disputes without force and in the spirit of negotiations."[18] China did not argue against total victory. Rather, Peking suggested that a negotiated settlement would open the way for the pursuit of victory by other, primarily political, means. As in Korea and the Straits of Formosa, China showed keen awareness of the value of negotiations and political settlements as a stage in the dialectical progression toward policy objectives that best could be achieved by a subtle combination of strategies. The long years of a difficult war encouraged Ho Chi Minh to adopt the Chinese approach and to adapt it to the situation in Indochina. At the end of November 1953 he proposed Franco-Vietnamese bilateral negotiations. The Chinese, for their part, insisted upon multilateral negotiations that would include the Big Four and China. China wanted peace on its frontier and wanted to participate in the achievement of this goal. Perhaps China feared a greater conflagration, including Korea and the Formosan Straits, at a time when Peking wanted to concentrate on economic and social development at home.

The Big Four foreign ministers met in Berlin in February 1954 and agreed to hold a conference on Korea and Indochina at Geneva in late spring and summer. In Southeast Asia, the situation grew more acute. By the middle of March 1954, Ho Chi Minh's Viet Minh forces had laid seige to the French at Dien Bien Phu. The Chinese supported the Vietnamese with materiel and occasional air sorties. The United States, true to the pattern of behavior it had exhibited in Korea and the Formosan Straits, decided to support the French with air power; as the Chinese delivered increased amounts of military hardware to the Viet Minh, the Americans threatened to bomb bases in South China if Peking intervened directly in Indochina. American aircraft carriers moved out of Manila into the South China Sea toward the Indochinese coast. The Americans implied that they were prepared to employ nuclear weapons if the French called upon them to do so, but Paris rejected the idea. Peking declared that American intervention would elicit an appropriate Chinese response. Once again, the United States was deeply involved in a struggle directly on China's frontier and made no bones about the fact that its primary target was China. The Chinese made it clear that they now felt completely encircled by American power. On May 7, however, one day before the Geneva conference was to take up the question of Indochina, Dien Bien Phu fell in the worst French military defeat since the fall of France in 1940.

The Geneva conference marked Communist China's entry into the world of great power diplomacy. China took part in the negotiations as one of the great powers, increasing their number from four to five. The demonstration of Chinese military power in Korea and China's ability to support an ally in Southeast Asia established China's great power status, to which participation in the Geneva conference only gave diplomatic confirmation. The Empire was regaining the world status appropriate to it. But, as was to become clear years later, the Sino-Soviet alliance could not survive this recognition; for one thing, great power status meant participation in more conferences and situations that would increasingly reveal the depths of disagreement between Peking and Moscow.

The Geneva Agreement, announced on July 24, 1954, which the United States pledged to support but refused to sign, divided Vietnam (like Korea) into two parts at the seventeenth parallel. Ho Chi Minh's Viet Minh constituted the government of North Vietnam. The South Vietnamese government, originally composed chiefly of native agents of the French, moved, under the premiership of the independent-minded Ngo Dinh Diem, progressively away from French authority and placed itself increasingly under the protection of the United States. According to the Geneva Agreements, none of the four Indochinese states—North Vietnam, South Vietnam, Laos, or Cambodia—was to enter any military alliances. Neither Vietnamese regime could receive foreign military aid, except on a one-for-one replacement basis. The North Vietnamese were to withdraw their forces from South Vietnam, Laos, and Cambodia, and a small French military mission was permitted to remain in Laos. In order to insure international supervision of the Geneva accords, an international control commissions was established for each Indochinese country, Vietnam (North and South), Cambodia and Laos (India, Canada, and Poland each chaired one), with particular responsibility for the military arrangements specified at Geneva. General elections were to be held in both North and South Vietnam in July 1956, and most informed observers fully expected that fair elections would be won overwhelmingly by the Communists. The Chinese Communists participated in every aspect of the negotiations that led to this Indochina settlement. After the Geneva conference, China contributed significantly to the reconstruction and further development of North Vietnam, hoping to win it as an ally.

Like Vietnam, Laos had undergone a civil war in which the right and left were represented, respectively, by the royal Laotian government and the Pathet Lao. The Geneva accords provided for collaboration between the two sides in those areas that had experienced civil conflict. An international control commission was responsible for overseeing the Laotian settlement, which included the same conditions that applied to Vietnam. As in Vietnam, the next step in Laos—the merging of the territories held by the two parties—never took place. The United States made it clear that, in its opinion, Laos represented a Communist victory. Cambodia's independence and neutrality were also recognized by the Geneva conference. Its government, under Prince Norodom Sihanouk, had not fought the French during the first Indochina war; now Cambodia pursued a neutralist policy, moving more to the center and then, gradually, to the left.

The United States soon betrayed its own declaration that it would support the Geneva accords. On November 23, 1954, President Eisenhower promised the South Vietnamese considerable American aid to build a strong state that could resist aggression, which, obviously, could come only from North Vietnam or China. The South Vietnamese government, following American guidance, had refused to sign the Geneva accords and declared that it would not be bound by the provision for an election in July 1956. On November 26, only three days after Eisenhower had made his promises, Premier Diem declared South Vietnam an independent republic, whereupon the United States agreed to provide military and economic aid and to send some six hundred military advisors, ostensibly to help suppress guerrilla activity and other forms of resistance in South Vietnam.

The United States further violated the intent of the Geneva Agreements by proceeding to create the Southeast Asia Collective Defense Treaty and SEATO. At Washington's behest, Great Britain, France, Australia, New Zealand, the Philippines, Thailand, Pakistan, and the United States met in Manila and, on September 8, 1954, signed the treaty that set up SEATO; the treaty came into effect on February 19, 1955. The Geneva accord forbade the Indochinese states from becoming members of such an organization, but the United States had created SEATO deliberately to bring Indochina under its military and political protection. Despite the international agreements providing for neutrality in the region, the United States insisted on keeping Indochina in the Cold (and sometimes hot) War. With an American protectorate firmly established over South Vietnam, the North Vietnamese government had to protect itself by pursuing a middle course between China and the Soviet Union, which were gradually cooperating less and less with each other; Ho accepted aid from both.

The focus of attention in Indochina now shifted to Laos. The premier, Souvanna Phouma, who was a neutralist, asked the Soviet Union toward the end of 1960 to send military equipment to both the Pathet Lao and the neutralist military forces. In response to Soviet action on this request, the

United States directly sponsored a rightist coup in December; the Laotian capital, Vientiane, was occupied and a new right wing government was established. China expressed concern over these developments and, together with North Vietnam and the Soviet Union, called for the Geneva conference to reconvene in order to consider the Laotian situation. Inside Laos, the Pathet Lao expanded the region under its control, and China announced that if SEATO intervened it would retaliate.

The Geneva conference on Laos met from May 1961 to July 1962. Early in the conference, the participants accepted China's insistence on Laotian neutrality, but the Pathet Lao and Peking retained favorable geographical and political positions. The Soviet Union, which continued to airlift military and economic support to the revolutionary forces in Laos, obtained the cooperation of China, over whose territory Soviet supply planes had to fly. While these two powers were cooperating in the military reinforcement of their Laotian friends, they also cooperated at the Geneva conference in the political neutralization of Laos and in Vientiane in the development of a coalition government under neutralist Premier Souvanna Phouma.

In Vietnam, the increased participation of the United States in Saigon's internal affairs led the Chinese to escalate their support for the North Vietnamese government, and the more Peking supported Hanoi the more Washington supported Saigon. The two powers were locked into the consequences of a classic strategy of militant rivalry. As great power involvement increased, the activities of guerrilla and other resistance groups in South Vietnam increased, too. Political and economic unrest in the south led to a succession of coups. Washington further increased its support of Saigon in an effort to bring about reforms that were intended to stabilize the regime and enable it to resist what the Americans viewed more and more alarmingly as Communist Chinese aggression. Toward the end of January 1964, the American secretary of defense, Robert McNamara, announced that American military advisors in South Vietnam had increased to at least six thousand; however, he believed it would be possible to withdraw them within eighteen months. Three days later, another coup took place, and the activities of the guerrillas intensified. In March, Washington reversed McNamara's statement and promised to support the South Vietnamese government as long as necessary. The die was cast.

A little more than fourteen years after the beginning of direct American participation in the Korean War, the United States intervened in South Vietnam and, to all intents and purposes, transformed a civil war between two governments in one nation into a war of major international proportions; this step led to the worst defeat American diplomacy and arms had ever suffered. The North Vietnamese government announced on August 2, 1964, that American planes had struck a village along its border with Laos and that American ships had bombarded a North Vietnamese island in the

Gulf of Tonkin. On the evening of August 2, three North Vietnamese torpedo boats and an American destroyer exchanged fire in the gulf. On August 3, the United States declared that it had repelled an unprovoked North Vietnamese attack in international waters, and President Lyndon Johnson issued orders to destroy anyone attacking American installations, ships, or planes. On August 5, the United States charged that two American ships sailing sixty-five miles from land (and, therefore, in international waters) had been attacked by North Vietnamese torpedo boats. Washington ordered retaliation and American planes bombed an oil depot and four torpedo boat staging areas in North Vietnam. The North Vietnamese admitted the incident of August 2 but resolutely denied the August 5 incident.

The United States revealed its real intentions by immediately dispatching reinforcements to the battle area even as Washington turned to the United Nations and asked for a meeting of the Security Council. Moreover, Johnson requested Congress to authorize him to take whatever steps would prove necessary to assist any Southeast Asian nation to defend its freedom, as American rhetoric put it. China entered the picture on August 6, accusing the United States of having carried out a surprise attack on North Vietnam and thereby beginning an international war in Southeast Asia. The North Vietnamese lodged protests with the international control commission, but they refused to go to New York to discuss the crisis at the United Nations. The next several days were characterized by military activities in the air around North Vietnam, political unrest in Saigon, and Chinese accusations of active U.S. aggression. On September 18, Washington announced that four unidentified ships had disappeared after an American destroyer had fired on them in the Gulf of Tonkin. Both Peking and Hanoi declared that the American charge was pure fabrication. Nonetheless, the crisis now escalated rapidly. By December 1964, President Johnson, operating under the authority granted him by the U.S. Senate, had increased the American commitment of personnel in South Vietnam to over twenty-three thousand troops. That was only the beginning.

Faced once again with American military action on a significant scale in a region that was both traditionally and currently well within its own sphere of interest and influence, China had to decode American intentions. American involvement in Vietnam steadily escalated toward the end of 1964 and throughout 1965, and after March 1965 the Americans regularly bombed North Vietnam. Nonetheless, the implications of the U.S. actions remained unclear. Korea, for example, could have served as a precedent for predicting Washington's behavior, but neither Hanoi nor Peking could determine whether the United States would cross the seventeenth parallel as it had the thirty-eighth parallel in Korea; nor was it clear whether the United States would attack China as it had threatened to do during the Korean conflict.

Uncertain about American military objectives in Southeast Asia, the Chinese leadership in 1965 debated the question of an appropriate strategic response to the escalation. By September 1965, the basic outlines of a Chinese strategic response were clear. These were explained by Lin Biao, the minister of defense, in a famous and widely disseminated article, entitled "Long Live the Victory of the People's War!" Guerrilla warfare, or "people's war," was the appropriate strategy to employ against the Americans and South Vietnamese, Lin explained, and the conduct of this kind of war was the responsibility primarily of the people under attack. Moreover, the rural countryside had to serve as the base from which to attack and undermine the urban centered and advanced technological military establishment of the Americans. This strategy accomplished three objectives. First, it took maximum advantage of the population and resources of the battle area, placing the burden of combat on them. Second, it maximized the advantages to be gained from the glaring differences in technology and its associated forms of organization that divided advanced industrial societies such as the United States and peasant populated, rural societies such as South Vietnam. In this context, Lin Biao's statements became a standard reference in the late 1960s and the 1970s for the strategy of national liberation wars throughout the Third World. Third, Lin's strategy maximized, and stated clearly, China's interest in the war while minimizing and circumscribing China's actual participation in it. If the United States attacked China, he warned, Peking would be free to respond as it saw fit. In the meantime, China had no intention of intervening directly in the people's war, the brunt of which had to be borne by the National Liberation Front in South Vietnam, using Maoist strategy and tactics with Chinese material assistance. China would send troops into action only if the Americans or the South Vietnamese invaded North Vietnam or attacked Chinese territory. Lin also made it clear that Peking did not expect the Americans to make that mistake.[19]

The Americans, for their part, tried to reassure the Chinese. The Secretary of State, Dean Rusk, testified in March 1966 before a subcommittee of the House of Representatives' Committee on Foreign Affairs and made it clear that the United States was concerned to contain, not to isolate, China. In April Washington announced that Chinese scholars and scientists could visit the United States if they wished; Peking rejected this gesture. In April, too, the Secretary of State issued a long statement that contained no threats of attack but did suggest the possibility of better Sino-American relations.

Meanwhile, the war continued to escalate. Toward the end of April, American planes encountered North Vietnamese MIGs north of Hanoi in what was to be the first important air battle of the Vietnam War. Rusk repeated an earlier statement that there were no sanctuaries in the Vietnam War, and at the end of the month Washington announced that the president reserved to himself the right to decide whether American planes would pursue Chinese aircraft over China itself; this was an obvious warning to Peking. Throughout the rest of the year, military activity was interspersed with attempts by each side to make it clear that it did not intend to threaten the other. In 1967, China became consumed by the turmoil of the Cultural Revolution, and foreign affairs seemed to move into the background of Chinese attention. In May 1968, as the upheaval inside China receded, the United States once again tried to reassure the Chinese. In a major statement Washington repeated America's desire for more contacts and the assurance that the United States posed no threat to China's security. Inside the United States, the turmoil that accompanied the decline of the Johnson administration in the latter half of 1968 made an aggressive initiative on Washingon's part highly unlikely. Internal developments in each country had decreased considerably the probability of mutual armed conflict in Vietnam or elsewhere along the rim of China, but the tragedy of Vietnam grew with each passing month. The new American administration of Richard Nixon and the consequences of the Cultural Revolution inside China, together with other important developments on the international scene, created the conditions for an entirely new departure in China's foreign policy in the 1970s.

Empire versus Oikoumene Again

CHINA AS EMPIRE REVIVED did not resume immediately in 1949 the world role its geography, size, and historical tradition and experience assigned it. Indeed, in the decade between the reestablishment of the Chinese state in October 1949 and the emergence of China as an independent, self-standing world power at the end of the 1950s and beginning of the 1960s, the Oikoumene, at least in its East bloc guise, still sought to absorb China within its own network of relationships, in pre-1949 fashion. The traditional Empire's growing weakness, which had led after the middle of the nineteenth century to its victimization at the hands of an aggressive Oikoumene and, between 1911 and 1949, to the virtual disappearance of the Chinese state, was not immediately overcome by the victory of the Communist Party. The ensuing decade was spent under the protective umbrella of Soviet power while the Soviet Union tried to draw China into the structure of the Oikoumene as a permanently subservient extension of one of the Oikoumene's centers, the Soviet Union. The process whereby China distanced itself from the Soviet Union and the Oikoumene and reasserted its own status in the world, resuming its character of Empire in distinction to, and in contrast with, the Oikoumene, was the Sino-Soviet dispute and the consequent disintegration of the alliance. In a real sense, both the causes and the effects of the dispute were built into the structure of the Sino-Soviet relationship. At the same time, the relationship, and its dialectical opposite, the dispute, were themselves elements in a world that differed greatly from the world in which China last had been Empire.

The Sino-Soviet Dispute

The world into which the Chinese state reemerged at the end of 1949 was profoundly different from the world in which it had experienced its most recent disintegration. In that now distant age, the last decade before World War I, the Oikoumene, confronting the Empire, had been a congeries of states grouped into something akin to a headless organism, with one state or another assuming a preponderant role, depending upon place, time, and issue, and with coordination of policy developing when a common front was needed to advance the interests of all. By 1949, however, the Oikoumene had split into two sharply defined camps: the Western bloc, headed by the United States, and the Eastern bloc, led by the Soviet Union. Each bloc consisted of a superpower surrounded by its client and satellite states, which interacted with the superpower in different ways depending upon structures of power, mutual needs, historical relationships, leaders' personalities, and a vast array of other factors. The two blocs had already engaged in various types of warfare, which is to say that their combat took different forms in accordance with the particular conditions of any given historical conjuncture. These forms of combat ranged from the mutual interbloc restriction of commerce in economic warfare through civil harassment, such as the Berlin airlift, to proxy wars, that is, wars in which each bloc fought the other through the agency of one of its clients or satellites, as in Greece's civil war. The superpowers usually measured their own and their opponent's strength in three different ways. First, and probably most important, each power gauged the other side's present and potential future military strength in terms of men and conventional weapons and materiel and, increasingly important, in terms of nonconventional nuclear weapons, and warning systems. Second, it measured strength by the number of the other side's clients and satellites, taking into account their military, political, and social conditions. Third, economic production and the material well-being of the population of each power constituted an important measure. Thus, for example, the Soviet drive to catch up with American production of all kinds, including that of consumer goods, during the administration of Nikita Khrushchev, was part of an Eastern bloc challenge to the power of the Western bloc.

The Communist government of the new Chinese state clearly recognized the nature of this new and different world in Mao's three-zone analysis of the international scene, with its two blocs and large intermediate zone. Moreover, "leaning to one side" was an appropriate policy for the reemerging state to follow in such a world. The powers of the Oikoumene, on the other hand, misunderstood both the policy of the Chinese and the conceptual context out of which the policy grew, and this misunderstanding led to political and analytical errors.

The leaders of both East and West blocs perceived the Chinese Communist victory in terms of the Western historical experience and conceptual framework. Even the Soviet Union was conceptually and historically in the West, as were its European satellites. With the exception of a few scholars well versed in Chinese affairs, observers outside the region understood the momentous revolutionary events taking place in East Asia in terms of a combat between rivals for power, the victor seizing the government in an emerging nation-state and proceeding to consolidate his power in the country. The superpowers recognized that China possessed characteristics that distinguished it from other nation-states, but they perceived them as characteristics of exaggeration, such as an enormous geographical area and population, abysmal poverty, and vast production potential. Or they perceived them as characteristics of complexity, such as multi-ethnicity, the juxtaposition of the old and traditional (quaint) and the modern (Western and recognizable), or the difficulties of an obscure but highly sophisticated language, which resulted in great illiteracy. But these characteristics of exaggeration and complexity were not perceived by the Oikoumene's analysts in either bloc as characteristics of difference. They did not understand that China was a state of a different kind in a world in which there were many different kinds of states, not just the Western nation-state and the "tribal units" of a not yet fully emerged or self-conscious Africa. Consequently, in dealing with China, both the East bloc and the West bloc used definitions of problems, methods of approach, forms of analysis, and propositions for solution, that were familiar from their own interactions.

What Mao's three-zone analysis of the world had failed to make explicit, although it was certainly implicit, was that in actuality there was a fourth position, namely, the *locus* of the Empire, that is, China. The specification of the three zones—the Eastern bloc, the Western bloc, and the intermediate zone of neutral, underdeveloped, colonial societies—did not expose the obvious: semicolonial China, upon whose originality and distinction Mao had long insisted, was a fourth zone in the world; this zone's very existence made the existence of the other three zones apparent. In this context, the policy of "leaning to one side" encompassed the view of the world in which the new government saw itself and, arrayed across from it like mountains with a valley between them, the three zones of the analysis. China, the policy concluded, wanted relations with the entire world so described, although it would, for reasons of ideology and mutual interest, tend to lean toward the Soviet bloc.

Neither East bloc nor West bloc understood this conceptual context. The Soviet Union, which at the time meant Stalin, undoubtedly saw China as a real and important, if somewhat problematic, addition to Moscow's group of satellites and clients, and the United States saw the potential and reality of China's relationship with the Soviet Union in precisely the same terms, as membership in a bloc. Moreover, the two superpowers shared the same conception of the nature of a bloc: a superpower surrounded by its clients and satellites, whose real relationships with the center were structured by the inequality of power but were described in the language of sovereign equality. Membership in a bloc had to be exclusive; neutrality, or nonmembership, was a suspect condition. The blocs were held together by ties of military, political, economic, and, not the least, ideological importance. There were some exceptions, such as Finland, which was theoretically neutral, internally bourgeois and democratic, but in fact almost a member of the Eastern bloc. Finally, each superpower recognized, however reluctantly with regard to its opponent, the right of a superpower to intervene in the internal affairs of its clients and satellites. The United States, for example, could overthrow a government in Guatemala or Chile that it did not find to its liking, and the Soviet Union could do the same in Hungary or Czechoslovakia, each with a fair degree of impunity from the possibility of countermoves by its opponent. Finally, the politics of the age taught each superpower to heap calumny on its opponent for behaving just as it itself did.

The reemerging Chinese state, with its theoretical sympathy for the Eastern bloc, understood that it would make an alliance with the latter, but Peking at no time assumed that an alliance implied any of the characteristics of bloc membership as understood in the Oikoumene. Moreover, the structure of relationships Peking did understand by alliance was reinforced by psychological imperatives born of recent Chinese experience. For example, the state-Empire did not enter a relationship of subservient inequality with the Soviet Union because of Chinese historical tradition and conceptual structure; China's very recent experience at the hands of the Oikoumene, particularly of those states that were now members of the Western bloc, such as Britain, France, and the United States, would not have permitted the Chinese to accept a similar humiliation at the hands of the Soviet Union. This does not mean that Mao, in his negotiations in Moscow between December 1949 and February 1950, did not have to make some concessions to the Soviet Union; however, when he did so, he was aware that such concessions were an almost intolerable transgression of his, and the Empire's, view of the world. Therefore, the Soviet Union saw in China a potentially extraordinarily powerful, if troublesome, satellite; the United States saw only China's entry into the Soviet bloc, which, *ipso facto*, was an exclusive relationship that made Peking an enemy of Washington and a real danger to American interests. Peking, however, saw its Moscow alliance as, at best, a difficult and unnatural compromise, as Mao made clear when he described his negotiations with Stalin. That he thoroughly understood the Western concept of a bloc, and equally thoroughly disagreed with it, was also clear:

> Stalin was a bad teacher for a lot of people. They had a very metaphysical approach and their thinking became rigid, which is why politically they made mistakes. If someone did not agree with them they proscribed him; all they could do with counterrevolutionaries was to cut off their heads; if anyone had a different opinion from the Soviet Union, they called him anti-Soviet.[1]

Because most analysts and policy planners of both the Western and the Eastern bloc failed to understand this Chinese view, the Sino-Soviet dispute took them by surprise. Actually, the dispute is better understood as the resolution, in antagonistic terms, of a fundamental contradiction that was built into the alliance from its very beginning: Moscow and Peking did not share even the vocabulary of ideological expression; the words may have sounded the same in each capital, but they meant something different to each speaker. When all is said and done, the alliance, not the dispute, should have caught the Oikoumene's observers by surprise. Undoubtedly, there are lessons in the tale to be learned by those who thought that at the end of the 1970s China was joining the Western bloc.

THE ALLIANCE TURNS INTO ITS
DIALECTICAL OPPOSITE

The causes of the breakdown of the Sino-Soviet alliance have been discussed far and wide since at least 1959–1960, when Western analysts began to be aware that something unexpected was happening in the Eastern bloc. Indeed, Western analysts could never quite agree on the causes or, at the beginning, even on the existence of the dispute. For many years, some maintained that it was nothing more than a camouflage for a grotesque communist plot. Furthermore, by using the term "dispute" they immediately defined this espisode as a set of discrete issues that could be resolved if historical circumstances or political conditions changed. In fact, they missed the point. On the one hand, the event was not a dispute but a conflict of the most profound proportions between the distinct world views embodied in the political structures of China and the Soviet Union; on the other hand, political necessity may lead to an alliance of opposites in which disagreement is temporarily submerged in the need for collaboration (it happened in 1949–1950 and could happen again). To reject or to take too lightly the Chinese leaders' use of the Marxist dialectical model as a mode of analysis is to fail to perceive the richness of the strategic and tactical fabric in which they had clothed themselves.

The Empire's foreign policy, at least since the beginning of the nineteenth century, has exhibited a dialectical alternation in the paramountcy of the Oikoumene's Eastern or Western bloc in China's consciousness. To be sure, the characteristics of the two poles of the Oikoumene have themselves changed over time, but the Empire never saw the Oikoumene as an undifferentiated, much less a unified, whole. On the contrary, the very application of the traditional Chinese strategy of "using the barbarian to control the barbarian" to the Empire's relations with the Oikoumene depended upon the Empire's foreign policy planners' ability to perceive differences among the powers or groups of powers in the Oikoumene. To the Chinese mind, Russia (later the Soviet Union) was always one of the two poles; the other was Britain or, later, the United States. The Soviet alliance was only the latest in the series of periodic reorientations of the Empire's policy from the Oikoumene's west to the Oikoumene's east; by the middle of the 1970s China was once again in the process of reorienting itself between East and West, this time toward the West. Nothing in any state's foreign policy is forever.

Care must be taken, in light of all this, to distinguish between the immediate causes of the dispute and the profound differences in world view that still divide the Chinese and the Soviets. The causes include all those *types* of disagreement that characterize disputes between many allies, such as rival claims to pieces of territory, disagreement or disappointment over issues of aid and trade, or lack of agreement over specific policy issues that results from differences in each party's "natural interest." These causes are not less important for being more immediate, but they can be resolved or overcome if each party finds that a collaborative relationship is preferable, under certain conditions, to a combative one. For example, disputes over the long Sino-Soviet border, extending from the middle of Central Asia almost to the Pacific shore, antedated the Sino-Soviet dispute and continue to this day. Peking used territorial disputes not as a serious attempt to regain large tracts of land but rather as an alternative means of communication, an additional language in which the two sides could express their disapproval of each other. On occasion, rival claims to a piece of territory gave either side or both an opportunity to translate verbal disagreement into physical action, which by virtue of the real unimportance of the territory in dispute severely limited the arena of military activity and effectively prevented an escalation of the confrontation. A border skirmish, however long it may be sustained, is still a border skirmish, which serves a specific political and communications purpose but is easily contained, presenting no real danger to the central political concerns of the parties to the dispute.

Specific policy disagreements were more immediately important as causes of the dispute. The Soviet Union's conservative use of its military and political power, for instance, was dangerous to China's own national interests, which required that Washington be challenged and kept busy everywhere possible in the world, thus lessening the pressure on China. Although America posed a threat to both Peking and Moscow, for Peking the threat was more acute. China, not the Soviet Union, had fought a war with the United States in Korea; Chinese territory, not Soviet territory, was still "occupied" by the United States on the island of Formosa and on the offshore islands; China, not the Soviet Union, had just gone through a revolution in which the old regime had been supported strongly by the United States, whereas the American and Allied intervention against the Soviet revolution had occurred more than three decades earlier; and finally, Peking's attempts to establish some kind of relationship with the United States had been turned back and, instead, the United States was constantly expressing hostility to the new China. Thus, the Soviet Union's failure to act decisively in the Middle East in the summer of 1958, Mos-

cow's relative lack of enthusiasm for China's effort to match American military moves with her own, and Soviet unwillingness in the late 1950s and
early 1960s to act more decisively in Africa, all were policy disputes that
China saw as inimical to its self-interest. Similarly, Peking was never satisfied either with Soviet aid (which was never given *gratis*) or with the
terms of the trade agreements, which required that China make deliveries
of goods that were needed within China itself. Both the terms and the
prices exacted for them, not to mention the difficult negotiations that always surrounded Sino-Soviet agreements, were galling to Peking. As important a source of conflict as the terms were, equally important was the
use the Soviet Union made of the negotiations themselves to give expression to the structure of inferiority-superiority that, in Moscow's view, characterized the Chinese relationship with the Soviet Union. The language of
international diplomacy did not permit Stalin to say to Mao, "You are inferior to us," but Mao's journeying to Moscow in 1950 and again in 1957
to conduct the most important negotiations in the history of the alliance
was such a transgression of Chinese tradition that no one in the sinitic
world could have failed to receive the message. If China was to be a member of the bloc, Peking wanted the bloc to act as a unit, with the Soviet
Union using its political and military power in terms of the bloc's, not
Moscow's own, interests. Manifestly, this was not the way the Soviet
Union saw things. China's needs and the Soviet Union's abilities to satisfy
them, along with China's ambitions and the Soviet Union's ambitions—all
within the tangled skein of the history of Sino-Russian relations—could not
fail to be causes of serious political disagreement between the two powers.

There were broad and deep reasons why the alliance was a temporary
political feature of the international landscape and not a "world historical"
feature with the permanency of, say, the Anglo-American "special relationship"; these reasons must be sought in the particularities of the Chinese
view of themselves in the world and in their relationship with the Soviet
bloc. China was different and, therefore, not simply an element in the
Soviet bloc but a distinct entity: from the very beginning this was one of
the constant themes of Mao Zedong's public and private thinking about
foreign policy as well as other matters. That distinctness led the Chinese
to question in almost every way Moscow's insistence that the Soviet Union
was the tutor, the leader, and the model that all members of the East bloc
had to follow as a condition of membership in the bloc and as a condition
of Marxist identity.

The definition of the unity of the bloc (and the actual content of the
term) was one of the roots of Sino-Soviet disagreement from the outset of
the alliance. In fact, Mao made clear that it was an issue in the first significant Sino-Soviet negotiations early in 1950. To begin with, for China unity
did not mean subservience. Unity meant a coordination of policy but not
the subordination of China's policy to the Soviet Union's. In Korea, for

example, policy coordination had taken place. And unity in the sense of a degree (even if limited) of cooperation was certainly characteristic of the Sino-Soviet aid and trade arrangements and of the activities of Soviet advisory personnel inside China.

Two areas in which unity in the *Soviet* sense—subservience and subordination—were an impossibility for China were political behavior and policy. China simply could not adopt Soviet political patterns. Cultural differences were too great, historical experience too disparate. The monolithic, totalitarian police state that Stalin, who ruled more by terror than by collegiality, had created was utterly foreign to general Chinese and specific Chinese Communist experience. From the beginning, Mao sought to use education and persuasion rather than terror as the means for exerting internal political and ideological control. In contrast to Stalin, with his concentration camps and liquidation of real or supposed enemies, Mao believed in thought reform and reeducation. At no time did the Chinese party adopt the tactics of terror with which the Soviets ruled through their secret police. This is not to say that Chinese Communist rule has not been as authoritarian and dogmatic as that of the Soviets, but the cultural style of politics differed so greatly that there was no way in which China could fit into the Soviet political culture as had, to one extent or another, the East European "people's democracies." This difference in political culture and style between China and the Soviet Union made the internal differences between them obvious; moreover, Stalin's whole style of leadership carried over into the conduct of the Soviet Union's foreign relations and created further problems.

Mao profoundly disagreed with Stalin's style, but he equally profoundly recognized Stalin's historical role, and in his thinking Mao tried to distinguish clearly between the two. He fully understood that without Stalin the Soviet Union might not have survived until World War II, much less been able to weather that storm. Such admiration did not carry over to Stalin's style of politics. This distinction, which Mao made clearly in his own mind, led him to question the rapidity and the degree to which de-Stalinization took place after the Soviet leader's death and, therefore, to make Stalin a symbol in China's political vocabulary that he could use to oppose those developments in Soviet policy with which he disagreed. (The reevaluation of Stalin's historical role and the removal of his picture from various displays in China in the very late 1970s and early 1980s indicated that China, developing a new relationship with the Oikoumene's Western bloc, no longer needed Stalin as a symbol for discourse within the Marxist camp. The Soviet Union was no longer perceived as the enemy *within* the camp but, rather, as the enemy outside, and Stalin's image became not so much distasteful as unnecessary. Moreover, its close association with Mao Zedong's policies implied that the reevaluation of those policies had to include a reevaluation of the symbols that had been used to represent them.)

Stalin's style of rule, rooted in Russian and Soviet political culture and applied to interstate and international relations, meant that the parity essential to the Chinese concept of unity with the East bloc was outside the Soviet conceptual scheme. Despite the temporary appearance of equality when Khrushchev and Bulganin visited Peking during the relatively liberal period in Soviet history after Stalin, the Stalinist political style continued to be operative when Khrushchev, without prior consultation with Mao and the Chinese, gave his famous de-Stalinization speech at the twentieth congress of the Communist Party of the Soviet Union on February 14, 1956. In 1958, at a conference in the Chinese city of Chengtu, Mao expressed his feelings about this:

> When Chinese artists painted pictures of me with Stalin, they always made me a bit shorter than him. They blindly bowed to the moral pressure of the Soviet Union at that time. But Marxism-Leninism makes all men equal, and one should treat them all equally. . . .Khrushchev's gunshot assassination of Stalin was another kind of pressure, with which most people in the Chinese Communist Party disagreed.[2]

Mao was acutely aware that the Soviet style of leadership in a superior-inferior relationship could lead to a very considerable error in specific policy decisions. In the 1950s he was not yet ready to expose such cases inside China, but in March 1957, reviewing events in Eastern Europe on the eve of the short liberal period known as the Hundred Flowers inside China, Mao pointed out that the 1956 revolt in Hungary had been a direct consequence not of the activities of the counterrevolutionaries, as the Soviets claimed but, rather, of incorrect policies adopted by the government in power, particularly a policy of enforced industrialization, which had led directly to a profound social crisis. "Those countries," Mao had noted earlier, in 1956, "did not do their work well; they copied Soviet methods to the hilt without any regard for their own concrete circumstances, and this caused the illness."[3]

On occasion, the Chinese felt they had to step into intrabloc relationships in order to save the bloc from the Soviet Union's errors. In 1956, Zhou Enlai visited Eastern Europe in order to preserve the bloc at a moment when overbearing Soviet leadership had led to such mistakes in some Eastern European countries that internal disintegration seemed a real possibility. The Chinese Communists argued stoutly that constructive criticism, not obedience, was required. As Mao said in 1957: "As for relations between China and the Soviet Union, the skin always has to be torn off; one cannot expect skin never to get torn off in the world. That is what Marxism means . . . because there are always contradictions and there must be struggle."[4]

In 1961, after China had been severely criticized at the 1960 Moscow conference of communist parties, Mao stated:

We must not mind if they have cursed us a bit; we should not be afraid of it; every Communist Party has been cursed at since the day it began, if not it would not be a Communist Party. It does not matter how they behave, we should adopt a policy of unity. When it is necessary, for instance at conferences, in cases where they violate principles we should criticize them for it, no matter who is responsible.[5]

The Soviet Union insisted from the beginning that Soviet experience was the basis on which internal policy in the satellites had to be fashioned. Industrialization, political control, and even art were to be modeled upon Soviet experience and practice. In China this meant the use of the Soviet model for everything from the adoption of the Soviet single-manager system in industrial administration to, as Chairman Mao once remarked facetiously, the prohibition in his own diet of eggs and chicken soup because of a Soviet article on health and food. Consequently, when China began to experiment in the field of agricultural organization, for example, with forms that developed from China's own experience and set its own objectives, the Soviet Union found this kind of independence both incomprehensible and intolerable. Throughout, Mao was prepared to learn from the Soviet Union; he never wanted to imitate the Soviet Union. The Soviet Union perceived, perhaps correctly, that the Chinese position on intrabloc relations was a direct challenge to Soviet primacy. In June 1960 at Bucharest, Nikita Khrushchev, now both premier and party secretary, surprised the communist world by launching a major attack on China. Two months later the Soviet Union withdrew its aid from China. Obviously, despite a change in personalities, the Stalinist style of political culture continued to be the style both inside the Soviet Union and in its relations with the other members of the bloc.

The specific theoretical differences that divided the two powers, profoundly significant in and of themselves, were yet more important in that they provided a wide range of conceptual issues in the discussion of which the Soviet Union expected China to follow Moscow's line. These issues all concerned what the West calls ideology but what is, more accurately, conceptual constructions of the world. However, as with specific political issues, Chinese political theory grew out of Chinese culture, experience, and history. In Soviet and Western experience, revolution was fundamentally an urban phenomenon that spread to the countryside, but the Chinese revolution had been based upon peasant organization and warfare in the countryside, with cities functioning as military prizes. This difference contributed to the ideological or theoretical conflict between Peking and Moscow. For example, Mao's concept of contradictions, rooted in Chinese thought and history, was understood as a fundamental rule of the world. Thus, for Peking contradictions existed even *inside* socialist societies. This idea was an implicit—even an explicit—denial of the Stalinist style of leadership. It also called into question the absoluteness of the Soviet model. For Mao, contradictions were not simply a passive characteristic; they were a feature that could be exploited. The contradictions inside the capitalist and imperialist powers and between them were opportunities for the socialist camp. Furthermore, the contradictions in the colonial and semicolonial world were more pronounced and sharper because of imperialism than were the contradictions in the advanced industrial world. Therefore, it was possible that the revolution would succeed in the more backward areas of the globe before it came to the most advanced industrial areas. This view represented, on the one hand, a distinct modification of Marxist theory, though Lenin sometimes made allusions to the possibility; on the other hand, however, it represented China's bid not only for equality but also for leadership. China belonged to the so-called backward world, and yet the revolution had come to China second only after the Soviet Union. With the example of China before them, other parts of the Third World might move toward socialism before, say, Western Europe. This theory had, for the Soviet Union, profound political implications: the Soviets saw it, not incorrectly, as a threat to their own leadership in Asia, Africa, and Latin America. The Chinese claimed that their own revolutionary experience was both theoretically and strategically more applicable to these areas than was the Soviet Union's.

Warfare, in Mao's view, was a contradiction. Indeed, it was the major form on the international scene of that contradiction called "class struggle." While no one wanted war, war could not be defined as an absolutely negative phenomenon. The possibility or desirability of war between the capitalist and the socialist camp could not be ruled out completely. Furthermore, the stronger the socialist camp became, the less likely a ruinous war became. Consequently, at the very time when the Soviet Union and the United States were seeking ways in which the world could be set on a course of arms control and détente, China appeared to be pursuing war as an end in itself. Of course, that was not the case. The Chinese were arguing that theory did not require timidity in world affairs, as their own experience had shown. They had faced down the United States in Korea and the Formosa Straits; they had gained access to great power status through the negotiations over the Indochina conflict. Warfare was not good, but it was not to be avoided at all costs. The Soviet Union could not accept this attack on its foreign policy.

Mao's theory posited two types of contradictions: "antagonistic contradictions," which could be resolved by warfare, and "nonantagonistic contradictions," which could be resolved by politics. Nonantagonistic contradictions, he argued, were part of life itself, such as the contradictions between men and women, mountains and valleys, land and sea, or city and countryside; moreover, these contradictions continued to exist in socialist society in the very nature of things. This, of course, was an intolerable position for the Soviet Union since it implied that the socialist stage of development was itself subject to internal conflicts, which in turn implied that the leadership of a socialist state (Soviet leadership) was capable of making errors and even of being overcome by positions that were more correct than its own. Moscow saw this argument as a direct theoretical attack on Soviet leadership and considered it a danger because it undermined the very basis upon which the state's authority in the socialist period rested. For the Chinese, far more conscious of the totality of the social experience, including culture and technology, movement from one period of history to another was a revolution that, by definition, affected every facet of existence. As Mao wrote in 1961:

> To move from socialism to communism is revolution; to move from communism to yet another stage is also revolution. One still has technological revolutions, cultural revolutions, and communism must certainly pass through very many stages, have many revolutions. . . . In socialist society there must still be the advanced and the backward; there must still be those who are dedicated and committed and enthusiastic toward the collective enterprise, and there are those who are ambitious, selfish and moody.[6]

This statement denied ultimate validity to any system, including the Soviet system; moreover, it opened the way for internal criticism as an element in the dialectical process, which, of course, Soviet political culture could not tolerate.

The theory of contradictions within socialist society led, logically, to still another issue: the nature of the transition from socialism to communism. In the Soviet Union, the experience of the revolution and of the period of collectivization in the late 1920s and early 1930s had taught Stalin that the peasantry was basically reactionary. The appropriate form of property in a communist society was state ownership; the state was, by definition, the whole people. Collective ownership was by and large a socialist period phenomenon since collective ownership meant ownership by a group, not by the whole people. From Stalin's point of view, therefore, the transition from socialism to communism required that the countryside be restructured socially and economically to fit the model of urban ownership and management. This meant, for example, movement from the collective farm system of organization to the state farm system, in which the peasants were transformed into agricultural workers who were employed by the state on the same basis as workers in urban factories, thus being transformed from peasants into (proletarian) workers. China's revolutionary experience and the preponderance of peasants in China's social landscape had given Mao and his colleagues a very different view of the peasantry. They had been the basis upon which the Chinese Revolution had taken place, and since 1949 they had proven themselves to be not only supportive of the regime but ingenious in their ability to respond creatively to the regime's needs and demands. Mao accepted the basic Marxist (and non-Marxist) thesis that transition from one to another stage of social development required changes in material culture, which meant that in China, as elsewhere, economic growth was necessary if the country were to move toward communism. Mao, however, was far less of a materialist, in the vulgar sense of the term, than Stalin; he fully recognized the importance of attitude and mind and saw the transition to communism not in terms simply of material progress but of consciousness as well. Therefore, the transition to communism could be effected in the countryside, as well as in the city, perhaps even first in the countryside, because the peasants were a revolutionary force. Moreover, changes in consciousness could compensate for lacks in material progress, so that the structure of property ownership and of social relationships could be altered through cultural revolution even while the society was making economic progress. The material economy was not the sole causative factor in history. This was the fundamental theoretical insight behind the Great Leap Forward and, later, the Cultural Revolution. To the Soviet Union, it was a direct challenge.

The Soviets understood, not incorrectly, that Mao's viewpoint undermined the theoretical basis of Soviet social development policy. They also correctly understood that Mao was arguing that China, and other societies as well, could develop toward communism without progressing through the stage of material development under socialism that the Soviet Union insisted was necessary. Finally, Mao was suggesting that China might enter communism without having fulfilled all the tasks laid down for it by the Soviet Union. In response to Mao's challenge, the Soviet Union, particularly under Khrushchev, justified its positions by denying the validity of Mao's theoretical formulations and their policy implications. The legitimacy of Soviet power required this reaction.

The dispute was not, then, a set of isolated disagreements, the cumulative effect of which disrupted Sino-Soviet relations. Rather, the dispute encompassed almost every aspect of theory and policy, and those two domains were not as distinct in either Chinese Communist or Soviet minds as they were in the minds of many Westerners, who tended to underplay the importance of ideology. Theory and policy were extensions of each other for the Chinese Communists, while for the Soviet Union policy had to rest upon theory. It can be well argued that in the Soviet Union theory changes to suit policy. The distinction between the two in the Soviet mind, nevertheless, is greater than in the Chinese. Either way, two world views were in conflict. The Soviet alliance had been a temporary arrangement of convenience. The Chinese and the Russians shared neither long years of joint revolutionary struggle nor fundamental assumptions about the world. The history of the Chinese Revolution shows not only how little the Soviet Union contributed to it but also how many mistakes the Soviet Union committed against it. Thus, the alliance, not the dispute, was the surprise. The conflict worked itself out in political history.

THE POLITICS OF THE DISPUTE

By 1960, the basis of the Soviet alliance had been undermined by developments in almost every field of real or potential common endeavor. Inadequate Soviet aid, combined with Chinese insistence on pursuing their own, agriculturally based, program of development and path to communism, created little of the economic edifice that could have provided the relationship with some depth. The Soviet Union's insistence that sophisticated armaments had changed the conditions of the international political process and required fundamental revisions in the way in which the two world blocs dealt with each other—that is, some measure of détente—destroyed the strategic purposes of the alliance as far as China was concerned. Territorial disagreements, which the alliance had glossed over, were a continuing, if minor, source of irritation. And public admission, in the bitter polemics that were carried on in a variety of Chinese and Soviet publications, of the absence of any ideological unity removed the last vestige of meaning or structural basis for the Soviet relationship.

The dispute unfolded mainly through exchanges in Chinese and Soviet journals and newspapers and in international conferences and congresses at which the two sides directly, or through partisan proxies, faced each other in angry debate. It all came out in the open during 1960. In February, the Chinese were present as observers at a meeting of the Warsaw Pact powers in Moscow, where Khrushchev mounted a major attack on Chinese foreign and military policy and announced that the Soviet Union had refused to provide China with nuclear arms. Moscow was pursuing détente with the United States, and proliferation of nuclear weapons would not have been productive for such a policy. Actually, Khrushchev did not admit at the time that the Soviet Union previously had promised China an example of an atomic bomb that the Chinese could copy but then had withdrawn the offer. In April, on the anniversary of Lenin's birth, *Red Flag*, the theoretical organ of the Central Committee of the Chinese Communist Party, published a very long article—"Long Live Leninism!"—that the Soviets polemically ascribed to Mao Zedong himself. The article thoroughly condemned Soviet "revisionism." The leading Soviet ideologist, Otto Kuusinen, responded that Soviet foreign policy rested on "the Leninist Principle of Peaceful Co-existence of States regardless of the differences in their social and political systems."[7] On May 1, the Soviet position on peaceful coexistence (détente) received a rude shock when an American U-2 plane was shot down deep inside Soviet territory; the Chinese tried to use the incident to drive their argument against détente home. Early in June, at a meeting of the World Federation of Trade Unions in Peking, the Chinese delivered a strong attack on Soviet policy. Later that month, a meeting of the twelve ruling communist parties was held in Bucharest. Khrushchev himself was present, and China was represented by Peng Zhen, a member of the Politburo of the Chinese party, who was considered particularly close to Mao. Khrushchev delivered a powerful attack on China, in the course of which he reportedly attacked Chairman Mao personally and compared him with Stalin; he accused him of living in a world of theoretical unreality, detached from the realities of modern life. Peng Zhen did not hold back in his response. In late September, the Chinese and the Soviets again attacked each other at the third congress of the North Vietnamese Communist Party in Hanoi. It was a repetition of the Bucharest meeting.

In November 1960, after the anniversary celebrations of the Russian Revolution, a congress of eighty-one communist parties met in Moscow. It may have been, as one observer put it, "the most important gathering of its kind in the entire history of communism."[8] Relations between the U.S.S.R. and China had reached the point that survival of the alliance itself was in question, and communism as an international movement was about to enter into schism on the grounds of disagreements over both theory and practice. This was no new development in the history of the left, which had always taken theory seriously; indeed, the left's organizational structures were constantly fracturing and regrouping because of theoretical disputations. Never before, however, had an intra-left dispute been fraught with such worldwide significance. The Moscow conference aired the full range of issues that were in contention. The question of authority within the bloc, the nature of the current historical period, the theoretical and strategic advantages of war and peace, peaceful coexistence, armaments, policy toward and in the Third World, the Yugoslav heresy—all these and more furnished the foci of the debate. The conference ended with a declaration that was, to all intents and purposes, a restatement of the Soviet position on almost every issue; Moscow's orthodoxy was amended only slightly by some insignificant modifications introduced in the course of debate. To a certain extent, the Soviets had had to purchase the support of other parties by adopting harsher positions than they would have adopted otherwise. The internal authority of each communist party was so much a part of the intrabloc international structure that the member parties found it difficult to tolerate moves within the bloc that might undermine their authority within their own territories. There was nothing in the declaration with which the Soviets could not live. They had emerged victorious, although the Chinese were not yet completely defeated. Nonetheless, nothing was hidden from view and nothing had been kept in reserve.

The final break between Moscow and Peking occurred, almost ritualistically, at the twenty-second congress of the Soviet Communist Party in October 1961. The issue was Albania. This small country on the Adriatic Coast had long been a thorn in the side of the Soviet Union. By far the most backward corner of Europe, Albania was socially almost incomprehensible to the Soviets, and it seemed to absorb relatively large amounts of aid without demonstrating significant economic development. On top of the tribal structure of Albanian society and the kinship relationships that provided the ruling party with a significant infrastructure that escaped traditional Marxist analysis, the Albanian ruler, Enver Hoxha, had built a powerful personal security apparatus, eliminating his rivals and preventing Soviet penetration of Albanian state institutions. Speaking at the party congress, Khrushchev criticized Albania sharply for having departed from the line the communist parties had agreed upon the year before; he talked about Albania, but he meant China. On October 19, Premier Zhou Enlai, who headed the Chinese delegation to the Soviet party congress, addressed the delegates and referred to Albania as one of the "fraternal countries" in the socialist camp.[9] This was a direct counterattack against the Soviet party. Zhou did not stop there, however. In addition, he voiced China's view that interparty disagreements should not be aired in public. In other words, he moved from counterattack to attack by criticizing not only the substance of Soviet policies but the Soviet party's political style as well.

The Soviet leadership responded to Zhou with one of the loudest silences in communist history. The speakers who followed him, including Anastas Mikoyan and Mikhail Suslov, both members of the innermost circles of the Soviet party and government, ignored the Chinese warnings and continued to attack Albania. This constituted nothing less than a direct rejection of Peking's last attempt to save at least the appearance of a fraternal relationship with the Soviet Union. Zhou Enlai now performed the last ritual act in the drama that was sundering the East bloc. On October 20, with great ceremony, he laid a wreath on Stalin's tomb; the wreath bore the inscription "To the Great Marxist-Leninist, J. Stalin." Having paid tribute to Stalin as a way of indicating Peking's total rejection of the Khrushchevian line—the ritual rejection was the more acute because Khrushchev had led the attack on Stalin's historical role—the Chinese premier left Moscow for home. Little Albania simply had been the straw that had broken the camel's back.

The Sino-Soviet relationship had already begun to deteriorate seriously in 1960. In that year, Moscow had withdrawn its engineers and advisors from China and had restricted severely all forms of economic aid to Peking. Now interparty relations had been broken, and only formal state-to-state relations remained. The polemics increased in intensity. In 1962, China and India engaged in a difficult and rather confused border war, and the Soviet Union supported the Indian side with both words and military aid. In October 1962, at the time of the Cuban missile crisis, the Chinese accused the Soviets of adventurism for having tried to place missiles in Cuba; they then accused them of weakness for having withdrawn the missiles under the threat of an American response. Peking added "capitulationism"[10] to the list of Moscow's errors. Khrushchev's signature of a test-

426

ban treaty with the United States in July 1963 furnished further proof of Peking's charges, if any more proof were needed. Moscow and Peking were going their own ways on the international scene.

Mao Zedong now developed an analysis of the Soviet Union that has remained the basis of Chinese attitudes toward Moscow to the present time. He argued that the Sino-Soviet dispute and the Soviet-American efforts at peaceful coexistence (détente) had exposed the internal contradictions in Soviet society. The socially rooted contradictions were reflected in policies that turned the Soviet Union into a danger no less than capitalist imperialism. In May 1964 he declared that "the present-day Soviet Union is a dictatorship of the bourgeoisie, a dictatorship of the big bourgeoisie, a dictatorship like German fascism, a Hitler type of dictatorship, they are a pack of ruffians, even worse than de Gaulle."[11] The polemics of dispute did not abate. Other communist parties tried to mediate the conflict but to no avail. On almost no issue did the two former allies find any area of agreement.

More profoundly than the language of the debate indicated, the Sino-Soviet dispute and the consequent end of the alliance were, in historical terms, the event by means of which the Chinese state-Empire reasserted its existence as an independent entity on the world scene. Part of this process was the redefinition of the world in terms of the Empire's conceptual constructs. By calling the Soviet Union "a dictatorship of the bourgeoisie, a dictatorship of the big bourgeoisie," Mao had reestablished the sharp distinction between Empire and Oikoumene and placed the Soviet Union squarely within the Oikoumene. To drive the point home and avoid any misunderstanding, he had used Hitler and de Gaulle as analogies to deepen the characterization of the Soviet Union as capitalist. This conceptual re-reorganization of the world, which was the intellectual manifestation of the self-assertion of the state-Empire, marked China's maturation in international relations; henceforth Peking would be the arbiter of its own foreign policy. In the history of the decline and fall of imperialism in the Far East, the Sino-Soviet dispute marked the final end of the long period, beginning with the Treaties of Peking of 1860, in which China's foreign policy had been subservient to one or another of the powers in the Oikoumene.

The powers of the Oikoumene were, by definition, imperialist and the Soviet Union was no exception. In Marxist terms, according to the Chinese, the Soviets were revisionists and renegades who had converted the Soviet Union into a "Paradise for a handful of bureaucrat-monopoly-capitalists of a new type, a prison for the millions of working people."[12] Obviously, the argument continued, the Soviet Union was not a bourgeois society in the same sense as the United States; therefore, the Soviet Union was guilty of an imperialism that in many ways was more insidious than the capitalist imperialism of the United States because it fooled people into thinking that the Soviet Union was friendly to revolution. The Soviet invasion of Czechoslovakia was greeted by Peking, in no uncertain terms, as a "monstrous crime." This was an invasion of one socialist state by another and perfectly fitted Mao's description of Soviet policy. China could not but completely reject the Soviet move, and this episode occasioned the entry into the Chinese political lexicon of the term "social[ist] imperialism" to describe Soviet foreign policy. Perhaps Peking saw that, but for its size, China could have stood in Czechoslovakia's place. In China's view, the Soviet Union had betrayed socialism.[13]

The Soviet Union was also guilty of "hegemonism"; in Chinese ideological statements, the term was used to refer to Soviet insistence upon Moscow's predominant leadership. Neither American capitalist imperialism nor Soviet social imperialism was acceptable to the Chinese, but Peking was free to choose alliances with one or the other power as opportunity and advantage dictated. Although a radical change in Peking's relationship with the United States was still far in the future, Mao's analysis of the Soviet Union and restructuring of the Chinese world view were preparing the way, however unintentionally, for a new departure in Sino-American relations.

In the mid-1960s and later, the Sino-Soviet conflict continued at an intense polemical level; from time to time, it took more immediate forms. A Soviet ship was detained in port by the Chinese at Dairen. A fight between Chinese students and Soviet bystanders took place in Red Square in Moscow. Demonstrations against each other's policies were held in Moscow and Peking. Rumors of Soviet troop movements along the Chinese border appeared from time to time. Many incidents or rumors of incidents kept the pot boiling.

American involvement in Vietnam and the war's consequent escalation led to limited cooperation between Moscow and Peking in pursuit of the common objective of defeating American imperialism. Soviet supplies were permitted to move through China to North Vietnam, but this did not change the nature of the relationship in any way. Indochina had been one of the many arenas of dispute between the two powers. Russian influence was growing in Vietnam, and when Ho Chi Minh died, Zhou Enlai went to Hanoi to pay his respects but stayed only one day and did not attend the Vietnamese leader's funeral. Apparently Zhou wanted to avoid meeting Soviet Premier Aleksei Kosygin. In an unexpected development, Kosygin flew to Peking from Hanoi, where he held a six-hour conference with Zhou. As a result of this conference, border clashes, which had reached serious proportions in 1969, by and large came to an end, and the level of the polemics that the two countries were hurling at each other diminished.

The decline in the dispute's intensity meant that each side had come to recognize that there was no longer an alliance and, therefore, the dispute could pass into a new stage. The Soviet-Chinese relationship now resembled the relationships between each of them and the other powers. Paradoxically, this made it possible for trade and other economic agreements to be negotiated despite deteriorating ideological and party relations. In August 1971, June 1972, and January 1974, various agreements governing trade, payments, and air service between Peking and Moscow were signed. Although Sino-Soviet trade had declined with the public outbreak of the dispute, by the 1970s it was climbing again.

China and the Third World

The Chinese three-zone analysis provided Peking with a powerful analytical tool for understanding the international political position of the less developed countries, or the Third World. Chinese ideology and the historical experience of the Chinese Revolution in the particular conditions of China as an underdeveloped country gave Peking insight into the historical, political, economic, and social processes of other countries undergoing modernization and liberation. Neither China's understanding of the Third World's international position nor its comprehension of the historical experience of underdevelopment implied that China had the political, economic, or military means with which to effect its objectives as clearly as Peking saw them. In this China differed significantly from the United States and the Soviet Union, both of which had the resources to establish leadership (however tentative) in one or another part of Asia, Africa, and Latin America. China, in contrast, had to rely on example and persuasion as a means of providing Third World leadership.

As in other areas of activity, China's specific policies in the Third World derived from underlying assumptions that were always present, even if they changed from period to period. These underlying assumptions themselves derived their richness from a broader view of the world, the theory of contradictions, which was fundamental to Chinese thinking. Consequently, what seem like vagaries in policy decisions and changes in the party line should be understood as adjustments of policy that took into account the realities of any specific historical situation against the background of a broad theory about the way the world runs.

The Chinese Revolution was the first major, and victorious, revolution in the underdeveloped world that took its primary analytical perspective and rhetoric from Marxism. The pot was just beginning to boil in Africa; in Latin America and those other parts of Asia that had obtained their independence, the Chinese experience made possible a certain perspective on revolutions and political systems in the Third World. Thus, for example, India, Indonesia, and Burma were all newly independent countries, but the Chinese spoke of them as "the feeble-minded bourgeoisie of the East" and identified their leaders as imperialist agents.[14] Independence alone, in other words, was insufficient; a socialist led social revolution was required if independence were not to become merely a screen for imperialism. Consequently, from the beginning the Chinese gave verbal support to revolutionary movements in the Philippines and Malaya. There is no evidence that Peking extended material aid to any revolutionary groups in the years immediately before or after 1949, but beginning at least by 1947 the Communist leadership was encouraging the development of armed struggle wherever possible. Moreover, the Chinese model of revolution was held out as an example to be studied. At the same time, it was a source of dispute among revolutionaries, particularly communists in other parts of Asia. In India, for example, the Communist Party claimed that the Maoists relied too heavily on the peasantry, although in the very early years even the Soviets agreed with Peking's position.

Peking's revolutionary sentiments did not prevent it from seeking diplomatic relations wherever possible, and in the first six months of its existence the new regime established formal ties with Afghanistan, Pakistan, India, Burma, Ceylon, and Indonesia. Peking's sole criterion for rejecting diplomatic relations with another state was the principle that no country could maintain relations with both Peking and Taipei; at the same time, China felt free to encourage revolution wherever possible. Clearly, this perspective on international relations differed from that in the West. In the world of the late 1940s and early 1950s, revolution generally meant national liberation from colonialism or semicolonialism, but China had not yet achieved international maturity, and what this meant for Peking's foreign policy was still unclear.

Within the context of broad historical and theoretical assumptions, Chinese foreign policy in the Third World developed through the analysis attendant upon the necessity to make concrete decisions in particular situations. The wars in Korea and Indochina, for example, provided opportunities for significant clarification of China's policies toward the Third World. In Korea there were two governments, ostensibly independent of each other, with radically different intentions. South Korea was obviously a client of the United States; North Korea was a Soviet satellite. South Korea was concerned almost solely with the issue of political independence narrowly construed; North Korea was far more concerned with social change and the creation of a new society. These two governments confronted each other politically, economically, and militarily, quite independently of their superpower sponsors. Other determinants of its foreign policy aside (such as the relationship with the Soviet Union), China found in the Korean situation the necessity to begin developing a more acute intellectual and theoretical appreciation of the contradictions inherent in the Third World. The Indochina war presented a very different situation. Here a strictly anticolonial battle was being waged, and its leader was well acquainted with China and China with him. China could appreciate, within the context of its own revolutionary experience, the strategy of a war of national liberation like the one Ho Chi Minh was fighting. China's policies toward Korea and Indochina derived from a single political and moral source, but the policies differed in pragmatic terms to the extent the situations themselves differed. In Korea, therefore, China became a direct participant in a land war, committing great numbers of men and amounts of treasure to the conduct of a war along fairly traditional lines. In Indochina, on the other hand, China provided important political and limited material aid; the experience of China's own revolution suggested that direct mass intervention was not called for. Moreover, the long history of Vietnamese suspicion of Chinese intentions—a suspicion rather lacking in Korea's perception of her great continental neighbor—suggested further that a massive Chinese intervention might be counterproductive to China's political objectives in the region.

In both cases, the struggles, however different they were in themselves, elicited American intervention in support of one side. This intervention inevitably sharpened the contradictions and showed that the United States was prepared to continue its own interventionist policy, wherever necessary, to hold the line of the so-called free world against communism. It was obvious, however, that a simple dichotomous analysis and policy according to which any given country or party was forced to choose between the United States and the communists would be insufficiently responsive to the needs of the moment. Many, including some American allies and some national liberation movements, opposed America's policy in Asia and, by extension, in other parts of the world, but they could not afford to join the communists, either for ideological or for political reasons of their own. The development of a third position, neutralism, became increasingly imperative because it allowed a choice against American imperialism without forcing a choice for the Sino-Soviet bloc.

Neutralism created a space in which the bourgeois leaders of newly independent states could stand, and it allowed national liberation movements not yet in power to garner support from a wider spectrum of sources than membership in the communist camp permitted. Neutralism, furthermore, was a political position that refracted developments in Europe, where many Western European countries looked hopefully toward some form of détente between the Soviet Union and the United States. China itself sought an environment of peace in Asia so that Peking could shift its attention away from international crises like Korea, the Formosa Straits, and Indochina to internal development. In China's eyes, it was possible to pursue at one and the same time peaceful coexistence and armed struggle for national liberation, depending on historical circumstances and strategic and tactical considerations. The likelihood of success was also no small matter to be taken into account in the choice of one or another strategy. To Americans who saw the world strictly in the dichotomous terms of the

Cold War—freedom versus communism, America versus Russia, us versus them—Chinese policy seemed self-contradictory. The Chinese, however, were developing policy in a different world, and their choices were based upon the pursuit of more than one objective; policy was dictated by the pragmatic consideration of potential success or failure. With the breadth of theoretical and practical choices available to the Chinese, therefore, a policy of entertaining active diplomatic relations with nations of differing social systems was not only feasible but also perfectly reasonable.

NEUTRALISM AND COEXISTENCE

In April 1954, China and India signed an agreement on Tibet that included, for the first time, the Five Principles of Peaceful Coexistence, or, as they became known in South and Southeast Asia, the *"Panch Shila."* These principles, considered the guide to the development of relations between China and India, included mutual respect for each other's territorial integrity and sovereignty, nonaggression, noninterference in each other's internal affairs, equality and mutual benefit, and peaceful coexistence. In June 1954, Zhou Enlai visited India and Burma in order to advance the cause of peaceful relations between China and those two South Asian nations, and on June 28, 1954, India's prime minister, Jawaharlal Nehru, and Zhou signed an agreement affirming once again their two countries' adherence to the five principles. Burma also signed such an agreement, and to further cement mutual relations Nehru and the Burmese prime minister, U Nu, visited Peking. This visit coincided with the Geneva conference on Korea and Indochina. Thus, at the same time that China was becoming a functional big power at Geneva, it was moving forward on its own frontiers, breaking out of diplomatic inactivity and American attempts to isolate China, and developing a forward and peaceful foreign policy that differed significantly from the policies of the other big powers. India and Burma, in these and other discussions, agreed that they would pursue a policy of neutrality in the Cold War between the East bloc and the West bloc and would maintain amicable relations with Peking. China, in turn, agreed that any outstanding differences among China, Burma, and India, including frontier disagreements, would be resolved by negotiations, not by military actions.

The next step in this departure in international relations was the convening of a conference of Asian and African nations at Bandung, Indonesia, in April 1955. The meeting was intended to create a nonbloc bloc of nations that wished to remain outside the Cold War and membership in either one or the other superpower camp. China sought to assume leadership of these nonaligned states. China was, after all, the largest underdeveloped country; the Chinese had demonstrated in Korea and the Formosa Straits that imperialism could be resisted; and China was, racially and culturally, part of the Afro-Asian, not the European, world. In a speech to the conference, Zhou Enlai added to the five principles considerations that could not but appeal directly to the participants: recognition of racial equality and respect for the rights of the people of all nations to choose their own ways of life and their own political and economic systems. This gave neutrality a positive content, introduced the idea of social change, and reminded the participants that one of the factors binding them was race, that is to say, they were all nonwhite. The conference issued a declaration calling upon the members of the new nonbloc bloc to "practice tolerance and live together in peace with one another as good neighbors and develop friendly cooperation."[15]

Peaceful coexistence by no means implied an end to armed struggle. The Bandung conference clearly intended colonialism and imperialism to be understood as a form of aggression and interference; therefore, resistance to them was necessary. Moreover, the nonaligned, neutral powers were not expected to avoid conflict with the imperialists by cooperating with, or being co-opted by, them. "Nonalignment," as neutrality came to be known, was intended to be a moral position, but it was a moral position that, like China itself, would "lean to one side" in favor of independence for colonies. This emphasis, little appreciated by Western policy planners, led to a strong antipathy in Washington toward the position of neutralism. First, the Bandung policy declared neutrality a third position standing between, and outside, the two great power blocs, but it did not call for neutrality toward the independence struggles of colonial peoples. Because the United States, more often than not, allied itself with the colonial powers, it correctly interpreted Bandung neutrality as inimical to Washington's own interests. Second, the Bandung position did not call for one social system in member countries to the exclusion of others. Quite the contrary, it recognized the possibility of diversity and specified noninterference in each other's internal affairs; no member of the nonaligned bloc would promote revolution within the territory of another. Consequently, it was possible to include under the umbrella of neutralism a great variety of historical stages of development, ranging from feudal aristocracies to communist societies. Washington saw this as cynicism, but for Peking it was a subtle, and suitable, move against imperialism. Moreover, this position defined more clearly for Peking the range of nations with which China could hope to conduct fruitful diplomatic exchanges. Peking endeavored to actualize the Bandung spirit even in its relations with the United States by urging negotiations over the Formosa Straits and other outstanding issues, but Washington rejected these overtures.

China's relations with Burma put into practice the Bandung spirit. Great Britain, as the colonial power in Burma for more than half a century, had negotiated agreements with one or another Chinese government to define the frontier between China and Burma, but as a rule these agreements had been drawn up in relative ignorance of the regions concerned and they had never proven satisfactory. The new Chinese state had problems with Burma. Burma was one of those countries of "the feeble-minded bourgeoisie of the East." Moreover, Nationalist Chinese army units continued to raid into China from bases in Northern Burma. The Chinese Communists, for their part, expressed sympathy for various dissident ethnic and political groups in the region. China and Burma recognized the possibility of conflict between them, and they sought to resolve their problems on the basis of the five principles. On November 9, 1955, they announced that a resolution was in sight, and in the spring of 1956, Zhou Enlai and the Burmese leader U Nu, meeting in Southwest China, signed a new Sino-Burmese border agreement, which included the exchange of minor pieces of territory, in sum to the benefit of Burma.

The Bandung conference and the spirit of cooperative neutrality that emerged from it did not preclude disagreements among the members of the neutral camp. And there were many. Bandung established principles on the basis of which these conflicts were to be resolved. For example, China and Indonesia disagreed sharply about the status of overseas Chinese in Indonesia. Over 2.5 million Chinese lived in the Indonesian islands, where they maintained a separate existence, acted as a petty bourgeois class of shopkeepers, merchants, and wholesalers, and enjoyed the benefits of both Chinese and Indonesian citizenship. The Indonesian government, responding to nationalist emotions within the indigenous population—emotions that were at times directed against this widespread foreign element, which by and large, lived off profit made from the Indonesian economy—began in 1957 to attempt to control Chinese financial activities and to resettle Chinese so as to break up foreign population nuclei. China made strong objections to Indonesian regulations that curtailed the activities of Chinese merchants in the countryside and obtained modifications of Indonesian policies through an intensive diplomatic and political campaign; at the same time, Peking demonstrated that it was prepared to make concessions when necessary.

China's diplomatic opportunities in South and Southeast Asia were the greater since the Soviet Union's priorities lay elsewhere. In the autumn and winter of 1956–1957, Zhou Enlai tried to expand Chinese influence by visiting Afghanistan, Pakistan, India, Burma, Ceylon, Nepal, Cambodia, and North Vietnam. It was a time of great international crisis, with Soviet actions in Hungary and Anglo-French actions at the Suez Canal occupying much of the world's attention. As China made its presence more and more felt in South and Southeast Asia by means of state visits, cultural exchanges, and the like, a Sino-Soviet rivalry for political influence and control of local communist and related parties began to develop. By the end of the 1950s it was openly acknowledged throughout the region that a conflict between the two great communist powers was taking place.

THE INDIAN WARS

India provided the exception to the growth of Chinese influence, and there were two primary reasons for this. First, with the Communists in power in Asia's largest state and the world's most populous society, the West (particularly the United States) needed an example of successful noncommunist economic development to provide an alternative to the appeal that a successful China would have for developing countries. India, the second largest country in Asia and the second most populous country in the world, was ruled by a European educated socioeconomic aristocracy with which the United States could communicate. Washington considered India the best possible alternative to the Chinese example and selected it as the model and example of noncommunist economic development. The rivalry that grew between India and China after the mid-1950s derived, therefore, not from major issues that divided them but, rather, from the conditions of the world that surrounded them. The international power struggle provided the general framework within which specific and relatively minor problems became causes of conflict. Second, despite what at times appeared to be a honeymoon period for Peking and Delhi in the early 1950s, India feared a growing Chinese power on its frontier. This fear increased in proportion to China's success in mobilizing its society for economic and social change at the same time that India's development never quite got off the ground. As early as 1951, rumors circulated that the Chinese Communists were attempting to infiltrate Nepal through Tibet; Nepal was important to India as a buffer zone between India and China. Moreover, a Communist Party became active in Nepal, which was an unwelcome political development both for the Nepalese government and for India; predictions of a Chinese Communist takeover in the Himalayas were even more unsettling. As Chinese influence spread in Afghanistan, Nepal, Sikkim and Bhutan—all astride India's northern frontiers—India felt increasingly unsettled and insecure.

Developments in Tibet were of particular concern to the New Delhi government, which always had looked upon that remote country as an area of special interest to India for geographical, political, and religious reasons. Indian commercial ties with Tibet were strong, if not significant in India's total trade picture, and India considered Tibet an important northern buffer. (The British Indian government had also feared the establishment of any strong third power in Tibet.) Tibet remained, therefore, a potential issue between India and China. This issue was the more poignant since the Tibetans themselves did not acquiesce in the reassertion of Chinese authority over Tibet, and between 1951 and 1958 discontent grew considerably. Nevertheless, at the end of April 1954, Peking and Delhi reached an agreement recognizing Chinese claims over "the Tibet region of China."[16] The agreement included the five principles but did not contain any description of the Sino-Indian border. By and large, relations between China and India seemed friendly, and perhaps neither party felt the need to define the frontier precisely.

However, the situation began to change toward the end of the 1950s. Continuing unrest in Tibet and, perhaps, the growing acerbity of the Sino-Soviet conflict seemed to make the Chinese anxious about Indian intentions. In April 1958, Nehru announced he would visit Tibet in order symbolically to support Tibet's ruler, the Dalai Lama, in the latter's attempt to moderate Chinese policy in the country. Peking, however, insisted that Nehru cancel his plans; he did. Now Peking began to call attention to the Sino-Indian frontier problem by publishing a map indicating China's territorial claims. The map also suggested that China had constructed a military highway through territory that New Delhi claimed as part of India. The region in question, Ladakh, now entered into contention as the Indians verified the existence of the road. India sent patrols into the Aksai Chin area to determine how far the Chinese had intruded and to reassert claims over what the Indians insisted was historically their territory. The Chinese captured some of the patrols. In November 1959, Peking proposed that both sides withdraw from the territory and, to demonstrate their goodwill, the Chinese released the Indians they had captured on patrol. India agreed, and the two powers arrived at a local settlement that resulted in territorial gains for China. However, Nehru now began to express public doubts about China, raising the question of the sincerity of China's adherence to the five principles. This was only the first unfriendly exchange.

Inside Tibet, the situation worsened as Tibetan opposition to the exercise of Chinese authority to change Tibetan society increased rapidly. In March 1959, an armed rebellion broke out against the Chinese in Lhasa, the Tibetan capital in the central part of the country, and in eastern Tibet. Peking rushed in troops and reinforcements, and the rebellion in Lhasa and central Tibet was suppressed by the end of March. Some reports claimed that as many as sixty-five thousand Tibetans had been killed. The Dalai Lama fled to India, as had his predecessor in a similar situation. The Indian government and people received him enthusiastically, while China began to exert pressure on, and according to reports even to penetrate, Indian territory all along the Northeastern frontier.

China and India had moved from friendly relations to open hostility. Indian crowds, used to chanting "Indians and Chinese are brothers," now regarded China as an enemy. In Peking, Nehru's image underwent a metamorphosis after he began expressing sympathy for the Tibetan plight. India, China said, was behaving just as the traditional imperialists did. Furthermore, Peking accused New Delhi of interfering in China's internal affairs because India was giving support to the "reactionary" Tibetan rebels. The issue of the precise border between India and Tibet (China) became more and more aggravated as Tibetan refugees sought sanctuary in Indian territory. The transport of supplies for the Tibetan guerrillas through India and Nepal worsened the situation even more. Border clashes occurred, and New Delhi accused China of aggression. The Soviet Union, not without some irony, declared its own neutrality, which did not endear Moscow any the more to Peking. Common sense prevailed, however, and the conflict did not escalate at the time. Zhou Enlai and Nehru met in April 1960 for inconclusive negotiations, while small, localized border clashes continued.

Toward the end of 1962, the Indian prime minister evidently became convinced, finally, that the situation of continuing low-level confrontation and recurring border skirmishes needed to be resolved once and for all. On October 12, Nehru announced that he had sent military units to drive the Chinese out of territory that India claimed as its own. The Chinese countered on October 20 by mounting major offensives that had as their objective driving the Indians out of those territories that Peking claimed traditionally belonged to China. India declared a state of national emergency and called for the reestablishment of the *status quo ante*, but the Chinese offensive continued. The Indian government asked for help from the United States and Great Britain, while the Soviet Union moved to a position of pro-Indian neutrality. Moscow demonstrated this stance by not interrupting its aid to India.

China's objectives in this second Sino-Indian war were limited: Peking wanted to demonstrate to New Delhi that it could bring military power to bear on India, even across the vast wastes of Tibet and the Himalayas; China also wanted to establish its position in the disputed territories and to show the world that the Indian model for development was no match for the Chinese. India's inability to ward off the Chinese advances and to field military forces adequate for its defense, despite a great outpouring of popular support for the government, proved China's points. Consequently, Peking proposed a cease-fire and a border settlement along the lines of the 1959 proposal, but India rejected this. In the middle of November Chinese forces took to the offensive again, but on November 21 Peking unexpectedly announced a unilateral cease-fire and a withdrawal to the borders China had always claimed. The withdrawal began within a week. China had made its point and needed to go no further. At an international conference held in Colombo, Ceylon, the Chinese moderated their position more, and on January 9, 1963 China and India signed agreements ending the war. China emerged the clear victor; Peking's leadership in Asia was uncontested. Furthermore, Chinese moderation, holding to those positions Peking had claimed originally, China's good treatment of Indian prisoners of war, and its general international deportment won the Chinese considerable respect throughout the world and in India too.

CHINA, THE MIDDLE EAST, AFRICA, AND LATIN AMERICA

The Bandung conference was the point of departure for the development of China's relations with the countries and independence movements of the Middle East and Africa. The conference provided China and those regions with their first coherent regional exposure to each other. A second such conference, the Afro-Asian People's Solidarity Conference, was held in Cairo in September 1957. Many observers considered it the occasion for the great awakening of African nationalism and of Africanism. Between the two conferences, China opened an embassy in Cairo, and through it Peking pursued the development of active relations not only with Egypt but also with the other Arab countries and with Africa. Gradually, diplomatic, economic, and cultural relations were established with most of the nations in the area.

In the Middle East as elsewhere, China's analysis concluded that regional conflicts were the refraction in local terms of global contradictions. The Palestinian-Israeli conflict, for example, was considered a consequence of the American-British attempt to control the Middle East. China consistently took the side of those whom it identified as opponents of capitalist imperialism, and Peking was the first non-Arab government to extend diplomatic recognition to the Palestine Liberation Organization (PLO). In 1964–1965 Peking moved further by extending the Palestinians economic and military assistance, providing training to Palestinian guerrilla groups and supporting the PLO's political budget. Where China considered the Soviet Union insufficiently aggressive for China's own anti-imperialist tastes, Peking attempted to take the lead.

China's activities in the Middle East were not all revolutionary. In January 1958 Peking and Yemen signed a ten-year agreement under which China would send technicians and skilled workers to Yemen, primarily for road construction. After the success of its own atomic weapons development program, China was prepared, in 1965, to advise the Egyptians in atomic research. Peking stood ready to help both revolutionary movements and established governments, always depending upon circumstances. Peking's policies here were the same as in South and Southeast Asia.

In Africa and Latin America Peking pursued the same policies. China lent arms support to revolutionary movements, cooperated with states that recognized Peking and not Taipei, and received endless visits from African leaders. In Latin America, where most of the established governments were American clients, the field for China's activities was more limited. Throughout the region, however, as the Sino-Soviet dispute led to splits in local communist parties, China began supporting the splinter groups that were pro-Peking.

Throughout Asia, Africa, and Latin America, China had several foreign policy objectives. First, Peking sought political advantage for itself. This was expressed primarily in the establishment of diplomatic relations between Peking and various countries. Every recognition of Peking meant one less recognition of Taipei and one more vote against Formosa and for China's membership in the United Nations. Second, Peking sought to help revolutionary movements and political parties throughout the underdeveloped world that favored Chinese positions, particulary within the context of the Sino-Soviet dispute. Third, China sought to develop those economic relationships that would be profitable to its own interests. In pursuit of these objectives, Peking utilized a limited amount of resources to develop a broad program of foreign aid to countries less developed than China. Before 1960, Peking spent about $30 million a year in some seven countries, extending from Cambodia to Egypt. This amount increased in the 1960s to about $125 million per annum in twenty-one countries, including eight in Asia, three in the Middle East, and ten in Africa. Chinese aid had both political and economic purposes, and through it Peking tried to create an image of China as an industrializing country that was a model for the less developed nations of the world. Moreover, the conditions of Chinese aid were both politically and financially far more favorable to the recipients than were those of aid extended by the United States or the Soviet Union.

In 1964, Premier Zhou Enlai visited Africa. During the trip, which was widely publicized at the time, he enunciated eight principles of foreign aid: (1) equality and mutual benefit, (2) respect for the sovereignty of other countries, (3) extension of interest-free or low-interest loans with flexible time limits for repayment, (4) encouragement of self-reliance and independent economic development, (5) emphasis on building projects requiring less investment and yielding quicker results, (6) provision of quality equipment and material of Chinese manufacture, (7) the mastering of techniques by the personnel of the recipient country, and (8) the restriction of Chinese Communist experts and advisory personnel to the standard of living to which their counterparts in the recipient countries were accustomed.[17] These eight principles of foreign aid obviously were an extension, to this field of the Five Principles of Peaceful Coexistence. After 1960, China increased the number of technicians going abroad on assistance programs. By 1965 Peking had about half as many advisors in the field as did Moscow, although Chinese aid accounted for only ten percent of the total communist aid to the developing world. In marked contrast to the Soviets, Chinese advisors and technicians in the Third World lived close to the host populations, and Chinese projects, such as road construction in Yemen and railway construction in Tanzania, tended to focus on infrastructural development. Furthermore, the Chinese often brought Chinese workers in to provide the labor force on large-scale projects, whereas the Soviets used local labor. This meant that not only could the Chinese control the labor force themselves but, also, they did not have to enter into superior-inferior relations with the local population and thus avoided many of the cross-cultural and interpersonal problems that frequently plagued American and Soviet aid programs.

Chinese analyses of appropriate strategies in the Third World were summarized in 1965 in Lin Biao's famous essay "Long Live the Victory of the People's War!" The Third World, Lin said, constituted the "country-side" of the world and stood in sharp contrast to the advanced capitalist nations and, by extension, to the Soviet Union, which were the world's urban centers. In this view, the strategy of the Chinese Revolution provided a model for study in and emulation by the Third World, whose societies could achieve national liberation only by their own efforts. (The course of the war in Vietnam was to provide further evidence supporting Lin's thesis.) Chinese economic aid and political behavior throughout the Third World had an indirect objective that, in the final analysis, was more important than direct action upon, and interference in, Third World affairs: Peking clearly intended to create an atmosphere in which the Chinese model would be studied as an encouragement to self-reliance and self-help and as a guide to action.

Foreign Policy in the Age of Radicalism: Revolutionary Reprise

Although the Cultural Revolution, the period of extreme radicalism extending roughly from the mid-1960s to the mid-1970s, originally was intended to be a movement for internal cultural, psychological, and political change focused primarily but not exclusively on the Communist Party itself, this event had a strong impact—often with unexpected consequences—on both the direction and the content of China's foreign policy. In many respects the Cultural Revolution was directed against the increasingly entrenched bureaucracy of the party and the state. The era was characterized by conflicts among individuals and groups, all claiming to be the executors of Chairman Mao Zedong's will and ideas but each interpreting those ideas in its own, often radical, terms. The Cultural Revolution's primary instruments were the groups generically called Red Guards—informal bands of radical youths and other members of society who were doing battle with the Communist establishment—and the People's Liberation Army, at the time a highly egalitarian organization that, as an institution, was deeply rooted in the masses and in work as well as in military training. These two groups were not synonymous, however, and conflict often surfaced between Red Guard organizations and units of the People's Liberation Army. While such conflict was basically ideological and political, it all too often took personal forms, and many individuals were killed or

wounded in armed battles or consigned to reeducation centers in the countryside or simply sent to the country to live and learn from the peasants,
often for long periods of time.

The Cultural Revolution was not a purge in the Stalinist sense of the
term. It was a highly self-conscious attempt to change the mind, and therefore the culture, of the Chinese people. It is important not to forget the
revolution's intentions and purposes in the almost frenetic analyses of its
failures and costs that followed the death of Mao himself in 1976 and the
subsequent fall from power of the Cultural Revolution's leading ideologue,
Jiang Qing, Mao's widow. The Cultural Revolution may be judged in a
variety of perspectives, but its goals must be understood both in and of
themselves and in the context of a China striving mightily to find its own
way in the world.

The immediate and most startling foreign policy consequences of the
Cultural Revolution were its effects on the conduct of foreign relations.
The disintegration of policymaking and policy executing bodies and institutions characterized the period. By middle or late 1966, the movement
had spread to many agencies of the government and the economy, so that
the entire country seemed swept up in the fever and fervor of dramatic
change. In November 1966, the foreign minister, Chen Yi, became an
object of Red Guard attack for ideological deviations. Soon China's whole
foreign policy establishment was involved, and the Foreign Ministry at
home, together with Chinese diplomats stationed abroad, turned its attention to self-analysis, ideological rectification, and reeducation—in short, to
the problems the Cultural Revolution presented to a very great number of
Chinese as individuals. In Peking, the Ministry of Foreign Affairs practically ceased to function as its personnel increasingly became involved in
the process. According to reports from foreign diplomats, ministry personnel changed rapidly and often no one seemed to be in charge. In China's
embassies and other diplomatic organizations overseas, ambassadors and
other staff often were summoned home to participate in, or become the
objects of, the Cultural Revolution. The diplomatic structure sometimes
developed strange forms. As one observer in Paris half-humorously noted,
the most significant Chinese diplomat in France at the height of the Cultural Revolution seemed to be the proprietor of a Chinese restaurant off
the Boulevard St. Michel whose cousin was ambassador in Prague, except
that the proprietor had been assigned to wash dishes when the workers
had taken over the cash register. In short, China's foreign policy and its
conduct were thrown into confusion as the Cultural Revolutionaries assaulted the strongholds of bureaucratic power and process.

The ideological impact of the Cultural Revolution on foreign policy centered on the Sino-Soviet dispute, particularly on the Soviet Union and its
role in the world and on China's response to the challenge, or threat, the
Soviet Union presented. Peking had already identified the Soviet Union as

a socialist society that had slid back into capitalism and that was behaving internationally as an imperialist power. This attack was now intensified as the Chinese began conceptually to construct a world that was immeasurably more complicated than the seemingly simple bipolar world of the 1950s. There was, after all, a profound qualitative difference between a Soviet Union whose interests were not in complete harmony with China's but that nonetheless played a vital role in support of China and a Soviet Union that was a major enemy in a world already inhabited by another major enemy, the United States. The Sino-Soviet dispute gave rise to a world that the Chinese interpreted no longer as bipolar but as tripolar or polycentric. This new world had three major international actors, China, the Soviet Union, and the United States. It also contained an increasing number of varieties of communism or communist parties, ranging from splinter Marxist-Leninist (that is, pro-Chinese) parties in Australia and New Zealand to great European communist parties that were no longer willing to follow blindly Moscow's dictates. Even among socialist states the situation now was vastly more complicated: there were East European countries like Albania, which allied itself with China, and Rumania, which increasingly sought a quasi-neutralist status both between Peking and Moscow and between the two of them and the West.

The complications produced by the Sino-Soviet dispute were only one aspect of an international scene in the 1960s that a host of developments made immensely confusing: the growing importance, both politically and economically, of the European Common Market; the unexpected influence of Cuba, whose international status and global reach had increased with surprising speed, despite Cuba's relatively small size; the increasing restiveness of client and satellite states; and growing doubts about American political, military, and moral power as a consequence of the misconceived, badly executed, and blatantly immoral Vietnam War. These developments, among others, produced a new world context in which China had to make and pursue foreign policy. Surprising events, such as the great change in Sino-American relations in the late 1970s, perhaps best can be understood as a consequence of the dialectical interaction of the Sino-Soviet dispute and the Cultural Revolution in the context of the new, and rather unexpected, world. Any attempt at understanding must include, however, the recognition that narrative history perforce imposes upon both events and processes an apparent rationality or direct relationship of cause and effect that the events and processes did not possess, or did not seem to possess, at the time.

HEIGHTENED ACTIVITY

Until the mid-1960s, China's policy in the Third World of Asia, Africa, and Latin America focused on winning friends among both established governments (Peking's friendship with which would help its case for entrance into the United Nations and would harm Taipei) and revolutionary movements (where the growth of China's influence was important in its contest with the Soviet Union). Lin Biao's "Long Live the Victory of the People's War!" summarized Chinese policy up to 1965, particularly insofar as the essay provided an explanatory model and strategic foreign policy program for established Third World governments in their relations with the advanced industrial societies of the Oikoumene in both the West and the East bloc. Just as the revolutionary strategy appropriate to conditions in the Third World called for the development of a rural base from which the cities would be captured, so in the international scene, this reasoning suggested, the Third World constituted the rural base for the struggle against the urbanized and highly industrialized imperialist world of the two superpowers.

Although Lin Biao's essay preceded the Cultural Revolution, it indicated the direction Chinese foreign policy would take. The radicalization of Chinese political, social, and cultural life implied the radicalization of China's foreign policy interests. Several governments now became potential objects of Chinese sponsored revolutionary activity. Some maintained formal diplomatic relations with China, such as India, Indonesia, and Burma; others were identified as imperialist (Israel) or racist (Rhodesia). The consequences of China's policy included disaffection from China among former friends, anti-Chinese demonstrations in various parts of the Third World, expulsion of Chinese diplomats, and, beginning in January 1967, counterdemonstrations aimed at foreign diplomatic establishments in Peking. These demonstrations were themselves part of the Cultural Revolution. As the movement gained momentum, activities and attitudes stemming from Peking impinged upon normal relations with every country except China's sole European ally, Albania.

China conducted its foreign relations on two levels—the formal diplomatic level and the level of revolutionary activity—throughout the Cultural Revolution. This gave Peking a breadth of actions and responses that was lacking in most countries that pursued foreign policy along more traditional lines. For example, events in Indonesia, at least until the last part of 1965, were by and large favorable to Peking's interests, and China's influence with the government of President Sukarno remained strong. However, by the end of October, in the midst of a Moslem revolt against the government, the Chinese embassy in Djakarta was subjected to infringements of its diplomatic immunities, and anti-Chinese activities aimed both at Communist China and at Indonesia's Overseas Chinese community spread throughout the islands. In some areas, bands of Indonesians killed thousands of Chinese and conducted bloody persecutions with the active or passive support of the police and governmental agencies. Despite all this activity, however, which resulted in the almost complete loss of Chinese influence in that populous Southeast Asian nation, China limited itself to strong statements of protest and outrage; perhaps out of inability but also from lack of inclination, no overt action was taken against Indonesia. Nor did the "loss" of Indonesia lead to the subjection of Chinese policy planners and diplomats to the kind of witch hunt that had swept the American diplomatic establishment after the "loss" of China in the years after 1949.

The same evenhandedness characterized Chinese behavior in the war between India and Pakistan in 1965. Here a radicalizing China demonstrated the catholicity of its foreign policy by supporting the Pakistanis against India, although the Pakistani government was far to the right of the Indian in internal affairs. The Soviet Union, of course, supported the Indians.

China's relations with Cuba also suffered during the Cultural Revolution. This development is much more problematic than the others since Cuban revolutionary theory and experience most closely resembled China's, as Chinese and other observers recognized. Moreover, an important Cuban-Chinese trade had developed in which Cuban sugar was exchanged for Chinese rice. With the high state of antagonism and antipathy that existed between Havana and Washington, on the one hand, and between Washington and Peking, on the other, and with great Cuban interest in revolutionary developments elsewhere in Latin America, a Cuban-Chinese relationship supposedly would have been important to Peking. Nevertheless, in November 1965 China informed Cuba that rice exports would diminish in 1966, officially because of Chinese commitments to North Vietnam but actually, many thought, as a goad to Castro to encourage him to distance himself further from Moscow and to make closer approaches to Peking. Castro, in common with the leaders of many other secondary communist states, now was forced to engage in the delicate diplomacy required to maintain a position between the two communist superpowers so as to benefit from both, and in May a Chinese-Cuban trade agreement resulted in an increase in Chinese rice exports to Cuba. Nonetheless, in a short time Cuba firmly entered the lists of the pro-Moscow, anti-Peking East bloc.

By the latter part of 1969 the high tide of the Great Proletarian Cultural Revolution had passed. Although the radicals stayed in power, generally speaking, until Mao Zedong's death in 1976, by 1970 China was beginning to assert, through its foreign policy, the calm strength of world leadership. It was as though the turmoil of the Cultural Revolution had served only to reinforce the image of China's power and stability. China conveyed the image of a great nation sincerely searching for new ways to solve old problems. The ability of the Chinese to mobilize themselves in vast numbers was broadcast to the world by words and images depicting great demonstrations in Peking's Square of Heavenly Peace. Third and even First World countries began to recognize the power, real or potential, that China possessed. Chinese embassies abroad became active once again as Chinese diplomatic personnel, having passed through the cauldron of the Cultural Revolution, returned to their posts; diplomatic relations were established with countries that previously had not recognized Peking. Leaders in Pakistan, Tanzania, Libya, and elsewhere began to use one or another aspect of China's Cultural Revolution to build loyalties inside their own countries. Numerous foreign delegations, ranging from heads of state to leaders of small pro-Chinese, or Marxist-Leninist, splinter parties visited Peking.

A NEW PRAGMATISM

The revival of Chinese diplomacy contributed to the development of a certain pragmatism in China's view of the world. In October 1972, for example, the Chinese in the United Nations declared that they were opposed to "adventurist activities of terrorism" and thereby placed themselves squarely on the side of international order in the world.[18] At the same time, new international responsibilities led them to make refinements in their analyses of world politics. The Chinese insisted on the importance of national liberation and resistance to aggression, which meant that imperialist repression and aggression had to be distinguished from the violence of the oppressed and the victims of aggression. On the one hand, this distinction represented a restatement on a more theoretical plane of the same dichotomy that had characterized Chinese Communist views of the international scene from the very beginning in 1949. On the other, it placed the Chinese, within the context of the Cultural Revolution and the Sino-Soviet dispute, squarely on the side of those who opposed the Soviet Union. The latter, increasingly adventuristic in Africa, for example, now became the imperialist aggressor against which China supported popular opposition. The new position was, in fact, a Chinese transformation of the concept of just and unjust wars. Ironically, this transformation in both theory and practice was made possible by the Cultural Revolution and the strength it portrayed, regardless of whether the Cultural Revolution was a failure in other terms.

Peking's relations with Japan exemplified the new pragmatism in Chinese policy within the structure of a complex view of the world. Throughout the 1950s and 1960s, despite many and frequent goodwill visits to China by a great variety of Japanese groups, including representatives of the ruling Liberal Democratic Party, China had persisted in perceiving Japan as nothing more than an extension of the American imperialist military and economic presence in East Asia. The U.S. occupation of the Japanese Ryukyu chain until 1972 and Japan's diplomatic relations with, and very active economic presence in, Formosa, which was America's primary client state in the Far East, confirmed China's analysis of Japan's international position. By the late 1960s, Peking's view of Japan contained a new and disturbing element: the "economic miracle" in Japan had increased that nation's industrial and commercial potential and consequent political power to the point that Japan began to assume, in the Chinese mind, the proportions of a possible aggressor against China or Chinese interests in Asia as an agent of American imperialism. This fear was expressed in frequent Chinese statements about the supposed revival of militarism in Japanese government and industrial circles.

The Diaoyu Islands affair added to China's public suspicions of Japanese intentions. Peking feared that South Korea and Formosa would join Japan as American agents in economic aggression against the interests of the People's Republic of China. Considerable resources, particularly oil, lay beneath the waters around islands to the north of Formosa and to the south of the Ryukyus; these islands became the focus of a three-way tug-of-war in which Peking, Taipei, and Tokyo each claimed them and their adjacent resources. Peking saw collusion among Japan, Formosa, and the United States in an attempt to prevent Chinese access to the potential riches of the area.

At the same time that Peking pursued a verbally antagonistic policy toward Japan, China also laid the groundwork for the development of positive and mutually beneficial relations with Tokyo. At the end of September 1972, the Japanese government recognized Communist China and withdrew recognition from Formosa. In a joint communiqué, Peking declared that Formosa was "an inalienable part of the territory of the People's Republic of China," and the Tokyo government announced that it fully understood and respected Peking's position.[19] In return, China abandoned reparations claims against Japan, and the two governments entered into negotiations for the purpose of normalizing and regulating the wide range of interactions that they expected to develop between their countries.

In the aftermath of the Cultural Revolution, the Chinese analysis of the Third World identified three major negative forces that had to be combated: the imperialism of the advanced industrial West; the hegemonism, or imperialism, of the Soviet Union; and colonialism, which apparently takes two forms—direct colonial control, which is decreasing throughout the world, and indirect colonial control, in which racist governments made up of local agents of imperialism and hegemonism are in power. In this analysis, China is "a developing socialist country belonging to the Third World," and the Third World itself is the primary arena for the struggle with the three negative forces.[20] This analysis was spelled out during a conference of foreign ministers of the nonaligned countries that was held in Georgetown, Guiana, in August 1972. "Imperialism," "colonialism," "racial oppression," and "the big powers' monopoly over the handling of international affairs" were the identification tags for the various forms that imperialism takes in the Third World. However, not all revolutionary activity against these factors is positive. Some of it may be the consequence of "deviationism," "revisionism," or other tendencies that tend to negate or inhibit the struggle against imperialism. On the other hand, that struggle may be carried on by an established government. In short, the same rubrics China applied in the analysis of its own internal condition were applied abroad as well, and the significance of a particular government or political movement had to be defined and measured in terms of its orientation and activities within the dialectical structure of international politics. Peking's grant to Sri Lanka in May 1971 of an interest-free loan of 150 million rupees that carried extremely favorable repayment conditions was intended to encourage the Sinhalese government's suppression of revolutionary opposition to a friendly, and therefore anti-imperialist, state.

Chinese policy toward the Bangladesh revolution against Pakistan, and toward India's complicated involvement in it, provided further evidence of policy evolution in Peking. Increasingly, the division of the Indian subcontinent into two entities, Pakistan and India, gave Peking and Moscow opportunity for actions of mutual hostility as they responded to the imperatives of Indian and Pakistani bilateral politics over local issues. Peking's support of Pakistan and Soviet support for India increased throughout the 1960s. Now, Peking supported Pakistan against the Bangladesh independence struggle. Expressions of this support took the form of state visits and an interest-free loan to Pakistan, with highly favorable repayment terms, to aid that country's fourth five-year plan.

When Bangladesh declared its independence from Pakistan at the end of March 1971, and as India, the Soviet Union's friend, became more deeply involved on the side of Bangladesh, Peking increased its support for Pakistan. On April 12, 1972, China declared that it would support Pakistan if India took offensive action. Six months later, the Soviet Union countered by signing a treaty of peace, friendship, and cooperation with India. The Soviet Union also provided military equipment to India, which had invaded East Pakistan (Bangladesh) toward the end of 1971. Peking increased its verbal support of Pakistan and at the United Nations leveled indirect charges against the Soviet Union. The United States, in this complicated situation, seemed to favor Pakistan, if only because of India's flirtation with the Soviet Union.

Bangladesh gained its independence with India's support, which had depended in turn on military equipment and supplies provided by the Soviet Union. India had also assumed a considerable economic burden by providing for the large number of Bengali refugees who had crossed into India to avoid the fighting. China's support for Pakistan had rested on the presupposition that the Pakistani government, whatever its internal policies may have been, was fighting Soviet hegemonism in South Asia. Taken together, the complex events and relationships surrounding the Bangladesh revolution provided the occasion for the first major confrontation among the three superpowers: the United States and China found them-

selves arrayed against the Soviet Union. The Indian-Bangladeshi victory
over Pakistan implied gains for the Soviet Union, including diplomatic advantages in India and Bangladesh and an extension of the ring of Soviet
influence around China. Indeed, in December 1971 the Chinese delegate
to the Security Council, Huang Hua, accused the Soviet Union of plotting
to encircle China. In the middle of December, the United States proposed
a Security Council resolution calling for an immediate cease-fire in South
Asia and the withdrawal of both Indian and Pakistani forces into their own
national boundaries. The Soviet Union, for the third time in ten days,
vetoed the American resolution, demonstrating its diplomatic strength in
the area.

For China, the Bangladeshi war had profound importance. It was the
first occasion on which China and the United States openly had found
themselves allies, however unwitting the mutuality of their interests may
have been, against the Soviet Union; Soviet analysts were quick to point
out this alliance. Moreover, it was the first time that China and the Soviet
Union had fought a "proxy war," that is, a war in which the two powers
were participants by proxy through the agency of the actual combatants.
Finally, China recognized the necessity for a more active campaign to
break out of Soviet encirclement. Over the next several years this effort
would take a variety of forms. The development of a new relationship with
the United States in 1972 was one. A severe border clash with India in
1975, in which China reasserted its military power on India's frontier, was
another. Chairman Hua Guofeng's visit to Iran in 1978 was a third. In all
three instances, China directly challenged the Soviet Union. In Peking's
view, India continued to be an agent of Soviet hegemonism. The United
States was still an imperialist power, although it was useful for China to
encourage imperialist opposition to hegemonism. The shah's government
in Iran, certainly by no means progressive from the Chinese point of view,
similarly needed encouragement to oppose Soviet hegemonism. In the
same way and for at least some of the same reasons, the Soviet Union
maintained friendly relations with Nepal and Afghanistan, both feudal type
societies with repressive political systems.

The same principles guided Chinese policy in Southeast Asia. Rapid
changes in the region led to new alignments. The Vietnam War ended
with the rout of the Americans in 1976, and Vietnam was reunified under
the North Vietnamese government. Communist regimes were installed in
Cambodia and Laos. American power throughout Asia had been damaged
severely by these reverses. Both the Soviet Union and China, despite their
mutual antagonism, had supported the North Vietnamese, the Pathet Lao,
and the Khmer Rouge. Now the dialectical contradictions between Moscow and Peking, on the one hand, and between each of them and Washington, on the other, resolved themselves with remarkable speed into a
new contradiction.

With the end of the war and the disappearance of the immediate American threat, Vietnam pursued, with more attention than ever, its traditional policy of balancing Soviet influence from afar with Chinese power across its own frontier. The ancient antagonism between the Cambodians and the Vietnamese, which had been visible throughout the Vietnam War, now reasserted itself in more strident terms as a new and almost shockingly radical Cambodian Communist government and the Communist government of the Democratic Republic of Vietnam went to war along the former South Vietnam's frontier with Cambodia. The Southeast Asian international scene was further complicated in 1978 as the Vietnamese, in a characteristic and almost traditional expression of nationalism in the region, initiated a serious persecution of the country's overseas Chinese. This involved attacks on persons and property, confiscation of property, and expulsion of large numbers to China. The persecution, combined with Hanoi's use of Soviet influence to balance China's, placed Vietnam in the category of agent of Soviet hegemonism and led China to increase its verbal and material support for Cambodia, whose war with Vietnam made it a combatant against Soviet hegemonism. Thus China allied itself with Cambodia in the latter's conflict with Vietnam, which was the Soviet Union's ally. The United States, whose relations with China were growing increasingly close, sympathized strongly with the Cambodian regime that it had previously condemned as illegitimate, uncivilized, and inhumane. In the beginning of the 1980s, China and the United States combined to support the anti-Vietnamese (and therefore anti-Soviet) forces in Cambodia, which had been displaced by a more moderate, pro-Hanoi government that relied heavily on Vietnamese military support within Cambodia itself.

In sum, Chinese policy throughout Asia in the 1970s was firmly guided by the concepts of contradiction and dialectic, which had been central to the Chinese Communist conceptual construction of the world from the beginning. Foreign observers trying to pass judgment on the changes in Chinese policy tended to undervalue the importance of ideology in the conduct of Peking's foreign affairs and to ascribe the dramatic changes in the Empire's diplomacy after the middle of the 1970s to interpretations and reinterpretations by Peking of its self-interest. However that may be, even China's interpretation of its self-interest took place well within its ideological construction of the world. China was demonstrating that what the West, particularly the Americans, took to be a rigid and increasingly irrelevant ideological structure was, in fact, a versatile analytical tool that could account for the remarkable pragmatism that China was exhibiting on an increasing scale in its relations with the United States and Western Europe.

China's policy in the Middle East, Africa, and Latin America rested on the same principles as its policy in Asia. Just as Peking considered Formosa the primary agent of imperialism in the Far East, so it considered Israel its primary agent in the Middle East. Therefore, China established relations with the Palestine Liberation Organization in the early 1960s, and Mao Zedong received a PLO delegation in 1965. The Arab-Israeli conflict and the larger struggle against Soviet hegemonism were the focal points of Chinese policy in the Middle East. Peking's main objective was to keep the Soviet Union out of the Middle East, an objective shared with the United States. Consequently, as the PLO became increasingly dependent upon Soviet economic and military support either directly or indirectly through intermediaries such as Syria and Iraq, China decreased its aid to the Palestinians and actively sought increased political, economic, and cultural relations with the governments of the various Arab states. Unlike Asia and Africa, however, the Middle East did not present China with many opportunities for direct intervention.

Africa, on the other hand, gave Peking further confirmation of the validity of China's theoretical analysis and its application to the execution of policy. Rhodesia, South Africa, and Angola were foci of China's attention. Rhodesia belonged to the category of colonial-settler regimes of the racist type, as did South Africa. In these cases, the Chinese accused the United States, itself a racist power in Peking's view, of protecting and supporting the white regimes in power. At the same time and in both instances, support for African national liberation movements was a matter of conflict with the Soviet Union, which was able to provide more aid more directly than could China.

The Angolan revolution provided China with an especially sharply defined problem to be solved. The Angolan national liberation movement against Portuguese colonialism consisted of three major groups: the Popular Movement for the Liberation of Angola (MPLA), the Front for the National Liberation of Angola (FNLA), and the National Union for the Total Independence of Angola (UNITA). At first, these three revolutionary groups were united in a loose coalition, and China extended support to all three. In the course of 1975, however, the coalition began to dissolve, and China withdrew its support in the hope of forcing a re-formation of the coalition. The dissolution was occasioned by several developments, including the departure of the Portuguese colonial government—a consequence of the revolution in Portugal in 1974—and the subsequent exodus of great numbers of Portuguese residents from the colony. The revolution now disintegrated into a struggle among the formerly allied anticolonial movements, and the resultant civil war had strong tribal overtones. As in Southeast Asia, so in Angola: the armed struggle within the country became a war by proxy between the superpowers. The MPLA obtained significant support from the Soviets in treasure and materiel and, supported by Cuban military personnel (Havana actually sent troops in considerable numbers to fight for the MPLA), it successfully campaigned against the UNITA and the FNLA. Just as the MPLA had turned to the Soviets for support, the UNITA became an extension of American interests and the FNLA placed itself under the aegis of the Chinese. As Soviet and Cuban influence over the MPLA increased and the MPLA made military progress against its opponents, Peking sought Washington's cooperation in joint support of the FNLA-UNITA front. The American administration, however, recognized that it would be unable to arouse popular support in the United States for intervention in Angola so soon after the Vietnam fiasco; therefore, Washington encouraged South African intervention but did not support the direct involvement China proposed. The Chinese, faced with the participation in the Angolan struggle of the racist government of South Africa, could only withdraw from the scene completely. The Soviet Union's clients won the day.

The same dialectic informed Chinese policy in 1978, when exiled Katangan troops invaded the Congo from Angola with MPLA and Russian support. The United States and the Chinese participated in a general anti-Soviet move to support the government of Congolese President Joseph Mobutu, the Chinese finding themselves once again, by the very logic of their analysis, in an unofficial alliance with the United States and, this time, with France and Belgium as well.

In Latin America, China's analysis led it to the support not of revolutionary movements and activities but, rather, of Latin American economic independence from the United States, that is to say, China opposed imperialism in the region. Distance and preoccupation with other parts of the world, combined with Peking's continued disaffection with Havana and improving relations with Washington, inhibited the development of Chinese activity in the region beyond a minimal level. Nonetheless, Peking gave active verbal support to those governments and forces that opposed both the Soviet Union and American domination. When the contradiction between Washington and Moscow required Peking to take the side of one in opposition to the other, it favored Washington. This logic led the Chinese into some very peculiar moves, such as Peking's quick recognition of the violently anticommunist military regime that emerged from the coup against the government of Salvador Allende in Chile.

Throughout the 1970s in Asia, Africa, and Latin America, economic aid was a significant Chinese diplomatic tool and, as a West German analyst remarked, China's aid programs were models of a progressive approach to economic assistance. Moreover, China was, both by self-definition and in reality, an underdeveloped country and a member of the Third World. Consequently, Chinese aid programs had an ideological and public relations impact that neither the United States nor the Soviet Union could muster. China provided interest-free loans with repayment terms more favorable than those required by the Oikoumene's capitalist and socialist members. Moreover, as we saw earlier, Chinese technicians and advisors overseas were required to live at the same standard of living as their counterparts in the host country, which stipulation had important propaganda value. As Sino-American relations improved, more countries became willing to entertain the possibility of receiving aid from China, since Washington no longer perceived such a development to be inimical to America's interests. (For a discussion of changes in Sino-American relations, see Chapter 11.) China's future ability to maintain and increase the level of economic assistance throughout the Third World now depends greatly on its economic performance at home.

China and Europe

Throughout the early 1960s and early 1970s, China had perceived Europe as a simple addendum to the United States and the Soviet Union. In the context of the strategic reorientation of its foreign policy, however, China began to understand that Europe was the main locus of the conflict between the two great imperialist superpowers. According to Peking's analysis, Moscow sought complete domination of Europe. Therefore, pursuing the logic of its own foreign policy, China now supported the North Atlantic Treaty Organization (NATO) and America's military and economic presence in Western Europe and the Mediterranean. Furthermore, Peking broadly attacked the Soviet Union for its exploitation of Eastern Europe. In order to develop their own relations with Western Europe, the Chinese actively began to promote visits to China by West European heads of state, foreign ministers, politicians of all political persuasions, scholars, and tourists. Within the socialist camp, they broadly applauded the disintegration of Soviet power over the communist parties in Western Europe and generally supported Eurocommunism, the independence of West European communist parties from Soviet domination.

Washington and Peking both recognized that it would be next to impossible for the United States to supply China with the materiel, including weapons, that China needed to build up its own military capabilities. Europe, however, provided a convenient source for the same kinds of goods that China wanted to purchase from the United States. Consequently, in 1978 Chinese military procurement missions began to visit various European countries, particularly France, West Germany, and Italy, with a view to exploring the possibility of Western Europe's supplying China with necessary items.

China's position also led Peking to support those leaders and parties in Europe that most strongly opposed the expansion of Soviet power and influence. Ironically, this meant that in Europe, as in the United States of Richard Nixon, China felt more comfortable with leaders of the conservative and even far right wings, as defined in domestic politics, than with either liberals or socialists. In the summer of 1978, Chairman Hua Guofeng visited Rumania and Yugoslavia. Rumania, strongly Stalinist internally

but increasingly neutral in its foreign policy, and Yugoslavia, liberal internally and strongly neutral, received Hua in the same spirit in which he
came: the visit was intended to demonstrate to the Soviet Union that it no
longer commanded the allegiance of countries in its own front yard.

China at the United Nations

As American policy toward China changed in 1971 and afterward, and as
the number of governments recognizing Peking increased, it became apparent that the time had arrived for the U.S. government to end its policy
of opposition to China's admission to the United Nations. During the
spring and summer of 1971, Washington made clear that it had withdrawn
its objections to China's entry into the United Nations but that it would
oppose the expulsion of the Nationalist government on Formosa. After a
great deal of parliamentary maneuvering and politicking, intended to save
face for everyone to the extent possible, the General Assembly voted on
October 25, 1971, to admit China and, over the United States' formalistic
objections, to expel the Chinese Nationalist government. China's admission was considered a great victory for the Third World and another sign
of improvement in Sino-American relations.

For Peking, the United Nations served four purposes. First, it provided China with an arena for the development of its leadership of the
Third World. As the United Nations became a locus in which the North-
South contradiction received greater and greater attention, particularly in
economic matters, China, as the world's largest poor country and as the
recognized antagonist of the superpowers, both of which were advanced
industrial states, found itself in a position to develop its leadership by consistently supporting the interests of the poor, or Southern, nations of the
world. Second, the United Nations provided China with a continuous opportunity to expound its policies toward the Soviet Union and its analysis
of Soviet objectives before representatives of all the governments of the
world. Third, China's presence at the United Nations enabled Peking to
pursue discussions even with governments with which it had no formal
relations. Membership also provided China with access to the many specialized agencies of the United Nations. Finally, China's admission to the
United Nations was the ultimate symbolic recognition of its international
status. China was now a great, if not yet a super, power.

China and Peace

The Chinese Communist attitude toward war and peace has always been
more complex than Washington, in either its analytical or its propagandis-

tic mode, has been willing to understand. Throughout the 1950s and 1960s, this very complexity of China's analysis of the issues enabled Washington repeatedly to accuse Peking of seeking war as a means of advancing its national and revolutionary purposes. The Chinese position, however, was a direct application of its conceptual or ideological construction of the world.

Mao Zedong never suggested that war was preferable to peace. Peace, obviously, was desirable in itself; moreover, China needed peace to attend to its domestic agenda. In 1955, speaking about the transition to socialism, Mao said: "For us to achieve this task, we must have a time of peaceful construction. Can we gain this time or not?"[21] Furthermore, China never suggested that war was a satisfactory means to achieve national objectives. Rather, Peking viewed war as the consequence of historical forces that could be controlled only with the greatest difficulty, if at all. The logic of the theory and reality of class conflict, translated on the international scene into the contradiction between the advanced industrial powers and the people, demonstrated, as Marxists had known all along, that the ruling classes, or on the international scene the ruling powers, would not willingly surrender their power. The United States confirmed this view when it responded militarily to verbal attacks in the Formosa Straits or intervened in, and escalated, the Vietnam War.

As the Soviet Union became the greater menace, in Peking's opinion, Mao's theory of antagonistic contradictions—contradictions whose resolution depended upon armed conflict—indicated that war between the United States and the Soviet Union might well be unavoidable. In such a case, China would prefer an American victory. This accounts for Chinese emphasis on the likelihood of war and Peking's insistence on the maintenance by the United States of its military capabilities against the Soviet Union. China did not seek war, but Maoist reasoning told Peking that war was highly likely.

At the Moscow conference of communist parties in the middle of November 1957, Mao Zedong argued that a nuclear war would be devastating but not final. It would, in fact, be progressive: "If the worst came to the worst, and half of mankind dies, the other half would remain while imperialism would be razed to the ground and the whole world would become Socialist." This was not the first time, nor was it to be the last, that the Chinese leadership argued that nuclear war was not to be feared, and Washington and its allies concluded that China's attitude toward nuclear weapons was irresponsible at best and, more likely, dangerous. Several months later, back in China, Mao spoke again:

If they are going to do [start a nuclear war] they will just do it. It will sweep the world clean of imperialism, afterwards we can rebuild again, and from that time onwards there can never be another world war. Since there is a possibility of a world war, we must be prepared and not caught asleep. Nor should we be terrified of having to fight a war. For you cannot have a battle without people getting killed.

If the contradictions between the two superpowers were more likely than not to lead to war, and if either or both were armed with nuclear weapons, there was every likelihood, Mao thought, that the war would start as, or become, a nuclear war. In that case, Mao envisioned tremendous devastation and killing. While sane minds might prevent such developments, one could not count on their prevailing in a crisis. Consequently, China had to be prepared for any eventuality; possession of nuclear weapons was essential both to China's security, and, by extension, to the interests of the Third World.[22]

Mao often said, although he was not often heard, that nuclear war was against the very logic of the capitalist system and, for that matter, the Soviet. Both systems required people for exploitation; without people, there could be no production of the wealth upon which the ruling classes in those two societies thrived. Therefore, China ought to strive to persuade the superpowers that it would be against their own self-interest to use nuclear weapons. That is why, for example, the Chinese in the mid-1960s proposed a no-first-use agreement with the United States. When the United States, in turn, asked China to sign a partial test-ban treaty, Peking interpreted this move not as an agreement not to use nuclear weapons but, rather, as a way to prevent China from developing those weapons it felt it needed to protect Chinese interests in case the United States and the Soviet Union went to war. Mao was aware that the possession of nuclear weapons operated as a deterrent. He had learned that lesson from the United States if from nowhere else.

When all was said and done, however, China could not depend upon the imperialist powers voluntarily to reject the use of the most powerful weapons in their arsenals. China and its allies, primarily in the Third World, should not be terrified into surrendering to the interests of the imperialists, however. This was the meaning of Mao's insistence that if nuclear war did come, it would be a progressive moment and socialism would survive. If the imperialist powers destroyed each other, the world would be rebuilt on the basis of socialism since the foundations of capitalism would be destroyed by the imperialists' conflict. The Maoist position, therefore, was by no means reckless or belligerent. China's attitude toward nuclear weapons was defined by the broader logic of the dialectical contradictions upon which China's analysis of the world rested.

China in the World:
The Next Stage

ON THE EVENING BEFORE October 1, 1975, China marked the twenty-sixth anniversary of the victorious revolution and the establishment of the new state. Premier Zhou Enlai, the official host for the gathering of over four thousand people in the Great Hall of the People on the Square of Heavenly Peace in Peking, was too ill to attend. Zhou was represented by Vice-premier Deng Xiaoping, who was also vice-chairman of the Central Committee of the Chinese Communist Party. Among the members of the leadership present were Jiang Qing, Chairman Mao's wife and the forceful leader of the Cultural Revolution, and Zhu De, the great military hero.

Within a year of that reception, a series of major events ushered China into a new stage in the dialectical development of its foreign policy. On January 8, 1976, Zhou Enlai died. His death opened the way for a sharp radicalization of China's internal politics. The Cultural Revolution had been characterized by tension between a so-called moderate, pragmatic approach to the restructuring of China's institutions and culture and the more radical, often extreme, policies supported by Jiang Qing and her followers. Zhou had been leader of the pragmatists, and his death removed the brakes on the radicals' drive for the total imposition of their line on both party and society. Very quickly after Zhou's death, his primary colleague and supporter, Deng Xiaoping, came under sharp attack for failing to understand the nature and process of the Cultural Revolution. Deng was accused of being a "capitalist roader," that is, a right-wing deviationist who advocated capitalist policies and looked toward the restoration of some degree of capitalism in China; the attacks were widely publicized on wall posters. As this campaign developed, Hua Guofeng, minister for public security, was appointed acting premier to replace Zhou. On April 4 and 5 popular demonstrations at the Memorial to the Revolutionary Martyrs startled Peking and the government. These demonstrations, together with those in other cities, were unusual in post-1949 Chinese political behavior. Even more unusual was the obvious sympathy the demonstrators expressed for Zhou Enlai and, by extension, for Deng Xiaoping and the policies they had pursued and advocated. By implication, the demonstrators were criticizing Jiang Qing and the radical direction in which she and her supporters were leading the Cultural Revolution and China. The government responded to the demonstrations by dismissing Deng from all his positions and appointing Hua permanent premier. Criticism of the Zhou-Deng line of moderation increased.

Mao Zedong stopped receiving foreign visitors in June, which indicated the gravity of his condition, and he died on September 6, 1976. By the middle of October it became apparent that Hua Guofeng had been named to succeed Mao as chairman of the Central Committee and of the Military Control Commission. Moreover, Jiang Qing and her immediate supporters, who later became known as the Gang of Four, were accused of attempting to carry out a coup d'etat and were placed under arrest. (They were not brought to trial, however, until November 1980).

China's new leaders confronted two primary problems from the outset. First, they had to establish their legitimacy in the party, the bureaucracy, and the country as the appropriate successors to Chairman Mao. This they accomplished in a variety of ways, among the more significant being Hua Guofeng's appointment to edit and publish Mao's works, the publication of numerous references to Mao's faith in Hua and his distrust of the Gang of Four, and an intensive campaign to discredit Hua's rivals. Second, they had to attend to the economic legacy of the period of radicalism. The intensive concentration on ideology and politics and on mass participation in the Cultural Revolution's processes of demonstration, reeducation, and popular control of institutions had left China in a state of economic, and therefore military, weakness. The new leaders believed that China was more exposed to potential threats from abroad, particularly from the Soviet Union, than before. The need to repair the economy both in order to build a healthy socialist society in China and in order to provide for the defense of the country against its enemies increasingly became the central concern of the leadership in its public utterances and in its party and government convocations. In mid-August 1977, almost a year after Mao's death, the party held its eleventh congress. It adopted a new party constitution and elected a new Central Committee, from which the Gang of Four and its supporters were notably absent. Hua Guofeng's appointments were confirmed, and Deng Xiaoping was reappointed vice-chairman, also confirming the swing away from the radical policies of the preceding period. The party and government focused their attention, at the congress and after, on the repair, reform, and development of the economy, in terms not only of production but of institutions and procedures as well.

The Cultural Revolution affected the conduct of China's foreign policy more than that policy itself. Even during Mao's last years, when Jiang Qing and her supporters were in the ascendency, Zhou Enlai and significant members of the party and government bureaucracy, such as Deng, pursued policies, particularly in foreign affairs, that did not mirror substantively the apparently radical characteristics of China's internal life. This is not to say that foreign policy was unrelated to events within China (except in the most obvious Western style cause-and-effect fashion). Rather, China's foreign policy provided the necessary dialectical variation to internal policy that permitted the Cultural Revolution to develop internally, for good or ill, without external interference in a process that certainly disturbed the equanimity of many who watched China from the position of either friend or foe. What appeared in a certain light to be a discontinuity between internal Chinese politics and China's foreign policy was, rather, a structure of acceptable, even productive, contradictions that laid the groundwork in the arena of international relations for the policies China pursued in the late 1970s and 1980s as Peking attempted to repair the damage to internal politics and to develop agriculture, industry, science and technology, and national defense. This "four modernizations campaign" provided the keynote for China's internal and external policy from the end of 1977 on.

Certain distinctions should be kept in mind in considering the course of China's foreign affairs from the beginning of the 1970s. First, immediate events and the explanations of them given by participants provide the content of any historical conjuncture we describe as a period or a situation. Such explanations contribute to, but are not the same as, the significance of the conjuncture under consideration; nor do they explain the processes that operate in the conjuncture. Second, the historical actors' behavior is rooted in the immediate historical conjuncture of their activities and in the immediate cause-and-effect relationships in which they are enmeshed. These cause-and-effect relationships certainly are a determining factor in the actors' immediate decisions, actions, and reactions; however, they cannot explain the broader historical significance of immediate actions. The actors are not guilty of bad faith in their declarations and explanations; rather, they are acting in two contexts simultaneously, and the two contexts are not completely coextensive. The first is the immediate historical conjuncture; the second is the broad historical field within which, and by which, historical conjunctures articulate with each other. A particular event's significance within a historical conjuncture is not necessarily its significance in the broader historical field within which the conjuncture itself becomes but one event. Furthermore, what may appear contradictory within a conjuncture loses its contradictory character when perceived within the broader historical field. Both Marxist ideology and its Maoist variant recognize, indeed insist upon, these distinctions. Finally, every historical conjuncture includes contradictions as well as consistencies, just as a fissure may be an integral part of a comprehensive, coherent, and even composed landscape. The emphasis on contradictions in Mao Zedong's theories and analyses reflects this perception. In this light, the contradiction internal to the Cultural Revolution between the moderate pragmatism of Zhou Enlai and the extreme ideological and behavioral radicalism of Jiang Qing is both tolerable and explicable; moreover, this contradiction existed as a consequence of the very nature of history as perceived through the lens of Marxist-Maoist theory. In the same way, the fact that China's relations with the United States took an unexpected turn toward improvement in the midst of the Cultural Revolution can be a surprise only within the time frame of the immediate historical conjuncture and the perceptions that conjuncture imposes upon those who act within it. In the broader historical field, however, the event acquires a reason that is its explanation.

The Antithesis in the Thesis:
China and the United States

The theory that contradictions are inherent in the world and in historical and, therefore, political processes provided the theoretical basis for the immediate contradiction between the Empire and the Oikoumene, on the one hand, and between the two superpowers of the Oikoumene, the Soviet Union and the United States, on the other. In this view, the sharpening of the contradictions between the two superpowers was, and is, historically inevitable and politically necessary. The notions of inevitability and necessity in this context are often misunderstood or misstated, however, and a brief clarification is required if the visit of the American president, Richard Nixon, to China in 1972 and the departure in Sino-American relations that event signified are to be perceived within the framework of Chinese policy.

     The theory of contradictions—which is a specification of the theory of the dialectic—is not a policy but an explanatory device that efficiently reconstructs the actual processes of history for the purposes of understanding and of action. Contradiction is inevitable in history not because Marxist-Maoist theory says so but because it is. The speed with which contradictions develop and deepen is a separate question: that is, the existence of contradictions and the rate of their growth are distinct issues. The concept of the speed with which contradictions develop provides the beginning of an outline of the space in which policy develops. Contradictions exist; their speed makes them apparent to observers—in short, contradictions that develop very slowly may escape the notice of the immediate observer, which does not mean that they do not exist. The detection of contradictions makes policy possible by enabling the activist to attempt to take advantage of the contradiction to further his objectives. In one sense, then, history becomes an instrument of the policymaker. The policymaker is free to act within the framework set by history in order to maximize opportunities to achieve goals by using contradictions to good effect (those contradictions providing the historical framework of action), but at the same time a dialectical relationship exists between the historical actor and history, which means that the actor can move history ahead, can take advantage of history, and can be defeated by history all within the framework of history itself. In this perspective, the deepening of the contradictions in a historical conjuncture becomes both a source of optimism about the conjuncture and an obligation placed by history on the historical actor within the conjuncture. The issue that confronts the policymaker is how to fulfill the historical obligation to maximize the advantages to be derived from the contradictions in the immediate historical conjuncture without, in the field of international relations, destroying history itself through the provocation of a globally destructive atomic war.

The two contradictions that are primary in the present conjuncture—the contradiction between China (Empire) and Oikumene and that between the two superpowers, the United States and the Soviet Union—are not equally determinative in the current historical period. The more significant contradiction is that between the United States and the Soviet Union, both because of their superior military, economic, and political power and because historical analysis predicts that they will lead each other to decline and even destruction as a consequence of the contradictions inherent in their competitive systems, competitive against each other for mastery of the rest of the world. The contradiction between China and the Oikoumene (the world of the two superpowers) is immanent; that is, it is already present in the current conjuncture but neither that contradiction nor China has developed to the point that it can supersede the primary contradiction between the United States and the U.S.S.R. That will happen only when two requirements are satisfied. First, the United States and the Soviet Union must exhaust or destroy each other. Second, China must develop to the point that it can control the consequences of the U.S.-U.S.S.R. contradiction. That point will be reached when China is modernized, and the internal vehicle for that process is the four modernizations campaign. In the meantime, the present historical conjuncture, with its primary contradiction between the United States and the Soviet Union, places certain historical (and consequently theoretical) obligations on China.

First, China must promote, and therefore contribute to the deepening of, the contradiction between the superpowers. In practical terms this means the pursuit of policies that will encourage the United States and the Soviet Union to exhaust their peoples and economies in preparation for mutual conflict and even the encouragement of conflict itself (albeit short of a conflict that would destroy the world). China can and indeed must encourage the deepening of this contradiction by taking sides with one against the other superpower when taking sides satisfies both this first objective and makes it possible for China to turn the primary contradiction to its own advantage.

Second, at the same time that it is fulfilling its first obligation in the present historical conjuncture, China must prepare itself for the new historical conjuncture that will follow without becoming so involved in the present conjuncture that Peking becomes a victim of one or the other (or both) superpowers. Therefore, China must encourage the mutual hostility of the Soviet Union and the United States and, furthermore, prevent them from finding sufficient common ground to lead them into a mutual alliance against China. That possibility assumes nightmarish proportions in the minds of Chinese policymakers both because China, at its present stage of development, would be unable to protect itself against a Soviet-American anti-Chinese alliance and because such an alliance would represent China's ultimate historical failure: the inability to turn history to China's advantage, to work with, rather than against, history. (Incidentally, such a failure would impugn the validity of the policies the Chinese have evolved to manage history in the present conjuncture; it would not impugn the historical analysis itself. Failure in this context is man's failure, not history's, and it arises from inaccurate theoretical and historico-political analysis).

This second obligation—to prepare for the future while encouraging the present contradiction to develop further and faster—takes three forms. First, China must develop its military strength, and its economic support, so that China can serve as a catalyst but avoid destruction in the conflict. The optimal fulfillment of this obligation would be a Soviet-American war at a subnuclear level at a time when China is so strong that the superpowers would agree to prevent its entering the lists on the side of either lest its strength weigh decisively against the other. A more realistic goal is the development of increasingly exhausting conflicts in Europe, Southeast Asia, Africa, and Latin America, in which the superpowers would use up their resources in military and economic competition. In any event, China must participate in the process not as a competitor but as an encourager. Chinese presence in the crucial areas has to be political; it need not be economic or military. Second, China must take advantage of one side or the other to strengthen itself, given the fact that it suffers from serious, historically induced, economic and productive inadequacies at the present time. This is a very realistic perception of the problem of development today. What distinguishes the present world of development from the past is that developing societies such as China can take advantage of the capital accumulation and technological knowledge of the advanced industrial societies to speed up their own development and do not have to depend wholly upon their own resources for the accumulation of capital and knowledge that development requires. (In the hindsight of history, one of Mao's great errors was to pursue self-reliance, that is, to insist that China develop through its own accumulation of capital and develop its own development technology *sui generis* at a time when both history and immediate political advantage suggested that China would better profit from using one or the other superpower as a basis for its own development.) Third, China must prepare for leadership in the world and contribute to the decline and destruction of the superpowers by widening its own ties throughout the world. Peking must broaden and deepen Chinese ties with the members of the Oikoumene both in order to take advantage of them for China's own economic and military growth and in order to encourage the heightening of contradictions within the Oikoumene. For example, trade with Western Europe contributes to China's growth but also heightens the contradictions within the Oikoumene by encouraging competition between Europe and the United States and by denying the United States advantages from trade with China that would help America in its present economic difficulties. Since the primary contradiction within the Oikoumene is between the United States and the Soviet Union, and since the United States seeks to encourage China to stay close to the West and to continue to oppose the Soviet Union, the Americans will not prevent the development of China's relations with Western Europe even if they find them less than advantageous to American interests and would prefer China to direct all its trade to the American market. At the same time, China must broaden and deepen its relations throughout Asia, Africa, and Latin America both to promote superpower rivalry in those areas and to provide leadership through the present conjuncture into the next one.

Chinese commentaries at the beginning of 1972 made it clear that this analysis underlay current policy and future policy planning. In an editorial on New Year's Day the *Peking People's Daily* declared:

> The world has been in a state of great upheaval in the past year. The basic contradictions in the contemporary world have sharpened. In particular, the contradictions between U.S. imperialism and Soviet revisionism on the one hand and the people of the world including the American and Soviet people on the other, and the contradictions between the two super-powers in their scramble for world hegemony and spheres of influence have become even more acute and widespread.[1]

All this was cause for immediate political and long-term historical optimism and rested firmly on historical analysis:

> The world is definitely moving towards progress and light, not towards reaction and darkness. This general trend of history can be checked by nobody. Stepping into the third year of the 70s, the people of the world see more clearly that the United States and the Soviet Union, the two overlords which have

been over-bearingly arrogant for a time, are bound to head for decline and
complete defeat. In the 50s U.S. imperialism was swashbuckling as the sole
world overlord, claiming wildly that the whole world must be put under U.S.
"leadership." In the 60s, the United States and the Soviet Union contended
for world hegemony and domination. The Soviet revisionists once alleged that
given an agreement between the leaders of the United States and the Soviet
Union, "there will be a solution of international problems on which mankind's
destinies depend." Today in the 70s, the medium-sized and small countries are
uniting against hegemony and this situation is developing; the revolutionary
struggle of the world's people against imperialism and colonialism has been
mounting as never before; the basic contradictions in the international arena
are sharpening and all the political forces are regrouping in a process of great
upheaval, great division and great reorganization.[2]

This analysis tied past Chinese policy to the present and the future. In
the 1950s, when American imperialism was "the sole world overlord,"
China's alliance with the Soviet Union was a historical necessity both for
China and for the development of the contradiction between the superpowers. Not a balance of power (or terror) but the continuity of conflict
was the consequence, and it was a progressive consequence. In the 1960s,
however, the two superpowers achieved some degree of parity in power;
that is, the conflict persisted on the basis of their own relative strengths.
Furthermore, the growth of Soviet power had led the U.S.S.R. into the
same historical role that the United States was playing. Consequently, not
only was the Sino-Soviet alliance historically no longer either justifiable or
necessary, but also the combat between the United States and the Soviet
Union now arose from their similarities and their attempts to achieve the
same objective, worldwide hegemony. China had to oppose both powers.
In the 1970s, a new situation arose that was to become clearer as the decade passed. The revolutionary situation—the contradictions in the rest of
the world—was sharpening, and China would have to provide leadership.
This meant modernizing. At the same time, it became apparent that the
Soviet Union was becoming too strong militarily and politically and that
the American side of the contradiction ("America's will to fight") was weakening. China had to weigh in on the American side by encouraging, without joining, the Americans in their opposition to the Soviet Union.
    This was the theoretical and analytical context within which a radical
departure in Sino-American relations was not only reasonable but even
required. The fact that this shift developed at the very time of American
escalation of the war in Vietnam—a war in which the Chinese were
strongly engaged politically—only emphasizes the degree to which
Chinese policy was, and is, based not upon immediate passions and advantages but upon long-range in-depth analysis and determination of historical
and, therefore, dialectical advantages.

China and the United States: A New Departure

The increasing dialectical opposition between China and the Soviet Union did not diminish the imperialistic nature of the United States in the opinion of Peking's foreign policy planners, nor did it force them to reexamine their fundamental conclusions concerning American policy. In fact, no theoretical imperative required a reevaluation either of the United States or of its foreign policy. On the contrary, as the Sino-Soviet dispute increased in acerbity and China recognized Soviet behavior as imperialist, Peking began to perceive a resemblance between American and Soviet imperialism. China understood full well that the United States and the Soviet Union were both part of the Oikoumene, even if they were in conflict with each other. From the point of view of China's historical experience with the Oikoumene, there was nothing new in this situation. Chinese policy planners did not have to ask themselves which one, the Soviet Union or the United States, was imperialist. Rather, the question was: which of the two superpowers posed a greater threat to China and its policy objectives under the present circumstances?

China's recognition of the similarity between Soviet and American foreign policy also made the Chinese aware that an American-Soviet alliance against China was not beyond the realm of possibility. The Soviet Union could no longer be considered a socialist society; it had backslid into capitalism. Therefore, any particular Soviet policy derived not from socialist ideology and values but from the requirements of the immediate historical conjuncture in which policy was being made. What was true of all capitalist states was true of the Soviet Union: foreign policy served narrow self-interest. Accordingly, China concluded that if Moscow and Washington found it to their mutual benefit, they could arrive at an understanding that would allow them to put aside their rivalry in the interest of overcoming a third power, China. Should they arrive at such an understanding and succeed in vanquishing China, they would return to their combat. Consequently, dialectical logic itself dictated in the late 1960s and the 1970s one of Peking's major foreign policy objectives, the prevention of collusion between the United States and the Soviet Union, that is, opposition to détente. In January 1975, for example, Zhou Enlai remarked: "Their fierce contention is bound to lead to war someday. The people of all countries must be prepared."[3] China could achieve its objective of preventing Soviet-American détente by entering the lists on the side of the United States. By the same token, however, China's analysis allowed it, and continues to allow it, to repair Sino-Soviet relations if such a move would benefit China's, and its friends', interests and would promote world peace without détente. In the late 1970s and early 1980s, the purpose of preventing détente seemed to China to be served best by an improvement in Sino-American relations. At another time, under different circumstances, that same purpose might be served best by an improvement in Sino-Soviet relations to the detriment of the United States. The fundamentals of China's reasoning about international relations permitted Peking great latitude in the formulation of policy. Throughout the 1970s, China perceived the Soviet Union and its social imperialism to be a greater threat to the world than was the United States. The major contradiction in the world was between the people and the superpowers. This major contradiction contained two subcontradictions, as it were: the people *versus* the United States and the people *versus* the Soviet Union. The "overdetermining contradiction" in that temporal conjuncture was the people *versus* the Soviet Union. The latter was the "main danger" for two primary reasons. First, Soviet military strength, in Chinese opinion, now surpassed the Americans'; second, the Soviet Union, clothing itself in socialist language, was far more capable than the United States of leading parts of the Third World astray. The logic of the Chinese analysis, as it developed from the late 1950s on, led Peking to conclude that a reorientation of Sino-American relations was in order. Moreover, at the beginning of the 1960s Peking judged that the election of John Kennedy, the first new American president since the Korean War, had created a good opportunity for improvement. In October 1961, therefore, Chen Yi, the Chinese foreign minister, signaled the United States that Peking continued to be interested in Sino-American discussions at the ministerial level. The new American president and his secretary of state, Dean Rusk, responded that China and the United States were already engaged in conversations at the ambassadorial level at Warsaw. Indeed, the Chinese had badly misjudged the foreign policy potential of the Kennedy administration, as the Cuban imbroglio and Kennedy's injection of the United States into the Vietnam situation demonstrated. Indeed, from China's point of view the Kennedy administration's foreign policy, at least as it pertained to China, was no less reactionary than the previous administration's, and at moments it seemed to contain greater threats to world peace. Moreover, at the United Nations the Kennedy administration continued the policy of preventing the entry of China into the United Nations. At the beginning of August 1963, Kennedy himself made it clear that the United States viewed China with great alarm:

> I would regard that combination, if it is still in existence in the 1970's, of weak countries around it, 700 million people, a Stalinist internal regime, and nuclear powers, and a government determined on war as a means of bringing about its ultimate success, as potentially a more dangerous situation than any we have faced since the end of the Second War, because the Russians pursued in most cases their ambition with some caution.[4]

President Kennedy's assassination and the succession of Lyndon Johnson did not appreciably change American policies and attitudes. America's continued support for Formosa and its constantly escalating role in Vietnam were facts, in China's eyes, that no American words could change. Clearly, the Chinese were waiting for a change in the United States. Foreign Minister Chen Yi explained on September 29, 1965, "It is up to the U.S. President and the Pentagon to decide whether the United States wants a big war with China today. . . . For sixteen years we have been waiting for the U.S. imperialists to come in and attack us. My hair has turned grey in waiting."[5] Each side was trying to contain the other. Each side rejected verbal gestures of moderation from the other. Well into the next administration, moreover, the U.S. government continued to insist that the major enemy in Vietnam was China, and China certainly needed no proof that the United States was the primary combatant on the other side in South Vietnam. The Vietnam War and American activities in Southeast Asia were barriers that neither China nor Washington could overcome.

The election of Richard Nixon, a conservative Republican whose political career had been made as an anticommunist, provided the opportunity for a shift in America's China policy. The receding of the high tide of the Cultural Revolution and the return of the Chinese diplomatic establishment to full activity opened up similar opportunities for new departures in China's America policy. The ninth congress of the Chinese Communist Party, held in April 1969, brought the Cultural Revolution to a formal, if not a real, end. In July, on the island of Guam, President Nixon enunciated the Nixon Doctrine, according to which the United States henceforth would not allow itself to become involved in situations like Vietnam. The Nixon administration next signaled Peking that it was eager to find a new basis for conversations. It had become clear that Chinese participation would be necessary for any solution to the Vietnam War, and Washington indicated this by slightly reducing the size of the American military forces in Vietnam at the same time that it relaxed restrictions on travel to, and trade with, China. In a major foreign policy address to Congress in February 1971, Nixon stated that China had to be brought into a "constructive relationship with the world community."[6]

THE BREAKTHROUGH

Indications of significant change in Chinese policy came gradually, tentatively, and subtly in the course of 1971, before Peking published its January 1, 1972 theoretical analysis (see above). In April 1971, during the world championship ping-pong games in Japan, the U.S. team was included, with Washington's approval, in an invitation to several teams to visit mainland China. Premier Zhou Enlai himself received the group, explaining that "your visit to China on invitation has opened the door to friendly contacts between the people of the two countries. We believe that such friendly contacts will be favored and supported by the majority of the two peoples."[7] The message could not have been clearer, and on April 14, only four days after the ping-pong team arrived in China, Washington relaxed the embargo on trade with China. Three American scientists visited China in May after going to North Vietnam, and in June a group of American students and their wives were granted Chinese visas. On June 10, the Americans published a list of goods that could be traded freely to China, and on July 15, the American president, in a nationwide television broadcast, announced that he had accepted an invitation to visit the People's Republic. All this occurred without diplomatic recognition.

The euphoria with which the sudden change in the Sino-American relationship was greeted in the United States was matched by cold realism in China. The Chinese analysis of American policy had not changed, as Peking continued to indicate throughout the rest of 1971, reminding the United States that Formosa remained a central issue dividing the two powers. Nonetheless, the Chinese moves created an atmosphere in which both Washington and Peking began to consider the possibility and advisability of a visit by President Nixon to China, even though formal diplomatic relations between the two did not exist and the United States continued to recognize and support the Chinese Nationalist regime on Taiwan. Henry Kissinger, the American president's primary foreign affairs adjutant, made two visits to China to lay the groundwork for the president's visit. Kissinger's first trip was secret, evidently arranged through the Pakistani government. The president's visit was announced for February 21, 1972, and while the Chinese were extremely modest in their expectations, the trip excited considerble anticipation and interest in the United States. In January, an advance party arrived in Peking to make final preparations; the group included General Alexander Haig, the deputy assistant for national security affairs.

Nixon's historic visit to China took place February 21-28, 1972 and was formal and fairly low-key. Nixon was accompanied by a broad spectrum of American officials, including the secretary of state, William Rogers. The president met most of China's top leaders and spent an hour with Mao Zedong in what was described by official spokesmen as a frank and serious "exchange of views." Zhou Enlai and Nixon held long discussions, as did the Chinese foreign minister and the American secretary of state. A short tour of eastern China preceded the Americans' departure from Shanghai on February 28. Discussions took place throughout the week at various levels, covering the broad range of topics that divided the two countries. Zhou went to great pains to explain the Chinese perception of the world

to the Americans. For example, in a toast to President Nixon at a ceremonial banquet, he stated:

> The social systems of China and the United States are fundamentally different,
> and there exist great differences between the Chinese government and the
> United States government. However, these differences should not hinder
> China and the United States from establishing normal state relations on the
> basis of the Five Principles of mutual respect for sovereignty and territorial
> integrity, mutual non-aggression, non-interference in each other's internal af-
> fairs, equality and mutual benefit, and peaceful co-existence; still less should
> they lead to war.[8]

This was a clear statement, unencumbered by ideological vocabulary,
of the theory of dialectical contradictions and its application to foreign
policy.

The conclusions of the Sino-American discussions were published in
the now famous joint *Shanghai Communiqué*, which set the stage for the
new relationship's further development. The communiqué followed a pattern that both fitted the Chinese analysis of historical and international
reality and avoided creating situations in which the two parties, by trying
to agree, would have to conclude that consensus was impossible. It described the essential policies of each government, on the basis of which
further relations would be developed. Peking reiterated its position on
Formosa, and the United States, for its part, recognized that there was
only one China, that Formosa was a part of that China, and that it was
interested in a peaceful settlement of the question by the Chinese themselves. Moreover, Washington affirmed "the ultimate objective of the
withdrawal of all U.S. forces and military installations from Taiwan."[9] The
two sides also agreed to a set of general principles on the basis of which
they would try to improve their relationship. These principles were not
identical with, but derived from, the famous Five Principles of Peaceful
Coexistence. Finally, Washington and Peking agreed on future steps, including the development of exchanges and trade and the maintenance of
official contact through the dispatch, from time to time, of a senior American official to Peking. The entire communiqué was a refraction, in the
1970s, of the history of China's relations with the rest of the world. The
historical echoes were powerful. For example, the declaration by each side
of its position in parallel but nonconflicting form recalled the arrangements
developed in long negotiations in the first two decades of the eighteenth
century to manage Sino-Russian relations through Kyakhta. The pursuit of
exchanges and trade, together with the dispatch of a senior American official to Peking from time to time, resembled nothing less than the traditional tribute system. This is not to suggest that the Chinese, and certainly
not the Americans, had these models in mind but, rather, that the struc-

tures of behavior characteristic of Chinese political culture naturally reasserted themselves in the ambiguous situation Washington and Peking confronted in this new stage of their relationship.

In the months and years immediately following the Nixon visit, China and the United States explored more and more forms of contact, and the traffic between the two countries grew considerably, even if, at the beginning, very tentatively. Scholars, journalists, athletes, and merchants visited China. Secretary of State Kissinger returned to Peking in the middle of February 1973, at which time he visited Chairman Mao. Contact had now reached a level requiring more permanent arrangements even while the fiction of non-recognition had to be maintained if only because of the continuing American relationship with Taiwan. Immediately after Kissinger's visit, the two governments announced that each would establish a liaison office in the other's capital. With time these offices assumed all the structures and functions of embassies, although the official designation could come only with formal diplomatic recognition. Indeed, the formal act of recognition that would change their status from liaison offices to embassies would not affect their internal structures or functions. Increased travel between the two countries, official and semi-official visits, and a general opening of communications characterized Sino-American relations for the rest of the 1970s. All this began before the death of Mao Zedong, while the Cultural Revolution continued to affect China's internal institutions and while the leadership group later excoriated as The Gang of Four was still in power. New departures in Sino-American relations obviously did not depend upon changes in China's ideological commitments, much less upon Peking's abandonment of its analysis of world politics.

With the establishment of the liaison offices, which both resulted from, and contributed to, the growth of Sino-American interaction on all levels, the full range of institutions necessary for the pursuit of normal relations between Peking and Washington was in place, lacking only Western style formalization. In Western practice the relations still lacked legitimacy insofar as formal diplomatic recognition had not been exchanged. This ambiguity was worth tolerating, however, since it permitted constructive interaction with China along with continued American commitment to the regime on Formosa. There was nothing strange or discomfiting in these arrangements from the point of view of traditional Chinese diplomatic practice. President Gerald Ford's trip to Peking in December 1975 demonstrated just how regularized, if not warm, the two countries' relationship had become. From the Chinese perspective, the visit was a tributary mission from a new ruler announcing his accession to power. In the American view, it was a traditional presidential visit abroad. The vicissitudes of the Sino-American relationship now exhibited "normality," and, of course, as in any bilateral diplomatic relationship, certain issues from time to time strained relations; in the Sino-American case, these were, primarily, the

Vietnam War and continued American recognition of the Taipei government. In this regard, the Sino-American relationship was no different from, for example, a relationship as old and close as the American relationship with Canada, which also showed occasional strain over long-term issues of profound disagreement. The structure, in other words, functioned precisely as it was supposed to function; it mediated the communication of problems and provided for interaction leading to their resolution or postponement. Similarly, internal political developments were often refracted through the diplomatic relationship onto the international scene. Sino-American relations in general, and exchanges in particular, showed signs of strain induced by the radicalization of China's internal politics in the last years of Mao Zedong's life, particularly as he became less active on the political scene. This international refraction of internal developments is a normal function of the diplomatic apparatus, however, as the impact of the election of Ronald Reagan to the American presidency in November 1980 demonstrated in the case of both China and the Soviet Union, when the prospect of a different leadership in Washington had an unsettling effect on Washington's relations with the other two powers.

Despite the improvement in relations between Washington and Peking, the Chinese continued to make clear their consciousness that the United States was an imperialist power with which improvement of relations was a strategic move that in no way altered China's fundamental perception of the world. Chinese criticisms of American policy and behavior in Vietnam, as well as criticisms of American-Soviet détente, were not softened by the improvement of relations at the formal level. Nevertheless, Peking was aware that a strong United States was the only force capable of dealing with the primary threat, the Soviet Union, and China urged the United States to maintain its defenses around the world, to improve its economic situation, to strengthen the dollar, and to preserve its military alliances.

NORMALIZATION

Despite the normality of Sino-American intercourse, the diplomatic struture's lack of legitimacy in traditional Western terms gave the Chinese an instrument with which to achieve one of Peking's most cherished political objectives, the resolution, in China's favor, of the status of Taiwan. That resolution required that the United States withdraw recognition from Taipei and transfer it to Peking. Diplomatic recognition was nothing more, and nothing less, than a vehicle for Washington's acceptance of Peking's legitimacy. The term "normalization" came to denote this development. Once again Peking was to use, as it had in the 1860s and after, Western law and diplomatic practice to achieve Chinese objectives.

Before normalization could take place, certain "objective conditions" had to be satisfied. First, the Vietnam War, long an issue in Sino-American relations, had to be resolved in a fashion acceptable to China, and, by virtue of the American rout, it was. Second, and paradoxically, new leadership, less wedded to the Taipei regime, was needed in Washington. The paradox lay in the ambiguities not of the Sino-American relationship but of Republican President Richard Nixon's own politics and commitments. As noted widely at the time, it was precisely Nixon's long record of conservatism and anticommunism that made it possible for him to begin a sharp departure away from Sino-American animosity without being accused in his domestic backyard of being "soft on communism." At the same time, the Republican Party and Nixon himself had strongly supported Chiang Kaishek's and the Guomindang's interests in the United States, so Nixon could take bold measures to open the *possibility* for normal relations between the United States and China, but he could not normalize those relations in the Western sense, as the Chinese insisted, without creating serious political difficulties at home and transgressing a major principle of his own political career. (His career suggests that he would have done the latter if it would not have had serious political consequences for him, but it would have and he did not.) The election of Jimmy Carter to the presidency in November 1976 resolved this problem by providing new leadership in Washington.

Almost immediately following the Carter election, members of the U.S. Senate began calling for normalization of relations with Peking. This was important both politically and legally since the Senate was responsible for foreign policy insofar as the legislative branch of the American government was concerned. Moreover, some senators, with Chinese encouragement, began to create the rationale that would make such a move possible. This rationale had two components. During Carter's campaign, and in subsequent pronouncements by both the president-elect and various other leaders, reference was made to the need for normalizing relations with Peking while not "abandoning" Taiwan. The use of this last term created an opportunity to define an American relationship with Taiwan that, like the prenormalization relationship with Peking, would have the substance of diplomatic ties without the formal legitimacy conferred by recognition. International precedence existed for this in Japan's transfer of recognition from Taipei to Peking in the fall of 1972. This first component, which made normalization possible, had to be accompanied by a second, a reason for the action that would override the American commitment to Taiwan. That reason was the growth of Soviet strength and power, perceived as an increasing threat to the United States. In the weeks after the American presidential election the Chinese succeeded in convincing at least one group of U.S. senators that the Soviet threat had grown so great that it took precedence over the issue of Taiwan. While China would never surrender its position on Taiwan, it would agree, in the face of a threat that increasingly endangered both the United States and China, not to insist on the return of the island to Chinese control as part of an arrangement that would permit the United States and China to cooperate more closely. Nothing in the existing arrangement, of course, precluded cooperation, but American desire to legitimate the Washington-Peking relationship allowed the Chinese to move a step closer to their goal in the Formosa Straits and, at the same time, to encourage the United States to oppose the Soviet Union more vigorously. Now it became apparent to the Americans that China was more important to the interests of the United States than was Taiwan.

Little real progress was made toward normalization in the first two years of the Carter administration. In fact, a visit by Secretary of State Cyrus Vance to Peking in August 1977 was widely regarded as a setback, primarily because of American inability to come to terms with the Taiwan problem. At the same time, the presence of Zbigniew Brzezinski in the position of assistant to the president for national security affairs contributed to the development of the rationale for normalization. Brzezinski was widely regarded as anti-Soviet, doubtful about détente with the Soviet Union, and eager to cooperate with China in the development of a forceful approach to Moscow. He visited Peking in May 1978 and apparently made common cause with the Chinese. Indeed, the difference between the attitudes of Vance and Brzezinski toward Peking, as shown both by their receptions in China and by their statements about U.S.-China relations, reflected their divergence in Washington over issues like détente and strategic arms limitation agreements with Moscow.

The Brzezinski position won the day. On December 16, 1978, a joint Sino-American communiqué announced to the world the establishment of formal diplomatic relations between Washington and Peking as of January 1, 1979, and the exchange of ambassadors on March 1, 1979. The announcement was so sudden—negotiations evidently continued right up to the last moment—that Chiang Chingkuo, the president of the Nationalist Chinese regime in Taipei, was informed of this development by phone at 2:00 A.M. that very morning.

The communiqué spelled out the conditions for normalization. Washington recognized the government of the People's Republic of China as the sole legitimate government of all China. Furthermore, Washington acknowledged (agreeing, again, to set aside final resolution until a later date) Peking's claim that Taiwan was an integral part of China. The United States agreed to break all official relations with the Taipei regime but planned to continue economic relations on an unofficial basis. In return for this major victory, Peking made three concessions that Washington could use to defend itself against criticism. The Americans could end their relationship with Taiwan on the basis of the stipulations in the legal documents embodying that relationship, primarily a treaty of mutual defense and friendship. Peking did not contradict the unilateral American statement regarding expectations of a peaceful resolution to the Taiwan problem. Finally, Peking did not note, thereby allowing normalization to proceed, an American statement that Washington would continue to supply Taiwan with defensive weapons even beyond the termination of the Washington-Taipei relationship. The Carter administration received relatively minor criticism for the move. China had scored a major victory by using tactics that were well tested in its historical experience. And the United States apparently had succeeded in legitimating its relationship with Peking without in any way substantively changing that relationship.

DENG IN THE UNITED STATES

Slightly more than one year after normalization, a high-ranking Chinese official made the first formal Chinese visit to the United States since 1949. Deng Xiaoping was rapidly emerging as the real power in Peking. Equally important, he played the role of Zhou Enlai's successor, carrying out reforms and instituting programs that were extensions of the late premier's pragmatism and emphasis on economic development; he also wished to liquidate the negative consequences of the Cultural Revolution. Deng's importance in the evolution of China's internal politics must not be minimized, but the real significance of his visit to the United States lay elsewhere.

In the dialectical progression of Chinese history, particularly the history of China after 1949, the era of pragmatism and economic growth that followed upon the Cultural Revolution was a logical development for two reasons. First, the Cultural Revolution had cost China dearly in terms of personnel—the loss of education and training among cadres who had had to spend years in political retraining or in agricultural labor—and in terms of economic growth and modernization. This loss had to be overcome through a rigorous pragmatism in economic development, which required that the social and political conditions necessary to encourage development be created. This was one hallmark of the new era, and Deng Xiaoping's power rested to no small extent on his advocacy of this position. Second, the era of the Cultural Revolution had been marked—overdetermined in Marxist terms—by the struggle for cultural change, involving social order, political institutions, culture in the narrower sense of the term (the arts), and individual mental attitudes. Mao Zedong believed that this overdetermination was historically necessary to avoid bureaucratization of Chinese government and party life, which would stifle and deform the genius of the revolution. In this sense, the Cultural Revolution was the dialectical consequence of the form and content of change during the preceding period of construction, and its emblem was Mao himself and, with radicalization, his wife, Jiang Qing. It is next to impossible to determine, at this time, the degree to which the Cultural Revolution achieved its objectives in terms of the definition of those objectives from within the period of the Cultural Revolution itself and as defined against the structures of the previous period that Mao wished to dismantle or change. Future historians may argue that without the Cultural Revolution, China in an age of pragmatic enonomic development based upon capital and technology from the capitalist world would itself have run the risk of a return to capitalism, much as China has accused the Soviet Union of returning, for other reasons, to a capitalist way of life and culture. On the other hand, the baleful influences of the Cultural Revolution on China's economic and social life were apparent for all to see, and—still arguing within the framework of Marxist theory—it was the function of the next (now the present) period to liquidate the negative results and reverse the trends of the previous dialectical period. In this sense, the post–Cultural Revolution period had a real historical legitimacy within Marxist-Maoist theory, and the drive to liquidate the immediate past and its leaders was neither a betrayal nor an arbitrary reversal; nor could it be described, in any sense, as China's coming to its senses. This next phase was reasonable, logical, and legitimate.

Deng Xiaoping, the historical emblem and leader of the new era, derived his legitimacy from the Marxist-Maoist view of history, as both his career and his political behavior showed. As the primary figure in Zhou Enlai's entourage during the last years of his life and as the expositor of Zhou's ideas and inheritor of his mantle, Deng, even in the course of the Cultural Revolution, was clearly a flag bearer of one-half of the thesis-antithesis dichotomy whose other half was, eventually, Jiang Qing and her Gang of Four. The thesis and antithesis are always present in each other, Marxism-Maoism argues, and the vicissitudes of Deng's career charted the course of the antagonism between them. Deng's emergence as the new leader signified both a dialectical turn in Chinese affairs and the legitimacy of that turn within the structure of the Chinese philosophy of history and politics. Furthermore, his visit to the United States signified, to China, that the new era was to be marked by Chinese development based fully upon the resources of the advanced capitalist-technological world within the contemporary structure of world politics, in which the primary contradiction centered on the United States and the U.S.S.R. Americans, in their optimism, interpreted the visit as indicative of China's coming to its senses and turning toward a reasonable approach to economic organization. They defined "reasonable" as something approaching capitalism and American values. American commentators did not understand that, in the Marxist-Maoist mind, history is a process whose purposes the United States could serve, if it would; Deng's visit was intended to encourage Washington to do so.

Vice-Premier Deng arrived in the United States on January 29, 1979, and he stayed until February 4. His activities during this period focused on his purpose of turning the United States into an instrument of Chinese history in its present phase. On January 31 he and President Carter signed agreements that, in their sum, described Chinese desiderata during the first stage of cooperation and laid the institutional groundwork for that co-operation. Provisions covered cultural exchanges and scientific and tech-nological cooperation in "agriculture, energy, space, health, environment, earth sciences, engineering and other areas of science and technology,"[10] as well as in high-energy physics. Two institutional structures were agreed upon. First, a joint commission on cooperation in the scientific and tech-nological fields was established to meet annually, alternately in the United States and in China. Second, consular establishments were to be set up by each country in the other. Deng clearly emphasized the close relationship, in the Chinese view, between science and politics. Speaking to the Senate Foreign Relations Committee during his stay in Washington, the vice-pre-mier said that China would collect intelligence information about the So-viet Union and share it with Washington if the Americans would provide the advanced technology necessary for the task. The international impli-cations of the new relationship were apparent in Deng's statement that the United States must not place its faith in the Salt-II agreement as a means of containing Soviet expansion. Deng clearly wanted to deflect the Ameri-cans from détente. During the rest of his trip Deng visited Atlanta, Hous-ton, and Seattle, cultivating in each place industrial and business interest in participation in China's development. Most striking was his style, which combined the rigorous pragmatism of a powerful businessman with a touch of the burlesque that could easily have been interpreted as the mark of an unsophisticated tourist (Deng visited a rodeo in Texas and donned a ten-gallon hat). This approach could not have been better calculated to spark the imagination of Americans from many walks of life.

Deng's visit stimulated American participation in China. In April, an agreement between the University of California and Peking University gave formal structure to many kinds of academic exchange, and universi-ties like Stanford began to receive significant numbers of Chinese students at advanced graduate and research levels, primarily in scientific and tech-nological fields. A Sino-American trade agreement was signed on July 7, 1979, and in October the Carter administration requested Congress to ap-prove the agreement and, by direct implication, to grant China "most fa-vored nation" status. This meant that the Americans now were prepared to develop their relationship with China despite, and even because of, Amer-ican-Soviet relations. Washington was no longer evenhanded, to quote of-ficial rhetoric, in its attitude toward Moscow and Peking. The relationship with China had become a major element in the American posture in the world and in Washington's global strategy. This was precisely what Peking had wanted, because both political necessity and dialectical reasoning re-quired the deepening of the contradiction between the United States and the Soviet Union.

Opposition to Hegemonism: Moscow and Peking

The stormy conditions characteristic of the relationship between China and the Soviet Union in the 1960s can be seen, from the perspective of the next period, as a process through which the Chinese government and party leadership sought to define the Soviet Union's contemporary historical role. The broad consistency of China's analysis of the Soviet Union in the world, despite dramatic changes in China's internal politics in the mid-1970s, suggests once again the profundity of the historico-ideological roots of China's view of the world and of itself in the world.

The term that became the sign of China's analysis of the Soviet Union was hegemonism. In the dichotomy China (Empire)-Oikoumene, in which both the United States and the Soviet Union were politically, economically, and technologically part of the same First World, the two superpowers were struggling for hegemony both within the Oikoumene and throughout the world. In this context the Soviet Union and the United States were behaving in a remarkably similar fashion, although, obviously, neither recognized this. At the same time, the particular condition of a society's "being in the world" and the policies that actualized that condition had, according to Marxist-Maoist theory, to refract the nature, the structure, of the society. The Soviet Union, according to the Chinese, had backslid into capitalism, but it was not, or at least was not yet, a capitalist country in the sense that the United States was capitalist. This meant that however much Soviet policy in the world resembled American policy, and however synonymous the two states' political intentions may have been, there was an objective difference between them; that is, the objective conditions of each society differed and this objective difference was necessarily refracted in their respective international policies. A terminological distinction must indicate this difference. Both the United States and the Soviet Union were struggling for world domination, including domination over each other. The first arena in which the struggle was being waged was the First World itself, the Oikoumene. The second was the broader world, primarily the Third, or developing, World, itself containing a subset of societies, the socialist camp. Both superpowers were imperialist, or sought world domination within these various arenas. The United States was imperialist pure and simple, if only because imperialism was the way in which an advanced industrial power of the Oikoumene was in the world, by very definition; capitalism, with all its internal contradictions, dictated this. The Soviet Union was also imperialist, but because it was not a wholly capitalist society, its imperialism was of a different kind, although no less pernicious; indeed, if anything it was more pernicious because the Soviet Union's "being in the world" was described by Moscow in language that tried to make the U.S.S.R. appear nonimperialistic. As we saw previously, this particular Soviet form of imperialism was designated hegemonism or social imperialism. In many ways, Soviet imperialism was far more dangerous than American imperialism precisely because it masked Moscow's true intentions behind a screen of Marxist terminology. The Soviets attempted to use the national liberation struggles of the Third World for their own purposes, while the United States, for its part, opposed directly the national liberation movements and represented itself to the world more honestly, with less deception. This did not make American policy in the world any more acceptable, only more honest. There was a difference. Sometimes the use of terminology became sloppy, and one term could spill over into a reference to the other reality, so that the United States might also be guilty of hegemonism. But the distinction nonetheless remained valid.

The objectivity of this distinction, as represented by these terms, combined with the perception of history as a process that can be described and—if the will, analysis, and strategies are present—managed, explained how China could vociferously oppose American imperialism while seeking American cooperation and participation in Chinese economic development. It also explained how the continuing conflict between China and the Soviet Union could appear most striking in the domain of ideology and in interparty relationships while the two states, as governments, maintained normal, even though not friendly, relationships. The course of Sino-Soviet relations in the last years of Mao's rule and in the new stage illustrated this as clearly as did Sino-American relations.

The Chinese analysis of the Soviet Union and its intentions derived from a philosophical position that underlay both the Cultural Revolution and the next, pragmatic, period of Chinese politics. Consequently, China's perspective on the Soviet Union did not change. China was, and remained, fully aware of the military threat the Soviet Union posed to China directly, as a consequence of Soviet social imperialism and hegemonism. This threat constituted a real and present danger to China. China's policy toward the Soviet Union at the state-to-state (government-to-government) level had the primary objective, therefore, of avoiding the deterioration of relations to the point that the Soviet Union would feel that it should, or could, attack China. China was equally aware of its own weakness, and détente with the United States, beginning in 1971–1972, served the purpose of making a potential Soviet attack on China seem so costly to the Soviet Union that Moscow would not consider the possibility. The concept of cost to the Soviet Union had to rest on two assumptions. First, sufficient doubt had to be raised concerning American intentions in case war broke out between Moscow and Peking that Moscow would think twice before initiating such an attack. Moscow had to be kept in doubt concerning the probability of an American attack on the Soviet Union at precisely the time the Soviet Union would have committed its military power to the very difficult task (the Japanese had shown how difficult a task it would be) of conquering China. The growth of a Sino-American relationship would serve to increase the scope of doubt in Moscow's thinking. Second, China had to modernize so that Peking itself could make a Soviet attack appear so costly that the Soviet Union would resist temptation. The development of Chinese nuclear weaponry certainly was important for China's self-esteem in a world in which military power was defined largely in terms of the possession of nuclear arsenals. More immediately significant, however, was the fact that the greater China's nuclear potential, the more costly a Soviet attack on China would appear to Soviet interests.

Moscow, in all probability, shared China's objective of avoiding conflict. The Soviet Union did not intend to become involved in the long and exceedingly painful process of attempting to conquer China. Certainly the U.S.S.R. lacked the economic resources to engage in prolonged conflict, and the inability to improve significantly the performance of Soviet agriculture left Moscow little margin for large-scale foreign adventures. The growth of the Sino-American relationship fostered the intended doubt in Soviet planning, too. As Moscow suggested in 1971, "Western commentators consider that Peking has started a complicated diplomatic game. However . . . there is nothing complicated about it."[11]

Throughout the 1970s, therefore, Moscow and Peking continued to keep the potential of armed conflict to a minimum by engaging in negotiations over specific issues in contention. These issues were, by and large, the kind over which governments traditionally have contended. For example, the two governments conducted negotiations by joint commissions and visiting teams about delineation of the Sino-Soviet frontier and resolution of conflicting territorial claims along the frontier. Trade continued at a minimal level necessary to avoid total rupture. Even incidents of espionage were contained by confining the dispute to invective. For example, in March 1974 Moscow announced that a Soviet helicopter had strayed accidentally over the border with Xinjiang. Although Moscow claimed the helicopter had been on a humanitarian mission, Peking insisted that it was an armed reconnaissance vehicle that had actually landed on Chinese territory. This kind of incident was of the sort that normally occurs between hostile but nonbelligerent powers.

Chinese accusations against Soviet policy greatly resembled accusations Peking had made against Washington in the 1950s and 1960s. In one medium or another Peking accused Moscow of trying to encircle China and of building up its various forms of military strength for the purposes of aggression against China and for the pursuit of imperialist designs in the Third World. As the 1970s progressed, Chinese attacks on the Soviet Union broadened to include arguments similar to those being made by the Americans. In January 1974, for example, the Chinese press began to comment on dissidence in the Soviet Union, attacking Moscow in terms strongly reminiscent of those used by American sources critical of the

U.S.S.R. for oppressing workers and peasants and for using psychiatric hospitals to handle dissidents.

Throughout this same period China refined its analysis of the roots of Soviet policy. In the first part of 1974, *Red Flag*, the Chinese Communist Party's ideological journal, defined the Soviet system as "state monopoly capitalism" whose international expression was "Soviet revisionist social imperialism." On March 6, the *People's Daily*, using a more popular language, stated that "the present Soviet Union is a dictatorship of the bourgeoisie, a dictatorship of the big capitalists, a German fascist dictatorship and a Hitler type dictatorship." Claiming to quote Mao directly the newspaper strongly reflected the emphasis Maoist thought gave to intention and mental constructs. Since the Soviet Union was "state monopoly capitalism," the statement that the U.S.S.R. was a bourgeois and big capitalist dictatorship referred directly to the state of mind induced by that socioeconomic system—a state of mind and, consequently, behavior that belonged in the same category as American capitalism.[12]

China's analysis of Soviet society and behavior was by no means rigid and inflexible, however. Marxism, as well as its Maoist variant, has always been an evolving system of analysis, responding to external change and to greater accuracy of observation and definition. Thus, for example, in November 1979 Peking said the Soviet Union was a socialist country because the means of production in the Soviet Union were owned by the state; consequently, Soviet policy fell within the analysis of socialism and was not necessarily revisionist (that is, formerly socialist). However, Soviet foreign policy was still considered social imperialism; that is, the structure of the U.S.S.R.'s international relationships and the definition of Moscow's political objectives on the international scene were imperialist, albeit within the Oikoumene's socialist camp. This analytical modification took place at a time when the Sino-Soviet state-to-state relationship was not as tense as it had been at other periods, but the two developments were not necessarily related in a cause-and-effect fashion. State relationships may be influenced by theoretical analysis, just as theoretical analysis may be influenced by changes in state relationships, but there is no necessary connection between the two. Failure to recognize this point often has led Western observers either into overreading ideological pronouncements in terms of political import or into undervaluing the import of political events because of ideological considerations.

China and Western Europe

Far removed though Europe may be from the Far East, the crucial role of Western Europe in Chinese foreign policy reflects both the global analysis that underlies that policy and the global reach of the immediate concerns that China's policy reflects. Several considerations guided the development of China's policy toward Western Europe, all of them direct spinoffs of China's policy toward the Soviet Union and the United States. First, China saw Western Europe as a potential third force against the Soviet Union, allied with, but distinct from, the United States and China itself. Western Europe obviously had emerged from the client status that may have defined its relationship with the United States in, for example, the 1950s. Economically and, potentially, militarily, it now occupied a position of strong independence from Washington. Therefore, the strength of Western European opposition to Soviet interests was a crucial factor in Chinese global strategy. Second, the depth and steadfastness of the American commitment to oppose the Soviet Union anywhere and everywhere was subject to doubt; moreover, the mental consequences of the American defeat in Vietnam and the economic consequences for America both of the Vietnam War and of the exacerbation of the contradictions within capitalism, particularly American capitalism, inhibited American policy. China needed to be assured that Western Europe could compensate for potential American weakness on the Soviet Union's western flank. Third, Western Europe was also a part of the Oikoumene since it belonged to the world of advanced industrial technology. Moreover, it was economically successful and capable of contributing to Chinese development in cooperation or competition with the United States. Indeed, China might be able to satisfy its needs for foreign capital and technology less expensively in Europe than in the United States; at the very least Western Europe was an additional source of development capital for China. For all these reasons, therefore, throughout the 1970s Peking very actively cultivated its relationships with Western Europe in various ways. This policy encompassed relations with individual states, relations with the European Economic Community (the EEC or the Common Market), and strong support for the maintenance and expansion of NATO as the primary European military formation opposed to the Soviet Union.

The first Western head of state to visit China was Georges Pompidou, president of France, who arrived in Peking on September 11, 1973, for a one-week stay. The importance the Chinese attached to this event was indicated by the fact that Pompidou and Chairman Mao Zedong spent two hours together, longer than Mao was accustomed to receive foreign visitors. Despite numerous broad areas of disagreement between China and France, particularly over policy toward the Soviet Union, Peking made it clear that it considered European unity extraordinarily desirable in the face of the Soviet menace. Zhou Enlai, speaking at a banquet for Pompidou on September 11, declared, "We . . . support the people of European countries in uniting themselves to safeguard their independence. We are for the view that the cause of European unity, if it is carried out well, will contribute to the improvement of the situation in Europe and the whole world."[13] China cultivated relations with individual European states toward the end of gaining not only their increased participation in an anti-Soviet coalition but also Chinese access to their capital and technology. Thus, for example, in February 1975 France began development of a petrochemical project in China. Helmut Schmidt, chancellor of West Germany, visited China at the end of October and beginning of November 1975. Having expressed support for many of each other's policies, including Chinese support for German policy toward Berlin and the reunification of Germany, the two sides signed agreements for the training of Chinese engineers and technicians in West Germany and for the manufacture in China of such West German machines as industrial turbines. European companies were encouraged to invest, or establish branches, in China. Frequent visits to China by European leaders from various political, economic, and military domains and return visits by Chinese leaders promoted military and political cooperation between China and individual European states. European countries began, in the late 1970s, to sell certain military goods to China, as well as to increase their economic investments in China or in joint ventures with Chinese enterprises.

At the same time that China developed state relations with European governments on a bilateral basis, Peking pursued relations with the Common Market both to obtain economic advantage and to encourage European unity. At the beginning of 1975, for example, the Dutch foreign minister returned from a visit to Peking to announce that China wanted to establish permanent relations with the Common Market. In September 1975 China formally recognized the Common Market when the Chinese ambassador to Belgium presented his credentials to the president of the Council of Ministers of the European Economic Community (EEC). In contrast, Moscow had no diplomatic relations with the EEC and sharply accused China of trying to injure the economic development of the socialist camp by encouraging the Common Market. In February 1978, China and the Common Market signed a trade agreement according to which China was granted "most favored nation" status. The agreement also stipulated the establishment of an EEC-Chinese commission to encourage trade and resolve differences between the Common Market and China. At the end of February 1979, Roy Jenkins, president of the EEC Commission, visited China and met with both Premier Hua Guofeng and Vice-Premier Deng Xiaoping. Jenkins announced that the first meeting of the China-EEC joint committee would take place in May. By 1980, therefore, China was well embarked upon a policy of close economic relations with Western Europe as an alternative to reliance solely upon the United States. Moreover, there were, throughout the late 1970s, signs that the United States, far from being averse to this development, encouraged it; Europe could serve as a source of goods for China, particularly military goods, that the United States could not provide for reasons of international politics, especially American relations with Moscow.

China was no less interested in the strengthening of NATO, particularly as American resolve or ability to maintain a powerful presence in Europe came into question. In declaration after declaration, the Chinese leadership encouraged the United States to maintain its strength in Europe, as well as elsewhere in the world, and urged the strengthening of NATO as a countervailing force in Europe to the Warsaw Pact.

China and the Third World

For China, the Third World is the arena of the future in the present. This has two meanings. First, the Third World is one of the environments in which the two superpowers, the United States and the Soviet Union, struggle for world domination. It is not necessarily, or always, the most important field of battle, but it is always a field of battle. Each superpower needs the resources and productive capacities of the Third World for the satisfaction of its own economic and industrial needs, that is, each exploits the Third World, and in ways that are not dissimilar. Thus, for example, American capitalist economic exploitation of Third World resources parallels Soviet exploitation of resources through interest-bearing (and therefore profit-making) loans that often have to be repaid in raw materials or manufactured goods. Moreover, each needs to dominate the Third World in order to deny it to the other in the military contest that will engage them. The United States and the Soviet Union will compete, therefore, for military domination of the Indian Ocean or Angola not only because they require territory to exploit but also because domination gives strategic advantage. In this context, China's policies toward the Third World oppose both superpowers but use one against the other whenever it is to the advantage of China and the immediate countries concerned. Nevertheless, China has maintained, with a fair degree of consistency, that Europe is the primary focus of the contradiction between the two superpowers. Second, as the two superpowers decline and disintegrate in the course of their struggle for supremacy, the Third World, engaged in the meantime in its own development, will become the power center of the world and the arena of primary importance in the next stage of history. This will be the case because the Third World has vast resources and because, as the relative weight of power shifts from a declining Oikoumene to the Third World, the latter will be able to use its resources to control the superpowers (which, of course, will no longer be super). China's role in the Third World is to provide leadership and to protect the Third World from the depredations of the superpowers, while, at the same time, it must contribute to the development of the Third World's capacity for production and future leadership.

The theoretical basis of China's policy toward the Third World was spelled out at length by Deng Xiaoping in a speech he delivered on April

10, 1974, at a special session of the United Nations General Assembly.[14] A socialist camp had existed as a factor in world politics for a period after World War II, but as a consequence of social imperialism that camp no longer exists. The Western imperialist camp is also in the process of disintegration. The world is now divided into three parts. First there is the world of the two superpowers, the United States and the Soviet Union. This First World is, in effect, according to Deng's description, the latest avatar of the Oikoumene. Then there is the Third World, consisting of the developing countries of Asia, Africa, and Latin America (and elsewhere, such as the Pacific). Finally, there is a Second World, whose members are the developed countries of Europe, Asia, Africa, Latin America, and elsewhere. These countries are, on the one hand, subject to imperialist socio-economic relationships with the superpowers and therefore often stand opposed to them; at the same time, they may maintain imperialist relationships with the Third World. For example, Portugal was exploited by the United States at the same time that it was an imperialist-colonial power in Angola, Mozambique, and elsewhere in Africa, the Far East, and the Pacific. The countries of the Second World participate in the process of history to the extent that they oppose the superpowers, and they hold back the historical process to the extent that they try to maintain their colonial and imperialist relations with Third World regions. Their very ambiguity gives them historical potential in the future to the extent that they can be encouraged to forego their negative position *vis-à-vis* the Third World and to join forces with the Third World in opposition to the superpowers. Portugal in 1974 and 1975, after its revolution but before it began moving to the political right, would be a case in point.

The superpowers depend on exploitation of the population and resources of the Third World. With its vast extent and its great potential for power, this region constitutes, by virtue of the ability to deny its resources to the First World, the primary revolutionary force in the world today. As Deng put it: "[The Third World countries] constitute a revolutionary motive force propelling the wheel of world history and are the main forces combating colonialism, imperialism, and particularly the superpowers." Deng cited the OPEC nations' use of their oil resources on the international scene as an example of the revolutionary potential of the Third World *vis-à-vis* the superpowers. By seizing control of their own resources they place themselves in an advantageous position to combat the superpowers and to reverse the power relationships the superpowers must try to impose upon the world.

China's program for the Third World derives directly from its analysis of the structure of power relationships in the world. First, the Third World countries must maintain their political independence, which is a prerequisite for the establishment and maintenance of economic independence. In fact, political independence without economic independence is a sham;

economic independence without political independence is an impossibility. The two are inseparable. Second, the Third World countries must develop, but they must do so on the basis of self-reliance. Deng carefully defined the concept of self-reliance in such a way that its applicability transcended the immediate forms and sources of capital investment available to a developing country:

> By self-reliance we mean that a country should mainly rely on the strength and wisdom of its own people, control its own economic lifelines, make full use of its own resources, strive hard to increase food production and develop its national economy step by step and in a planned way.

Self-reliance requires that national policy be based upon the "actual conditions" of a country; "the distinction must be made between different circumstances, and . . . each country should work out its way of practicing self-reliance in the light of its specific conditions." This is the application to the grand arena of international politics and to economic development of the same strategy China had recommended for use in Vietnam. It also means that Third World countries are free to use capital investment from advanced industrial countries. The issue is not the source of investment but, rather, who controls the Third World countries' economies and the decisions that have to be made:

> We have always considered it beneficial and necessary for the development of the national economy that countries should carry on economic and technical exchanges on the basis of respect for state sovereignty, equality and mutual benefit, and the exchange of needed goods to make up for each other's deficiencies.

Third, the Third World must demand that the structure of economic relations between the developed and the developing countries change. In this regard, China joined the voices around the world that have called periodically, through various agencies and international forums, for radical restructuring of existing economic relationships. Fourth, relations between countries must be based upon the Five Principles of Peaceful Coexistence, which include the right of every people to choose and to manage their own social and economic system. Finally, technology transfers from developed to developing countries

> must be practical, efficient, economical and convenient for use. The experts and other personnel dispatched to the recipient countries have the obligation to pass on conscientiously technical know-how to the people there and to respect the laws and national customs of the countries concerned.

China itself is both a socialist country and a developing country. By definition, therefore, China belongs to the Third World. China is not a superpower and has no pretensions to such status. China's leadership role, therefore, can be defined in terms of the program Peking has established for the Third World:

> Consistently following Chairman Mao's teachings, the Chinese Government and people firmly support all oppressed peoples and oppressed nations in their struggle to win or defend national independence, develop the national economy and oppose colonialism, imperialism and hegemonism. This is our bounden internationalist duty.

Furthermore, China is aware of the dangers of the restoration of capitalism in a socialist country:

> If capitalism is restored in a big socialist country, it will inevitably become a superpower. . . .If one day China would change her colour and turn into a super-power, if she too should play the tyrant in the world, and everywhere subject others to her bullying, aggression and exploitation, the people of the world should identify her as social-imperialism, expose it, oppose it and work together with the Chinese people to over-throw it.

Several points in this analysis are striking and provide clues to an understanding of what otherwise appears to be a contradictory Chinese policy and pattern of behavior toward various Third World countries. First, the definition of a country's status in the structure of the world depends completely upon its level of economic development and its relationship to the superpowers. These are objective analytical categories, not subjective ideological (in the Western sense of that term) categories. Accordingly, there are only two superpowers by virtue of their economic and military potential and policies. There are advanced industrial or at least relatively developed countries that are not superpowers but that both are objects of the superpowers' imperialism and hegemonism and are themselves potential imperialist powers. Poland would be an example in the Soviet bloc; England, France, or Portugal, in the American bloc. Finally, the category of Third World countries also is defined strictly in objective terms. At no point in Deng's speech or in other Chinese discussions of the Third World is the political attitude of a specific government toward China a factor in the definition of that country's position in the world. A Third World country may oppose China (and be pursuing erroneous policies, therefore) but still be a Third World country. Chinese policy toward any Third World country begins with the objective status of that country as a member of the Third World, and that is the primary and determining factor in China's approach. Whether the government of the country in question is progressive or reactionary in its internal structure, class relationships, and policies is another question, but these features do not determine Third World status, and it is from that status that Chinese policy begins. Consequently, what to external observers appears inconsistent in Chinese policy toward particular governments in the Third World—China has dealt productively with both reactionary and progressive regimes, benefiting such varied societies and localities as "feudal" Afghanistan in 1976 and the "progressive" Congo (Brazaville)—is from the Chinese viewpoint completely consistent with China's theory of world politics and history. China's membership in, and leadership of, the Third World, as China itself has defined it, finds expression in two primary areas of activity: economic aid and political action.

ECONOMIC AID

China extends aid to Third World countries based upon considerations that can be defined along two axes: the needs of the country in question and China's ability to extend aid in terms of those needs. The most productive form of aid that satisfies Peking's considerations along both axes is the development of medium- and small-scale projects in which minimal investment can yield significant returns for the planned economic development of the country. China does not want to build projects that will need imported raw materials, thus making the country in question dependent upon external sources of materiel and contributing to that country's economic and political vulnerability. China wants to turn these countries from exporters of their raw materials into utilizers of those materials, and when they lack the necessary raw materials China gives priority to finding a solution to the raw materials problem: "We proceed to help construct sugar refineries only after the growth of sugar cane proves a success."[15]

In sponsoring development projects, China also insists upon the acquisition of the technical skills necessary for the venture. Chinese personnel participate in projects only to the extent of teaching the necessary skills and operating the project during the instruction process; once this phase is completed, Chinese participation and responsibility come to an end.

Chinese aid "is either gratis or in the form of loans on favorable terms."[16] Offering either interest-free or very low interest loans, the Chinese since 1964 have tended to concentrate almost entirely on interest-free loans.

Chinese aid to Third World countries also has tended to focus on specific categories: light industry, transport, agriculture, water control and irrigation, public health and medical care training, power and communications, sports and cultural complexes, and, finally, heavy industry. Although Albania, Pakistan, and Vietnam have been involved in the construction of steel mills and machine tool plants and other heavy industry ventures, Chinese aid has focused largely on areas that contribute directly to the quality of life of the recipient population and on the construction of cultural and communications infrastructures. This approach has accorded both with China's abilities and with its policies. In the category of light industry, for example, Chinese aid has contributed to the development of textile mills, sugar mills and refineries, rice mills, paper mills and printing plants, brick and cement works, and chemical plants.[17]

POLITICAL RELATIONS

Over the years China has established or maintained diplomatic relations with Third World countries on the same basis as Peking has given economic aid. The primary consideration is their status as members of the Third World, not their internal policies or their policies *vis-à-vis* China itself. Only two issues have inhibited the development of diplomatic relations. First, the question of Taiwan has always been thorny, and over the years a variety of formulae have been used, ranging from outright recognition of China's claim to Taiwan to agreement not even to mention the subject. Second (and this is perhaps the only exception to the rule of Third World status), some states simply have been beyond the pale of Chinese recognition by virtue of their internal racist policies, such as South Africa and Rhodesia. The list of states with which China has established diplomatic relations since 1949 is too long to enumerate here. By 1980 China had relations with all but a handful of countries that insisted for one or another reason on maintaining relations with Taiwan. The speed with which China has extended the net of its relationships increased significantly after the early 1970s, when the change in U.S. policy toward China removed one of the barriers many of America's client states faced in trying to develop relations with Peking.

VIETNAM AND CAMBODIA

Indochina presents an excellent example of the dynamics of China's policies in the Third World. Throughout the Vietnam War, China strongly supported North Vietnam and the Viet Cong revolution against the government of South Vietnam. To be sure, Chinese support was stronger in words than in deeds, but Peking gave the Vietnamese, both in the north and in the revolutionary south, a limited amount of material and technical aid, including technical support personnel in the north. It is important to note that China did not permit its dispute with the Soviet Union to interfere with the extension of aid to Vietnam, even though the dispute at times made difficulties. The Soviet Union also extended aid to Vietnam, and as often as not the Chinese facilitated, or at least did not hinder, the passage of that aid through or over China. This was so despite the continual jockeying of Moscow and Peking for the dominant position in Hanoi, while Hanoi walked a tightrope between the two socialist giants. Similarly, when the time came, China did not allow the fact that the United States was waging active war against Peking's North Vietnam and Viet Cong allies and clients to prevent the development of bilateral Chinese-American relations. Here as elsewhere, China's touch in international affairs was delicate and subtle.

After the Vietnam War, however, relations between Peking and Hanoi began to deteriorate. Numerous issues divided them, including conflicting Vietnamese and Chinese territorial claims along their common frontier; Vietnamese treatment of the Chinese minority in Vietnam; conflicting claims over islands in the South China Sea; and incursions by the troops of each country into the territory of the other. Underlying all these specific issues was the growth of Soviet influence in Hanoi at the expense of China. A crisis developed in 1978, when the Vietnamese started to persecute the Chinese resident minority. As Chinese from Vietnam began to flee to China or to apply for permission to emigrate legally, Hanoi accused China and other "reactionary elements" of subverting Vietnam and inciting Vietnamese to oppose the regime or to flee. At first China attempted to resist Vietnam by refusing to accept the victims of Vietnamese persecution. More important from the perspective of international relations, Peking specifically accused Hanoi and Moscow of collusion and the Soviet Union of turning Vietnam into a "forward post" in its attempt to penetrate the Indian and Pacific oceans.[18]

In the meantime, Hanoi, acting in China's eyes as Moscow's agent, moved into Cambodia to overthrow China's client, the Pol Pot regime, which had come to power with the failure of the American war effort. In December 1979, as Vietnam pushed its invasion of Cambodia, China thoroughly denounced Vietnam. Rumors began to circulate concerning Chinese preparations for a move into Indochina. Peking did not help prevent the circulation of the rumors. In February 1979, for example, Deng Xiaoping told foreigners in Peking that China "may have to do something that we do not want to do, if people deny us the wish" to live in a peaceful environment.[19] He had said much the same thing to the United States Senate during his visit to Washington a few weeks earlier. Toward the end of February, China attacked Vietnam in order to "punish" Hanoi for its invasion of Cambodia, as Peking put it. Hostilities lasted about a month, and while Chinese forces made some headway, even capturing a Vietnamese provincial capital, they did not acquit themselves well; nor did they succeed in forcing the Vietnamese to abandon Cambodia. Negotiations, including negotiations over the exchange of prisoners, took place in the middle of 1979. Vietnamese-Chinese relations had been damaged beyond repair, and the two countries continued to snipe at each other verbally, though no further major outbreak of military hostilities occurred. The Chinese withdrew to their side of the border and the Vietnamese remained in Cambodia.

The Vietnamese attack on Cambodia (Kampuchea) at the end of 1978 is, in historical perspective, simply one more stage in an agelong incursion of ethnic Vietnamese into Cambodian territory. The Vietnamese now tried to justify their attack on Cambodia in terms of humanitarian concern for the suffering of the Cambodian people at the hands of the draconian Pol Pot regime. Indeed, considerable concern for the suffering of the Cambodians had been expressed around the world, not the least by the American government. Inhumane policies resulting in famine and the death of at least hundreds of thousands of Cambodians were the focus of the American propaganda attack on Pol Pot and the rationale for the Vietnamese invasion. In relatively short order the Pol Pot regime was driven from Pnom Phenh and, as hostilities declined, it was left in control of only small enclaves along the Thai border, where the remnants of the regime's armed forces functioned as guerrilla bands. China's invasion of Vietnam was insufficient to the task of reversing the Vietnamese action.

The significance of these very confused events lies in the fact that they provided a touchstone for the public realignment of major forces on the international scene. In a sense, the Vietnamese government acted as Moscow's proxy in attacking Peking's client, the Cambodian regime of Pol Pot. China's limited military engagement with Vietnam was intended to support Peking's own client but, at the same time, it was a proxy attack on the Soviet Union in a situation in which neither the Soviet Union nor China wanted to confront each other directly. The United States, increasingly China's ally in reality if not in formal treaty arrangements, shifted from utter condemnation of the Pol Pot regime on humanitarian grounds to deep support for it on legal grounds; that is, as inhumane as the regime may have been, it was the legal government of Cambodia, even if the United States did not recognize it as such. Hanoi's status as Moscow's client was not really crucial in China's consideration, however. Peking maintained reasonable relations with many states that fell within the Soviet Union's power penumbra. What was crucial, however, was first Hanoi's persecution of a Chinese minority, which Peking could not tolerate given the fact that throughout Southeast Asia there were large concentrations of ethnic Chinese whose support China wanted and needed, and, second, the fact that Hanoi had behaved toward Cambodia as an imperialist power. Washington's switch from condemnation to support of the Pol Pot regime was crucial not because of some sudden accretion of merit in the Pol Pot government but because Washington could *indirectly* show its support for Peking and its growing distance from Moscow by expressing support for Peking's client, which was under attack by Moscow's client. The situation was only apparently complicated. Moscow and Peking thoroughly understood what was happening.

ANGOLA

The complex struggle for national liberation in Angola is another example of the parameters controlling Chinese foreign policy. The struggle

among the three revolutionary movements, each supported by one of the
great powers (the Soviet Union, China, and the United States), provided
a context within which China and the Soviet Union could oppose each
other in a region and in a conflict in which, in an earlier age, cooperation
would have been logical. The MPLA, clearly the Soviet Union's agent,
equipped with Soviet arms and aided by Soviet advisors and Cuban troops,
had won the field by the end of 1975. China had supported the FNLA and
had sought American cooperation in bringing the FNLA and the American
supported movement, UNITA, into cooperation against the MPLA. The
Americans believed that the Vietnam trauma precluded a further foreign
adventure and so they invited, or at least permitted, South African troops
to enter the fray in support of UNITA. South Africa, ostensibly to protect
hydroelectric installations along the Angolan frontier with Namibia (South
West Africa), occupied a strip inside the Angolan frontier about one
hundred miles in depth. In October China decided on two grounds to
withdraw its support from the FNLA: first, it was already apparent that
the Soviet Union's MPLA had won with Cuban and Soviet support; second, the entry of South Africa, apparently with American approbation and
even on American invitation, made impossible further participation by
China in the struggle in support of any movement even remotely allied to
South Africa. Instead, China called in November for the Organization of
African Unity to bring an end to foreign intervention in Angola and to
establish some kind of structure incorporating all three Angolan national
liberation movements.

Peking's public analysis of these events directly reflected China's general foreign policy positions and analysis of the international world. Peking
accused Moscow of harboring ulterior objectives in Southern Africa, including the economic exploitation of the region, and charged that Soviet
support of the MPLA was primarily anti-American, not pro-Angolan. Finally, Peking warned the United States that Angola was an example of
Soviet policy that, if not countered and stopped, would extend to other
areas. China obviously saw Angola not as a potential ally but as one more
example of China's own need to bolster American willingness to resist the
Soviet Union. China considered Angola not in terms of immediate political
advantage but in terms of the context of the forces at work in contemporary
history, in which China itself had to play a leading role according to its
own philosophical assumptions and the policies that derived from them.

THE MIDDLE EAST AND NORTH AFRICA

China's policies in other parts of the Third World have reflected many
of the same assumptions and concerns that its policies in Indochina and
Angola have exhibited. This was the case in the Middle East, for example.
Although China possesses a significant indigenous Moslem population, par-

ticularly in the southwestern province of Yunnan and in Gansu and Xin-jiang in the northwest, this minority is not sufficiently large or important politically to dictate China's policy toward Iran or its pro-Arab, anti-Israeli position. However, China's policies in that region have remained remark-ably consistent over time because of the powerful assumptions of the Chinese analysis.

Throughout the Middle East, from Iran to Israel and Egypt, China has been concerned primarily with the contest between the superpowers and the necessity of opposition to the Soviet Union, both as superpower and as ersatz socialist state. As elsewhere, China's assumptions and the policies that derive from them have led Peking to lie with strange bedfellows, strange in the light of Peking's broad social policies as they apply to China and to the world. For example, Chairman Hua Guofeng visited Iran be-tween August 29 and September 1, 1978. Significantly, this was the first visit by a Chinese leader to a country outside the socalist bloc. Even more significant was the timing of the visit, coming as it did as the shah's gov-ernment and the shah himself were facing increasing attack from many quarters outside Iran for oppression of legitimate opposition and for the use of inhumane measures, including torture, against dissidents. More-over, the revolutionary movement within Iran was gaining no little mo-mentum. China's broad global concerns overrode, however, what must have been its repugnance, or at least its distaste, for the shah and his government. Hua's visit was motivated primarily by concern about bolster-ing Iran's stand against the Soviet Union.

The shah's government was quickly becoming the regional superpower, thanks to American political, military, and economic aid, and China sought to insure that this regional power would play its appropriate role in the struggle between the superpowers and against the Soviet Union. The visit ended without a joint communiqué, evidently more reflective of Iran's sen-sitivities about its relations with the Soviet Union than of any Chinese concern. Nonetheless, the signing of a cultural agreement indicated accord between the two governments, and various signs around the Persian Gulf demonstrated that Hua had spoken clearly to the shah and his advisors about China's position, which included apprehension about Soviet ad-vances into, and threats against, the Indian Ocean. China wanted Iran to help defend the security of the Indian Ocean; Peking also worried that Soviet power could increase throughout the region to the point that it would challenge American domination of the Persian Gulf. China and Iran apparently agreed that regional security should be the "sole responsibility of the littoral states."[20] Hua and the shah evidently also discussed the re-cent coup in Afghanistan, in which a conservative government on friendly terms with China had been turned out by a Soviet sponsored left-wing party. The Afghan situation undoubtedly was, for Chinese policy planners, a foretaste of what could happen in the Persian Gulf if the shah, and his American allies, did not stand firm.

Throughout this region, as elsewhere, China has based its policy upon the assumption that the problems internal to the region are the consequence primarily of the contradictions between the superpowers and their intervention in the contradictions that are internal to the region. For example, China noted in May and June 1974 that the thrust of American Secretary of State Kissinger's Middle East diplomacy was the replacement of Soviet with American power. Thus, an agreement for limited military disengagement between Israeli and Syria was interpreted as a disengagement between the superpowers, and Egypt's break with Moscow as a Soviet defeat to which Moscow would not reconcile itself. The Arab-Israeli conflict in general is a proxy conflict between the superpowers. "The root cause of the Middle East upheaval lies in the rivalry between the two hegemonic powers, and the so-called 'just and everlasting peace' is nothing but deceitful rubbish," the Chinese official news agency commented on May 31, 1974. By the same token, the Arab and Palestinian struggle against Israel has been interpreted as "an important component of the Third World struggling against imperialism and hegemonism," that is, against both the United States and the Soviet Union.[21]

China's policy objectives have concentrated on the strengthening of local powers capable of withstanding both superpowers and especially the Soviet Union. This is, in a certain fashion, a reverse of the content of Mao Zedong's original policy of "leaning to one side"; China wants local forces to oppose both superpowers but to lean to one side away from and against the Soviet Union. China is prepared to encourage such a posture in any way that lies within its means. When Anwar el-Sadat, president of Egypt, abrogated the Soviet-Egyptian Treaty of Friendship and Cooperation in the first part of 1976, thus ending the comparatively short but intense Soviet attempt to establish a dominant relationship with Cairo, China hailed the move as signifying "the bankruptcy of Soviet hegemonism in Egypt."[22] But Peking did more. The Chinese moved quickly to step into the breach created by the Soviet Union's ouster in order to bolster Egypt's resolve, and in March Peking and Cairo announced that China would supply Egypt with engines and spare parts, *gratis*, for Egyptian owned MIG fighter planes. Peking was so delighted to be able to do this that, according to reports, it turned back an Egyptian offer to purchase the engines and parts with the remark, "We are no arms merchants."[23] Betweeen April 18 and 24, the Egyptian vice-president, Hosny Mubarak, visited China; China attached such importance to the visit that Mubarak was met at the airport by no less an official than Chairman Hua himself—an exaggeration of protocol in order to register a political point. The Peking government gave Mubarak a banquet to welcome him to China, and making their own point, the representatives of the Soviet Union and its satellites refused to attend. Their nonappearance underscored the strain between Peking and Moscow and gave it expression with reference to a particular geopolitical region. During Mubarak's visit, Egypt and China signed agreements for Egyptian purchase of strategic materials and for trade in a variety of consumer goods. The visit and its results were reported in moderate and controlled terms, indicating not China's aim to win Egypt over to its side but, rather, Peking's desire to insure that Egypt, like Iran, played the role it had to play in world politics. This point was made doubly, and subtly, clear when China gave considerable publicity to President Sadat's tour of Europe in the spring of 1976 and even reported approvingly that Egypt was purchasing considerable quantities of consumer goods from the West. Neither Sadat's European progress nor Egypt's foreign trade would have merited much note in the Chinese press had it not been for China's specific desire to build Sadat's strength and image.

China does not depend upon Middle Eastern oil and does not have to fear an eruption of Moslem fundamentalism within Chinese borders. In fact, China has had no reason to adopt the resolutely anti-Israel position it has, other than its desire to turn all available forces against the Soviet Union. China's anti-Israel policy is simply the reverse side of the policy and analysis that led Peking to strong support of Iran and Egypt. In a very real sense, Chinese opposition to Israel is predicated on the Israeli-Arab contradiction and the combination of both the great threat to the Arabs from Soviet attempts to penetrate the region and the great potential for Arab resistance to the Soviets. Peking's global policies dictate not that it oppose Israel but that it support the Arabs, and if encouragement of the Arabs to oppose the Soviet Union means taking sides in the Arab-Israeli conflict, so be it. Actually, there is greater ambiguity in Peking's policy toward Israel than observers generally recognize. Israel, like Iran, has been a client of the United States (indeed, Israel and Iran shared common concerns, including the Soviet Union and the Arabs and, consequently, cooperated in several ways before the overthrow of the shah by fiercely anti-Israel Shiite Moslem fundamentalists), and China, paralleling its policy toward Iran, could have pursued the same logic it used in the Persian Gulf to the conclusion that it should support Israel. The primary internal regional contradiction, however, poses the Arabs against the Israelis, and this contradiction dictates China's policy toward the regional manifestations of the global U.S.-U.S.S.R. contradiction. China has to respond to the ferocity of Arab opposition to Israel by supporting the Arabs because Peking needs to encourage the Arabs to adopt a correct attitude toward the superpowers.

Chinese policy toward Israel reflects the ambiguities of the region. China cultivates, to the extent possible, the Palestinian movement, even supplying it with small arms and ammunition when asked. In November 1979, Chairman Hua received a Palestinian delegation, and throughout the period there were frequent reports that Palestinian terrorists had received training in China. President Sadat's peace initiative—his trip to Jerusalem in November 1977—was vehemently opposed by the Palestinians and the other Arab states. The Chinese, however, viewing the peace initiative as a way of limiting the potential of both superpowers for further involvement in the Middle East, quietly supported Sadat and gave no play to the Arab objections to his move.

The Arab states quickly noted the ambiguity in China's response to Sadat's initiative. In August 1978, a Libyan delegation visited China—Libya was a "rejectionist" state, that is, it opposed Egypt and Sadat's new policy toward Israel—and publicly expressed "regret" at China's support of Sadat's "betrayal."[24] China did not report the Libyan remarks and increased its support for Sadat. In fact, Deng Xiaoping publicly supported the Camp David accords between Egypt and Israel in remarks he made to a visiting French leader. In the same way, a high Chinese official visiting Syria in July 1978 subtly urged the Arabs to support Egypt. He specifically argued for the validity of the Chinese global analysis: "The reason why Israeli Zionism is so stubborn and reactionary is because it enjoys covert or overt connivance and support of the superpowers which have been bolstering it with manpower and materials. This is the root cause of the prolonged turmoil in the Middle East and the lack of a solution to the problem."[25] Keeping to this position, China extended further aid to Egypt. On June 5, 1979, President Sadat announced that Egypt and China had concluded an agreement for the sale by China of military equipment to Egypt, including perhaps sixty Chinese modified MIG-19s. Evidently, the planes were a gift to Egypt, and reports circulated that Egypt would buy an additional forty or more planes at low cost. The very size of this transfer of military equipment made China a major military participant in Middle Eastern affairs, if only for a short time. Conclusion of this deal in a period when Egypt's primary enemy was no longer Israel but the other Arab states (indeed, the Arab states had withdrawn military subsidies from Egypt as a consequence of Sadat's peace policy) carried what in other circumstances would have been a clear message about Peking's policy in the region. In light of Egypt's policy toward Israel, Israel obviously was not the enemy against which China was supporting Egypt. The ambiguities in China's policy, however, were already clear in mid-May 1979 when the Chinese ambassador in Beirut told Yasir Arafat, the leader of the Palestinian movement, that China would not recognize Israel and would not deal with that nation. A year later, however, during the summer of 1980, strong rumors began to circulate that China was preparing to purchase military equipment from Israel. By the end of 1980 these rumors gained considerable credence, though they were never substantiated.

ALBANIA

The primary casualty of the resumption by China of an active foreign policy in late 1971 and 1972 was Peking's only European ally throughout the 1960s and perhaps the only European country that could properly be called a member of the Third World, Albania, located on the western coast of the Balkan Peninsula. Albania had broken with Moscow in the late 1950s, partly as a consequence of the Soviet Union's attempts to repair its relations with Albania's archenemy, Yugoslavia. Albania's own internal situation, moreover, seemed to resist Soviet attempts to penetrate or to restructure it (Khrushchev once remarked that he could not understand Albania or why Soviet aid seemed to have little or no effect there); accordingly, Moscow did not make great efforts to keep Albania within its orbit. The Albanian regime developed a highly organized and tightly knit society, and Tirana's foreign policy moved to strong, even violent, antipathy toward the Soviet Union. On the principle that friends from afar can protect one from enemies close at hand but do not constitute a threat, Albania and China proceeded to develop in the 1960s a strong friendship, in which China made considerable contributions to the maintenance of the Albanian economy and appeared, at times, to serve as a model for Albanian political, social, and economic change. As late as November 1976 relations between Peking and Tirana were, on the surface, warm, but rumors in the West hinted that China's new policies had strained the alliance.

The Albanian party newspaper published a lengthy open criticism of Chinese foreign policy theory and practice in July 1977. Interestingly, the criticism pinpointed some of the building blocks of Chinese policy. Although the editorial did not mention China by name, its attack on the three-zone theory and on the practice of conducting foreign policy on the basis of "my enemy's enemy is my friend" made China the obvious target. Since, by any measure Albania itself belongs to the Third World as described by China, it was fascinating that Albania rejected the theory precisely because, it claimed, the concept of the Third World as the primary revolutionary force in world affairs was a "flagrant violation of the teachings of Marxism-Leninism."[26] Albania, out in the socialist cold except for its Chinese friend, took refuge in a rigid and uncompromising Marxism-Leninism. Moreover, the priority assigned by China to the contradiction between the superpowers, which meant that China had to deal with any Third World or Second World regime that would play the role the primary contradiction assigned to it, itself came under attack in Albania as a betrayal of "the many oppressed millions." China's willingness to deal with Chile's Pinochet, Brazil's Geisel, and the shah of Iran was intolerable to purist Albania. Peking responded to the Albanian criticism in a somewhat offhanded fashion (reprinting already published materials) and continued to maintain good state-to-state relations with Tirana. The Soviet Union, on the other hand, used the Albanian materials to attack China, the only surprise being the source of the criticism.

Throughout 1977, Chinese-Albanian government relations continued to prosper, at least ceremonially and publicly, although the Yugoslavs, ever eager to exploit anything that could annoy the Albanians, announced that Chinese aid to Albania had been cut back as early as 1976 and that, consequently, Albania faced an economic crisis. In 1978 Albania's theoretical criticism of China deepened. Moreover, the disagreement now came out in the open. Albania publicly supported Vietnam against China, and on May Day 1978 slogans attacking China and its policies appeared at a rally in Tirana. On July 7 the Chinese Ministry of Foreign Affairs informed Tirana that all economic and military aid was being canceled and claimed that Albania's anti-Chinese policy had included sabotage of China's aid program to the country. Albania, in response, recalled its citizens studying in China. A year later, in April 1979, China sent a new ambassador to Tirana; however bad Chinese-Albanian relations had become, formal diplomatic relations were maintained. In this respect, China's relations with Albania resembled China's relations with the Soviet Union; diplomatic contact continued despite the acerbity of ideological criticism and the ending of economic and military support.

The case of Albania in Chinese foreign policy is relatively uninteresting in itself. However important China may have been in Albania's calculations, for China Albania was a convenient stick with which occasionally to beat the Soviet Union. It never became a major Chinese diplomatic or military base in Europe. It never played a major role in China's global plans.

China in East Asia

China's relations with, and its policies toward, the countries along its maritime perimeter were in certain respects much more complex than they were in other parts of the world, for both historical and political reasons.

NORTH KOREA

Like Vietnam, Korea found itself in the 1960s caught politically between the two great socialist powers. Korea's situation was further complicated because both these powers were its immediate neighbors; moreover, the Soviet Union had a strong and immediate interest, political and strategic, in Korea's future.

Historically, of course, Korea had fallen well within the traditional sinocentric tribute system, from which it was removed, in effect, only by Japan's victory over China in the war of 1894–1895 (a war motivated to a certain extent by increased Russian interest in the peninsula). The division of the country into two parts after World War II meant that, for China, the first factor to be considered in the development of a policy toward the Koreas was the United States as South Korea's primary political protector and military ally, especially after the Korean War, when America maintained a strong military presence in South Korea. The second factor was the Soviet Union's sponsorship of the North Korean regime, a sponsorship that had roots in the history of the Korean Communist Party (many of whose leaders were Soviet tutees) and in Soviet strategic concerns that derived from the American presence in South Korea, close to Soviet territory, particularly to the Soviet Union's one warm-water port on the Pacific, Vladivostok. The line of defense between the United States and the socialist bloc passed right through Korea at the thirty-eighth parallel; moreover, as Moscow and Peking distanced themselves from each other, Korea itself became a frontier territory between the two.

By the beginning of the 1960s, that is to say, by the time the Sino-Soviet dispute was a public factor in international affairs, North Korea had fallen once again within the Chinese sphere of influence. In effect, it had returned to the structure of the sinocentric Empire. There were several reasons for this development, not the least of which were the greater socioeconomic and cultural similarities betweeen China and North Korea, as opposed to the purely ideological and political commonalities shared by North Korea and the Soviet Union. The same factors that had made Korea part of the sinocentric Empire before 1895 now made it part of that Empire again. The clearest sign of North Korea's presence in the Chinese orbit was the internal development campaign it waged in the late 1950s—the Flying Horse campaign—which was organized largely on the model of, and at the same time as, China's Great Leap Forward. As before, so now, Korea's domestic socioeconomic life followed a pattern also exhibited by China.

With the radical change in Sino-American relations from 1972 on, the American presence in South Korea took on a completely different coloration for Peking. What had previously been a threat to China's security now began to appear, in light of American moderation and Soviet antagonism, a guarantee of China's northeastern flank from any Soviet attempt politically or militarily to encircle China. Both American and Chinese policy wanted to keep North Korea in the Chinese orbit. This goal evidently coincided with the interests of North Korea's leader, Kim Il-sung, who, with advancing age, had become by the beginning of the 1980s more intent upon internal affairs than upon Korea's international position. His primary concern was to assure internal stability in order to insure the succession of his son to the leadership of the country. Peking and Washington found in Korea an area in which their interests coincided; both wanted stability in the peninsula in order to discourage the growth of Soviet power.

JAPAN

America's defense perimeter in the Far East passed well to the west of Japan, and Washington after 1945 consciously used Japan as its primary base in the Far East. The American occupation of Japan was only the beginning of a powerful American Far Eastern presence; after the conclusion of the peace treaty with Japan, the American presence remained necessary to both Japan and the United States because of Japan's own defense needs, which were exacerbated by certain limitations imposed upon Japanese military development by the constitution Japan had adopted but the Americans had written. Furthermore, the continuing antagonism between Washington and Peking, on the one hand, and between Washington and Moscow, on the other, meant that America's presence in Japan had political significance in the Far East beyond the narrow needs of Japan's own military defenses.

Throughout the 1950s and the 1960s, Peking perceived Japan as a direct potential military threat to China. This perception was based both upon America's politico-military presence and upon Japan's attempts to provide for its own defense through the revival of "self-defense forces" as prescribed and limited by Japanese law. As late as the summer of 1971, Peking attacked the growing militarization of Japan. "Once Japanese militarism embarks on the old path of unleashing an aggressive war," China declared, "it may fight a conventional war as well as a nuclear war."[27] Japan, for its part, found it difficult to defuse its relationship with China. For example, in October 1971 Tokyo and Washington co-sponsored the American resolution at the United Nations that resulted finally in Chinese membership. However, because of the peculiar wording of the resolution and the complicated parliamentary maneuvers it had entailed—more to avoid domestic political problems within the United States than to prevent China's entrance into the U.N.—Peking disregarded Japanese Premier Sato Eisaku's statement that "the normalization of Japanese-Chinese relations is more important than the problem of Chinese representation in the United Nations."[28] Nonetheless, growing unofficial Sino-Japanese trade relations and the desire on the part of the Japanese business community and Chinese economic planners to increase trade led to the signing, on December 25, 1971, of a Sino-Japanese trade agreement. Moreover, the Japan-China Memorandum Trade Office in Peking began to function as a consular and semidiplomatic establishment. Traditional tributary patterns appeared again as a potential basis for the resolution of contemporary problems.

Sino-Japanese rapprochement was hastened by Japanese chagrin at the cavalier way in which the United States had prepared for, and carried out, the Nixon visit to Peking without keeping Japan, as one of America's chief allies, fully informed. Furthermore, America's new relationship with China weakened Japan's support for Taiwan—between 1895 and 1945 part of the Japanese empire—and its independence, thus removing a further obstacle in the path of new relations between Tokyo and Peking. Although China now began to attack Japan for trying to conduct a two-China policy, trade relations and other communications between the two powers continued to expand. However, both sides had to find an appropriate formula and instrument for the reestablishment of normal bilateral relations.

In the summer of 1972, Tokyo and Peking both publicly called for a resumption of Sino-Japanese relations. The occasion was the election of a new Japanese premier, Tanaka Kakuei, who, at the beginning of July, called for relations with China. A week later, Zhou Enlai, at a banquet in Peking, declared that Tanaka's statement "merits welcome."[29] In a pattern that strongly resembled the breakthrough in Sino-American relations, a Japanese volleyball team visited China and a Chinese dramatic troupe went to Japan. Thus, nondiplomatic means were again being used to conduct diplomacy. China's leaders now invited Premier Tanaka to visit Peking, which he did at the end of September, spending one hour with Chairman Mao. The two sides agreed to establish relations, and Japanese Foreign Minister Ohira Masayoshi announced that Japan's treaty with Taiwan had "lost the meaning of its existence and is declared to be terminated"[30]—Japan was breaking relations with Taiwan in exchange for relations with Peking. Japan, with powerful economic interests in Taiwan, would open a semi-official liaison office in Taipei, which could carry out consular functions; a regular embassy would be opened in Peking. Japan's first postwar ambassador to China presented his credentials on April 3, 1973, and China's first ambassador to Japan presented his on April 5 in Tokyo. Undoubtedly, the combination of the American demarche toward Peking and Tokyo's anger at Washington's disregarding Japanese feelings in the matter had both opened the way for a Sino-Japanese entente and goaded Japan into action, but Japan had taken the lead by working out with Peking an arrangement that was to serve as a precedent for the resumption of formal Sino-American relations at an appropriate time in the future. Japan's growing rapprochement with China adversely affected Moscow's campaign to bring Japan closer to its orbit of power by inviting Japan to participate in the economic development of Siberia's vast resources. Premier Tanaka visited Moscow in October, but no progress was made on any of the issues outstanding between Japan and the Soviet Union: the conclusion of a World War II peace treaty, the disposition of islands occupied by the Soviet Union but claimed by Japan, and Japanese participation in Siberian economic development.

The resumption of formal relations did not mean that Sino-Japanese interaction followed a smooth course. Several problems continually provided the substance of a sometimes unharmonious process of communication as the two powers sought an appropriate instrument for the development of the relationship. The frequent exchange of delegations of businessmen, politicians, cultural leaders, theatrical performers, and the like created a climate in which communication could take place, but communication did not necessarily occur. In the period before the resumption of normal relations, delegation exchanges had provided the occasions upon which conversation could proceed. Now, however, a more appropriate instrument had to be found, and the normalization of relations dictated that the appropriate instrument was treaty negotiation. Consequently, Japan and China entered almost immediately into long and torturous conversations covering all the various forms of interaction that would normally occur between two states, particularly two states finding themselves in such close geographical proximity. The first major negotiation concerned civil aviation; after great difficulties, a treaty was signed on April 20, 1974. The substance of the issues that divided China and Japan in this area were less important than was the use of negotiations to teach each side the diplomatic style of the other. Once the civil aviation agreement had been completed, the way was open for treaties covering a great many areas of mutual concern, such as shipping and fishing.

The conclusion of a treaty of peace and friendship was the ultimate objective of all the treaty negotiations that took place after the resumption of normal relations between Peking and Tokyo. Each new treaty dealing with a specific area of interaction was another building block in the edifice of Sino-Japanese relations, but the peace treaty had to be the keystone that held it all in place. Negotiations toward the desired objective were fraught with crises and interruptions. The Sino-Japanese Treaty of Peace and Friendship was not signed until August 12, 1978, after a three-year suspension of negotiations. One of the primary issues dividing the two powers—perhaps the most important—was the definition of hegemonism, opposition to which Peking insisted be made a part of the treaty text. A statement about this was obviously the instrument whereby Peking intended to bind Japan to its interests and to foreclose a Soviet-Japanese rapprochement. The Soviet Union well understood Peking's intentions and therefore became, as it were, a party to the Sino-Japanese negotiations. The Japanese were prepared to see a discussion of antihegemonism included in the preamble of the proposed treaty as a general principle; they did not want it to appear in the text of the treaty because, they claimed, it could be construed as a restraint on Japanese foreign policy and, therefore, unconstitutional in Japan. The Chinese, for their part, argued exactly the opposite position. Hegemonism was the greatest danger to peace in the world, they claimed, and both the Chinese constitution and Chinese foreign policy required rigorous opposition to it. The Soviets, however, insisted that the Sino-Japanese treaty make no mention of the Soviet Union, a point made forceably to the Japanese foreign minister by the Soviet foreign minister, Andrei Gromyko, in New York in September 1975, for example. Gromyko also visited Japan in January 1976, at which time he pushed the Soviet position further, making it clear that Moscow would have to reconsider its relations with Tokyo if Tokyo gave in to the Chinese demand for an antihegemony—that is, anti-Soviet—clause in the treaty.

Japan, seeking final legitimation of its new bilateral relationship with

China, found itself on the horns of a dilemma created by China's analysis of the structure of international relations. Japan's problem lay in the fact that it did not appear possible to complete negotiations with China without seriously damaging Japanese relations with the Soviet Union. The Japanese foreign minister, Miki Takeo, sought a way out in mid-January when he declared that "regardless of the terminology employed, the United States, China, the Soviet Union and Japan are unanimous in opposing hegemony. It is not contradictory, therefore, for Japan to incorporate that principle in the China-Japan treaty and at the same time pursue furtherance of better relations with the Soviet Union."[31] Japan agreed to accept the antihegemony clause in the treaty on four conditions: it could not be aimed at any third country (such as the Soviet Union); it could not require joint action by Tokyo and Peking; it should apply to all nations throughout the world (this condition was really a further application of the first); and it should be understood as a specification of a universal principle already embodied in the United Nations Charter.

The construction of a document that satisfied both Peking and Tokyo without damaging Soviet-Japanese relations beyond repair required delicate diplomatic surgery. To achieve that objective the issue of hegemony was discussed in two different articles of the treaty. The second article of the treaty declared that neither Japan nor China sought, or would seek, hegemony in the Far East or, for that matter, anywhere else; furthermore, they would both oppose the attempt by any other country to establish hegemony. This article reflected Chinese concerns. The fourth article, on the other hand, declared that the treaty would not require the modification of either country's policies toward third countries. This reflected Japan's concerns. Moscow of course reacted negatively but the Soviets stated that they would watch Japan's behavior in the future to see whether Tokyo could, under the new treaty, "pursue an independent foreign policy."[32]

The development and extension of bilateral Sino-Japanese relations was the most important of many means whereby Peking sought to make Japan part of the structure of anti-Soviet powers. Efforts in this direction also attempted to promote closer Japanese-American ties once the breakthrough between Washington and Peking had occurred. For example, a leading Japanese politician visited Peking in January 1975 and met with both Zhou Enlai (in the hospital) and Deng Xiaoping. Zhou told the Japanese that China "could understand the especially deep relations that had grown up between Japan and the United States because of the process following the Second World War." He also added, however, that "Japan and the United States should develop even more intimate ties" and reportedly said that he had insisted directly to Henry Kissinger that the American secretary of state "extend the time you spend in Tokyo." Zhou also urged Japan to strengthen its armed (so-called self-defense) forces and, on occasion, explored the possibility of purchasing arms or weapons components from Japanese manufacturers.[33]

The potential international significance of the relationship between Peking and Tokyo became clear almost immediately after the conclusion of the Sino-Japanese Treaty of Peace and Friendship. Deng made a three-day visit to Tokyo on his way back to China from the United States. Under the antihegemony clauses of the treaty, the Chinese had suggested that Japan join China to support Cambodia against Vietnam's aggression. Japan, with good relations with Hanoi, refused on the grounds that it believed unilateral diplomacy would be more effective a means to reduce tension in Southeast Asia. Japan, however, did suspend certain forms of aid to Vietnam and supported a call by the Association of South East Asian Nations (ASEAN) for the complete withdrawal of foreign troops from Cambodian territory. Deng interpreted this as satisfaction of the treaty's articles concerning hegemonism and expressed his thanks to Japan and his hope that Japan would "keep going on this road."[34] Japanese trade with China also increased rapidly, by forty-six percent in 1978. Projects for joint exploration for, and development of, Chinese natural resources, Japanese development loans to China, approval of Sino-Japanese commercial contracts—all these were signs of increasing cooperation between the two countries.

The combination of Japanese capital and technology with Chinese labor and low production costs, within the context of a cooperative political relationship, suggested, at the beginning of the 1980s, an economic and political potential that could make East Asia a center of power in the world to rival the North Atlantic and Western Europe. In a real sense, from this point of view, Japan itself served as a vehicle whereby China could become part of a major international economic power.

FORMOSA

The rapprochement between Washington and Peking and the eventual normalization of relations included American recognition that the disposition of the island of Formosa and its Guomindang regime was, fundamentally, a matter internal to China to be resolved by negotiations between the parties concerned. Japan had accepted the same formula in its earlier negotiations with Peking for normalization. In the perspective of Chinese foreign policy, Taiwan was a domestic matter that had been internationalized only by virtue of the interest shown in the Guomindang regime and the island by foreign powers such as the United States and Japan.

After the beginning of Sino-American rapprochement and normalization, however, Peking began to treat Formosa, in terms of diplomatic action (rather than theory and pronouncement), almost as if it were a foreign power and to deal with Taipei in a fashion that refracted, rather than reflected, the fluid techniques with which it dealt with other powers before normalization (that is, before the initiation of formal diplomatic relations). Throughout 1972, for example, Peking sought to persuade residents of Taiwan to visit, even if secretly, the mainland. This tactic was not remarkable in itself. More interesting, however, was China's attempt to apply diplomacy-through-sports to Taiwan, as Peking had done with the United States through ping-pong and with Japan through volleyball. On May 25, 1973, a Chinese ping-pong master champion, visiting Hong Kong, invited "table tennis players and coaches in Taiwan province as well as enthusiasts of the sport among the overseas Chinese from Taiwan province"[35] to make official visits to China. A cable followed from the president of the Chinese Table Tennis Association to his opposite number on Taiwan, formally confirming the invitation. Although the opportunity was not even acknowledged by Taiwan, Peking nevertheless had tried to apply to the island a diplomatic technique it had used in other interstate relations to great effect.

Evidence suggests that as relations between China and Taiwan's now former protector, the United States, improved, Peking sought American mediation in the resolution of the problems the island presented. In October and November 1976, for example, rumors circulated in the Far East that Taipei had sent a high official to Peking for discussions. Peking did not respond to a request by a Japanese news agency for further information with a denial, although Taipei denied this report so hotly that it almost lent the story credence. Such rumors frequently spread through Tokyo and Hong Kong. More interesting, in November and December 1976 a Guomindang official and former member of the executive branch of the Guomindang government, at the time resident in the United States, made an extensive tour of China and was received by at least one high Chinese official. Such a visit could not have been made without at least the cognition, if not the encouragement, of the American government.

As normalization of China's relations with Washington and Tokyo proceeded on the basis of American and Japanese acknowledgment of China's views on the status of the island, the immediate need to seek a resolution to the problem receded into the background. Moreover, it was obvious to Peking that China had more to gain from the development of positive relations with the United States and Japan than from the reacquisition of Formosa by force. Furthermore, the expulsion of the Guomindang regime from the United Nations and increasingly severe limitations on its diplomatic relationships denied the Taipei government platforms from which it could continue to attack China's interests. As the 1980s began, it was obvious that both Peking and Taipei were prepared to allow time a way to find an accommodation between them.

Formosa was the biggest and most important piece of Chinese *terra irredenta* in Peking's eyes, but it was not the only one. Others included the Diaoyu Islands between Formosa and Japan, the Hsi Hsa Islands in the South China Sea, and even smaller islands. Emotionally these islands represented for China parts of its territory that were occupied or claimed by states that not only lacked legitimate claims (Formosa, Japan, South Korea, Vietnam, and the Philippines) but were in illegal occupation. They had a further significance, however. As China's interest in offshore and seabed resources grew, these island groups became significant as potential bases for exploration and resource development; furthermore, particularly in the case of the Diaoyu and Hsi Hsa groups, they had a certain strategic importance *vis-à-vis* Formosa and Vietnam, respectively. The Hsi Hsa Islands would also provide China with a strategic base in the middle of the South China Sea. In all cases, possession of the islands would permit China to extend its claims over territorial waters and the seabed under them.

From the beginning of the 1970s, as China began to assume more and more of a major international role both at the United Nations and in bilateral diplomatic relations, Peking asserted its historical and legal claims to the islands in question. The extent to which Peking pursued these claims depended largely on costs and challenges. The issues would flare up from time to time. As late as 1978, however, China attempted, fairly unsuccessfully, to assert its claims over the Diaoyus by sending some one hundred fishing boats to the islands with signs claiming Chinese sovereignty. The Japanese protested and the Chinese boats soon withdrew. Peking claimed that the incident had been blown up by Japanese anti-Chinese hawks. At the same time, the Chinese claimed that the appearance of the fishing boats had been an accident. The Japanese accepted Peking's explanation and put an end to the incident. Two years earlier the Chinese, Vietnamese, Formosans, and Filipinos had seemed about to enter a very confused situation of armed hostilities in and around the Nan Sha (or Spratly) Islands in the South China Sea. Confrontation had been avoided, but there was no reason not to believe that these and similar areas could become foci of minor conflicts in the future.

China at the United Nations

Possession of the United Nations seat assigned to China by the U.N. Charter provided a major subject for dispute between Peking and Washington throughout the 1950s and 1960s. China's concerns were essentially fivefold. First, membership in the United Nations became, after 1945, an important mechanism for the legitimation of governments. Diplomatic recognition by other governments remained, of course, the primary means of legitimation, but U.N. membership served either to reinforce diplomatic recognition or to work around it. Thus, for example, a new nation or a new government come to power in an established nation by means of revolution or coup could achieve a large measure of legitimacy through U.N. membership even if one or another of the great powers, particularly the superpowers, denied it legitimacy by refusing to extend diplomatic recognition. China sought membership in the U.N.—in its case, possession of the seat assigned to China—for this very reason. Moreover, membership in the

U.N. would enable Peking to pursue discussions with governments with which it had no formal relations. Second, the occupation of that seat by the Guomindang regime conferred upon it a legitimacy China sought to deny. Third, membership in the United Nations would provide China with access to areas of the world and to international problems from which Peking was barred by its absence from the world organization. As a great power, if not a superpower, China needed a forum in which it could prove its status by pronouncement. Moreover, China's seat was a great power seat—it included permanent membership on the Security Council, which further testified to China's great power status. Membership would mean Chinese participation in U.N. bodies and commissions, access to which was blocked without membership. The various agencies of the United Nations would provide China with an arena for the development of its leadership of the Third World. As the United Nations became a locus in which the North-South contradiction received greater and greater attention, particularly in economic matters, China, as the world's largest poor country and as the recognized antagonist of the superpowers, both of which were advanced industrial states, found itself in a position to develop its leadership by consistently supporting the interests of the poor, or Southern, nations of the world. Her best access to the Third World as a body of nations, in other words, was through the United Nations. Fourth, Peking sought U.N. membership precisely because the United States insisted on using every diplomatic wile it could muster to deny China a seat. The achievement of membership became a necessary precondition to any improvement in Peking's relations with the United States. Finally, as China's relations with the Soviet Union worsened disastrously, Peking needed access to the one forum in which China could publicly oppose Moscow and, at the same time, provide diplomatic and political leadership to those countries China needed to recruit into an anti-Soviet alliance, however informal that alliance might be.

American opposition almost single-handedly kept China out of the world body. Washington's commitment to the Guomindang regime was one reason for this opposition. Internal political considerations also played a role, at least to the extent that any administration that let down its guard enough to permit China into the United Nations would suffer severe criticism from its opponents. Nevertheless, China finally won its seat, together with the expulsion of the Guomindang regime, on October 25, 1971. The actual maneuver whereby this was accomplished consisted of two resolutions. The first, which the United States and Japan co-sponsored, declared that Taiwan's expulsion from the United Nations was an "important question" and, therefore, a two-thirds' vote in the United Nations General Assembly was required for action. Because the question about an important question was not an important question itself, however, this resolution required only a simple majority to pass; it was defeated by a vote of fifty-five to fifty-nine, with fifteen abstentions. The second resolution, which restored to China all its lawful rights in the United Nations and immediately expelled "the representatives of Chiang Kaishek," was sponsored by twenty-two countries. Because it was not an important question according to the ruling of the first resolution, this resolution required a simple majority and passed seventy-six to thirty-five, with seventeen abstentions. Both the United States and Japan voted in the negative.[36] The complexity of this maneuver undoubtedly was intended to satisfy potential critics of the American administration within the United States. By the latter part of 1971 preparations were already under way for Nixon's visit to Peking, and American opposition to China's taking its seat in the United Nations now appeared more formalistic than real.

Hailing the vote as a great victory for Mao Zedong-thought and the Cultural Revolution, the new Chinese delegation reached New York on November 11 and took its place immediately. By the end of December Peking was participating in several United Nations councils and in several specialized agencies. On the one hand, the United Nations satisfied China's needs by giving it access, as a permanent great power member, to such varied international activities as conferences on international narcotic problems and conferences on the law of the sea. China participated actively, enthusiastically, and responsibly in all these, providing wherever possible leadership to the smaller Third World countries both in defining their own interests and positions and in opposing the policies of the two superpowers. At the same time, China took full advantage of the platform the United Nations afforded to air its views on all the problems that concerned the world's governments.

China's entry into the United Nations had three primary consequences. First, it drew China into the complex web of international relationships and problems and thereby contributed to the growth of both China's stature as a great power and its experience in the world of multilateral diplomacy. Second, U.N. membership removed a major block to the development of bilateral relationships between China and at least two major powers, Japan and the United States; the lack of these bilateral relationships had contributed heavily to international tension and unease. Finally, and at least as important, by giving China the opportunity to provide leadership to the Third World as a bloc, China's U.N. membership enabled the Third World to begin defining its own interests more precisely. This is not to suggest either that the Third World succeeded in functioning as a coherent bloc in world politics or that China succeeded in providing the kind of leadership that would have been required if the contradictions among the various members of the Third World were to be resolved in favor of some form of bloc unity. No coherent Third World bloc developed and one of the reasons for this lack was the persistence of major contradictions among Third World governments. Nonetheless, at the very least

China could deny to the Soviet Union the role it coveted as the spokesman for the underdeveloped regions of the globe, and as time went on Chinese opposition to the Soviet Union in the United Nations helped define the Soviet Union in the terms China wanted to assign to it, a superpower member of the First World, a leader of the Oikoumene.

IMPERIUM IRREDENTUM

During the period of Manchu rule both Tibet and Xinjiang had been integral parts of the Empire. During the period of polycentrism they had slipped away to a certain extent, but the new state brought them thoroughly back into the Empire in the course of the 1950s. Outer Mongolia, however, which had been intricately involved in the Empire, slipped away completely: as the Mongolian People's Republic it stoutly maintained its independence after 1921, under close Soviet supervision and with considerable Soviet military and economic support. As an independent member of the Soviet bloc, Mongolia remained far beyond the reach of China's power after 1949. Nevertheless, throughout the first two decades of the new state's existence, normal interstate relations developed between Peking and Ulan Bator.

Two factors significantly influenced the course of Sino-Mongolian relations. First, Mongolia was so closely allied to the Soviet Union that whatever the internal sentiments of the Mongol leadership and people may have been, relations with China had to reflect, and reflect almost immediately, all the vicissitudes of the Sino-Soviet relationship. Thus, for example, in the 1950s considerable trade took place between China and Mongolia, and China extended aid in certain forms, particularly road and railroad construction, to Mongolia. Peking sent several thousand Chinese workers into Mongolia to labor on construction projects in an economy that was chronically short of labor in the modern sector. Mongolia remained, even under its own form of communism, a largely nomadic society with a population insufficient to the needs of an economy with pretensions to modernization and expansion. The growing abrasiveness in relations between Peking and Moscow was echoed not only in government-to-government relations between China and Mongolia but also in people-to-people relations between the Chinese (largely Han) workers in Mongolia and the Mongolian populace. Throughout the late fifties and the sixties, incidents were not infrequent, and China eventually withdrew its aid and its workers from Mongolia. The second factor that influenced Peking's relations with Ulan Bator was Chinese policy toward those Mongols who inhabited territories on the Chinese side of the Sino-Mongolian frontier. While the Outer Mongols were, for the most part, Khalkhas and the Inner Mongols, as the inhabitants of the Mongolian lands inside China were known collectively, belonged to other tribes, strong ties of kinship and culture united these legally and politically divided peoples. Nationalism in the Mongolian People's Republic, therefore, found grist for its mill in the supposedly oppressive policies the Han majority in China pursued toward the Inner Mongols.

Relations between China and Mongolia were, by the beginning of the 1970s, to all intents and purposes a subset of the relations betweeen Peking and Moscow. On the one hand, normal state-to-state relations continued, as they did in almost every case in which Communist Party-to-Communist Party relations were sundered. For example, in April 1974 China and Mongolia signed a trade agreement, as they were accustomed to do annually or biannually. At the same time, Mongolia kept up its attacks on Peking: in June 1974 Ulan Bator accused China of trying to destroy all chances for international détente. However, the issues that gave real substance to the acrimony between Ulan Bator and Peking were largely local and far more interesting than the echoes of Moscow statements Ulan Bator's press and radio were usually wont to broadcast. In September 1973, for example, a Mongolian newspaper published materials that condemned the Chinese for various errors, including cartographic imperialism—errors in maps depicting the Sino-Mongolian frontier; the conduct of military exercises too close to the frontier, often accompanied by penetration of Mongolian territory; and the killing of "rare animals protected by law."[37] In August 1974, *Unen*, the Mongolian equivalent of Moscow's *Pravda*, accused the Chinese of having destroyed the Republic of Inner Mongolia in 1946, "exterminating to a man" the Mongolian freedom fighters who had been struggling for self-determination and autonomy. *Unen* also accused the Chinese of practicing hegemonism in Inner Mongolia and of systematically destroying the Inner Mongols' cultural heritage.[38]

One of the most interesting Mongolian attacks on China appeared as an editorial in *Unen* at the end of July 1975. Accusing Peking of revanchism and neofascism and of supporting militarism around the world, the newspaper declared that China's policies were "dictated by the 'arch-reactionary idea of Sino-centrism' which meant the transformation of China into the hub of a Maoist super-empire." China's weapons in this effort included an alliance with the imperialists and "colonies of Chinese emigrants" whom it planned to use as "a fifth column for the realization of [China's] hegemonic aspirations." This attack, which has been characterized as "remarkably bitter," could have been framed in such terms only by members of a culture well acquainted with the Empire but who had themselves become part of the Oikoumene. The conflict was bound to continue.[39]

A Perspective

THE STUDY OF CHINA's foreign relations—of the Empire's external policy—raises as many questions as it answers. Some phenomena are striking. Most recently, for example, even the casual observer cannot help but be impressed with the relative ease and rapidity with which China's foreign policy *appears* to have changed course and to have moved from utter antagonism to the United States to increasingly intense and close, even enthusiastic, interaction. Is this ease and rapidity of change real or apparent? If real, what made it possible? If merely apparent, what is behind it? The answer to these questions can be found only in hints and clues: there has been no real change in the sense of a change that was not allowed by the underlying coherent structures upon which China constructs the world and develops policy toward it.

The hints and clues point to the persistence of certain forms of behavior and certain views of the world. Historians sometimes are wont to talk about tradition *versus* change, as if the two were mutually exclusive. But within what context does tradition persist? To put the same question in different terms, within what context does change take place? Are there deep structures that are, or that give rise to, the construction of the world and of policy toward it, structures that permit change to take place, but only certain change and not all change? Can we define such structures or bring them sufficiently close to the surface so that we can see them and talk about them?

At the level of surface phenomena, the student cannot but be impressed by the repetition or reappearance of certain behaviors in the history of China's relations with other societies. For example, the red *versus* expert controversy of the Chinese Communists more than echoes the *t'i-yung* debate that was so central to the discussion of tradition and modern-

498

ization in the late Qing empire. The Chinese Communists have been deeply concerned with the question: Is it better to be techincally competent (expert) or ideologically correct (red), if the two come into conflict? This is a contemporary transformation of the problem that lay behind the late Qing slogan, "Chinese learning for substance, Western learning for instrument," in other words, use the technology of the "barbarians" to defend the purity of Confucian culture. Another example is the reversal from the extreme xenophobia of the Boxers to the extreme desire to learn from the West that characterized the court and many Han Chinese intellectuals after 1905, which certainly is paralleled by the reversal from the extreme xenophobia of the Cultural Revolution in the 1960s and the early 1970s to the extraordinary openness to the West that was the hallmark of the late 1970s and early 1980s. How can we explain the repetition of these surface phenomena? Are they more, or less, than the manifestation in history and sentiment of the deep structures to which the hints and clues we find in the record of Chinese foreign policy point? Are there some explanatory matrices that we can use to fit the pieces together into an intelligible whole? We may be unable to answer the question, but we can suggest some points for a perspective on it.

The whole history of the Empire's external relations—its relations with societies beyond the reach of imperial institutions and power—seems to be based on a fundamental dichotomy between "us" and "them." The dichotomy has persisted through changes in its more manifest content. In the traditional period, the dichotomy took the form of civilization *versus* barbarism, and the outsider who had not accepted the fundamental forms of sinitic culture was beyond the pale, a barbarian. In contemporary China a similar dichotomy characterizes the construction of the world, with the category "them" sometimes occupied by the Americans and their allies, sometimes by the Soviets and their allies. The dichotomy, not its content, persists at the deep level. At the level of broad institutional structures, the dichotomy appears again in the organization of the centralized, hierarchical Empire, ruled by a Confucian scholar-bureaucracy or a Communist Party bureaucracy, focused upon an emperor or a chairman, and held together by a deeply shared ideology, Confucianism or Marxism-Maoism. The other half of the dichotomy at this level has been, and is, the Oikoumene, a radically different institutional structure easily recognized as them and behaving according to its own imperatives. This same dichotomous structure appears in the dialectical relationship between Confucianism and modernism in the Qing empire and early interregnum and in the dialectical relationship betweeen the extreme Maoist thought promulgated during the Cultural Revolution and the Marxism-Maoism promulgated in the next period as a basis for modernization. Marxism-Maoism itself refracts the dichotomy in the dialectical opposition it posits between antagonistic and nonantagonistic contradictions. Indeed, this primary structure of dichotomy informs almost all major aspects of Peking's contemporary foreign policy.

Sensitivity to the specificities of the Empire's external policies may be heightened by some observations concerning the differences between Chinese and U.S. policies. China views the world in terms of dichotomies that are mutually contradictory, and it defines broad and specific policies in terms of these dichotomies. Furthermore, China views history as a progression through dichotomies. Regardless of whether history has an end or an objective, as some Marxists would insist it has, history *is* process, in the Chinese view, and correct policy is that which contributes to the foreward movement of history or uses history to achieve history's more immediate objectives. For example, justice for the Third World may be an intermediate objective in history regardless of whether an ultimate end to history exists. The best policy uses history to achieve this justice. Consequently, all policy and, ultimately, all judgments are relative to the immediate moment in which history, as process and structure, presents itself. The American view is quite different. American foreign policy is usually couched in terms of the national interest. In U.S. policy, values seem to derive from an assumption of the existence of an absolute definition of good and evil in the universe, and Washington does not seem to possess a concept of history as process in time. Rather, American foreign policy views history, and therefore politics, as a series of moments or events that are related to each other only in immediate cause-and-effect terms. This leads to a certain impatience with politics, while the Chinese appear to exhibit great patience, which the West often ascribes to a somewhat mystical view of the world that is supposedly characteristic of the Chinese but is really not mystical at all; Chinese "patience" is, rather, a consequence of a different philosophy of history and society.

Similar differences may be observed in the ways Chinese and Americans define the goals of, and values in, their policies. For China, both goals and values are present in history and process and are exhibited by them. The present is always read as a text that is defined by the future or by a structure of which history itself is but a manifestation. Americans, on the other hand, define goals and values in a much more immediate sense, not in history but in here-and-now events. For an American policy planner, therefore, victory or defeat is defined in terms of an immediate battle or diplomatic maneuver, while for the Chinese the immediate event is only a moment in a process, and victory or defeat is a consequence not of the event but of the process as a whole. The American policy planner thinks in terms of each battle as a war, while the Chinese thinks of each war as a battle in a dialectical process that is history itself. The American views foreign policy as a separate domain of human and inter-societal activity, while the Chinese sees it as history itself, without distinction between history and society or between domestic and foreign.

Mao Zedong captured the relationship between event and history, between phenomenon and structure, in "On Contradiction," an essay written in 1937. Contradictions in the form of mutually antagonistic, dichotomous phenomena are, in fact, integral parts of one and the same process. "In war, offence and defence, advance and retreat, victory and defeat are all contradictory phenomena," he wrote. But "without the one, the other cannot exist."[40] The process, too, can be described: "When the old unity and its constituent opposites yield place to a new unity and its constituent opposites, a new process emerges in place of the old. The old process is completed and the new one emerges. As the new process in its turn contains a new contradiction, the history of the development of its own contradiction begins."[41] That is not a bad description of the tranformation of the Sino-Soviet anti-American alliance through a period of disruption into a Sino-American anti-Soviet alliance. History is philosophically substantive.

But there is more. History does not develop evenly, and it is the very unevenness of history that propels it forward. Moreover, this unevenness has two aspects: first, there is the greater weight of one side of a dichotomy; second, more than one contradiction may exist at the same time, but one of the contradictions will be more significant than the other(s):

> We cannot treat all the contradictions in a process as being equal, but must distinguish between the principal and the secondary contradictions, and pay particular attention to grasping the principal one. But, in any contradiction, whether principal or secondary, can we treat the two contradictory aspects as being equal? No, we cannot. *In any contradiction, the development of the contradictory aspects is uneven. Sometimes there seems to be a balance of forces, but that is only a temporary and relative state; the basic state is unevenness. Of the two contradictory aspects, one must be the principal and the other the secondary.* The principal aspect is that which plays the leading role in the contradiction. The quality of a thing is mainly determined by the principal aspect of the contradiction that has taken the dominant position.[42]

The roots of Peking's concept of contradictions in the world of international politics and of the function of the primary contradiction of the superpowers and the secondary contradiction (secondary *only* at this state of history) between Empire and Oikoumene or between Third World and First World find literary expression in this statement. In slightly different terms, the primary contradiction between the superpowers is the overdetermining factor in this historical conjuncture. The immediate- and intermediate-range objective of Chinese policy must be to encourage the resolution of the primary contradiction by maintaining the unevenness within the contradiction—at this juncture by encouraging the United States against the Soviet Union—so that history may move forward.

Nothing is forever, however, in history or policy. Even war and peace are relative to each other. Mao wrote:

As everybody knows, war and peace transform themselves into each other. War is transformed into peace; for example, the First World War was transformed into postwar peace; the civil war in China has now also ceased and internal peace has come about. Peace is transformed into war; for example, the Kuomintang-Communist co-operation of 1927 was transformed into war, and the peaceful world situation today may also be transformed into a Second World War. Why? Because in a class society such contradictory things as war and peace are characterized by identity under certain conditions.[43]

In 1937 Mao outlined an analysis of the world, a construction of the world as history and process, that apparently provides a powerful explanatory instrument for Chinese policy in the world, and this is true regardless of the other uses to which his writings have been or may be put and regardless of Mao's own historical reputation. Mao was both Marxist and Chinese. The distinction is relevant, but more to philosophers than to historians or policy analysts. What is important is whether we can make some theoretical statements beyond policy itself that help illuminate the sources of Chinese foreign policy. Apparently we can.

Finally, thinking now as an American: are the Chinese constructions of the world and the policies Peking has developed toward the world any less valid than our own? Who is to say? One observation seems accurate, however: the Chinese construction of the world seems to lead to a modus operandi that gives Peking much greater maneuverability, perhaps because of the spatial relationship of goals and strategy the Chinese world view contains, than Washington seems to possess. In other words, China seems more flexible in the world than does the United States. That should give us some pause.

Notes

CHAPTER 1

[1] Ho-yun Hsu, *Ancient China in Transition: An Analysis of Social Mobility, 722–222 B.C.* (Stanford: Stanford University Press, 1965), p. 64.

CHAPTER 2

[1] Marcel Mauss, *The Gift: Forms and Functions of Exchange in Archaic Societies* (Glencoe: The Free Press, 1954), p. 78.

[2] On the concept of boundary mechanism, see Karl Polanyi, Conrad Arensberg, Harry W. Pearson, *ed., Trade and Market in the Early Empires: Economies in History and Theory* (Glencoe: The Free Press, 1957).

[3] On Bateson's theories and analysis of the perception process, see Jurgen Ruesch and Gregory Bateson, *Communication: The Social Matrix of Psychiatry* (New York: W. W. Norton, 1951). See especially Gregory Bateson, *Naven: A Survey of the Problems Suggested by a Composite Picture of the Culture of a New Guinea Tribe Drawn from Three Points of View* (Stanford: Stanford University Press, 1958), pp. 108–122.

[4] Joseph R. Levenson, "The inception and displacement of Confucianism: from history as the base of culture to historicism and shifting sands," *Diogenes* 42 (Summer 1963), pp. 65–80, especially 67–68.

[5] Vadime Elisseeff, "The middle empire, a distant empire, an empire without neighbors," *Diogenes* 42 (Summer 1963), pp. 60–64.

[6] *Kham-dinh Viet-su Thong-giam cuong-muc* (Texte et commentaire du miroir complet de l'histoire du Viet), *tr.* Maurice Durand, Ecole Francaise d'Extreme-Orient (Hanoi, 1950), pp. 24–27, 62–65.

[7] Kieu-Oanh-Mau, *Ban trieu ban nghich liet truyen* (Saigon, 1963), pp. 20–21.

[8] M. R. Seni Pramoj and M. R. Kukrit Pramoj, *King of Siam Speaks* (n.p., n.d.), p. 123. For examples of the use of Chinese seals by Mongkut, see *Ibid*, pp. 104, 107.

[9] H. G. Quaritch Wales, *Siamese State Ceremonies: Their History and Function* (London: Bernard Quaritch, 1931), pp. 84–90.

[10] *Ta-ch'ing Man-chou shih-lu* (Taipei, 1964), p. 287. I am indebted to Joseph Fletcher for the original translation upon which this version is based.

[11] S. E. Malov, *Pamiatniki drevnotiurskoi pis'mennosti: teksty i issledovaniia* (Moscow: Izdatel'stvo Akademii nauk SSSR, 1951), pp. 34–35.

¹² Max Gluckman, *Order and Rebellion in Tribal Africa: Collected essays, with an autobiographical introduction* (London: Cohen and West, 1963), p. 51.

¹³ For a discussion of a theoretical view of ritual as a mechanism for integration, see *Ibid*, pp. 50–83.

CHAPTER 3

¹ Hou Jen-chih, "Frontier horse markets in the Ming dynasty," in E-tu Zen Sun and John DeFrancis, *Chinese Social History: Translations of selected studies* (Washington: American Council of Learned Societies, 1956), pp. 309–332, esp. 322–324.

² Mauss, p. 3.

³ J. L. Cranmer-Byng, "Lord Macartney's Embassy to Peking in 1793," *Journal of Oriental Studies*, 4.1–2:133 (1957–1958).

⁴ Polanyi, p. 257.

⁵ *Ibid.*, pp. 240–257.

⁶ Philip L. Wagner, *The Human Use of the Earth* (Glencoe: The Free Press, 1960), pp. 58–71.

⁷ G. William Skinner, "Marketing and social structure in Rural China," *The Journal of Asian Studies*, 24.1:3–43 (November 1964), pp. 9–31.

⁸ *Ibid.*, p. 31.

⁹ Quoted in Li Chien-nung, "Price control and paper currency in Ming," in Sun, pp. 281–297, esp. p. 286.

¹⁰ *Ibid.*, p. 281.

¹¹ *Ibid.*, pp. 293, 287.

¹² On ports of trade see Polanyi, chapters IV, VII, and VIII. See esp. pp. 154ff.

¹³ Hou, pp. 323–329, esp. 323–324, 329.

¹⁴ For the text of this correspondence, see *Ch'ing T'ai-tsung Wen Huang-ti shih-lu*, *chuan* 3:41–42, 4:2b–6 (hereafter referred to as *SL-TT*). For a biography of T'ai-tsung (Abahai), see Arthur W. Hummel, *ed.*, *Eminent Chinese of the Ch'ing Period 1644–1912*, 2 vols. (Washington: Library of Congress, 1943), II, 394–395.

¹⁵ *SL-TT*, 14:13–15, 18b–20b.

¹⁶ *Ch'ing Sheng-tsu Jen Huang-ti shih-lu*, *chuan* 187.7 (hereafter this will be referred to as *SL-KH*).

¹⁷ On Hong Wu, see Hummel, I, 355.

¹⁸ *SL-KH*, 25:22.

¹⁹ See *SL-KH*, 116:18a–b.

²⁰ *Ibid.*, 232:4a–b. For instructions on surveillance measures, see *Ibid.*, 232:8b–9.

²¹ *SL-KH*, 270:14b–16, 271:6–7. On ironwood, see Morohashi Tetsuhi, *Dai Kanwa Jiten* (n.p., n.d.), vol. 11, p. 644.

[22] *SL-KH*, 298:3a–b.

[23] *Ch'ing Shih-tsung Hsien Huang-ti shih-lu, chuan* 81:20b–21 (hereafter referred to as *SL-YC*). For a biography of the Yung-cheng emperor, see Hummel, II, 915–920.

[24] On Kao Ch'i-cho, see Hummel, II, 735.

[25] Cranmer-Byng, p. 133.

CHAPTER 4

[1] Quoted in Immanuel Wallerstein, *The Modern World-System: Capitalist Agriculture and the Origins of the European World Economy in the Sixteenth Century* (New York: Academic Press, 1974), p. 128.

[2] Quoted in John K. Fairbank, Edwin O. Reischauer, and Albert M. Craig, *East Asia: The Modern Transformation, A History of East Asian Civilization*, volume 2 (Boston: Houghton Mifflin Company, 1965), p. 21.

[3] Lo-shu Fu, *ed.*, *A Documentary Chronicle of Sino-Western Relations (1644–1820)*, 2 vols. (Tucson: The University of Arizona Press, 1966), vol. I, p. 31.

[4] Marian Malowist, "The problem of the inequality of economic development in Europe in the latter Middle Ages," *Economic History Review*, 2nd series, XIX.1:15–28 (April 1966), p. 180, quoted in Wallerstein, p. 306.

[5] Fairbank *et al.*, *East Asia: The Modern Transformation*, p. 58.

[6] John K. Fairbank, Edwin O. Reischauer and Albert M. Craig, *East Asia: Tradition and Transformation* (Boston: Houghton Mifflin, 1978), p. 251.

CHAPTER 5

[1] Hsin-pao Chang, *Commissioner Lin and the Opium War* (Cambridge: Harvard University Press, 1964), p. 89.

[2] *Ibid.*, pp. 126–128.

[3] *Ibid.*, p. 135.

[4] Ssu-yu Teng and John K. Fairbank, *China's Response to the West: A Documentary Survey, 1839–1923* (New York: Atheneum, 1965), pp. 24–27.

[5] *Chang*, p. 141.

[6] *Ibid.*, p. 194.

[7] *Ibid.*, pp. 202ff.

[8] Quoted in *Ibid.*, p. 210.

[9] Fairbank *et al.*, *East Asia: The Modern Transformation*, p. 361.

[10] *Ibid.*, p. 376.

[11] *Ibid.*, p. 378.

[12] *Ibid.*, p. 477.

[13] Immanuel C. Y. Hsu, *China's Entrance into the Family of Nations:*

The Diplomatic Phase, 1858–1880 (Cambridge: Harvard University Press, 1960), p. 107.

14 Teng, pp. 47–49.

15 Fairbank *et al.*, *East Asia: The Modern Transformation*, p. 318.

16 Teng, p. 74.

17 *Ibid.*, pp. 74–75.

18 *Ibid.*, p. 101.

19 *Ibid.*, p. 28.

20 *Ibid.*, p. 29.

21 *Ibid.*, p. 31.

22 *Ibid.*, p. 38.

23 *Ibid.*, p. 39.

24 *Ibid.*, p. 63.

25 *Ibid.*, p. 51.

26 *Ibid.*, p. 69.

27 For excerpts from this essay, see *Ibid.*, pp. 166–174.

28 *Ibid.*, pp. 158–159.

29 *Ibid.*, p. 98.

30 Hsu, p. 126.

31 Mary Clabaugh Wright, *The Last Stand of Chinese Conservatism: The T'ung-Chih Restoration, 1862–1874* (Stanford: Stanford University Press, 1957), p. 237.

32 Hsu, p. 128.

33 Wright, p. 238.

CHAPTER 6

1 Teng, p. 196; Fairbank *et al.*, *East Asia: The Modern Transformation*, p. 615.

2 See, for example, Teng, pp. 197–205.

3 *Ibid.*, p. 209.

4 Quoted in Fairbank *et al.*, *East Asia: The Modern Transformation*, p. 630.

5 Wesley R. Fishel, *The End of Extraterritoriality in China* (Berkeley: University of California Press, 1952), p. 34.

6 *Ibid.*, p. 37.

7 *Ibid.*, p. 41.

8 *Ibid.*, p. 44.

9 *Ibid.*, p. 46.

10 *Ibid.*, p. 56.

11 *Ibid.*, p. 65.

12 *Ibid.*, p. 64.

13 See *Ibid.*, pp. 211–212 for a summary of this treaty.

14 Arthur N. Young, *China's Nation-Building Effort, 1927–1937: The*

Financial and Economic Record (Stanford: Hoover Institution Press, 1971), p. 325.

[15] *Ibid.*, pp. 326–329.

[16] Quoted in *Ibid.*, p. 362.

[17] *Ibid.*, p. 363.

[18] *Ibid*, p. 365.

[19] On this definition see *Ibid.*.

[20] *Ibid.*, p. 376.

[21] Quoted in *Ibid.*, p. 354.

[22] Fairbank *et al.*, *East Asia: The Modern Transformation*, pp. 616ff.

[23] Quoted in Young, p. 345.

[24] Quoted in Peter S. H. Tang, *Russian and Soviet Policy in Manchuria and Outer Mongolia, 1911–1931* (Durham: Duke University Press, 1959), pp. 137–138.

[25] For the text of this declaration, see Allen S. Whiting, *Soviet Policies in China, 1917–1924* (New York: Columbia University Press, 1954), pp. 269–271.

[26] Ho-t'ien Ma, *Chinese Agent in Mongolia, tr.* John De Francis (Baltimore: The Johns Hopkins Press, 1949), p. 74. This has to be a gross exaggeration.

[27] Quoted in Fairbank *et al.*, *East Asia: The Modern Transformation*, p. 666.

[28] Quoted in Whiting, p. 35.

[29] *Ibid.*, p. 201.

[30] *Ibid.*, p. 153.

[31] O. Edmund Clubb, *China and Russia: The "Great Game"* (New York: Columbia University Press, 1971), pp. 264–265.

CHAPTER 7

[1] O. Edmund Clubb, *20th Century China* (New York: Columbia University Press, 1965), pp. 166–167.

[2] *Ibid.*, p. 238.

[3] *Ibid.*, p. 241.

[4] Clubb, *China and Russia*, pp. 337–338.

[5] *Ibid.*, p. 341.

[6] Max Beloff, *Soviet Policy in the Far East, 1944–1951* (London: Oxford University Press, 1953), p. 30.

[7] Clubb, *China and Russia*, p 345.

[8] *Ibid.*, pp. 346–347.

[9] Arthur N. Young, *China and the Helping Hand, 1937–1945* (Cambridge: Harvard University Press, 1963), pp. 73–75.

[10] *Ibid.*, p. 83.

[11] Tang Tsou, *America's Failure in China, 1941–50* (Chicago: The University of Chicago Press, 1963), p. 33.

[12] *Ibid.*, p. 141.

CHAPTER 8

[1] Beloff, pp. 39–40.

[2] For "On New Democracy," see Mao Tse-tung, *Selected Works*, vol. 3: 1939–1941 (New York: International Publishers, 1954), pp. 106–156. For a discussion of this particular passage, see Tsou, p. 210, fn. 120.

[3] Clubb, *China and Russia*, pp. 360–361.

[4] Conrad Brandt, Benjamin Schwartz, and John K. Fairbank, *A Documentary History of Chinese Communism* (Cambridge: Harvard University Press, 1949), pp. 453–454.

[5] Beloff, p. 65.

[6] Tsou, pp. 443–444.

[7] *Department of State Bulletin*, January 16, 1950, p. 80, as quoted in Tsou, p. 531.

CHAPTER 9

[1] John Gittings, *The World and China, 1922–1972* (New York: Harper & Row, 1974), pp. 52–54.

[2] Theodore H. White and Annalee Jacoby, *Thunder out of China* (New York: William Sloane Associates, 1946), p. 289.

[3] Gittings, p. 165.

[4] Brandt *et al.*, p. 453.

[5] Gittings, p. 166.

[6] Tsou, p. 508.

[7] *Ibid.*, pp. 508–509.

[8] *Gittings*, pp. 175–176.

[9] *Ibid.*, p. 152.

[10] *Ibid.*, pp. 158–159.

[11] Beloff, p. 68.

[12] Gittings, p. 237.

[13] Beloff, pp. 73–76.

[14] *Ibid.*, p. 75.

[15] Gittings, p. 199.

[16] *Ibid.*, p. 202.

[17] Stuart Schram, *ed.*, *Chairman Mao Talks to the People. Talks and Letters: 1956–1971* (New York: Pantheon Books, 1974), p. 82.

[18] Gittings, p. 194.

[19] Lin Piao, "Long Live the Victory of the People's War!," in Samuel B. Griffith, *Peking and People's Wars* (New York: Frederick A. Praeger, 1966), pp. 51–114.

CHAPTER 10

[1] Gittings, p. 239.

[2] *Ibid.*, p. 240.

[3] *Ibid.*, p. 241.

[4] *Ibid.*, p. 242.

[5] *Ibid.*, p. 243.

[6] *Ibid.*, p. 251.

[7] Clubb, *China and Russia*, p. 441.

[8] Donald Z. Zagoria, *The Sino-Soviet Conflict, 1956–1961* (Princeton: Princeton University Press, 1962), p. 343.

[9] Clubb, *China and Russia*, p. 453.

[10] *Ibid.*, p. 456.

[11] Gittings, p. 256.

[12] Robert C. North, *The Foreign Relations of China*, 3rd ed. (North Scituate: Duxbury Press, 1978), p. 155.

[13] *Ibid.*, p. 158.

[14] Gittings, p. 208.

[15] North, p. 132.

[16] *Ibid.*, p. 135.

[17] *Ibid.*, p. 144.

[18] *Ibid.*, p. 183.

[19] *Ibid.*, p. 185.

[20] *Ibid.*, p. 186.

[21] Gittings, p. 223.

[22] *Ibid.*, pp. 230–231.

CHAPTER 11

[1] *The China Quarterly*, 50, (April/June 1972), p. 381.

[2] *Ibid.*, pp. 381–382.

[3] *The China Quarterly*, 62 (June 1975), p. 368.

[4] Roderick MacFarquhar, *ed.*, *Sino-American Relations, 1949–71* (New York: Praeger, 1972), p. 200.

[5] *Ibid.*, p. 222.

[6] *Ibid.*, p. 252.

[7] *Ibid.*, p. 253.

[8] *The China Quarterly*, 50 (April/June 1972), pp. 395–396.

[9] *Ibid.*, p. 402.

[10] *The China Quarterly*, 78 (June 1979), p. 436.

[11] Quoted in *The China Quarterly*, 47 (July/September 1971), p. 604.

[12] *The China Quarterly*, 58 (April/June 1974), p. 424.

[13] *The China Quarterly*, 56 (October/December 1973), p. 813.

[14] For the text of Teng's speech, see *The China Quarterly*, 59 (July/September 1974), pp. 641–646.

[15] *The China Quarterly*, 60 (December 1974), p. 837.

[16] *Ibid.*, p. 838.

[17] On Chinese foreign aid, see Gail A. Eadie and Denise M. Grizzell, "China's Foreign Aid, 1975–78," *The China Quarterly*, 77 (March 1979), pp. 217–234.

[18] *The China Quarterly*, 76 (December 1978), p. 965.

[19] *The China Quarterly*, 78 (June 1979), p. 439.

[20] *The China Quarterly*, 76 (December 1978), p. 948.

[21] *The China Quarterly*, 59 (July/September 1974), p. 653.

[22] *The China Quarterly*, 66 (June 1976), p. 440.

[23] *Ibid.*

[24] *The China Quarterly*, 76 (December 1978), p. 950.

[25] *Ibid.*

[26] *The China Quarterly*, 72 (December 1977), p. 897.

[27] *The China Quarterly*, 47 (July/September 1971), p. 601.

[28] *The China Quarterly*, 49 (January/March 1972), p. 197.

[29] *The China Quarterly*, 52 (October/December 1972), p. 776.

[30] *Ibid.*, p. 781.

[31] *The China Quarterly*, 66 (June 1976), pp. 441–442.

[32] *The China Quarterly*, 76 (December 1978), p. 949.

[33] *The China Quarterly*, 62 (June 1975), pp. 373–374.

[34] *The China Quarterly*, 78 (June 1979), p. 425.

[35] *The China Quarterly*, 55 (July/September 1973), p. 605.

[36] *The China Quarterly*, 49 (January/March 1972), pp. 202–203.

[37] *The China Quarterly*, 56 (October/December 1973), p. 813.

[38] *The China Quarterly*, 60 (December 1974), p. 842.

[39] *The China Quarterly*, 64 (December 1975), pp. 800–801.

[40] Mao Zedong, "On Contradiction," *Selected Works*, vol. 2, 1937–1938 (New York: International Publishers, 1954), p. 13–53, esp. p. 20.

[41] *Ibid.*, p. 21.

[42] *Ibid.*, p. 37.

[43] *Ibid.*, p. 45.

Suggested Reading

CHINAS FOREIGN RELATIONS have been a central theme in the study of East Asia since the middle of the nineteenth century, when Western interest in Chinese affairs deepened and broadened as a consequence of the Oikoumene's victory in the series of "Opium Wars" that have been called, in this book, the "Twenty-one Years' War." Great continents of source materials, surveys and monographic works have been published in Chinese, Japanese, Russian, French, German and English, not to mention the languages of the many countries that have interacted with China over the decades. No bibliography can hope to exhaust the resources for study of the field, even those in the English language. This list of titles, therefore, has two very modest purposes. First, it suggests, but only suggests, the range of material published in English and available for further study, and it contains ideas for further reading on specific topics in the history of China's foreign relations. I have tried to be selective and to bring to the reader's attention works that are relatively easily available. I have included only books; relevant articles are too numerous to begin to list in this format; moreover, many bibliographical guides exist that will help the reader locate items of interest. Second, it indicates those English-language works upon which the author has relied. I only hope that I have not omitted any work to which I owe a debt of gratitude for insight or information; if I have, I beg the author's forgiveness in advance.

CHINESE HISTORY

General background. The most thorough account of the grand sweep of East Asian history in general, and of Chinese history in particular, is contained in two volumes, Edwin O. Reischauer and John K. Fairbank, *East Asia: The Great Tradition* (Boston: Houghton Mifflin, 1960) and John K. Fairbank, Edwin O. Reischauer and Albert M. Craig, *East Asia: The Modern Transformation* (Boston: Houghton Mifflin, 1965). For a one volume modification of this two volume work, see John K. Fairbank, Edwin O. Reischauer and Albert M. Craig, *East Asia: Tradition and Transformation* (Boston: Houghton Mifflin, 1978). See also John K. Fairbank, *The United States and China*, 4th ed. (Cambridge, Mass.: Harvard University Press, 1979). For general histories of the three major periods covered in this book, see Frederic Wakeman, Jr., *The Fall of Imperial China* (New York:

511

The Free Press, 1975); James E. Sheridan, *China in Disintegration: The Republican Era in Chinese History, 1912–1949* (New York: The Free Press, 1975); Maurice Meisner, *Mao's China: A History of the People's Republic* (New York: The Free Press, 1977). For excellent bibliographies of suggested readings that cover China's internal history in the periods with which this book is concerned, consult the volumes in this series, which are listed above.

The most important journal for the study of contemporary China is *The China Quarterly*, published in London. It frequently contains important studies that pertain to China's international relations. Historical as well as contemporary studies are published in the *Journal of Asian Studies*, the *Harvard Journal of Asiatic Studies* and *Asian Survey*.

SOURCE MATERIALS

Documentary materials on China's international relations and foreign policies have been published primarily in Chinese and, to a lesser but still significant extent, in Japanese. Lo-shu Fu, *A Documentary Chronicle of Sino-Western Relations (1644–1820)*, 2 vols. (Tucson: University of Arizona Press, 1966) provides a broad survey of documents for the period indicated, however, and the second volume is an index that serves as an indispensable guide to the subjects and personae in the documents themselves. Earl Swisher, *China's Management of the American Barbarians: A Study of Sino-American Relations, 1841–1861* (New Haven: Far Eastern Association, Yale University, 1953) focusses on the Qing empire's policy toward the United States. The best survey of China's intellectual and political reaction to the new world that developed from the Twenty-one Years' War, and which combines documents with incisive and insightful commentary, is Ssu-yu Teng and John K. Fairbank, *China's Response to the West: A Documentary Survey, 1839–1923* (Cambridge, Mass.: Harvard University Press, 1954).

The history of Communism in China and its impact on international relations is represented by many documentary collections. The early history of Sino-Soviet interactions is documented in C. Martin Wilbur and Julie Lien-ying How, *eds., Documents on Communism, Nationalism, and Soviet Advisers in China, 1918–1927: Papers Seized in the 1927 Peking Raid* (New York: Columbia University Press, 1956). A broader documentary survey that provides important background information as well as materials on international relations is Conrad Brandt, *et al., A Documentary History of Chinese Communism* (Cambridge, Mass.: Harvard University Press, 1959).

Treaties and formal agreements provide the skeleton of a country's international relations. Two standard collections for China are John Van Antwerp MacMurray, *ed., Treaties and agreements with and concerning*

China, 1894–1919, 2 vols. (New York: H. Fertig, 1973); Ying-ching Ch'en, *Treaties and agreements between the Republic of China and other powers, 1929–1954, together with certain international documents affecting the interests of the Republic of China* (Washington: Sino-American Publication Service, 1957).

FOREIGN POLICY

General history. The classic survey of China's international relations during the late Qing and early Republican periods is Hosea Ballou Morse, *The International Relations of the Chinese Empire*, vol. I: The Period of Conflict, 1834–1860; vol. II: The Period of Submission, 1861–1893; vol. III: The Period of Subjection, 1894–1911 (London: Longmans, Green, 1910–1918). While detailed monographic studies and later surveys have made this work out of date in many respects, it remains useful both for its sweep and for many of the insights it gives from a time closer to the events. Several more contemporary works provide useful introductions: John Paton Davies, Jr., *Dragon by the Tail: American, British, Japanese, and Russian Encounters with China and One Another* (New York: W.W. Norton, 1972); Robert C. North, *The Foreign Relations of China* (North Scituate: Duxbury Press, 1978). John Gittings, *The World and China, 1922–1972* (New York: Harper and Row, 1974) is most useful for suggestions concerning the intellectual and theoretical foundations of Chinese Communist policy; it was particularly helpful in the writing of the present volume. For a Chinese Communist analysis of the history of China's foreign relations in the nineteenth and twentieth centuries, see Sheng Hu, *Imperialism and Chinese Politics* (Peking: Foreign Languages Press, 1955).

The Qing Dynasty. By far the most significant studies of the institutions of traditional China's interactions with other societies are contained in John K. Fairbank, *ed.*, *The Chinese World Order* (Cambridge, Mass.: Harvard University Press, 1968). The development of a transitional institutional framework in the period when "foreign policy" was a new concept is discussed in S. Meng, *The Tsungli Yamen: Its Organization and Functions* (Cambridge, Mass.: The East Asian Research Center, Harvard University Press, 1962). The process through which China entered the international community's formal institutional structures is the subject of Immanuel C.Y. Hsu, *China's Entrance into the Family of Nations: The Diplomatic Phase, 1858–1880* (Cambridge, Mass.: Harvard University Press, 1960).

The Oikoumene's approach to China is the subject of many monographs. Among the most outstanding and enlightening are Michael Greenberg, *British Trade and The Opening of China, 1800–42* (Cambridge: Cambridge University Press, 1951), and John King Fairbank, *Trade and Diplomacy on the China Coast: The Opening of the Treaty Ports, 1842–*

1854, 2 vols. (Cambridge, Mass.: Harvard University Press, 1953; Stanford: Stanford University Press, 1969). The latter, which is a classic in the field, pioneered the analysis of the early interactions between Oikoumene and Empire from the Chinese perspective, and it has not been surpassed. The beginning of the Twenty-one Year's War is the focus of Hsin-pao Chang, *Commissioner Lin and the Opium War* (Cambridge, Mass.: Harvard University Press, 1964). A direct consequence of the impact of the Oikoumene on the Empire was the great Taiping Rebellion in the middle of the 19th century. Its international dimension is studied in Ssu-yu Teng, *The Taiping Rebellion and the Western Powers: A Comprehensive Survey* (Oxford: Clarendon Press, 1971). Mary Clabaugh Wright, *The Last Stand of Chinese Conservatism: The T'ung-Chih Restoration, 1862–1874* (Stanford: Stanford University Press, 1957), which analyzes the Qing attempt to find a new basis for political and institutional life after the Taiping Rebellion and in light of the Oikoumene's challenge, provides useful information and insights about the relationship of domestic and foreign policy in the period. Chester C. Tan, *The Boxer Catastrophe* (New York: Columbia University Press, 1955), concentrates on the crisis at the turn of the century and is a useful parallel to Chang's study of Lin Zexu and the Opium War (see above).

Among the best studies of economic-institutional issues created by imperialism in China are Kwang-ching Liu, *Anglo-American Steamship Rivalry in China, 1862–1874* (Cambridge, Mass.: Harvard University Press, 1962), and En-han Lee, *China's Quest for Railway Autonomy, 1904–1911: A Study of the Chinese Railway-rights Recovery Movement* (Singapore: Singapore University Press, 1977). For a study of one Western company's activities in China, consult Edward LeFevour, *Western Enterprise in Late Ch'ing China: A Selective Survey of Jardine, Matheson and Company's Operations, 1842–1895* (Cambridge, Mass.: East Asian Research Center, Harvard University, 1968).

Studies of the political and intellectual impact of the West on Chinese society at large, i.e., that focus on a broader perspective than that provided by the Dynasty's institutions, are Frederic C. Wakeman, *Strangers at the Gate: Social Disorder in South China, 1839–1861* (Berkeley: University of California Press, 1966), and Paul A. Cohen, *China and Christianity: The Missionary Movement and the Growth of Chinese Anti-foreignism, 1860–1870* (Cambridge, Mass.: Harvard University Press, 1963). Yen-p'ing Hao, *The Compradore in Nineteenth Century China: Bridge between East and West* (Cambridge, Mass.: Harvard University Press, 1970), is a study of the development of a "contact group" that mediated between the Oikoumene and the Empire. Lin [William L.] Tung, *China and the Foreign Powers: The Impact of and Reaction to Unequal Treaties* (Dobbs Ferry: Oceana Publications, 1970), analyzes the structure and development of the Chinese response to the Empire's situation of inequality vis-à-vis the Oikoumene.

The Republic. By far the most confusing period in the history of China's modern international relations and foreign policy is the years 1912–1949. The best studies of foreign relations in this period concern specific problems. For examplé, the establishment and disestablishment of extraterritoriality are analyzed in a pair of works: George W. Keeton, *The Development of Extraterritoriality in China*, 2 vols. (New York: H. Fertig, 1969), and Wesley R. Fishel, *The End of Extraterritoriality in China* (Berkeley: University of California Press, 1952). Carl F. Nathan, *Plague Prevention and Politics in Manchuria, 1910–1931* (Cambridge, Mass.: The East Asian Research Center, Harvard University, 1967) studies an early example of international attempts to alleviate China's internal crises, while two works by Arthur N. Young, *China's Nation-Building Effort, 1927–1937: The Financial and Economic Record* (Stanford: Hoover Institution Press, 1971) and *China and the Helping Hand, 1937–1945* (Cambridge, Mass.: Harvard University Press, 1963), examine international participation in institutional construction and internal reconstruction during the era of the Guomindang regime.

The Communist Period. It is not surprising that material on the foreign policies and international relations of China since 1949 should bulk overwhelmingly large in the published bibliography of the field. It is almost unmanageable. One of the best guides is Anthony Ferguson, *Far Eastern Politics: China, Japan, Korea, 1950–1975. An Index to International Political Science Abstracts* (Paris: International Political Science Association, 1977).

A study of the formative years of Chinese Communist foreign policy is James Reardon-Anderson, *Yenan and the Great Powers: The Origins of Chinese Communist Foreign Policy, 1944–1946* (New York: Columbia University Press, 1980). A distinctive characteristic of survey studies of Chinese foreign policy since 1949 is the fact that they are written in, and necessarily reflect, periods of time that are powerfully influenced by immediate concerns; moreover, they often contain indications of the author's political perspective, even if it derives from interests that are not immediately tied to China and the study of it. Among the more interesting such surveys are: Harold C. Hinton, *Communist China in World Politics* (New York: Houghton Mifflin, 1966); A. M. Halpern, *ed.*, *Policies Toward China: Views from Six Continents*, Council on Foreign Relations (New York: McGraw-Hill, 1965); King C. Chen, *ed.*, *The Foreign Policy of China* (Roseland, N.J.: East-West Who? in cooperation with Seton Hall University Press, 1972); Michael B. Yahuda, *China's Role in World Affairs* (New York: St. Martin's Press, 1978); and Joseph A. Camilleri, *Chinese Foreign Policy: The Maoist Era and Its Aftermath* (Seattle: University of Washington Press, 1980). The impact and consequences of the Cultural Revolution are the point of departure for Robert G. Sutter, *Chinese Foreign Policy after the Cultural Revolution* (Boulder: Westview Press, 1977).

For some studies of the broad strategies of Chinese Communist foreign policy, see: Peter Van Ness, *Revolution and Chinese Foreign Policy: Peking's Support for Wars of National Liberation* (Berkeley: University of California Press, 1970); Vidya Prakash Dutt, *China's Foreign Policy, 1958–62* (New York: Asia Publishing House, 1964); Melvin Gurtov and Byong-Moo Hwang, *China under Threat: The Politics of Strategy and Diplomacy* (Baltimore: Johns Hopkins University Press, 1980).

The choice of issues upon which monographic studies concentrate also reflects the concerns of the community of specialists and informed citizens. Arms control, for example, has been, and remains, a primary issue in the study of Communist China's international relations. Some examples of work on this topic are: Alice Langley Hsieh, *Communist China's Strategy in the Nuclear Era* (Englewood Cliffs: Prentice-Hall, 1962). Morton H. Halperin and Dwight H. Perkins, *Communist China and Arms Control* (Cambridge, Mass.: East Asian Research Center and Center for International Affairs, Harvard University, 1965); Morton H. Halperin, *China and the Bomb* (New York: Frederick A. Praeger, 1965). A broader perspective is provided by Harry G. Gelber, *Technology, Defense, and External Relations in China, 1975–1978* (Boulder: Westview Press, 1979). Another area of great concern has been China's impact on the Third World, and this has given rise to a limited number of important studies. See, for example: Charles Neuhauser, *Third World Politics: China and the Afro-Asian People's Solidarity Organization, 1957–1967* (Cambridge, Mass.: East Asian Research Center, Harvard University, 1970); Alvin Z. Rubinstein, *Soviet and Chinese Influence in the Third World* (New York: Praeger, 1975); James David Armstrong, *Revolutionary Diplomacy: Chinese Foreign Policy and the United Front Doctrine* (Berkeley: University of California Press, 1977).

Communist China's "re-entry" into the international community has been another area of primary scholarly interest. Works too numerous to mention analyzed the problems posed by the potential recognition of the Chinese government by the United States, and they retained historical, but not really scholarly, interest after recognition took place. Once China had assumed its seat in the United Nations and had entered more fully into all aspects of international affairs, the study of institutional issues became more important. See, for example, Samuel S. Kim, *China, the United Nations, and World Order* (Princeton: Princeton University Press, 1979), and Jerome A. Cohen and Hungdah Chiu, *People's China and International Law: A Documentary Study* (Princeton: Princeton University Press, 1974).

REGIONAL RELATIONSHIPS

The primacy of China's continental orientation, the role of the United States as the major actor in the Oikoumene's interaction with China, the reassertion of the continental orientation as embodied, after 1949, in the Sino-Soviet relationship and, later, dispute, and the relatively lesser importance China attached, and attaches, to its relations with Western Europe, Africa and Latin America, are reflected in the weight of publication in each of these areas.

The Inner Asian Crescent. The work that established the primary theoretical framework for the study of the Empire's relations with the societies on its Inner Asian frontiers was Owen Lattimore, *Inner Asian Frontiers of China*, 2nd ed. (New York: American Geographical Society, 1951). It is unsurpassed. While there are some works that concentrate on Outer Mongolia, later called the Mongolian People's Republic, in the modern era, relatively few are primarily concerned with relations between China and Mongolia. Mongolia's legal status before its recognition by China and its later admission into the United Nations was defined in Gerard M. Friters, *Outer Mongolia and Its International Position* (London: George Allen and Unwin, 1951). There is almost no material reflecting Chinese observations in Mongolia. An exception, and a fascinating one at that, is Ho-t'ien Ma, *Chinese Agent in Mongolia*, tr. John De Francis (Baltimore: The Johns Hopkins Press, 1949). The disposition of Chinese Turkestan, more legitimately called Xinjiang, has been an issue in Chinese-Russian relations since their inception in Central Asia in the 17th century, but the subject has been little studied in English. Two important works, the first rather journalistic and the second more in the nature of a *memoire*, are Owen Lattimore, *Pivot of Asia: Sinkiang and the Inner Asian Frontiers of China and Russia* (Boston: Little, Brown and Company, 1950), and Allen S. Whiting and Shih-ts'ai Sheng, *Sinkiang: Pawn or Pivot?* (East Lansing: Michigan State University Press, 1958). General Sheng was himself an important figure in the modern history of Xinjiang. On Chinese policy toward Xinjiang since the establishment of Communist power in Peking, see Donald H. McMillen, *Chinese Communist Power and Policy in Xinjiang, 1949–1977* (Boulder: Westview Press, 1979).

Tibet too, despite the fascination its religion, arts and society hold for Western scholars in many fields, has not been a major focus of attention in the study of China's international relations. One exception is Luciano Petech, *China and Tibet in the Early 18th Century: History of the Establishment of Chinese Protectorate in Tibet* (Leiden: E.J. Brill, 1950). Throughout the 20th century, Tibet has figured in international affairs primarily in the context of British and independent India's defense problems along its northern frontier and its relations with China. A guide to the materials on this subject can be found in Julie G. Marshall, *Britain and Tibet, 1765–1947: The Background to the India-China Border Dispute: A Select Annotated Bibliography of Printed Material in European Languages* (Bundoora: La Trobe University Library, 1977). While travel literature about Tibet abounds and is often of high excitement, modern scholarly work on the

West's penetration of this region is relatively scant. An important exception is Alastair Lamb, *Britain and Chinese Central Asia: The Road to Lhasa, 1767 to 1905* (London: Routledge and Kegan Paul, 1960).

East Asia. The most important survey of Sino-Japanese relations from the last decades of the Qing through the first two decades of Communist power in China is Marius B. Jansen, *Japan and China: From War to Peace, 1894–1972* (Chicago: Rand McNally College Publishing Company, 1975). An interesting aspect of an early Japanese attempt to participate in Chinese politics is the subject of Marius B. Jansen, *The Japanese and Sun Yat-sen* (Cambridge, Mass.: Harvard University Press, 1954). The published literature on the Japanese in China during the Republican period is voluminous. Of particular interest as a case study of the development of Japanese policy is Sadako N. Ogata, *Defiance in Manchuria: The Making of Japanese Foreign Policy, 1931–1932* (Berkeley: University of California Press, 1964). Shao Chuan Leng, *Japan and Communist China* (Kyoto: Doshisha University Press, 1958), provides a standard analysis of Japan and China after 1949. A long range, and different geographical, perspective is offered by Rajendra Kumar Jain, *China and Japan, 1949–1976* (Atlantic Highlands, N.J.: Humanities Press, 1977).

Korea, once a full participant in the tribute system, was detached from it through the process of its "opening" by the United States. The basic study of this problem within the context of Chinese foreign policy is Foo Chien, *The Opening of Korea: A Study of Chinese Diplomacy, 1876–1885* (Hamden: Shoe String Press, 1967). After 1895 Korea moved into the Japanese orbit and, eventually, was occupied by Japan, but it again became a major issue for Chinese policy at the beginning of the 1950s, as demonstrated in Allen S. Whiting, *China Crosses the Yalu: The Decision To Enter the Korean War* (New York: Macmillan, 1960). A good survey of China's policies in East Asia is Doak A. Barnett, *China and the Major Powers in East Asia* (Washington: The Brookings Institution, 1977).

Taiwan presents special problems in the study of Chinese foreign policy and international relations, generally because of its ambiguous relationship to China as a whole and, more particularly, because of the claims of the Guomindang regime, domiciled on the island after 1949, to be *the* government of China. A good introduction to the problem is Ralph N. Clough, *Island China* (Cambridge, Mass.: Harvard University Press, 1978). The more immediate issue of Taiwan in Chinese foreign policy before the advent of Japan as the major foreign power interested in the island is studied in Sophia Su-fei Yen, *Taiwan in China's Foreign Relations, 1836–1874* (Hamden: Shoe String Press, 1965). After Taiwan reverted to Chinese control in 1945, it became an issue in Sino-American relations about which libraries were written. Three works that provide significant insights and materials about the subject are: William M. Bueler, *U.S. China Policy and The Problem of Taiwan* (Boulder: Colorado Associated University Press,

1971); Jerome A. Cohen *et al., Taiwan and American Policy: The Dilemma in U.S.-China Relations* (New York: Praeger, 1971); Hungdah Chiu, ed., *China and the Question of Taiwan: Documents and Analysis* (New York: Praeger, 1973).

Southeast Asia. Long within the penumbra of Chinese power and profoundly influenced by Chinese culture, Southeast Asia's relations with China have attracted surprisingly little scholarly concern in the English-speaking world, and this is the case despite the fact that in the 1960s and 1970s it was the locus of major military conflict. On China and the region as a whole, see Melvin Gurtov, *China and Southeast Asia—The Politics of Survival: A Study of Foreign Policy Interaction* (Baltimore: The Johns Hopkins University Press, 1975), and Jay Taylor, *China and Southeast Asia: Peking's Relations with Revolutionary Movements* (New York: Praeger, 1974). The consequences for Chinese policy of French colonial penetration of the region is the subject of Henry McAleavy, *Black Flags in Vietnam: The Story of a Chinese Intervention* (New York: Macmillan, 1968), one of the very few studies of Sino-Vietnamese relations in modern times. For studies of Sino-Vietnamese relations in more recent times, see King C. Chen, *Vietnam and China, 1938–1954* (Princeton: Princeton University Press, 1969); Melvin Gurtov, *The First Vietnam Crisis: Chinese Communist Strategy and United States Involvement, 1953–1954* (New York: Columbia University Press, 1967). There are also very few studies of Chinese policy toward other Southeast Asian lands, such as David P. Mozingo, *Chinese Policy toward Indonesia, 1949–1967* (Ithaca: Cornell University Press, 1976) and Sarasin Viraphol, *Tribute and Profit: Sino-Siamese Trade, 1652–1853* (Cambridge, Mass.: Harvard University Press, 1983).

South Asia. Separated from China by the Himalayan mountain range, South Asia in modern times has never been an object of primary interest for Chinese policy. Sino-Indian border disputes provide the one exception to this rule, and they became prominent after the Communist government in Peking asserted its control over Tibet. At that point, Tibet's relations with China lost their ambiguity and Lhasa lost any potential for independent action. The best works on this topic are: Alastair Lamb, *The China-India Border: The Origins of the Disputed Boundaries* (London: Oxford University Press, 1964); Neville Maxwell, *India's China War* (Garden City: Anchor Books, 1972); John Rowland, *A History of Sino-Indian Relations: Hostile Co-existence* (Princeton: Van Nostrand, 1967); Harish Kapur, *The Embattled Triangle: Moscow—Peking—New Delhi* (New York: Humanities Press, 1973). As China's relations with India took a turn for the worse, her relations with Pakistan improved. See Anwar Hussain Syed, *China and Pakistan: Diplomacy of an Entente Cordiale* (Amherst: University of Massachusetts Press, 1974).

West Asia. Despite China's often loud support for one or another party in one or another of the many Middle Eastern disputes, she has hardly been directly involved in the politics of the region and, therefore, has not had to develop significant policy toward it. Three studies that explore various aspects of Chinese policy in the Middle East are Yitzhak Shichor, *The Middle East in China's Foreign policy, 1949–1977* (Cambridge: Cambridge University Press, 1979); Michael Brecher, *Israel, the Korean War and China: Images, Decisions and Consequences* (Jerusalem: Jerusalem Academic Press, 1974); Joseph E. Khalili, *Communist China's Interaction with the Arab Nationalists since the Bandung Conference* (New York: Exposition Press, 1970). Consequential works on other facets of Chinese interest in the area remain to be written.

Russia, the Soviet Union, and the Eastern Bloc. Throughout almost the entire Qing period, Russia played a more significant role in China and in Chinese foreign affairs than most Western scholars recognized, and it would not be ungenerous to say that that condition still exists. A major survey of the history of Sino-Russian relations by a significant Chinese scholar and diplomat, who had personal knowledge of the subject, is available in English translation: T'ien-fang Ch'eng, *A History of Sino-Russian Relations* (Washington: Public Affairs Press, 1957). Several American scholars have written survey histories, the most readable of which is O. Edmund Clubb, *China and Russia: The "Great Game"* (New York: Columbia University Press, 1971).

The early history of Russian-Chinese relations may be studied in three monographic works: Mark Mancall, *Russia and China: Their Diplomatic Relations to 1728* (Cambridge, Mass.: Harvard University Press, 1971); Joseph Sebes, *The Jesuits and the Sino-Russian Treaty of Nerchinsk (1689): The Diary of Thomas Pereira* (Rome: Institutum Historicum S.I., 1962); Eric Widmer, *The Russian Ecclesiastical Mission in Peking during the Eighteenth Century* (Cambridge, Mass.: East Asian Research Center, Harvard University Press, 1976). The definitive survey of Sino-Russian relations before 1912 remains to be written, however.

Several monographs focus on particular aspects of Russian-Chinese relations in the last part of the 19th century. Richard A. Pierce, *Russian Central Asia, 1867–1917: A Study in Colonial Rule* (Berkeley: University of California Press, 1960) provides important background information for a consideration of the growth of the Russian challenge to the Empire in Central Asia. On specific issues see: Immanuel C.Y. Hsu, *The Ili Crisis: A Study of Sino-Russian Diplomacy* (Oxford: Oxford University Press, 1965); Don C. Price, *Russia and the Roots of the Chinese Revolution, 1896–1911* (Cambridge, Mass.: Harvard University Press, 1974); Peter S. H. Tang, *Russian and Soviet Policy in Manchuria and Outer Mongolia, 1911–1931* (Durham: Duke University Press, 1959).

The 1917 revolution in Russia inaugurated a new and more complicated period in Sino-Russian relations, which is discussed in a series of works: Sow-Theng Leong, *Sino-Soviet Diplomatic Relations, 1917–1926* (Honolulu: University Press of Hawaii, 1976); Robert C. North, *Moscow and Chinese Communists* (Stanford: Stanford University Press, 1963); Allen S. Whiting, *Soviet Policies in China, 1917–1924* (New York: Columbia University Press, 1954); Conrad Brandt, *Stalin's Failure in China, 1924–1927* (Cambridge, Mass.: Harvard University Press, 1958); Charles B. McLane, *Soviet Policy and the Chinese Communists, 1931–1946* (New York: Columbia University Press, 1958). One of the best surveys of Soviet policy toward China during the latter part of this period is contained in Max Beloff, *Soviet Policy in the Far East: 1944–1951* (London: Oxford University Press, 1953).

The Sino-Soviet relationship after 1949 and, more particularly, the Sino-Soviet dispute, attracted considerable attention in the English-speaking world because it both puzzled and challenged policy-makers. See, for example, Donald S. Zagoria, *ed.*, *Communist China and the Soviet Bloc*, The Annals of The American Academy of Political and Social Science, vol. 349 (September 1963). The best guide to the literature of the dispute, a most complicated subject, is Vimla Saran, *comp.*, *Sino-Soviet Schism: A Bibliography, 1956–1964* (London: Asia Publishing House, 1971), and the most thorough study of it remains Donald S. Zagoria, *The Sino-Soviet Conflict: 1956–1961* (Princeton: Princeton University Press, 1962). For a later analysis, see John Gittings, *Survey of the Sino-Soviet dispute: A Commentary and Extracts from the Recent Polemics, 1963–67* (London: Oxford University Press, 1968). On the territorial dimension of the problem, see Tai Sung An, *The Sino-Soviet Territorial Dispute* (Philadelphia: The Westminster Press, 1973). There are probably few issues (other than Taiwan) in Chinese international relations that have attracted such polemical writing as has the subject of Sino-Russian relations. For the "official" Guomindang point of view, written by one who was in a position to designate his point of view as official, see Chiang Kai-shek, *Soviet Russia in China, a Summing-up at Seventy* (New York: Farrar, Strauss and Cudahy, 1958). Victor E. Louis, *The Coming Decline of the Chinese Empire, with a dissenting introduction by Harrison E. Salisbury* (New York: Times Books, 1979) represents a Soviet perspective. See also Drew Middleton, *The Duel of the Giants: China and Russia in Asia* (New York: Scribner, 1978) for an example of non-disinterested American analysis.

The United States. The history of Sino-American relations is the subject of numerous monographs, and fewer surveys, mostly by Americans. Here there is room to indicate only some of the more significant ones. The ideology of America's China policy is the subject of Marilyn Blatt Young, *The Rhetoric of Empire: American China Policy, 1895–1901* (Cambridge,

Mass.: Harvard University Press, 1968), and Warren I. Cohen, *America's Response to China: An Interpretative History of Sino-American Relations* (New York: Wiley, 1971). Philip West, *Yenching University and Sino-Western Relations, 1916–1952* (Cambridge, Mass.: Harvard University Press, 1976) illustrates one form of American penetration of China—the "western" in the title refers primarily to the United States, and Wilma Fairbank, *America's Cultural Experiment in China, 1942–1949*, Cultural Relations Programs of the U.S. Department of State, Historical Studies: Number 1 (Washington: Bureau of Educational and Cultural Affairs, Department of State, 1976) is an important survey of a largely unstudied field of activity.

American involvement in Chinese affairs from the late 1930s to 1949 has been a major issue in the study of American foreign affairs. For background to the problem, see the masterful work by Dorothy Borg, *The United States and the Far Eastern Crisis of 1933–1938* (Cambridge, Mass.: Harvard University Press, 1964). The best in-depth survey of the topic is Michael Schaller, *The U.S. Crusade in China, 1938–1945* (New York: Columbia University Press, 1979). Two other standard works are Herbert Feis, *The China Tangle: the American Effort in China from Pearl Harbor to the Marshall Mission* (Princeton: Princeton University Press, 1953), written by an outstanding American scholar of American foreign policy, not a "China specialist," and Tang Tsou, *America's Failure in China, 1941–1950* (Berkeley: The University of California Press, 1963), by a Chinese scholar with access to both English and Chinese sources. A classic analysis of a primary American actor on the Chinese scene during World War II is Barbara Tuchman, *Stilwell and the American experience in China, 1911–1945* (New York: Macmillan, 1971). Roderick MacFarquhar, *Sino-American Relations, 1949–1971* (New York: Praeger, 1972), provides an introduction to the documentation of the first period of Sino-American relations after the establishment of the new regime in Peking.

American diplomats in China played a unique role in the annals of American foreign policy; they often became participants in the Chinese scene and paid the cost of that participation in the United States when the United States "lost" (as it used to be said) China in 1949. What amounted to a purge of State Department officials who were concerned with China was significant both in institutional and historical terms; it was also a personal tragedy for many. See Ely Jacques Kahn, *The China Hands: America's Foreign Service Officers and What Befell Them* (New York: Viking, 1975); Gary May, *China Scapegoat: The Diplomatic Ordeal of John Carter Vincent* (Washington: New Republic Books, 1979). On the role of the Guomindang regime in the formulation of American policy toward China, see Ross Y. Koen, *The China Lobby in American Politics* (New York: Macmillan, 1960). Ta-jen Liu, *A History of Sino-American Diplomatic Relations, 1840–1974* (Taipei: China Academy, 1978) presents a Chinese Nationalist (Guomindang) view of American-Chinese relations in light of the reorientation of American policy from Taipei to Peking in the 1970s.

Western Europe. Most studies of China's relations with the countries of Western Europe are in the relevant Western European languages and, therefore, outside the scope of these suggested readings. On Chinese policy toward France at the end of the 19th century, however, see Lloyd E. Eastman, *Throne and Mandarins: China's Search for a Policy during the Sino-French Controversy, 1880–1885* (Cambridge, Mass.: Harvard University Press, 1967). Several studies of British-Chinese relations have been mentioned above. On the institutional background to Great Britain's China policy, see Nathan Albert Pelcovits, *Old China Hands and the Foreign Office* (New York: Octagon Books, 1969). On the interaction of diplomacy and the Chinese reaction to Western intrusions, see Edmund S. Wehrle, *Britain, China and the Antimissionary Riots, 1891–1900* (Minneapolis: University of Minnesota Press, 1966). For Sino-British relations after 1949, consult Evan Luard, *Britain and China* (Baltimore: The Johns Hopkins Press, 1962); Robert Boardman, *Britain and the People's Republic of China, 1949–74* (London: Macmillan, 1976). For one of the few studies in English of Sino-German relations, see John E. Schrecker, *Imperialism and Chinese Nationalism: Germany in Shantung* (Cambridge, Mass.: Harvard University Press, 1971).

Africa and Latin America. Although from time to time much has been written in the popular press about Chinese activities in Africa and Latin America, relatively little attention has been paid to these areas by scholars, and this has been almost entirely centered on the period after 1949, when China's relations with the "Third World" became a matter of concern for Anglo-American policy-makers. On China's relations with Africa, see Bruce D. Larkin, *China and Africa, 1949–1970: The Foreign Policy of the People's Republic of China* (Berkeley: University of California Press, 1971). George T. Yu, *China's African Policy: A Study of Tanzania* (New York: Praeger, 1975) is a case study of one country, but it suggests implications for a broader consideration of Chinese policy in Africa. On Chinese concerns with Latin America, see Cecil Earle Johnson, *Communist China and Latin America* (New York: Columbia University Press, 1970), which is considerably out of date. Both Africa and Latin America still require their China-specialists.

Index